Advanced Praise

"As a federal criminal defense attorney for the past 28 years, this is one of the best books out there on federal prisons. It discusses not only each facility and what is available, but the process you go through when entering a federal prison. If you are facing a federal criminal case, working with an attorney familiar with the federal criminal justice system includes knowledge of the information contained in this book. It is an essential tool for lawyers and those who may face federal prison time. Work with a federal lawyer to get the best possible results and to find the best location to serve time should you be subjected to a prison sentence. This book will help ease the process. Knowledge is the key to dealing with these difficult situations." – **Marcia G. Shein, nationally recognized federal criminal defense attorney, Shein and Brandenburg (www.federalcriminallawcenter.com), Life Member of the National Association of Criminal Defense Lawyers (NACDL), and Past President of Georgia Association of Criminal Defense Lawyers**

"Once again, Christopher Zoukis displays why his perspective is unique, insightful, and simply different than what is available in the print media. This work provides clarity and will help combat the profiteers in the market who prefer to leave one in the dark to capitalize on this very information. You will simply not get this detail of information and analysis from what is currently available in the market. It's a must-read for advocates, attorneys, and academics to gain a better insight into the BOP." – **Jack Donson, nationally awarded retiree of the Federal Bureau of Prisons, Director of Case Management & Programs for FedCURE, Chairman of the American Bar Association's standing sub-committee on Federal Bureau of Prisons policy, and Marywood University adjunct professor of criminal justice**

"Going to prison is terrifying, and finding reliable information about what a federal facility is like can be daunting. The *Directory of Federal Prisons* is a useful source of information that is often otherwise very hard to find. It's the book you hope you never need, but if you need it, you'll be grateful it's there." – **Matthew Kaiser, Partner, KaiserDillon PLLC, 2018 Super Lawyer, Georgetown University Law Center adjunct professor, Past President of the DC Bar Association**

"With his *Directory of Federal Prisons*, Christopher Zoukis has provided an invaluable resource to federal criminal defense lawyers, their clients, client families, and federal judges. Holistic counseling requires informing clients who are going to be sentenced to prison about what to expect. Proper advocacy often requires requesting a non-binding — but-often-followed — judicial recommendation to the Bureau of Prisons about what prison facility is best suited for a particular individual's situation. Rich in detail, this Directory helps on both fronts, and will ease many minds." **– Subodh Chandra, white collar criminal defense attorney, Former Federal Prosecutor (AUSA), Former Executive Editor of Yale's *Law & Policy Review***

"Christopher Zoukis has written an invaluable guide to our federal prisons, from security levels, to health care information, to locations and news items concerning every federal prison facility." **– Brandon L. Garrett, L. Neil Williams Professor of Law, Duke University School of Law and author of *Federal Habeas Corpus: Executive Detention and Post-Conviction Litigation***

"*Directory of Federal Prisons* is an essential resource for anyone seeking information about the Bureau of Prisons and its facilities. It is detailed, concise, and meticulously researched. This is an invaluable handbook for federal inmates, attorneys, judges, consultants, journalists, or anyone seeking detailed information about the federal prison system." **– Chris Geel, federal criminal defense attorney, former Trial Attorney for Charleston County Public Defender's Office, and former Appellate Division Attorney for Georgia Public Defender's Office**

"I have been a prison and sentencing consultant for over 19 years and have relied on countless sources of information about particular federal prisons so as to properly advise my clients. Most third-party sources are either inaccurate or outdated -- until now. Christopher Zoukis' *Directory of Federal Prisons: The Unofficial Guide to Bureau of Prisons Institutions* is thorough, comprehensive, and accurate. Every federal criminal defense lawyer should have a copy on their desk when their client is facing a federal prison sentence." **– John B. Webster, Managing Director, National Prison & Sentencing Consultants**

"Christopher Zoukis has put together a very useful compendium of federal prisons across the United States. The *Directory of Federal Prisons* contains useful and hard-to-find information on each facility. It will be a valuable resource to researchers interested in following federal prison conditions, family members trying to stay involved with loved ones, and individuals who may be preparing for a prison stay themselves." **– Marc Morjé Howard, Professor of Government and Law, Director of Prisons and Justice Initiative, Georgetown University Law Center**

"With the Directory of Federal Prisons, Zoukis has built an incredible resource for prisoners, their families, advocates, and researchers alike. This book is a model of how to systematically analyze institutions, incorporating official statistics and policies, government and media reports, and first-hand experiences of those within every single federal prison institution across the United States. It provides a strong foundation for maintaining this important information going forward, as well as an important framework for rendering our prisons more transparent." – **Keramet Reiter, Associate Professor of Law, University of California Irvine, and author of *23/7: Pelican Bay Prison and the Rise of Long-Term Solitary Confinement and Mass Incarceration***

"The Directory of Federal Prisons is a remarkable achievement. Zoukis provides a wealth of important, detailed information about the facilities in the Bureau of Prisons, including demographics, security levels, and the availability of programming and services such as education, vocational training, medical and mental health care. Zoukis also interviewed inmates in many of the prisons to assess aspects like levels of violence, prison politics, gang activity, and vulnerability of certain inmates. The interviews provide invaluable insight about prison cultures. The combination of exhaustive profile information and the inside perspective from inmates themselves makes the *Directory* a must-read for attorneys, inmates, their families, and anyone interested in learning about the U.S. Bureau of Prisons." – **William R. Kelly, Professor of Law, University of Texas at Austin, and author of five books on criminal justice reform**

"The *Directory of Federal Prisons* is an important resource for federal criminal defense attorneys, as well as their incarcerated clients. The book starts by providing an overview of federal prison operations and policies, and then delves into detailed profiles of every institution. These profiles contain everything from basic information (e.g., contact information, security level, visitation information, etc.) to detailed information concerning programs available at each facility (e.g., medical care, psychological care, substance abuse treatment, education, recreation, etc.). One element of this book which is not seen elsewhere is the cultural information. Zoukis interviewed federal inmates at many facilities to discern the level of prison politics and violence amongst the inmate population, as well as whether it is safe for sex offenders, informants, and LGBT inmates to remain at each prison. Whether you have a client or loved one in federal prison, or are in federal prison yourself, this book is helpful in navigating a difficult situation." – **Mark Godsey, Daniel P. and Judith L. Carmichael Professor of Law, University of Cincinnati College of Law and Director of the Rosenthal Institute of Justice/Ohio Innocence Project**

"Although titled 'an unofficial guide' to the Bureau of Prisons, this latest 628-page book by Christopher Zoukis should more properly be called 'the definitive guide' to federal prisons. It builds on his earlier work, the *Federal Prison Handbook*, to provide an even more comprehensive examination of the BOP. Have questions about medical care, mental health services or educational, job and programming opportunities in federal prisons? This book has the answers. What are the guidelines for getting into RDAP, DRUG-ED or NR-DAP? What programs are available for sex offenders? Where can I find BOP facility addresses, phone numbers, available programs (including UNICOR), reviews and recent news reports? In this book. Questions about security points and classification? Same. Basically, the *Directory of Federal Prisons* is an exhaustive compilation of everything you could possibly want to know – and more – about the BOP, including things even federal prison officials likely don't know." – **Alex Friedmann, Managing Editor of *Prison Legal News*, Associate Director of the Human Rights Defense Center, and President of the anti-private prison Private Corrections Institute**

"This is essential reading for anyone who comes in contact with the federal prison system. Christopher Zoukis is not only an insider who spent time and learned the system from experience, but he shares federal prison information from the perspective of s writer who is dedicated to prisoners' rights advocacy." – **Jean Trounstine, professor, prison activist, and author, whose latest book is *Boy With a Knife: A Story of Murder, Remorse, and a Prisoner's Fight for Justice***

"This Directory is slam-bang essential for anyone entering federal prison, or anyone whose loved one is entering. The book should be on the desktop of any attorney who counsels and represents citizens entering the criminal 'justice' system, to educate them and prepare them for the realities. It's extensive, it's exhausting, and it's essential." – **Terri LeClercq, Ph.D., retired Professor of English Emerita, University of Texas at Austin and author of *Prison Grievances: When to Write, How to Write***

"What makes the *Directory of Federal Prisons* so impressive is how comprehensive it is. The first section is a detailed overview of the Federal Bureau of Prisons. A must-read for anyone (or the loved ones of anyone) about to enter the federal prison system. Even people incarcerated for years will find this section informative, as will attorneys. The bulk of the book provides descriptions of every prison within the Bureau of Prisons. Each prison profile provides official information. Policies, procedures, and what to expect is covered. Most importantly and uniquely, insights from the women and men serving time in every prison were gathered through interviews and questionnaires answered by hundreds of prisoners. This is an important one-of-a-kind resource. Congratulations to Christopher Zoukis and all whose dedication made it all possible." – **Lois Ahrens, Director of The Real Cost of Prisons Project and founding member of The National Council of Incarcerated and Formerly Incarcerated Women and Girls**

"Directory of Federal Prisons: The Unofficial Guide to Bureau of Prison Institutions is an invaluable resource for attorneys, families of inmates, and inmates themselves. The scope of this project is impressive, profiling every prison within the Bureau of Prisons from not only a programs and directory information perspective, but also from an inmate's perspective. Going beyond published information alone, incorporating experiences from inmates themselves makes this directory a one-of-a-kind resource." – **Dr. Marieke Liem, Associate Professor, Institute of Security and Global Affairs, Leiden University and author of *After Life Imprisonment***

"This is a must-have for anyone working with federal defendants and federal inmates. It is a comprehensive source of pertinent information that addresses the key questions defendants, inmates, and their families have regarding the federal prison system. This information will alleviate many of the concerns and much of the anxiety experienced by those facing incarceration." – **Richard Zaranek, President of Executive Prison Consultants**

"The federal prison system is a confusing and labyrinthian archipelago of prisons, camps and private institutions. In this excellent book, Christopher Zoukis provides a detailed guide to this system. He supplies general information about it, along with material about individual prisons throughout the United States. Importantly, Zoukis also includes the testimony of inmates who have experienced different institutions. This volume will be useful to policymakers and scholars studying the federal prison system. It will also be helpful to inmates and their families who are navigating a complex environment. I commend and admire Zoukis for his painstaking research and his deep knowledge of our penal system." – **Derek S. Jeffreys, Professor, Humanities and Religion, University of Wisconsin and author of *America's Jails: The Search for Human Dignity in an Age of Mass Incarceration***

"Directory of Federal Prisons is a resource that people in fed prisons and their loved ones need. As we know, the BOP transfers people to over 100 prisons throughout the country. This *Directory* will give you the 'heads up' info to know yourself before transfer as well as to share with your family and friends. – **Charles Sullivan, President of International CURE**

DIRECTORY OF FEDERAL PRISONS

The Unofficial Guide to Bureau of Prisons Institutions

BOOKS BY CHRISTOPHER ZOUKIS

Directory of Federal Prisons (Middle Street Publishing, 2019)

Federal Prison Handbook (Middle Street Publishing, 2017)

Prison Education Guide (Prison Legal News Publishing, 2016)

College for Convicts: The Case for Higher Education in American Prisons
(McFarland & Co., 2014)

DIRECTORY OF FEDERAL PRISONS

The Unofficial Guide to Bureau of Prisons Institutions

Christopher Zoukis, MBA

MIDDLE STREET
PUBLISHING

Charleston, South Carolina

Published in the United States by Middle Street Publishing in partnership with Zoukis Consulting Group.

Zoukis Consulting Group is a federal prison consultancy which assists attorneys, federal criminal defendants, and federal prisoners with prison preparation, in-prison matters, and reentry services.

Zoukis Consulting Group
Info@PrisonerResource.com

ISBN (pbk): 978-0-9913302-2-5
ISBN (ebk): 978-0-9913302-3-2

Middle Street Publishing, Charleston, South Carolina

Legal Notice to Readers

BRIEF TABLE OF CONTENTS

TABLE OF CONTENTS

Acknowledgements

First and foremost, I'd like to thank Mom and Dad for their impassioned support during these challenging years. They have stood by me while I've answered the call of prison education and prisoners' rights advocacy. Their support has been invaluable. This text could not have been completed without their integral support.

A huge debt of gratitude is owed to my research assistants and online team, Kamea Zelisko and Susan Mate at MKT Communications, Shauna Croom and Rondi Christopher. Their terrific assistance with everything technological, online, research and book marketing related have made this project what it is today.

Thanks to Dave Strauss at Dave Strauss Design. Dave has been phenomenal with the covers for this project and plenty of others.

A big thank you to my great legal team who have been with me for many years, Brandon Sample, Todd Bussert, Alan Ellis, and Chris Geel. You've been instrumental in my success for many years and have enabled me to engage in the work that calls me.

Also, thanks to the great team at *Prison Legal News* and *Criminal Legal News* for their support and encouragement all of these years. Paul Wright, Alex Friedmann, Richard Reich, and Betty Nerlander have very much helped me through the last few years by giving my life purpose and allowing me to follow my passion. I consider all of you brothers (and sisters) in arms.

Finally, thanks to the hundreds of prisoners who responded to my surveys, sat for interviews, and critiqued the prison profiles. You helped to add a real, boots-on-the-ground flavor to this project, which I hope will help countless others.

PART ONE

Federal Bureau of Prisons

This section presents an overview of the Federal Bureau of Prisons, with a special focus on custody and security scoring. Covered are matters of interest to inmates, security levels, medical and mental health care levels, and the designation and prison transfer process.

Federal Bureau of Prisons: An Overview

Introduction

The following is a brief overview of the issues most important to federal prisoners. This information is intended to complement the facility-specific information found in each of the prison profiles in this directory. For a more in-depth discussion of the subjects in this chapter, see our *Federal Prison Handbook: The Definitive Guide to Surviving the Federal Bureau of Prisons* (Middle Street Press, 2017) or our website PrisonerResource.com.

BOP Overview

The Bureau of Prisons is the arm of the U.S. Department of Justice that is tasked with the custody and care of all federal prisoners. Established by Congress in 1930, the Bureau began operations with 14 prisons, holding about 13,000 inmates. As of 2019, the federal prison population has grown to more than 180,000 prisoners, held in 127 stand-alone facilities, 68 satellite prison camps, and 12 private prisons across the nation. The Bureau has an annual budget of over seven billion dollars.

The Bureau is administratively organized in a top-down fashion. The Central Office, located in Washington, D.C., consists of the Director, the General Counsel, and the executive-level offices of the Health Services, Correctional Programs and Information, Policy and Public Affairs divisions. Under the Central Office are six geographically-organized Regional Offices. Regional Offices oversee the individual institutions in their geographic area.

At the institutional level, operations are generally divided between administrative functions and correctional/security functions. The Warden is the top administrator. Reporting to the Warden are various Associate Wardens, Unit Managers, Case Managers, Correctional Counselors and other administrators. The Captain is in charge of all correctional and security-related matters. Beneath the Captain are the lieutenants and front-line correctional officers.

Each Bureau facility is assigned one of five security levels. Minimum-security prisons, also known as camps, generally have no fences, few security measures and a low staff-to-inmate ratio. Low and medium-security prisons, also known as Federal Correctional Institutions (FCIs), have multiple barbed-wire fences, armed perimeter security patrols and a higher staff-to-inmate ratio. High-security federal prisons are known as United States Penitentiaries (USPs) and are usually surrounded by 40 to 50-foot walls, gun towers, and house violent or long-term prisoners.

Administrative prisons have a variety of missions. Federal Medical Centers (FMCs), Federal Detention Centers (FDCs), and Federal Transfer Centers (FTCs) handle major medical issues, pretrial detention and inmate movement, respectively. Inmates of all security levels may be held in these administrative facilities. The Administrative Maximum facility, also known as ADX Florence or ADMAX, is the Bureau's "supermax" prison. Only the highest security-level prisoners are held in this underground concrete bunker. See Chapter 2 for more information on BOP facility security levels.

The Designation and Sentence Computation Center (DSCC) is the stand-alone BOP office tasked with calculating an inmate's sentence and determining where he or she will be housed. Staff at the DSCC, located in Grand Prairie, Texas, consider a variety of factors when designating inmates. Such factors include inmate-specific information (e.g., history of violence, age, sentence length, medical needs, etc.) and Bureau-specific information (e.g., population considerations, specific security issues, etc.). See Chapter 3 for more information on DSCC and the designation process.

Demographics

As of May 1, 2019, the Bureau of Prisons housed 180,501 inmates in its institutions. Most inmates are held in either low- or medium-security FCIs (37.7 percent in low-security FCIs and 30 percent in medium-security FCIs). About 16.5 percent of all inmates live in minimum-security camps. United States Penitentiaries hold 11.9 percent of all federal prisoners.

The average age of a federal prisoner is 36. Almost all federal prisoners are male -- 93 percent. More than 58 percent of the Bureau's population is white or Hispanic, and 37.7 percent is black. Most federal inmates are serving a 5- to 10-year sentence (more than 25 percent) for a drug-related crime (more than 45 percent).

The Bureau employs over 35,000 individuals. Just under three quarters of all BOP staff are male. Most are white, non-Hispanic (62.8 percent). About 21.5 percent of all Bureau employees are black, and 12.2 percent are Hispanic.

About 83 percent of the Bureau's population is housed in BOP-operated facilities. The remaining inmates live in one of the 12 facilities owned or operated by for-profit contractors, such as CoreCivic or the GEO Group, or are in other types of housing (e.g., halfway house, home confinement, etc.).

Admissions and Orientation

Upon arrival at any Bureau institution, all newly committed prisoners and transferring inmates will go through the Admission and Orientation (A&O) process. During this period, which can last up to 30 days, inmates will be evaluated by staff members from Medical, Dental and Psychology Services. Ideally, inmates will also use their A&O time to become familiar with the institution and its workings, and to find a job. At some point during the A&O period, inmates will attend a town hall-style meeting during which heads of all relevant departments will make remarks and allow for questions. Once an inmate has attended the A&O meeting, his or her status is changed to reflect completion of the A&O process. The inmate is then officially part of the general population.

Housing

Housing in the BOP varies from institution to institution and is often determined by the security level of a given prison. Minimum- and low-security facilities generally house inmates in dormitory-style settings. These housing units are very large open spaces containing multiple cubicles, in which prisoners live. A typical dormitory will have a number of two-, three- and four-man cubicles, as well as communal showers and toilets. Showers in all Bureau facilities, including dormitories, are one-man showers with a door that allows for a modicum of privacy. Bathroom areas consist of long rows of toilets, generally separated by walls and often with a swinging door.

Medium-, high- and administrative-security institutions house inmates in cells with locking doors. Each cell holds anywhere from two to twelve inmates, with two-person cells being the most common. Cells contain a toilet, sink, desk, lockers and bunk beds. Rarely, a facility will also have in-cell showers, but for the most part, showers in higher security level institutions will be in a common area.

Housing units in nearly every Bureau institution include a communal day room. The day room generally has tables and chairs, a TRULINCS computer area, televisions (sometimes in separate TV rooms, sometimes mounted on the walls), a laundry area (if the institution still allows washing and drying machines in the housing units), and an area with either a microwave or a 200 degree hot water dispenser.

Contact with the Outside

Inmates in the Bureau of Prisons are provided several methods with which to stay in contact with family, friends and others on the outside. All communication between an inmate and anyone outside of the prison, other than an attorney, is subject to monitoring by Bureau staff.

Postal mail is the traditional mainstay of prison communication. Mail from friends and family should be addressed to the inmate at the facility's address and must include the inmate's registration number. Incoming mail is opened and inspected by staff; outgoing mail must be left unsealed for inspection at medium- and high-security institutions. Inmates at all facilities may also receive commercial publications, such as newspapers and magazines. For those inmates held at medium- or high-security institutions, all commercial publications (including books) must come directly from the publisher (or a book distributor like Amazon). At lows and camps, inmates may receive softcover publications (including books) from any source.

Inmates also have access to telephones in federal prison. All telephone contacts must be approved by staff, but this practice is mostly perfunctory. Inmates are permitted 300 minutes of telephone time per month, and each call is limited to 15 minutes. Direct dial calls are debited from the inmate's commissary account at a rate of $0.06 per minute for local calls and $0.21 per minute for long distance calls. Calls to Canada cost $0.35 per minute, calls to Mexico cost $0.55 per minute, and calls to other countries cost $0.99 per minute. The system also allows for an inmate to call collect, but depending on the receiving party's telecom provider, a prepaid account with Value Added Communications (1-800-913-6097) may be necessary. As of the date of this writing, both AT&T and Verizon no longer allow customers to accept collect calls from federal prisons. All telephone calls are recorded, and some are monitored in real-time or in retrospect. Telephone access is considered a privilege which may be revoked for disciplinary reasons.

As part of the computerized TRULINCS system, the Bureau also offers some inmates access to a text-based email system through the website Corrlinks.com. Authorized inmates can exchange emails of up to 13,000 characters with their approved contacts. Inmates are charged one TRU-Unit per minute while accessing the email service, whether composing or reading emails. Contacts outside of prison do not incur a cost for service use. TRU-Units currently cost $0.05 each. All messages are stored by the Bureau and are subject to monitoring. Sex offenders are often restricted from access to the TRULINCS email system, and access is subject to disciplinary revocation.

Visitation

According to federal regulation, "The Bureau of Prisons encourages visiting by family, friends, and community groups to maintain the morale of the inmate and to develop closer relationships between the inmate and family members or others in the community." While the accuracy of this statement is arguable, the Bureau does allow nearly every inmate in its custody visitation privileges, including inmates held in the Special Housing Unit for any reason, unless visitation privileges have been restricted for disciplinary reasons.

Visits in the Bureau of Prisons are contact visits. This means that the inmate and visitors sit in the same place, usually around a table of some sort, and may exchange a brief hug or kiss at the beginning and end of each visit. Visitation is frequently available, and Wardens are required to establish visiting hours on the weekends and federal holidays. The length of visits is determined by staff and the visitors themselves, but generally amounts to some period of hours.

While visiting, guests can usually purchase vending machine-style snacks and drinks for themselves and the inmate. Board games and playing cards are often available, as is a children's play area.

Inmates may only visit with those individuals approved by the Bureau. Immediate family can be approved by the Correctional Counselor without any documentation. Such family are typically verified through the inmate's Pre-Sentence Report. All others must submit a Visitor Information Form (BP-A0629), which is available on BOP.gov or through the prisoner. Inmates may only visit individuals that they knew prior to incarceration, with the exception of certain religious organization volunteers, such as those with Prisoner Visitation and Support (PVS).

Visitors are subject to search upon entering prison grounds. This is usually limited to passing through a metal detector or an Ion Spectrometer device that searches for trace amounts of drugs and explosives. Inmates are stripped naked and must expose all body cavities for search upon entrance and exit of the visitation room. Inmates housed in minimum-security institutions are not always subject to a strip search upon entering the visitation room.

Visitors should review the Bureau's visiting policies prior to arriving at an institution. It is important that all rules be followed to the letter. Visitors face restrictions on what they are allowed to wear, for instance, and will be turned away if they wear a disallowed style or color of clothing. Visiting policies for each institution can be found online at https://www.bop.gov.

Visitation days and times can be found both at the Bureau of Prisons' website and in each institution's profile in Part Two.

Medical, Dental and Mental Health Care

A core principle of the Bureau's Health Services Mission Statement is that "[a]ll inmates have value as human beings and deserve medically necessary health care." Perhaps more importantly, the U.S. Supreme Court held in *Farmer v. Brennan*, 511 U.S. 825 (1994) that the United States Constitution *requires* prison officials to provide inmates with adequate medical care. As such, all federal prisoners will receive some level of care for their medical needs, although the quality of the care is by no means guaranteed or consistent.

The Bureau considers the provision of medical care in five different ways. "Medically Necessary" care is always provided, whether at the institution or an outside hospital. In order to qualify as Medically Necessary, an inmate's condition must be acute or emergent, meaning that without care, the inmate would suffer rapid deterioration of health, significant irreversible loss of function, or loss of life. Medically Necessary conditions include heart attack, stroke, severe trauma and hemorrhage.

"Medically Necessary-Non-Emergent" care is normally provided to all inmates. These conditions are not life-threatening, but if not treated would present a significant risk of serious deterioration leading to premature death, a significant reduction in the possibility of later repair, or significant pain or discomfort which impairs the inmate's participation in activities of daily living. Examples of Medically Necessary-Non-Emergent conditions include diabetes, heart disease, schizophrenia, infectious diseases and cancer.

Conditions that the Bureau considers "Medically Acceptable-Not Always Necessary" may be treated, but often are not. The Bureau considers conditions in this category to require only elective care, which is not medically necessary. Prior to treatment of any condition falling in this category, the Utilization Review Committee (a group of institution-level staff members made up of the Clinical Director and various others) must give its approval. Medically Acceptable-Not Always Necessary conditions include a torn anterior cruciate ligament of the knee, failing joints and a variety of other orthopedic disorders.

Medical conditions for which care provides "Limited Medical Value" are unlikely to be treated by the Bureau. These conditions are often minor and include cosmetic conditions and non-cancerous skin lesions. Even less likely to be provided is treatment of a condition that the Bureau classifies as "Extraordinary." Medical interventions are deemed Extraordinary if they affect the life of another individual (i.e., organ transplantation) or are investigational in nature.

Inmates who are experiencing a medical issue will either submit a sick call triage form or report to the institution's health services center at an appointed time. Inmates should anticipate a lengthy and trying process when accessing the Bureau's health care apparatus. Patience and diligence are required; with a modicum of both, most conditions will be treated by Bureau medical personnel.

Dental care is provided in the Bureau of Prisons. According to Bureau policy, "[d]ental care will be conservative, providing necessary treatment for the greatest number of inmates within available resources." Routine dental care (treatment of cavities, root canals, etc.) is furnished to inmates who are on the "Dental Routine Treatment List." Routine care is administered in a chronological fashion.

Most inmates are placed on the routine treatment list by dental staff after the inmate has an A&O examination. Ideally, this comprehensive examination takes place within 30 days of the inmate's arrival at an institution. Inmates may also get on the list by submitting an Inmate Request to Staff, also known as a cop-out (Form BP-A0148).

Urgent dental care is provided by way of a dental sick call program. Urgent care includes treatment of severe, acute dental pain, traumatic injuries and acute infections. Urgent care may not be provided via a wait list; other than life-threatening emergencies, urgent dental care is the highest priority for Bureau dental services professionals and is provided promptly.

Bureau policy requires each institution to retain one dentist for every 1,000 inmates. In practice, most if not all federal prisons have a dentist and multiple dental services staffers. The dental services department of every institution is, as a rule, swamped. As such, just as when dealing with medical situations, it is advisable that inmates approach dental care with a patient attitude. The best bet is to utilize preventative brushing so as to limit the need for dental intervention.

Mental health care is provided to all Bureau inmates through the institutional psychology services department. In addition to assessing and treating mental disorders, psychology services plays an integral part in the Bureau's reentry efforts. Psychologists and other mental health professionals from psychology services also provide behavioral science expertise to other Bureau staff members.

Every inmate will receive an initial medical screening when arriving at a Bureau institution. If the inmate presents mental health concerns, psychology services is notified, and a prompt intervention is required. Otherwise, a psychologist will interview the inmate within 14 days of arrival.

Outside of the initial screening, psychology services are provided on an as-needed basis. Inmates may access the services of a psychologist by submitting a written or electronic request to psychology services, or by attending the psychology services department's weekly open house.

Services available to the general population include individual counseling, group therapy and crisis intervention. Group therapy is by far the most common treatment provided to inmates with mental health issues. Bureau psychologists employ the cognitive behavioral therapy model in most clinical interventions. Psychology services also offers specialty treatment programs for drug-addicted inmates and sex offenders.

Psychotropic medications are available to inmates in Bureau custody. While psychology services is responsible for the mental health care of inmates, medications are only prescribed and dispensed through the health services department. Any inmate receiving such medication will be monitored through the health services chronic care clinic.

Education, Work and Programming

Every inmate in the Federal Bureau of Prisons has access to educational, job and programming opportunities. Programming, for the most part, is entirely voluntary. Work, and in some cases education, however, is required for all Bureau inmates.

There are a wide variety of programs available to federal inmates. The psychology services department is responsible for the implementation and oversight of many of the Bureau's core programs. Drug and addiction treatment programs are a significant part of the psychology department's efforts.

The Bureau offers three drug treatment programs. The Residential Drug Abuse Program (RDAP) is the most well-known and well-established program. Authorized by Congress, RDAP is a nine-month plus, 500-hour program that is offered in multiple institutions. Inmates who successfully complete RDAP are eligible for a sentence reduction of up to one year. Many categories of inmates are ineligible for the sentence reduction, however. Most notably, any inmate convicted of what the Bureau considers a crime of violence will not receive a sentence reduction for completion of RDAP. This includes crimes involving a gun or the sexual abuse of a child.

Every Bureau institution offers the Drug Abuse Education Course (DRUG-ED) and the Non-Residential Drug Abuse Program (NR-DAP). The DRUG-ED course is 12 to 15 hours in duration and requires completion of a final examination. The NR-DAP program is primarily intended for inmates awaiting placement in RDAP, but also enrolls inmates who do not qualify for RDAP or are otherwise in need of drug treatment. The NR-DAP program consists of 90- to 120-minute weekly sessions over a period of 12 to 24 weeks.

Psychology services is also responsible for sex offender programming. There are two treatment options available for sex offenders: the Non-Residential Sex Offender Treatment Program (SOTP-NR) and the Residential Sex Offender Treatment Program (SOTP-R). SOTP-R is a high intensity, voluntary program lasting from 12 to 18 months, and is only available at FMC Devens and USP Marion. The SOTP-NR program is a less intense, 9- to 12-month program offered at all eight of the Bureau's Sex Offender Management Program (SOMP) facilities.

Other programs overseen by the psychology department include the Bureau Rehabilitation and Values Enhancement (BRAVE) Program, the Challenge Program, the Mental Health Step-Down Unit Program, the Resolve Program, the Skills Program, and the Steps Toward Awareness, Growth, and Emotional Strengths (STAGES) Program. These programs address a variety of intellectual and personality disorders, provide support services for mentally ill inmates and address issues faced by younger, first-time inmates serving shorter sentences.

In addition to the programs offered through psychology services, Bureau institutions offer a variety of local programming opportunities. These supplemental programs mostly focus on recidivism reduction and reentry issues.

Educational opportunities in the Bureau can be divided into two categories: required and voluntary. Those inmates who have not graduated high school or earned a GED must attend literacy or GED classes. Failure to attend these classes can result in the loss of good conduct time and other sanctions. Once an inmate has passed the GED, participation is no longer required.

Inmates who do not speak English are required to participate in the English-as-a-Second-Language (ESL) Program. Participants in the ESL Program may receive incentives for participation and completion, though such incentives are limited to small cash awards, certificates, etc. Inmates who are required to attend the ESL Program will be disciplined when failing to participate.

There are numerous voluntary educational opportunities available in the Bureau. Every institution offers a selection of Adult Continuing Education (ACE) classes, taught by inmates, for inmates. Additionally, secondary education is available to all Bureau inmates, though this is largely limited to correspondence courses, paid for by the inmate. The author of this Directory earned his bachelor's degree and MBA from the regionally accredited Adams State University through correspondence while he was incarcerated in the Federal Bureau of Prisons. To learn more about correspondence programs accessible to inmates, see our *Prison Education Guide* (Prison Legal News Publishing, 2016).

In addition to hosting ACE classes and the higher education program, each Bureau Education Department has a library. Libraries vary from institution to institution, but as a rule, provide inmates with a limited variety of resources. Most federal prison libraries provide inmates with access to a computer-based electronic law library, typewriters and a copy machine. Bureau libraries also stock a good selection of fiction and non-fiction books, magazines, newspapers, and reference material.

Federal regulations and Bureau policy dictate that every sentenced inmate who is physically and medically able must work while incarcerated. The jobs available to inmates fall into just about every category imaginable. A federal prison is essentially a self-sufficient, stand-alone city, and the inmates living there keep the city running.

Most jobs are low- to mid-level and pay next to nothing. Kitchen workers, groundskeepers, landscapers, barbers, clerks and maintenance workers earn anywhere from $0.12 an hour to $0.40 an hour, or a minimum of $5.25 per month. Specialized workers, such as commissary, facilities and UNICOR factory workers earn more. An inmate in federal prison can expect to earn from $5.00 to $250.00 per month, depending on the job and the inmate's work ethic. No-show, no-pay jobs are usually available as well, because most institutions have more inmates than available jobs.

Money Matters

Inmates in the Federal Bureau of Prisons may not possess U.S. currency at any time. However, it is possible to send, receive and spend money while in federal prison. Indeed, funds are required to access the TRULINCS public messaging system, to direct dial telephone contacts and to shop at the institutional commissary.

The Bureau operates a trust account in which all funds received on an inmate's behalf, as well as all of the inmate's earnings, are deposited. Outside contacts may send money to an inmate by mailing a postal money order to the Bureau's "Lockbox." Money orders should be made payable to the inmate's first and last name, followed by the inmate's eight-digit registration number. All funds submitted on an inmate's behalf through the U.S. mail must be addressed as follows:

Federal Bureau of Prisons
[Inmate's First and Last Name]
[Inmate's Eight-Digit Registration Number]
P.O. Box 474701
Des Moines, Iowa 50947-0001

The Bureau also accepts Western Union transfers on behalf of inmates. Western Union charges a fee for this service, but money transferred in this manner generally arrives in an inmate's account within two to four hours. WesternUnion.com processes online transfers, and also has information on physical Western Union locations. Money can be transferred using a credit or debit card through WesternUnion.com, calling 1-800-634-3422 (using option 2), or in-store using the blue Quick Collect form. When transferring funds, the following information must always be provided:

- The inmate's committed name
- The inmate's eight-digit registration number
- City code: FBOP
- State code: DC

Inmates may send money from their institutional account to outside contacts via U.S. Treasury Check. Requests to send funds are made with Form BP-199. Inmates can initiate and monitor outgoing money transfers through the TRULINCS computer system.

The Bureau operates the Inmate Financial Responsibility Program (IFRP) in order to encourage inmates to meet legitimate financial obligations. In most cases, the obligations covered by the IFRP are court-ordered fines, fees and restitution. Staff at the local institution (most likely the correctional counselor) will meet with an inmate who has such an obligation in order to set up a payment plan. Payments generally start at a minimum of $25.00 per quarter and are based on how much money an inmate has received in the last six months. The IFRP is considered a voluntary program, but inmates with an obligation who opt not to participate will be denied certain privileges, such as favorable housing and commissary purchases.

Each institution operates a commissary where inmates can purchase a variety of items for use or consumption while in Bureau custody. In most cases, inmates shop at the commissary once per week. The Bureau limits what an inmate can spend at the commissary in order to ensure parity amongst the population. Currently, the spending limit is $360.00 per month. Items available at most institutional commissaries include consumables (e.g., rice, beans, meats, cheeses, candy, sodas, etc.), hygiene products (e.g., soap, shampoo, razors, etc.), clothing (e.g., sweat suits, t-shirts, boxers, socks, etc.), electronics (e.g., radios, MP3 players, batteries, etc.), and over-the-counter medications (e.g., pain relievers, vitamins, etc.).

Recreation

Both federal regulation and Bureau policy encourage inmates to make use of the recreation options available in federal prisons. The importance of recreation to inmates cannot be overstated. Constructive use of time and maintaining physical, emotional and mental health are crucial to enduring a prison term.

Recreation opportunities available to inmates in federal prison can be divided into active and passive categories. Virtually every federal prison provides multiple active recreation options. Most federal prisons have a large outdoor recreation yard, which generally contains at least a track, basketball court, softball field, football/soccer field, handball wall, bocce ball courts and horseshoe pits. Free weights are no longer available in most federal prisons, but cardiovascular exercise equipment is often available. Most yards have multiple treadmills, ellipticals and stationary bicycles for inmate use.

Federal prisons also offer many passive recreation options, most of which take place in housing units or in enclosed, inside recreation areas. Art programs are common, as are other hobbycraft activities such as ceramics, leatherwork, models, crochet and woodworking. Most federal prisons also offer a music program, stocked with musical instruments of many kinds (e.g., guitars, bass guitars, drums, pianos, etc.). Other passive recreation options include card playing, institutional movies and board games.

Organized activities are a significant part of the Bureau's recreation program. Team activities, such as softball and football leagues are extremely popular among federal inmates. Bureau recreation departments also sponsor social and cultural clubs and programs, stage shows and holiday sports tournaments.

Religion

Both the United States Constitution and federal law prohibit governmental interference with an individual's religious practices. The right to hold religious beliefs and engage in religious practices extends to federal prisoners. As such, every federal prison has a religious center, often referred to as a chapel, staffed by trained (and usually ordained) religious personnel.

Organized religious services for every recognized belief are held in the chapel. Staff chaplains set the time for such services, and in some cases, lead services. The Bureau allows outside volunteers and contractors to enter the institution in order to interact with inmates of their faith, and to lead services.

In addition to supervising all religious activities, Bureau chaplains provide pastoral care and ensure that there is equity among the recognized religions. Chaplains handle inmate requests for religious accommodation and determine what religious items inmates may possess. Chaplains are also responsible for organizing ceremonial meals for each religion and ensuring that religious holidays and requirements (i.e., Ramadan) are accommodated.

Religious diets are generally available to federal inmates. Every federal chow hall operates a "certified" food option. Certified food is prepared and packaged off-site and is Kosher. In addition to what is served in the chow hall, Kosher and Halal shelf-stable entrees are available for purchase in every commissary.

CHAPTER 2:

Security, Medical and Mental Health Care Levels

Introduction

The Bureau of Prisons classifies every federal prison by security level, medical care level, and mental health care level. The Bureau also assigns each federal inmate a security, medical care and mental health care level. As a general rule, an inmate will be housed in an institution with classifications that correspond with his or her designation.

The federal prison experience can differ significantly from institution to institution. The biggest difference maker is the security level assigned to a given prison. High-security federal prisons tend to be extremely dangerous environments where abject violence at the hands of inmates and staff alike is relatively common. Minimum-security facilities, on the other hand, are usually quite safe and sane.

Medical and mental health care level classifications also impact life in federal prison, though to a lesser degree than security level classifications. In general, the higher the level, the better the care provided to inmates. For a federal inmate with a medical or mental health condition, the quality of care available at an institution can make a tremendous difference in the prison experience and quality of life. Sometimes the difference quite literally amounts to life or death.

Security Levels

Every federal prison is designated one of five security levels, which are described in detail below. The level assigned to a particular institution dictates the physical security parameters of the prison, the staff-to-inmate ratio, and the freedoms afforded to inmates. As a general rule, the higher the security level, the more restrictions are placed on inmates.

Every federal prisoner is assigned one of four security levels: minimum, low, medium or high. Absent unusual circumstances, an inmate will be housed in an institution with a security level that matches his or her assigned level.

Minimum Security

The least restrictive federal prisons are classified as minimum security and are also known as camps. While the Bureau operates some stand-alone Federal Prison Camps (FPCs), most minimum-security federal prisons are instead satellite camps. A satellite camp is located adjacent to a higher-security institution, and the campers provide services for the main institution.

Minimum-security federal prisons are different than higher-security prisons in many ways. Perhaps most significantly, there are often no barriers between the camp and the outside world. No fences, no walls -- federal prisoners housed in camps can simply walk away, if they choose. Due to the near certainty of recapture and the wealth of negative consequences associated with an escape from federal prison, very few campers ever walk away.

Most minimum-security federal prisons house inmates in dormitory-style settings. Violence is nearly unheard of in federal prison camps. Across the Bureau, between 220 and 250 "less serious" assaults (i.e., fights) were reported each month in 2017. Less than 5 percent of those fights took place in a camp.

Only prisoners with the lowest security point total and a custody assignment of OUT will be housed in a minimum-security federal prison (see Chapter 3 for more information on security point calculation and custody assignments). Camp inmates are generally low-level, nonviolent offenders who do not have a significant history of institutional disciplinary violations or escape. Inmates with more than ten years remaining on their sentence will not be housed in a camp. Sex offenders and other inmates the Bureau considers high risk are prohibited from placement in a camp.

Low Security

Low-security federal prisons, also known as Federal Correctional Institutions (FCIs), house the largest percentage of the Bureau's population. Low-security FCI's have fences and electronic security systems, a higher staff-to-inmate ratio, and tighter control over inmate movement.

Due to the size of the Bureau's low-security population, these facilities tend to be crowded. Inmates live in dormitory or cubicle-style settings, though some low-security institutions have a limited number of cells. Low-security federal prisons are generally safe, but the number of "less serious" inmate assaults reported in 2017 was about five times higher than that reported in minimum-security institutions.

In order to be designated to a low-security facility, a federal inmate must have less than 20 years left to serve. Sex offenders and higher-risk inmates are housed at low-security facilities. Low-security prisoners may have a history of violence, but those caught fighting, drinking, using drugs, or committing other serious infractions are generally sent to medium-security prisons.

Medium Security

Medium-security federal prisons are also referred to as Federal Correctional Institutions (FCIs). Medium-security prisons have strengthened perimeters, an even higher staff-to-inmate ratio, and greater control over inmates.

Medium-security institutions are nearly as crowded as low-security federal prisons, holding about 30 percent of the Bureau's population. Housing in medium-security facilities tends to consist of two- or three-person cells with locking doors. Some mediums house inmates in larger cells that hold up to twelve inmates.

Due to the nature of the population housed at the medium-security level, violence is more prevalent than in lower security settings. Levels of violence tend to vary significantly from medium to medium, however. Some medium-security institutions are run in a manner comparable to a federal penitentiary, while some are more laid back.

Inmates designated to a medium-security federal prison may have a history of violence. A history of escape, in-prison alcohol and substance abuse, and a lengthy disciplinary record will not preclude an inmate from being placed in a medium-security federal prison. Inmates designated to a medium generally must have less than 30 years left to serve, but often have more than 20 years remaining on their sentence.

High Security

High-security federal prisons, also known as United States Penitentiaries (USPs), house a smaller percentage of the Bureau's population. Federal penitentiaries tend to be very dangerous, and extreme violence is commonplace in these environments. Typically, a USP is surrounded by a 40-foot concrete wall, as well as gun towers staffed with rifle-wielding sharpshooters. Other than the federal ADX supermax (discussed below), high-security federal prisons have the highest staff-to-inmate ratio and closest control of inmates.

Despite only holding about 12 percent of the federal prison population, more than half of the 2017 "less serious" and "more serious" assaults on inmates, as well as most assaults on staff, took place in high-security institutions. Gangs tend to run USPs, and as a result, fights and stabbings are commonplace.

Inmates designated to high-security institutions will almost certainly have a history of violence. Federal prisoners with more than 30 years left to serve generally must be placed in a USP. Inmates housed in USPs tend to be younger and have very high security point totals. See Chapter 3 for more information on security point calculation.

Administrative Security

The Bureau of Prisons categorizes federal prisons with special missions as administrative-security institutions. These facilities are equipped to house inmates of any security level. Federal prisons that house pretrial detainees, such as Metropolitan Correctional Centers (MCCs) and Metropolitan Detention Centers (MDCs), are classified as administrative security, as are Federal Medical Centers (FMCs), Federal Transfer Centers (FTCs) and the Administrative Maximum (ADX), the Bureau's supermax, located in Florence, Colorado.

In terms of violence, data from 2017 puts administrative-security prisons between low- and medium-security institutions. Because of the variety of missions that administrative-security prisons serve, however, violence levels in these institutions tend to vary significantly. Federal Medical Centers, for example, see very little violence. The ADX, on the other hand, houses inmates that the Bureau has judged to be extremely dangerous, violent and virtually unmanageable.

Designation to an administrative-security prison is based almost entirely on the prison's mission, and not the inmate's security points or custody classification. For example, an inmate with serious medical needs may be designated to an administrative-security FMC regardless of his security point total, though the inmate's security level may influence the particular FMC to which he or she is designated.

Medical Care Levels

In an effort to better address and manage the health care needs of federal prisoners, the Bureau of Prisons assigns one of four medical care levels to each federal prison. The Bureau also designates every inmate with a medical care level classification. In most circumstances, an inmate will be housed in an institution with a medical care level classification that corresponds with, or is higher than, his or her medical care level.

Medical Care Level I

Bureau institutions classified as Care Level 1 are located one hour or more from a community medical center. Care Level 1 facilities provide on-site medical treatment for prisoners, and contract with local hospitals for inpatient care needs. As of March 2017, 21 Bureau institutions were classified as Care Level 1 prisons.

Inmates designated Care Level 1 are less than 70 years of age and are generally healthy. Care Level 1 inmates may have some limited medical needs requiring clinical evaluation and treatment every six months. Such medical needs may include asthma or diet-controlled diabetes, among other mild conditions. As of February 2019, about 71 percent of all federal inmates were classified as Medical Care Level 1.

Medical Care Level 2

Institutions classified as Care Level 2 provide the same on-site medical services as Care Level 1 facilities, but are located less than one hour from a major regional treatment center. The closer proximity of these prisons to major treatment centers permits more immediate attention to serious and life-threatening medical situations. As of March 2017, 96 Bureau facilities were classified as Medical Care Level 2.

Care Level 2 inmates are medically stable but require at least quarterly clinical evaluations. Inmates with this designation can be managed in chronic care clinics and do not regularly require enhanced medical resources. Inmates designated Care Level 2 may suffer from medication-controlled diabetes, epilepsy or emphysema. As of February 2019, 26 percent of all federal inmates were classified as Medical Care Level 2.

Medical Care Level 3

A Medical Care Level 3 facility is generally located near, or adjacent to, a Medical Care Level 4 facility. In rare instances, an institution that has greater on-site medical capabilities than typical Bureau institutions is classified as Care Level 3. As of March 2017, fewer than 20 Bureau institutions were classified as Medical Care Level 3.

Federal inmates designated as Care Level 3 have chronic conditions and are fragile outpatients who require frequent clinical contact and treatment. Care Level 3 inmates may require assistance with what the Bureau refers to as "activities of daily living" (bathing, dressing, etc.). Federal inmates suffering from advanced HIV, congestive heart failure and cancer in remission less than a year may be designated Care Level 3. As of February 2019, about 2 percent of the Bureau's population was designated as Medical Care Level 3.

Medical Care Level 4

The Bureau classifies seven institutions as Medical Care Level 4. All of these prisons are Federal Medical Centers, which provide enhanced medical services, including inpatient care. FMC Butner, North Carolina, is affiliated with Duke's medical school and provides advanced oncology services. FMC Devens, Massachusetts, provides dialysis services to the federal prison population. FMC Rochester, Minnesota, is affiliated with the Mayo Clinic and provides complex, inpatient medical care. FMC Carswell, Texas, is the Bureau's female-only Care Level 4 facility. FMC Lexington, Kentucky, provides complex medical services to lower -federal prisoners. MCFP Springfield, Missouri, provides Care Level 4 services to higher-security level inmates. FMC Fort Worth, Texas, is the Bureau's newest Care Level 4 facility, officially designated an FMC in December 2016.

Care Level 4 inmates are severely impaired and may require daily nursing care. Such inmates may be suffering from cancer (in active treatment), quadriplegia, may require dialysis, or may be undergoing or recovering from major surgery. Less than one percent of the Bureau's population is designated Medical Care Level 4.

Mental Health Care Levels

In recent years, the Bureau of Prisons has operationalized a Mental Health Care Level system. This system augments the Medical Care Level system. Similar to Medical Care Levels, each federal institution is assigned one of four Mental Health Care Levels. The Bureau also designates every inmate with a Mental Health Care Level and attempts to house inmates in corresponding institutions according to their designation.

Mental Health Care Level I

Federal prisons classified as Mental Health Care Level 1 are also classified as Medical Care Level 1. As such, an institution with this designation has no specialized services available to inmates with mental health care needs. As of February 2013, 17 Bureau institutions were classified as Mental Health Care Level 1.

Only inmates who show no significant level of functional impairment associated with mental illness will be designated Mental Health Care Level 1. An inmate with a history of serious functional impairment due to mental illness will only be designated at this level if the inmate consistently demonstrates appropriate help-seeking behavior in response to the reemergence of symptoms. If an inmate demonstrates the need for regular mental health interventions, he or she will not be designated Mental Health Care Level 1. As of February 2019, 96 percent of the federal prison population was designated Mental Health Care Level 1.

Mental Health Care Level 2

A Bureau institution classified as Mental Health Care Level 2 has a fully-staffed Psychology Services department. Such institutions also utilize dedicated Care Coordination and Reentry (CCARE) Teams. According to the Bureau, an institutional CCARE Team "identifies potential concerns affecting inmates with mental illness in a correctional environment" and develops "strategies and supports to mitigate potentially negative interactions between inmates with mental illness and the correctional environment." As of February 2013, there were 61 Bureau institutions classified as Mental Health Care Level 2.

Inmates assigned Mental Health Care Level 2 require moderate levels of intervention. Such inmates have a mental illness requiring routine outpatient mental health care on an ongoing basis. Mental Health Care Level 2 inmates may also require brief, crisis-oriented mental health care of significant intensity. This type of periodic crisis care is generally limited to placement on suicide watch. As of February 2019, about 4 percent of the Bureau's population was designated Mental Health Care Level 2.

Mental Health Care Level 3

The Mental Health Care Level 3 classification is different in that the Bureau does not classify entire institutions with this level. Rather, specific programs and psychologists are designated to provide this level of mental health care. However, if an institution provides such programs and psychologists, it is for all intents and purposes a Mental Health Care Level 3 facility. Mental Health Care Level 3 institutions also use CCARE Teams and are able to provide at least weekly interventions and more intensive outpatient care. As of 2013, 19 federal prisons were classified as Mental Health Care Level 3.

Inmates assigned Mental Health Care Level 3 require significant mental health interventions but not inpatient treatment. An inmate may also be designated as Mental Health Care Level 3 if he or she requires care in a residential treatment program, such as the STAGES program. As of February 2019, less than one percent of the Bureau's population was designated Mental Health Care Level 3.

Mental Health Care Level 4

Federal prisons classified as Mental Health Care Level 4 are also classified as Medical Care Level 4, meaning that all Mental Health Care Level 4 prisons are Federal Medical Centers. Mental Health Care Level 4 institutions are essentially inpatient psychiatric hospitals that provide a broad range of services for the most severely mentally impaired inmates. As of February 2013, five federal prisons were classified as Mental Health Care Level 4.

Inmates assigned Mental Health Care Level 4 have acute needs that require intense, inpatient care. Such inmates are gravely disabled and cannot function in general population in a Mental Health Care Level 3 institution. Very few inmates in the Bureau's custody are assigned Mental Health Care Level 4.

CHAPTER 3

Federal Inmate Classification, Designation and Transfer

Introduction

The Federal Bureau of Prisons utilizes a data-driven classification system designed to ensure that each federal inmate is placed in an institution commensurate with his or her security and program needs. The system is defined and illustrated in Program Statement P5100.08, Inmate Security Designation and Custody Classification (9/12/2006). Initial classification, designation and transfers are covered in PS P5100.08.

The initial classification and designation of all new and returning federal inmates is processed by the Designation and Sentence Computation Center (DSCC), located in Grand Prairie, Texas. Once in the system, an inmate's Unit Team may update his or her security and custody classification levels, but all redesignations and institutional transfers go through the DSCC.

The Bureau analyzes a variety of data in order to calculate an inmate's security point total and make a designation decision. Some of the data considered is subject to interpretation by DSCC officials and institutional case managers. As such, it is important that every incoming and long-term federal inmate understand what the Bureau considers when making security level and designation decisions.

DSCC Action: Security Points, Classification and Designation Using Form BP-337

When a federal criminal defendant is found guilty and sentenced to serve a prison term, court officers upload documents to the Bureau's eDesignate system. The most important documents are the judgment and commitment (J&C) order, and the Presentence Report (PSR). Other relevant documents may make their way onto the eDesignate system as well.

Using these documents, DSCC team members calculate an inmate's security point total, consider Public Safety Factors and Management Variables, and classify the inmate's security level as minimum, low, medium or high. A dedicated team of DSCC officials (the "Hotel Team") then designate the inmate to a particular facility.

Program Statement P5100.08 identifies the nine categories of information used by Bureau officials to classify and designate an inmate. The information is entered into Form BP-337, Inmate Load and Security Designation, which can be found in PS P5100.08, and which is reproduced at the end of this chapter. After all of the data required by Form BP-337 is entered, a software tool assigns a numerical security point value to each inmate. The scale is zero to forty-five; 0-11 equates to minimum security, 12-15 is low security, 16-23 is medium, and 24+ indicates that an inmate is classified as high security.

The first category is unusual in that it is the only category that allows for the deduction of security points. If the inmate had the option to voluntarily surrender to an institution, and did so, three security points are deducted. If no such option was available or the inmate did not self-surrender, nothing is deducted, but no points are added, either.

The second category assigns points based on the severity of the inmate's current offense. Points assessed in this category range from zero to seven. It is important to note that when determining the severity of the instant offense, the Bureau does not limit itself to the offense of *conviction*. Severity points are assessed based on *the most severe documented instant offense behavior* -- regardless of the conviction offense. This means that Bureau officials will consider what is in an inmate's PSR when determining and scoring the severity of the offense. The severity of the current offense is scored using the Offense Severity Scale, which is reproduced at the end of this chapter.

The third category scores points based on the inmate's criminal history. This information is lifted directly from the PSR or J&C and is based entirely on the United States Sentencing Guidelines (USSG) criminal history point total, as found by a judge at sentencing. A USSG criminal history point total between 0 and 1 nets zero security points; 2-3 results in the addition of two security points; 4-6 equates to four points; 7-9 gets an inmate six security points; 10-12 results in eight security points; and 13+ USSG criminal history points equates to 10 security points.

The fourth category scores points for the inmate's prior history of violence. Zero to seven points are assessed, depending on the seriousness and recency of the violent behavior. Minor violence is defined as "[a]ggressive or intimidating behavior which is not likely to cause serious bodily harm or death," while serious violence is defined as the same behavior, except that it was likely to cause serious bodily harm or death. Note that only behavior that resulted in a documented finding of guilt will be considered a prior act of violence. However, if such a finding was made, the severity of the violence is determined by the offense behavior, not necessarily the specific offense of guilt. The inmate's prior history of violence is scored using the History of Violence Scale, which is reproduced at the end of this chapter.

The fifth category assigns points for any history of escape or attempted escape. Zero to three points are assessed based on the seriousness and recency of the escape or attempted escape. A minor history of escape is defined as "[a]n escape from an open institution or program (e.g., minimum-security facility, Community Correction Center, furlough) not involving any actual or threat of violence." This includes violation of the Bail Reform Act and flight to avoid prosecution. A serious history of escape is defined as "[a]n escape from secure custody with or without threat of violence" and includes escape from an open facility that did include actual threat of violence. Only instances which involved documented findings of guilt will be counted. The inmate's history of escape or attempted escape is scored using the History of Escape or Attempts Scale, which is reproduced at the end of this chapter.

The sixth category contemplates the addition of zero to seven security points for outstanding detainers, charges or warrants. The number of points scored depends on the severity of the offense behavior associated with the detainer. The Bureau uses the Offense Severity Scale (reproduced at the end of this chapter) to determine severity; low severity detainers result in one security point, moderate severity detainers equate to three points, high severity detainers net five points, and greatest severity detainers, charges or warrants result in seven additional security points. Note that the Bureau takes a liberal approach to scoring points for a detainer on Form BP-337. Program Statement P5100.08 instructs staff members that "[i]f law enforcement officials indicate a firm intent to lodge a detainer, consider it lodged."

The seventh category scores between zero and eight security points depending on the inmate's age. The Bureau has determined that younger offenders require greater security, and as such, assigns those aged 24 or less eight points. An inmate between the ages of 25 and 35 is given four points; an inmate aged 36 through 54 gets two points. Those inmates aged 55 or over are assessed zero additional age-related security points.

A lack of documented education results in the assignment of security points pursuant to the eighth category. Inmates who have earned their GED or high school diploma are not given any points. Those who are enrolled in and are making satisfactory progress toward the procurement of a GED or high school diploma are scored one point. An inmate who does not have a GED or high school diploma, and who is not in a program to earn one, is assigned two security points.

The final category assigns security points when an inmate has a history of drug or alcohol abuse. Any conviction or finding of guilt for an offense related to drug or alcohol use within the previous five years results in one scored security point. Such offenses include DUI and positive drug tests. Note that the Bureau will also score this point based on an inmate's self-report of drug or alcohol abuse within the previous five years. Drug or alcohol abuse that took place more than five years prior to the inmate's classification is not scored.

Once an inmate's security point total is calculated, Bureau officials will consider two additional factors that override the security level classification indicated by security points: Public Safety Factors and Management Variables.

Public Safety Factors

According to the Bureau, a Public Safety Factor (PSF) is based on "relevant factual information regarding the inmate's current offense, sentence, criminal history or institutional behavior that requires additional security measures be employed to ensure the safety and protection of the public." Public Safety Factors are considered and applied by DSCC staff during an initial designation, and by institutional staff when completing the Custody and Classification Form (see below for more information concerning Form BP-338, Custody and Classification). Public Safety Factors may be waived, but only by the DSCC Administrator. There are currently 11 Public Safety Factors.

A male inmate who is a validated member of a *Disruptive Group* is assigned PSF Code B. Application of this PSF requires housing the inmate in a high-security institution, regardless of his security score. When this PSF is applied during an inmate's initial designation, the facility to which the inmate is designated must take steps to validate the inmate's membership in the disruptive group.

A male inmate whose current offense falls into the *Greatest Severity Offense* range on the Offense Severity Scale (reproduced at the end of this chapter) is assigned PSF Code C. Application of this PSF requires that the inmate be housed in at least a low-security facility.

A male or female inmate whose current offense or prior history indicates that he or she is a *Sex Offender* is assigned PSF Code F. A conviction is not required for the application of this PSF. The Bureau requires only documentation of any history of sexual assault, sexual abuse of a child, possession of child pornography, or any sexual act or contact that a Bureau official determines was "aggressive or abusive in nature" to apply this PSF. Application of the Sex Offender PSF requires that the inmate be housed in at least a low-security institution.

Any male or female inmate with a Bureau Central Inmate Monitoring (CIM) designation of *Threat to Government Official* is assigned PSF Code G. Only inmates who "have made threats to government officials or who have been identified, in writing, by the United States Secret Service as requiring special surveillance" are designated with this CIM status. Program Statement 5180.05, Central Inmate Monitoring System. Application of the Threat to Government Official PSF requires that the inmate be housed in at least a low-security institution.

A male or female inmate who is a *Deportable Alien* will be assigned PSF Code H. However, if immigration officials determine that the deportable alien inmate will not be subject to deportation proceedings upon release from custody, or if such proceedings have been held and the inmate found not deportable, the PSF should not be applied. Application of the Deportable Alien PSF requires that the inmate be housed in at least a low-security institution.

A male inmate with more than ten years remaining to serve is assigned PSF Code I, *Sentence Length*. A male inmate with between ten and 20 years remaining will be housed in at least a low-security prison. A male inmate with between 20 and 30 years left will be housed in at least a medium-security institution. Those male inmates with 30 or more years remaining to serve must be housed in a high-security institution. The Sentence Length PSF can be waived or over-ridden by a Management Variable.

A female inmate with a recent history of *Violent Behavior* is assigned PSF Code K. This PSF is only assigned to a female inmate whose current incarceration or history involves at least two convictions (including institutional violence convictions) for serious incidents of violence within the previous five years. A female inmate assigned the Violent Behavior PSF will be housed in at least a low-security institution.

A male or female inmate with a history of *Serious Escape* is assigned PSF Code L. A male inmate will be assigned this PSF if he has escaped from a secure facility at any time, with or without the threat of violence, or if he has escaped from an open institution at any time, with the threat of violence. A male inmate with this PSF must be housed in at least a medium-security facility. A female inmate is only assigned the Serious Escape PSF if she has been "involved in a serious escape" within the last ten years. Female inmates assigned this PSF will be housed at FMC Carswell, the administrative prison used to house female inmates who present special management concerns.

A male or female inmate who was involved in a *Prison Disturbance* is assigned PSF Code M. This PSF is only assigned to an inmate who engaged in, encouraged or acted in furtherance of a riot, and only when the inmate did so during an actual riot (also known as an "institution disruption"). A male inmate assigned a Prison Disturbance PSF will be housed in at least a high-security institution. A female inmate assigned PSF Code M must be housed at FMC Carswell.

A male or female inmate who is currently a juvenile, and has a history of *Juvenile Violence* is assigned PSF Code N. Any single instance of violent behavior will suffice, as long as it resulted in a conviction, delinquency adjudication or finding of guilt. Violent behavior is defined as "aggressive behavior causing serious bodily harm or death or aggressive or intimidating behavior likely to cause serious bodily harm or death (e.g., aggravated assault, intimidation involving a weapon, or arson)." A juvenile inmate assigned this PSF will be housed in at least a low-security institution.

A male or female inmate with a history of *Serious Telephone Abuse* is assigned PSF Code O. Such abuse consists of utilizing the telephone, whether in prison or out, to further criminal activities or to promote illicit organizations, if the inmate meets certain criteria. Such criteria includes documentation that the inmate is or was a leader or organizer, utilized the telephone to communicate threats of death or bodily injury, utilized the telephone to engage in significant fraud while housed in a prison, or used the telephone to arrange for the introduction of alcohol or drugs into an institution while confined in an institution. This PSF may also be applied when an inmate was found guilty of a 100 or 200 series offense for telephone abuse. Application of the Serious Telephone Abuse PSF results in an inmate being housed in at least a low-security facility.

Management Variables

A Management Variable is used when a Bureau administrator, often an institutional case manager, determines that an inmate should be housed at an institution with a security level that is inconsistent with the inmate's scored security level. While case managers often determine the need for a Management Variable, only the DSCC Administrator may actually apply one. The need for certain Management Variables will be clear to DSCC staffers during an inmate's initial classification and designation. In many cases, however, a Management Variable will only become necessary during the inmate's incarceration, in which case the Variable will be entered on Form BP-338. There are currently 11 Management Variables.

A *Judicial Recommendation* of a specific program or institution may result in the application of Management Variable Code B. While the Bureau is statutorily required to *consider* a judicial recommendation (see 18 U.S.C. § 3621(b)), there is no legal requirement that the Bureau *comply* with any such recommendation. As such, if a sentencing court recommends an institution with lesser security than the Bureau deems the inmate to require, the Judicial Recommendation

Management Variable will generally not be applied. When the Judicial Recommendation Management Variable is applied, it does not have an expiration timeframe.

Designation of an inmate to an institution that is reasonably close to the inmate's *Release Residence* may require the application of Management Variable Code D. The Bureau considers placement in an institution that is within 500 miles of an inmate's release residence "reasonably close." Security level considerations tend to trump release residence proximity concerns until an inmate is close to the end of his or her sentence. Thus, this Management Variable is most often requested by institutional case managers when an inmate is within 36 months of release. As of press time, Congress was considering the First Step Act, which may require that the Bureau house inmates within 500 miles of their release residence, and which could result in a significant increase in the use of this Management Variable. Once applied, the Release Residence Management Variable has no expiration.

Population Management concerns sometimes require the application of Management Variable Code E. Typically, this Management Variable is applied when institutions for which an inmate is qualified are all overcrowded, requiring that the inmate be designated to a higher-security facility. Sometimes the Population Management Variable is applied when gang or other security concerns restrict where an inmate may be housed. If this Management Variable is applied, it automatically expires after 18 months.

The need to keep an inmate separate from another inmate may require the application of Management Variable Code G, *Central Inmate Monitoring Assignment*. This Management Variable may be applied for any CIM-related reason, including the need to more closely supervise an inmate deemed a threat to government officials. A CIM Management Variable does not expire.

When an inmate presents special *Medical or Psychiatric* issues, Management Variable Code I may be applied. This assignment allows an inmate who ordinarily would not qualify for placement at a particular psychiatric or medical referral center to be housed at such a facility. This Management Variable is temporary, lasting no more than six months, and can only be assigned by the Central Office Medical Designator.

When an inmate requires designation at a particular facility for *Program Participation* reasons, Management Variable Code N is applied. This Management Variable is most often used when an inmate is participating in a program that is unique to one institution, and the inmate is reclassified to a different (almost always lower) security level. The Program Participation Management Variable expires after 18 months.

When a higher security Bureau institution does not have a satellite camp, institutional staff may request the application of the Code R *Work Cadre* Management Variable to certain inmates.

When this Management Variable is applied, an inmate who would otherwise be prohibited from such work will be authorized to work outside the perimeter of the institution. Work Cadre Management Variables do not expire.

When the DSCC Administrator has determined that an inmate's Public Safety Factor should be waived, Code S *PSF Waived* is entered as a Management Variable. Because a PSF overrides an inmate's scored security level, the application of this Management Variable requires that the DSCC Administrator determine and apply a new "Management Security Level" that is at least one level lower than the (waived) PSF level. The PSF Waived Management Variable does not expire.

Long-term alien detainees are given an initial custody and security level, but are never rescored at the institutional level using the BP-338, Custody and Classification Form. As such, transfers for positive or negative behavior require the application of Management Variable Code U, *Long-Term Detainee*. The Detention Services Branch of the Central Office Correctional Programs Division applies this Management Variable. Once applied, the Long-Term Detainee Management Variable does not expire.

When an inmate presents security concerns that are not reflected by the inmate's scored security level and custody classification, the Code V *Greater Security* Management Variable may be applied. Program Statement P5100.08 specifically refers to the use of this Management Variable when an inmate presents a greater security risk than their assigned level due to "pending charges, detainer, escape risk, etc." Because charges, detainers and escape risk are all already considered in the scoring of an inmate's security level, it is more likely that this Management Variable is used when an inmate's institutional behavior gives cause for concern. If the Greater Security Management Variable is applied, the DSCC Administrator must also apply a new (at least one level higher) Management Security Level. This Management Variable expires 24 months after application.

When an inmate presents *Lesser Security* concerns than those reflected by the scored security level, Management Variable Code W may be applied. This Management Variable allows institutional staff to adjust an inmate's security level downward when good institutional behavior is trumped by a more rigid and arbitrary security consideration, such as an inmate's age. When the Lesser Security Management Variable is applied, the DSCC Administrator must also apply a new (at least one level lower) Management Security Level. This Management Variable does not expire.

Institutional Action: Security Points and Custody Classification Using Form BP-338

The Bureau recognizes that an inmate's security and custody needs may change during a term of incarceration. Institutional staff use Form BP-338, Custody Classification, in order to assign and update an inmate's level of supervision according to his or her criminal history and institutional behavior/adjustments. A sample BP-338 is reproduced at the end of this chapter.

An inmate's case manager will complete Form BP-338 within seven months of the inmate's arrival at the institution, and will review and update the form every 12 months thereafter. The Custody Classification Form is also updated at any point when something that may change an inmate's overall security level has happened (e.g., incident reports, sentence changes, etc.).

The Custody and Classification Form is similar to the Inmate Load and Security Designation Form, BP-337. In fact, some of the nine BP-338 fields relating to an inmate's security level classification, which are identical to the nine BP-337 security point calculation fields, are populated with the data from Form BP-337. The BP-338 Criminal History Score field, for instance, uses the data from Form BP-337, because an inmate's Criminal History Score does not change during incarceration. However, much of what is used to score an inmate's base security level can change during incarceration, and requires institutional staff action.

The Custody Classification Form has three sections. Section A, Identifying Data, requires basic information about an inmate, but also includes fields for entry of Public Safety Factors and Management Variables. Section B, Base Scoring, requires information relating to the nine categories used on Form BP-337 to score an inmate's security point total. Section C, Custody Scoring, requires information relating to the inmate's institutional adjustment, and is unique to Form BP-338.

There are six categories in the Custody Scoring section of Form BP-338. Staff score each category and then apply a "custody variance" to the inmate's base security point total. The Custody Variance Table, which is included in Form BP-338, is designed to push well-behaved and adjusted inmates' security point total down, and less well-behaved and adjusted inmates' security point total up.

The first category that is measured in the Custody Scoring section of Form BP-338 is *Percentage of Time Served*. To determine the percentage, staff divide the number of months already served by the total number of months expected to be served. This calculation results in a percentage of time served. If the percentage totals 0-25 percent, three points are entered; 26-75 percent nets four points; 76-90 percent equates to five points; and 91+ percent results in six points. Note that in the custody scoring/variance context, the more points, the better.

The second category measured in the Custody Scoring section is *Program Participation*. Staff will enter between zero and two points depending on how the inmate is programming. "Good" inmate programming is defined as "active[] participat[ion] in multiple recommended programs," and results in two points. An inmate with "average" program participation, defined as "could be participating in multiple recommended programs but chooses to be involved in one at a time," is assigned one point. "Poor" program participation nets zero points.

An inmate's *Living Skills* are measured and scored in the third category of the Custody Scoring section. Zero to two points are awarded, based largely on staff's subjective evaluation of an inmate's "demeanor, attitude, personal accountability and nature of interactions with staff and other inmates." Sanitation and personal hygiene issues are also addressed in this category. Note that inmates who refuse to participate in the Financial Responsibility Program or required Reentry Preparation Programs automatically receive zero points for this and the Program Participation category.

The fourth category awards points based on an inmate's *Type and Number of Most Serious Incident Reports*. Between zero and five points are scored, depending on the severity of any incident reports and the amount of incident reports received in the previous ten years. Any greatest severity (100 series) incident report in the previous ten years results in zero points.

The fifth category scores points based on the *Frequency of Incident Reports*. An inmate with 6+ incident reports in the past year receives zero points. Between 2 and 5 incident reports in the past year nets an inmate one custody point. One incident report in the past year equates to two points, and zero incident reports result in three points.

The final category measured in the Custody Scoring section of Form BP-338 is *Family/ Community Ties*. Either three or four points are awarded, depending on "the inmate's efforts to build, maintain and strengthen family/community ties." An inmate who demonstrates no initiative to further or enhance relationships with supportive family is scored as "none or minimal," which nets three points. All others are scored as "average or good," and receive four points.

Once points for all six Custody Scoring categories are entered and totaled, staff adjust the inmate's security point total using the Custody Variance Table, which is included in Form BP-338. A lower custody score results in points being *added* to the security point total. A higher Custody Score results in points being *subtracted* from the security point total. The updated security point total is then used to determine the inmate's security level, which may now be different (higher or lower) than it was prior to completion of the Custody Classification Form. Note that the security point scale remains the same: 0-11 = minimum security, 12-15 = low security, 16-23 = medium security, and 24+ = high security.

In addition to altering an inmate's security point total, the Custody Variance Score may change the inmate's Custody Level. The Bureau classifies each inmate's Custody Level as Maximum, In, Out or Community. An inmate assigned Maximum Custody will be housed at a high-security institution, regardless of his security point total. An inmate classified as In Custody may be housed at a low, medium- or high-security prison, depending on his security point total, and is only eligible for work details inside the institution's perimeter. An inmate assigned Out Custody may be housed at a minimum-, low- or medium-security facility, depending on his security point total, but is eligible to participate in work details that go outside the fence. Those inmates designated Community Custody will only be housed in minimum-security camps or Community Corrections Centers.

If the Custody Variance Score is negative (meaning that it resulted in a lower security point total), then staff will consider a Custody Level decrease. If the Custody Variance Score is zero, the Custody Level remains the same. If the Custody Variance Score is positive (meaning that the inmate's security point total went up), then staff will consider a Custody Level increase. Any change in Custody Levels, up or down, will normally be a change of only one level.

Inmate Transfers

The Bureau routinely transfers inmates from one institution to another. While transfer decisions generally originate at the institution level, most transfer requests are processed and approved by the DSCC. According to the Bureau, each type of transfer has a specific objective. There are many reasons for a transfer, eight of which are outlined here.

The first and most common type of transfer is the *Institutional Classification Transfer*. When an inmate's security level changes as a result of an update to his or her Custody Classification Form, transfer is usually requested. For example, an inmate housed at a medium-security institution whose security points fall below 16 and whose time remaining is less than 20 years will ordinarily be transferred to a low-security facility. An Institutional Classification Transfer may also be requested based on a change to an inmate's Custody Level. For example, a medium-security inmate whose Custody Level is increased from In to Maximum will ordinarily be transferred to a high-security facility, since medium-security facilities cannot house Maximum Custody Level inmates.

Because the Bureau attempts to house inmates within 500 miles of their release residence, *Nearer Release Transfers* are sometimes necessary. Such transfers are only considered after an inmate has served 18 consecutive months of clear conduct time at an institution, and will only be to an institution consistent with the inmate's security level. Inmates subject to deportation do not qualify for Nearer Release Transfers.

An act of documented institution misconduct may result in a *Disciplinary/Close Supervision Transfer*. Normally, such transfers require the application of a Management Variable, because the transfer will invariably be to a higher-security institution. Institution staff are directed to apply "sound correctional judgment" before requesting such a transfer. A Close Supervision Transfer is normally associated with a Special Investigation Services (SIS) investigation.

Transfers for the purpose of placing an inmate in a new setting due to poor institutional adjustment or CIM concerns is accomplished through an *Adjustment Transfer*. This kind of transfer differs from a Close Supervision Transfer in that it accommodates CIM verified protection transfers.

Medical and Psychiatric Transfers are relatively common. These transfers are processed and approved by the Central Office Medical Designator, Office of Medical Designations and Transportation. Medical and Psychiatric Transfers are classified as Emergency, Routine/Urgent or Routine. Emergency Transfers involve the immediate transfer of an inmate to a medical referral center. Routine/Urgent Transfers require direct transfer to a medical referral center within two to three weeks of designation, and do not allow holdover at other Bureau institutions or county jails. Routine Medical and Psychiatric Transfers use the normal Bureau transportation apparatus and can take anywhere from a few weeks to several months.

Temporary Transfers are often used to move inmates subject to disciplinary sanctions from an institution without a Special Housing Unit (SHU) to one with a SHU. These transfers are usually between institutions in close proximity to one another.

The Bureau regularly *Transfers for Training Purposes or Program Participation*. This type of transfer is used when an inmate will participate in a national program, such as the Residential Drug Abuse Program (RDAP) or a sex offender treatment program, but the program is not available at the inmate's institution. When the inmate completes the program, he or she is transferred back to the sending institution, unless the inmate is very near release.

Transfers to Satellite Camps are used when higher-security inmates become eligible for camp placement, and the local Warden determines that the inmate should be housed at the satellite camp. This kind of transfer is also used in the other direction, when an inmate at a satellite camp is temporarily transferred to the higher-security institution for disciplinary purposes.

Inmates transferring from one Bureau institution to another should prepare themselves for a long and arduous journey. Other than the very few Minimum Security Level and Out Custody Level inmates, federal prisoners are treated as if they are Pablo Escobar during transfer. Inmates should expect belly chains, handcuffs and ankle restraints during any movement. Federal Transfer Centers are spartan, but fairly comfortable. The variety of local jails and detention centers that transferring inmates often find themselves in, however, are not.

Chapter Appendix A:
Inmate Load and Security Designation (Form BP-337)

BP-A0337
JUNE 10

INMATE LOAD AND SECURITY DESIGNATION CDFRM

U.S. DEPARTMENT OF JUSTICE   **FEDERAL BUREAU OF PRISONS**

INMATE LOAD DATA				
1. REGISTER NUMBER:				
2. LAST NAME		3. FIRST NAME	4. MIDDLE	5. SUFFIX
6. RACE	7. SEX	8.ETHNIC ORIGIN	9. DATE OF BIRTH	
10. OFFENSE/SENTENCE				
11. FBI NUMBER			12. SSN NUMBER	
13. STATE OF BIRTH		14. OR COUNTRY OF BIRTH	15. CITIZENSHIP	
16. ADDRESS-STREET				
17. CITY		18. STATE	19. ZIP	20. OR FOREIGN COUNTRY
21. HEIGHT FT IN		22. WEIGHT LBS	23. HAIR COLOR	24. EYE COLOR
25. ARS ASSIGNMENT:				

SECURITY DESIGNATION DATA			
1. JUDGE	2. REC FACILITY	3. REC PROGRAM	4. USM OFFICE

5. VOLUNTARY SURRENDER STATUS 0 = NO (-3) = YES	
IF YES, MUST INDICATE: 5a. VOLUNTARY SURRENDER DATE:	
5b. VOLUNTARY SURRENDER LOCATION:	
6. MONTHS TO RELEASE :	
7. SEVERITY OF 0 = LOWEST 3 = MODERATE 7 = GREATEST CURRENT OFFENSE 1 = LOW MODERATE 5 = HIGH	
8. CRIMINAL HISTORY 0 = 0-1 4 = 4-6 8 = 10-12 SCORE 2 = 2-3 6 = 7-9 10= 13 +	
8a. SOURCE OF DOCUMENTED - PRESENTENCE INVESTIGATION REPORT or - NCIC III	

9. HISTORY OF		NONE	>15 YEARS	10-15 YEARS	5-10 YEARS	<5 YEARS	
VIOLENCE	MINOR	0	1	1	3	5	
	SERIOUS	0	2	4	6	7	

10. HISTORY OF		NONE	>15 YEARS	>10 YEARS	5-10 YEARS	<5 YEARS	
ESCAPE OR	MINOR	0	1	1	2	3	
ATTEMPTS	SERIOUS	0	3(S)	3(S)	3(S)	3(S)	

11. TYPE OF 0 = NONE 3 = MODERATE 7 = GREATEST DETAINER 1 = LOWEST/LOW MODERATE 5 = HIGH	
12. AGE 0 = 55 and over 4 = 25 through 35 2 = 36 through 54 8 = 24 or less	
13. EDUCATION 0 = Verified High School Degree or GED LEVEL 1 = Enrolled in and making satisfactory progress in GED Program 2 = No verified High School Degree/GED and not participating in GED Program	
13.a HIGHEST GRADE COMPLETED	
14. DRUG/ALCOHOL ABUSE 0 = NEVER/>5 Years 1 = <5 Years	
15. SECURITY POINT TOTAL	0

16. PUBLIC   A-NONE   I-SENTENCE LENGTH (males only)
SAFETY   B-DISRUPTIVE GROUP (males only)   K-VIOLENT BEHAVIOR (females only)
FACTORS   C-GREATEST SEVERITY OFFENSE (males only)   L-SERIOUS ESCAPE
          F-SEX OFFENDER   M-PRISON DISTURBANCE
          G-THREAT TO GOVERNMENT OFFICIALS   N-JUVENILE VIOLENCE
          H-DEPORTABLE ALIEN O-SERIOUS TELEPHONE ABUSE	

17. REMARKS	
18. OMDT REFERRAL (YES/NO)	

FILE IN SECTION 2 UNLESS APPROPRIATE FOR PRIVACY FOLDER

SECTION 2

PDF   Prescribed by P5100   Replaces BP-S337 of FEB 02

Chapter Appendix B:
Offense Severity Scale

P5100.08
9/12/2006
Appendix A, Page 1

```
OFFENSE SEVERITY SCALE
```

GREATEST SEVERITY

Aircraft Piracy - placing plane or passengers in danger
Arson - substantial risk of death or bodily injury
Assault - serious bodily injury intended or permanent or
    life threatening bodily injury resulting)
Car Jacking - any
Drug Offense - see criteria below*
Escape - closed institution, secure custody, force or
    weapons used
Espionage - treason, sabotage, or related offenses
Explosives - risk of death or bodily injury
Extortion - weapon or threat of violence
Homicide or Voluntary Manslaughter - any
Kidnaping - abduction, unlawful restraint, demanding or
    receiving ransom money
Robbery - any
Sexual offenses - rape, sodomy, incest, carnal knowledge,
    transportation with coercion or force for commercial
    purposes
Toxic Substances/Chemicals: - weapon to endanger human life
Weapons - distribution of automatic weapons, exporting
    sophisticated weaponry, brandishing or threatening use of
    a weapon

* Any **drug offender** whose current offense includes the following
criteria will be scored in the Greatest severity category:

The offender was part of an organizational network and he or she
organized or maintained ownership interest/profits from **large-scale** drug
activity,

AND

The drug amount equals or exceeds the amount below:

Cocaine - greater than or equal to 10,000 gm, 10 K, or 22 lb
Cocaine Base "Crack" - greater than or equal to 31 gm
Hashish - greater than or equal to 250,000 gm, 250 K, or 551 lb
Marijuana - greater than or equal to 620,000 gm, 620 K, or 1,367 lb
PCP - greater than or equal to 100,000 mg, 100 gm, or 20,000 dosage units
Heroin or Opiates - greater than or equal to 2,000 gm, 2 K, or 4.4 lb
Methamphetamine - greater than or equal to 16,000 gm, 17 K, or 35 lbs
Other illicit drugs: - Amphetamine, Barbiturates, LSD, etc. greater than
or equal to 250,000 dosage units

P5100.08
9/12/2006
Appendix A, Page 2

HIGH SEVERITY

Arson - other
Cruelty to Children - any
Drugs (For Females only)
    Cocaine - greater than or equal to 10,000 gm, 10 K,
    Or 22 lb
    Cocaine Base "Crack" - greater than or equal to 31 gm
    Hashish - greater than or equal to 250,000 gm, 250 K,
    Or 551 lb
    Marijuana - greater than or equal to 620,000 gm, 620 K,
    Or 1,367 lb
    PCP - greater than or equal to 100,000 mg, 100 gm, or
    20,000 dosage units
    Heroin or Opiates - greater than or equal to 2,000 gm,
    2 K, or 4.4 lb
    Methamphetamine - greater than or equal to 16,000 gm,
    17 K, or 35 lb
    Other illicit drugs - Amphetamine, Barbiturates, LSD
    etc. - greater than or equal to 250,000 dosage units
Explosives - other
Extortion - other
Involuntary manslaughter - includes vehicular homicide
Residential Burglary - with evidence that occupants were in
    dwelling during the commission of the offense
Rioting - any
Sexual Offenses - sexual exploitation of children, unlawful
    sexual conduct with a minor, pornography
Stalking - any
Threatening Communications - with conduct evidencing intent to
    carry out such threat
Toxic Substances/Chemicals - other

P5100.08
9/12/2006
Appendix A, Page 3

MODERATE SEVERITY

Assault - other

Auto Theft - any

Breaking and Entering - any

Burglary - other

Child Abandonment - any

Contempt of Court - criminal contempt

Drugs Cocaine - greater than or equal to 400 gm, .4 K, or .88 lb

    Cocaine Base "Crack" - greater than or equal to 1 gm

    Hashish - greater than or equal to 11,000 gm, 11 K, or 24 lb

    Marijuana - greater than or equal to 25,000 gm, 25 K, or 55 lb

    PCP - greater than or equal to 4,000 mg, 4 gm, or .14 oz

    Heroin or Opiates - greater than or equal to 80 gm, .08 K, or .18 lb

    Methamphetamine - greater than or equal to 667 gm, .67 K, or 1.47 lb

    Other illicit drugs - Amphetamine, Barbiturates, LSD, etc. greater than or equal to 10,000 dosage units, .05 K, or .11 lb

Escape - walkaway from open institution, failure to appear/bail reform act, no threat of violence involved

Immigration Offenses - transportation of unlawful aliens

Obstruction of Justice - any

Property Offenses - over $250,000, includes theft, fraud, tax evasion, forgery, currency offenses

Sexual Offenses - other

Weapons - other

LOW-MODERATE SEVERITY

Bigamy - Polygamy

Drugs Cocaine - less than 400 gm, .4 K, or .88 lb

    Cocaine Base "Crack" - less than 1 gm

    Hashish - less than 11,000 gm, 11 K, or 24 lb

    Marijuana - less than 25,000 gm, 25 K, or 55 lb

    PCP - less than 4,000 mg, 4 gm, or .14 oz

    Heroin or Opiates - less than 80 gm, .08 K, or .18 lb

    Methamphetamine - less than 667 gm, .67 K, or 1.47 lb

    Other illicit drugs - Amphetamine, Barbiturates, LSD, etc., less than 10,000 dosage units, .05 K, or .11 lb

Indecent Exposure - indecent acts, lewd behavior

Immigration Offenses - other

Post-Release Supervision Violation - technical, administrative

Property Offenses - valued between $2,000 and $250,000)

P5100.08
9/12/2006
Appendix A, Page 4

LOWEST SEVERITY
Drugs – personal use **Gambling Law Violation** – any **Liquor Law Violation** – any **Property Offenses** – less than $2,000 **Suspicion** – any **Traffic Laws** – any **Vagrancy** – any **Vandalism** – any

MARIJUANA EQUIVALENT CHART	
DRUG	MARIJUANA EQUIVALENT
1 gm of Heroin	1000 gm
1 gm of Cocaine Powder	200 gm
1 gm of Methamphetamine	2000 gm
1 gm of LSD	100,000 gm
1 gm of "crack" cocaine	20,000 gm
1 gm of Hashish Oil	50 gm
For other drug equivalents, please refer to the U.S. Sentencing Commission Guidelines Manual.	

MEASUREMENT CONVERSION TABLE	
1 oz = 28.35 gm 1 lb = 453.6 gm 1 lb = 0.4536 kg 1 gal = 3.785 liters 1 qt = 0.946 liters	1 gm = 1 ml (liquid) 1 liter = 1,000 ml 1 kg = 1,000 gm 1 gm = 1,000 mg 1 grain = 64.8 mg

Chapter Appendix C:
History of Violence Scale

6. HISTORY OF		NONE	>15 YEARS	10-15 YEARS	5-10 YEARS	<5 YEARS	
VIOLENCE	MINOR	0	1	1	3	5	
	SERIOUS	0	2	4	6	7	

Chapter Appendix D:
History of Escape or Attempts Scale

5. HISTORY OF ESCAPE		NONE	>15 YEARS	10-15 YEARS	5-10 YEARS	<5 YEARS	
OR ATTEMPTS	MINOR	0	1	1	2	3	
	SERIOUS	0	3(S)	3(S)	3(S)	3(S)	

Chapter Appendix E:
Custody Classification (Form BP-338)

BP-A0338   **CUSTODY CLASSIFICATION** CDFRM
JUNE 10
U.S. DEPARTMENT OF JUSTICE   **FEDERAL BUREAU OF PRISONS**

A. IDENTIFYING DATA

1. INSTITUTION CODE	2. UNIT	3. DATE

4. NAME	5. REGISTER NUMBER

6. MANAGEMENT VARIABLES			
A - NONE	G - CIMS	S - PSF WAIVED	
B - JUDICIAL RECOMMENDATION	I - MED/PSYCH TREATMENT	U - LONG TERM DETAINEE	
D - RELEASE RESIDENCE/PLANNING	N - PROGRAM PARTICIPATION	V - GREATER SECURITY	
E - POPULATION MANAGEMENT	M - WORK CADRE	W - LESSER SECURITY	

7. PUBLIC SAFETY FACTORS		
A - NONE	I - SENTENCE LENGTH (males only)	
B - DISRUPTIVE GROUP (males only)	K - VIOLENT BEHAVIOR (females only)	
C - GREATEST SEVERITY OFFENSE (males only)	L - SERIOUS ESCAPE	
F - SEX OFFENDER	M - PRISON DISTURBANCE	
G - THREAT TO GOVERNMENT OFFICIALS	N - JUVENILE VIOLENCE	
H - DEPORTABLE ALIEN	O - SERIOUS TELEPHONE ABUSE	

B. BASE SCORING

1. TYPE OF DETAINER	0 = NONE	3 = MODERATE	7 = GREATEST	
	1 = LOWEST/LOW MODERATE	5 = HIGH		

2. SEVERITY OF CURRENT OFFENSE	0 = LOWEST	3 = MODERATE	7 = GREATEST	
	1 = LOW MODERATE	5 = HIGH		

3. MONTHS TO RELEASE

4. CRIMINAL HISTORY SCORE	0 = 0-1	4 = 4-6	8 = 10-12	
	2 = 2-3	6 = 7-9	10 = 13 +	

5. HISTORY OF ESCAPE OR ATTEMPTS		NONE	>15 YEARS	10-15 YEARS	5-10 YEARS	<5 YEARS	
	MINOR	0	1	1	2	3	
	SERIOUS	0	3(S)	3(S)	3(S)	3(S)	

6. History of Violence		NONE	>15 YEARS	10-15 YEARS	5-10 YEARS	<5 YEARS	
	MINOR	0	1	1	3	5	
	SERIOUS	0	2	4	6	7	

7. VOLUNTARY SURRENDER STATUS	0 = NOT APPLICABLE	(-3) = VOLUNTARY SURRENDER	

8. AGE	0 = 55 and over	4 = 25 through 35	
	2 = 36 through 54	8 = 24 or less	

9. EDUCATION LEVEL	0 = Verified High School Degree/GED	
	1 = Enrolled in and making satisfactory progress in GED Program	
	2 = No verified High School Degree/GED & not participating in GED Program	

10. DRUG/ALCOHOL ABUSE	0 = Never/>5 Years	1 = <5 Years	

11. BASE SCORE (ADD § B. ITEMS 1 - 10)	0

C. CUSTODY SCORING

1. PERCENTAGE OF TIME SERVED	3 = 0-25%	5 = 76-90%	
	4 = 26-75%	6 = 91+%	

2. PROGRAM PARTICIPATION	0 = POOR	1 = AVERAGE	2 = GOOD	

3. LIVING SKILLS	0 = POOR	1 = AVERAGE	2 = GOOD	

4. TYPE & NUMBER OF MOST SERIOUS INCIDENT RPT	0 = ANY GREAT (100) IN PAST 10 YRS	3(A) = 1 MOD (300) IN PAST YR	
	1 = > 1 HIGH (200) IN PAST 2 YRS	3(B) = >1 LOW MOD (400) IN PAST YR	
	2(A) = 1 HIGH (200) IN PAST 2 YRS	4 = 1 LOW MOD (400) IN PAST YR	
	2(B) = > 1 MOD (300) IN PAST YR	5 = NONE	

5. FREQUENCY OF INCIDENT REPORTS (IN PAST YEAR)	0 = 6+	2 = ONE	
	1 = 2 THRU 5	3 = NONE	

6. FAMILY/COMMUNITY TIES	3 = NONE OR MINIMAL	4 = AVERAGE OR GOOD	

7. CUSTODY TOTAL (ADD § C. ITEMS 1 - 6)	0

8. CUSTODY VARIANCE (FROM APPROPRIATE TABLE ON TABLE ON BP-338, PAGE 2)	

9. SECURITY TOTAL (ADD OR SUBTRACT CUSTODY VARIANCE (§ C.8) TO BASE SCORE (§ B.11))	0

10. SCORED SECURITY LEVEL	11. MANAGEMENT SECURITY LEVEL

PDF   Prescribed by P5100   Replaces BP-S338.051 of FEB 02

D. INSTITUTION ACTION	
1. TYPE OF REVIEW: (EXCEPTION OR REGULAR)	
2. CURRENT CUSTODY: (MAXIMUM, IN, OUT, COMMUNITY)	
3. NEW CUSTODY: (MAXIMUM, IN OUT, COMMUNITY)	
4. ACTION: (APPROVE, DISAPPROVE)	
5. DATE OF NEXT REVIEW	

6.CHAIRPERSON

NAME AND SIGNATURE

7. EXCEPTION REVIEW

NAME(WARDEN OR DESIGNEE) AND SIGNATURE

8. SUMMARY OF FINAL ACTION	SECURITY LEVEL	
	CUSTODY	

CUSTODY CHANGE RECOMMENDATIONS BASED ON CUSTODY VARIANCE	
IF CUSTODY VARIANCE IS IN THE (+) RANGE	CONSIDER A CUSTODY INCREASE
IF CUSTODY VARIANCE IS IN THE (-) RANGE	CONSIDER A CUSTODY DECREASE
IF CUSTODY VARIANCE IS ZERO	CONTINUE PRESENT CUSTODY

MALE CUSTODY VARIANCE TABLE — CUSTODY

BASE SCORE		6	7	8	9	10	11	12	13	14	15	16	17	18	19	20	21	22
S C O R E	0-11	+4	4	+3	+3	+2	+1	+1	+1	0	0	-1	-1	-2	-3	-4	-5	-5
	12-15	+4	+4	+3	+3	+2	+1	+1	+1	0	0	0	-1	-2	-3	-4	-5	-5
	16-23	+8	+6	+5	+4	+4	+3	+2	+1	+1	0	0	0	-1	-1	-2	-2	-3
	24 +	+8	+6	+5	+4	+4	+3	+2	+1	+1	+1	0	0	0	-1	-1	-2	-3

FEMALE CUSTODY VARIANCE TABLE — CUSTODY

BASE SCORE		6	7	8	9	10	11	12	13	14	15	16	17	18	19	20	21	22
S C O R E	0-15	+15	+11	+7	+4	+3	+2	+1	+1	0	0	0	0	-2	-4	-8	-12	-16
	16-30	+15	+11	+7	+4	+3	+2	+1	+1	0	0	0	0	0	-4	-8	-12	-16
	31 +	+15	+11	+7	+4	+3	+2	+1	+1	0	0	0	0	0	0	-1	-5	-8

FILE IN SECTION 2 UNLESS APPROPRIATE FOR PRIVACY FOLDER

SECTION 2

PDF

Prescribed by P5100

Page 2 of 2
Replaces BP-S338.051 of FEB 02

PART TWO

Prison Profiles

This section presents profiles of every federal prison within the Bureau of Prisons.

The information in these profiles was obtained from both official and non-official sources. Official sources include Admission and Orientation handbooks for each facility, data obtained from the Department of Justice and BOP via Freedom of Information Act requests, a variety of documentation available at https://www.bop.gov, and a series of Government Accountability Office reports. A complete listing of all official sources relied upon in creating these profiles can be found in the bibliography of this book.

Unofficial sources were utilized to obtain much of each prison's cultural information. Many hundreds of federal inmates provided information to me through personal interviews and survey responses. These individuals, who have actually experienced life in these profiled prisons, have been kind enough to share with me details that only a prisoner would know.

Every effort has been made to verify the contents of these profiles, but a cautionary note is in order. Information relating to prison politics, levels of violence, and the status of vulnerable populations was, for the most part, obtained from prisoners. As such, all cultural information reflects the general opinion of inmates currently housed at each institution, and will not necessarily reflect the experience of every prisoner at a particular institution. The cultural status of each prison, including who can walk the yard and who cannot, is provided here for informational purposes only.

Most of what is provided in each profile is self-explanatory. However, some sections require background.

Prison Politics: "Politics" in the prison setting refers to the inmate-imposed social structure on a particular compound. The political situation at an institution is not a Bureau position, though how local staff deal with local inmates impacts prison politics. At highly political yards, inmates are only allowed to cell, eat and associate with members of their own race, geographic area or gang. These highly segregated groups check the paperwork of all new arrivals in order to confirm that the new inmate is not a sex offender or informant. Anyone who is not "clean" will be given the opportunity to "check-in" to protective custody, or will simply be attacked.

Cars: In prison, a car is a group of similar inmates who band together for safety or other reasons. Cars are often based on race or geography (e.g., the Aryan car or the Florida car). Cars are also organized by gangs. At federal prisons where cars are prevalent, new inmates will generally need to join one. This will usually require showing the car's "shot caller" (e.g., the CEO of the car) clean paperwork. Sometimes "independents" -- those who stand alone and are not part of a car -- are allowed at more political yards. Note that at lower-security institutions, cars may exist, but are usually not associated with violence.

Level of Violence: The level of violence at each institution is based entirely on the experience of prisoners who lived or live there. The Bureau of Prisons is not forthcoming with data related to violence at each institution.

Vulnerable Inmates: This information must be considered in the context from which it is derived -- inmates serving time at each institution. Regardless of what other inmates say, new arrivals at any institution should exercise care and diligence. The culture of a yard can (and does) shift from time to time, so anyone with cause for concern should proceed with caution. I believe, however, that the information provided correctly captures the culture of each profiled prison.

Quotes from Inmates: Anything appearing in quotation marks is a direct quote from an interviewee or survey respondent, unless otherwise indicated.

Chapter 4: Central Office

Chapter 5: Mid-Atlantic Region Prisons

Chapter 6: North Central Region Prisons

Chapter 7: Northeast Region Prisons

Chapter 8: South Central Region Prisons

Chapter 9: South East Region Prisons

Chapter 10: Western Region Prisons

Chapter 11: Private Contract Facilities

CHAPTER 4:

Central Office

Central Office

The Bureau of Prisons' Central Office oversees all BOP operations and regions. This is the headquarters for the federal prison system.

Acting Director: Hugh J. Hurwitz, Acting Director
BOP Population: 180,501

Facility Address & Contact Information

Central Office
Federal Bureau of Prisons
320 First Street, NW
Washington, DC 20534

Email: Info@bop.gov
Phone: 202-307-3198
Fax: n/a

BOP Website: https://www.bop.gov/locations/central_office/
Wikipedia: https://en.wikipedia.org/wiki/Federal_Bureau_of_Prisons
ZCG Website: https://prisonerresource.com/resources/federal-prison-profiles/federal-prison-central-office/

Staff Mail

Staff Name
Central Office
Federal Bureau of Prisons
320 First Street, NW
Washington, DC 20534

The Central Office serves as the headquarters for the Bureau of Prisons, which is overseen and managed by Director Hugh J. Hurwitz. Here, national programs are developed, and functional support is provided by the following divisions:

Administrative Division
Correctional Programs Division
Health Services Division
Human Resource Management Division
Federal Prison Industries
Information, Policy & Public Affairs Division
National Institute of Corrections
Office of General Counsel
Program Review Division
Reentry Services Division

The Central Office campus is located in Washington, DC near the U.S. Capitol, federal courts, and the Department of Justice headquarters. The Central Office oversees the operations of all six regional offices:

Mid-Atlantic Regional Office (MXR)
North Central Regional Office (NCR)
Northeast Regional Office (NER)
South Central Regional Office (SCR)
Southeast Regional Office (SER)
Western Regional Office (WXR)

CHAPTER 5:

Mid-Atlantic Region Prisons

═══════════════════════════════════════

Mid-Atlantic Regional Office

The Mid-Atlantic Regional Office is an administrative office providing oversight and support to facilities located in the Mid-Atlantic Region (MXR). The Mid-Atlantic Region covers Federal Bureau of Prison facilities located in Delaware, Kentucky, North Carolina, Maryland, Tennessee, West Virginia, and Virginia. These facilities are overseen by a regional office that provides oversight, technical assistance, and other types of operational support. In addition, they conduct training programs for staff in their region and assist state and local criminal justice agencies.

Regional Director: D.J. Harmon
MXR Population: 27,435

Facility Address & Contact Information

Mid-Atlantic Regional Office
Federal Bureau of Prisons
302 Sentinel Drive
Annapolis Junction, MD 20701

Email: MXRO/ExecAssistant@bop.gov
Phone: 301-317-3100
Fax: 301-317-3119

BOP Website: https://www.bop.gov/locations/regional_offices/mxro/
Wikipedia: n/a
ZCG Website: https://prisonerresource.com/resources/federal-prison-profiles/federal-prison-regional-offices/mid-atlantic-regional-office-mxr/

Staff Mail

Staff Name
Mid-Atlantic Regional Office
302 Sentinel Drive, Suite 200
Annapolis Junction, MD 20701

Freight and Non-USPS Parcels

Staff Name
Mid-Atlantic Regional Office
ATTN: Warehouse
302 Sentinel Drive, Suite 200
Annapolis Junction, MD 20701

Mid-Atlantic Region Prisons

FPC Alderson (WV)

FCI Ashland (KY)

FCI Beckley (WV)

USP Big Sandy (KY)

FCI Butner Low (NC)

FCI Butner Medium 1 (NC)

FCI Butner Medium 2 (NC)

FMC Butner (NC)

FCI Cumberland (MD)

FCI Gilmer (WV)

FCI Hazelton (WV)

FCI Hazelton Secure Female Facility (WV)

USP Hazelton (WV)

USP Lee (VA)

FMC Lexington (KY)

FCI Manchester (KY)

USP McCreary (KY)

FCI McDowell (WV)

FCI Memphis (TN)

FCI Morgantown (WV)

FCI Petersburg Low (VA)

FCI Petersburg Medium (VA)

FPC Alderson

Federal Prison Camp Alderson | FPC Alderson

Facility Address & Contact Information

Federal Prison Camp Alderson
Glen Ray Road, Box A
Alderson, WV 24910

Phone: 304-445-3300
Fax: 304-445-3320
Email: ALD/ExecAssistant@bop.gov

BOP Website: http://www.bop.gov/locations/institutions/ald
Wikipedia: https://en.wikipedia.org/wiki/Federal_Prison_Camp,_Alderson
ZCG Website: https://www.prisonerresource.com/resources/federal-prison-profiles/
mid-atlantic-region-mxr/federal-prison-camp-alderson-
fpc-alderson/

Inmate Correspondence Address

Inmate Name and Registration Number
FPC Alderson
Federal Prison Camp
Glen Ray Road, Box A
Alderson, WV 24910

NOTE: Funds cannot be sent directly to federal inmates. See Chapter 1 for more information on sending funds to federal inmates.

Sex: Female

Security Level: Minimum Security

Location: FPC Alderson is located in the city of Alderson, West Virginia in the southeastern part of the state.

BOP Region: Mid-Atlantic Region (MXR)

BOP Institution Code: ALD for FPC Alderson

Judicial District: Southern District of West Virginia

Medical Care Level: Level 2. See Chapter 2 for more information on Medical Care and Mental Health Care Levels.

Mental Health Care Level: Level 2.

Population (as of May 1, 2019): 880

Background: Federal Prison Camp Alderson is a minimum-security federal prison in Alderson, West Virginia, which houses female prisoners. It was opened in 1928.

Formerly known as the Federal Reformatory for Women, FPC Alderson was the first federal prison exclusively for women. Serving as a model for prison reform at the time, it was styled after a boarding school and offered education with no armed guards. It originally consisted of cottages built in a horseshoe pattern. While there is no razor wire on the fence surrounding the camp, the prisoners have schedules and each must work if medically able. Most of the inmates at FPC Alderson have been convicted of non-violent or white-collar crimes. News media members nicknamed the prison "Camp Cupcake" when Martha Stewart served her time there.

FPC Alderson is one of six federal and state prisons participating in the paws4people/paws4prisons service dog training program. This program offers college-level classes and instruction in the raising and training of dogs for placement with disabled, active duty, and veteran military service members, as well as adolescents with physiological, developmental, and other challenges. This program works as a reentry program for FPC Alderson inmates, who are in demand as dog trainers upon release.

Notable inmates include Billie Holliday; Manson family member Lynette "Squeaky" Fromme (attempted assassination of President Gerald Ford); Chicago Alderman Sandi Jackson (public corruption); Detroit Councilwoman Monica Conyers; Michigan Supreme Court Justice Diane Hathaway (mortgage fraud); Esther Reed (fraud and identity theft); and Chicago Public Schools CEO Barbara Byrd-Bennett (bribery scandal). Celebrity homemaker Martha Stewart served five months in 2004 at FPC Alderson for obstruction of justice in connection with insider trading, telling Katie Couric in 2017 that it was "a *horrible* experience. Nothing is good about it. Nothing."

Media reports indicate that numerous prison guards, including a former captain, have been charged with sexually assaulting female inmates at the institution.

In 2017, Insider Monkey named FPC Alderson one of the ten easiest federal prisons in which to do time. In 2012, CNBC named the institution one of the 12 best federal prisons in which to do time. And in 2009, *Forbes* magazine named the facility one of the ten cushiest prisons in America.

Housing: Inmates are housed in dormitories which are divided into two-person cubicles. There is a total of eight housing units.

Health Services: Upon arrival at FPC Alderson, inmates are provided an intake screening complete with TB testing. Each inmate is assigned to a medical provider and associated support staff, according to the inmate's register number. Clinical appointments, call-outs, emergency services, dental examinations, eyeglasses and contact lenses, physical examinations and medications are provided to inmates. Insulin line is held during breakfast and dinner. Pill line is conducted from 7:00 to 7:30 a.m. and 2:00 to 2:30 p.m.

Psychology Services: FPC Alderson provides individual counseling, group counseling, and intake evaluations. The Resolve Program offers workshops and processing groups for survivors of physical and sexual abuse and is available to interested inmates. FCP Alderson also offers a number of groups and courses including individual crisis counseling, Psychology of Achievement, Positive Mental Attitude, Pre-Release Syndrome, Anger Management, Dissolving Stress, Domestic Violence, Progressive Meditation, Problem Solving, Self-Relaxation, Stress Relief, and Self-Image.

Residential Drug Abuse Program (RDAP): FPC Alderson houses a Residential Drug Abuse Program (RDAP). A Drug Education Class, the Non-Residential Drug Abuse Program (NR-DAP), Alcoholics Anonymous (AA), Narcotics Anonymous (NA), and Gamblers Anonymous (GA) are also available.

Education Services: FPC Alderson offers literacy, GED, and English-as-a-Second Language (ESL) programs. High school diplomas and post-secondary programs are available through paid correspondence programs.

Advanced Occupational Education: FPC Alderson offers advanced occupational education in Cosmetology, Customer Service Representative, Horticulture, Library Clerk, Medical Office Clerk, and Receptionist.

Vocational Training: FPC Alderson does not offer any vocational training aside from its advanced occupational education and apprenticeship programs.

Apprenticeship: FPC Alderson offers apprenticeships in Air Conditioning/Refrigeration, Cooking, Electrician, Plumbing, Powerhouse, Teacher's Assistant, and Welding.

Library Services: The FPC Alderson law library provides typewriters for legal use and a copying machine is available at a cost. The leisure library collection includes fiction, nonfiction, basic legal reference materials, literary works in Spanish, current magazines, major newspapers, medical reference materials, and audio/video cassettes.

UNICOR: FPC Alderson houses UNICOR factories which provide data services, warehousing, distribution and fulfilment, assistance and help desk, and custom printing.

Commissary: An account is established for the inmate's committed name and register number. Inmates can spend up to $360.00 each month. Inmates are permitted to shop once a week on their housing units designated shopping day. An Inmate Identification Card is issued to each inmate. This card must be presented when shopping at the FPC Alderson Commissary Sales Unit. Inmates must submit their orders several days in advance of their actual shopping day. Inmates can purchase food items, drink mixes, sodas, clothing, and other items.

Recreation: Recreation programs range from individualized arts and crafts programs to intramural team sports (basketball, softball, and volleyball). Activities include but are not limited to arts and crafts classes, aerobics, step aerobics, country line aerobics, Pilates, sweating to the oldies, fusion, low impact spinning, volleyball (indoor/outdoor), billiards, basketball, ping pong, jogging, brisk walking, softball, roller skating, table games, bingo, bocce ball, game shows, progressive relaxation and talent shows. Tournaments are held periodically, with prizes awarded to winners. The yarn project is a volunteer project where inmates crochet hats, sweaters, scarves, mittens, and lap afghans for local needy children and women's resource centers.

Visitation: On Sunday, Monday, and Saturday visitation is held between 8:15 a.m. and 3:15 p.m. On Friday visitation is held between 11:30 a.m. and 6:30 p.m. On federal holidays visitation is held between 8:15 a.m. and 3:15 p.m. See Chapter 1 for more information on visitation.

Prison Politics: Because FPC Alderson is a camp, there are virtually no prison politics.

Level of Violence: There is virtually no violence. Anyone caught engaging in violence is typically sent to a higher-security prison.

Vulnerable Populations: While sex offenders can't be placed at a camp due to Bureau policy precluding such placement, inmates report that both informants and LGBT inmates can remain.

Good: "The land is beautiful."

In the News: In June 2018, Captain Jarred Grimes, who was in charge of all security and correctional functions at Federal Prison Camp Alderson, pleaded guilty to having sex with four female prisoners and abusive sexual contact with two others between November 2016 and December

2017. Grimes resigned his position in 2017 and will face up to 10 years in prison when he is sentenced in October 2018.

In August 2017, Chicago Public Schools CEO Barbara Byrd-Bennett reported to FPC Alderson to begin her four-and-a-half-year sentence for her involvement in a bribery scandal.

In November 2016, Christina Kimble, who walked away from FPC Alderson without authorization in November 2015, was sentenced to a year in prison for her escape.

In 2014, FPC Alderson work supervisor Jeffrey S. Walton was sentenced to ten months of incarceration for touching the breasts of a female prisoner.

In June 2013, Michigan Supreme Court Justice Diane Hathaway, who pleaded guilty to mortgage fraud, was recommended by her sentencing judge to be sent to the Federal Prison Camp at Alderson.

FCI Ashland

Federal Correctional Institution Ashland | FCI Ashland

Facilities: FCI Ashland with an adjacent minimum-security satellite prison camp.

Facility Address & Contact Information

Federal Correctional Institution Ashland
State Route 716
Ashland, KY 41105

Phone: 606-928-6414
Fax: 606-929-4395
Email: ASH/ExecAssistant@bop.gov

BOP Website: http://www.bop.gov/locations/institutions/ash
Wikipedia: https://en.wikipedia.org/wiki/Federal_Correctional_Institution,_Ashland
ZCG Website: https://www.prisonerresource.com/resources/federal-prison-profiles/mid-atlantic-region-mxr/federal-correctional-institution-ashland-fci-ashland/

Inmate Correspondence Address

For FCI Ashland

Inmate Name and Registration Number
FCI Ashland
Federal Correctional Institution
P.O. Box 6001
Ashland, KY 41105

For Satellite Prison Camp

FCI Ashland
Satellite Prison Camp
P.O. Box 6000
Ashland, KY 41105

NOTE: Funds cannot be sent directly to federal inmates. See Chapter 1 for more information on sending funds to federal inmates.

Sex: Male

Security Level: Main: Low Security; Camp: Minimum Security

Location: FCI Ashland is located 5 miles southwest of the city of Ashland in northeastern Kentucky.

BOP Region: Mid-Atlantic Region (MXR)

BOP Institution Code: ASH for FCI Ashland

Judicial District: Eastern District of Kentucky

Mental Health Care Level: Level 2

Medical Care Level: Level 2. See Chapter 2 for more information on Medical Care and Mental Health Care Levels.

Population (as of May 1, 2019): Main: 1,056; Camp: 201

Background: Federal Correctional Institution Ashland is a low-security federal prison in Ashland, Kentucky, which houses male inmates. It was opened in 1940. Federal Correctional Institution Ashland Camp, which also houses male inmates, was opened in 1991 and is adjacent to the main institution.

Originally designed for bootleggers and revenue violators, FCI Ashland now houses adult males and serves as a phasing down program for inmates who are nearing the end of their sentences in one of the regional penitentiaries.

Notable inmates include former Luzerne County (PA) Judge Mark A. Ciavarella, Jr. (serving 28 years for racketeering, fraud, money laundering, extortion, bribery, and tax evasion in the infamous cash-for-kids scandal); David Kernell (unauthorized access to a computer and obstruction of justice); Azamat Tazhayakov (lying to federal investigators regarding the Boston Marathon bombing); and Spencer Reinhard, Eric Borsuk, and Warren Lipka whose book heist was memorialized in the movie *American Animals*.

Media reports indicate that at least one guard has been charged with smuggling contraband into the institution and at least one inmate has been charged with stabbing a fellow inmate.

In 2009, *Forbes* magazine ranked FCI Ashland Camp one of the ten cushiest federal prisons in America.

Housing: FCI Ashland has two-person cells, two-person dorms, and two- to six-person rooms. There is also one unit of one-person rooms. There is a total of 12 housing units, five of which house dorms. The camp at FCI Ashland has dormitory style housing, which consists of two-person cubicles.

Health Services: At FCI Ashland, inmates will complete an admission physical, including but not limited to a hands-on physical exam, urinalysis, serology, PPD skin test (Tuberculosis), Tetanus Toxoid, dental examination, an EKG (for inmates age 50 and older), hearing and vision screening, and testing for HIV. Emergency medical care, medical and dental sick call, and medications are provided. Health Services hours of operation are 6:30 a.m. to 3:30 p.m. In order to submit a triage form, inmates must place their form in the box outside of the department at 7:30 a.m. Pill and insulin line are held at 7:30 a.m. and 6:00 p.m. Emergency medical care is available 24 hours a day.

Psychology Services: FCI Ashland offers assessment and treatment of mental health problems, individual and group counseling, as well as psycho-educational classes, supportive services, and self-help and chronic care clinics for inmates with mental illnesses. Current classes offerings include Anger Management, Criminal Thinking, Basic Cognitive Skills, Smart Recovery, Emotional Regulation, and Suicide Watch Companion.

Residential Drug Abuse Program (RDAP): FCI Ashland does not house the Residential Drug Abuse Program (RDAP). A Drug Abuse Education Course, the Non-Residential Drug Abuse Program (NR-DAP), Alcoholics Anonymous (AA), and Narcotics Anonymous (NA) are available. Some inmates are required to participate in the Drug Abuse Education Course, while others can opt-in to the program if so desired.

Education Services: FCI Ashland's Education Department is open from 6:45 to 10:30 a.m., 11:45 a.m. to 3:30 p.m., and 4:30 to 8:30 p.m., Monday through Friday with the exception of the Friday evening closure. The Department is also open on Sundays from 6:05 to 9:30 a.m. and 10:30 a.m. to 3:30 p.m. The Department offers GED (in English and Spanish languages) and the English-as-a-Second Language (ESL) program. Classes are separated into pre-GED, Advanced GED, and Special Learning Needs levels. Incentive awards are provided to recognize inmates making satisfactory progress toward completing the literacy (i.e., GED and ESL) program. Inmates may also receive incentives ($25.00) for completing the GED or ESL programs. Graduation ceremonies recognize GED, ESL, and Occupational Education completions. Adult Continuing Education (ACE) courses and a parenting program are also available. Current ACE offerings include Baseball, Jazz, Rock & Roll, Japanese, Arabic, Spanish, Math

Refresher, Grammar Refresher, and Math for Welders. High school diplomas and post-secondary programs are available through paid correspondence programs.

Advanced Occupational Education: FCI Ashland offers advanced occupational education in Autobody and Car Care. The FCI Ashland camp offers a Gardener Program and Welding.

Vocational Training: No vocational training programs are offered aside from the advanced occupational education and apprenticeship programs.

Apprenticeship: FCI Ashland offers apprenticeships in Baking, Cooking, Dental Assistant, Maintenance Electrician, and Welding. The camp offers apprenticeships in Baking and Cooking.

Library Services: The FCI Ashland leisure library offers inmates a variety of reading materials which include periodicals, newspapers, fiction, nonfiction, and reference books. Also available is a DVD viewing room where inmates can watch educational movies. Both institutions participate in an interlibrary loan program with local, state, and college libraries and available bookmobile services. The TRULINCS Electronic Law Library offers inmates access to legal materials, case law, and Bureau program statements. Resources, including typewriters, are available for inmates to prepare legal materials, at the inmate's expense. A copying machine is available to reproduce materials needed for research.

UNICOR: FCI Ashland's UNICOR factory manufactures office furniture. In addition to FCI Ashland's furniture factory products, there are three support sections: Quality Assurance, Business Office, and Warehouse. The FCI Ashland camp does not house a UNICOR factory.

Commissary: Inmates can spend up to $360.00 each month. Commissary and validation schedules are posted on the inmate bulletin boards. Inmates are allowed to shop Monday through Thursday on their housing unit's assigned day, which rotates quarterly. Hours of operation are 10:15 to 11:45 a.m. and 1:00 to 2:00 p.m. UNICOR inmates shop from 3:00 to 3:30 p.m. An account is established for the inmate's committed name and register number and an Inmate Identification Card is issued to each inmate. This card must be presented when shopping. Inmates can purchase include food items, drink mixes, sodas, clothing, and other items.

Recreation: FCI Ashland's recreation offerings include physical fitness and leisure programs. The yard is open from 6:00 a.m. to 3:30 p.m., and 4:30 to 8:00 p.m. Leisure activities include organized and informal games, sports, physical fitness, table games, hobbycrafts, music programs, intramural activities, social and cultural organizations, and movies. Art activities include paintings and sketches rendered using traditional methods (e.g., oils, pastels, crayons, pencils, inks, and charcoal). Softball, basketball, flag football, soccer, tennis, Ultimate Frisbee, volleyball, bocce ball, cornhole, horseshoes, and handball are available on the yard, as is a weight pile and a track. Indoors, inmates can participate in yoga, spin classes, over 40 cardio, chess, and guitar. The gym has pool tables, board games, basketball, handball, cardio equipment, and TVs. Hobbycraft activities include ceramics, leatherwork, models, clay, mosaics, crochet, knitting, sculptures, air brushing, and woodworking. The Recreation Department also has a library which has a broad selection of books. It is available to inmates from 12:00 to 3:00 p.m. In the camp, recreation offerings include three pool tables, cable television, and exercise equipment. Each housing unit is equipped with cable television and card tables for playing board games.

Prison Politics: There is a very low level of prison politics at this facility. According to one inmate, "The yard is not political." Another explained, "not many politics here."

Level of Violence: Minimal violence, which, according to inmate respondents, usually involves the TV. One respondent stated that the prison is "very safe" and that of the few fights that he had witnessed, "they were over quickly and usually only involving two people." Another inmate explained, "There is almost zero violence here. There has been one stabbing in the last decade and one rape. Otherwise, a few fights occur on occasion. Generally, this is a very safe compound."

Vulnerable Populations: Sex offenders, informants, and LGBT inmates can walk this yard. One inmate noted that "certain staff target sex offenders." Another inmate explained, "While I am a sex offender, I have zero problems here. I am only restricted from the white TV room in the unit." Another respondent stated, "Sex offenders are the majority here. So, no issues on the yard; even the weight pile is open to them."

Good: "There really isn't anything good about this place." "The good things are the safety and the yard. The library is fairly stocked as well." "The commissary is ok, but does seem to be getting better." "They took out the metal detectors, so that is good."

Bad: "The harassment from certain CO's; petty shots." "The prison is poorly organized." "Extremely petty guards." "No air conditioning, and it's over 105 degrees as I write this." "They took away our pillows." "The food is terrible, but better than transit or most county jails." "It's a dump."

Other Comments: "If you have a choice to go anywhere, I would not come here unless FCI Ashland gets you closer to home." "It's very safe here, but the guards can be very disrespectful and sometimes denigrating towards inmates."

In the News: In July 2018, Beverly Sharp, a former guard and employee trainer at Federal Correctional Institution Ashland, was hired as the criminal justice program coordinator at Ashland Community and Technical College.

In April 2016, former Luzerne County Judge Mark A. Ciavarella, Jr., who was sentenced to 28 years for racketeering, money laundering and fraud in the infamous kids-for-cash scandal, was transferred to the low-security FCI Ashland.

In 2014, Azamat Tazhayakov, friend and roommate of the man known as the Boston Bomber, was found guilty of obstructing a terrorism investigation by disposing of the bomber's backpack full of fireworks, and designated to FCI Ashland to serve his three-and-a-half-year sentence.

In 2013, James Lewis, a guard at FCI Ashland, was accused of working with a prisoner, Gary Musick, and the prisoner's girlfriend, Cindy Gates, to smuggle contraband into the facility, which included marijuana, pornography and cell phones.

In August 2010, one prisoner was stabbed by another prisoner, both unnamed, at FCI Ashland and was taken to a local hospital for treatment.

In June 2006, Spencer Reinhard, Eric Borsuk and Warren Lipka -- whose rare-book heist was made into the 2018 movie *American Animals* -- were sent to FCI Ashland to serve their sentences.

Visitation Information: On Sunday, Monday, and Saturday visitation is held between 8:00 a.m. and 3:00 p.m. On federal holidays visitation is held between 8:00 a.m. and 3:00 p.m. See Chapter 1 for more information on visitation.

In the News: In May 2018, reality TV celebrity Kim Kardashian West met with President Donald Trump to advocate for a presidential pardon of Alice Marie Johnson, who was serving a life sentence at the Federal Correctional Institution at Aliceville for a first-time drug conspiracy offense. Johnson was subsequently pardoned by President Trump.

Also in May 2018, Jesse Bailey, a guard at FCI Aliceville, was sentenced to a year-and-a-half in prison for having sex with a female prisoner and lying about it to federal investigators.

In April 2017, Eric C. Walker, a materials handling supervisor at FCI Aliceville, was arrested and accused of smuggling tobacco and other contraband into the prison for cash bribes.

In January 2017, Patricia Bradley became warden of FCI Aliceville after serving as an associate warden at Federal Correctional Complex Yazoo City.

In September 2016, Brenda Montgomery and Cindy Tate were sentenced to 57 months in federal prison for stealing nearly $4 million from the bank where they were employed. Both were sent to FCI Aliceville.

In February 2016, a tornado tore through FCI Aliceville, ripping the roof off of a dorm building and leaving the female prisoners hiding under their bunks on the top floor and standing in four inches of water on the bottom floor.

FCI Beckley

Federal Correctional Institution Beckley | FCI Beckley

Facilities: FCI Beckley and an adjacent minimum-security satellite prison camp.

Facility Address & Contact Information

Federal Correctional Institution Beckley
1600 Industrial Road
Beaver, WV 25813

Phone: 304-252-9758
Fax: 304-256-4956
Email: BEC/ExecAssistant@bop.gov

BOP Website: http://www.bop.gov/locations/institutions/bec
Wikipedia: https://en.wikipedia.org/wiki/Federal_Correctional_Institution%2C_Beckley
ZCG Website: https://www.prisonerresource.com/resources/federal-prison-profiles/mid-atlantic-region-mxr/federal-correctional-institution-beckley-fci-beckley/

Inmate Correspondence Address

For FCI Beckley

Inmate Name and Registration Number
FCI Beckley
Federal Correctional Institution
P.O. Box 350
Beaver, WV 25813

For Satellite Prison Camp

Inmate Name and Registration Number
FCI Beckley
Satellite Prison Camp
P.O. Box 350
Beaver, WV 25813

NOTE: Funds cannot be sent directly to federal inmates. See Chapter 1 for more information on sending funds to federal inmates.

Sex: Male

Security Level: Main: Medium Security; Camp: Minimum Security

Location: FCI Beckley is located in Raleigh County, West Virginia, approximately 51 miles southeast of Charleston.

BOP Region: Mid-Atlantic Region (MXR)

BOP Institution Code: BEC for FCI Beckley

Judicial District: Southern District West Virginia

Medical Care Level: Level 2. See Chapter 2 for more information on Medical Care and Mental Health Care Levels.

Mental Health Care Level: Level 2

Population (as of May 1, 2019): Main: 1,521; Camp: 141

Background: Federal Correctional Institution Beckley is a medium-federal prison in Beaver, West Virginia, which houses male inmates. It was opened in 1974. Federal Correctional Institution Beckley Camp, which also houses male inmates, is located adjacent to the main institution.

Established as the Beckley Work Release Center, the facility was reorganized in 1997 and renamed the Beckley Correctional Center. In March 2011, the center expanded into the Jackie Withrow Hospital to incorporate a Residential Substance Abuse Treatment Unit on the grounds of the hospital.

Notable inmates include founder of Berkeley Nutraceuticals Steven Warshak (served nine years for fraud and money laundering); James Kopp (serving a life sentence for murder); and Eric DeWayne Boyd (serving an 18-year sentence for carjacking in order to elude law enforcement).

Media reports indicate that at least five inmates have been charged with weapons possession in the past several years, one was indicted for drug possession, and a former inmate was indicted for threatening to blow up the prison. News reports also indicate that one transgender inmate was subjected to ongoing harassment, sexual assaults by inmates and staff, threats, and other abuse while incarcerated.

Housing: FCI Beckley is comprised of two-person cells. The camp consists of open-bay dorms with two-person cubicles.

Health Services: Medical and dental sick call, medications, medical and dental open house, routine dental care, physical examinations, eyeglasses, and emergency medical and dental care are available at FCI Beckley. In order to be evaluated for non-emergency care, inmates must submit a triage form and wait to be placed on the call-out list.

Psychology Services: FCI Beckley offers the BRAVE (Bureau Rehabilitation and Values Enhancement) Program, which is a self-improvement program for young offenders serving lengthy terms of incarceration. Other programming groups for anger management and stress management are also available.

Residential Drug Abuse Program (RDAP): FCI Beckley houses a Residential Drug Abuse Program (RDAP). Additional services include a Drug and Substance Abuse Education Program and a Non-Residential Drug Abuse Treatment Program (NR-DAP). The camp does not offer RDAP.

Education Services: FCI Beckley offers GED classes and English-as-a-Second Language (ESL) classes. Adult Continuing Education (ACE) courses and parenting programs are also available. High school diplomas and postsecondary education is available through paid correspondence programs.

Advanced Occupational Education: FCI Beckley offers advanced occupational education in Business Retail Management, Customer Service, Appliance Repair & Refrigeration, Blueprint Reading, Carpentry, HVAC, Masonry, and Residential Wiring. The camp offers Appliance Repair & Refrigeration, HVAC, and Welding. Advanced occupational college classes are offered through New River Community and Technical College.

Vocational Training: There are no vocational training programs aside from their advanced occupational education programs.

Apprenticeship: There are no apprenticeship programs.

Library Services: The Education Department offers a video library, where inmates may check-out videos to watch during scheduled times. Videos are educational in nature and include a variety of topics related to health, wellness, leisure, athletics, and sports. Inmates may also check out various periodicals, magazines, literature, and other wellness and leisure reading materials. The law library is located in the Education Department and contains a variety of legal reference materials for use in preparing legal papers. Reference materials include the United States Code Annotated, Federal Reporter, Supreme Court Reporter, Bureau of Prisons Program Statements, institutional supplements, indexes, and other legal materials.

UNICOR: The FCI Beckley UNICOR facility produces ergonomic chairs and office furniture. The FCI Beckley camp does not have a UNICOR facility.

Commissary: Inmates are permitted to spend up to $360.00 each month for purchases. Inmates shop once a week on their assigned day. On this day, inmates go to the Commissary, turn in their slip, and wait for their order to be filled. Funds from an individual account may be withdrawn by use of a commissary card for personal spending in the institution Commissary. Funds may also be withdrawn from the account for family support, or other approved purposes, using Form BP-199. Accumulated institution earnings and funds sent from outside are given to the inmate upon release or may be mailed home.

Recreation Services: Recreation programs at FCI Beckley include indoor and outdoor activities, though recreation time is divided based on housing units and only accessible through one-way moves. Musical instruments and classes are available for inmates. The Recreation Department offers a variety of organized league sports, including softball, flag football, basketball, soccer, and volleyball. A variety of health and wellness classes, including NFPT, yoga, calisthenics, aerobics, and pre-release wellness are also offered. The FCI Beckley Recreation Department offers a variety of hobbycraft activities, including drawing, painting, leather, and ceramics. Weekend movies, weekend pictures, musical lessons, group bands, and holiday tournaments and competitions are also available.

Prison Politics: This is a very political yard. This applies to all races. While not everyone is required to join a gang or car, most do. There are also some independents.

Level of Violence: According to inmate respondents, there are lots of fights, though not many stabbings at this facility. Another inmate stated that "it does tend to be fairly violent."

Vulnerable Populations: Sex offenders, informants, and LGBT inmates are not allowed to walk the yard.

Good: "Good food."

Bad: "Lots of old, broken recreation equipment." "They recently changed rec to a split schedule where only certain units can rec at a time."

Other Comments: "Don't go there." "This is not a safe yard."

In the News: In April 2018, two prisoners at the Federal Correctional Institution in Beckley were each sentenced to 12 months of additional prison time for weapons possession.

In July 2017, Michael Camp, an inmate at FCI Beckley, was caught with a sharpened toothbrush in his work boot.

In June 2017, Daqone Lance, a prisoner at FCI Beckley, was found with an improvised weapon -- a sock tied to a combination lock -- hidden in the waistband of his pants.

In December 2017, FCI Beckley prisoners James Broadhurst and David Harsley were sentenced to additional time in prison after pleading guilty to unlawful possession of a prohibited object, namely, drugs. Broadhurst received five extra months and Harsley received three extra months in prison.

In November 2016, Larry Antoine Smith, a prisoner at FCI Beckley, was sentenced to 21 months for the possession of a weapon in a federal institution -- a combination lock attached to a belt.

In February 2016, Scotty Rose, a physician's assistant at FCI Beckley, was sentenced to two years in prison for unwittingly tampering with an FBI investigation. Rose had previously received reprimands for being too nice to the prisoners.

In 2015, Paris Leibelson, a transgender woman who was convicted of purse snatching in 2005 and imprisoned at FCI Beckley, filed a lawsuit against the prison alleging that officials failed to protect her from assault, threats and harassment which she was subjected to between late 2013 and early 2014. According to the suit, prison gangs controlled most of the dining tables and demanded sexual favors in return for allowing her to eat, resulting in her going for days at a time without eating. It also stated that when Leibelson was sent to the SHU, guard Christopher Cook performed an illegal strip search and digitally anally raped her. In January 2018, after Leibelson was found dead of an apparent drug overdose at her family's home, her father, Michael Leibelson, decided to pursue the lawsuit in the name of justice. William Bruce DelValle, who represented Paris and now her father, said she was in prison far too long for purse snatching. "She was not a menace to society," DelValle said. "She was not dangerous."

In October 2003, Roger Hager, who had previously served time at the Federal Correctional Institution at Beckley, was indicted for threatening to blow up the prison.

Visitation Information: On Sunday, Monday, and Saturday visitation is held between 8:00 a.m. and 3:00 p.m. On federal holidays visitation is held between 8:00 a.m. and 3:00 p.m. See Chapter 1 for more information on visitation.

USP Big Sandy

United States Penitentiary Big Sandy | USP Big Sandy

Facilities: USP Big Sandy and an adjacent minimum-security satellite prison camp.

Facility Address & Contact Information

United States Penitentiary Big Sandy
1197 Airport Road
Inez, KY 41224

Phone: 606-433-2400
Fax: 606-433-2577
Email: BSY/ExecAssistant@bop.gov

BOP Website: http://www.bop.gov/locations/institutions/bsy
Wikipedia: https://en.wikipedia.org/wiki/United_States_Penitentiary%2C_Big_Sandy
ZCG Website: https://www.prisonerresource.com/resources/federal-prison-profiles/mid-atlantic-region-mxr/united-states-penitentiary-big-sandy-usp-big-sandy/

Inmate Correspondence Address

For USP Big Sandy

Inmate Name and Registration Number
USP Big Sandy
U.S. Penitentiary
P.O. Box 2068
Inez, KY 41224

For Satellite Prison Camp

Inmate Name and Registration Number
USP Big Sandy
Satellite Prison Camp
P.O. Box 2068
Inez, KY 41224

NOTE: Funds cannot be sent directly to federal inmates. See Chapter 1 for more information on sending funds to federal inmates.

Sex: Male

Security Level: Main: High Security; Camp: Minimum Security

Location: USP Big Sandy is located in eastern Kentucky, 133 miles from Frankfort.

BOP Region: Mid-Atlantic Region (MXR)

BOP Institution Code: BSY for USP Big Sandy

Judicial District: Eastern District of Kentucky

Medical Care Level: Level 1. See Chapter 2 for more information on Medical Care and Mental Health Care Levels.

Mental Health Care Level: Level 1

Population (as of May 1, 2019): Main: 1,267; Camp: 86

Background: United States Penitentiary Big Sandy is a high-security federal prison in Inez, Kentucky, which houses male inmates. It was opened in 2003. United States Penitentiary Big Sandy Camp, which also houses male inmates, is located adjacent to the main institution.

USP Big Sandy is known for housing dangerous, high-profile inmates. The prison has experienced numerous violent incidents over the years.

Notable inmates include Roy Belfast, Jr. (serving a 97-year sentence for acts of torture on political and military opponents in Liberia), and former acting boss of the Bonanno crime family Vincent Basciano (serving two life sentences for murder, conspiracy, and racketeering).

Media reports indicate that at least one inmate has been killed by guards, one guard was transported to a local area hospital after being stabbed by an inmate, at least 13 inmates have been indicted for weapons possession and assaulting guards, two inmates have been murdered by fellow prisoners, and one guard has been indicted for smuggling contraband into the institution.

Housing: USP Big Sandy is comprised of one and two-person cells. The camp has dormitory housing.

Health Services: Sick call, dental call, emergency medical care, medications, physical examinations, immunizations, TB screening, and dental care are available to inmates. Emergency case is available 24 hours a day.

Psychology Services: USP Big Sandy offers individual counseling, group therapy, and a self-help library. The Challenge program is available to address the psychological, cognitive, and behavioral health factors that may hinder an inmate's ability to live life as a responsible citizen. All inmates can attend classes in anger management, criminal thinking, stress management, impact of crime on victims, values, and more. Various psychological services and psychiatric treatments are also available.

Residential Drug Abuse Program (RDAP): USP Big Sandy houses a Residential Drug Abuse Program (RDAP). Groups are offered for Alcoholics Anonymous (AA), Narcotics Anonymous (NA), and Drug Education. The Non-Residential Drug Abuse Program (NR-DAP) is also available.

Education Services: USP Big Sandy offers GED instruction and the English-as-a-Second Language (ESL) program. Classes are separated into Pre-GED, GED, Advanced GED, and Special Learning Needs levels. A parenting program is also available. High school diplomas and post-secondary education is available through paid correspondence programs.

Advanced Occupational Education: USP Big Sandy offers advanced occupational education in Data Entry, Major Appliance Repair, and Receptionist.

Vocational Training: USP Sandy does not offer any vocational training aside from its advanced occupational education programs.

Apprenticeship: USP Big Sandy does not offer any apprenticeship programs.

Library Services: A law library and leisure library are available for inmates at both USP Big Sandy and the camp. The leisure library offers magazines, newspapers, fiction, nonfiction, and reference books. The law library provides inmates with access to legal materials and an opportunity to prepare legal documents.

UNICOR: The USP Big Sandy UNICOR facility produces clothing and textiles. The USP Big Sandy satellite camp does not have a UNICOR facility.

Commissary: Inmates are permitted to spend up to $90.00 per week with a total of $360.00 per month. The following items are available by special purchase order (SPO) and excluded from the spending limitation: Nicotine Replacement Therapy (NRT) patches and Kosher/Halal shelf stable entrees.

Recreation Services: USP Big Sandy offers indoor and outdoor activities. A gym with various sports and intramural programs is available to inmates. A hobbycraft program with classes in the arts and table games is also offered.

Visitation Information: On Sunday and Saturday visitation is held between 8:30 a.m. and 3:00 p.m. On federal holidays visitation is held between 8:30 a.m. and 3:00 p.m. See Chapter 1 for more information on visitation.

In the News: In May 2018, prisoner Andy Cox, currently housed at the United States Penitentiary in Big Sandy, was featured in a news story because he had reached ten years of his mandatory life sentence for a third non-violent marijuana offense.

In 2009, a guard at USP Big Sandy shot and killed Warren Lee Back, a prisoner who was stabbing another prisoner and who ignored warnings to stop.

In October 2008, a guard at USP Big Sandy was stabbed in the head and lower back by a prisoner. The guard was taken to the hospital for treatment and released the same day.

In 2007, a USP Big Sandy guard, Alice Stapleton, was sentenced to a 78-month prison term for smuggling in heroin, marijuana and cell phones to a prisoner, Personne McGhee.

In 2007, 13 prisoners were indicted for crimes that included heroin and weapons possession and assaults on guards.

In October and November 2006, two prisoners, Shamoni Peterson and Calvin Speight, were stabbed and killed, the first murders since the prison opened in 2003.

In July 2002, prison officials announced that the new $170 million USP Big Sandy, which was built on top of an abandoned mine, was sinking, with one guard tower leaning.

FCC Butner

Federal Correctional Complex Butner | FCC Butner

Facilities: FCC Butner houses FMC Butner, FCI Butner Medium 1 with an adjacent minimum-security satellite prison camp, FCI Butner Medium 2, and FCI Butner Low.

FMC Butner

Federal Medical Center Butner | FMC Butner

Facility Address & Contact Information

Federal Medical Center Butner
Old North Carolina Highway 75
Butner, NC 27509

Phone: 919-575-3900
Fax: 919-575-4801
Email: BUH/ExecAssistant@bop.gov

BOP Website: http://www.bop.gov/locations/institutions/buh
Wikipedia: https://en.wikipedia.org/wiki/Federal_Medical_Center%2C_Butner
ZCG Website: https://www.prisonerresource.com/resources/federal-prison-profiles/mid-atlantic-region-mxr/federal-correctional-complex-butner-fcc-butner/federal-medical-center-butner-fmc-butner/

Inmate Correspondence Address

Inmate Name and Registration Number
FMC Butner
Federal Medical Center
P.O. Box 1600
Butner, NC 27509

NOTE: Funds cannot be sent directly to federal inmates. See Chapter 1 for more information on sending funds to federal inmates.

Sex: Male

Security Level: Multiple Security Levels

Location: FMC Butner is located in North Carolina near the Research Triangle area of Durham, Raleigh, and Chapel Hill. It is 5 miles off I-85 on Old Highway 75.

BOP Region: Mid-Atlantic Region (MXR)

BOP Institution Code: BUH for FMC Butner, BUX for Butner Federal Correctional Complex

Judicial District: Eastern District of North Carolina

Medical Care Level: Level 3/4. See Chapter 2 for more information on Medical Care and Mental Health Care Levels.

Mental Health Care Level: Level 4

Population (as of May 1, 2019): 992

Background: Federal Medical Center Butner is an administrative-security federal prison in Butner, North Carolina, which houses male inmates. It was opened in 1995 and is part of the Butner Federal Correctional Complex.

FMC Butner is a medical referral center that treats significant medical conditions which normal federal prisons are not equipped to handle. Inmates either referred to or assigned to FMC Butner can receive treatments that include routine and emergency health care and dental care.

Notable inmates include John Hinckley, Jr. (released to a psychiatric hospital in 1981 after attempting to assassinate President Ronald Reagan); hitman for the Chicago Outfit Frank Calabrese, Jr. (died while serving a life sentence for racketeering conspiracy); cult leader Tony Alamo (serving a life sentence for transporting minors across state lines for sexual purposes); and president of the Outlaws Motor Club Harry Bowman (serving a life sentence for directing a racketeering enterprise).

Housing: Cadre inmates are housed in dorms consisting of two- and three-person cubicles. Inmate patients are housed primarily in two- and three-person cells.

Health Services: Inmates receive a medical screening upon arrival at FMC Butner. Inmates are then scheduled for routine physical examinations, laboratory studies, physical and dental examinations, and assessment of health needs. Sick call, dental sick call, emergency care, medications, chronic care, physical examinations, periodic health screenings for HIV, TB, colon cancer (for inmates over 50 years of age), diabetes and cholesterol screening (for inmates over 45), and vaccinations as recommended are available to the inmate population. Other preventive health services may be available based on the inmate's age and needs. Inmates can present to sick call Monday, Tuesday, Thursday, and Friday at 7:00 a.m. to be evaluated for routine care needs.

Psychology Services: Individual and group therapy, including stress management, and anger management are offered at FMC Butner. A residential psychiatric hospital is also available at the facility.

Residential Drug Abuse Program (RDAP): FMC Butner does not house a Residential Drug Abuse Program (RDAP). However, a Non-Residential Drug Abuse Program (NR-DAP) is offered. Programs also include a Drug Education Class, Transitional Drug Treatment, Alcoholics Anonymous (AA), Narcotics Anonymous (NA), and others.

Education Services: FMC Butner offers GED and English-as-a-Second Language (ESL) programs to inmates. A parenting program and Adult Continuing Education (ACE) courses are also available. Hours of operation are 7:30 to 10:30 a.m., 12:30 to 3:30 p.m., and 5:30 to 8:30 p.m., Monday through Thursday and Saturday. On Fridays, the hours are 7:30 to 10:30 a.m. and 12:30 to 2:30 p.m. High school and post-secondary education is available through paid correspondence programs.

Advanced Occupational Education: FMC Butner offers advanced occupational education in Horticulture 1, 2 and 3, and Logistics. An Office System Technology (OST) one-year certification program is also available.

Vocational Training: FMC Butner does not offer any vocational training programs aside from its advanced occupational training and apprenticeship programs.

Apprenticeship: FMC Butner offers apprenticeships in Biomedical Technician, Commercial Cleaning, and Health and Sanitation.

Library Services: FMC Butner offers a legal and leisure library to inmates. The leisure library has numerous books and other reading materials available, including magazines and newspapers, career planning, multicultural studies and parenting materials, and fiction and nonfiction selections. A DVD program is also available. The law library consists of the TRULINCS Electronic Law Library.

UNICOR: FMC Butner does not house a UNICOR facility.

Commissary: The monthly spending limit is $360, which is divided into two $180 biweekly spending limitations. Inmates may shop only once per week and are assigned a specific shopping day based on their inmate number. The Commissary is currently open on Monday, Tuesday,

Wednesday, and Thursday. Items available for purchase include drinks, food, over-the-counter medications, clothing, and other items.

Recreation: The FMC Butner Recreation Department offers intramural sports, leisure activities, passive and non-competitive activities, unit-based activities, hobbycrafts, a CD program, movie program, wellness program, and many other activities. Inside, inmates have access to pool tables, stair steppers, ellipticals, treadmills, stationary bikes, and a piano. Outside, inmates have access to a track, softball, basketball, bocce ball, handball, volleyball, and horseshoes. Yard time is scheduled based on housing unit.

Visitation Information: On Sunday and Saturday visitation is held between 8:30 a.m. and 3:00 p.m. On Friday visitation is held between 2:30 and 8:00 p.m. On federal holidays visitation is held between 8:30 a.m. and 3:00 p.m. See Chapter 1 for more information on visitation.

Prison Politics: There are no politics in either general population or in the work cadre.

Level of Violence: There is no violence in either general population or the work cadre.

Vulnerable Populations: Sex offenders, informants, and LGBT inmates can stay at this facility.

Good: "Female medical staff members, not a political yard, staff respectful and care."

Bad: "Lots of rats."

Other Comments: "If you need serious medical care, then this is the place for you." "Very soft yard due to its medical mission." "The prison has pretty much gone to shit since the new administration has come in."

In the News: In December 2017, Eric Brown, who was accused of kidnapping and killing Ashanti Billie and found incompetent to stand trial, was moved to Federal Medical Center Butner.

FCI Butner Medium 1

Federal Correctional Institution Butner Medium 1 | FCI Butner Medium 1

Facilities: FCI Butner Medium 1 with an adjacent minimum-security prison camp.

Facility Address & Contact Information

Federal Correctional Institution Butner Medium 1
Old North Carolina Highway 75
Butner, NC 27509

Phone: 919-575-4541
Fax: 919-575-5023
Email: BUF/ExecAssistant@bop.gov

BOP Website: http://www.bop.gov/locations/institutions/but
Wikipedia: https://en.wikipedia.org/wiki/Federal_Correctional_Complex%2C_Butner
ZCG Website: https://www.prisonerresource.com/resources/federal-prison-profiles/mid-atlantic-region-mxr/federal-correctional-complex-butner-fcc-butner/federal-correctional-institution-butner-medium-1-fci-butner-medium-1/

Inmate Correspondence Address

For FCI Butner

Inmate Name and Registration Number
FCI Butner Medium 1
Federal Correctional Institution
P.O. Box 1000
Butner, NC 27509

For Satellite Prison Camp

Inmate Name and Registration Number
FCI Butner Medium 1
Satellite Prison Camp
P.O. Box 1000
Butner, NC 27509

NOTE: Funds cannot be sent directly to federal inmates. See Chapter 1 for more information on sending funds to federal inmates.

Sex: Male

Security Level: Main: Medium Security; Camp: Minimum Security

Location: FCI Butner Medium 1 is located in North Carolina near the Research Triangle area of Durham, Raleigh, and Chapel Hill. It is 5 miles off I-85 on Old Highway 75.

BOP Region: Mid-Atlantic Region (MXR)

BOP Institution Code: BUT for Butner Medium 1, BUX for Butner Federal Correctional Complex

Judicial District: Eastern District of North Carolina

Medical Care Level: Level 3. See Chapter 2 for more information on Medical Care and Mental Health Care Levels.

Mental Health Care Level: Level 1

Population (as of May 1, 2019): Main: 661; Camp: 301

Background: Federal Correctional Institution Butner Medium 1 is a medium-security federal prison in Butner, North Carolina, which houses male inmates. The facility has an inpatient psychiatric hospital which houses mental patients. All federally committed sex offenders are also housed at the institution. It was opened in 1976 and is part of the Butner Federal Correctional Complex. Federal Correctional Institution Butner Camp, which also houses male inmates, is located adjacent to the main institution.

Notable inmates include Bernie Madoff (serving a 150-year sentence for fraud, money laundering, perjury, and theft), and former Colombo family crime boss Carmine Persico (serving a 139-year sentence for murder, loansharking, bribery and extortion).

Media reports indicate that at least one guard has been convicted of attempting to obtain drugs from an inmate.

Housing: FCI Butner Medium 1 houses inmates in a variety of styles. Georgia Tech, North Carolina, Duke, and Maryland housing units consist of primarily two-person cells. Wake Forest, State, Clemson, and Virginia all have cubes and cells with occupancy ranging from 6 to 10 people, though with some area dividers. The Maryland Commitment & Treatment Unit is where civilly committed sex offenders are housed. Those participating in treatment are single-celled, while those refusing to participate are double-celled. The camp houses inmates in two-person rooms. Deaf inmates are housed in two-person cells which have special fire alert systems.

Health Services: Inmates receive a medical screening upon arrival at FCI Butner Medium 1. Inmates are then scheduled for routine physical examinations, laboratory studies, physical and dental examinations, and assessment of any health needs. Sick call, dental sick call, emergency care, medications, chronic care, physical examinations, periodic health screenings for HIV, TB, colon cancer (for inmates over 50 years of age), diabetes and cholesterol screening (for inmates over 45), and vaccinations as recommended are available. Other preventive health services may be available based on the inmate's age and needs. Inmates can attend sick call on Monday, Tuesday, Thursday, and Friday mornings at 6:30 a.m. Pill and insulin line are held at 6:00 a.m., 10:30 a.m., 5:00 p.m., and 7:30 p.m. On the weekends, pill and insulin line are held at 7:00 a.m., 11:30 a.m., and 7:30 p.m.

Psychology Services: Each housing unit at FCI Butner Medium 1 has a psychologist assigned to provide counseling and other mental health services to inmates. These services include individual counseling and group therapy. Groups include stress management, anger management, Thinking for a Change, victim impact, violence prevention, and others. There is also a self-help library and DVD program. Civilly committed individuals do not have access to regular psychology services.

Residential Drug Abuse Program (RDAP): FCI Butner Medium 1 houses a Residential Drug Abuse Program (RDAP). The Drug Education Class, the Non-Residential Drug Abuse Program (NR-DAP), Alcoholics Anonymous (AA), and Narcotics Anonymous (NA) are also offered.

Education Services: FCI Butner Medium 1 offers GED, Spanish GED, GED in American Sign Language, and English-as-a-Second Language (ESL) courses to inmates. Adult Continuing Education classes are available in 24 different subjects. High school diplomas and post-secondary education programs are available through paid correspondence programs. A local community college also offers lectures on business topics. Hours of operation are Monday through Friday from 7:45 a.m. to 3:30 p.m., and 5:30 to 8:10 p.m., except for Friday nights, when the department is closed. Education is also open on Saturday from 8:00 a.m. to 3:15 p.m. Civilly committed inmates do not have access to the Education Department.

Advanced Occupational Education: FCI Butner Medium 1 offers advanced occupational education in Carpentry, Electrical, Horticulture 1, 2 & 3, and Logistics. The camp offers Horticulture 1 & 2.

Vocational Training: FCI Butner Medium 1 does not offer any vocational training programs aside from the advanced occupational training and apprenticeship programs.

Apprenticeship: FCI Butner Medium 1 offers an apprenticeship in Logistics Coordinator.

Library Services: FCI Butner Medium 1 offers a legal and leisure library to inmates. The leisure library has numerous books and other reading materials available, including magazines and newspapers, career planning, multicultural studies and parenting materials, and fiction and nonfiction selections. At FCI Butner Medium 1 and the camp the law library is located in the Education Department, which contains a variety of legal reference materials for use in preparing legal papers. Inmates have access to the Trust Fund Limited Inmate Communication System (TRULINCS) law library computers for legal research needs.

UNICOR: FCI Butner Medium 1 has a UNICOR facility which makes eyeglasses for BOP inmates.

Commissary: Inmates may shop in the commissary only once per week. The monthly spending limit is $360, though this is further divided into a $180 biweekly spending limitation. Inmates are assigned a specific shopping day when they may shop. The commissary is open Monday through Thursday from 12:30 to 1:00 p.m. and 5:30 to 6:00 p.m. When shopping, inmates turn in their commissary slips, receive a number, wait until their number is called, then collect their purchases.

Recreation: Recreation programs at FCI Butner Medium 1 include both indoor and outdoor components. Inside, inmates have access to arts and crafts, air brush, ceramics, pool tables, leather room, band room, TVs, basketball, ellipticals, treadmills, stationary bikes, and pull-up bars. Outside, inmates have access to a weight pile, track, softball, soccer, basketball, yoga, horseshoes, bocce ball, handball, racquetball, and football. The Recreation Department's hours of operation are 6:30 to 10:30 a.m., 12:30 to 3:30 p.m., and 4:30 to 8:30 p.m., Monday through Friday, and 7:00 to 9:30 a.m., 10:30 to 3:30 p.m., and 4:30 to 8:30 p.m. on the weekends.

Visitation Information: On Sunday and Saturday visitation is held between 8:30 a.m. and 3:00 p.m. On Friday visitation is held between 2:30 and 8:00 p.m. On federal holidays visitation is held between 8:30 a.m. and 3:00 p.m. See Chapter 1 for more information on visitation.

Prison Politics: This is not a political yard. One inmate reported this being a "drop-out yard," while another referred to it as a "safe yard."

Level of Violence: Violence is minimal and rare at this prison. According to one inmate, "We do have our typical fights that break out, but it is not very frequent." Another respondent pegged the number at one fight a month.

Vulnerable Populations: Sex offenders, informants, and LGBT inmates can stay at the facility. According to one inmate, "This is a hideout yard which has a lot of sex offenders, informants, gang drop-outs, and gay and transgender inmates. Most of the time all of these are allowed to walk the yard. It is rare for a sex offender get run off."

Good: "Very laid back and friendly. No politics. Plants and trees around the compound." "The yard is very relaxed and its run like a Low custody yard. No locked doors on the cells. No violence. There are many programs and accommodations for the deaf community such as VRS, VRI, interpreters, visual alerts, and employment options."

Bad: "There are very few good things about this yard. The bad thing is that this is a split compound due to the housing of committed sex offenders who have to be separated from the general population. It creates a lot of stress, anger, frustration, and hatred from staff and general population inmates." "Nothing is on schedule and the staff isn't great."

Other Comments: "A very good place to be. Good place to do time." "This facility was once a very good place, but after the passage of the Adam Walsh Child Protection and Safety Act of 2006, this facility really went downhill." "This facility is not bad." "It's a good place to do time if you can get here."

In the News: In 2017, it was reported that Bernie Madoff, who was sentenced to 150 years in prison for stealing $17.5 billion from investors, had monopolized the hot chocolate market at Federal Correctional Institution Butner Medium 1.

In 2011, Nathan Prady, a kitchen supervisor at FCI Butner Medium 1, was sentenced to six years in prison after encouraging a prisoner to obtain heroin for him.

FCI Butner Medium 2

Federal Correctional Institution Butner Medium 2 | FCI Butner Medium 2

Facility Address & Contact Information

Federal Correctional Institution Butner Medium 2
Old North Carolina Highway 75
Butner, NC 27509

Phone: 919-575-8000
Fax: 919-575-8020
Email: BTF/ExecAssistant@bop.gov

BOP Website: http://www.bop.gov/locations/institutions/btf
Wikipedia: https://en.wikipedia.org/wiki/Federal_Correctional_Complex%2C_Butner
ZCG Website: https://www.prisonerresource.com/resources/federal-prison-profiles/mid-atlantic-region-mxr/federal-correctional-complex-butner-fcc-butner/federal-correctional-institution-butner-medium-2-fci-butner-medium-2/

Inmate Correspondence Address

Inmate Name and Registration Number
FCI Butner Medium 2
Federal Correctional Institution
P.O. Box 1500
Butner, NC 27509

NOTE: Funds cannot be sent directly to federal inmates. See Chapter 1 for more information on sending funds to federal inmates.

Sex: Male

Security Level: Medium Security

Location: FCI Butner Medium 2 is located in North Carolina near the Research Triangle area of Durham, Raleigh, and Chapel Hill. It is 5 miles off I-85 on Old Highway 75.

BOP Region: Mid-Atlantic Region (MXR)

BOP Institution Code: BTF for Butner Medium 2, BUX for Butner Federal Correctional Complex.

Judicial District: Eastern District of North Carolina

Medical Care Level: Level 3. See Chapter 2 for more information on Medical Care and Mental Health Care Levels.

Mental Health Care Level: Level 2

Population (as of May 1, 2019): 1,516

Background: Federal Correctional Institution Butner Medium 2 is a medium-security federal prison located in Butner, North Carolina, which houses male inmates. It is part of the Butner Federal Correctional Complex.

Notable inmates include co-founder of the Cali Cartel Gilberto Rodriguez Orejuela (serving a 30-year sentence for importing cocaine), and Lee Farkas (serving a 30-year sentence for fraud).

Media reports indicate that at least one guard has been convicted of smuggling contraband into the facility.

Housing: Inmates are housed in two-person cells. There is a total of 12 housing units.

Health Services: Inmates receive a medical screening upon arrival at FCI Butner Medium 2. Inmates are then scheduled for routine physical examinations, laboratory studies, physical and dental examinations, and assessment of any health needs. Sick call, dental sick call, emergency care, medications, chronic care, physical examinations, periodic health screenings for HIV, TB, colon cancer (for inmates over 50 years of age), diabetes and cholesterol screening (for inmates over 45), and vaccinations as recommended are available to the inmate population. Other preventive health services may be available based on the inmate's age and needs. Sick call is held between 6:15 and 7:00 a.m., which is also when pill line and insulin line are conducted.

Psychology Services: The FCI Butner Medium 2 Psychology Department offers both individual therapy and group treatment options. On the group side, inmates can participate in anger management, stress management, and other programs. FCI Butner Medium 2 also has a fully staffed Mental Health Hospital with full-time psychiatrists who are medical doctors and can be seen by appointment after referral by a psychologist. The facility also has a Mental Health Step Down Program for inmates with serious mental health issues who need to develop functional skills.

Residential Drug Abuse Program (RDAP): FCI Butner Medium 2 houses a Residential Drug Abuse Program (RDAP). It also offers Narcotics Anonymous (NA), Alcoholics Anonymous (AA), the Drug Education Program, and the Non-Residential Drug Abuse Program (NR-DAP).

Education Services: FCI Butner Medium 2 offers GED and English-as-a-Second Language (ESL) courses to inmates. Adult Continuing Education (ACE) classes are also available. High school diplomas and post-secondary degrees are available through paid correspondence programs.

Advanced Occupational Education: FCI Butner Medium 2 offers advanced occupation education in Automotive Electrical, Culinary Arts, Drivetrain, Engine Repair and Undercarriage, Office System Technology (OST), Carpentry, Electrical, and Automotive Technology.

Vocational Training: FCI Butner Medium 2 does not offer any vocational training programs aside from the advanced occupational training and apprenticeship programs.

Apprenticeship: FCI Butner Medium 2 offers an apprenticeship in Commercial Cleaning.

Library Services: FCI Butner Medium 2 has a legal and leisure library available to inmates six days a week. The leisure library has numerous books and other reading materials available, including magazines and newspapers, career planning, multicultural studies and parenting materials, and fiction and nonfiction selections. The law library is located in the Education Department, where a variety of legal reference materials for use in preparing legal papers can be found.

UNICOR: FCI Butner Medium 2 houses a UNICOR facility which makes eyeglasses for federal inmates.

Commissary: The commissary is available to prisoners, who shop only once per week on their assigned shopping day. Inmates must submit their order the day prior to shopping. Currently, sales are conducted Monday through Thursday from 9:00 to 10:00 a.m., 12:00 to 2:00 p.m., and 5:00 to 7:00 p.m. The monthly spending limit is $360. Inmates can purchase a variety of items, including food, beverages, electronics, shoes, and more.

Recreation: Recreation programs at FCI Butner Medium 2 include indoor and outdoor activities, and range from individualized arts and crafts programs to intramural team sports such as softball, basketball, handball, soccer, tennis, racquetball, bocce ball, and volleyball. Weights, a track, and benches are available outside. Indoors, inmates will find basketball, aerobics classes, pool tables, ellipticals, stationary bikes, treadmills, TVs, band room, and art and leather rooms. Physical fitness, weight reduction, hobbycraft, and musical programs are available to inmates.

Visitation Information: On Sunday and Saturday visitation is held between 8:30 a.m. and 3:00 p.m. On Friday visitation is held between 2:30 and 8:00 p.m. On federal holidays visitation is held between 8:30 a.m. and 3:00 p.m. See Chapter 1 for more information on visitation.

Prison Politics: While all respondents stated that this is not a political yard, one did highlight that there is some level of politics in chow hall seating and another noted that there are racial-oriented unit shot callers. There are also a lot of gang drop-outs.

Level of Violence: There is very minimal violence at this prison, with the exception of Hispanic inmates, who have a higher rate of violence, according to respondents. One inmate stated that he'd rate the safety as a 4 out of 10.

Vulnerable Populations: Sex offenders, informants, and LGBT inmates can stay at the prison. According to one inmate, there is even a specific gay table in the chow hall. Another agreed but clarified that "some sex offenders have problems."

Good: "There are weights, everything is clean, trees and flowers around the prison, and real mattresses."

Bad: "Some small level of politics in the Chapel and chow hall." "Poor quality musical instruments." "The food is terrible, and staff are always having a bad day." "Staff act as though they can do no wrong, and the new Warden backs them up on it."

Other Comments: "Good place, go there." "Not a hard yard, but not the best place either." "Since it is a Care Level 3 institution, it has great health care. Great prison if confined to a wheelchair or walker."

In the News: Between 2011 and 2012, William Neville Dowe, a guard at Federal Correctional Institution Butner Medium 2, earned about $15,000 for smuggling contraband to prisoners. He was caught and charged with the smuggling and sentenced to three years in prison.

FCI Butner Low

Federal Correctional Institution Butner Low | FCI Butner Low

Facility Address & Contact Information

Federal Correctional Institution Butner Low
Old North Carolina Highway 75
Butner, NC 27509

Phone: 919-575-5000
Fax: 919-575-5023
Email: BUF/ExecAssistant@bop.gov

BOP Website: http://www.bop.gov/locations/institutions/buf
Wikipedia: https://en.wikipedia.org/wiki/Federal_Correctional_Complex%2C_Butner
ZCG Website: https://www.prisonerresource.com/resources/federal-prison-profiles/mid-atlantic-region-mxr/federal-correctional-complex-butner-fcc-butner/federal-correctional-institution-butner-low-fci-butner-low/

Inmate Correspondence Address

Inmate Name and Registration Number
FCI Butner Low
Federal Correctional Institution
P.O. Box 999
Butner, NC 27509

NOTE: Funds cannot be sent directly to federal inmates. See Chapter 1 for more information on sending funds to federal inmates.

Sex: Male

Security Level: Low Security

Location: FCI Butner Low is located in North Carolina near the Research Triangle area of Durham, Raleigh, and Chapel Hill. It is 5 miles off I-85 on Old Highway 75.

BOP Region: Mid-Atlantic Region (MXR)

BOP Institution Code: BUF for Butner Low, BUX for Butner Federal Correctional Complex

Judicial District: Eastern District of North Carolina

Medical Care Level: Level 3. See Chapter 2 for more information on Medical Care and Mental Health Care Levels.

Mental Health Care Level: Level 2

Population (as of May 1, 2019): 1,020

Background: Federal Correctional Institution Butner Low is a low-security federal prison in Butner, North Carolina, which houses male inmates. It was opened in 1995 and is part of the Butner Federal Correctional Complex.

Notable inmates include former real estate investor Troy Titus (serving a 30-year sentence for orchestrating a Ponzi scheme), and founder of the now-defunct Bayou Hedge Fund Group Samuel Israel (serving 22 years for defrauding investors).

Media reports indicate that at least one guard has been convicted of sexually assaulting a transgender inmate.

In 2017, Insider Monkey named FCI Butner Low one of the ten easiest federal prisons to do time. In 2012, CNBC named FCI Butner Low one of the 12 best federal prisons in which to do time. And in 2009, *Forbes* magazine named the facility one of the ten cushiest federal prisons in America.

Housing: Inmates are housed in two-person and three-person cubicles, along with a central dormitory area with eight bunks. There are eight total housing units, four upstairs and four downstairs.

Health Services: Inmates at FCI Butner Low receive a medical screening upon arrival. Inmates are then scheduled for routine physical examinations, laboratory studies, physical and dental examinations, and assessment of any health needs. Sick call, dental sick call, emergency care, medications, chronic care, physical examinations, periodic health screenings for HIV, TB, colon cancer (for inmates over 50 years of age), diabetes and cholesterol screening (for inmates over 45), and vaccinations as recommended are available. Other preventive health services may be available based on the inmate's age and needs.

Psychology Services: The FCI Butner Low Psychology Department offers individual counseling and group therapy opportunities for inmates in need. Group therapy topics include stress management, anger management, and many others. A self-help video program is available on Tuesday and Friday mornings from 7:30 to 10:30 a.m. A fully staffed Mental Health Hospital with full-time psychiatrists who are all medical doctors is available. If an inmate feels that they need psychiatric treatment, they are advised to seek a referral through a psychologist in the Psychology Department.

Residential Drug Abuse Program (RDAP): FCI Butner Low does not house a Residential Drug Abuse Program (RDAP). It does offer Alcoholics Anonymous (AA), Narcotics Anonymous (NA), a Drug Education Course, and a Non-Residential Drug Abuse Treatment Program (NR-DAP).

Education Services: FCI Butner Low offers GED and English-as-a-Second Language (ESL) courses to inmates. Adult Continuing Education (ACE) classes are also available. High school diplomas and post-secondary degrees are available through paid correspondence programs. Hours of operation are 7:30 to 10:30 a.m., 12:30 to 3:30 p.m., and 5:30 to 8:30 p.m.

Advanced Occupational Education: FCI Butner Low offers advanced occupational education in HVAC 1 & 2, Logistics, Office System Technology (OST), Carpentry, Electrical, and Automotive Technology.

Vocational Training: FCI Butner Low does not offer any vocational training programs aside from the advanced occupational training and apprenticeship programs.

Apprenticeship: FCI Butner Low offers apprenticeships in Commercial Cleaning and HVAC.

Library Services: FCI Butner Low has a legal and leisure library available to inmates. The law library is located in the Education Department, which contains a variety of legal reference materials for use in preparing legal papers. Most legal research is conducted through the TRULINCS Electronic Law Library computers. The leisure library has numerous books and reading materials available, including magazines and newspapers, career planning, multicultural studies and parenting materials, and fiction and nonfiction selections. A movie program is also available where inmates can watch older DVDs.

UNICOR: FCI Butner Low houses a UNICOR facility that makes clothing, textiles, and industrial products.

Commissary: The monthly spending limit for inmates is $360, which is divided into a biweekly limit of $180. The commissary is available to each inmate only once per week.

Inmates must submit their order form prior to 9:30 a.m. on the day they shop. They can then collect their purchases at 12:30 p.m. Currently, shopping is conducted Monday through Thursday. Items such as food, snacks, shoes, over-the-counter medications, drinks, and more can be purchased by inmates.

Recreation: Recreation programs at FCI Butner Low include indoor and outdoor activities, and range from individualized arts and crafts programs to intramural team sports such as softball, basketball, soccer, bocce ball, football, horseshoes, and volleyball. Physical fitness, track walking and running, weight reduction, hobbycraft, and musical programs are also available. The music program offers inmates access to guitars, drums, bass, piano, percussion, saxophone, trumpet, trombone, flute, accordion, banjo, and a mandolin. Inside inmates also have access to seven pool tables, stationary bikes, four treadmills, two ellipticals, and two stair climbers. The Recreation Department is open from 6:30 to 10:30 a.m., 11:30 a.m. to 3:30 p.m., and 4:30 to 8:30 p.m., Monday through Friday, and 7:30 to 9:30 a.m., 11:30 a.m. to 3:30 p.m., and 4:30 to 8:30 p.m. on Saturday and Sunday.

Visitation Information: On Sunday, Monday, and Saturday visitation is held between 8:00 a.m. and 3:00 p.m. On Thursday and Friday visitation is held between 2:30 and 8:00 p.m. On federal holidays visitation is held between 8:00 a.m. and 3:00 p.m. See Chapter 1 for more information on visitation.

Prison Politics: This is not a political yard. There is no car requirement.

Level of Violence: There is minimal, if any, violence. According to one inmate, violence is "mostly [the result of] lovers' quarrels and TV room issues (chair, channel, etc.) or gambling issues."

Vulnerable Populations: Sex offenders, informants, and LGBT inmates can walk the yard.

Good: "Clean facility and good medical care." "Very nice landscaping with neatly manicured grass on the compound with something in bloom from early March to late December."

Bad: "The food could be better." "Petty nitpicking staff." "Security is run more like a medium than a low."

Other Comments: "Great place to do time." "This is an easy place to do time." "This place will take some getting used to if you are coming from a higher-security spot or if this place is your first prison." "Common expressions around the compound include 'They don't do this anywhere else,' 'You cannot make this stuff up,' and 'Only at Butner.'"

In the News: In October 2017, Calvin Terrance Davis, a guard at Federal Correctional Institution Butner Low, was sentenced to 13 months in prison for forcing a transgender prisoner to perform oral sex on him. The official charge was criminal sexual abuse of a ward, which occurred in May 2016.

FCI Cumberland

Federal Correctional Institution Cumberland | FCI Cumberland

Facilities: FCI Cumberland and an adjacent minimum-security satellite prison camp.

Facility Address & Contact Information

Federal Correctional Institution Cumberland
14601 Burbridge Road SE
Cumberland, MD 21502

Phone: 301-784-1000
Fax: 301-784-1008
Email: CUM/ExecAssistant@bop.gov

BOP Website: http://www.bop.gov/locations/institutions/cum
Wikipedia: https://en.wikipedia.org/wiki/Federal_Correctional_Institution%2C_Cumberland
ZCG Website: https://www.prisonerresource.com/resources/federal-prison-profiles/mid-atlantic-region-mxr/federal-correctional-institution-cumberland-fci-cumberland/

Inmate Correspondence Address

For FCI Cumberland

Inmate Name and Registration Number
FCI Cumberland
Federal Correctional Institution
P.O. Box 1000
Cumberland, MD 21501

For Satellite Prison Camp

Inmate Name and Registration Number
FCI Cumberland
Satellite Prison Camp
P.O. Box 1000
Cumberland, MD 21501

NOTE: Funds cannot be sent directly to federal inmates. See Chapter 1 for more information on sending funds to federal inmates.

Sex: Male

Security Level: Main: Medium Security; Camp: Minimum Security

Location: FCI Cumberland is located in western Maryland, 130 miles northwest of Washington, D.C.

BOP Region: Mid-Atlantic Region (MXR)

BOP Institution Code: CUM for FCI Cumberland

Judicial District: District of Maryland

Medical Care Level: Level 2. See Chapter 2 for more information on Medical Care and Mental Health Care Levels.

Mental Health Care Level: Level 2

Population (as of May 1, 2019): Main: 1,042; Camp: 224

Background: Federal Correctional Institution Cumberland is a medium-security federal prison located in Cumberland, Maryland, which houses male inmates. It was opened in 1994. Federal Correctional Institution Cumberland Camp, which also houses male inmates, is located adjacent to the main institution.

FCI Cumberland has a license plate manufacturing center where inmates produce license plates for use on federal government vehicles.

Notable inmates include leader of the Virginia jihad network Masoud Khan (serving a life sentence for seditious conspiracy); former U.S. Army doctor Jeffrey MacDonald (serving a life sentence for murdering his wife and children); boss of the Lucchese crime family Vittorio

Amuso (convicted of racketeering in 1992); and lobbyist Jack Abramoff (served 42-months for fraud, tax evasion, and conspiracy).

Media reports indicate that at least one guard and one prison visitor have been convicted of smuggling contraband into the institution.

Housing: Inmates are housed in two-person and three-person cells. Inmates at the camp are housed in dormitories.

Health Services: All inmates at FCI Cumberland receive a physical examination within 14 days of arrival. A complete physical examination is required for inmates who are out of BOP custody for more than 30 days (e.g. furlough, writ, or Residential Reentry Center failure). Periodic health examinations, including age-specific preventive health examinations (e.g. cancer screening), are provided at the Clinical Director's discretion. Other health services include sick call, chronic care clinics, routine dental care, medical and dental emergency care, medications, age-appropriate preventive care to promote optimal health and functional status, restorative care to promote achievable functional status, long-term care and end-of-life care. Additional treatments may be available depending on staff referrals.

Psychology Services: FCI Cumberland offers screening, assessment, and treatment of mental health problems, individual and group counseling, psychoeducational classes, self-help and supportive services, along with referral to Health Services for medical treatment of a mental illness. Groups for anger management and stress management, as well as crisis intervention, are available.

Residential Drug Abuse Program (RDAP): Both FCI Cumberland and the satellite camp offer a Residential Drug Abuse Program (RDAP). The facilities also offer a Drug Education Course and the Non-Residential Drug Abuse Program (NR-DAP).

Education Services: FCI Cumberland offers GED and English-as-a-Second Language (ESL) programs. Classes are separated into Pre-GED, GED, Advanced GED, and Special Learning Needs levels. Parenting, Pre-Release classes, the Hope House Book Reading Program, and employment preparation classes are also available. High school diplomas and post-secondary degrees are available through paid correspondence programs.

Advanced Occupational Education: FCI Cumberland offers advanced occupational education in Carpentry and Drywall. The camp offers Dog Trainer, Pet Grooming, and Veterinary Assistant programs.

Vocational Training: FCI Cumberland does not offer any vocational training aside from the advanced occupational education and apprenticeship programs.

Apprenticeship: FCI Cumberland offers apprenticeships in Baker, Carpentry, Maintenance, Peripheral Equipment Operator, Cook, and Electrical Maintenance. The camp offers Automobile Mechanic, Computer Peripheral Equipment Operator, and Powerhouse Mechanic. Both facilities offer apprenticeships in Cook, Electrical Maintenance, Heating, Ventilation and Air Conditioning, Landscape/Gardener, Painter, and Welder Fitter.

Library Services: FCI Cumberland Inmates are provided access to legal materials through the TRULINCS Electronic Law Library, which can be used to prepare legal documents. Inmates can also check out newspapers, magazines, and a wide variety of nonfiction and fiction books.

UNICOR: The FCI Cumberland UNICOR produces signs and license plates used on government vehicles.

Commissary: Inmates are permitted to spend up to $360.00 per month. Inmates may use funds in their account to purchase items at the institution commissary, place funds on their inmate phone account, purchase TRU-Units for their TRULINCS account, and may also send funds out of the institution using Form BP-199. Inmates shop by completing a commissary form with their selections, submitting the form, and then using a laundry bag to carry their purchases back to their housing unit.

Recreation Services: FCI Cumberland provides physical fitness and leisure programs. Leisure activities include organized and informal games, sports, physical fitness, table games, hobby-crafts, music programs, intramural activities, social and cultural organizations, and movies. Art activities include paintings and sketches using traditional methods (e.g., oils, pastels, crayons, pencils, inks, and charcoal). Hobbycraft activities include ceramics, leatherwork, models, clay, mosaics, crochet, knitting, sculptures, and woodworking. Wellness programs include screening, assessments, goal setting, fitness/nutrition planning, and counseling.

Visitation Information: On Sunday and Saturday visitation is held between 8:45 a.m. and 3:00 p.m. On Friday visitation is held between 4:30 and 8:30 p.m. On federal holidays visitation is held between 8:45 a.m. and 3:00 p.m. See Chapter 1 for more information on visitation.

In the News: In January 2018, the National Telecommunications and Information Administration tested its "micro-jamming technology" at the Federal Correctional Institution in Cumberland aimed at disrupting cell phone signals inside prison.

In April 2017, the BOP turned a prisoner-created and prisoner-run rehabilitation and reentry program, Young Men Incorporated (YMI), into a pilot program at FCI Cumberland. The founder of the program, Dominic Henry, founded the Community Economic Development program while serving life plus 40 years at USP Allenwood, and established YMI at FCI Otisville. Henry was released in 2015 after serving 35 years in prison.

Robb Phillips, a guard at FCI Cumberland, pleaded guilty in 2007 to receiving over $14,000 to smuggle tobacco into the facility for prisoners.

In 2004, a visitor to FCI Cumberland, Lilvon Johnson, was arrested for smuggling heroin and marijuana into the prison in certain body cavities.

FCI Gilmer

Federal Correctional Institution Gilmer | FCI Gilmer

Facilities: FCI Gilmer with an adjacent minimum-security satellite prison camp.

Facility Address & Contact Information

Federal Correctional Institution Gilmer
201 FCI Lane
Glenville, WV 26351

Phone: 304-626-2500
Fax: 304-626-2693
Email: GIL/ExecAssistant@bop.gov

BOP Website: http://www.bop.gov/locations/institutions/gil
Wikipedia: https://en.wikipedia.org/wiki/Federal_Correctional_Institution,_Gilmer
ZCG Website: https://www.prisonerresource.com/resources/federal-prison-profiles/mid-atlantic-region-mxr/federal-correctional-institution-gilmer-fci-gilmer/

Inmate Correspondence Address

For FCI Gilmer

Inmate Name and Registration Number
FCI Gilmer
Federal Correctional Institution
P.O. Box 6000
Glenville, WV 26351

For Satellite Prison Camp

Inmate Name and Registration Number
FCI Gilmer
Satellite Prison Camp
P.O. Box 7000
Glenville, WV 26351

NOTE: Funds cannot be sent directly to federal inmates. See Chapter 1 for more information on sending funds to federal inmates.

Sex: Male

Security Level: Main: Medium Security; Camp: Minimum Security

Location: FCI Gilmer is located in central West Virginia, 12 miles west of Burnsville, 85 miles northeast of Charleston, and 150 miles west of Pittsburgh, Pennsylvania.

BOP Region: Mid-Atlantic Region (MXR)

BOP Institution Code: GIL for FCI Gilmer

Judicial District: Northern District of West Virginia

Medical Care Level: Level 2. See Chapter 2 for more information on Medical Care and Mental Health Care Levels.

Mental Health Care Level: Level 2

Population (as of May 1, 2019): Main: 1,326; Camp: 89

Background: Federal Correctional Institution Gilmer is a medium-security federal prison in Glenville, West Virginia, which houses male inmates. It was opened in 2003. Federal Correctional Institution Gilmer Camp, which also houses male inmates, is located adjacent to the main institution.

FCI Gilmer has had an ongoing history of attempted escapes, riots, and assaults.

Notable inmates include Floyd Lee Corkins (serving a 25-year sentence for terrorism-related offenses); former pharmacist Robert Courtney (serving a 30-year sentence for diluting cancer drugs, now housed at FCI Big Spring); Hector Rivera (serving a 32-year sentence for stealing diamonds and other jewels); Lee (MA) Police Chief Joseph Bluffis (convicted of extortion); and East Haven (NH) Police Chief Jason Zullo (sentenced for intentionally crashing into a motorcycle three times while in pursuit of the vehicle).

Media reports indicate that at least one inmate has escaped, one guard has been convicted of smuggling contraband into the institution, and on at least one occasion guards had to use chemical munitions to stop a riot which included at least 75 prisoners.

Housing: Inmates are housed in two-person and three-person cells. There is a total of 12 housing units. At the camp, inmates are housed in dormitories.

Health Services: Medical and dental sick call, urgent care, and medications are provided to inmates at FCI Gilmer. Inmates over the age of 50 may request a physical exam every year. Inmates under the age of 50 may request a physical exam every two years. Emergency medical services are available 24 hours a day. Inmates may request to be evaluated for non-emergency care by submitting a triage form and waiting to be placed on the call-out list. Pill and insulin lines are conducted during meals.

Psychology Services: FCI Gilmer psychology services include basic mental health care such as screening, assessment, and treatment of mental health problems, individual and group counseling, psychoeducational classes (e.g., anger management, basic cognitive skills, etc.), self-help and supportive services, and referral to Health Services for medical treatment of a mental illness. Inmates are notified of new class and group offerings through notices posted on housing unit bulletin boards.

Residential Drug Abuse Program (RDAP): FCI Gilmer does not offer RDAP. However, FCI Gilmer offers a Drug Abuse Education course, the Non-Residential Drug Abuse Program (NR-DAP), Alcoholics Anonymous (AA), Narcotics Anonymous (NA), the Resolve Program, and the Challenge Program.

Education Services: FCI Gilmer Education Services include literacy, GED, and English-as-a-Second Language (ESL) programs. Incentive awards are provided to recognize inmates making satisfactory progress and successfully completing the literacy (i.e., GED and ESL) program. Inmates may also receive incentives for progressing to various levels in the GED or ESL programs. Graduation ceremonies recognize GED, ESL, and Occupational Education completions. Adult Continuing Education (ACE) classes and a parenting program are also offered. Current ACE classes include Intro to Business, Intro to Stock Market, Marketing and Advertising, College Algebra, Basic Algebra, Trigonometry, CDL, and Basic Construction. A Resume/Job Skills class is also available. A college program sponsored by Glenville State College allows inmates to earn an associate's or bachelor's degree in business management. High school diplomas and post-secondary degrees are available through paid correspondence programs.

Advanced Occupational Education: FCI Gilmer offers advanced occupational education in Residential Wiring. The camp does not offer any advanced occupational education programs.

Vocational Training: FCI Gilmer does not offer any vocational training aside from the advanced occupational education and apprenticeship programs.

Apprenticeship: FCI Gilmer offers apprenticeships in Automobile Mechanic, Cabinet maker, Carpenter, and Electrician Maintenance. Both facilities offer Automobile Mechanic, Baker, Cook, Heating and Air Conditioning Installation Service, Painter, Plumber, Polished Concrete and Floor Coverings, Quality Control Inspector, Teacher Aide, and Welder/Fitter Apprenticeship. The camp also offers an apprenticeship in Powerhouse Mechanic.

Library Services: The FCI Gilmer leisure library offers inmates a variety of reading materials which include periodicals, newspapers, fiction, nonfiction, and reference books. Inmates are afforded access to legal materials through the TRULINCS Electronic Law Library. Typewriters and a copy machine are also available in the law library.

UNICOR: The FCI Gilmer UNICOR facility handles metal fabrication and customization of U.S. Customs and Border Patrol vehicles.

Commissary: Inmates may use funds in their account to purchase items at the institution commissary, place funds on their inmate phone account, purchase TRU-Units for their TRULINCS account, or send funds in another manner. Inmates are permitted to spend up to $360.00 per month. Popular items for inmate purchase include food, soda, ice cream, clothing, and shoes. Inmates are allowed to shop once a week on their housing unit's assigned day. Inmates who have certain work details (e.g., food service, UNICOR, etc.) are allowed to shop first thing in the morning in addition to their regular shopping time. First-time shoppers and those only purchasing over-the-counter medications are permitted to shop during the noon meal.

Recreation: Leisure activities at FCI Gilmer include organized and informal games, sports, physical fitness, table games, hobbycrafts, music programs, intramural activities, social and cultural organizations, and movies. Art activities include paintings and sketches using traditional methods (e.g., oils, pastels, crayons, pencils, inks, and charcoal). Hobbycraft activities include ceramics, leatherwork, models, clay, cross stitch, manga art, mosaics, crochet, knitting, sculptures, and woodworking. Wellness programs include screening, assessments, goal setting, fitness/nutrition prescriptions, and counseling. Inside, inmates have access to basketball, band room, art room, ping pong, treadmills, stationary bikes, pool tables, TVs, audio CDs, ellipticals, tables, foosball, and stair steppers. Outside, inmates have access to basketball, softball, soccer, football, cornhole, bocce ball, handball, volleyball, and a track. Hours of operation are 6:00 a.m. to 8:15 p.m., excluding meals and counts.

Visitation Information: On Sunday, Friday, and Saturday visitation is held between 8:00 a.m. and 3:00 p.m. On federal holidays visitation is held between 8:00 a.m. and 3:00 p.m. See Chapter 1 for more information on visitation.

Prison Politics: This is a very political yard. Inmates are required to be part of a car.

Level of Violence: While some respondents felt that there is a moderate level of violence, others felt that there was a low level of violence. The general feel is that fights are common and stabbings periodically occur, but that these tend to be focused amongst the DC car.

Vulnerable Populations: While some inmates report that sex offenders and LGBT inmates cannot stay and informants can remain if they are under the radar, others report that all three of these groups can't walk the yard. As explained by one respondent, "Sex offenders and informants are usually driven off, but there is a significant population of gay/trans inmates who receive no problems."

Good: "Nothing." "Good portion and quality of food. "

Bad: "Mostly everything." "Staff attitude very poor, inmate politics, dirty and crowded housing units." "Staff, in general, are not at all responsive. The re-entry coordinator does almost nothing related to her job description. In short, if you want something done here you have to do it yourself or go through unofficial channels to do so."

Other Comments: "Don't go unless you like harder, political time." "If you're LGBT, a sex offender, or non-political, don't go. If you want the USP experience at a Medium, go."

In the News: In October 2017, Joseph Carter, a prisoner at Federal Correctional Institution Gilmer, escaped from the facility and was captured walking along the road the same day.

In May 2016, Lee, Massachusetts, Police Chief Joseph Buffis was sentenced to 27 months for extortion and sent to FCI Gilmer to serve his sentence.

In December 2013, East Haven, New Hampshire, Police Officer Jason Zullo was sentenced to two years in prison for intentionally colliding with a motorcycle with a passenger three times during a pursuit, causing a crash. He was designated to FCI Gilmer.

In 2013, a guard at FCI Gilmer, Jason Noel Squires, and his girlfriend, Nikole Monique Watkins, were sentenced to 18 and 12 months in prison, respectively, for their tobacco-smuggling operation that resulted in $44,000 in profits.

In September 2010, a riot resulted in a several-week lockdown. Approximately 75 prisoners were involved. Guards regained control using "chemical munitions."

FCC Hazelton

Federal Correctional Complex Hazelton | FCC Hazelton

Facilities: USP Hazelton with an adjacent minimum-security satellite prison camp, FCI Hazelton with a secure female facility.

USP Hazelton

United States Penitentiary Hazelton | USP Hazelton

Facility Address & Contact Information

United States Penitentiary Hazelton
1640 Sky View Drive
Bruceton Mills, WV 26525

Phone: 304-379-5000
Fax: 304-379-5039
Email: HAZ/ExecAssistant@bop.gov

BOP Website: http://www.bop.gov/locations/institutions/haz
Wikipedia: https://en.wikipedia.org/wiki/United_States_Penitentiary,_Hazelton
ZCG Website: https://www.prisonerresource.com/resources/federal-prison-profiles/mid-atlantic-region-mxr/federal-correctional-complex-hazelton-fcc-hazelton/united-states-penitentiary-hazelton-usp-hazelton/

Inmate Correspondence Address

For USP Hazelton

Inmate Name and Registration Number
USP Hazelton
U.S. Penitentiary
P.O. Box 2000
Bruceton Mills, WV 26525

For Satellite Prison Camp

Inmate Name and Registration Number
USP Hazelton
Satellite Prison Camp
P.O. Box 3000
Bruceton Mills, WV 26525

NOTE: Funds cannot be sent directly to federal inmates. See Chapter 1 for more information on sending funds to federal inmates.

Sex: Male

Security Level: Main: High Security; Camp: Minimum Security

Location: USP Hazelton is in the mountains of Preston County, West Virginia, in the community of Bruceton Mills, approximately 35 minutes from Morgantown; 45 minutes from Uniontown, PA; and 45 minutes from Cumberland, MD.

BOP Region: Mid-Atlantic Region (MXR)

BOP Institution Code: HAZ for USP Hazelton, HAX for Hazelton Federal Correctional Complex

Judicial District: Northern District of West Virginia

Medical Care Level: Level 2. See Chapter 2 for more information on Medical Care and Mental Health Care Levels.

Mental Health Care Level: Level 3

Population (as of May 1, 2019): Main: 1,050; Camp: 111

Background: United States Penitentiary Hazelton is a high-security federal prison in Bruceton Mills, West Virginia, which houses male inmates. It was opened in 2004 and is part of the Hazelton Federal Correctional Complex. United States Penitentiary Hazelton Camp, which also houses male inmates, was opened in 2004 and is located adjacent to the main institution.

USP Hazelton was built due to the need for modern facilities to house the growing number of high-security inmates. Along with 768 general population cells, the prison contains 120 Special Housing Unit (SHU) cells for those confined to segregation. USP Hazelton has a history of violence and inmate deaths.

Notable inmates at the camp include former Kentucky Agriculture Commissioner and University of Kentucky basketball player Richie Farmer (served 27 months for corruption).

Media reports indicate that at least three inmates have been murdered at USP Hazelton and that one guard has been convicted of sexually abusing an inmate.

Housing: Inmates are housed in one-person and two-person cells. At the camp, inmates are housed in dormitories.

Health Services: Urgent care, medications, preventive care, and diagnosis or treatment of chronic infectious diseases are provided at USP Hazelton. Emergency medical and dental care is available 24-hours a day. Routine care is available through the submission of triage forms at the Health Services Unit.

Psychology Services: All inmates are screened by Psychology Services staff upon arrival at USP Hazelton and the camp. Psychologists are available for individual and/or group psycho-therapy. Inmates are notified of new classes and groups through postings on inmate bulletin boards. The Challenge Program, an intensive, residential program for inmates with drug abuse and/or mental health problems is available. A self-help lending library is also accessible to the inmate population.

Residential Drug Abuse Program (RDAP): USP Hazelton and the satellite camp do not provide a Residential Drug Abuse Program (RDAP). Both institutions do offer Alcoholics Anonymous (AA), the Drug Education class, and the Non-Residential Drug Abuse Program (NR-DAP).

Education Services: USP Hazelton provides GED, English-as-a-Second Language (ESL), and parenting programs. Adult Continuing Education (ACE), career counseling/Pre-Release Program (RPP) courses, and Microsoft Office 2010 are also offered. High school diplomas and post-secondary education are available through paid correspondence programs.

Advanced Occupational Education: USP Hazelton does not offer any advanced occupational education programs.

Vocational Training: No vocational training is offered at USP Hazelton aside from the apprenticeship programs.

Apprenticeship: The camp offers apprenticeships in Electrician and Powerplant Mechanic.

Library Services: The law library is located in the USP Hazelton Education Department and contains a variety of legal reference materials for use in preparing legal papers. Inmates have access to the TRULINCS Electronic Law Library, typewriters, and a copy machine. The Education Department also maintains a leisure library. The library stocks reference books, such as encyclopedias, dictionaries, medical encyclopedias, college listings and synopses, recent volumes of "Books in Print," etc. Reference books are available for use only in the Library. Magazines, newspapers, and both fiction and nonfiction books are available for checkout, as is a DVD movie program.

UNICOR: USP Hazelton manufactures Army Combat Uniform (ACU) trousers, Diplomatic Bags, and GSA Tarps.

Commissary: Inmates may withdraw money for family support, to purchase publications or for other approved purposes, using Form BP-199. Inmates are permitted to spend up to $360.00 each month, which does not include stamps or funds transferred from commissary to their inmate telephone account. This is further restricted to $180 every two weeks. Soda, food, clothing, shoes, and other items are available for inmate purchase. Inmates submit their orders in the morning, then collect their purchases in the afternoon.

Recreation Services: USP Hazelton offers formal and informal recreation programs with a combination of competitive, recreational, and fitness type activities. The Institution Hobbycraft program is available in the Recreation Department, and includes canvas painting, watercolor painting, crocheting, drawing, and paper art. Indoors, inmates have access to treadmills, stationary bikes, ellipticals, basketball, tables, band room, art room, TVs, and a barbershop. Outdoors, inmates have access to basketball, softball, soccer, football, handball, horseshoes, bocce ball, and a track.

Visitation Information: On Sunday and Saturday visitation is held between 8:00 a.m. and 3:00 p.m. On federal holidays visitation is held between 8:00 a.m. and 3:00 p.m. See Chapter 1 for more information on visitation.

Prison Politics: This is a very political yard where all inmates must belong to a car and clean paperwork is required.

Level of Violence: Inmates report significant violence with weekly fights and monthly stabbings. There are also frequent lockdowns as a result of the violence.

Vulnerable Populations: While some respondents said that sex offenders, informants, and LGBT inmates are not allowed to stay, others reported that only sex offenders can't stay, and that informants and LGBT inmates are severely ostracized if they do remain.

Good: "Respect and great rec."

Bad: "Violence, politics, and frequent lockdowns." "There are frequent lockdowns due to violence on the yard."

Other Comments: "Depends on their time. Good for harder, political time." "Sex offenders, informants, and LGBT inmates would be killed if they stayed." "Gangbangers should go there, and that's about it. Those who want to put in work will like it."

In the News: In April 2018, Ian Thorne, a prisoner at the United States Penitentiary at Hazelton, was killed by another prisoner in a fight between the two which included the use of homemade weapons. Richard Heldreth, president of the local guards union, and Senator Joe Manchin blamed the fight and death on a shortage of guards.

In December 2009, a racially-motivated fight among six prisoners at USP Hazelton resulted in the death of one of the prisoners, Jimmy Lee Wilson.

Also in 2009, Lori Sue Helmick, a nurse at USP Hazelton, engaged in sex with a prisoner and was sentenced to five months in prison.

In 2007, USP Hazelton prisoners Kevin Bellinger and Patrick Andrews stabbed fellow prisoner Jessie Harris to death. Bellinger and Andrews, who were already serving life sentences, were later sentenced to additional life sentences. Bellinger was sentenced in October 2014 and Andrews was sentenced in April 2015.

FCI Hazelton

Federal Correctional Institution Hazelton | FCI Hazelton

Facilities: FCI Hazelton with a Secure Female Facility.

Facility Address & Contact Information

Federal Correctional Institution Hazelton
1640 Sky View Drive
Bruceton Mills, WV 26525

Phone: 304-379-1500
Fax: 304-379-1531
Email: HAX/ExecAssistant@bop.gov

BOP Website: http://www.bop.gov/locations/institutions/haf
Wikipedia: https://en.wikipedia.org/wiki/Federal_Correctional_Institution,_Hazelton
ZCG Website: https://www.prisonerresource.com/resources/federal-prison-profiles/mid-atlantic-region-mxr/federal-correctional-complex-hazelton-fcc-hazelton/federal-correctional-institution-hazelton-fci-hazelton/

Inmate Correspondence Address

For FCI Hazelton

Inmate Name and Registration Number
FCI Hazelton
Federal Correctional Institution
P.O. Box 5000
Bruceton Mills, WV 26525

For Secure Female Facility

Inmate Name and Registration Number
FCI Hazelton
Federal Correctional Institution
Secure Female Facility
P.O. Box 3000
Bruceton Mills, WV 26525

NOTE: Funds cannot be sent directly to federal inmates. See Chapter 1 for more information on sending funds to federal inmates.

Sex: Main: Male; Secure Female Facility: Female

Security Level: Main: Medium Security; Secure Female Facility: Medium Security

Location: FCI Hazelton is located in the mountains of Preston County, West Virginia, in the community of Bruceton Mills, approximately 35 minutes from Morgantown; 45 minutes from Uniontown, PA; and 45 minutes from Cumberland, MD.

BOP Region: Mid-Atlantic Region (MXR)

BOP Institution Code: HAZ for USP Hazelton, HAX for Hazelton Federal Correctional Complex

Judicial District: Northern District of West Virginia

Medical Care Level: Level 2. See Chapter 2 for more information on Medical Care and Mental Health Care Levels.

Mental Health Care Level: Level 2

Population (as of May 1, 2019): Main: 1,419; Secure Facility: 598

Background: Federal Correctional Institution Hazelton is a medium-security federal prison in Bruceton Mills, West Virginia, which houses male inmates. It is part of the Hazelton Federal Correctional Complex. The complex also houses a separate Secure Female Facility for medium-security female inmates.

Media reports indicate that the local guards' union has picketed at least once to protest staff shortages and other concerns.

Housing: Inmates are housed in two- and three-person cells. In the housing units there are six TVs, a typing room, and a law library room.

Health Services: Health services at FCI Hazelton and the Secure Female Facility include episodic visits for new or recurring medical or dental symptoms through a sick call system, chronic care clinics, routine dental care, medical and dental emergency care for injuries and sudden illness, age-appropriate preventive care to promote optimal health and functional status, restorative care to promote achievable functional status, long-term care, and end-of-life care. Dental sick call and regular sick call are held several times a week. Pill line and insulin line coincide with meals.

Psychology Services: Inmates at FCI Hazelton receive a mental health screening, assessment, and treatment, individual and group counseling, psycho-educational classes (e.g., anger management, stress reduction, etc.), self-help and supportive services, and referral to Health Services for medical treatment of a mental illness. The female facility also offers the Resolve Program, a non-residential program for female inmates who have a history of physical and/or sexual abuse.

Residential Drug Abuse Program (RDAP): A Residential Drug Abuse Program (RDAP) is available in the FCI Hazelton Secure Female Facility. Alcoholics Anonymous (AA), Narcotics Anonymous (NA), the Non-Residential Drug Abuse Treatment Program (NR-DAP), and the Drug Education Class are available at both facilities.

Education Services: FCI Hazelton and the Secure Female Facility provide GED and English-as-a-Second Language (ESL) programs. Incentive awards are provided to recognize inmates making satisfactory progress and successfully completing the literacy (i.e. GED and ESL) program. Inmates may also receive incentives for progressing to various levels in the GED or ESL programs. Graduation ceremonies recognize GED, ESL, and Apprenticeship completions. FCI Hazelton and the female facility offer parenting, Adult Continuing Education (ACE) and career counseling/Pre-Release Program (RPP) courses, and Microsoft Office 2010. High school diplomas and post-secondary degrees are available through paid correspondence programs.

Advanced Occupational Education: Neither facility offers any advanced occupational education programs.

Vocational Training: No vocational training is offered at FCI Hazelton or the female facility aside from the education services and apprenticeship programs.

Apprenticeship: The FCI Hazelton Secure Female Facility offers apprenticeships in Electrician, HVAC, Maintenance Repairer Industrial, Plumber, and Welder.

Library Services: The law library is located in the Education Department and contains a variety of legal reference materials on the ten law library computers for use in preparing legal papers. Electronic typewriters and a copy machine are also available. The Education Department maintains a leisure library which is available to the general population. Reference books, such as encyclopedias, dictionaries, medical encyclopedias, college listings and synopses, recent volumes of "Books in Print," etc. are available. These reference books are only available for use within the Resource Library. Magazines, fiction and nonfiction books, and newspapers are available. Inmates may also participate in an interlibrary loan program with a community library.

UNICOR: FCI Hazelton does not house a UNICOR facility.

Commissary: Inmates are permitted to spend up to $360 each month on commissary items. Copy cards, postage stamps, and certain over-the-counter medications are spending limit exempt. Shopping is permitted once a week on a designated day for each inmate. Schedules are posted in the housing units. Shoes, clothing, electronics, food, drinks, and more can be purchased in the commissary.

Recreation Services: Both facilities offer physical fitness and leisure programs, including organized and informal games, sports, physical fitness, table games, hobbycrafts, music programs, intramural activities, social and cultural organizations. Movies, artwork (e.g., oils, pastels, crayons, pencils, inks, and charcoal), and hobbycraft activities (e.g., ceramics, leatherwork, models, clay, mosaics, crochet, knitting, sculptures, woodworking, and lapidary, etc.) are also available. Wellness programs are provided. Softball, soccer, football, handball, and basketball are popular league sports.

Visitation Information: On Sunday and Saturday visitation is held between 8:00 a.m. and 3:00 p.m. On federal holidays visitation is held between 8:00 a.m. and 3:00 p.m. See Chapter 1 for more information on visitation.

Prison Politics: This is a moderately political yard where most inmates belong to cars and check paperwork.

Level of Violence: The level of violence is high at this prison. According to one respondent, "The officers here do not make any attempt to locate shanks, drugs, or other contraband." The respondent continued, "The biggest group subjected to violence here are the 'exposed' sex offenders who are made to sit at one certain set of two tables, a total of 12 seats for approximately 210 exposed sex offenders." A number of sex offenders have been attacked. There is also a problem with gang violence.

Vulnerable Populations: Sex offenders, informants, and LGBT inmates are present, though many are driven off through violence. Generally speaking, this is not a very forgiving yard for such inmates, even if they can stay.

Good: "I honestly would have a hard time coming up with many good things about Hazelton."

Bad: "The list of bad is endless here. They allow sex offenders to be assaulted and battered. They lock us down constantly without any real apparent reason. If you begin to file grievances, the staff immediately start retaliating against you relentlessly. If you check-in because you feel you are in danger, the staff will throw you in a cell with someone they know you will have issues with and will provoke a fight between the two of you." "They have a track record of locking us down for every holiday. Each time they claim that they are short on staff."

Other Comments: "This is seriously the worst prison I have seen in the BOP. Of course, it could always be worse."

In the News: In May 2018, Terence O'Brien, who was warden for six years at Federal Correctional Institution Hazelton before his retirement in 2016, was appointed to chair the West Virginia Parole Board.

In August 2015, the local chapter of the American Federation of Government Employees, which represents FCI Hazelton guards, picketed as the result of staff shortages and other employee concerns.

USP Lee

United States Penitentiary Lee | USP Lee

Faculties: USP Lee with an adjacent minimum-security satellite prison camp.

Facility Address & Contact Information

United States Penitentiary Lee
Lee County Industrial Park
Hickory Flats Road
Pennington Gap, VA 24277

Phone: 276-546-0150
Fax: 276-546-9115
Email: LEE/ExecAssistant@bop.gov

BOP Website: https://www.bop.gov/locations/institutions/lee/
Wikipedia: https://en.wikipedia.org/wiki/United_States_Penitentiary,_Lee
ZCG Website: https://www.prisonerresource.com/resources/federal-prison-profiles/mid-atlantic-region-mxr/united-states-penitentiary-lee-usp-lee/

Inmate Correspondence Address

For USP Lee

Inmate Name and Registration Number
USP Lee
U.S. Penitentiary
P.O. Box 305
Jonesville, VA 24263

For Satellite Prison Camp

Inmate Name and Registration Number
USP Lee
Satellite Prison Camp
P.O. Box 644
Jonesville, VA 24263

NOTE: Funds cannot be sent directly to federal inmates. See Chapter 1 for more information on sending funds to federal inmates.

Sex: Male

Security Level: Main: High Security; Camp: Minimum Security

Location: USP Lee is located in southwest Virginia in Lee County, 8 miles east of Jonesville.

BOP Region: Mid-Atlantic Region (MXR)

BOP Institution Code: LEE for USP Lee

Judicial District: Western District of Virginia

Medical Care Level: Level 1. See Chapter 2 for more information on Medical Care and Mental Health Care Levels.

Mental Health Care Level: Level 1

Population (as of May 1, 2019): Main: 1,341; Camp: 88

Background: United States Penitentiary Lee is a high-security federal prison located in Pennington Gap, Virginia, which houses male inmates. Construction was completed in August 2001 and the institution began receiving inmates in 2002. United States Penitentiary Lee Camp, which also houses male inmates, is located adjacent to the main institution.

Native American artifacts such as arrowheads and pottery have been found on the prison grounds and are believed to date as far back as 10,000 years. There have been numerous incidents of violence at USP Lee, including several homicides.

Notable inmates include former assassin for the now-defunct Medellin Drug Cartel Dandeny Munoz-Mosquera (serving a life sentence for blowing up an airplane); hitman for Loz Zetas Gerardo Castillo-Chavez (serving a life sentence for racketeering, drug trafficking conspiracy, and weapons charges); former U.S. Air Force intelligence analyst Brian Patrick Regan (serving a life sentence for espionage); and Somali pirate leader Mohammed Modin Hasan (serving a life sentence for attacking an American warship).

Media reports indicate that at least five guards were federally indicted for falsifying reports and that in 2015 eight inmates and one guard were transported to a local hospital for treatment following a brawl at the prison.

Housing: Inmates are housed one- and two-person cells. The camp has dormitories.

Health Services: USP Lee inmates receive an initial routine health screening shortly after being admitted. Health examinations, dental care, specific preventive health examinations (e.g., cancer screening), routine care, medications, vaccinations, and specialty care are provided. Inmates can request to be seen by a provider by attending sick call at 8:30 a.m. Appropriate medical care will be provided by institution health services staff. Emergency medical care is available 24 hours a day. Pill and insulin line are held at 6:30 a.m. and 5:15 p.m.

Psychology Services: USP Lee offers screening, assessment, and treatment of mental health problems, individual and group counseling, self-help and supportive services, and referral to Health Services for medical treatment of a mental illness. Additional programs and groups are available for anger management and stress management, as well as crisis intervention. A self-help library is available. The facility also houses the Challenge Program for inmates who are prone to substance abuse, mental illness, and violence.

Residential Drug Abuse Program (RDAP): USP Lee does not have a Residential Drug Abuse Program (RDAP). It does offer Alcoholics Anonymous (AA), Narcotics Anonymous (NA), the Non-Residential Drug Abuse Treatment Program (NR-DAP) and a Drug Education Class.

Education Services: USP Lee offers GED instruction and an English-as-a-Second Language (ESL) program. Classes are separated into Pre-GED, GED, Advanced GED, and Special Learning Needs levels. Parenting and Adult Continuing Education (ACE) classes are also available. High school diplomas and post-secondary degrees are available through paid correspondence programs.

Advanced Occupational Education: USP Lee offers advanced occupational education in Basic Home Construction and Residential HVAC. The camp offers Horticulture/Gardening.

Vocational Training: USP Lee does not offer any vocational training programs, aside from its advanced occupational education programs.

Apprenticeship: USP Lee does not offer any apprenticeships programs.

Library Services: USP Lee inmates have access to the TRULINCS Electronic Law Library, a copy machine, and electronic typewriters. A leisure library is also available where fiction and nonfiction books, newspapers, and magazines can be checked out by the inmate population.

UNICOR: USP Lee does not have a UNICOR factory.

Commissary: Each inmate is allowed to spend $90 per week. All items count against this limit, including Special Purchase Orders (SPO's), with the exception of kosher meals, stamps, over-the-counter medications, and copy cards. Commonly purchased items include drink mixes, candy, food, snacks, and clothing. Inmates are only permitted to shop on their assigned shopping day.

Recreation Services: Recreation programs at USP Lee include indoor and outdoor activities, individualized arts and crafts programs, and intramural team sports such as softball, basketball, soccer, and volleyball. Bocce ball, horseshoes, and a track are also available. Physical fitness and weight reduction programs are available for inmates. A hobbycraft program is available, which includes activities such as painting, leather, art, and drawing. Indoors, inmates also have access to tables, an art room, TVs, stationary bikes, basketball, volleyball, and ping pong.

Visitation Information: On Sunday and Saturday visitation is held between 8:15 a.m. and 3:00 p.m. On federal holidays visitation is held between 8:15 a.m. and 3:00 p.m. See Chapter 1 for more information on visitation.

Prison Politics: This is a very political yard. Inmates are required to be part of a car.

Level of Violence: There is a very high level of violence at this prison. Inmates report several fights per week and monthly stabbings. One respondent explained, "Since the new warden got here, the level of violence has increased greatly."

Vulnerable Populations: Sex offenders, informants, and LGBT inmates cannot stay at this facility. According to one inmate, "None of those kinds of inmates are here; if they are, they have yet to be 'exposed.'"

Good: "Nothing. I cannot think of anything that was good about that place."

Bad: "Inmate-on-inmate and staff-on-inmate violence." "There is nothing good about this prison. It's constantly locked down, which means that guys can't get what little programs they do offer and guys who are trying to get their GEDs can't attend classes."

Other Comments: "Go there if you want to die or make a name for yourself by killing somebody." "If you're young and wild, Lee is the place for you."

In the News: In March 2018, the warden at United States Penitentiary Lee announced "heightened mail monitoring protocols" that severely restricted where prisoners could purchase books, which included a cumbersome ordering process and a 30 percent markup. Bureau of Prisons officials reversed this policy in May 2018.

In January 2018, USP Lee was instructed to eliminate 62 staff positions, bringing the total number down from 427 to 365.

In November 2017, federal charges against five USP Lee guards -- Michael Bernette, Jerry Shuler, Charles Carter, Ryan Sluss, and William Marshal -- accused of falsifying reports, and who admitted their guilt, were dropped by Assistant U.S. Attorney Zachary T. Lee.

In July 2015, multiple fights broke out at USP Lee, resulting in eight people being treated at a local hospital for cuts, stab wounds, and broken teeth. It was reported that a guard also had his wrist broken.

Camp in the News: In February 2008, Edward Porta, an inmate at USP Lee Camp, walked away from the prison. He was incarcerated for defrauding the U.S. Department of Agriculture of more than $400,000. He was recaptured in May 2016.

FMC Lexington

Federal Medical Center Lexington | FMC Lexington

Facilities: FMC Lexington with an adjacent minimum-security satellite prison camp.

Facility Address & Contact Information

Federal Medical Center Lexington
3301 Leestown Road
Lexington, KY 40511

Phone: 859-255-6812
Fax: 859-253-8821
Email: LEX/ExecAssistant@bop.gov

BOP Website: https://www.bop.gov/locations/institutions/lex/
Wikipedia: https://en.wikipedia.org/wiki/Federal_Medical_Center,_Lexington
ZCG Website: https://www.prisonerresource.com/resources/federal-prison-profiles/mid-atlantic-region-mxr/federal-medical-center-lexington-fmc-lexington/

Inmate Correspondence Address

For FMC Lexington

Inmate Name and Registration Number
FMC Lexington
Federal Medical Center
P.O. Box 14500
Lexington, KY 40512

For Satellite Prison Camp

Inmate Name and Registration Number
FMC Lexington
Satellite Prison Camp
P.O. Box 14525
Lexington, KY 40512

NOTE: Funds cannot be sent directly to federal inmates. See Chapter 1 for more information on sending funds to federal inmates.

Sex: Main: Male; Camp: Female

Security Level: Main: Multiple Security Levels; Camp: Minimum Security

Location: FMC Lexington is located seven miles north of Lexington on U.S. Highway 421.

BOP Region: Mid-Atlantic Region (MXR)

BOP Institution Code: LEX for FMC Lexington

Judicial District: Eastern District of Kentucky

Medical Care Level: Level 4. See Chapter 2 for more information on Medical Care and Mental Health Care Levels.

Mental Health Care Level: Level 3

Population (as of May 1, 2019): Main: 1,259; Camp: 228

Background: Federal Medical Center Lexington is an administrative-security federal prison located in Lexington, Kentucky, which houses male inmates. It was opened in 1974. Federal Medical Center Lexington Camp, which houses female inmates, is located adjacent to the main institution.

Opening in 1935, the site was initially named the United States Narcotic Farm, but was subsequently renamed the United States Public Health Service Hospital. In 1967, the facility changed its name once again to the National Institute of Mental Health, Clinical Research Center. Its original purpose was to treat people who voluntarily admitted with drug abuse problems, using experimental methods -- the first facility of its kind in the United States. In 1974, the institution became a federal prison, but maintained its psychiatric hospital title until 1998, when the facility's psychiatric function was transferred to a new Federal Medical Center in Devens, Massachusetts.

Notable inmates include leader of the Universal Divine Saviors religious cult Narseal Batiste (convicted of terrorism conspiracy); white supremacist Daniel Cowart (convicted of plotting to assassinate then-Presidential nominee Barack Obama); former Democratic campaign treasurer Kinde Durkee (convicted of mail fraud); and Leona Helmsley (served 18 months for tax fraud).

Media reports indicate that one inmate was federally indicted for assaulting another inmate and at least two guards have been charged with accepting bribes and smuggling contraband into the facility. At the camp, at least two guards have been charged with sexually assaulting female prisoners.

Housing: Inmates are housed in one-, two-, four-, six-, ten-, and twelve-person rooms. The camp houses inmates in dormitories, which are divided into two-, four-, six-, eight-, and sixteen-person rooms.

Health Services: Sick call, physical examinations, medications, and dental care are all provided to inmates at FMC Lexington. Additional services such as physical therapy, medical laboratory, radiology, nutritional services, and vaccinations are available. Sick call is held Monday, Tuesday, Wednesday, and Friday between 6:30 and 7:00 a.m. Pill line and insulin line are held during breakfast and dinner, with self-carry medication pick-up during lunch.

Psychology Services: Individual services such as crisis intervention, brief counseling, and individual psychotherapy are available at FMC Lexington. Groups are offered in stress management, anger management, sexual abuse issues, and values clarification. Programs such as the Suicide Prevention Program, Hospice Volunteer and Compassion Program, and HIV/AIDS Education are offered. Furthermore, several housing units have particular missions, for example Forensic Studies or Behavioral Medicine. In addition, the camp offers behavioral medicine programs (weight loss/control, chronic pain management, and biofeedback). The camp also houses the Resolve Program for inmates who are dealing with mental illness as a result of trauma.

Residential Drug Abuse Program (RDAP): FMC Lexington offers a Residential Drug Abuse Program (RDAP). A Non-Residential Drug Abuse Program (NR-DAP), Drug Education class, Alcoholics Anonymous (AA), and Narcotics Anonymous (NA) are also available. The camp does not offer RDAP.

Education Services: FMC Lexington offers GED instruction and English-as-a-Second Language (ESL). Classes are separated into pre-GED, Advanced GED, GED, and Special Learning Needs levels. A Career Resource Center and a guidance counselor are available to assist inmates in exploring and learning more about potential careers. Parenting and Adult Continuing Education (ACE) programs are also available to inmates. Current ACE classes include Commercial Real Estate, Interviewing, Journaling, Small Business, and Spanish (1 & 2). High school diplomas and post-secondary degrees are available through paid correspondence programs. In addition to the above, the camp offers the following stand-alone classes: Dave Ramsey's Financial Peace, Money Smart, AARP Financial Planning, Parenting, Job Interviewing, Resume Writing, and Lean Sigma Six.

Advanced Occupational Education: Both facilities offer advanced occupational education in Small Business Management.

Vocational Training: FMC Lexington and the satellite camp offer vocational training in Carpentry, Culinary Arts VT, Greenhouse, Masonry, Residential Electrical, and Welding. The camp offers Computer Applications. Both facilities offer Horticulture.

Apprenticeship: FMC Lexington offers apprenticeships in Electromechanical Wire Harness Assembler, Building Maintenance Service and Repair, Carpentry, Construction Craft Laborer, Cook, Customer Service Representative, Electrician, Healthcare Sanitation, Heating & Air Conditioning Installer & Servicer, Horticulturist, Machinist, Maintenance Mechanic (any industry), Material Coordinator, Office Manager/Administrative Services, Painter, Pipefitter-Steamfitter, Plumber, Power Plant Operator, Quality Assurance Inspector, and Welder. The camp offers apprenticeships in Automobile Mechanic, Building Maintenance Service and Repair, Cook, Material Coordinator, and Small-Engine Mechanic.

Library Services: The FMC Lexington Education Department maintains a leisure and law library. The leisure library has numerous books, magazines, and newspapers available for circulation and reference. There are also NEO word processors, DVD movies, and an interlibrary loan program. The law library provides law books, policy statements, institution supplements, and other materials. Inmates also have access to typewriters in the law library, though there currently isn't a copy machine.

UNICOR: The FMC Lexington UNICOR facility houses an electronic cable factory, quality control department, business office, customer service center, and an accounts receivable operation. The camp does not have a UNICOR facility.

Commissary: Inmates may withdraw funds for family support, legitimate debt payment or to purchase personal items from the institution Commissary. Inmates have a monthly spending limitation of $360 for food, drinks, clothing and other commissary items. This set dollar amount of purchases allowed is increased for November and December. A biweekly spending limit of $180 is also imposed. Inmates are assigned a specific shopping day when they are allowed to buy items in the commissary. Inmates who work at UNICOR and Facilities can shop weekdays between 6:15 and 7:30 a.m. Other inmates can shop on their assigned day at 7:30 a.m., 8:30 a.m., 11:30 a.m., and 1:30 p.m. At the camp, inmates are allowed to shop on Tuesday and Thursday between 7:00 a.m. and 2:00 p.m.

Recreation Services: Recreation at FMC Lexington includes structured fitness classes, such as circuit training, step aerobics, yoga, jump rope, and spinning. Equipment, exercise books, track, health education classes, and a health resource area are also available. The Recreation Department also offers intramural sports leagues. Outdoor leagues include basketball, soccer, flag football, softball, handball, volleyball, and bocce ball. Indoor leagues include basketball, volleyball, and billiards. Hobbycraft programs includes a unit Art Program, ceramics, painting, crochet, leather works, and t-shirt design. Movies on DVD are rented weekly. Inside, inmates have access to handball, tables, art rooms, TVs, foosball, ellipticals, weight machines, treadmills, and stationary bikes. Outside, inmates have access to weights, a track, pull-up bars, and tables. Hours of operation are 6:00 a.m. to 8:30 p.m., excluding counts and meals.

Visitation Information: On Sunday and Saturday visitation is held between 8:30 a.m. and 3:00 p.m. On Thursday and Friday visitation is held between 2:25 and 8:30 p.m. On federal holidays visitation is held between 8:30 a.m. and 3:00 p.m. See Chapter 1 for more information on visitation.

Prison Politics: This is not a political yard.

Level of Violence: There is virtually no violence at this facility. As explained by one inmate, "It is very safe here with hardly any violence."

Vulnerable Populations: Sex offenders, informants, and LGBT inmates are ok to say. According to one respondent, "The yard is open to anyone." Another inmate agreed, stating, "Sex offenders and gays can walk anywhere. There is also one trans person who doesn't seem to have any problems."

Good: "Staff really respectful, no politics, great medical, and good food." "It is very laid back here as if it were a Camp."

Bad: "Some buildings don't have air conditioning." "It is very unorganized, and nothing is consistent." "Medical is shut down a lot." "You can never get a straight answer from anyone." "It's a very old place with a lot of damage and outdated equipment." "The food sucks."

Other Comments: "Absolutely try to go. Great place!" "There are a lot of Mental Health Care Level 3 and 4 people here. This can both be interesting and problematic due to the psych issues."

Camp Prison Politics: There are no politics at this facility.

Camp Level of Violence: There is virtually no amount of violence at this prison.

Camp Vulnerable Populations: While sex offenders are precluded from Camp placement, informants and LGBT inmates are allowed to walk the yard.

Camp Good: "The living arrangements are good, as is the consideration given to the elderly (e.g., the elevator). There is also a pilot program where we can video chat with family for $6 for 25 minutes."

Camp Bad: "Lots of informants who don't mind being vocal about it." "This is not home."

Camp Other Comments: "This is the best Camp that I've been to by far."

In the News: In July 2018, Kevin Labracio Frazier, a prisoner at the Federal Medical Center in Lexington, was sentenced to an additional nine years and seven months in prison after being convicted of repeatedly punching another prisoner in the head and face.

In December 2017, Eric Brown, the man accused of kidnapping and murdering Ashanti Billie, was temporarily housed at FMC Lexington.

In July 2017, James Carrington, a guard at FMC Lexington, pleaded guilty to accepting bribes from a woman named Stephanie Dukes in exchange for smuggling contraband such as cigarettes and cell phones to Dukes' boyfriend, FMC Lexington prisoner Keith Griffith.

In October 2015, Michael Hardin, an employee at FMC Lexington, was federally indicted for accepting $22,000 in bribes and supplying contraband to prisoners.

Camp in the News: In January 2015, writer and peace activist Kathy Kelly was sent to the women's satellite prison camp at Federal Medical Center Lexington again. Kelly was sentenced to a year in federal prison in 1988 for planting corn on nuclear missile sites, and to three months in 2014 for trying to deliver a loaf of bread to an Air Force base commander with a request that drone flights over Afghanistan be stopped. Her writing, which is critical of the prison industrial complex, has been featured at *Huffington Post*, Progressive.org, and ConsortiumNews.com.

In March 2005, Reginald Wilson, a guard at FMC Lexington Camp, was sentenced to probation for sexually assaulting a female prisoner.

In January 2005, Gregory Goins, a guard at FMC Lexington Camp, was sentenced to nine years in prison for sexually abusing a prisoner and lying to a federal agent.

FCI Manchester

Federal Correctional Institution Manchester | FCI Manchester

Facilities: FCI Manchester and an adjacent minimum-security satellite prison camp.

Facility Address & Contact Information

Federal Correctional Institution Manchester
805 Fox Hollow Road
Manchester, KY 40962

Phone: 606-598-1900
Fax: 606-599-4115
Email: MAN/ExecAssistant@bop.gov

BOP Website: https://www.bop.gov/locations/institutions/man/
Wikipedia: https://en.wikipedia.org/wiki/
Federal_Correctional_Institution%2C_Manchester
ZCG Website: https://www.prisonerresource.com/resources/federal-prison-profiles/mid-atlantic-region-mxr/federal-correctional-institution-manchester-fci-manchester/

Inmate Correspondence Address

For FCI Manchester

Inmate Name and Registration Number
FCI Manchester
Federal Correctional Institution
P.O. Box 4000
Manchester, KY 40962

For Satellite Prison Camp

Inmate Name and Registration Number
FCI Manchester
Satellite Prison Camp
P.O. Box 4000
Manchester, KY 40962

NOTE: Funds cannot be sent directly to federal inmates. See Chapter 1 for more information on sending funds to federal inmates.

Sex: Male

Security Level: Main: Medium Security; Camp: Minimum Security

Location: FCI Manchester is located in eastern Kentucky, approximately 75 miles south of Lexington, the state's second-largest city.

BOP Region: Mid-Atlantic Region (MXR)

BOP Institution Code: MAN for FCI Manchester

Judicial District: Eastern District of Kentucky

Medical Care Level: Level 1. See Chapter 2 for more information on Medical Care and Mental Health Care Levels.

Mental Health Care Level: Level 1

Population (as of May 1, 2019): Main: 967; Camp: 157

Background: Federal Correctional Institution Manchester is a medium-security federal prison located in Manchester, Kentucky, which houses male inmates. It was opened in 1992. Federal Correctional Institution Manchester Camp, which also houses male inmates, is located adjacent to the main institution.

Very little information is available to the public regarding this facility. In February 2018, an agreement was reached between the prison and Eastern Kentucky University for criminal justice students to take classes at the prison with inmates. In May 2014, a Prison Rape Elimination Act audit summary reported that all inspected elements of the facility met or exceeded compliance requirements.

Notable inmates include former Missouri State Senator Jeff Smith (served 8 months for obstruction of justice), and computer hacker Jeremy Hammond (convicted of conspiracy).

Housing: Inmates are housed in two-person cells within the eight housing units. The camp houses inmates in dormitories, which are divided into two-person cubicles. While there are four dormitories at the camp, two have been closed down.

Health Services: The FCI Manchester Health Services Unit provides emergency and routine ambulatory health care services. The outpatient clinic provides diagnostic and support services used by the health care providers in the provision of urgent and ambulatory care services. Included are examination rooms, treatment rooms, a medication room, dental clinic, radiology and laboratory areas, waiting areas, storage areas, and administrative offices. At the main facility there are two rooms used for suicide watch and custodial purposes. Medical and dental sick call are also provided. Sick call is held at 7:00 a.m., while pill line and insulin line are conducted at 7:30 a.m. and 6:00 p.m.

Psychology Services: FCI Manchester provides screening, assessment, and treatment of mental health problems, individual and group counseling, psycho-educational classes, self-help and supportive services, and referrals to Health Services for medical treatment of a mental illness. The Psychology Services Department offers community mental health services. Many services are designed to help inmates manage depression, anxiety, and serious mental illness like schizophrenia or bipolar disorder. Groups are available, and typically focus on topics like learning to manage emotions, stopping depressive thoughts, learning new communication skills, and wellness. Inmates who are identified as having mental health needs will have an appointment with a psychologist to discuss their needs and identify what types of groups and services would be most helpful. The Psychology Services department also offers groups for all inmates who want to learn skills that will help keep them out of prison and get along with others more effectively.

Residential Drug Abuse Program (RDAP): FCI Manchester does not offer a Residential Drug Abuse Program (RDAP). However, there are group programs including Alcoholics Anonymous (AA), Narcotics Anonymous (NA), a Drug Education class, and the Non-Residential Drug Abuse Program (NR-DAP).

Education Services: FCI Manchester provides literacy, GED, and English-as-a-Second Language (ESL) programs. Incentive awards are provided to recognize inmates making satisfactory progress and successfully completing the literacy (i.e., GED and ESL) program. Inmates may also receive incentives for progressing to various levels in the GED or ESL programs. Graduation ceremonies recognize GED, ESL, and Occupational Education completions. Parenting and Adult Continuing Education (ACE) classes are also available. High school diplomas and post-secondary degrees are available through paid correspondence programs.

Advanced Occupational Education: FCI Manchester offers advanced occupational education in Carpentry, Electrical, and Masonry Bricklayer. Both facilities offer Culinary Arts, and the camp offers Horticulture and Hydroponics.

Vocational Training: No vocational training is offered at FCI Manchester or the satellite camp aside from the advanced occupational education and apprenticeship programs.

Apprenticeship: FCI Manchester offers apprenticeships in Cabinetmaker, Carpentry, Drafting, Machine Operator I (Sewing), Painter, and Plumber. Both facilities offer Baker, Electrician, HVAC, and Landscape Management Technician. The camp offers Baker, Boiler Room Operator, Combination Welder, and Cook.

Library Services: The leisure library offers inmates a variety of reading materials which include periodicals, newspapers, fiction, nonfiction, and reference books. FCI Manchester also participates in an interlibrary loan program. Inmates are afforded access to legal materials and an opportunity to prepare legal documents. Legal research is primarily conducted on the electronic law library computers. Typewriters and a copy machine are also available for legal work.

UNICOR: FCI Manchester houses a UNICOR facility that makes clothing and textiles. The camp does not have a UNICOR facility.

Commissary: Inmates may use funds in their account to purchase items at the institution commissary (e.g., food, clothing, snacks, shoes, etc.), place funds on their inmate phone account, purchase TRU-Units for their TRULINCS account, or send funds outside of the institution using Form BP-199. Inmates are permitted to spend up to $360.00 per month. When shopping on their designated day, inmates must go to the commissary building, submit their order form, and wait for their order to be filled.

Recreation Services: Leisure activities at FCI Manchester include organized and informal games, sports, physical fitness, table games, hobbycrafts, music programs, intramural activities, social and cultural organizations, and movies. Art activities include paintings and sketches using traditional methods (e.g., oils, pastels, crayons, pencils, inks, and charcoal). Hobbycraft activities include leatherwork, models, crochet, drawing, card making, etc. Wellness programs include screening, assessments, goal setting, fitness/nutrition plans, and counseling. Inside, inmates have access to an art room, TVs, and a basketball court. Outside, inmates have access to a track, basketball, soccer, softball, horseshoes, and a weight pile.

Visitation Information: On Sunday, Friday, and Saturday visitation is held between 8:00 a.m. and 3:00 p.m. On federal holidays visitation is held between 8:00 a.m. and 3:00 p.m. See Chapter 1 for more information on visitation.

Prison Politics: This is a somewhat political yard. Inmates are required to be part of a car.

Level of Violence: Violence is minimal at this facility.

Vulnerable Populations: Sex offenders may not be allowed to walk the yard.

Good: "Quantity and quality of food; good dessert (e.g., ice cream, popsicles, etc.)."

Bad: "Politics, very rainy weather, and lots of fog counts."

Other Comments: "Sex offenders wouldn't do well here."

Camp Prison Politics: Due to being a Camp, there are virtually no politics. According to one respondent, the facility is "not political at all."

Camp Level of Violence: There is a very low level of violence. One inmate explained, "There is no violence; it is very safe." Another respondent agreed, stating, "There is just a bunch of talk, but no action."

Camp Vulnerable Populations: While informants and LGBT inmates can walk the yard, sex offenders are precluded from Camp placement by Bureau of Prisons policy.

Camp Good: "The wildlife. There are skunks, foxes, cats, dogs, raccoons, deer, and turkeys." "The COs are fairly friendly and not aggressive."

Camp Other Comments: "It's a good facility, though a bit boring." "Very green and outdoors." "We call it a 'daddy daycare.'"

In the News: In February 2018, a new program was announced that allows criminal justice students from Eastern Kentucky University and prisoners at Federal Correctional Institution Manchester to take a college course together in a prison environment.

USP McCreary

United States Penitentiary McCreary | USP McCreary

Facilities: USP McCreary with an adjacent minimum-security satellite prison camp.

Facility Address & Contact Information

United States Penitentiary McCreary
330 Federal Way
Pine Knot, KY 42635

Phone: 606-354-7000
Fax: 606-354-7190
Email: MCR/ExecAssistant@bop.gov

BOP Website: https://www.bop.gov/locations/institutions/mcr/
Wikipedia: https://en.wikipedia.org/wiki/United_States_Penitentiary%2C_McCreary
ZCG Website: https://www.prisonerresource.com/resources/federal-prison-profiles/mid-atlantic-region-mxr/united-states-penitentiary-mccreary-usp-mccreary/

Inmate Correspondence Address

For USP McCreary

Inmate Name and Registration Number
USP McCreary
U.S. Penitentiary
P.O. Box 3000
Pine Knot, KY 42635

For Satellite Prison Camp

Inmate Name and Registration Number
USP McCreary
Satellite Prison Camp
P.O. Box 3000
Pine Knot, KY 42635

NOTE: Funds cannot be sent directly to federal inmates. See Chapter 1 for more information on sending funds to federal inmates.

Sex: Male

Security Level: Main: High Security; Camp: Minimum Security

Location: USP McCreary is located approximately 88 miles north of Knoxville, Tennessee. 125 miles south of Lexington, Kentucky; and 208 miles south of Cincinnati, Ohio.

BOP Region: Mid-Atlantic Region (MXR)

BOP Institution Code: MCR for USP McCreary

Judicial District: Eastern District of Kentucky

Medical Care Level: Level 2. See Chapter 2 for more information on Medical Care and Mental Health Care Levels.

Mental Health Care Level: Level 2

Population (as of May 1, 2019): Main: 1,399; Camp: 142

Background: United States Penitentiary McCreary is a high-security federal prison located in Pine Knot, Kentucky, which houses male inmates. It was opened in 2003. United States Penitentiary McCreary Camp, which also houses male inmates, is located adjacent to the main institution.

As is the case with many high-security facilities, little information about this prison is available to the public. However, the media has reported on numerous violent incidents at USP McCreary, including inmate-on-inmate and inmate-on-staff assaults. Some staff members from the prison have been quoted by local media as being in fear of their lives due to the risks involved in their jobs at the facility. In October 2013, a controversial story aired on a local television station concerning the prison staff working without pay due to the 2013 federal government shutdown, while the prison inmates still collected pay from their work. While not reported in the story, the inmates were paid not from federal government budgets, but from an internal trust fund which is funded by inmate commissary purchases.

Notable inmates include gang leader Ronell Wilson (serving life for the murder of two New York City police detectives); former hitman for the Bonanno crime family Thomas Pitera (serving a life sentence for murder, murder conspiracy, and racketeering); white supremacist Ricky Mungia (serving a life sentence for civil rights violations); lawyer and financier Tim Durham (serving a 50-year sentence for conspiracy to commit mail fraud and securities fraud); and Otis Jackson (confessed to the crimes that political activist Jamil Al-Amin is currently serving a life sentence for).

Media reports indicate that at least one inmate has been stabbed on the orders of the Nuestra Familia gang.

Housing: Inmates are housed in one-person and two-person cells within the twelve housing units. Camp inmates are housed in dormitories.

Health Services: Medical and dental sick call, preventive health care services, emergency services, diagnosis and treatment of chronic infectious diseases, medications, dental care, eyeglasses, physical examination, and chronic care are available to inmates. Inmates must submit a triage form in order to receive routine care.

Psychology Services: USP McCreary and the satellite camp have psychologists who are available to provide counseling and other mental health services. All inmates meet with a psychologist for an intake screening interview during their first 14 days at the institution. The Challenge Program is available to inmates interested in making positive lifestyle changes. Group therapy, personal counseling, and a self-help library are also available. Groups are regularly offered in stress management, anger management, and self-image, amongst others.

Residential Drug Abuse Program (RDAP): Neither facility offers the Residential Drug Abuse Program (RDAP). Inmates can be referred to other facilities that provide the program. Both facilities offer Alcoholics Anonymous (AA), Narcotics Anonymous (NA), the Non-Residential Drug Abuse Program (NR-DAP), and a Drug Education Class.

Education Services: USP McCreary offers GED, English-as-a-Second Language (ESL), Adult Continuing Education (ACE), and parenting programs to inmates. High school diplomas and post-secondary degrees are available through paid correspondence programs.

Advanced Occupational Education: USP McCreary and the camp do not offer any advanced occupational education programs.

Vocational Training: The main facility offers vocational training in Office Clerk, Residential Wiring, and Web Page Designer. The camp offers Master Gardener.

Apprenticeship: USP McCreary offers apprenticeships in HVAC, Painter, Cook, and Electrical. The camp offers Auto Mechanic, Cook, Landscape Management, Landscape Technician, Powerhouse Mechanic, and Welding.

Library Services: A leisure library is available in the Education Department. Inmates may check out books, magazines, reference materials, and a number of newspapers. The law library is located in the Education Department and contains a variety of legal reference materials and the TRULINCS Electronic Law Library for use in preparing legal papers. Reference materials include the United States Code Annotated, Federal Reporter, Supreme Court Reporter, and Bureau of Prisons Program Statements, institution supplements, indexes, and other legal materials.

UNICOR: USP McCreary's UNICOR facility conducts Automated Data Processing (ADP), processing patents for the U.S. Patent Office.

Commissary: The total value of an inmate's accumulated commissary items must stay within the monthly spending limitation of $360.00. In addition, an inmate is authorized to have 60 postage stamps in his possession. At the commissary, inmates can purchase items such as snacks, food, drinks, clothing, electronics, and shoes.

Recreation Services: Recreation programs at USP McCreary include indoor and outdoor activities and range from individual arts and crafts programs to intramural team sports, such as softball, basketball, soccer, and volleyball.

Visitation Information: On Sunday and Saturday visitation is held between 8:30 a.m. and 3:00 p.m. On federal holidays visitation is held between 8:30 a.m. and 3:00 p.m. See Chapter 1 for more information on visitation.

In the News: Otis Jackson, the man who confessed, on three separate occasions, to the crime that political activist Jamil Al-Amin is serving a life sentence for, is being held at United States Penitentiary McCreary on unrelated charges.

In March 2013, a prisoner at USP McCreary was stabbed on the orders of Andrew Cenrantes, a leader of the Nuestra Familia gang who was imprisoned at USP Lewisburg.

FCI McDowell

Federal Correctional Institution McDowell | FCI McDowell

Facilities: FCI McDowell with an adjacent minimum-security satellite prison camp.

Facility Address & Contact Information

Federal Correctional Institution McDowell
101 Federal Drive
Welch, WV 24801

Phone: 304-436-7300
Fax: 304-436-7318
Email: MCD/ExecAssistant@bop.gov

BOP Website: https://www.bop.gov/locations/institutions/mcd/
Wikipedia: https://en.wikipedia.org/wiki/Federal_Correctional_Institution,_McDowell
ZCG Website: https://www.prisonerresource.com/resources/federal-prison-profiles/mid-atlantic-region-mxr/federal-correctional-institution-mcdowell-fci-mcdowell/

Inmate Correspondence Address

For FCI McDowell

Inmate Name and Registration Number
FCI McDowell
Federal Correctional Institution
P.O. Box 1009
Welch, WV 24801

For Satellite Prison Camp

Inmate Name and Registration Number
FCI McDowell
Satellite Prison Camp
P.O. Box 1009
Welch, WV 24801

NOTE: Funds cannot be sent directly to federal inmates. See Chapter 1 for more information on sending funds to federal inmates.

Sex: Male

Security Level: Main: Medium Security; Camp: Minimum Security

Location: FCI McDowell is located in southern West Virginia, four miles north of Welch and 48 miles southwest of Beckley, West Virginia.

BOP Region: Mid-Atlantic Region (MXR)

BOP Institution Code: MCD for FCI McDowell

Judicial District: Southern District of West Virginia

Medical Care Level: Level 1. See Chapter 2 for more information on Medical Care and Mental Health Care Levels.

Mental Health Care Level: Level 1

Population (as of May 1, 2019): Main: 1,261; Camp: 62

Background: Federal Correctional Institution McDowell is a medium-security federal prison in Welch, West Virginia, which houses male inmates. It was opened in 2011. Federal Correctional Institution McDowell Camp, which also houses male inmates, is located adjacent to the main institution.

The facility was completed in 2010 at an approximate cost of $233 million. The first inmates to arrive were assigned to the minimum-security prison camp and were immediately put to work in maintenance jobs. McDowell County residents had voted almost unanimously to allow the construction of the prison at its location because of the assertion that it would create many job opportunities for the economically challenged county. However, in July 2010, West Virginia Public Broadcasting reported that local people were not landing as many prison jobs as was expected. Out of the first 87 hires, only 12 were from McDowell County and five from the bordering Wyoming County. The McDowell County Animal Shelter sends some of its dogs to FCI McDowell and Federal Prison Camp Alderson as part of a program to help train and socialize the dogs before finding them forever homes.

Notable inmates include former Trenton, New Jersey, Mayor Tony F. Mack (serving a 58-month sentence for bribery, mail fraud, wire fraud, and extortion).

Media reports indicate that at least five inmates have been charged with weapons possession and three other prisoners have been charged with smuggling over the past several years.

Housing: Inmates are housed in two-, three-, and four-person cells. There is a total of 12 housing units. Inmates at the camp are housed in dormitories.

Health Services: Dental sick call, sick call, routine dental care, physical examinations, emergency services, eyeglasses, diagnosis and treatment of chronic infectious diseases, preventive health care services, and medications are provided to inmates. Sick call is held at 6:45 a.m. on Monday, Tuesday, Thursday, and Friday. Pill line is conducted twice a day.

Psychology Services: The FCI McDowell Psychology Department provides a variety of services. Individual counseling is available for inmates experiencing family, interpersonal, adjustment, or other personal concerns. Educational and therapeutic groups are offered as well. Group topics are determined based on population needs, interests, and staff availability. The self-help library program includes books and audio and video materials. A psychiatrist, who is a medical doctor, is available for regular consultation for those needing medications or medication monitoring. There are many alternatives for inmates who have personal problems and desire to correct them. These options include self-image groups and other voluntary groups conducted by correctional counselors.

Residential Drug Abuse Program (RDAP): FCI McDowell does not house a Residential Drug Abuse Program (RDAP), but referrals can be made to institutions that do provide RDAP. The facility provides a Drug Education Class and the Non-Residential Drug Abuse Program (NR-DAP), however.

Education Services: FCI McDowell and the satellite camp provide literacy, English-as-a-Second Language (ESL), and parenting programs. Adult Continuing Education (ACE) classes are also available. High school diplomas and post-secondary degrees are available through paid correspondence programs.

Advanced Occupational Education: FCI McDowell and the camp do not offer advanced occupational education programs.

Vocational Training: FCI McDowell offers vocational training in Carpentry, Masonry, and Residential Wiring. The camp offers Business Marketing.

Apprenticeship: FCI McDowell offers an apprenticeship in Dental Assistant. Both facilities offer apprenticeships in Cook, Electrical, HVAC, Plumber, and Teacher Assistant. The camp offers Welding.

Library Services: The law library is located in the Education Department and contains a variety of legal reference materials for use in preparing legal papers. Reference materials include the United States Code Annotated, Federal Reporter, Supreme Court Reporter, Bureau of Prisons Program Statements, institutional supplements, indexes, and other legal materials. Most of these materials are available on the TRULINCS Electronic Law Library computers. Inmates can also check out fiction and nonfiction books, newspapers, and magazines. DVD movies are also available for viewing.

UNICOR: FCI McDowell does not have a UNICOR facility.

Commissary: The total value of an inmate's accumulated commissary items (including special purchases) is limited to the monthly spending limit of $360.00. Inmates are allowed to purchase items such as candy, snacks, food, drinks, clothing, and shoes once per week. Inmates must submit their order form by 8:00 a.m. the day before they are scheduled to shop. On their designated shopping day, inmates are called unit-by-unit to pick up their orders.

Recreation Services: Leisure activities and recreation programs at FCI McDowell include indoor and outdoor activities, and range from individualized arts and crafts programs to intramural team sports. Physical fitness and weight reduction programs are also available. Indoors, inmates have access to treadmills, stair climbers, stationary bikes, ellipticals, indoor basketball, TVs, art room, leather room, band rooms, musical equipment, and tables. Outdoors, inmates have access to softball, football, soccer, handball, basketball, and a track.

Visitation Information: On Sunday, Monday, and Saturday visitation is held between 8:00 a.m. and 3:00 p.m. On federal holidays visitation is held between 8:00 a.m. and 3:00 p.m. See Chapter 1 for more information on visitation.

Prison Politics: This is a very political yard. Inmates have to be part of a racially-oriented car to stay. According to one respondent, the races and cars "claim everything from TVs and tables to cells."

Level of Violence: While most respondents stated that there is a moderate level of violence, a few suggested that "violence is pretty low, and safety overall is pretty good." Most agreed that there are lots of fights and that stabbings are not unusual.

Vulnerable Populations: Sex offenders and LGBT inmates cannot stay. If informants can fly under the radar, then they can walk the yard. According to one inmate, "sex offenders are usually run up top the day they get here, and informants are usually beat off. There are a few gay inmates here, but they are pretty much shunned. They have nowhere to sit in the chow hall."

Good: "Nine TVs per housing unit." "The food is really good."

Bad: "Lots of car meetings. Very political." "We get locked down every time the Warden breaks a nail. They have made it very hard to get mail from your family by only allowing white paper, white envelopes, and even rejecting mail based on the color of ink used to write the letters." "No microwaves." "The prison is in poor condition even though it is relatively new."

Other Comments: "Stand-up white guys who aren't homosexual will like it. Such inmates will like how time is done here. If not, stay away." "Not the best prison around, especially if your paperwork isn't good."

In the News: In December 2017, three prisoners at Federal Correctional Institution McDowell -- Scott Finnell, Misael Santana-Rivera and Antonio R. Azpeitia -- were each sentenced to a year and three months, and prisoners Ernest Shields and Diego Ninos were each sentenced to two years for the possession of handcrafted weapons known as shanks.

In November 2017, Marcus Buggs, Frederick Griggin and Scotty Pullum, prisoners at FCI McDowell, were sentenced to between five and six additional months in prison for separate incidents of attempting to smuggle drugs into the facility.

In June 2017, Christopher Williams, a prisoner at FCI McDowell, pleaded guilty to possessing a weapon -- a handmade shank -- while in prison, and faces up to five additional years.

Camp in the News: In June 2014, the former mayor of Trenton, New Jersey, Tony Mack, reported to Federal Correctional Institution McDowell Camp to begin his 58-month sentence for public corruption.

FCI Memphis

Federal Correctional Institution Memphis | FCI Memphis

Facilities: FCI Memphis with an adjacent minimum-security satellite prison camp and a detention center.

Facility Address & Contact Information

Federal Correctional Institution Memphis
1101 John A Denie Road
Memphis, TN 38134

Phone: 901-372-2269
Fax: 901-380-2462
Email: MEM/ExecAssistant@bop.gov

BOP Website: https://www.bop.gov/locations/institutions/mem/
Wikipedia: https://en.wikipedia.org/wiki/Federal_Correctional_Institution%2C_Memphis
ZCG Website: https://www.prisonerresource.com/resources/federal-prison-profiles/mid-atlantic-region-mxr/federal-correctional-institution-memphis-fci-memphis/

Inmate Correspondence Address

For FCI Memphis

Inmate Name and Registration Number
FCI Memphis
Federal Correctional Institution
P.O. Box 34550
Memphis, TN 38184

For Satellite Prison Camp

Inmate Name and Registration Number
FCI Memphis
Satellite Prison Camp
P.O. Box 2000
Millington, TN 38083

NOTE: Funds cannot be sent directly to federal inmates. See Chapter 1 for more information on sending funds to federal inmates.

Sex: Male

Security Level: Main: Medium Security; Camp: Minimum Security

Location: FCI Memphis is located in the northeast section of Memphis, Tennessee.

BOP Region: Mid-Atlantic Region (MXR)

BOP Institution Code: MEM for FCI Memphis

Judicial District: Western District of Tennessee

Medical Care Level: Level 2. See Chapter 2 for more information on Medical Care and Mental Health Care Levels.

Mental Health Care Level: Level 2

Population (as of May 1, 2019): Main & Detention Center: 1,086; Camp: 229

Background: Federal Correctional Institution Memphis is a medium-security federal prison located in Memphis, Tennessee, which houses male inmates. It was opened in 1977. Federal Correctional Institution Memphis Camp, which also houses male inmates, is located adjacent to the main institution.

In addition to housing medium-security federal prisoners, FCI Memphis also contains a unit designated for the housing of pre-trial and pre-sentence federal detainees. In 2012, a joint investigation conducted by the FBI, the Bureau of Prisons, and the Department of Justice Inspector General exposed a drug distribution ring run by several inmates with the assistance of corrupt prison staff members.

Media reports indicate that at least 11 prisoners have been transported to local area hospitals following brawls at the prison. At least three prisoners have escaped from the camp in the past several years.

In 2009, *Forbes* magazine named FCI Memphis one of the ten cushiest federal prisons in America.

Housing: Inmates are housed in two-person cells within the five housing units. In the camp there are dormitories of two-and four-person cubicles within the four housing units.

Health Services: The FCI Memphis Health Services Department offers a wide variety of services and is staffed by physicians, mid-level practitioners, nurses, pharmacists, dentists, and administrative staff. All inmates are assigned a primary care provider (PCP) and may not change PCPs. Health services include an initial screening, sick call, periodic health examinations, eyeglasses, dental services, medications, emergency medical services, and diagnosis and treatment of chronic infectious diseases. Emergency care is available 24 hours a day.

Psychology Services: Every inmate at FCI Memphis must complete a Psychology Services Inmate Questionnaire within 14 days of his arrival. Inmates who are experiencing major psychological symptoms such as depression or anxiety, as well as those with significant interpersonal difficulties, are encouraged to seek services. Available services to inmates include individual counseling and crisis intervention, simple advice concerning personal issues, psychological testing (only by proper referral), and specialty groups such as anger management and stress management.

Residential Drug Abuse Program (RDAP): FCI Memphis has the Residential Drug Abuse Program (RDAP). It also offers Alcoholics Anonymous (AA), Narcotics Anonymous (NA), a Drug Education class, and the Non-Residential Drug Abuse Program (NR-DAP). The camp screens inmates for the Residential Drug Abuse Program (RDAP) but does not have its own RDAP facility.

Education Services: FCI Memphis offers literacy, Pre-GED, GED, Spanish GED, English-as-a-Second Language (ESL), and parenting programs to inmates. Career counseling, educational advisement, Adult Continuing Education (ACE) courses, and a Pre-Release Program are also available to inmates. High school diplomas and post-secondary degrees are available through paid correspondence programs.

Advanced Occupational Education: Both facilities offer advanced occupational education in Logistics/Transportation Management and Quality Assurance and Supervision. FCI Memphis also offers occupational education in Building Trades.

Vocational Training: FCI Memphis does not offer any vocational training.

Apprenticeship: Both facilities offer apprenticeships in Career Development Technician, Carpenter (Maintenance), Cook (Hotel and Restaurant), Dental Assistant, Electrician, HVAC, Landscape Gardener, and Teacher Aide. The main facility offers apprenticeships in Drafter (Architectural), Electronics Tester, Machinist, Maintenance Electrician, Painter, Plumber, Purchasing Agent, and Quality Control Technician. The camp offers apprenticeships in Engraver, Golf Course Management, Printer-Slotter and Operator, and Welder (Combination).

Library Services: A leisure and law library is available to FCI Memphis inmates. An Interlibrary Loan Program associated with the Memphis/Shelby County Library is also available. In the leisure library, inmates can check out books, magazines, and newspapers. A DVD movie program is also available. In the law library inmates can use the TRULINCS Electronic Law Library, a copy machine, and typewriters.

UNICOR: FCI Memphis houses a UNICOR factory producing and servicing electronic cable assemblies and a printing operation.

Commissary: Inmates may withdraw money for reasons of personal spending in the institution's commissary, for family support, or other approved purposes. Inmates are permitted to spend up to $360.00 per month on items such as shoes, food, drinks, clothing, electronics, and other items. Copy cards, postage stamps, and over-the-counter medications do not count against the spending limitation. Inmates may only shop once a week on their designated shopping day.

Recreation: The Recreation Department offers intramural sports where inmates can participate in softball, basketball, soccer, volleyball, handball, and flag football. The Wellness Program offers instruction on various health/fitness topics. Activities available include structured classes, exercise programs and fitness clubs. Participants can receive certificates for program completion. A variety of activities are available on the recreation yard, softball field, and in the gymnasium for "off-duty" inmates, including bocce ball, volleyball, handball, racquetball, basketball, soccer, shuffleboard, horseshoes, stationary bikes, and football. There is a jogging/walking track which is approximately 1/3 mile in length and an activity room available for ping pong. Recreation also offers a music room for individual practice and for use by groups. The Hobbycraft Program provides tools, a work room and instruction in various crafts including leather craft, woodworking, painting, and beading. The recreation yard also has a weight pile.

Visitation Information: On Sunday, Monday, and Saturday visitation is held between 8:00 a.m. and 3:00 p.m. On federal holidays visitation is held between 8:00 a.m. and 3:00 p.m. See Chapter 1 for more information on visitation.

Prison Politics: There is some level of politics at this prison, but not much. Somewhat racially divided, but not truly political.

Level of Violence: There is a low level of violence at this facility.

Vulnerable Populations: Most respondents stated that sex offenders, informants, and LGBT inmates can stay, though they may be ostracized. One respondent in particular stated that "sex offenders are not generally allowed and are typically run off."

Good: "The recreation offerings are really good. The art program is particularly good. There is also air conditioning in the buildings."

Bad: "There is a large Hispanic population which tries to run the yard." "The drug problem is really bad."

Other Comments: "It's a good place." "Nice yard."

In the News: In April 2018, a brawl in the recreation yard at Federal Correctional Institution Memphis resulted in eleven prisoners being transported to an outside medical facility for treatment.

Camp in the News: In March 2018, three prisoners at Federal Correctional Institution Memphis Camp escaped and were recaptured the next day, making it the third escape from the prison camp since 2013.

In November 2017, Travon Gardner, a prisoner at FCI Memphis Camp, walked away from the camp without authorization. He was subsequently taken back into custody.

FCI Morgantown

Federal Correctional Institution Morgantown | FCI Morgantown

Facilities: FCI Morgantown with a detention center.

Facility Address & Contact Information

Federal Correctional Institution Morgantown
446 Greenbag Road, Route 857
Morgantown, WV 26501

Phone: 304-296-4416
Fax: 304-284-3600
Email: MRG/ExecAssistant@bop.gov

BOP Website: https://www.bop.gov/locations/institutions/mrg/
Wikipedia: https://en.wikipedia.org/wiki/Federal_Correctional_Institution%2C_Morgantown
ZCG Website: https://www.prisonerresource.com/resources/federal-prison-profiles/mid-atlantic-region-mxr/federal-correctional-institution-morgantown-fci-morgantown/

Inmate Correspondence Address

Inmate Name and Registration Number
FCI Morgantown
Federal Correctional Institution
P.O. Box 1000
Morgantown, WV 26507

NOTE: Funds cannot be sent directly to federal inmates. See Chapter 1 for more information on sending funds to federal inmates.

Sex: Male

Security Level: Minimum Security

Location: On the southern edge of Morgantown, in north central West Virginia.

BOP Region: Mid-Atlantic Region (MXR)

BOP Institution Code: MRG for FCI Morgantown

Judicial District: Northern District of West Virginia

Medical Care Level: Level 2. See Chapter 2 for more information on Medical Care and Mental Health Care Levels.

Mental Health Care Level: Level 2

Population (as of May 1, 2019): 853

Background: Federal Correctional Institution Morgantown is a minimum-security federal prison located in Morgantown, West Virginia, which houses male inmates. It was opened in 1969. The facility also contains a detention center.

Notable inmates include the first winner of the reality TV show Survivor Richard Hatch (convicted of tax evasion); former Arizona Congressman Rick Renzi (convicted of extortion, bribery, insurance fraud, money laundering, and racketeering); former mayor of Charlotte, North Carolina, Patrick Cannon (convicted of services fraud); and former Ohio Congressman Bob Ney (convicted of services fraud).

In 2017, Insider Monkey named FCI Morgantown one of the ten easiest federal prisons to do time. In 2012, CNBC named the facility one of the 12 best federal prisons in which to do time.

Housing: Inmates are housed in dormitories, consisting primarily of two-person cubicles and rooms. There are several inmate housing units.

Health Services: FCI Morgantown's Health Services Department offers a variety of healthcare services including initial evaluation, treatment of chronic conditions, and emergency medical care. Sick call is conducted Monday, Tuesday, Wednesday, and Friday at 6:45 a.m. Pill and insulin line are held during breakfast and dinner.

Psychology Services: During the admission and orientation program inmates will have a chance to be interviewed individually by a member of the psychology staff. Psychology Services provide crisis intervention and brief counseling.

Residential Drug Abuse Program (RDAP): FCI Morgantown houses the Residential Drug Abuse Program (RDAP). It also offers a Drug Education Class and the Non-Residential Drug Abuse Program (NR-DAP).

Education Services: FCI Morgantown provides GED and English-as-a-Second Language (ESL) programs. Adult Continuing Education (ACE) courses are also available, with classes including Microsoft Office and a Job Search Class introducing inmates to various employment skills. This program covers a variety of topics including career explorations, resume writing, portfolio development, job market search, networking, and interview techniques. Other ACE classes include space travel, introduction to auto body, civil rights, CDL, and finance. A Mock Job Fair is also held once a year in the spring. Local employers and transitional services come into the institution and perform "mock" interviews. It is an all-day event and inmates prepare for the event by attending a 10-week Job Search Class. High school and post-secondary education are available through paid correspondence programs.

Advanced Occupational Education: FCI Morgantown does not offer any advanced occupational education programs.

Vocational Training: No vocational training is offered at FCI Morgantown.

Apprenticeship: FCI Morgantown offers an apprenticeship in Welding.

Library Services: A leisure library and an electronic law library are available for inmates. Fiction and nonfiction books, newspapers, and magazines can be checked out. An interlibrary loan program is available. Inmates also have access to the TRULINCS Electronic Law Library. Typewriters and a copy machine are available for inmate use.

UNICOR: FCI Morgantown has a UNICOR facility that offers call center/help desk services.

Commissary: Inmates are permitted to shop once per week on their designated day. Currently, sales are conducted Monday through Thursday. Inmates are permitted to spend up to a $360.00 each month for regular purchases and special purchase items. Stamps, over-the counter medications, TRULINCS credits, and phone calls are not counted against this spending limit.

Recreation Services: FCI Morgantown's Recreation Department includes an auditorium, multi-purpose room, gymnasium, and a range of indoor/outdoor sports and activities. While some recreational activities are organized, others are available on a leisure-time basis. Recreation programs include indoor/outdoor sports and activities, hobbycraft programs, health/fitness promotion, and disease prevention programs. Leisure time may be spent watching television, playing table games, or participating in sports. Hobbycraft activities are offered daily. The hobby shop includes crafts such as drawing, painting, leather craft, crochet, and beading. Outside, inmates have access to a weight pit, handball, Frisbee, soccer, track, softball, cornhole, and a track. After 4:00 p.m., inmates can walk to a second track which encircles a duck pond. Hours of operation for outdoor recreation are 6:30 to 10:00 a.m., 11:00 a.m. to 3:30 p.m., and 5:00 to 8:30 p.m. Hours of operation for indoor recreation are 12:45 a.m. to 3:30 p.m. and 5:45 to 7:30 p.m.

Visitation Information: On Sunday and Saturday visitation is held between 8:00 a.m. and 3:00 p.m. On Friday visitation is held between 5:00 and 9:00 p.m. On federal holidays visitation is held between 8:00 a.m. and 3:00 p.m. See Chapter 1 for more information on visitation.

Prison Politics: Little to no prison politics. According to one inmate, "There are no politics at all on the yard. Everyone houses with everyone else for the most part." Another respondent agreed, stating that this is "not a political yard."

Level of Violence: There is very little violence at this facility. According to one respondent, "The safety is a 10 out of 10. While there are a few fist fights from time to time, these are never serious and more like what you would see in middle school." Another inmate stated that there is "zero violence."

Vulnerable Populations: Due to not having a fence, sex offenders are not allowed by Bureau policy. Informants and LGBT inmates can stay. According to one respondent, "EVERYONE can walk the yard with no issue, this extends to informants and homosexuals."

Good: "No 10-minute moves." "The setting is beautiful and serene here."

Bad: "The compound is run more like a Low than a Camp."

In the News: In February 2017, former Buffalo police officer Robert Eloff reported to Federal Correctional Institution Morgantown to begin his three-month prison term for falsifying an arrest.

In November 2014, the former mayor of Charlotte, North Carolina, Patrick Cannon, arrived at FCI Morgantown to begin his 44-month sentence for bribery.

FCC Petersburg

Federal Correctional Complex Petersburg | FCC Petersburg

Facilities: FCC Petersburg houses FCI Petersburg Medium and FCI Petersburg Low, with an adjacent minimum-security satellite prison camp.

FCI Petersburg Medium

Federal Correctional Institution Petersburg Medium | FCI Petersburg Medium

Facility Address & Contact Information

Federal Correctional Institution Petersburg Medium
1060 River Road
Hopewell, VA 23860

Phone: 804-504-7200
Fax: 804-504-7204
Email: PEM/ExecAssistant@bop.gov

BOP Website: https://www.bop.gov/locations/institutions/pem/
Wikipedia: https://en.wikipedia.org/wiki/Federal_Correctional_Institution%2C_Petersburg
ZCG Website: https://www.prisonerresource.com/resources/federal-prison-profiles/mid-atlantic-region-mxr/federal-correctional-complex-petersburg-fcc-petersburg/federal-correctional-institution-petersburg-medium-fci-petersburg-medium/

Inmate Correspondence Address

Inmate Name and Registration Number
FCI Petersburg Medium
Federal Correctional Institution
P.O. Box 1000
Petersburg, VA 23804

NOTE: Funds cannot be sent directly to federal inmates. See Chapter 1 for more information on sending funds to federal inmates.

Sex: Male

Security Level: Medium Security

Location: FCI Petersburg is located 25 miles southeast of Richmond, Virginia.

BOP Region: Mid-Atlantic Region (MXR)

BOP Institution Code: PEM for FCI Petersburg Medium, PEX for Petersburg Federal Correctional Complex

Judicial District: Eastern District of Virginia

Medical Care Level: Level 2. See Chapter 2 for more information on Medical Care and Mental Health Care Levels.

Mental Health Care Level: Level 2

Population (as of May 1, 2019): 1,588

Background: Federal Correctional Institution Petersburg Medium is a medium-security federal prison in Hopewell, Virginia, which houses male inmates. It was opened in 2002 and is part of the Petersburg Federal Correctional Complex.

The institution is a Sex Offender Management Program (SOMP) facility. As such, around 40 percent of the inmate population is incarcerated for current or past sexual offenses. The facility has begun to house transgender male-to-female inmates who have been moved from other Bureau of Prisons facilities. This enables the protection and enhanced management of this vulnerable population. In both 2015 and 2018, transgender inmates committed suicide by hanging themselves.

Notable inmates include Jewish Rabbi David A. Kaye (convicted of illicit sexual conduct); former mayor of Newark, New Jersey, Sharpe James (convicted of fraud); and NFL safety Darren Sharper (convicted of multiple counts of sexual assault).

Media reports indicate that at least two guards have been convicted of smuggling contraband into the institution. News reports also indicate that Darren Sharper was transferred from the institution as a result of unauthorized donations of sports equipment made to the recreation department. At least one recreation department guard was also disciplined as a result of facilitating the donations. At least three inmates have committed suicide while housed at the institution.

Housing: Inmates are housed in two, three, and four-person cells. There is a total of twelve housing units. E-North is the RDAP unit.

Health Services: FCI Petersburg offers sick call, medications, treatment of medical emergencies, dental sick call, routine dental care, eyeglasses, hearing aids, and physical examinations to inmates. For routine health care, inmates must attend sick call, which is held Monday, Tuesday, Thursday, and Friday at 8:30 a.m. For emergency dental care, inmates must attend dental sick call, which is held Monday, Tuesday, Thursday, and Friday at 6:30 a.m. Insulin line is conducted before breakfast and dinner. Pill line is held at 6:30 a.m. and 5:30 p.m., with self-carry medication pickup conducted during the noon meal.

Psychology Services: All inmates are screened by a psychologist during the institution's admission and orientation program. Crisis counseling, coping skills, suicide prevention, mental health counseling, and spiritual counseling are all available to inmates. FCI Petersburg Medium also offers the Non-Residential Sex Offender Treatment Program (SOTP-NR).

Residential Drug Abuse Program (RDAP): FCI Petersburg Medium houses a Residential Drug Abuse Program (RDAP). A Non-Residential Drug Abuse Program (NR-DAP) and a Drug Education Class are also offered.

Education Services: FCI Petersburg Medium provides literacy, GED, and English-as-a-Second Language (ESL) programs. Adult Continuing Education (ACE) classes and a parenting program are also available. Current ACE classes include bookkeeping, CDL, creative writing, auto sales, payroll accounts, and CDL business. High school diplomas and post-secondary degrees are available through paid correspondence programs

Advanced Occupational Education: FCI Petersburg Medium does not offer any advanced occupational education programs.

Vocational Training: FCI Petersburg Medium offers vocational training in AutoCAD and Carpentry.

Apprenticeship: FCI Petersburg Medium offers apprenticeships in HVAC, Landscape, and Plumbing.

Library Services: A general library includes a variety of magazines, newspapers, reference materials, and fiction and nonfiction books necessary for meeting inmates' educational, cultural, and leisure needs. An Interlibrary Loan Program is available in conjunction with the Appomattox Regional Library. Inmates also have access to a number of DVD movies. Inmates are able to prepare legal documents and have reasonable access to legal materials via TRULINCS the Electronic Law Library (LexisNexis). Additionally, the law library contains required legal publications, general legal reference materials, and a selection of Bureau of Prisons policies. Inmates have access to typewriters and a copy machine.

UNICOR: FCI Petersburg Medium houses a UNICOR facility that receives, sorts, and repackages clothes hangers for private vendors.

Commissary: Inmates may use funds in their account to purchase items at the institution commissary, place funds on their inmate phone account, purchase TRU-Units for their TRULINCS account, or send funds out of the institution using Form BP-199. It is the responsibility of the inmate to know the amount of money available in his account. Items such as ice cream, snacks, food, candy, clothing, shoes, and electronics in the commissary are available for purchase. Inmates are permitted to spend up to $360 per month in the commissary. Sales are conducted Monday through Thursday at 9:00 a.m., 11:00 a.m., and 2:00 p.m. UNICOR inmates shop at 3:00 p.m.

Recreation: FCI Petersburg Medium's recreation facilities include basketball courts, athletic fields, a handball & racquetball court, a volleyball court, soccer field, a tennis court, a bocce ball court, softball field, horseshoe pits, and a walking track area. The facility also offers organized intramural leagues throughout the calendar year including soccer, volleyball, softball, basketball, Ultimate Frisbee, and flag football. The hobbycraft programs include drawing, painting, leather craft kits, crochet, and cross stitch. Inmates can also play pool, watch TV, and participate in the band program, which offers guitars, bass, drums, piano, violin, and other musical equipment.

Visitation Information: On Sunday and Saturday visitation is held between 8:00 a.m. and 3:00 p.m. On Monday, Thursday, and Friday visitation is held between 5:00 and 9:00 p.m. On federal holidays visitation is held between 8:00 a.m. and 3:00 p.m. See Chapter 1 for more information on visitation.

Prison Politics: This is not a political yard at all. While there is no car requirement, there are groups of inmates who elect to join cars and gangs. Within these groups there can be some politics. These groups sometimes claim tables in the chow hall, housing units, or on the recreation yard. For those not a part of these groups, there is no checking of paperwork. As reported by one respondent, "You have a few fringe groups who every now and then try something, but nothing significant, and usually confined within their groups."

Level of Violence: There is very little violence at this prison. Inmates report that any violence is typically of an interpersonal nature, not group-oriented. There tends to be one or so fistfights a week. One respondent stated that "the safety level is really high." Another agreed, stating, "This is a very safe yard, especially for sex offenders and those of alternative lifestyles." Another respondent explained, "I would rate the safety of this yard as a 9 out of 10. If you know how to carry yourself in a prison setting, you will have no problems on this yard." The belief that this yard is safe was repeated by many other respondents.

Vulnerable Populations: Sex offenders, informants, and LGBT inmates can walk the yard. Generally, all of these groups are welcome and are not harassed by fellow inmates. According to one inmate, "This is a SOMP yard, so there are sex offenders, informants, gang drop-outs, and PC inmates. There is a large gay and transgender population as well." Another respondent echoed this, stating, "Sex offenders almost run this yard. This is primarily a P.C. yard." One inmate stated, "Sex offenders, informants, and gay and transgender inmates casually interact in general population."

Good: "Pretty lenient yard for the most part." "Some guards are prejudiced towards gays, transgender inmates, and sex offenders." "Safe." "Clean facility, good food." "Almost anyone can walk the yard." "Very easy and laid-back yard." "You can be yourself here and people will leave you be." "Lots of K2 and Suboxone." "Overall the staff is good." "The population is very casual. Everyone generally seems to get along."

Bad: "Lack of respect between inmates." "The officers treat inmates very poorly because of the large sex offender population." "Lots of gay drama." "Not a whole lot in the way of training and education." "There are a handful of bad lieutenants and compound officers." "The good things are few and far between." "While some of the staff is alright, others take it upon themselves to be jerks." "Bad medical care."

Other Comments: "For vulnerable populations, Petersburg can be a life saver." "Strange facility, very strange." "If you are a softer sort or a sex offender, transfer here. This is a safe yard where time isn't too bad." "For what it is, it isn't too bad." "Sex offenders, informants, and LGBT folks are perfectly safe here." "The facility is referred to on the compound as 'Sweetersburg' because of the overall safety and diversity here." "Nice yard. Good safety."

In the News: In September 2018, two prisoners at Federal Correctional Institution Petersburg Medium died: one of a suicide and the other an accidental death.

In February 2017, U.S. Marshals arrested Matthew Ezekiel Stager, a sex offender who was released from FCI Petersburg Medium but failed to report to his designated halfway house in Texas. While at the facility, Stager, who was known as "Bird Man," continuously engaged in erratic behavior such as asking guards if they had any bath salts and making loud bird sounds. While incarcerated, he had multiple tattoos added to his face and body.

In May 2015, Jermaine Brown, a guard at FCI Petersburg Medium, was federally indicted on charges of accepting money to smuggle heroin, marijuana and cigarettes into the facility for prisoners.

Between September and October 2012, FCI Petersburg Medium recreation specialist Jeffrey T. Jones was paid $1,500 in a scheme that involved prisoners Alvin Dewayne Hall and Patrick Gregory to smuggle marijuana and cigarettes.

FCI Petersburg Low

Federal Correctional Institution Petersburg Low | FCI Petersburg Low

Facilities: FCI Petersburg Low and an adjacent minimum-security satellite prison camp.

Facility Address & Contact Information

Federal Correctional Institution Petersburg Low
1100 River Road
Hopewell, VA 23860

Phone: 804-733-7881
Fax: 804-863-1510
Email: PET/ExecAssistant@bop.gov

BOP Website: https://www.bop.gov/locations/institutions/pet/
Wikipedia: https://en.wikipedia.org/wiki/Federal_Correctional_Institution%2C_Petersburg
ZCG Website: https://www.prisonerresource.com/resources/federal-prison-profiles/mid-atlantic-region-mxr/federal-correctional-complex-petersburg-fcc-petersburg/federal-correctional-institution-petersburg-low-fci-petersburg-low/

Inmate Correspondence Address

For FCI Petersburg Low

Inmate Name and Registration Number
FCI Petersburg Low
Federal Correctional Institution
P.O. Box 1000
Petersburg, VA 23804

For Satellite Prison Camp

Inmate Name and Registration Number
FCI Petersburg Low
Satellite Prison Camp
P.O. Box 1000
Petersburg, VA 23804

NOTE: Funds cannot be sent directly to federal inmates. See Chapter 1 for more information on sending funds to federal inmates.

Sex: Male

Security Level: Main: Low Security; Camp: Minimum Security

Location: FCI Petersburg Low is located 25 miles southeast of Richmond, Virginia.

BOP Region: Mid-Atlantic Region (MXR)

BOP Institution Code: PET for FCI Petersburg Low, PEX for Petersburg Federal Correctional Complex

Judicial District: Eastern District of Virginia

Medical Care Level: Level 2. See Chapter 2 for more information on Medical Care and Mental Health Care Levels.

Mental Health Care Level: Level 2

Population (as of May 1, 2019): Main: 986; Camp: 288

Background: Federal Correctional Institution Petersburg Low is a low-security federal prison located in Hopewell, Virginia, which houses male inmates. It was opened in 1932 and is part of the Petersburg Federal Correctional Complex. Federal Correctional Institution Petersburg Camp, which also houses male inmates, was opened in 1978.

FCI Petersburg Low and the camp primarily house inmates who are to be released in the mid-Atlantic region of the United States. In 2017, the basement portions of the inmate housing units were deemed a health hazard and closed.

Notable inmates include former Tennessee police officer Richard Chandler (serving 25 years for child pornography offenses); Roger Loughry, Sr. (serving a 30-year sentence for advertising and distributing child pornography); and former Washington (DC) mayor Marion Barry.

Media reports indicate that at least two guards have been charged with sexually assaulting an inmate; one of the two was also convicted of bribery and smuggling contraband into the institution.

Housing: Inmates are housed in dormitories in two- or four-person cubicles. Most of the six housing units do not have air conditioning. Two of the older housing units have ten- and twelve-person rooms.

Health Services: Sick call, medications, treatment of medical emergencies, dental sick call, routine dental care, eyeglasses, hearing aids, physical examinations, and mandatory HIV testing are provided at the prison. Inmates must attend sick call in order to be seen by their primary health care provider. Sick call is conducted at 8:30 a.m. Monday, Tuesday, Thursday, and Friday.

Psychology Services: FCI Petersburg Low offers counseling and a variety of treatment groups including stress management, anger management, criminal thinking, and additional groups. Treatment offerings change quarterly based upon inmate population need. The Religious Services Department also offers the Life Connections Program for inmates who desire to grow as responsible persons.

Residential Drug Abuse Program (RDAP): FCI Petersburg Low houses the Residential Drug Abuse Program (RDAP). It also offers the Non-Residential Drug Abuse Program (NR-DAP), a Drug Education class, Smart Recovery, Alcoholics Anonymous (AA), and Narcotics Anonymous (NA).

Education Services: FCI Petersburg Low and the camp provide GED, English-as-a-Second Language (ESL), Adult Continuing Education (ACE), and parenting programs. Current ACE offerings include couponing, algebra, math, statistics, aviation history, and real estate. High school diplomas and post-secondary degrees are available through paid correspondence programs.

Advanced Occupational Education: FCI Petersburg Low and the camp do not offer advanced occupational education programs.

Vocational Training: FCI Petersburg Low offers vocational training in Carpentry, Machinist and Masonry. No vocational training is available at the camp.

Apprenticeship: FCI Petersburg Low offers apprenticeships in Binder, Cook, HVAC, Landscape, Machinist, Maintenance Electrician, and Plumbing. No apprenticeships are available at the camp.

Library Services: A general library includes a variety of magazines, newspapers, reference materials, and fiction and nonfiction books necessary for meeting inmates educational, cultural, and leisure needs. A DVD movie program is also available. An Interlibrary Loan Program is available. Inmates are able to prepare legal documents and have reasonable access to legal materials via the TRULINCS Electronic Law Library (LexisNexis). Additionally, the law library contains required legal publications, general legal reference materials, and a selection of Bureau of Prisons policies. Typewriters and a copy machine are also available for inmate use. Hours of operation are 7:30 a.m. to 8:30 p.m., Monday through Thursday and 7:30 a.m. to 3:30 p.m., Friday and Saturday, excluding meals, recalls, and counts.

UNICOR: FCI Petersburg Low UNICOR houses a printing plant.

Commissary: Inmates may use funds in their account to purchase items at the institution commissary, place funds on their inmate phone account, purchase TRU-Units for their TRULINCS account, and send funds out of the institution using Form BP-199. Inmates must have their commissary card in their possession at all times for identification purposes. Inmates can purchase a variety of items in the commissary, including beverages, food, snacks, clothing, and electronics. Inmates can spend up to $360 per month in the commissary. Shopping is conducted Monday through Thursday between 9:00 and 11:00 a.m. and 11:45 a.m. to 2:00 p.m. Inmates can only shop once a week on their designated shopping day.

Recreation: Recreation facilities at FCI Petersburg Low include a gymnasium, outdoor weight-lifting pavilion, athletic fields, a handball & racquetball court, basketball courts, a tennis court, a bocce ball court, and a walking track area. The recreation program offers both structured and leisure time activities as well as organized intramural leagues throughout the calendar year, including soccer, volleyball, softball, Frisbee, basketball, and flag football. All intramural teams are organized by housing units. Additional programs include an Institutional Movie Program, an Inmate Photo Program, a Band & Music Program, activities on recognized federal holidays, and various other programs. The hobbycraft programs include drawing, painting, leather craft kits, crochet, and cross stitch. Inmates also have access to pool tables and tables where Role Playing Games (RPG) can be played.

Visitation Information: On Sunday and Saturday visitation is held between 8:00 a.m. and 3:00 p.m. On Monday, Thursday, and Friday visitation is held between 5:00 and 9:00 p.m. On federal holidays visitation is held between 8:00 a.m. and 3:00 p.m. See Chapter 1 for more information on visitation.

Prison Politics: This is not a political yard. Inmates are not required to join a car or gang in order to stay.

Level of Violence: There is a very minimal level of violence at this prison. According to one respondent, "As a whole, this is a place where you are safe from people hurting you." Another inmate agreed, stating, "There is no violence here."

Vulnerable Populations: Sex offenders, informants, and LGBT inmates can walk the yard. Due to the Petersburg Medium being a SOMP institution, there are a number of sex offenders at this facility. According to one inmate, "All of these groups can easily walk this yard."

Good: "Our yard is pretty laid back. The guards leave inmates alone most of the time, but then again you can't get anything from them when needed since they are so lazy." "You can watch TV all night." "Cell phones and drugs aren't too hard to get a hold of." "Sometimes you can get a second tray of food in the chow hall." "Food is good." "Officers are generally polite." "It's a slack place, which is generally a good thing."

Bad: "Very boring." "Not many programs." "Rundown inmate housing units. You see cockroaches every day. All of the roofs leak." "No air conditioning and the weather gets very hot in the summer."

Other Comments: "It's a good go-home spot."

In the News: In 2016, Federal Correctional Institution Petersburg Low guard Catandra M. Chavis was accused of having sex with a prisoner in January 2015 and lying to federal authorities over plans to smuggle contraband into prison for him.

In 2007, Alfreda Best, another FCI Petersburg Low guard, pleaded guilty to accepting several thousand dollars in bribes to smuggle contraband to one prisoner, Miguel Cabrera, and having a consensual sexual relationship with another, Rodney Simmons.

Camp in the News: In January 2015, former Virginia Governor Bob McDonnell was sentenced to two years in federal prison for false declaration of bankruptcy and was expected to serve his term of imprisonment at Federal Correctional Institution Petersburg Camp.

CHAPTER 6:

North Central Region Prisons

North Central Regional Office

The North Central Regional Office is an administrative office providing oversight and support to facilities located in the North Central Region (NCR). The North Central Region covers Federal Bureau of Prison facilities located in Colorado, Iowa, Kansas, Illinois, Indiana, Michigan,

Minnesota, Missouri, Nebraska, North Dakota, South Dakota, and Wisconsin. These facilities are overseen by a regional office that provides oversight, technical assistance, and other types of operational support. In addition, they conduct training programs for staff in their region and assist state and local criminal justice agencies.

Regional Director: Jeffrey E. Krueger
NCR Population: 28,686

Facility Address & Contact Information

North Central Regional Office
Federal Bureau of Prisons
400 State Avenue, Suite 800
Kansas City, KS 66101

Email: NCRO/ExecAssistant@bop.gov

Phone: 913-621-3939

Fax: 913-551-1175

BOP Website: https://www.bop.gov/locations/regional_offices/ncro/

Wikipedia: n/a

ZCG Website: https://prisonerresource.com/resources/federal-prison-profiles/federal-prison-regional-offices/north-central-regional-office-ncr/

Staff Mail

Staff Name

North Central Regional Office

400 State Avenue, Suite 800

Kansas City, KS 66101

Freight and Non-USPS Parcels

Staff Name

North Central Regional Office

ATTN: Warehouse

400 State Avenue, Suite 800

Kansas City, KS 66101

North Central Region Prisons

MCC Chicago (IL)
FPC Duluth (MN)
FCI Englewood (CO)
FCI Florence (CO)
USP Florence (CO)
ADX Florence (CO)
FCI Greenville (IL)
USP Leavenworth (KS)
USP Marion (IL)
FCI Milan (MI)
FCI Oxford (WI)
FCI Pekin (IL)
FMC Rochester (MN)
FCI Sandstone (MN)
MCFP Springfield (MO)
FCI Terre Haute (IN)
USP Terre Haute (IN)
AUSP Thomson Camp (IL)
FCI Waseca (MN)
FPC Yankton (SD)

MCC Chicago

Metropolitan Correctional Center Chicago | MCC Chicago

Facility Address & Contact Information

Metropolitan Correctional Center Chicago
71 West Van Buren Street
Chicago, IL 60605

Phone: 312-322-0567
Fax: 312-347-4012
Email: CCC/ExecAssistant@bop.gov

BOP Website: https://www.bop.gov/locations/institutions/ccc/
Wikipedia: https://en.wikipedia.org/wiki/Metropolitan_Correctional_Center,_Chicago
ZCG Website: https://www.prisonerresource.com/resources/federal-prison-profiles/north-central-region-ncr/metropolitan-correctional-center-chicago-mcc-chicago/

Inmate Correspondence Address

Inmate Name and Registration Number
MCC Chicago
Metropolitan Correctional Center
71 West Van Buren Street
Chicago, IL 60605

NOTE: Funds cannot be sent directly to federal inmates. See Chapter 1 for more information on sending funds to federal inmates.

Sex: Male and Female Prisoners

Security Level: Administrative Security (Multiple Security Levels)

Location: MCC Chicago is located in downtown Chicago, at the intersections of Clark Street and Van Buren Street.

BOP Region: North Central Region (NCR)

BOP Institution Code: CCC for MCC Chicago

Judicial District: Northern District of Illinois

Medical Care Level: Level 2. See Chapter 2 for more information on Medical Care and Mental Health Care Levels.

Mental Health Care Level: Level 2

Population (as of May 1, 2019): 636

Background: Metropolitan Correctional Center Chicago is an administrative-security federal prison located in Chicago, Illinois, which houses both male and female inmates. It was opened in 1975.

The 26-story high-rise primarily houses pre-trial and pre-sentence detainees. In recent years, MCC Chicago has been in the news due to women performing strip shows on the roof of an adjacent parking garage for inmate viewing.

Notable inmates include high-ranking members of the Sinaloa Cartel Alfredo Vasquez-Hernandez and Tomas Arevalo-Renteria (facing charges of drug trafficking); radio personality Kevin Trudeau (sentenced to 10 years for criminal contempt); Thomas Zajac (serving 35 years for using a destructive device); former U.S. Representative Mel Reynolds (convicted of failure to file taxes); Mumbai terror attack conspirator David Headley; and author Piper Kerman (incarcerated for drug trafficking and money laundering).

Media reports indicate two inmates escaped by rappelling down 17 stories, one guard has been convicted of violating security procedures, at least two guards have been charged with smuggling contraband into the institution, one inmate was hospitalized after being assaulted by two other prisoners, and one case manager was held hostage by an inmate.

Housing: There are cells and dormitories for both male and female inmates.

Health Services: The Health Services Unit includes dental, medical, x-ray, and laboratory testing capabilities. Inmates receive a physical examination if they are at the prison for at least 10 days. The possible exception to this rule concerns inmates who are being transferred to MCC Chicago from another BOP facility. Inmates with chronic medical conditions are enrolled in a clinic to see a Primary Care Practitioner and a supervising physician. Inmates may retain non-metal, non-tinted, prescription glasses in their possession at the time of arrival. Repairs for non-Bureau of Prisons supplied glasses are at the inmate's expense. The Health

Services Administrator approves contact lenses only when an MCC Chicago clinician or one of their providers documents that standard prescription glasses will not address visual deficits. Preventive health care services, emergency services, dental services, and medications are also provided.

Psychology Services: MCC Chicago provides initial evaluations, along with group therapy. Typical offerings include anger management. Emergency psychological care is also available.

Residential Drug Abuse Program (RDAP): This facility does not house a Residential Drug Abuse Program (RDAP). The Drug Education class, the Non-Residential Drug Abuse Program (NR-DAP) and Alcoholics Anonymous (AA) are available.

Education Services: MCC Chicago provides literacy, GED, and English-as-a-Second Language (ESL) programs. The facility also offers a parenting program and Adult Continuing Education (ACE) classes. High school diplomas and post-secondary degrees are available through paid correspondence programs.

Advanced Occupational Education: MCC Chicago does not offer any advanced occupational education programs.

Vocational Training: MCC Chicago does not offer any vocational training programs.

Apprenticeship: There are no apprenticeship programs available at MCC Chicago.

Library Services: The TRULINCS Electronic Law Library, which is located in the Education Department, is where inmates can access legal materials and prepare legal documents. A leisure library is also available, where inmates can check out fiction and nonfiction books, newspapers, and magazines.

UNICOR: MCC Chicago does not house a UNICOR facility.

Commissary: The commissary spending limit is $360.00 per month. Inmates can purchase hygiene items, food, drinks, electronics, and other items.

Recreation Services: Recreation equipment is available within each housing unit at MCC Chicago. Though space is limited, there is full opportunity to maintain physical fitness with available equipment and scheduled recreational activities. Various board games are also available in the housing units. Hobbycraft classes are held twice a week and supplies are provided for all participants.

Visitation Information: On Sunday, Monday, Friday, and Saturday visitation is held between 9:00 a.m. and 3:00 p.m. On federal holidays visitation is held between 9:00 a.m. and 3:00 p.m. See Chapter 1 for more information on visitation.

In the News: In August 2018, former U.S. Representative Mel Reynolds reported to Metropolitan Correctional Center Chicago to begin serving his six-month sentence for failure to file his taxes.

In July 2018, David Headley, who was sentenced to 35 years in prison as one of the main conspirators of the Mumbai terror attacks, was attacked by two prisoners at MCC Chicago and hospitalized.

In March 2018, Rafael Lizak, a guard at MCC Chicago, was indicted for bribery and conspiracy to smuggle drugs, cell phones and other contraband into the facility.

In June 2017, the *New York Post* reported that the rooftop of a parking garage across the street from MCC Chicago "is the unlikely stage for gyrating women who perform dances and other sex acts" for the prisoners.

In April 2017, Carleous Clay, who was being held at MCC Chicago on federal charges of kidnapping and attempted murder, attacked a female case manager and held her at knifepoint before he was subdued with pepper spray.

In 2017, Tommy Haire, a religious services worker at MCC Chicago, was sentenced to two years of probation for violating several security measures, including allowing prisoners to make calls on his unmonitored cell phone, sending out prisoners' letters, and letting prisoners surf the internet on his computer.

In 2013, Tony Henderson, a guard at MCC Chicago, was sentenced to two years in prison after being convicted of smuggling food and cigarettes into the facility for bribes of up to $10,000.

In 2012, prisoner Jose Banks and his cellmate made a rope out of bed sheets and dental floss and rappelled 17 stories down the side of the MCC Chicago building. In order to aid the escape attempt, the pair had first managed to remove their cell's external window and the metal bar securing it. This resulted in the national implementation of a weekly "bar tap" where guards go into every cell and beat the window and metal housing with a mallet to ensure that it is still intact.

FPC Duluth

Federal Prison Camp Duluth | FPC Duluth

Facility Address & Contact information

Federal Prison Camp Duluth
4464 Ralston Drive
Duluth, MN 55811

Phone: 218-722-8634
Fax: 218-733-4701
Email: DTH/ExecAssistant@bop.gov

BOP Website: https://www.bop.gov/locations/institutions/dth/
Wikipedia: https://en.wikipedia.org/wiki/Federal_Prison_Camp,_Duluth
ZCG Website: https://www.prisonerresource.com/resources/federal-prison-profiles/north-central-region-ncr/federal-prison-camp-duluth-fpc-duluth/

Inmate Correspondence Address

Inmate Name and Registration Number
FPC Duluth
Federal Prison Camp
P.O. Box 1000
Duluth, MN 55814

NOTE: Funds cannot be sent directly to federal inmates. See Chapter 1 for more information on sending funds to federal inmates.

Sex: Male

Security Level: Minimum Security

Location: FPC Duluth is located on the southwest tip of Lake Superior, halfway between Minneapolis-St. Paul and the U.S.-Canadian Border; 7 miles north of Duluth, off Highway 53 at Stebner Road.

BOP Region: North Central Region (NCR)

BOP Institution Code: DTH for FPC Duluth

Judicial District: District of Minnesota

Medical Care Level: Level 2. See Chapter 2 for more information on Medical Care and Mental Health Care Levels.

Mental Health Care Level: Level 2

Population (as of May 1, 2019): 581

Background: Federal Prison Camp Duluth is a minimum-security federal prison located in Duluth, Minnesota, which houses male inmates. It was opened in 1983. FPC Duluth was previously the Duluth Air Force Base.

Notable inmates include former MLB player Jerry Koosman (convicted of federal tax charges), and political campaign contributor Stuart Levine (convicted of money laundering and mail fraud).

Media reports indicate that at one point at least 18 prisoners contracted MRSA at the institution and that at least two inmates have escaped.

In 2017, Insider Monkey named FPC Duluth one of the ten easiest federal prisons to do time.

Housing: Inmates are housed in two-person, three-person, and four-person cubicles within the five dormitories.

Health Services: Health services available to inmates include sick call, x-rays, lab, dental services, and a pharmacy. While emergency medical care is available 24 hours a day, inmates must attend sick call at 6:30 a.m. to be seen by a health care provider for non-emergency needs.

Psychology Services: The FPC Duluth Psychology Services Department consists of two psychologists and five drug treatment specialists available Monday through Friday. Inmates can reach them via cop-out (inmate request to staff), open-door policy, mainline, and through referral from staff. Individual appointments are scheduled by call-out, and inmates are required to check the call-out schedule daily for appointments. If there is an emergency, staff may be contacted at any time, and a psychologist will be contacted.

Residential Drug Abuse Program (RDAP): A Residential Drug Abuse Program (RDAP) is available at FPC Duluth. The facility also offers a drug education program and a Non-Residential Abuse Program (NR-DAP).

Education Services: FPC Duluth provides GED and English-as-a-Second Language (ESL) programs. Incentives are provided for continued effort and excellence as well as to reward the successful completion of an educational activity. The facility also offers a parenting program and Adult Continuing Education (ACE) classes. The ACE Program offers classes in the areas of foreign languages, math, business, and real estate, although classes vary from quarter to quarter. High school diplomas and post-secondary degrees are available through paid correspondence programs.

Advanced Occupational Education: FPC Duluth offers advanced occupational education courses in Construction Tech/Carpentry.

Vocational Training: No vocational training is offered at FPC Duluth aside from its advanced occupational education and apprenticeship programs.

Apprenticeship: FPC Duluth offers apprenticeships in Dentistry, Electrical, HVAC, and Plumbing.

Library Services: The leisure and law libraries are open daily for inmate use. The leisure library has daily newspapers, periodicals, reference books, and magazines for inmates to read and view. Inmates can also check out books. The law library is electronic, and inmates have access to typewriters and a copy machine.

UNICOR: FPC Duluth does not have a UNICOR facility.

Commissary: Inmates can spend up to $360.00 per month in the commissary, where they can buy food, snacks, candy, sodas, drink mixes, clothing, electronics, and shoes. Inmates are only allowed to shop once a week on their designated shopping day. Currently, sales are conducted Tuesday, Wednesday, and Thursday at 10:00 to 11:30 a.m. and 1:00 to 2:30 p.m.

Recreation Services: FPC Duluth offers a gymnasium with basketball, volleyball, racquetball, indoor soccer, handball, and cardiovascular conditioning equipment. A theater screens movies, and an activity center houses pool tables, ping pong table, a card room, and some casual literature. A hobbycraft area offers ceramics, painting, drawing, and leathercraft. Many outside amenities are available, including a softball field, soccer field, bocce courts, hockey, horseshoes, handball, and a walking track. Inmates may listen to selected CDs using a personal radio through a system that broadcasts within the Activity Center, Gymnasium, and outdoor recreation areas. Hours of operation are 6:00 a.m. to 8:30 p.m., excluding recalls and counts.

Visitation Information: On Sunday, Monday, and Saturday visitation is held between 8:15 a.m. and 3:15 p.m. On federal holidays visitation is held between 8:15 a.m. and 3:15 p.m. See Chapter 1 for more information on visitation.

Prison Politics: There is a very low level of prison politics at this facility.

Level of Violence: There is little to no violence at this facility. According to one inmate, "There is very little violence." Another respondent agreed, stating that violence is "rare."

Vulnerable Populations: While informants and LGBT inmates can remain, sex offenders are precluded from Camp placement due to Bureau of Prisons policy.

Good: "There is a movie theater."

Bad: "Everything is spread out. Phones, computers, and laundry are all in separate buildings. So, you have to walk to do anything."

Other Comments: "It's not really a Camp-like atmosphere; it feels more like a Low. Staff is not focused on rehabilitation or trying to assist inmates in transitioning to the outside world."

In the News: In March 2013, prisoners Michael Kezyzaniak, 64, and Gerald Greenfield, 67, escaped from the Federal Prison Camp in Duluth, and were caught by the U.S. Marshals six days later.

In the summer of 2006, at least 18 prisoners at FPC Duluth were found to have contracted MRSA, a highly contagious and potentially fatal skin disease.

FCI Englewood

Federal Correctional Institution Englewood | FCI Englewood

Facilities: FCI Englewood with an adjacent minimum-security satellite prison camp, and a detention center.

Facility Address & Contact Information

Federal Correctional Institution Englewood
9595 West Quincy Avenue
Littleton, CO 80123

Phone: 303-763-4300
Fax: 303-763-2553
Email: ENG/ExecAssistant@bop.gov

BOP Website: https://www.bop.gov/locations/institutions/eng/
Wikipedia: https://en.wikipedia.org/wiki/Federal_Correctional_Institution%2C_Englewood
ZCG Website: https://www.prisonerresource.com/resources/federal-prison-profiles/north-central-region-ncr/federal-correctional-institution-englewood-fci-englewood/

Inmate Correspondence Address

For FCI Englewood

Inmate Name and Registration Number
FCI Englewood
Federal Correctional Institution
9595 West Quincy Avenue
Littleton, CO 80123

For Satellite Prison Camp

Inmate Name and Registration Number
FCI Englewood
Satellite Prison Camp
9595 West Quincy Avenue
Littleton, CO 80123

NOTE: Funds cannot be sent directly to federal inmates. See Chapter 1 for more information on sending funds to federal inmates.

Sex: Male

Security Level: Main: Low Security; Camp: Minimum Security

Location: FCI Englewood is located 15 miles southwest of Denver, off Interstate 285.

BOP Region: North Central Region (NCR)

BOP Institution Code: ENG for FCI Englewood

Judicial District: District of Colorado

Medical Care Level: Level 2. See Chapter 2 for more information on Medical Care and Mental Health Care Levels.

Mental Health Care Level: Level 2

Population (as of May 1, 2019): Main & Detention Center: 1,010; Camp: 142

Background: Federal Correctional Institution Englewood is a low-security federal prison in Littleton, Colorado, which houses male inmates. It was opened in 1940. Federal Correctional Institution Englewood Camp, which also houses male inmates, was opened in 1990 and is located adjacent to the main institution. An adjacent detention center houses federal pre-trial and pre-sentence detainees.

FCI Englewood is a Sex Offender Management Program (SOMP) facility. As such, approximately 40 percent of the inmate population has either a current or past sexual offense.

Notable inmates include former governor of Illinois Rod Blagojevich (serving a 14-year sentence for wire fraud, bribery, and extortion); former Subway spokesperson Jared Fogle (serving 15 years for child pornography offenses); former CIA officer Jeffrey Sterling; and former University of Southern California professor Walter Lee Williams (served five years for illicit sexual conduct).

Media reports indicate that at least one inmate was attacked as a result of having a notorious sexual offense case. Another inmate filed suit against the prison, calling the medical staff "unresponsive and dismissive."

In 2005, *The Kansas City Star* named FCI Englewood Camp one of the five best federal prisons for white collar offenders.

Housing: Inmates are housed in four-person cubicles and two-person cells. In the detention center, inmates are housed in two-person cells. The camp houses inmates in two dormitories of four-person rooms.

Health Services: The FCI Englewood Health Services Department conducts an intake screening examination upon arrival at the institution. Within 14 days inmates are also given a complete physical examination. Routine sick call and dental sick call, emergency care, preventive health screening, and medications are provided. While emergency care is available 24 hours a day, inmates must submit a triage form for routine care needs.

Psychology Services: The Psychology Services Department provides mental health services to the inmate population. These services include initial screenings, suicide prevention, crisis intervention, psychiatric medication referrals, psycho-educational groups, providing self-help materials, and individual counseling. FCI Englewood also offers a Non-Residential Sex Offender Treatment Program (SOTP-NR).

Residential Drug Abuse Program (RDAP): FCI Englewood offers the Residential Drug Abuse Program (RDAP) and a Drug Education Program. The main facility also offers a Non-Residential Drug Program (NR-DAP). The camp offers Alcoholics Anonymous (AA) and Narcotics Anonymous (NA).

Education Services: FCI Englewood and the satellite camp provide GED, English-as-a-Second Language (ESL), and parenting programs. Adult Continuing Education (ACE) and Release Preparation Program classes are also available. High school diplomas and post-secondary degrees are available through paid correspondence programs.

Advanced Occupational Education: FCI Englewood offers advanced occupational education courses in Customer Service and General Business.

Vocational Training: No vocational training is offered at FCI Englewood aside from its advanced occupational education programs.

Apprenticeship: FCI Englewood does not offer any apprenticeship programs.

Library Services: Leisure and law libraries are available at both facilities. The TRULINCS Electronic Law Library is maintained and coordinated by the Education Department and is located in the Education Building adjacent to the leisure library. The leisure library has fiction and nonfiction books, a video collection, newspapers, and magazines for inmates to read and view. The library also has various tapes and video courses in finance, budgeting, psychology, self-help, and job searches. The Education Department also provides the opportunity for inmates to obtain leisure library materials not otherwise available at FCI Englewood, through the Jefferson County Public Library Interlibrary Loan System.

UNICOR: The UNICOR facility at FCI Englewood produces clothing and textiles.

Commissary: Inmates can spend $360.00 per month on a variety of commissary items. Popular items include snacks, ice cream, food, over-the counter medications, and clothing. Radios and MP3 players can also be purchased.

Recreation Services: FCI Englewood has a recreation yard, gymnasium, weight room, hobby shop, music room, and wellness center. The Arts and Crafts Program includes leather, fine arts, pottery, painting, beading and ceramics. The camp has a walking track with a fitness trail, softball field, soccer field, volleyball court, horseshoe pit, basketball area, bocce ball court, weight room, and hobby shop. Special events, tournaments, and entertainment are sponsored by the Recreation Department on each holiday at both FCI Englewood and the camp.

Visitation Information: On Sunday and Saturday visitation is held between 8:30 a.m. and 3:30 p.m. On Monday and Friday visitation is held between 5:00 and 9:00 p.m. On federal holidays visitation is held between 8:30 a.m. and 3:00 p.m. See Chapter 1 for more information on visitation.

In the News: In December 2015, Jared Fogle, the former face of Subway television ads, began serving his 16-year sentence at Federal Correctional Institution Englewood for child pornography. In January 2016, he was attacked by a fellow inmate. His injuries were non-life-threatening.

In 2015, former CIA officer and whistleblower Jeffrey Sterling was sentenced to three years in federal prison and sent to FCI Englewood. Sterling filed a complaint in August 2016 accusing the medical personnel at the prison of being "unresponsive and dismissive."

In March 2012, former Illinois Governor Rod Blagojevich turned himself in to FCI Englewood to begin serving his 14-year prison sentence for corruption.

FCC Florence

Federal Correctional Complex Florence | FCC Florence

Facilities: FCC Florence houses USP Florence Administrative Maximum, USP Florence High, and FCI Florence with an adjacent minimum-security satellite prison camp.

USP Florence ADMAX

United States Penitentiary Florence Administrative Maximum | USP Florence ADMAX

Facility Address & Contact Information

United States Penitentiary Florence-Administrative Maximum Facility
5880 Highway 67 South
Florence, CO 81226

Phone: 719-784-9464
Fax: 719-784-5290
Email: FLM/ExecAssistant@bop.gov

BOP Website: https://www.bop.gov/locations/institutions/flm/
Wikipedia: https://en.wikipedia.org/wiki/ADX_Florence
ZCG Website: https://www.prisonerresource.com/resources/federal-prison-profiles/north-central-region-ncr/federal-correctional-complex-florence-fcc-florence/united-states-penitentiary-florence-administrative-maximum-usp-florence-admax/

Inmate Correspondence Address

Inmate Name and Registration Number

USP Florence ADMAX
U.S. Penitentiary
P.O. Box 8500
Florence, CO 81226

NOTE: Funds cannot be sent directly to federal inmates. See Chapter 1 for more information on sending funds to federal inmates.

Sex: Male

Security Level: Administrative Security (Highest, AKA Supermax)

Location: USP Florence-Administrative Maximum is located on State Highway 67, 90 miles south of Denver, 45 miles south of Colorado Springs, and 40 miles west of Pueblo.

BOP Region: North Central Region (NCR)

BOP Institution Code: FLM for USP Florence-Administrative Maximum, FLF for Florence Federal Correctional Complex

Judicial District: District of Colorado

Medical Care Level: Level 2. See Chapter 2 for more information on Medical Care and Mental Health Care Levels.

Mental Health Care Level: Level 2

Population (as of May 1, 2019): 384

Background: Federal Administrative Maximum Florence (ADMAX) is an administrative-security federal prison in Florence, Colorado, which houses male inmates. It was opened in 1994 and is part of the Florence Federal Correctional Complex.

Florence ADMAX, which is also known as ADX and "The Alcatraz of the Rockies," is the nation's only level 6 supermax prison and was designed to house the most dangerous offenders. *Mother Jones* once described the prison as "pretty close to hell." At one point in time, both of then-President Barack Obama's books were banned by prison administrators, who called them "potentially detrimental to national security."

Notable inmates include former Al-Qaeda operative and 9/11 conspirator Zacarias Moussaoui (serving six life sentences); Dzhokhar Tsarnaev (sentenced to death by lethal injection for his participation in the 2013 Boston Marathon bombings); Terry Nichols (serving 161 life sentences for the 1995 Oklahoma City bombing); former FBI counterintelligence agent Robert Hanssen (serving 15 life sentences for espionage); Aryan Brotherhood prison gang leader Thomas Silverstein (serving a life sentence for murdering a prison guard); Aryan Brotherhood leader Barry Mills; Unabomber Ted Kackynski; and Shoe Bomber Richard Reid.

Media reports indicate that a member of the Bureau's elite Special Operations Response Team (SORT) was convicted of stealing and selling flash-bang grenades on the black market. At least one inmate has committed suicide, three inmates have been murdered by fellow prisoners, and numerous inmates have mutilated themselves at the facility. Class action lawsuits have also been filed which allege lack of medical and psychological treatment.

In 2018, InmateSurvival.com named ADX Florence one of the ten worst, toughest, deadliest, and most dangerous prisons in America. Also in 2018, Trendrr named the facility one of the 11 most dangerous prisons in the United States. In 2016, The Richest named the institution one of the 15 most dangerous prisons in America. And in 2011, News One named ADX Florence one of the ten most notorious prisons in the United States.

Housing: Inmates are housed in one-person cells, where they shower, participate in programming through a TV, and have all other human interactions, with the exception of recreation and some health care needs. There are 10 housing units that range from control unit, to special housing unit, to high security, to general population, to pre-transfer unit.

Health Services: Sick call, dental sick call, physical examinations, medications, eyeglasses, chronic care, preventive health services, emergency services, diagnosis and treatment of chronic conditions, and mental health care are provided to inmates. Mandatory HIV testing is performed when there are risk factors and the test is clinically indicated and/or surveillance testing is required. MRSA and TB screening are also conducted annually. Inmates typically file a paper sick call request, then are evaluated in their cell via a video camera by Health Services staff.

Psychology Services: After admission into USP Florence ADMAX, inmates are interviewed by a representative of Psychology Services, usually within 14 days. Psychology Services offers a variety of programs through the in-cell closed circuit TV, in coordination with the inmate's Unit Team, in place of group counseling. These programs include Stress Management, Anger Management, and various other topics. These classes are sometimes completed by using paper packets that inmates fill out and return. If an inmate successfully completes a formal program, he will receive a certificate. For psychiatric care, inmates have the services of a psychiatrist at MCFP Springfield via teleconferencing equipment. Tele-psychiatry clinics are held twice a month.

Residential Drug Abuse Program (RDAP): USP Florence ADMAX does not house a Residential Drug Abuse Program (RDAP). A Drug Education Program, the Non-Residential

Drug Abuse Program (NR-DAP), and other drug abuse programming is available. All education programming and testing is conducted in an inmate's cell, with instruction primarily facilitated through the use of closed-circuit television.

Education Services: USP Florence ADMAX provides GED and English-as-a-Second Language (ESL) programs. Adult Basic Education (ABE) and Adult Continuing Education (ACE) classes are also available. High school diplomas and post-secondary programs are available through paid correspondence programs. All classes are conducted via a TV screen in the inmate's cell.

Advanced Occupational Education: USP Florence ADMAX offers an advanced occupational education program in Restaurant Management/Culinary Arts.

Vocational Training: USP Florence ADMAX does not provide any vocational training aside from its advanced occupational education courses.

Apprenticeship: USP Florence ADMAX does not provide any apprenticeship training.

Library Services: Leisure and law libraries are available through the Education Department, though most programming is available only through closed circuit televisions in the inmate's cell. If a certain item is not available via the TV network, the inmate can file a paper request for an item to be retrieved and delivered to their cell.

UNICOR: USP Florence ADMAX does not house a UNICOR facility.

Commissary: Spending limits are $90.00 per week and up to $360.00 per month. Inmates can purchase a variety of commissary items, though some restrictions are in place due to the security level of the facility. Inmates shop by turning in their commissary form from their cell. Items are then delivered to the cell. While inmates can first only purchase hygiene items, they can work their way up to food and other items.

Recreation Services: The USP Florence ADMAX Recreation Department provides a variety of approved organized and free form activities. According to the BOP, some of these activities are basketball, handball, and special holiday activities such as table games, tournaments, and contests. In contrast to the official position, inmates at the facility describe being chained to a poll where they can walk in circles but not actually reach any other inmates. Regardless, communal recreation is highly controlled.

Visitation Information: On Sunday, Thursday, Friday, and Saturday visitation is held between 8:00 a.m. and 3:00 p.m. On federal holidays visitation is held between 8:30 a.m. and 3:00 p.m. See Chapter 1 for more information on visitation.

Prison Politics: ADX is very political, but due to most inmates being in total isolation, this doesn't tend to be an issue.

Level of Violence: There is only staff-on-inmate violence due to most inmates being isolated from one another.

Vulnerable Populations: Sex offenders, informants, and LGBT inmates can stay due to being isolated from one another.

Good: "You're alive and away from all politics." "Reputation from being there."

Bad: "Lonely existence, very limited contact with the outside world, only legal calls allowed, letters are read through a television screen in the cell, and the guards treat everyone the same (poorly) regardless of why you are there."

Other Comments: "Do not go. Now you have to attack a prison guard in order to go." "Very safe since you are isolated from everyone else."

In the News: In July 2018, white supremacist and Aryan Brotherhood leader Barry Mills was found dead of natural causes at Administrative Maximum Security Florence.

In 2013, the publication *Mother Jones* called ADX Florence one of America's worst prisons: "pretty close to hell."

In June 2012, a class-action lawsuit was filed against federal officials for failing to provide basic medical treatment for mentally ill prisoners at ADX Florence.

In May 2012, federal prison officials were sued over the suicide of Jose Martin Vega, a prisoner at ADX Florence who hanged himself after failing to receive proper mental health treatment.

Between 2009 and 2010, a guard and member of the Special Operations Response Team (SORT) at ADX Florence allegedly stole flash-bang grenades from the armory to sell on the black market.

In 2009, officials at ADX Florence banned two of President Barack Obama's books because they were considered "potentially detrimental to national security."

In 2005, Manual Torrez was murdered by fellow prisoners at ADX Florence. ADX Florence is the most restrictive and secure section of USP Florence.

Also in 2005, prisoner Gregory Joiner was held by James Duckett as Dominic Stewart beat him to death in ADX Florence.

In 1997, prisoner Maynard Campbell was stabbed to death near his cell at ADX Florence. Campbell's cellmate was also injured in the attack.

USP Florence

United States Penitentiary Florence | USP Florence

Facility Address & Contact Information

United States Penitentiary Florence
5880 Highway 67 South
Florence, CO 81226

Phone: 719-784-9454
Fax: 719-784-5157
Email: FLP/ExecAssistant@bop.gov

BOP Website: https://www.bop.gov/locations/institutions/flp/
Wikipedia: https://en.wikipedia.org/wiki/United_States_Penitentiary,_Florence_High
ZCG Website: https://www.prisonerresource.com/resources/federal-prison-profiles/north-central-region-ncr/federal-correctional-complex-florence-fcc-florence/united-states-penitentiary-florence-usp-florence/

Inmate Correspondence Address

Inmate Name and Registration Number
USP Florence
United States Penitentiary
P.O. Box 7000
Florence, CO 81226

NOTE: Funds cannot be sent directly to federal inmates. See Chapter 1 for more information on sending funds to federal inmates.

Sex: Male

Security Level: High Security

Location: USP Florence is located on State Highway 67, 90 miles south of Denver, 45 miles south of Colorado Springs, and 40 miles west of Pueblo.

BOP Region: North Central Region (NCR)

BOP Institution Code: FLP for USP Florence, FLF for Florence Federal Correctional Complex

Judicial District: District of Colorado

Medical Care Level: Level 2. See Chapter 2 for more information on Medical Care and Mental Health Care Levels.

Mental Health Care Level: Level 2

Population (as of May 1, 2019): 827

Background: United States Penitentiary Florence is a high-security federal prison in Florence, Colorado, which houses male inmates. It was opened in 1994 and is part of the Florence Federal Correctional Complex.

Notable inmates include Silk Road founder and operator Ross Ulbricht (serving a life sentence for money laundering, computer hacking, and conspiracy to distribute narcotics), and Walli Mujahidh (serving 17 years for conspiracy to commit murder of U.S. military officers).

Media reports indicate that at least two staff members have been assaulted by inmates, at least two prisoners have been murdered by fellow prisoners, and one guard was indicted for beating a handcuffed inmate.

Housing: Inmates are housed in one- and two-person cells.

Health Services: Sick call, dental sick call, physical examinations, medications, chronic care, preventive health services, emergency services, diagnosis and treatment of chronic conditions, and mental health care are provided to inmates. Emergency medical care is available 24 hours a day. Inmates must submit a triage form for routine health care needs.

Psychology Services: Psychology services at USP Florence include screening, assessment, and treatment of mental health and drug abuse problems, individual and group counseling, psycho-educational classes, self-help and supportive services, and referral to Health Services for medical treatment of a mental illness. Inmates can request treatment either through cop-out or by visiting the Psychology open house. The facility also offers the STAGES Program for inmates with serious mental illness and personality disorders.

Residential Drug Abuse Program (RDAP): USP Florence does not have the Residential Drug Abuse Program (RDAP), but referrals can be made to institutions that do provide RDAP. A

Drug Abuse Education Class and the Non-Residential Drug Abuse Program (NR-DAP) are available.

Education Services: USP Florence provides GED and English-as-a-Second Language (ESL) programs. Incentive awards are provided to recognize inmates making satisfactory progress and successfully completing the literacy (i.e., GED and ESL) program. Inmates may also receive incentives for progressing to various levels in the GED or ESL programs. Graduation ceremonies recognize GED, ESL, and Occupational Education completions. Courses are also available in Adult Continuing Education (ACE) and parenting. High school diplomas and post-secondary degrees are available through paid correspondence programs.

Advanced Occupational Education: USP Florence does not offer any advanced occupational education programs.

Vocational Training: USP Florence does not offer any vocational training programs.

Apprenticeship: USP Florence does not offer any apprenticeship programs.

Library Services: The leisure library offers inmates a variety of reading materials including periodicals, newspapers, fiction, nonfiction, and reference books. An interlibrary loan program is also available. Inmates are provided legal materials and an opportunity to prepare legal documents through the use of the TRULINCS Electronic Law Library. Inmates also have access to typewriters and a copy machine.

UNICOR: USP Florence does not house a UNICOR facility.

Commissary: Inmates may use funds in their trust fund account to purchase items at the institution commissary, place funds on their inmate phone account, purchase TRU-Units for their TRULINCS account, or send funds out of the institution using Form BP-199. Inmates are permitted to spend up to $360.00 per month and can only shop once a week on their designated shopping day. Items such as food, beverages, clothing, electronics, and over-the-counter medications can be purchased in the USP Florence commissary. When shopping, inmates must go to commissary, turn in their order form, and wait for their order to be filled.

Recreation Services: Leisure activities include organized and informal games, sports, physical fitness, table games, hobbycrafts, music programs, intramural activities, social and cultural organizations, and movies. Art activities include paintings and sketches using traditional methods (e.g., oils, pastels, crayons, pencils, inks, and charcoal). Hobbycraft activities include ceramics, leatherwork, models, clay, mosaics, crochet, knitting, sculptures, woodworking, and lapidary, etc. Wellness programs include screening, assessments, goal setting, fitness/nutrition plans, and counseling. Indoors, inmates have access to step machines, treadmills, ellipticals, basketball, volleyball, tables, and a band room. Outside, inmates have access to softball, horse-shoes, basketball, pull-up bars, handball, and soccer.

Visitation Information: On Sunday and Saturday visitation is held between 8:00 a.m. and 3:00 p.m. On federal holidays visitation is held between 8:00 a.m. and 3:00 p.m. See Chapter 1 for more information on visitation.

Prison Politics: This is a very political yard where inmates are required to be part of a car.

Level of Violence: There is a significant level of violence at this facility. Inmate respondents report daily fights and weekly stabbings.

Vulnerable Populations: Sex offenders and informants can't walk the yard. LGBT inmates can remain if they are willing to fight.

Good: "Great recreation, education, and library."

Bad: "Politics, staff indifference, and psychology offerings."

Other Comments: "Very violent and political prison. No independence due to safety concerns. You have to go with your people everywhere. Avoid going here at all costs."

In the News: In December 2010, United States Penitentiary Florence was temporarily locked down after a prisoner struck two staff members in the face.

In August 2008, a prisoner at USP Florence was stabbed to death.

In 1998, Stephen Mills, a guard at USP Florence, was convicted and sentenced for beating a prisoner, Fred Davis, who was handcuffed and restrained at the time. His 33-month sentence was the lowest possible.

In 1997, prisoner Frank Melendez was murdered in USP Florence's Special Housing Unit (SHU). *Prison Legal News* reported more than half of BOP deaths in fiscal year 1997 occurred at USP Florence.

FCI Florence

Federal Correctional Institution Florence | FCI Florence

Facilities: FCI Florence with an adjacent minimum-security satellite prison camp.

Facility Address & Contact Information

Federal Correctional Institution Florence
5880 Highway 67 South
Florence, CO 81226

Phone: 719-784-9100
Fax: 719-784-9504
Email: FLF/ExecAssistant@bop.gov

BOP Website: https://www.bop.gov/locations/institutions/flf/
Wikipedia: https://en.wikipedia.org/wiki/Federal_Correctional_Institution,_Florence
ZCG Website: https://www.prisonerresource.com/resources/federal-prison-profiles/north-central-region-ncr/federal-correctional-complex-florence-fcc-florence/federal-correctional-institution-florence-fci-florence/

Inmate Correspondence Address

For FCI Florence

Inmate Name and Registration Number
FCI Florence
Federal Correctional Institution
P.O. Box 6000
Florence, CO 81226

For Satellite Prison Camp

Inmate Name and Registration Number
FCI Florence
Satellite Prison Camp
P.O. Box 5000
Florence, CO 81226

NOTE: Funds cannot be sent directly to federal inmates. See Chapter 1 for more information on sending funds to federal inmates.

Sex: Male

Security Level: Main: Medium Security; Camp: Minimum Security

Location: FCI Florence is located on State Highway 67, 90 miles south of Denver, 45 miles south of Colorado Springs, and 40 miles west of Pueblo.

BOP Region: North Central Region (NCR)

BOP Institution Code: FLF for FCI Florence, FLF for Florence Federal Correctional Complex

Judicial District: District of Colorado

Medical Care Level: Level 2. See Chapter 2 for more information on Medical Care and Mental Health Care Levels.

Mental Health Care Level: Level 2

Population (as of May 1, 2019): Main: 949; Camp: 431

Background: Federal Correctional Institution Florence is a medium-security federal prison in Florence, Colorado, which houses male inmates. It was opened in 1993 and is part of the Florence Federal Correctional Complex. Federal Correctional Institution Florence Camp, which also houses male inmates, was opened in 1992 and is located adjacent to the main institution.

Inmates at FCI Florence have access to a college degree program through a partnership with Greenville College.

Notable inmates include Francisco Duran (serving a 40-year sentence for attempting to assassinate then-U.S. President Bill Clinton), former Baltimore police detective William King (serving a life sentence for stealing money and narcotics), and Brant Beckley (convicted of unlawful internet gambling, wire fraud, and bank fraud).

Media reports indicate that at least two inmates have been murdered at the facility and one guard has been federally indicted for sexually assaulting an inmate. There have been at least two escapes from the camp.

Housing: Inmates are housed in two-, six-, and eight-person cells within the eight housing units. In the camp, inmates are housed in dormitories within the two housing units.

Health Services: Sick call, dental sick call, physical examinations, medications, eyeglasses, chronic care, preventive health services, emergency services, diagnosis and treatment of chronic conditions, and mental health care are provided to inmates at FCI Florence. Mandatory HIV testing is performed when there are risk factors and the test is clinically indicated and/or surveillance testing is required. MRSA and TB screening are also conducted annually. Dental and medical sick call are held at 7:00 a.m. on Monday, Wednesday, and Friday. Pill and insulin lines are at breakfast and 6:00 p.m. Medication pick-up is at 1:00 p.m.

Psychology Services: Psychologists are available by submitting an Inmate Request to Staff Member form, or in an emergency, by alerting a staff member. Psychology Services at FCI Florence perform a variety of functions for the inmate population. Some of these functions include sponsoring psycho-educational classes on anger and stress management, along with sexual abuse/assault prevention and intervention. Counseling alternatives include anger management, self-image groups, and other voluntary groups. Inmate participation in these activities is encouraged upon staff assessment of inmate needs, but participation in such activities is voluntary. Self-help library is also available. Unit staff is available for informal counseling sessions and can also conduct formal group counseling activities in housing units.

Residential Drug Abuse Program (RDAP): Both FCI Florence and the satellite camp have the Residential Drug Abuse Program (RDAP). A Drug Education class, the Non-Residential Drug Abuse Program (NR-DAP), Alcoholics Anonymous (AA), Narcotics Anonymous (NA), and People In Prison Entering Sobriety programs are also provided.

Education Services: FCI Florence provides GED and English-as-a-Second Language (ESL) programs. Courses are also offered in Social Education-Life Skills, Parenting, Adult Continuing Education (ACE), and Career Counseling/Release Preparation. High school diplomas and post-secondary degrees are available through paid correspondence programs. Hours of operation are 7:40 to 10:30 a.m., 12:40 to 3:30 p.m., and 5:00 to 8:30 p.m. Monday through Friday, with the exception of Friday after 4:00 p.m. The Education Department is also open until 3:00 p.m. on Saturday, but closed Sunday.

Advanced Occupational Education: FCI Florence offers advanced occupational education programs in Building Trades, Cabinet/Furniture Maker, Computer Assisted Drafting, and Restaurant Management/Culinary Arts. Both facilities offer Green Energy.

Vocational Training: FCI Florence does not offer any vocational training aside from its advanced occupational education programs.

Apprenticeship: FCI Florence does not offer any apprenticeships.

Library Services: A leisure and law library is available through the Education Department. Inmates can check out fiction and nonfiction books, magazines, and newspapers. DVD movies and NEO word processors are also available for inmate use. In the law library, inmates can use the TRULINCS Electronic Law Library computers, typewriters, and copy machine.

UNICOR: FCI Florence does not have a UNICOR facility.

Commissary: The spending limit is $360.00 per month and is further restricted to $180 every two weeks. Postage stamps, copy cards, and photo tickets are not included in the spending limit. Inmates are permitted to shop once a week in the commissary on a designated day. Shopping is currently conducted Monday through Thursday at 7:00 a.m. and 1:00 p.m. Various food, drink, hygiene, clothing, and electronic items are available for purchase. If an inmate is only purchasing hygiene items, he can go at lunch without a commissary form, otherwise the order form must be submitted two days prior to shopping. SHU inmates shop on Friday.

Recreation: At FCI Florence, inmates have access to both indoor and outdoor recreation facilities where personal fitness, group sports, and hobbycraft projects can be undertaken. Inside, inmates have access to pool tables, art and leather rooms, tables, treadmills, ellipticals, stationary bikes, stair steppers, and a music program. Outside, inmates have access to weights, basketball, soccer, handball, softball, pull-up bars, tennis, bocce ball, horseshoes, volleyball, and a track. Hours of operation are 6:30 to 10:30 a.m., 1:00 to 3:00 p.m., and 5:30 to 8:00 p.m.

Visitation Information: On Sunday and Saturday visitation is held between 8:00 a.m. and 3:00 p.m. On federal holidays visitation is held between 8:00 a.m. and 3:00 p.m. See Chapter 1 for more information on visitation.

Prison Politics: This is a very political yard where inmates must be part of a car. According to one inmate, "All new arrivals must provide their paperwork to prove that they aren't an informant or a sex offender." Another respondent explained that "cells and the dining room are segregated by race."

Level of Violence: There is a moderate to high level of violence at this prison. Inmates report several fights per month, though cars largely keep violence controlled and out of staff view. According to one inmate, when the violence does spill into plain view, lockdowns occur. Another respondent explained, "There are many prisoners who transferred from the USP across the street. They tend to bring the USP mentality with them." Another inmate stated,

"The fighting is usually over dope or debt, and sometimes over insults or scores from other prisons. Lockdowns are frequent but not long-lasting."

Vulnerable Populations: Sex offenders and informants can't stay. LGBT inmates can stay if they are willing to fight, but they are still ostracized. One inmate stated that "sex offenders are usually 'asked' to check in." Another agreed, stating, "Sex offenders are not allowed to walk the yard." He further explained, "While gays are ok to stay, I don't think there are any transgender inmates." One respondent cautioned, "Don't rely on the assurances of SIS at intake that you can walk the yard. If you are a sex offender and others find out, they will take violent actions against you. If you are part of certain racial groups (e.g., Native Americans, etc.) and are found out, they don't even give a chance for the person to check in, they take physical action immediately after you get off the bus."

Good: "Scenery of surrounding mountains; good quality and quantity of food." "They feed real meals in the Styrofoam containers during lockdowns (no bologna sandwiches)." "Incredible mountain vistas all around; medical trips to Pueblo or Colorado Springs are awesome." "Guards are mellow." "Clothing handout is responsive and good." "Washers and dryers are still in the housing units, which also have three microwaves and 11 TVs per unit."

Bad: "Politics." "There are metal detectors everywhere." "Lunches are real filling, but the suppers are skimpy."

Other Comments: "If you can walk there, definitely go." "If you stay away from dope and gambling, and you are not a sex offender, the chances of you getting involved in violence is slim. Having said that, the chow hall is organized by cars -- collections of inmates from specific geographic regions or belonging to certain gangs. Car and racial support are expected of all inmates. You roll with your people." "The administration is slowly empty-ing out the units in order to reduce the prison population." "There are very few real jobs, most inmates work on job rosters for "ghost" jobs where no work is required or expected, but pay is also bad."

In the News: In 2011, four members of a prison gang -- Jose Augustin Pluma, Juan Martin Ruelas, Mark Rosalez and Justin Hernandez -- were convicted of murdering prisoner Pablo Zuniga-Garcia at Federal Correctional Institution Florence.

In 2010, Donald Denney was arrested trying to smuggle black tar heroin, which was concealed in his rectum, into FCI Florence for his son of the same name who was a pris-oner there.

In 2004, Rebecca Miller, a nurse at FCI Florence, was charged with two counts of having sex with a male prisoner.

In 1996, FCI Florence prisoner Charles Morrison was murdered.

Camp in the News: In July 2008, Edward Davidson escaped from Federal Correctional Institution Florence Camp when his wife drove him away. A few days later, Davidson killed her and his three-year-old daughter.

In 2006, John Reynolds was sentenced to an additional 16 months in prison after escaping from FCI Florence Camp in 1999.

FCI Greenville

Federal Correctional Institution Greenville | FCI Greenville

Facilities: FCI Greenville with an adjacent minimum-security satellite prison camp.

Facility Address & Contact Information

Federal Correctional Institution Greenville
100 U.S. Highway 40
Greenville, IL 62246

Phone: 618-664-6200
Fax: 618-664-6372
Email: GRE/ExecAssistant@BOP.GOV

BOP Website: https://www.bop.gov/locations/institutions/gre/
Wikipedia: https://en.wikipedia.org/wiki/Federal_Correctional_Institution,_Greenville
ZCG Website: https://www.prisonerresource.com/resources/federal-prison-profiles/north-central-region-ncr/federal-correctional-institution-greenville-fci-greenville/

Inmate Correspondence Address

For FCI Greenville

Inmate Name and Registration Number
FCI Greenville
Federal Correctional Institution
P.O. Box 5000
Greenville, IL 62246

For Satellite Prison Camp

Inmate Name and Registration Number
FCI Greenville
Satellite Prison Camp
P.O. Box 6000
Greenville, IL 62246

NOTE: Funds cannot be sent directly to federal inmates. See Chapter 1 for more information on sending funds to federal inmates.

Sex: Main: Male; Camp: Female

Security Level: Main: Medium Security; Camp: Minimum Security

Location: FCI Greenville is approximately 43 miles east of St. Louis, Missouri and 63 miles from Springfield, Illinois.

BOP Region: North Central Region (NCR)

BOP Institution Code: GRE for FCI Greenville

Judicial District: Southern District of Illinois

Medical Care Level: Level 2. See Chapter 2 for more information on Medical Care and Mental Health Care Levels.

Mental Health Care Level: Level 3

Population (as of May 1, 2019): Main: 1,020; Camp: 350

Background: Federal Correctional Institution Greenville is a medium-security federal prison located in Greenville, Illinois, which houses male inmates. It was opened in 1994. Federal Correctional Institution Greenville Camp, which houses female inmates, is located adjacent to the main institution.

Inmates at FCI Greenville have access to a college degree program through Greenville College.

Notable inmates include former LAPD officer David Mack (served 12 years for armed robbery), Animal Liberation Front member Walter Bond (serving 12 years for arson), and Derrick Shareef (serving 35 years for attempted use of a weapon of mass destruction).

Media reports indicate that at least two inmates have been charged with drug smuggling, three inmates have been charged with drug possession, one inmate has been charged with assaulting another inmate, one inmate has been charged with assaulting a guard, and one inmate has been charged with weapons possession. In addition, one guard was charged with bribery and smuggling, while the prison union's president was federally indicted for writing himself unauthorized checks.

Housing: Inmates are housed in two-, three-, and eight-person cells within the four housing units. Inmates in the camp are housed in dormitories consisting of two-person cubicles.

Health Services: FCI Greenville's Health Services Department provides medical care, dental care, and support services to all inmates. These services include sick call, dental sick call, emergency medical treatment, medications, eye care, and preventive treatment. Sick call is held Monday, Tuesday, Thursday, and Friday mornings. Pill and insulin line are conducted three times a day. Open house is on Friday.

Psychology Services: Inmates at FCI Greenville and the camp receive an initial psychological screening, assessment, and treatment of mental health and drug abuse problems, individual and group counseling, psycho-educational classes, self-help supportive services, crisis intervention, and referral to Health Services for medical treatment of a mental illness. The camp offers the Resolve Program, which is a non-residential program for female inmates who have a history of physical and/or sexual abuse, and a Trauma in Life Workshop, which addresses the challenges individuals face following exposure to traumatic life events and the strategies these individuals may use to enhance their resilience or ability to survive and thrive following these events.

Residential Drug Abuse Program (RDAP): FCI Greenville does not have the Residential Drug Abuse Program (RDAP), but it does have the Drug Abuse Education Program. The satellite camp offers RDAP as well as a drug abuse education course and the Non-Residential Drug Abuse Treatment Program (NR-DAP).

Education Services: FCI Greenville provides GED and English-as-a-Second Language (ESL) programs. Adult Continuing Education (ACE), parenting, release preparation, and offender placement programs are also available. Currently, ACE classes include framing, typing, Spanish, and physiology. High school diplomas and post-secondary degrees are available at both institutions through paid correspondence programs. Hours of operation are 8:30 to 10:30 a.m., 1:30 to 3:30 p.m., and 5:30 to 8:30 p.m. Monday through Friday, with the exception of Friday evenings, when the Education Department is closed.

Advanced Occupational Education: FCI Greenville offers advanced occupational education in Microsoft Office. The camp offers advanced occupational education in Horticulture, Microsoft Office, and Sewing.

Vocational Training: FCI Greenville and the camp offer vocational training in Cabinet Making 1 & 2.

Apprenticeship: FCI Greenville offers apprenticeships in Electrician, Landscape Management, Machinist Wood, Sewing, Teacher's Aide, HVAC, and Quality & Assurance. The camp offers

Animal Trainer, HVAC, Landscape Management, Teacher's Aide, Welding, and Prisoners Assisting with Support Personal Care and Service Dogs (PAWS).

Library Services: The library is designed to support leisure reading, independent study, and academic programs. Resources include a variety of printed materials in various forms, as well as audiotapes, videotapes, and reference materials. An active interlibrary loan program is available to supplement the inventory of available reading materials. The law library also provides access to legal research materials via the TRULINCS Electronic Law Library. Typewriters and a copy machine are also available for inmate use.

UNICOR: The FCI Greenville UNICOR facility produces clothing and textiles.

Commissary: Inmates at FCI Greenville and the camp are permitted to spend up to $360.00 per month for commissary purchases. This is further restricted to $180 every two weeks. Items that do not count against an inmate's monthly spending limitation include phone credits, postage stamps, and over-the-counter medications. Popular items include food, ice cream, candy drinks, and clothing. Inmates are only allowed to shop once a week on their designated shopping day.

Recreation Services: Recreation offerings at both facilities include indoor and outdoor activities and range from individualized arts and crafts programs to intramural team sports such as softball, basketball, volleyball, and more. Physical fitness, weight reduction, and hobbycraft leisure activities are available (e.g., art, yarn and crochet, beads, music, foosball, a variety of card and board games, chess, checkers, dominoes, scrabble, etc.). FCI Greenville also offers structured leagues in basketball, softball, soccer, football, Frisbee, tennis, volleyball, handball, horseshoes, racquetball, ping pong, bocce ball, beanbag toss, badminton, and paddle ball. A wellness room provides weights, treadmills, bikes, a row machine, and other equipment, as well as yoga classes, aerobics class, afternoon calisthenic and nutrition classes, and structured walking and jogging programs. The main facility also has a photo program, TVs, movies shown weekly via television in all housing units, and a Music Program with a variety of leisure bands.

Visitation Information: On Sunday, Monday, and Saturday visitation is held between 8:00 a.m. and 3:00 p.m. On federal holidays visitation is held between 8:00 a.m. and 3:00 p.m. See Chapter 1 for more information on visitation.

Prison Politics: While some inmate say that this is a very political yard, others disagree, feeling that it is not very political at all. Inmates are required to be part of a car. According to one respondent, "All races know where they stand and have a hands-off policy." Another respondent stated that the yard has progressively grown softer over the past decade.

Level of Violence: Inmates report a low level of violence, but a number of check-ins.

Vulnerable Populations: Inmates report mixed beliefs of sex offenders, informants, and LGBT inmates. Some say that sex offenders can't walk the yard and informants can possibly stay if they are undercover, while others believe that sex offenders and informants can remain. According to one inmate, "Sex offenders used to be ran up top, but due to the number of them and threats from staff, they are allowed to stay. Even so, the ones that remain know their place and stay out of the way. Same with rats, basically."

Good: "Large portions of food, soda/juice fountains in the chow hall, and good commissary selection."

Bad: "Prison politics and car requirement." "Staff get so bored that they make up new policies just to have something to complain about." "Child molesters and rats." "No pool tables." "They took out the microwaves."

Other Comments: "If you do go, make sure your paperwork is clean." "Unless you are clean, this is probably not a safe yard." "Oddly enough, people sometimes get shots (i.e., incident reports) in order to say and not go to a low."

In the News: In December 2017, James Leroy Gary, a prisoner at Federal Correctional Institution Greenville, was sentenced to ten years in prison for his role in smuggling meth into the prison in 2014.

In August 2017, Cody Delao and David Montalvo, prisoners at FCI Greenville, were indicted on charges of possessing contraband drugs -- suboxone --in federal prison.

In March 2017, Mario L. Gordon, a prisoner at FCI Greenville, was sentenced to six months for the possession of K2, a form of synthetic marijuana.

In December 2016, FCI Greenville prisoner Billy Evans pleaded guilty to assaulting another prisoner with a lock tied to a belt.

Also in December 2016, prisoner Antonio M. Green was sentenced to 18 months on top of his current sentence after he was found in possession of an icepick-style weapon while incarcerated at FCI Greenville.

In November 2016, Joshua Demery, a prisoner at FCI Greenville, was sentenced to five additional years in prison for assaulting guards, destruction of property and trying to stab a guard in March 2015.

In August 2014, Greenville College and FCI Greenville launched an educational program that allowed prisoners to earn college credit through classes taught by college professors.

In June 2011, Druex M. Perkins, a guard at FCI Greenville, pleaded guilty to receiving $2,000 to smuggle tobacco and other contraband into the facility. Prisoner Khalat J. Alama was charged with bribing federal officials.

In 2009, Dan Padgett, an official with the FCI Greenville guards' union, pleaded guilty to writing himself unauthorized checks for nearly $200,000 between 2001 and 2008.

USP Leavenworth

United States Penitentiary Leavenworth | USP Leavenworth

Facilities: USP Leavenworth, with an adjacent minimum-security satellite prison camp.

Facility Address & Contact Information

United States Penitentiary Leavenworth
1300 Metropolitan
Leavenworth, KS 66048

Phone: 913-682-8700
Fax: 913-578-1010
Email: LVN/ExecAssistant@BOP.GOV

BOP Website: http://www.bop.gov/locations/institutions/lvn
Wikipedia: https://en.wikipedia.org/wiki/United_States_Penitentiary%2C_Leavenworth
ZCG Website: https://www.prisonerresource.com/resources/federal-prison-profiles/north-central-region-ncr/united-states-penitentiary-leavenworth-usp-leavenworth/

Inmate Correspondence Address

For USP Leavenworth

Inmate Name and Registration Number
USP Leavenworth
U.S. Penitentiary
P.O. Box 1000
Leavenworth, KS 66048

For Satellite Prison Camp

Inmate Name and Registration Number
USP Leavenworth
Satellite Prison Camp
P.O. Box 1000
Leavenworth, KS 66048

NOTE: Funds cannot be sent directly to federal inmates. See Chapter 1 for more information on sending funds to federal inmates.

Sex: Male

Security Level: Main: Medium Security; Camp: Minimum Security

Location: USP Leavenworth is located 25 miles north of Kansas City on Highway 73.

BOP Region: North Central Region (NCR)

BOP Institution Code: LVN for USP Leavenworth

Judicial District: District of Kansas

Medical Care Level: Level 2. See Chapter 2 for more information on Medical Care and Mental Health Care Levels.

Mental Health Care Level: Level 2

Population (as of May 1, 2019): Main: 1,319; Camp: 354

Background: United States Penitentiary Leavenworth is a medium-security federal prison located in Leavenworth, Kansas, which houses male inmates. It was opened in 1906. United States Penitentiary Leavenworth Camp, which also houses male inmates, was opened in 1960 and is located adjacent to the main institution.

USP Leavenworth was one of the first federal prisons.

Notable inmates include rap artist Troy Deon Reddick (served four years for robbery); Ponzi schemer Tom Petters (serving a 50-year sentence for conspiracy, wire fraud, mail fraud, and money laundering); leader of the Latin Kings gang Antonio Fernandez (convicted of conspiracy to distribute heroin and cocaine); and NFL quarterback Michael Vick (served 23 months for operating an interstate dog fighting ring).

Media reports indicate that at least one guard has been assaulted and had to be transported to a hospital for treatment, three guards have been charged with smuggling contraband into the institution, one inmate has been murdered by fellow prisoners, one inmate died of unreported causes, and one inmate died as a result of negligent medical care which led to organ failure. In addition, at least one inmate from the camp has escaped. News reports indicate that handicapped visitors have been denied access to the institution due to the prison not being handicap accessible.

In 2011, News One named USP Leavenworth one of the ten most notorious prisons in the United States.

Housing: Inmates are housed in one-person and two-person cells. The camp houses inmates in open dormitories with about 50 inmates per dorm.

Health Services: Available health services include intake screenings, stress management, nutrition counseling, dental hygiene, urgent care, medical and dental care, chronic care, physical examinations, and medications. While emergency care is available 24 hours a day, inmates must submit a triage form for routine health care needs.

Psychology Services: The USP Leavenworth Psychology Services Department is available to inmates Monday through Friday from 7:30 a.m. to 4:00 p.m. by appointment only. Appointments can be made by submitting a cop-out to Psychology Services or through the Unit Team or Health Services staff. Inmates experiencing an emergency situation (e.g., serious depression or suicidal thoughts) should report this to the nearest staff member and are generally seen immediately by Psychology staff. An on-call psychologist is available after hours to deal with emergency situations which may arise on evenings or weekends. Various services provided include individual counseling, crisis intervention, and special group programs. Among the group programs offered is Diversity in a Prison/Correctional Setting, which is offered several times a year. Through the Religious Services Department, the Life Connections Program is offered for inmates who desire to grow as responsible persons.

Residential Drug Abuse Program (RDAP): USP Leavenworth has the Residential Drug Abuse Program (RDAP). A Drug Education class and the Non-Residential Drug Abuse Program (NR-DAP) is also available. The satellite prison camp also offers RDAP.

Education Services: USP Leavenworth provides GED and English-as-a-Second Language (ESL) programs. Parenting and Adult Continuing Education (ACE) classes are also available. High school diplomas and post-secondary degrees are available through paid correspondence programs.

Advanced Occupational Education: USP Leavenworth offers advanced occupational education in Hospitality Employment and Retail Therapy (HEART) and Janitorial.

Vocational Training: USP Leavenworth offers two vocational training programs, Graphic Arts and Custodial Maintenance.

Apprenticeship: USP Leavenworth and the satellite camp do not offer any apprenticeship programs.

Library Services: The law library is located in the Education Department and contains a variety of legal reference materials for use in preparing legal papers. Reference materials include the United States Code Annotated, Federal Reporter, Supreme Court Reporter, Bureau of Prisons Program Statements, institution supplements, indexes, and other legal materials. Most of these are available on the TRULINCS Electronic Law Library. A copy machine and typewriters are available for use at the law library. The leisure library is available for inmates to check out leisure reading material, including both fiction and nonfiction books. Reference books, magazines, and newspapers are located in the library for reading in the Education Department only. Cassette players for language programs (audiobooks on cassette), and video monitors for the video library program are also available for inmate use. An interlibrary loan service is available.

UNICOR: The UNICOR facility handles recycling activities and services, and produces clothing and textiles.

Commissary: Inmates at USP Leavenworth are allowed to spend up to $360.00 per month in the commissary on such items as food, clothing, drinks, over-the-counter medications, and electronics. Inmates tend to use laundry bags to carry their purchases back to their housing units.

Recreation Services: A variety of activities are available on the USP Leavenworth recreation yard, second/third floor recreation, and in the gymnasium. Special events, including unit or institution-wide tournaments, are held throughout the year. The Recreation Department also allows inmates to take photographs through the Inmate Photograph Program at designated areas. The Recreation Department has a Movie Program, which screens movies in the Auditorium. The list of movies and schedule of showings is posted outside the Auditorium. The Recreation Department also offers a Music Program that allows inmates to utilize musical equipment or listen to CDs.

Visitation Information: On Sunday, Monday, Friday, and Saturday visitation is held between 8:00 a.m. and 3:00 p.m. On federal holidays visitation is held between 8:00 a.m. and 3:00 p.m. See Chapter 1 for more information on visitation.

In the News: In June 2017, a prisoner at United States Penitentiary Leavenworth physically assaulted a guard, resulting in a temporary lockdown. The guard was transported to a local hospital for treatment.

In 2017, USP Leavenworth prison guard Marc Buckner was sentenced to three years in prison for taking more than $200,000 in bribes over a ten-year period to smuggle tobacco and rolling papers into the facility.

In December 2016, investigative reporters at the local Fox 4 News reported that disabled relatives of prisoners at USP Leavenworth have been unable to visit on numerous occasions because the accessibility lift for the front steps is frequently broken.

In November 2016, Nicole English became warden at USP Leavenworth, replacing Claude Maye who retired as warden in June 2016. English was previously the warden at Federal Correctional Institution Marianna and Federal Correctional Institution Waseca.

In November 2016, Benjamin Johnson, a prisoner at USP Leavenworth, was found unresponsive and taken to the hospital where he died. The cause of death was undetermined at the time of news reports.

In May 2016, Michael Harston, a guard at USP Leavenworth, pleaded guilty to smuggling tobacco into the facility.

In February 2015, Otis Bradley, a prisoner at USP Leavenworth who was ignored by prison medical staff until he was vomiting blood and sent to the hospital where he was diagnosed with gallstones, diabetes and pancreatitis, died after his organs shut down and he had a heart attack.

In 2009, USP Leavenworth recreation specialist Jacob Roscoe was sentenced to a year and a day for agreeing to a payment of $1,400 to smuggle marijuana and jewelry into the prison.

In January 1997, three letter bombs addressed to USP Leavenworth's prison parole office were intercepted and disarmed. The letters were sent from Alexandria, Egypt.

In February 1979, Thomas Silverstein, an Aryan Brotherhood prison gang member serving 15 years for armed robbery, stabbed prisoner Danny Atwell to death.

Camp in the News: In November 2016, Timothy Taylor, a prisoner at the United States Penitentiary Leavenworth Camp, walked away without authorization but later returned to turn himself in.

USP Marion

United States Penitentiary Marion | USP Marion

Facilities: USP Marion with an adjacent minimum-security satellite prison camp.

Facility Address & Contact Information

United States Penitentiary Marion
4500 Prison Road
Marion, IL 62959

Phone: 618-964-1441
Fax: 618-964-2058
Email: MAR/ExecAssistant@BOP.GOV

BOP Website: https://www.bop.gov/locations/institutions/mar/
Wikipedia: https://en.wikipedia.org/wiki/United_States_Penitentiary,_Marion
ZCG Website: https://www.prisonerresource.com/resources/federal-prison-profiles/north-central-region-ncr/united-states-penitentiary-marion-usp-marion/

Inmate Correspondence Address

For USP Marion

Inmate Name and Registration Number
USP Marion
U.S. Penitentiary
P.O. Box 1000
Marion, IL 62959

For Satellite Prison Camp

Inmate Name and Registration Number
USP Marion
Satellite Prison Camp
P.O. Box 1000
Marion, IL 62959

NOTE: Funds cannot be sent directly to federal inmates. See Chapter 1 for more information on sending funds to federal inmates.

Sex: Male

Security Level: Main: Medium Security; Camp: Minimum Security

Location: USP Marion is located 300 miles from Chicago, 120 miles from St. Louis, 9 miles south of Marion, off I-57 via Highway 148 North; east on Little Grassy Road.

BOP Region: North Central Region (NCR)

BOP Institution Code: MAR for USP Marion

Judicial District: Southern District of Illinois

Medical Care Level: Level 2. See Chapter 2 for more information on Medical Care and Mental Health Care Levels.

Mental Health Care Level: Level 2

Population (as of May 1, 2019): Main: 1,156; Camp: 222

Background: United States Penitentiary Marion is a medium-security federal prison located in Marion, Illinois, which houses male inmates. It was opened in 1963. United States Penitentiary Marion Camp, which also houses male inmates, was opened in 1971 and is located adjacent to the main institution.

USP Marion was designed as a replacement for Alcatraz. It was once the Bureau of Prisons' control unit and housed high-profile offenders such as John Gotti. While still retaining the USP Marion moniker, the facility was transitioned to a medium-security federal prison in 2017 and is currently a Sex Offender Management Program (SOMP) facility.

Notable inmates include leader of the Alaska Peacemakers Militia Francis Schaeffer Cox (serving 25 years for murder conspiracy), Russian arms dealer Viktor Bout (serving a 25-year sentence for conspiring to kill Americans and supplying antiaircraft missiles), and MLB player Pete Rose (served five months at the camp for filing false tax returns).

Media reports indicate that at least three guards have been assaulted, two guards killed, and two inmates murdered at the institution. At least one inmate was charged with weapons possession. In addition, at least one inmate has escaped from the camp.

In 2011, News One named USP Marion one of the ten most notorious prisons in the United States.

Housing: Inmates are housed in one-, two-, and three-person cells. In the Communication Management Unit (CMU), inmates are single-celled. Inmates in RDAP are housed in two-person cells, while those in the Residential Sex Offender Treatment Program (SOTP-R) are single-celled. In the camp prisoners are held in dormitories which are divided into two-person cubicles.

Health Services: Intake screening, medical and dental sick call, emergency services, medications, physical examinations, chronic care, eye care and eyeglasses, immunizations as necessary, and pre-release examinations are available for prisoners. Prisoners are assigned a primary care provider who is their primary point of contact with Health Services. Inmates must attend sick call at 7:15 a.m. on Monday, Tuesday, Thursday, or Friday to be evaluated. Pill and insulin line are held at 6:00 a.m. and 4:55 p.m.

Psychology Services: Psychology Services at USP Marion provides counseling and a variety of programs to assist inmates who are experiencing mental health issues. Psychology Services assesses, treats, and monitors inmates with mental health problems, and provides crisis counseling, suicide prevention, sex offender management programming, and various groups such as a Non-Residential Sex Offender Treatment Program (SOTP-NR), Residential Sex Offender Treatment Program SOTP-R), anger management, communication skills, criminal thinking, rational behavior therapy, and values clarification. Individual and group counseling is available for the mentally ill. A self-help library containing books, audio CDs, and DVDs is also available. Psychology offerings in the CMU are minimal and don't include any classes.

Residential Drug Abuse Program (RDAP): USP Marion has the Residential Drug Abuse Program (RDAP). The camp does not have a RDAP facility. Other drug programs include a Non-Residential Drug Abuse Program (NR-DAP) and a Drug Education Program.

Education Services: USP Marion provides GED and English-as-a-Second-Language (ESL) programs. Adult Continuing Education (ACE) and parenting classes are also available. A robust computer lab, where inmates can learn Microsoft Excel, Word, and PowerPoint, is also available. High school diplomas and post-secondary degrees are available through paid correspondence programs. Inmates in the CMU have access to some movies and educational DVDs, but are otherwise highly restricted from library and education access.

Advanced Occupational Education: USP Marion offers advanced occupational education in Building Trades, Certified Production Technician, and Information Processing. CMU inmates are not allowed to participate in advanced occupational education.

Vocational Training: USP Marion and the satellite camp do not offer any vocational training programs.

Apprenticeship: USP Marion offers apprenticeships in Electrical, HVAC, Painting, and Residential and Commercial Plumbing. CMU inmates are not allowed to participate in any apprenticeships. The camp offers Electrical, Waste Water Treatment, and Water Treatment apprenticeships.

Library Services: USP Marion has a leisure library containing a selection of educational books and leisure reading materials (e.g., magazines, newspapers, and both fiction and nonfiction books). Inmates are discouraged from removing some reading materials from the library due to living area sanitation conditions and to promote the availability of reading materials for everyone. Movies, educational DVDs, and an interlibrary loan program are also available. The contents of the law library assist inmates in basic research and document preparation. The law library also houses law books that are from donated sources and are not required by policy to be replaced when lost or destroyed. A copy machine and typewriters are available for use in the law library. Paper supplies such as carbon paper and typing paper may be supplied. Most legal research is conducted on the TRULINCS Electronic Law Library computers. While allowed access to the electronic law library, CMU inmates have limited access to other library offerings.

UNICOR: The USP Marion UNICOR facility is an Electronics Cable Factory. The cable factory produces various electronic work including cables, cable assemblies, etc. Inmates in the CMU are not allowed to work in UNICOR. The camp does not have a UNICOR facility.

Commissary: Inmates are permitted to shop once a week on a designated day, which is determined by their registration number. A monthly spending limit of $360.00 is imposed. Food, snacks, drinks, clothing, shoes, and electronics can be purchased. UNICOR and facilities inmates can shop at 6:15 a.m. on their designated days. All other inmates shop at 9:00 a.m. and 1:00 p.m. on their designated day. Inmates in the CMU turn in their commissary order forms on Friday and it is delivered on Monday.

Recreation Services: Scheduled activities at USP Marion include sports, arts, crafts, music, and entertainment. Leisure activities include organized and informal games, sports, table games, hobbycrafts, music program, intramural activities, cultural events, movies, and talent and stage shows. Hobbycraft includes leather kits, wood crafts with craft sticks, painting, and other hobbies consistent with institution guidelines. In-cell Hobbycraft includes crocheting, knitting, drawing with pens and pencils, bead work, and card making. No leather crafts or oil painting is authorized in housing units. Art activities, a wellness program, running events, and outdoor entertainment including concerts and inspirational and motivational speakers, as well as musical instruments are available. Inside, inmates have access to stationary bikes, treadmills, ellipticals, four pool tables, 11 TVs, foosball, ping pong, stair steppers, a gym where basketball and handball are played, and a band room. Outside, inmates have access to a track, basketball, bocce ball, handball, volleyball, horseshoes, softball, Frisbee, soccer, and tables. In the CMU, recreation is highly restrictive and separate from general population. The most popular activities are movies and monthly tournaments in volleyball, ping pong, basketball, and darts.

Visitation Information: On Sunday and Saturday visitation is held between 8:30 a.m. and 3:00 p.m. On federal holidays visitation is held between 8:30 a.m. and 3:00 p.m. See Chapter 1 for more information on visitation.

Prison Politics: The level of politics is very low at this prison. According to one inmate, "The races mix somewhat." Another respondent explained, "This is the dumping ground of the BOP. It's a protective custody yard where all can walk."

Level of Violence: There is minimal to no violence at this facility. One inmate referred to the compound as "safe." Another explained, "Most fights are the result of personal problems and are few and far between. This institution is safe." Another inmate agreed, stating that there is only a fight "every now and then."

Vulnerable Populations: Sex offenders, informants, and LGBT inmates can stay on the yard. According to one respondent, "Pretty open yard, both sex offenders and transgender walk easily here." Another agreed, stating "the sex offenders are not harassed" and that the inmate population is "indifferent to the gender and orientation of others." Another respondent explained, "This is a drop-out yard, so sex offenders and informants are basically all that is here. So, everyone is allowed to walk the yard." He continued, "In the past year, the number of gay and transgender inmates has increased."

Good: "Very respectful staff, great and caring psychology staff, soft yard, lots of grass, and well-maintained." "Some one-man cells are available." "The good thing about this prison is that it is safe." "Lots of things to keep you occupied (e.g., work, rec, etc.)."

Bad: "Quality and quantity of food; no air conditioning in single-man cells or SHU." "Food is terrible, and commissary is mediocre." "Nothing good in the Communications Management Unit (CMU)." "Only two phone calls each week and no contact visits in the CMU." "The prison is like 55 years old. As such, the roof leaks and other parts are falling apart." "The food has gotten increasingly bad." "Some staff still want to treat the prison like it is a high." "The food could be better, and the guards could be more respectful."

Other Comments: "Go there 100%." "If I could transfer back, I would." "This yard is for everyone; it is very safe."

In the News: In 2014, Erick Roman, a prisoner serving a 60-year sentence at the United States Penitentiary in Marion, assaulted three guards in three separate incidents.

In 2013, David J. Pederson was on his way to a halfway house upon nearing the end of his sentence at USP Marion when he carjacked two motorists at gunpoint, for which he was sentenced to 40 years in prison.

In 2007, USP Marion was converted from the federal government's highest-security prison -- a maximum-security lockdown prison that replaced Alcatraz in 1963 -- to a medium-security prison.

In 2005, the Bureau of Prisons doubled the capacity of USP Marion to 900 prisoners.

In 2000, prisoner Joseph Tokash was convicted of possessing weapons in prison after x-ray exams on two occasions detected knives hidden in his rectum.

In October 1983, Aryan Brotherhood prison gang members Thomas Silverstein and Clayton Fountain killed guards Merle Clutts and Robert Hoffman at USP Marion, then the toughest penitentiary in the federal system, sending the prison into lockdown for 23 years.

In November 1981, Thomas Silverstein and Clayton Fountain, prisoners at USP Marion, strangled prisoner Robert Chappelle to death, then, fearing retribution from Chappelle's friend Raymond Smith, Silverstein and Fountain stabbed him 67 times and dragged his body up and down the tier for everyone to see.

Camp in the News: In 2000, Donald E. Bruce, a 75-year-old prisoner at Federal Correctional Institution Marion Camp, escaped and was caught in Oakland, California.

FCI Milan

Federal Correctional Institution Milan | FCI Milan

Facilities: FCI Milan with a detention center.

Facility Address & Contact Information

Federal Correctional Institution Milan
4004 East Arkona Road
Milan, MI 48160

Phone: 734-439-1511
Fax: 734-439-0949
Email: MIL/ExecAssistant@bop.gov

BOP Website: https://www.bop.gov/locations/institutions/mil/
Wikipedia: https://en.wikipedia.org/wiki/Federal_Correctional_Institution,_Milan
ZCG Website: https://www.prisonerresource.com/resources/federal-prison-profiles/north-central-region-ncr/federal-correctional-institution-milan-fci-milan/

Inmate Correspondence Address

Inmate Name and Registration Number
FCI Milan
Federal Correctional Institution
P.O. Box 1000
Milan, MI 48160

NOTE: Funds cannot be sent directly to federal inmates. See Chapter 1 for more information on sending funds to federal inmates.

Sex: Male

Security Level: Low Security

Location: FCI Milan is located in the town of Milan, off of U.S. 23 (Exit 27). It is 45 miles south of Detroit and 35 miles north of Toledo.

BOP Region: North Central Region (NCR)

BOP Institution Code: MIL for FCI Milan

Judicial District: Eastern District of Michigan

Medical Care Level: Level 2. See Chapter 2 for more information on Medical Care and Mental Health Care Levels.

Mental Health Care Level: Level 2

Population (as of May 1, 2019): 1,373

Background: Federal Correctional Institution Milan is a low-security federal prison in Milan, Michigan, which houses male inmates. It was opened in 1933.

Besides being a traditional federal prison, FCI Milan also contains a detention center for pre-trial and pre-sentence detainees, as well as holdover inmates.

Notable inmates include alleged leader of the Sinaloa Cartel Vincent Zambada-Niebla (awaiting trial on charges of cocaine importation and drug-related murders).

Media reports indicate that one guard was indicted for bribery in connection with smuggling contraband and one inmate was charged with drug possession. In addition, at least one guard has been fired for assaulting an inmate. There has also been at least one inmate suicide. According to news reports, in the mid-1990s, more than 100 prisoners engaged in a brawl.

Housing: Inmates are housed in dormitories containing two- and four-person rooms. C Unit houses new arrivals. G Unit is the RDAP unit. H Unit is the RISE unit for those with mental health issues. A Unit houses Life Connections Program inmates. At the FDC, inmates are housed in two-person cells.

Health Services: Services available to inmates at FCI Milan include medical sick call, chronic care, specialty clinics, X-rays, lab, dental, pharmacy, medical records, preventive health care services, emergency services, and the diagnosis and treatment of chronic infectious diseases. While emergency medical care is available 24 hours a day, inmates must submit a sick call form to be evaluated for non-emergency medical needs.

Psychology Services: All new arrivals at FCI Milan are provided a brief clinical interview, during which they are made aware of available treatment opportunities and the process involved in requesting services from the Psychology Department. Treatment is typically offered in a group therapy format and includes anger management, wellness classes, and other groups. Notices of new and upcoming offerings are posted on inmate bulletin boards. The Religious Services Department also offers the Life Connection Program for inmates who desire to grow as a responsible persons. The residential RISE program is also available for mentally ill inmates.

Residential Drug Abuse Program (RDAP): FCI Milan offers the Residential Drug Abuse Program (RDAP). Additional programs include the Non-Residential Drug Abuse Program (NR-DAP), the Drug Education Class, Alcoholics Anonymous (AA), and Narcotics Anonymous (NA).

Education Services: FCI Milan provides GED and English-as-a-Second Language (ESL) programs. Adult Continuing Education (ACE) courses (e.g., creative writing, effective communications, etc.), a parenting program, and a Reading is Fundamental program are also offered. High school diplomas and post-secondary degrees are available through paid correspondence programs. Jackson Community College allows inmates to earn an associate's degree in business administration. Hours of operation are 7:30 a.m. to 7:30 p.m. Monday through Friday (excluding Friday evening) and 7:30 a.m. to 2:30 p.m. Saturday and Sunday, excluding inmate counts and meals.

Advanced Occupational Education: FCI Milan offers advanced occupational education in Automotive Service Technician, Janitorial Maintenance, National Federation of Professional Trainers (NFPT), and Parks & Recreation Worker.

Vocational Training: FCI Milan does not offer any vocational training aside from its advanced occupational education and apprenticeship programs.

Apprenticeship: FCI Milan offers apprenticeships in Carpentry, Computer Operator, Dental Assistant, Electrician, HVAC, Millwright, Pipefitter, Plumber, Quality Assurance, Stationary Engineer, Tool & Die, and Welding.

Library Services: Reference material are available in the law library, as well as typewriters and a copy machine. Inmates are allowed to check out fiction and nonfiction books, magazines, and newspapers. The TRULINCS Electronic Law Library allows inmates to conduct legal research. A robust CD and DVD program is available where inmates can listen to audio books and watch movies, including a robust selection of The Greatest Courses offerings.

UNICOR: The FCI Milan UNICOR operates a Metal Specialty Plant. There is a pre-industrial training program for inmates awaiting hire in the plant.

Commissary: Inmates are allowed to spend up to $360.00 monthly in the commissary. Postage stamps, copy cards, photo tickets, and over-the-counter medications do not count against this spending limit. Popular items include ice cream, soda, food, candy, and snacks. Inmates can shop once a week on their designated shopping day. Currently, sales are conducted Monday through Thursday from 6:00 a.m. to 2:30 p.m. Inmates at the FDC shop once every two weeks on Mondays. A $180 biweekly spending limitation is enforced.

Recreation Services: Indoor and outdoor recreation programs are provided to FCI Milan inmates, including a gymnasium and recreation yard. Hobbycraft and sports league activities are available to the inmate population. Popular sports include basketball, soccer, and flag football. Indoors, inmates have access to hobbycraft (crochet, drawing, painting, cross-stitch, ceramics, and leathercraft), a gym, treadmills, rowing machines, ellipticals, stair climbers, basketball, weight room, handball, and volleyball. Outdoors, inmates have access to bocce ball, horseshoes, hooverball, softball, soccer, football, a weight pile, chairs, tables, and a track. Hours of operation are 6:00 a.m. to 8:30 p.m., excluding counts and meals. In the FDC, inmates have access to an indoor area with cards, chess, and TVs. Outdoors at the FDC, there is a small enclosed yard with a basketball net.

Visitation Information: On Sunday and Saturday visitation is held between 8:15 a.m. and 3:00 p.m. On Thursday visitation is held between 4:30 and 8:00 p.m. On Friday visitation is held between 12:45 and 8:00 p.m. On federal holidays visitation is held between 8:15 a.m. and 3:00 p.m. See Chapter 1 for more information on visitation.

Prison Politics: This is not a political yard. According to one respondent, "No one cares what race you are or where you come from."

Level of Violence: There is a low level of violence at this prison. A common phrase on the compound is: "You don't get to Milan by being a badass."

Vulnerable Populations: Sex offenders, informants, and LGBT inmates can walk the yard. According to one inmate, while there are haters, "they bark more than bite." There is also a large gay population on the compound.

Good: "The food is pretty good." "The best run area is Facilities."

Bad: "Like most places, you can always depend on it being undependable." "New officers come through and try to make their mark, but in a few months, they get squared away." "The new captain sucks." "The worst run area is Education."

Other Comments: "The place isn't bad. You just have to expect the unexpected and realize that this place is consistently inconsistent."

In the News: In October 2015, Federal Correctional Institution Milan prison guard Jake John Froehly was indicted for accepting bribes in exchange for smuggling contraband into the prison.

In July 2010, Donald Brelje, a prisoner at FCI Milan, was charged with possession of contraband after more than three grams of marijuana was found in his cell.

In October 2007, pretrial detainee John Atchison, a federal prosecutor from Florida, killed himself while he was in isolation on suicide watch at FCI Milan as he was awaiting trial on charges that he flew to Michigan to have sex with a five-year-old girl.

In 2004, Marcus Johnson, a guard at FCI Milan, slammed a cell-door food slot shut on the arms of prisoner Yousseff Hmimssa and was fired after prosecutors refused to press charges against him.

In 1994, a riot erupted involving more than 100 prisoners and lasting more than 20 minutes before order was restored.

FCI Oxford

Federal Correctional Institution Oxford | FCI Oxford

Facilities: FCI Oxford, with an adjacent minimum-security satellite prison camp and a detention center.

Facility Address & Contact Information

Federal Correctional Institution Oxford
County Road G & Elk Avenue
Oxford, WI 53952

Phone: 608-584-5511
Fax: 608-584-6371
Email: OXF/ExecAssistant@bop.gov

BOP Website: https://www.bop.gov/locations/institutions/oxf/
Wikipedia: https://en.wikipedia.org/wiki/Federal_Correctional_Institution,_Oxford
ZCG Website: https://www.prisonerresource.com/resources/federal-prison-profiles/north-central-region-ncr/federal-correctional-institution-oxford-fci-oxford/

Inmate Correspondence Address

For FCI Oxford

Inmate Name and Registration Number
FCI Oxford
Federal Correctional Institution
P.O. Box 1000
Oxford, WI 53952

For Satellite Prison Camp

Inmate Name and Registration Number
FCI Oxford
Satellite Prison Camp
P.O. Box 1085
Oxford, WI 53952

NOTE: Funds cannot be sent directly to federal inmates. See Chapter 1 for more information on sending funds to federal inmates.

Sex: Male

Security: Main: Medium Security; Camp: Minimum Security

Location: Located in central Wisconsin, 60 miles north of Madison, off I-39 at the intersection of County Road G and Elk Avenue.

BOP Region: North Central Region (NCR)

BOP Institution Code: OXF for FCI Oxford

Judicial District: Western District of Wisconsin

Medical Care Level: Level 1. See Chapter 2 for more information on Medical Care and Mental Health Care Levels.

Mental Health Care Level: Level 1

Population (as of May 1, 2019): Main & Detention Center: 820; Camp: 126

Background: Federal Correctional Institution Oxford is a medium-security federal prison in Oxford, Wisconsin, which houses male inmates. It was opened in 1973. Federal Correctional Institution Oxford Camp, which also houses male inmates, was opened in 1985 and is located adjacent to the main institution.

Notable inmates include former Illinois Congressman Dan Rostenkowski (served 17 months for mail fraud), Jesus Cortez Zambrano (serving a 27-year sentence for murder), and former Illinois Governor George Ryan (convicted of corruption).

Media reports indicate that two guards have been charged with sexually assaulting inmates; one of them was also charged with lying to federal investigators, while the other was also charged with smuggling contraband. Another guard was charged with filing fraudulent mileage claims for reimbursement. News reports also state that one guard has been killed by an inmate at the institution.

Housing: Inmates are housed in one- and two-person cells in four units. Inmates at the camp are housed in dormitories containing four-person cubicles.

Health Services: Medical and dental sick call, emergency services, medications, physical examinations, health promotion and disease prevention, diagnosis and treatment of chronic infectious diseases, and eyeglasses are provided to inmates. While emergency care is available 24 hours a day, routine care must be requested through attending sick call, which is conducted at 7:15 a.m. Monday through Thursday.

Psychology Services: FCI Oxford has three psychologists who provide counseling and other mental health services to inmates. A psychiatrist also visits the institution on a regular basis. There are many alternatives for inmates who have personal problems and a desire to correct them. These options include self-image, PMA (Positive Mental Attitude), anger management, and other voluntary groups. Unit staff are available for informal counseling sessions, and they conduct formal group counseling activities in the inmate housing units.

Residential Drug Abuse Program (RDAP): FCI Oxford houses the Residential Drug Abuse Program (RDAP). The camp does not house the Residential Drug Abuse Program (RDAP). Both facilities offer the Drug Abuse Education course and a Non-Residential Drug Abuse Treatment Program (NR-DAP).

Education Services: FCI Oxford provides literacy, GED, and English-as-a-Second Language (ESL) programs. Various incentives are provided to inmates who pursue these educational objectives. Adult Continuing Education (ACE) and parenting classes are also available. High school diplomas and post-secondary degrees are available through paid correspondence programs.

Advanced Occupational Education: FCI Oxford does not offer any advanced occupational education programs.

Vocational Training: FCI Oxford offers vocational training in Certified Production Technician and Culinary Arts.

Apprenticeship: The main facility offers apprenticeships in Carpentry, Culinary Arts, and Dental Assistant. The camp offers Maintenance Repair, Painter, Stationary Engineer, Waste Water Treatment, and Welding. Both facilities offer apprenticeships as a Bricklayer, Electrician, HVAC, Painter, Pipefitter, and Plumbing.

Library Services: The TRULINCS Electronic Law Library is located in the Education Department. The legal library contains all materials required by BOP policy for the preparation and submission of federal questions of law, beginning with the Administrative Remedy process through the U.S. District Court, the U.S. Court of Appeals, and the U.S. Supreme Court. Typewriters, a copy machine, legal forms, and supplies for use in preparing legal documents are available as well. The resource/leisure library offers a wide range of reading materials. Books are also available for research as needed for college classes. In addition to books, the library subscribes to a wide variety of magazines and newspapers.

UNICOR: There are no UNICOR facilities at FCI Oxford or the satellite camp.

Commissary: Inmates are permitted to spend up to $360.00 per month ($180 biweekly) on regular purchases and $300.00 per quarter on special purpose items (e.g., religious items, art materials, etc.). This limit does not include telephone credits, postage stamps, or over-the-counter medications. In the commissary, inmates are allowed to buy a variety of items, including electronics, food, clothing, drinks, and shoes.

Recreation Services: FCI Oxford offers both structured and leisure time recreational activities. The gymnasium offers basketball, handball, racquetball, volleyball, soccer, and the ACE Wellness classes. Also available inside are weightlifting, a billiards room, and table game area (Ping-Pong, darts, etc.). The outside recreation yard offers a softball field, a running track, tennis courts, bocce ball, horseshoes, and shuffleboard. The Hobbycraft Center is open to inmates interested in ceramics and leather work. Drawing and painting activities are available to inmates through the art program. Musical instruments are available in the recreation area.

Visitation Information: On Sunday and Saturday visitation is held between 8:15 a.m. and 3:00 p.m. On federal holidays visitation is held between 8:15 a.m. and 3:00 p.m. See Chapter 1 for more information on visitation.

Prison Politics: This is a somewhat political yard. According to one respondent, "different cars and groups claim tables in the chow hall." New arrivals typically have to show their racial group shot caller their paperwork.

Level of Violence: There is a moderate level of violence at this prison. According to one respondent, "There was an accused informant who got stabbed a little while ago."

Vulnerable Populations: While sex offenders, informants, and LGBT inmates can walk the yard, they tend to have some problems. According to one inmate, "There are separate groups of sex offenders for each race. Each has its own table in the chow hall. We are all persona non grata, treated as non-people." Another respondent agreed, stating, "sex offenders are often extorted, robbed, and assaulted by members of their own race." Another inmate provided a personal example of how sex offenders are treated: "My paperwork was requested to be seen a few times when I came in. Instead of showing it, I opted to join the Native sex offender car. We are not allowed in the TV rooms." As it concerns LGBT inmates, another inmate expressed that "gays and transgenders are inconspicuous if they exist here."

Bad: "There is only air conditioning in the TV rooms and the cops' offices."

In the News: In February 2017, Stacy L. Lenorud, an SIS official at Federal Correctional Institution Oxford, was sentenced to two years of probation after pleading guilty to engaging in sexual acts with a prisoner and smuggling in contraband for him. In a related case, FCI Oxford employee Amy Ziemann was indicted on charges of engaging in sexual acts with a prisoner and trying to persuade Lenorud to testify falsely before a grand jury.

In 2014, Christopher A. Seifer, an electronics technician at FCI Oxford, was sentenced to 15 months in prison for filing 1,380 false mileage claims amounting to more than $100,000.

In 2007, former Illinois Governor George Ryan served time at FCI Oxford for corruption.

In January 1984, FCI Oxford guard Boyd Spikerman was killed by an inmate.

FCI Pekin

Federal Correctional Institution Pekin | FCI Pekin

Facilities: FCI Pekin with an adjacent minimum-security satellite prison camp.

Facility Address & Contact Information

Federal Correctional Institution Pekin
2600 South Second Street
Pekin, IL 61554

Phone: 309-346-8588
Fax: 309-477-4685
Email: PEK/ExecAssistant@bop.gov

BOP Website: https://www.bop.gov/locations/institutions/pek/
Wikipedia: https://en.wikipedia.org/wiki/Federal_Correctional_Institution,_Pekin
ZCG Website: https://www.prisonerresource.com/resources/federal-prison-profiles/north-central-region-ncr/federal-correctional-institution-pekin-fci-pekin/

Inmate Correspondence Address

For FCI Pekin

Inmate Name and Registration Number
FCI Pekin
Federal Correctional Institution
P.O. Box 5000
Pekin, IL 61555

For Satellite Prison Camp

Inmate Name and Registration Number
FCI Pekin
Satellite Prison Camp
P.O. Box 5000
Pekin, IL 61555

NOTE: Funds cannot be sent directly to federal inmates. See Chapter 1 for more information on sending funds to federal inmates.

Sex: Male

Security Level: Main: Medium Security; Camp: Minimum Security

Location: FCI Pekin is located on Route 29 South in Pekin, about 10 miles south of Peoria, 170 miles southwest of Chicago, and 170 miles northeast of St. Louis.

BOP Region: North Central Region (NCR)

BOP Institution Code: PEK for FCI Pekin

Judicial District: Central District of Illinois

Medical Care Level: Level 2. See Chapter 2 for more information on Medical Care and Mental Health Care Levels.

Mental Health Care Level: Level 2

Population (as of May 1, 2019): Main: 969; Camp: 246

Background: Federal Correctional Institution Pekin is a medium-security federal prison located in Pekin, Illinois, which houses male inmates. It was opened in 1994. Federal Correctional Institution Pekin Camp, which also houses male inmates, is located adjacent to the main institution.

Notable inmates include former Chicago police officer Joseph Miedzianowski (serving a life sentence for conspiracy and racketeering); Iowa machinist John Toimkins (serving 37 years for mailing threatening letters and two pipe bombs); former Petunia City Comptroller Rita Crundwell (sentenced to 20 years for embezzling $54 million); and Shon Hopwood (now a Georgetown University Law Center professor).

Media reports indicate that there has been one death at the institution in recent years for which the cause of death was not released. Additionally, two guards have been charged with drug smuggling.

Housing: Inmates are housed in two-, four-, and eight ten-person cells within the four housing units. Inmates at the camp are housed in dormitories containing two-person cubicles.

Health Services: FCI Pekin provides medical and dental sick call, emergency care, medications, eyeglasses, physical examinations, and emergency and routine dental care. Inmates are assigned to a Mid-Level Practitioner, who treats them for the duration of their stay. In order to be evaluated by Health Services staff, inmates must submit a written sick call request.

Psychology Services: The Psychology Department at FCI Pekin provides professional services in the area of evaluation, counseling, group programs, crisis assistance, drug treatment, and self-help programs. Each new arrival is interviewed and provided a summary of current psychological programs available for enrollment. Treatment groups include anger management, criminal thinking, and Smart Recovery.

Residential Drug Abuse Program (RDAP): Neither FCI Pekin nor the satellite camp offer the Residential Drug Abuse Treatment Program (RDAP). Both facilities offer a Drug Education Program, the Non-Residential Drug Abuse Program (NR-DAP) and Alcoholics Anonymous (AA).

Education Services: FCI Pekin provides GED and English-as-a-Second Language (ESL) programs. An Adult Continuing Education (ACE) program is taught by other inmates. Various incentives are provided for completing Pre-GED, ACE, and parenting courses. Topics such as Spanish, Real Estate, Public Speaking, and Drawing are offered. A parenting program is also available. High school diplomas and post-secondary degrees are available through paid correspondence programs.

Advanced Occupational Education: FCI Pekin offers advanced occupational education in Certified Production Technician and Computer Applications. The camp offers training in Computer Applications.

Vocational training: No vocational training is provided at FCI Pekin or the satellite camp aside from the advanced occupational education and apprenticeship programs.

Apprenticeship: FCI Pekin offers apprenticeships in Institutional Cook, Maintenance Electrician, Quality Control Technician, and Sheet Metal Worker. The camp does not offer any apprenticeship programs.

UNICOR: The FCI Pekin UNICOR facility produces industrial products and handles fleet management and vehicular components. The camp does not house a UNICOR facility.

Library Services: The Education Department maintains a leisure and law library. The leisure library has numerous books and other reading materials available for circulation and reference. This includes fiction and nonfiction books, newspapers, and magazines. The law library is located in the Education Department. Electric typewriters and a copy machine are available for inmates use. The TRULINCS Electronic Law Library is also available for inmate usage, which allows access to Bureau program statements, federal case law, and much more.

Commissary: Inmates are allowed to shop one day per week based on their housing unit or work assignments. The spending limit at FCI Pekin is $360.00 per month. The spending limit in the camp is also $360.00 per month. Inmates are allowed to purchase a wide variety of food and non-food items in the commissary.

Recreation Services: Scheduled activities at FCI Pekin include sports, athletics, arts, crafts, music, and entertainment. New programs are introduced as interest and participation warrant. The FCI Pekin recreation yard offers a track, horseshoes, bocce ball, basketball, handball, and volleyball courts, as well as softball fields, a soccer/flag football field, and a weight pile. Billiard tables, bumper pool tables, table tennis, art room, leather room, treadmills, ellipticals, tables, TVs, and weight training equipment are also available.

Visitation Information: On Sunday and Saturday visitation is held between 8:15 a.m. and 3:00 p.m. On Monday visitation is held between 1:00 and 8:00 p.m. On federal holidays visitation is held between 8:15 a.m. and 3:00 p.m. See Chapter 1 for more information on visitation.

Prison Politics: This is a very political yard. While most inmates belong to cars, independents are allowed.

Level of Violence: There is significant violence at this prison. Inmates report lots of fights and monthly stabbings.

Vulnerable Populations: Sex offenders and informants can't stay. LGBT inmates can remain, but it can be a challenging and unfriendly experience.

Bad: "Serious racial segregation. Inmates even have car-imposed color-coded chairs for their race."

Other Comments: "If not a rat or a sex offender, they'll be ok. Better for harder sorts."

In the News: In April 2018, Rita Crundwell, the former city comptroller of Petunia City who embezzled $54 million to fund her lavish lifestyle for 20 years, was moved from Federal Correctional Institution Waseca to Federal Correctional Institution Pekin to serve out the remaining 14 years of her sentence closer to her family.

In December 2016, the death of a prisoner at FCI Pekin, who was not identified, was being investigated to determine the cause.

In 2003, Cassandra Cooper was charged with bringing cocaine, marijuana and amphetamines to a prison staff member at FCI Pekin over a two-year period, who would smuggle the drugs inside to prisoner Beau Hansen to distribute within the facility.

In 2002, Leann Serrano, a nurse at FCI Pekin, was caught in a sting, purchasing two ounces of cocaine from an undercover agent to smuggle into the prison.

FMC Rochester

Federal Medical Center Rochester | FMC Rochester

Facility Address & Contact Information

Federal Medical Center Rochester
2110 East Center Street
Rochester, MN 55904

Phone: 507-287-0674
Fax: 507-287-9601
Email: RCH/ExecAssistant@bop.gov

BOP Website: https://www.bop.gov/locations/institutions/rch/
Wikipedia: https://en.wikipedia.org/wiki/Federal_Medical_Center,_Rochester
ZCG Website: https://www.prisonerresource.com/resources/federal-prison-profiles/north-central-region-ncr/federal-medical-center-rochester-fmc-rochester/

Inmate Correspondence Address

Inmate Name and Registration Number
FMC Rochester
Federal Medical Center
P.O. Box 4000
Rochester, MN 55903

NOTE: Funds cannot be sent directly to federal inmates. See Chapter 1 for more information on sending funds to federal inmates.

Sex: Male

Security Level: Administrative Security (Multiple Security Levels)

Location: Located in southern Minnesota, 2 miles east of downtown Rochester.

BOP Region: North Central Region (NCR)

BOP Institution Code: RCH for FMC Rochester

Judicial District: District of Minnesota

Medical Care Level: Level 3/4. See Chapter 2 for more information on Medical Care and Mental Health Care Levels.

Mental Health Care Level: Level 4

Population (as of May 1, 2019): 686

Background: Federal Medical Center Rochester is an administrative-security federal prison in Rochester, Minnesota, which houses male inmates. It was opened in 1984.

FMC Rochester was formerly a state mental hospital. Today it is a psychiatric and medical referral center for the Bureau of Prisons.

Notable inmates include Jared Lee Loughner (serving a life sentence for murder and an attempted assassination of a Congresswoman); Luke Helder (planted pipe bombs in five states); founder of Praise the Lord Ministries Jim Bakker (served five years for fraud); former House Speaker Dennis Hastert (served 13 months for structuring bank withdrawals to evade bank reporting requirements); former U.S. Representative Dan Rostenkowski; and fringe presidential candidate Lyndon LaRouche.

Housing: Inmates are housed in various settings ranging from individual cells to open dormitories. Most inmates are housed in two-person cells. There are four housing unit buildings, each with a different purpose: Hospital, Outpatient, Psychiatric, and Work Cadre.

Health Services: Health Services staff at FMC Rochester includes physicians, a dentist, dental assistants, nurse practitioners, physician assistants, nurses, pharmacists, pharmacy technicians, a radiological technician, physical therapists, laboratory technologists, and a respiratory therapist. Physical examinations, immunizations, sick call, dental care, emergency services, medications, health and wellness programs, preventive health care, and reading glasses are provided to inmates.

Psychology Services: Mental Health Services through the Psychiatry and Psychology Departments are available to all inmates at FMC Rochester. These include screening, assessment, and treatment of mental health problems, individual and group counseling, psychoeducational classes, self-help and supportive services, and referral to Health Services (Psychiatry) for medical treatment of a mental illness.

Residential Drug Abuse Program (RDAP): FMC Rochester does not offer the Residential Drug Abuse Program (RDAP). It does offer other drug abuse programs, a Drug Abuse Education class, and a Non-Residential Drug Abuse Program (NR-DAP).

Education Services: FMC Rochester provides literacy, GED, and English-as-a-Second Language (ESL) programs. Incentive awards are provided to recognize inmates making satisfactory progress and successfully completing the literacy (i.e., GED and ESL) program. Inmates may also receive incentives for progressing to various levels in the GED or ESL programs. Graduation ceremonies recognize GED, ESL, and Occupational Education completions. Adult Continuing Education (ACE) and a parenting program are also available. Classes are available in Spanish, typing, and different types of Microsoft software. High school diplomas and post-secondary degrees are available through paid correspondence programs.

Advanced Occupational Education: FMC Rochester does not offer any advanced occupational education programs.

Vocational Training: FMC Rochester offers vocational training in Landscape Management through Rochester Community and Technical College (RCTC).

Apprenticeship: FMC Rochester offers apprenticeships in Biomedical Equipment Repair, Electrical, HVAC, Painting, and Plumbing.

Library Services: The leisure library offers inmates a variety of reading materials, including periodicals, newspapers, fiction, nonfiction, and reference books. An interlibrary loan program is also available. Inmates are provided access to legal materials and an opportunity to prepare legal documents through the use of the TRULINCS Electronic Law Library. Inmates also have access to electric typewriters and a copy machine.

UNICOR: FMC Rochester does not house a UNICOR facility.

Commissary: Inmates are allowed to shop in the commissary one day per week. Items such as clothing, shoes, food, sodas, drink mixes, radios, MP3 players, and more can be purchased. A $360.00 monthly spending limit is imposed.

Recreation Services: Physical fitness and leisure programs at FMC Rochester are provided to promote positive lifestyle changes. Leisure activities include organized and informal games, sports, physical fitness, table games, hobbycrafts, music programs, intramural activities, social and cultural organizations, and movies. Art activities include paintings and sketches using traditional methods (e.g., oils, pastels, crayons, pencils, inks, and charcoal). Hobbycraft activities include ceramics and leatherwork. Wellness programs include screening, assessments, goal setting, fitness/nutrition plans, and counseling.

Visitation Information: On Sunday, Monday, Friday, and Saturday visitation is held between 8:15 a.m. and 2:30 p.m. On federal holidays visitation is held between 8:15 a.m. and 2:30 p.m. See Chapter 1 for more information on visitation.

Prison Politics: This prison is not political.

Level of Violence: There is a very low level of violence at this prison. One respondent stated that the prison was "safe."

Vulnerable Populations: Sex offenders, informants, and LGBT inmates can walk the yard. According to one inmate, "This is a very soft yard where informants, sex offenders, and gays can stay."

Good: "Peaceful and calm."

Bad: "There is very little structured programming or vocational training." "There are a lot of snitches who will openly and unashamedly go straight to the cops to tell on you."

Other Comments: "If you are a sex offender, you'll probably be very comfortable living here. If you don't mind sex offenders and snitches, and you like quiet, safe, boring, and peaceful prison time, you'll do well here. I personally love it here."

In the News: In June 2016, former Speaker of the House Dennis Hastert reported to Federal Medical Center Rochester to begin his 15-month sentence for federal bank violations related to sexual misconduct against boys when he was a high school wrestling coach.

FCI Sandstone

Federal Correctional Institution Sandstone | FCI Sandstone

Facility Address & Contact Information

Federal Correctional Institution Sandstone
2300 County Road 29
Sandstone, MN 55072

Phone: 320-245-2262
Fax: 320-245-0385
Email: SST/ExecAssistant@bop.gov

BOP Website: https://www.bop.gov/locations/institutions/sst/
Wikipedia: https://en.wikipedia.org/wiki/Federal_Correctional_Institution%2C_Sandstone
ZCG Website: https://www.prisonerresource.com/resources/federal-prison-profiles/north-central-region-ncr/federal-correctional-institution-sandstone-fci-sandstone/

Inmate Correspondence Address

Inmate Name and Registration Number
FCI Sandstone
Federal Correctional Institution
P.O. Box 1000
Sandstone, MN 55072

NOTE: Funds cannot be sent directly to federal inmates. See Chapter 1 for more information on sending funds to federal inmates.

Sex: Male

Security Level: Low Security

Location: Located 100 miles northeast of Minneapolis/St. Paul, 70 miles southwest of Duluth, off I-35.

BOP Region: North Central Region (NCR)

BOP Institution Code: SST for FCI Sandstone

Judicial District: District of Minnesota

Medical Care Level: Level 1. See Chapter 2 for more information on Medical Care and Mental Health Care Levels.

Mental Health Care Level: Level 1

Population (as of May 1, 2019): 1,223

Background: Federal Correctional Institution Sandstone is a low-security federal prison in Sandstone, Minnesota, which houses male inmates. It was initially opened in 1939, closed in 1949, but then reopened in 1959.

Notable inmates include former NHL player Mike Danton (convicted of conspiracy to commit murder), serial bank robber David Brankle (serving a 21-year sentence), and disbarred attorney Marc Dreier (serving 20 years for securities fraud, wire fraud, and money laundering).

In 2017, Insider Monkey named FCI Sandstone one of the ten easiest federal prisons to do time. In 2012, CNBC named the institution one of the 12 best federal prisons in which to do time.

Housing: Inmates are housed in dormitories, which are divided into two- and four-person cubicles.

Health Services: Health services at FCI Sandstone include episodic visits for new or recurring medical or dental symptoms through a sick call system, chronic care management for chronic and infectious diseases through enrollment in chronic care clinics for regular care, routine dental care, medical and dental emergency care for injuries and sudden illness, age-appropriate preventive care to promote optimal health and functional status, prescription glasses, and medications. Sick call is held at 6:15 a.m. Pill line is conducted at 6:00 a.m., noon, and 4:45 p.m. Insulin line is before breakfast and dinner.

Psychology Services: Psychology services at FCI Sandstone include screening, assessment, and treatment of mental health problems, individual and group counseling, psycho-educational classes, self-help and supportive services, and referral to Health Services for medical treatment of a mental illness. Psychology Department offerings include Values Training and other voluntary groups. Consultation, crisis intervention-type counseling sessions, relaxation training sessions, self-study, and meditative techniques are also available.

Residential Drug Abuse Program (RDAP): FCI Sandstone houses the Residential Drug Abuse Program (RDAP). Other drug abuse programs, a Drug Abuse Education course, a Non-Residential Drug Abuse Program (NR-DAP) and groups for Alcoholics Anonymous (AA) and Narcotics Anonymous (NA) are also available.

Education Services: FCI Sandstone provides literacy, GED, and English-as-a-Second Language (ESL) programs. Incentive awards are provided to recognize inmates making satisfactory progress and successfully completing the literacy (i.e., GED and ESL) program. Inmates may also receive incentives for progressing to various levels in the GED or ESL programs. Graduation ceremonies recognize GED, ESL, and Occupational Education completions. Adult Continuing Education (ACE) courses and a parenting program are also available. High school diplomas and post-secondary degrees are available through paid correspondence programs.

Advanced Occupational Education: FCI Sandstone does not offer any advanced occupational education programs.

Vocational Training: FCI Sandstone offers vocational training in Auto and Building Trades.

Apprenticeship: FCI Sandstone offers apprenticeships in Culinary and Welding.

Library Services: The leisure library offers inmates a variety of reading materials including periodicals, newspapers, fiction, nonfiction, and reference books. Inmates in college classes have access to computer word processors, while everyone else has access to NEO word processors. There is also a DVD movie program. Inmates are provided access to legal materials and an opportunity to prepare legal documents. The TRULINCS Electronic Law Library provides inmates access to case law, prison policy, federal rules of court, and other information of a legal nature. A copying machine and typewriters are available for inmate use.

UNICOR: The FCI Sandstone UNICOR facility produces clothing and textiles.

Commissary: Inmates can spend up to $360.00 per month in the commissary. A bi-weekly spending limitation of $180 is enforced at FCI Sandstone. A wide variety of items are available for inmate purchase, including radios, MP3 players, food, drinks, ice cream, clothing, and shoes. Commissary is open Monday through Thursday and inmates can shop between 6:00 and 7:30 a.m., and 10:30 a.m. to 12:00 p.m. on their designated shopping day.

Recreation: Leisure activities at FCI Sandstone include organized and informal games, sports, physical fitness, table games, hobbycrafts, music programs, intramural activities, social and cultural organizations, and movies. Art activities include paintings and sketches rendered in pastels, crayons, pencils, inks, and charcoal. Hobbycraft activities include leatherwork, air brushing, clay, mosaics, crochet, knitting, etc. Wellness programs include screening, assessments, goal setting, healthy living, diabetic education, fitness/nutrition plans, and counseling. Inside, inmates have access to basketball, street hockey, card tables, TVs, darts, pool tables, handball, and a band room. Outside, inmates have access to weights, basketball, handball, soccer, softball, pickleball, volleyball, horseshoes, bocce ball, and a track.

Visitation Information: On Sunday, Monday, and Saturday visitation is held between 8:30 a.m. and 3:30 p.m. On federal holidays visitation is held between 8:30 a.m. and 3:30 p.m. See Chapter 1 for more information on visitation.

Prison Politics: This is not a political yard. According to inmates, politics are only prevalent in the old housing units due to there being so few TV areas, but this isn't the case in the newer units, which have both TV rooms and TVs in the day room. One respondent made a surprising comment, stating, "Staff are very political and are known to both run inmate's paperwork and [tell] fellow inmates if they are a member of a vulnerable population."

Level of Violence: There is minimal violence at this facility. According to one inmate, "most of the small amount of violence is due to interpersonal issues regarding the placement of chairs and television channels."

Vulnerable Populations: Sex offenders, informants, and LGBT inmates can walk the yard. One respondent explained that some sports teams and areas will exclude sex offenders, but that this is the exception to the rule.

Good: "Great indoor recreation, good ACE classes." "I like the Chapel and Library a lot." "Great food due to the culinary arts program." "You can get through the day without a lot of BS." "Food is decent."

Bad: "Cold weather." "No air conditioning, phones, computers, or laundry in the old housing units."

Other Comments: "One of the better spots in the BOP." "This really is a decent place to spend time."

MCFP Springfield

Medical Center for Federal Prisoners Springfield | MCFP Springfield

Facility Address & Contact Information

Medical Center for Federal Prisoners Springfield
1900 West Sunshine Street
Springfield, MO 65807

Phone: 417-862-7041
Fax: 417-837-1717
Email: SPG/ExecAssistant@bop.gov

BOP Website: https://www.bop.gov/locations/institutions/spg/
Wikipedia:https://en.wikipedia.org/wiki/United_States_Medical_Center_for_Federal_Prisoners
ZCG Website: https://www.prisonerresource.com/resources/federal-prison-profiles/north-central-region-ncr/medical-center-federal-prisoners-springfield-mcfp-springfield/

Inmate Correspondence Address

Inmate Name and Registration Number
MCFP Springfield
Federal Medical Center
P.O. Box 4000
Springfield, MO 65801

NOTE: Funds cannot be sent directly to federal inmates. See Chapter 1 for more information on sending funds to federal inmates.

Sex: Male

Security Level: Administrative Security (Multiple Security Levels)

Location: MCFP Springfield is located at the corner of Sunshine Street and the Kansas Expressway, off I-44.

BOP Region: North Central Region (NCR)

BOP Institution Code: SPG for MCFP Springfield

Judicial District: Western District of Missouri

Medical Care Level: Level 3/4. See Chapter 2 for more information on Medical Care and Mental Health Care Levels.

Mental Health Care Level: Level 4

Population (as of May 1, 2019): 1,042

Background: United States Medical Center for Federal Prisoners Springfield is an administrative-security federal prison in Springfield, Missouri, which houses male inmates. It was opened in 1933.

The facility was initially called the United States Hospital for Defective Delinquents and was designed to remove mentally deficient criminals from the general prison population. Currently, it provides major medical, mental health, and dental services for the Bureau of Prisons. It also houses a 20-bed psychiatric hospital.

Notable inmates include former officer of the Holy Land Foundation Mohammad El-Mezain (serving 15 years for providing material support to terrorists); publisher of *Hustler* magazine Larry Flint (served six months for contempt of court in 1984); crime boss John Gotti (died while serving a life sentence for murder, conspiracy to commit murder, loansharking, illegal gambling, obstruction of justice, bribery, and tax evasion); and the Birdman of Alcatraz Robert Stroud.

Media reports indicate that at least two inmates have been murdered at the facility, one guard has been internally disciplined for assaulting an inmate and a supervising lieutenant was internally disciplined for trying to bribe the inmate to cover up the assault, and one guard was convicted of attempting to hire an inmate as a hitman.

Housing: Inmates are housed in one-person and two-person cells to open dormitories.

Health Services: All newly committed general population inmates receive a complete physical examination within 14 days of admission. As part of the admission and annual physical exams for inmates over the age of 50, each inmate is offered a glaucoma test, electrocardiogram, tonometry, and colorectal cancer screening. Periodic health examinations are available based on age-specific guidelines. Sick call, emergency care, immunizations, medications, dental sick call, and prescription eyeglasses are also available to inmates.

Psychology Services: All inmates at MCFP Springfield are screened by Psychology Services staff during the institution's A&O Program. Screening may include an individual interview. Each unit has a psychologist assigned or available to provide counseling and other mental health services to unit inmates. In some cases, the psychologist has an office in the unit where he or she can be easily reached by the inmates, help develop ongoing counseling programs, or provide personal crisis intervention. Mental health services are offered for behavioral and emotional problems. There are many alternatives for inmates who have personal problems and a desire to correct them. These options include self-image groups and other voluntary groups. In addition, MCFP Springfield has professional staff who are trained in the various social science fields.

Residential Drug Abuse Program (RDAP): MCFP Springfield houses the Residential Drug Abuse Program (RDAP). It also offers a Drug Education Program and a Non-Residential Drug Abuse Program (NR-DAP).

Education Services: MCFP Springfield provides GED and English-as-a-Second Language (ESL) programs. The facility also offers Adult Continuing Education (ACE) classes, a parenting program, and a release preparation program. High school diplomas and post-secondary degrees are available through paid correspondence programs.

Advanced Occupational Education: MCFP Springfield offers advanced occupational education in Advanced Small Engine Repair and Landscape Maintenance.

Vocational Training: MCFP Springfield does not offer any vocational training aside from its advanced occupational education and apprenticeship programs.

Apprenticeship: Baker, Barber, Biomedical Equipment Technician, Carpenter, Dental Assistant, Electrician, Housekeeping, HVAC, Machinist, Masonry, Meat Cutter, Orthotics Technician, Painter, Plumber, Prosthetic Technician, Sheet Metal, Stationary Engineer, and Steamfitter are all offered as apprenticeship programs at MCFP Springfield.

Library Services: A law library is available with a copy machine and typewriters. A leisure/reading library holds daily newspapers and monthly magazines, as well as fiction and nonfiction books, and a listening library holds video and audio tapes, DVDs, and CDs. Inmates also have access to the TRULINCS Electronic Law Library.

UNICOR: MCFP Springfield does not have a UNICOR facility.

Commissary: Inmates are permitted to shop once a week on a designated day. Food, clothing, drinks, electronics, shoes, over-the-counter medications, and other items can be purchased. A monthly spending limit of $360.00 is imposed.

Recreation Services: The Recreation Center at MCFP Springfield provides fitness equipment, pool tables, games, and a craft workshop (crafts include leather, ceramics, painting, and stick art). The main yard provides a softball field, horseshoes, bocce ball courts, volleyball court, basketball court, pavilion and tables, walking track, soccer, handball, and flag football. The gymnasium houses a music room, limited fitness equipment, and intramural activities.

Visitation Information: On Sunday and Saturday visitation is held between 8:15 a.m. and 3:00 p.m. On federal holidays visitation is held between 8:15 a.m. and 3:00 p.m. See Chapter 1 for more information on visitation.

In the News: In 2015, U.S. Medical Center for Federal Prisoners Springfield Lieutenant James C. Myrick, who witnessed another guard hit prisoner Shawn Springer, admitted to offering Springer a better cell assignment if he wouldn't report the assault and reporting that Springer's head injury was pre-existing.

In August 2014, prisoner Jerry Scott Hill was charged with murdering Cyprian Adoh at USMCFP Springfield by hitting his head against a wall.

In June 2014, Wesley Paul Coonce and Charles Michael Hall, prisoners at USMCFP Springfield, were sentenced to death for the January 2010 murder of fellow prisoner Victor Castro-Rodriguez.

In March 2014, Robert W. Jones, a guard at USMCFP Springfield, was sentenced to six years in prison after being convicted of asking a prisoner to kill his wife's ex-husband.

FCC Terre Haute

Federal Correctional Complex Terre Haute | FCC Terre Haute

Facilities: FCC Terre Haute houses USP Terre Haute and FCI Terre Haute with an adjacent minimum-security satellite prison camp.

USP Terre Haute

United States Penitentiary Terre Haute | USP Terre Haute

Facility Address & Contact Information

United States Penitentiary Terre Haute
4700 Bureau Road South
Terre Haute, IN 47802

Phone: 812-244-4400
Fax: 812-244-4791
Email: THA/ExecAssistant@bop.gov

BOP Website: https://www.bop.gov/locations/institutions/thp/
Wikipedia: https://en.wikipedia.org/wiki/United_States_Penitentiary%2C_Terre_Haute
ZCG Website: https://www.prisonerresource.com/resources/federal-prison-profiles/
north-central-region-ncr/federal-correctional-complex-terre-haute-fcc-terre-haute/
united-states-penitentiary-terre-haute-usp-terre-haute/

Inmate Correspondence Address

For USP Terre Haute

Inmate Name and Registration Number
USP Terre Haute
U.S Penitentiary
P.O. Box 33
Terre Haute, IN 47808

NOTE: Funds cannot be sent directly to federal inmates. See Chapter 1 for more information on sending funds to federal inmates.

Sex: Male

Security Level: High Security

Location: USP Terre Haute is located on Highway 63, 2 miles south of the City of Terre Haute, which is 70 miles west of Indianapolis on I-70.

BOP Region: North Central Region (NCR)

BOP Institution Code: THP for USP Terre Haute, THA for Terre Haute Federal Correctional Complex

Judicial District: Southern District of Indiana

Medical Care Level: Level 2/3. See Chapter 2 for more information on Medical Care and Mental Health Care Levels.

Mental Health Care Level: Level 3

Population (as of May 1, 2019): 1,407

Background: United States Penitentiary Terre Haute is a high-security federal prison in Terre Haute, Indiana, which houses male inmates. It was opened in 1940 and is part of the Terre Haute Federal Correctional Complex.

USP Terre Haute was hailed as a monument to progressive ideals when it opened. Prisoners were to be called "inmates" rather than "criminals," and were to be called by their names rather than their prisoner numbers. It was also the first federal prison to have an open structure instead of the old massive steel cell blocks. Silence at meals was no longer imposed, and USP Terre Haute was one of the first prisons to offer prisoners the chance to learn a trade. Today, USP Terre Haute also contains the Special Confinement Unit, which houses federal inmates sentenced to death.

Notable inmates include Timothy McVeigh (executed in 2001 after being convicted of planning and executing the bombing of the Oklahoma federal building); Louis Jones, Jr. (executed in 2003 after being convicted of the kidnapping, sexual assault, and murder of U.S. Army Private Tracie Joy McBride); Joseph Edward Duncan (sentenced to death in 2008 for kidnapping and quadruple murder); leader of the Dixie Mafia Kirksey Nix (serving a life sentence for ordering murders and operating a blackmail scheme); and Charleston church shooter Dylann Roof (placed on death row in 2017).

Media reports indicate that at least one inmate has been indicted for assaulting a fellow inmate and that at least two inmates have been transported to local area hospitals as the result of either being stabbed by fellow inmates or shot by guards. In addition, in one incident, four guards were stabbed by one inmate as they were searching for contraband.

Housing: Inmates are housed in four housing units, which consists of two-person cells.

Health Services: Health services include medical and dental sick call, emergency care, medications, annual and bi-annual physical examinations, health promotion and disease prevention programs, and diagnosis and treatment of chronic infectious diseases. Emergency care is available by approaching any staff member. A sick call form must be submitted to Health Services in order for routine care to be rendered.

Psychology Services: All inmates at USP Terre Haute are screened by Psychology Services staff during the first 14 days of admission. Psychology services are offered for behavioral and emotional problems. Inmates confined in special housing units are seen by a psychologist at least once per month, though these interactions usually last less than a minute. There are many alternatives for inmates who have personal problems and desire to correct them, such as self-image groups, anger management, and other voluntary groups. The facility also offers the Challenge Program for inmates who are prone to substance abuse, mental illness, and violence. The Life Connections Program is also offered through Religious Services for inmates who desire to grow as responsible persons.

Residential Drug Abuse Program (RDAP): USP Terre Haute does not have the Residential Drug Abuse Program (RDAP). The facility does offer the Drug Education class, the Non-Residential Drug Abuse Program (NR-DAP), Alcoholics Anonymous (AA), and Narcotics Anonymous (NA).

Education Services: USP Terre Haute provides GED, English-as-a-Second Language (ESL), parenting, and Adult Continuing Education (ACE) programs. High school diplomas and post-secondary degrees are available through paid correspondence programs.

Advanced Occupational Education: USP Terre Haute does not offer any advanced occupational education programs.

Vocational Training: USP Terre Haute offers vocational training in Computer Applications.

Apprenticeship: USP Terre Haute offers apprenticeships in Baker, Barbering, Cook, Housekeeping, Office Manager, and Tutor.

Library Services: The Reference Library provides nonfiction materials and reference books for inmates pursuing studies in specific areas. The TRULINCS Electronic Law Library is located in the Education Department and in the Special Housing Unit. The library contains a variety of legal reference materials for use in preparing legal papers. Inmates can check out fiction books, newspapers, and magazines from the library. An interlibrary loan program is also available.

UNICOR: The USP Terre Haute UNICOR facility produces clothing and textiles.

Commissary: The total value of an inmate's accumulated commissary purchases (except for postage stamps, copy cards, and over-the-counter medications) is limited to $360.00. Special limits may apply. Commissary items such as food, drinks, electronics, ice cream, and shoes are available. Inmates are only allowed to shop on their designated shopping day.

Recreation Services: Programs include indoor and outdoor activities, and range from individualized arts and crafts programs to intramural team sports such as softball, basketball, and volleyball. Physical fitness and weight reduction programs are also available. Hobbycraft programs at USP Terre Haute include activities such as painting, leather, and art. Inside, inmates have access to two gyms, basketball, art and band rooms, tables, ellipticals, treadmills, stationary bikes, and pool tables. Outside, inmates have access to three yards, handball, basketball, horseshoes, pull-up bars, soccer, softball, and a track.

Visitation Information: On Sunday and Saturday visitation is held between 8:00 a.m. and 3:00 p.m. On Friday visitation is held between 2:00 and 8:30 p.m. On federal holidays visitation is held between 8:00 a.m. and 3:00 p.m. See Chapter 1 for more information on visitation.

Prison Politics: This is a very political yard with a car requirement.

Level of Violence: There is a high level of violence at this prison. Inmates report fights several times a week and one or two stabbings per month.

Vulnerable Populations: While inmates say that sex offenders, informants, and LGBT inmates cannot walk the yard, they report that LGBT inmates can stay.

Good: "Education offerings, recreation."

Bad: "Inmates ran everything." "Really unprofessional and disrespectful staff; dirty cops."

Other Comments: "As far as USPs go, not a bad one, though still violent." "If you have clean paperwork, go. If not, avoid."

In the News: In April 2017, Dylann Roof, the man who killed nine people in a South Carolina church in 2015, was moved to death row at United States Penitentiary Terre Haute.

In March 2010, Adam G. Orr, a prisoner at the United States Penitentiary at Terre Haute, beat and stabbed another prisoner, who suffered rib and facial fractures, puncture wounds and a collapsed lung, because the other prisoner called him a liar and a snitch. He was sentenced to an additional 20 years in prison.

In 2009, guards at USP Terre Haute shot at prisoners in the recreation yard after they ignored warnings to stop fighting. Two of the prisoners were sent to the hospital for injuries, one for treatment of a gunshot wound.

In July 2004, Thomas Walker, a prisoner at USP Terre Haute, stabbed four guards -- Gregory Brummett, Terry Ray, Joseph Sims, and Lloyd McPherson -- with two metal shanks as the guards were conducting searches for contraband.

In 2001, Oklahoma City bomber Timothy McVeigh was executed at USP Terre Haute.

FCI Terre Haute

Federal Correctional Institution Terre Haute | FCI Terre Haute

Facilities: FCI Terre Haute with an adjacent minimum-security satellite prison camp.

Facility Address & Contact Information

Federal Correctional Institution Terre Haute
4200 Bureau Road North
Terre Haute, IN 47808

Phone: 812-238-1531
Fax: 812-238-3301
Email: THA/ExecAssistant@bop.gov

BOP Website: https://www.bop.gov/locations/institutions/tha/
Wikipedia: https://en.wikipedia.org/wiki/Federal_Correctional_Institution,_Terre_Haute
ZCG Website: https://www.prisonerresource.com/resources/federal-prison-profiles/north-central-region-ncr/federal-correctional-complex-terre-haute-fcc-terre-haute/federal-correctional-institution-terre-haute-fci-terre-haute/

Inmate Correspondence Address

For FCI Terre Haute

Inmate Name and Registration Number
FCI Terre Haute
Federal Correctional Institution
P.O. Box 33
Terre Haute, IN 47808

For Satellite Prison Camp

Inmate Name and Registration Number
FCI Terre Haute
Satellite Prison Camp
P.O. Box 33
Terre Haute, IN 47808

NOTE: Funds cannot be sent directly to federal inmates. See Chapter 1 for more information on sending funds to federal inmates.

Sex: Male

Security Level: Main: Medium Security; Camp: Minimum Security

Location: FCI Terre Haute is located on Highway 63, 2 miles south of the City of Terre Haute, which is 70 miles west of Indianapolis on I-70.

BOP Region: North Central Region (NCR)

BOP Institution Code: THA for FCI Terre Haute, THA for Terre Haute Federal Correctional Complex

Judicial District: Southern District of Indiana

Medical Care Level: Level 2/3. See Chapter 2 for more information on Medical Care and Mental Health Care Levels.

Mental Health Care Level: Level 3

Population (as of May 1, 2019): Main: 988; Camp: 336

Background: Federal Correctional Institution Terre Haute is a medium-security federal prison in Terre Haute, Indiana, which houses male inmates. It is part of the Terre Haute Federal Correctional Complex. Federal Correctional Institution Terre Haute Camp, which also houses male inmates, is located adjacent to the main institution.

Notable inmates include Earth Liberation Front member Daniel McGowan (served seven years for terrorism conspiracy); Al-Quaeda supporter Rezwan Ferdaus (serving 17 years for terrorism conspiracy); Al-Quaeda supporter Farooque Ahmed (serving 23 years for performing surveillance as part of a bombing plot); scientist and NASA consultant Stewart Nozette (serving a 13-year sentence for attempted espionage); former CIA counterintelligence agent

Aldrich Ames (serving a life sentence for espionage); and Peregrine Financial Group founder Russell Wasendorf (serving a 50-year sentence for embezzlement and mail fraud).

Media reports indicate that one prison guard was indicted for bribery, permitting escape, and smuggling contraband into the institution. Another guard was required to register as a sex offender after sexually assaulting an inmate.

Housing: Inmates are housed in two-person cells. Inmates at the camp are housed in dormitories consisting of two-, eight-, and twelve-person rooms.

Health Services: Health services include medical and dental sick call, emergency care, medications, annual and bi-annual physical examinations, health promotion and disease prevention programs, and diagnosis and treatment of chronic infectious diseases. In order to be evaluated by a healthcare provider, inmates must submit a triage form. Emergency medical care is available 24 hours a day.

Psychology Services: All inmates at FCI Terre Haute are screened by Psychology Services staff within 14 days of admission. Psychology services are offered for behavioral and emotional problems. Inmates confined in special housing units are evaluated by a psychologist at least once per month. There are many alternatives for inmates who have mental health problems and desire to correct them, which include self-image groups and other voluntary groups. The facility also offers the STAGES Program for inmates with serious mental illness and personality disorders.

Residential Drug Abuse Program (RDAP): FCI Terre Haute has the Residential Drug Abuse Program (RDAP). The Drug Education class, the Non-Residential Drug Abuse Program (NR-DAP), and Alcoholics Anonymous (AA) are also available.

Education Services: FCI Terre Haute provides GED and English-as-a-Second Language (ESL) programs. Parenting, release preparation, and Adult Continuing Education (ACE) programs are also available. High school diplomas and post-secondary degrees are available through paid correspondence programs.

Advanced Occupational Education: FCI Terre Haute does not offer any advanced occupational education programs.

Vocational Training: FCI Terre Haute offers Building Trades and Computers vocational training. The camp offers Diesel Mechanic and Computer Applications vocational training.

Apprenticeship: FCI Terre Haute offers apprenticeship in Baker, Barbering, Cook, Housekeeping, Office Manager, and Tutor. The camp offers Electronic Automotive, Fish Hatchery Worker, and Office Manager.

Library Services: The Reference Library provides nonfiction materials and reference books for inmates pursuing studies in specific areas. Fiction and nonfiction books, magazines, and newspapers are also available, as are CD players and DVD movies. The inmate law libraries are located in the Education Department library and in the Special Housing Unit. They contain a variety of legal reference materials for use in preparing legal papers. Most legal research is conducted via the TRULINCS Electronic Law Library computers. Typewriters and a copy machine are also available for inmate use.

UNICOR: The FCI Terre Haute and satellite camp UNICOR facilities handle fleet management and vehicle components.

Commissary: Inmates are permitted to spend up to $360.00 per month in the commissary on items such as food, drinks, electronics, clothing, and shoes. It is customary for inmates to use a laundry bag to carry their purchases back to their housing unit. Inmates are only allowed to shop once a week on their designated shopping day.

Recreation Services: Recreation programs at FCI Terre Haute include indoor and outdoor activities, and range from individualized arts and crafts programs to intramural team sports such as softball, basketball, and volleyball. Physical fitness and weight reduction programs are also available. Hobbycraft programs include activities such as painting, leather, and art. Inside, inmates have access to basketball, treadmills, stationary bikes, ellipticals, weights, pool tables, TVs, band room, and art room. Outside, inmates have access to basketball, weights, miniature golf, softball, soccer, handball, racquetball, horseshoes, and a track.

Visitation Information: On Sunday, Monday, and Saturday visitation is held between 8:00 a.m. and 3:00 p.m. On federal holidays visitation is held between 8:00 a.m. and 3:00 p.m. See Chapter 1 for more information on visitation.

Prison Politics: This is a very political yard with a car requirement.

Level of Violence: This facility is extremely violent. According to inmate respondents, it is common to have several fights a day and weekly stabbings.

Vulnerable Populations: While some inmates report that sex offenders, informants, and LGBT inmates cannot walk the yard, others say that LGBT inmates can stay if under the radar.

Good: "Gofers that eat from your hand." "Good cells, big chow hall."

Bad: "People, politics, really old facility, no air conditioning, 'shit hole.'" "Politics, racism."

Other Comments: "Absolutely don't go unless you are a solid white dude and like harder, political time." "It's a gang yard. If you're not affiliated, don't go."

In the News: In March 2017, Jeffrey E. Krueger, who was previously warden at Federal Prison Camp Duluth, Federal Correctional Institution Schuylkill and Federal Correctional Institution Pekin, was named the warden of the Terre Haute Federal Correctional Complex.

Camp in the News: In December 2017, Leon Perry III, the Reservation Patrol Officer at Federal Correctional Institution Terre Haute Camp, was charged with bribery, permitting escape and smuggling contraband into the prison. He allowed prisoners to have sexual relations with women both inside and outside of the prison.

In 2012, Lynsey Stangel, a guard at FCI Terre Haute Camp, will have to register as a sex offender after pleading guilty to having sex with a prisoner in a patrol car while on duty.

AUSP Thomson

Administrative United States Penitentiary Thomson | AUSP Thomson

Facilities: Administrative U.S. Penitentiary Thomson with an adjacent minimum-security satellite prison camp.

Facility Address & Contact Information

AUSP Thomson
1100 One Mile Road
Thomson, IL 61285

Phone: 815-259-1000
Fax: 815-259-0186
Email: TOM/ExecAssistant@bop.gov

BOP Website: https://www.bop.gov/locations/institutions/tom/
Wikipedia: https://en.wikipedia.org/wiki/Thomson_Correctional_Center
ZCG Website: https://www.prisonerresource.com/resources/federal-prison-profiles/north-central-region-ncr/administrative-united-states-penitentiary-thomson-ausp-thomson/

Inmate Correspondence Address

For Satellite Prison Camp

Inmate Name and Registration Number
AUSP Thomson
Satellite Prison Camp
P.O. Box 1002
Thomson, IL 61285

NOTE: Funds cannot be sent directly to federal inmates. See Chapter 1 for more information on sending funds to federal inmates.

Sex: Male

Security Level: Main: Administrative Security (Multiple Security Levels); Camp: Minimum Security

Location: AUSP Thomson is located near the western border of Illinois, 70 miles west of Rockford, Illinois and 52 miles east of Davenport.

BOP Region: North Central Region (NCR)

BOP Institution Code: TOM for Thomson

Judicial District: Northern District of Illinois

Medical Care Level: Level 2. See Chapter 2 for more information on Medical Care and Mental Health Care Levels.

Mental Health Care Level: Level 1

Population (as of May 1, 2019): Main: 320; Camp: 89

Background: Administrative United States Penitentiary Thomson is an administrative-security federal prison in Thomson, Illinois, which houses male inmates. The facility has yet to fully activate. AUSP Thomson Camp, which also houses male inmates, has activated and is located adjacent to the main institution.

Originally named Thomson Correctional Center, the facility was built as a state prison in 2001. It was purchased by the U.S. Government and became a Bureau of Prisons property in 2012. As of 2017, AUSP Thomson is being used to house low-security deportable aliens until the facility can be brought fully online, which is projected for late 2018 or early 2019.

Housing: Inmates are housed in cells. At the camp, inmates are housed in dormitories.

Health Services: New inmates receive a complete physical examination within 14 days of arrival at the institution. The Health Services Unit at AUSP Thomson functions as an ambulatory outpatient clinic. The medical staff consists of physicians, dentists, mid-level practitioners, and medical and administrative ancillary support staff. Medical and dental sick call, emergency medical treatment, preventive health care services, chronic care, medications, and eyeglasses are provided to inmates. Inmates may request a screening for infectious diseases. Inmates must be in the proper uniform and must show their assigned commissary ID card in order to be seen.

Psychology Services: New inmates and inmates who have previously identified mental health or drug abuse programming needs are scheduled for an interview with AUSP Thomson Psychology services staff. A psychologist may make recommendations to support the inmate's successful adjustment to prison and prepare them for their eventual release. Residential mental health programs designed to help inmates with severe emotional, cognitive, and behavioral problems are also available. These programs are for inmates who are having difficulty functioning in a mainline institution due to a psychological disorder. They are designed to improve the day to day functioning of inmates with the goal of helping them return to a mainline institution or preventing the need for hospitalization. Referrals can be made to other institutions with such treatment programs.

Residential Drug Abuse Program (RDAP): AUSP Thomson does not house the Residential Drug Abuse Program (RDAP), but a referral can be made to an institution that does offer the program. A drug abuse program, Drug Abuse Education course, and the Non-Residential Drug Abuse Program (NR-DAP) are available.

Education Services: AUSP Thomson provides literacy, GED, and English-as-a-Second Language (ESL) programs. Incentive awards are provided to recognize inmates making satisfactory progress and successfully completing the literacy (i.e., GED and ESL) program. Inmates may also receive incentives for progressing to various levels in the GED or ESL programs. Graduation ceremonies recognize GED, ESL, and Occupational Education completions. A parenting program and Adult Continuing Education (ACE) classes are also available. High school diplomas and post-secondary degrees are available through paid correspondence programs.

Advanced Occupational Education: AUSP Thomson does not offer any advanced occupational education programs.

Vocational Training: AUSP Thomson does not offer any vocational training programs.

Apprenticeship: AUSP Thomson does not offer any apprenticeship programs.

Library Services: Inmates are afforded access to legal materials and an opportunity to prepare legal documents through the use of the TRULINCS Electronic Law Library. The leisure library offers inmates a variety of reading materials, including periodicals, newspapers, fiction, nonfiction, and reference books. Typewriters and a copy machine are also available.

UNICOR: AUSP Thomson does not house a UNICOR facility.

Commissary: Inmates are permitted to shop once per week on a designated day. The commissary spending limit is $360.00 per month. Inmates can purchase food, sodas, ice cream, snacks, radios, MP3 players, clothing, shoes, and more.

Recreation Services: Leisure activities at AUSP Thomson and the satellite camp include organized and informal games, sports, physical fitness, table games, hobbycrafts, music programs, intramural activities, and social and cultural organizations. Wellness programs include screening, assessments, goal setting, classes, fitness/nutrition plans, and counseling. An inmate photo program is also available. The Recreation Department also offers movies and electric instruments.

Visitation Information: On Sunday and Saturday visitation is held between 8:00 a.m. and 3:00 p.m. On Friday visitation is held between 5:00 and 8:30 p.m. On federal holidays visitation is held between 8:15 a.m. and 3:00 p.m. See Chapter 1 for more information on visitation.

FCI Waseca

Federal Correctional Institution Waseca | FCI Waseca

Facility Address & Contact Information

Federal Correctional Institution Waseca
1000 University Drive, SW
Waseca, MN 56093

Phone: 507-835-8972
Fax: 507-837-4547
Email: WAS/ExecAssistant@bop.gov

BOP Website: https://www.bop.gov/locations/institutions/was/
Wikipedia: https://en.wikipedia.org/wiki/Federal_Correctional_Institution%2C_Waseca
ZCG Website: https://www.prisonerresource.com/resources/federal-prison-profiles/north-central-region-ncr/federal-correctional-institution-waseca-fci-waseca/

Inmate Correspondence Address

Inmate Name and Registration Number
FCI Waseca
Federal Correctional Institution
P.O. Box 1731
Waseca, MN 56093

NOTE: Funds cannot be sent directly to federal inmates. See Chapter 1 for more information on sending funds to federal inmates.

Sex: Female

Security Level: Low Security

Location: Located in southern Minnesota, 75 miles south of Minneapolis on I-35; 13 miles west of Owatonna on State Highway 57.

BOP Region: North Central Region (NCR)

BOP Institution Code: WAS for FCI Waseca

Judicial District: District of Minnesota

Medical Care Level: Level 2. See Chapter 2 for more information on Medical Care and Mental Health Care Levels.

Mental Health Care Level: Level 3

Population (as of May 1, 2019): 661

Background: Federal Correctional Institution Waseca is a low-security federal prison in Waseca, Minnesota, which houses female inmates. It was opened in 1995.

Formerly a University of Minnesota campus, FCI Waseca opened as an all-male federal prison in 1995. It was converted to an all-female facility in 2008. In 2014, Riverland Community College started offering cosmetology training to interested inmates.

Notable inmates include former CEO of Enron Corporation Jeffrey Skilling (serving a 24-year sentence for insider training and securities fraud and was a holdover at the facility), Catherine Greig (convicted of harboring a fugitive and identity fraud for assisting Irish Mob figure James "Whitey" Bulger evade capture), and Shelly Shannon (serving 20 years for firebombing six abortion clinics).

Media reports indicate that at least one prisoner has been prosecuted for assaulting a fellow inmate.

Housing: Inmates are housed in dormitories consisting of two- and four-person cubicles, along with four-person rooms.

Health Services: Health services at FCI Waseca include medical sick call, dental sick call, emergency medical services, treatment of infectious diseases, periodic health assessments, routine dental care, chronic care, medications, TB testing, immunizations, physical and periodic health examinations, eye care, health promotion, and disease prevention. While emergency medical care is available 24 hours a day, inmates must submit a triage form to be evaluated for routine health care needs.

Psychology Services: Inmates at FCI Waseca are screened by Psychology Services staff within 14 days of arriving at the prison. Inmates who have family or personal problems or are in a crisis may be seen for individual therapy. Psychology groups include Trauma and Life Workshop, Resolve (Trauma and Recovery), Basic Cognitive Skills, Criminal Thinking, and Emotional Self-Regulation. Additionally, Illness Management and Recovery is offered to inmates who are identified as needing additional assistance in self-care due to a mental illness. Open house is held on Monday, Wednesday, and Friday.

Residential Drug Abuse Program (RDAP): FCI Waseca offers the Residential Drug Abuse Program (RDAP). It also offers a Drug Education Program and a Non-Residential Drug Abuse Program (NR-DAP). Some inmates are mandated to take Drug Education classes based on their documented use history, judicial recommendations, and/or violation behavior, but all other programs are voluntary.

Education Services: FCI Waseca provides literacy, GED, and English-as-a-Second Language (ESL) programs. Current ACE offerings include insurance, accounting, Money Smart, basic math, grammar, creative writing, and business management. The Education Department also sponsors Adult Continuing Education (ACE) classes and a parenting program. High school diplomas and post-secondary degrees are available through paid correspondence programs.

Advanced Occupational Education: FCI Waseca offers advanced occupational education in Business Office Specialist, Cosmetology, and the P.A.W.S. (Prisoners Assisting With Service Dogs) Program.

Vocational Training: FCI Waseca offers vocational training in Horticulture and Woodworking.

Apprenticeship: FCI Waseca offers apprenticeship training in Landscape Technician.

Library Services: A leisure and law library are available to inmates. The leisure library offers fiction and nonfiction books, newspapers, and magazines. An interlibrary loan program is also available to the inmate population. The law library contains a variety of legal reference materials for use in preparing legal papers. Reference materials include the United States Code Annotated, Federal Reporter, Supreme Court Reporter, Bureau of Prisons Program Statements, institution supplements, indexes, and other legal materials. Most of these, plus federal case law, are available on the TRULINCS Electronic Law Library computers. Inmates also have access to typewriters and a copy machine.

UNICOR: The FCI Waseca UNICOR facility produces clothing and textiles.

Commissary: Inmates are allowed to buy commissary items such as food, drinks, clothing, electronics, and other items. A $360.00 monthly spending limit is imposed, which does not include the purchase of copy cards, postage stamps, or over-the-counter medications. This spending limit is further restricted to $180 every two weeks. Inmates are allowed to shop once a week.

Recreation Services: FCI Waseca offers a wide variety of athletic and leisure time activities for the inmate population. In addition to a full-sized gymnasium, there are indoor workout areas for aerobics, exercise machines, spin bikes, stretching, and yoga. There is a large DVD library with workout and fitness videos available for check out, as well as basic nutrition DVDs. Outdoor recreation areas offer a variety of activities, including racquetball, volleyball, bocce ball, tennis, frisbee golf, basketball, horseshoes, a multi-purpose field, and a large walking track which is open year-round. A variety of wellness classes are offered in the Recreation Department to address general wellness, nutrition, and fitness. In season, the Recreation Department offers an opportunity to participate in a Community Flower Garden. Hours of operation are 6:30 a.m. to 8:30 p.m., excluding meals and counts.

Visitation Information: On Sunday and Saturday visitation is held between 8:30 a.m. and 3:00 p.m. On Friday visitation is held between 4:30 and 8:30 p.m. On federal holidays visitation is held between 8:30 a.m. and 3:00 p.m. See Chapter 1 for more information on visitation.

Prison Politics: There is a very low level of prison politics at this facility.

Level of Violence: There is almost no violence at this prison. According to one inmate, "This place is safe, just a lot of bullying which staff put a stop to when reported."

Vulnerable Populations: Sex offenders, informants, and LGBT inmates are allowed to walk the yard. According to one respondent, "There are an enormous amount of gay people here. There are also a few transwomen here as well."

Good: "In the Resolve Program, most staff are here to help no matter how big or little the issue is. The staff don't give up on you." "The Camp Cadre unit is peaceful." "The Warden is good and is trying to make the place better."

Bad: "The food isn't very good at all. Lots of fatty foods." "Some of the staff are intimidating; they scare me."

In the News: In 2014, Federal Correctional Institution Waseca began a program with Riverland Community College to provide female prisoners with cosmetology training.

In January 2013, Felecia Thomas, who was serving 17 years at FCI Waseca for arson and the use of explosives, pleaded guilty to assault with a deadly weapon after choking another prisoner with a rope.

In October 2008, FCI Waseca began its transition from a men's prison to a women's prison.

FPC Yankton

Federal Prison Camp Yankton | FPC Yankton

Facility Address & Contact Information

Federal Prison Camp Yankton
1016 Douglas Avenue
Yankton, SD 57078

Phone: 605-665-3262
Fax: 605-668-1113
Email: YAN/ExecAssistant@bop.gov

BOP Website: https://www.bop.gov/locations/institutions/yan/
Wikipedia: https://en.wikipedia.org/wiki/Federal_Prison_Camp%2C_Yankton
ZCG Website: https://www.prisonerresource.com/resources/federal-prison-profiles/
north-central-region-ncr/federal-prison-camp-yankton-fpc-yankton/

Inmate Correspondence Address

Inmate Name and Registration Number
FPC Yankton
Federal Prison Camp
P.O. Box 700
Yankton, SD 57078

NOTE: Funds cannot be sent directly to federal inmates. See Chapter 1 for more information on sending funds to federal inmates.

Sex: Male

Security Level: Minimum Security

Location: Located in southeastern South Dakota, 60 miles northwest of Sioux City, IA and 85 miles southwest of Sioux Falls, SD; off U.S. Highway 81.

BOP Region: North Central Region (NCR)

BOP Institution Code: YAN for FPC Yankton

Judicial District: District of South Dakota

Medical Care Level: Level 1. See Chapter 2 for more information on Medical Care and Mental Health Care Levels.

Mental Health Care Level: Level 1

Population (as of May 1, 2019): 476

Background: Federal Prison Camp Yankton is a minimum-security federal prison in Yankton, South Dakota, which houses male inmates. It was opened in 1988.

FPC Yankton opened on the shuttered campus of Yankton College, which operated from 1881 to 1984. The facility houses inmates who do not have a history of escape, violence, sexual offenses, or major medical or psychiatric problems. As of 2011, prisoners can participate in a certified apprenticeship program or work towards an associate's degree in business, accounting, or horticulture. In 2017, the prison partnered with the Heartland Humane Society to offer the Federal Inmate Dog Obedience (FIDO) training program.

Notable inmates include former Mormon Bishop Shawn Merriman (serving 12 years for mail fraud), and film director John McTiernan (served 328 days for perjury).

In 2017, Insider Monkey named FPC Yankton one of the ten easiest federal prisons to do time. In 2012, CNBC named the facility one of the 12 best federal prisons in which to do time. In 2009, *Forbes* magazine rated FPC Yankton as one of the ten cushiest federal prisons in America. And in 2005, *The Kansas City Star* named FPC Yankton one of the five best federal prisons for white collar offenders.

Housing: Inmates are housed in dormitories consisting of four to twelve-person cubicles.

Health Services: Health services at FPC Yankton include medical and dental sick call, emergency services, medication, routine dental care, chronic care, eyeglasses, and eye exams. In order to be examined by a healthcare professional, inmates must submit a triage form and wait to be placed on call-out. Emergency medical care can be obtained by approaching any staff member and requesting assistance.

Psychology Services: The Psychology Services Department offers basic mental health care to inmates. This care includes screening, assessment, and treatment of mental health problems, individual and group counseling, psycho-educational classes, self-help and supportive services, and referral to Health Services for medical treatment of a mental illness. Care can be sought either at open house or by submitting an Inmate Request to Staff.

Residential Drug Abuse Program (RDAP): FPC Yankton offers the Residential Drug Abuse Program (RDAP). It also offers drug abuse programs, CHOICES (a drug awareness program), a Drug Abuse Education course, and the Non-Residential Drug Abuse Program (NR-DAP).

Education Services: FPC Yankton provides literacy, GED, and English-as-a-Second Language (ESL) programs. An incentive award system has been established which recognizes achievement at intervals within the literacy program with special recognition upon achievement of functional literacy. Incentives include consumable items, such as popcorn and sodas, for satisfactory progress toward literacy goals or for periodic classroom achievements (e.g., hardest worker, best test score, perfect attendance), $25.00 award for successful completion of the GED or ESL program, and public recognition, with name and picture placed on a plaque within the Education Department. High school diplomas and post-secondary degrees are available through paid correspondence programs.

Advanced Occupational Education: FPC Yankton offers advanced occupational education in Accounting, Business and Financial Administration, Science, and AWS Certified Welding.

Vocational Training: FPC Yankton does not offer any vocational training aside from its advanced occupational education and apprenticeship programs.

Apprenticeship: FPC Yankton offers apprenticeships in Baker, Boiler Operator/Mechanic, Building Maintenance, Carpentry, Cook, Dental Assistant, Electrician Maintenance, Human Services Direct Support Professional, HVAC, Industrial Housekeeper, Landscape Management Technician, Landscape Technician, Painting, Plumbing, Refrigeration Mechanic, and Tape Recorder Repairer.

Library Services: The leisure library offers inmates magazines, newspapers, and fiction and nonfiction books. The law library is located in the Education Department and contains a variety of legal reference materials for use in preparing legal papers. Reference materials include the United States Code Annotated, Federal Reporter, Supreme Court Reporter, Bureau of Prisons Program Statements, institution supplements, indexes, and other legal materials. Inmates also have access to a copy machine, typewriters, and the TRULINCS Electronics Law Library.

UNICOR: FPC Yankton does not house a UNICOR facility.

Commissary: The monthly spending limit is $360.00 with the exception of postage stamps, copy cards, phone credits, and over-the-counter-medications. Food, snacks, candy, ice cream, sodas, drink mixes, clothing, shoes, and electronics can be purchased from the commissary. Inmates are assigned a particular day of the week to shop.

Recreation Services: Programs at FPC Yankton include indoor and outdoor activities and range from individualized arts and crafts programs to intramural team sports such as softball, basketball, and volleyball. Physical fitness and weight reduction programs are also available. Musical instruments are available in the recreation area for the inmate population. The musical instruments are to remain in the music room. Hobbycraft programs include activities such as painting, leather, art, and beadwork.

Visitation Information: On Sunday and Saturday visitation is held between 8:15 a.m. and 3:00 p.m. On Friday visitation is held between 4:30 and 9:15 p.m. On federal holidays visitation is held between 8:15 a.m. and 3:00 p.m. See Chapter 1 for more information on visitation.

In the News: In January 2017, Yankton's Heartland Humane Society created the Federal Inmate Dog Obedience (FIDO) program, allowing prisoners at Federal Prison Camp Yankton to train dogs that are available for adoption.

In August 2016, Richard Hudgins became warden of FPC Yankton, replacing Gregory Kizziah who was the warden since May 2015.

CHAPTER 7:

Northeast Region Prisons

Northeast Regional Office

The Northeast Regional Office is an administrative office providing oversight and support to facilities in the Northeast Region (NER). The Northeast Region covers Federal Bureau of Prison facilities located in Connecticut, Maine, Massachusetts, New Hampshire, New Jersey, New York, Ohio, Pennsylvania, Rhode Island, and Vermont. These facilities are overseen by a regional office that provides oversight, technical assistance, and other types of operational support. In addition, they conduct training programs for staff in their region and assist state and local criminal justice agencies.

Regional Director: J. Ray Ormond
NER Population: 24,977

Facility Address & Contact Information

Northeast Regional Office
Federal Bureau of Prisons
U.S. Custom House, 7th Floor
200 Chestnut Street
Philadelphia, PA 19106

Email: NERO/ExecAssistant@bop.gov

Phone: 215-521-7301

Fax: 215-597-1893

BOP Website: https://www.bop.gov/locations/regional_offices/nero/

Wikipedia: n/a

ZCG Website: https://prisonerresource.com/resources/federal-prison-profiles/
federal-prison-regional-offices/northeast-regional-office/

Staff Mail

Staff Name

Northeast Regional Office

U.S. Custom House, 7th Floor

200 Chestnut Street

Philadelphia, PA 19106

Freight and Non-USPS Parcels

Staff Name

Northeast Regional Office

ATTN: Warehouse

U.S. Custom House, 7th Floor

200 Chestnut Street

Philadelphia, PA 19106

Northeast Region Prisons

FCI Allenwood Low (PA)
FCI Allenwood Medium (PA)
USP Allenwood (PA)
FCI Berlin (NH)
MDC Brooklyn (NY)
USP Canaan (PA)
FCI Danbury (CT)
FSL Danbury (CT)
FMC Devens (MA)
FCI Elkton (OH)
FSL Elkton (OH)
FCI Fairton (NJ)
FCI Fort Dix (NJ)
USP Leavenworth (PA)
FCI Loretto (PA)
FCI McKean (PA)
MCC New York (NY)
FCI Otisville (NY)
FDC Philadelphia (PA)
FCI Ray Brook (NY)
FCI Schuylkill (PA)

FCC Allenwood

Federal Correctional Complex Allenwood | FCC Allenwood

Facilities: FCC Allenwood houses USP Allenwood, FCI Allenwood Medium and FCI Allenwood Low.

USP Allenwood

United States Penitentiary Allenwood | USP Allenwood

Facility Address & Contact Information

United States Penitentiary Allenwood
Route 15
Allenwood, PA 17810

Phone: 570-547-0963
Fax: 570-547-9201
Email: ALX/ExecAssistant@bop.gov

BOP Website: https://www.bop.gov/locations/institutions/alp/
Wikipedia: https://en.wikipedia.org/wiki/United_States_Penitentiary%2C_Allenwood
ZCG Website: https://www.prisonerresource.com/resources/federal-prison-profiles/northeast-region-ner/united-states-penitentiary-allenwood-usp-allenwood/

Inmate Correspondence Address

Inmate Name and Registration Number
USP Allenwood
U.S. Penitentiary
P.O. Box 3000
White Deer, PA 17887

NOTE: Funds cannot be sent directly to federal inmates. See Chapter 1 for more information on sending funds to federal inmates.

Sex: Male

Security Level: High Security

Location: USP Allenwood is located 197 miles north of Washington, DC; 11 miles south of Williamsport, PA; 2 miles north of Allenwood, on U.S. Route 15.

BOP Region: Northeast Region (NER)

BOP Institution Code: ALP for USP Allenwood, ALX for Allenwood Federal Correctional Complex

Judicial District: Middle District of Pennsylvania

Medical Care Level: Level 3. See Chapter 2 for more information on Medical Care and Mental Health Care Levels.

Mental Health Care Level: Level 3

Population (as of May 1, 2019): 841

Background: United States Penitentiary Allenwood is a high-security federal prison in Allenwood, Pennsylvania, which houses male inmates. It was opened in 1993 and is part of the Allenwood Federal Correctional Complex.

USP Allenwood features a Special Management Unit (SMU), a multi-level program designed to teach self-discipline, pro-social values, and the ability to successfully coexist with members of other geographical, cultural, and religious backgrounds. SMUs are restrictive programs used to house and control inmates who have shown to be management problems.

Notable inmates include Howard Mason (serving a life sentence on racketeering charges, ordered the murder of a New York City police officer); former acting boss of the Lucchese crime family Louis Daidone (serving a life sentence for murder, murder conspiracy, racketeering, and loansharking); Somali pirate leader Mahamud Salad Ali (serving a life sentence for hijacking a civilian yacht); former physician Jorge A. Martinez (serving a life sentence for health care fraud); and James Eagan Holmes (serving 12 life terms for the 2012 Aurora, Colorado, theater shooting).

Media reports indicate that inmates have been charged with weapons possession and that at least two inmates have been charged with murder. News reports also indicate that at least one mass fight has occurred at USP Allenwood in which eight inmates were transported to a local area hospital for treatment of their injuries.

Housing: Inmates are housed in two-person cells.

Health Services: All inmates entering USP Allenwood will receive a mandatory, complete physical examination within 14 days of arrival. This examination may include laboratory studies, hearing and sight screening, dental examination, medical history, and physical examination. Sick call, dental sick call, physical examinations, annual immunizations/screenings, health promotion/disease prevention, and medications are provided to inmates. While emergency medical care is available 24 hours a day, inmates must submit a sick call form for non-emergency care.

Psychology Services: USP Allenwood provides psychological, psycho-educational, and consultative services to inmates. Psychologists conduct psychological assessments for new inmates and address their needs through crisis intervention services and other therapeutic approaches. SMU inmates are required to participate in, and complete, a psychoeducational group on Social/Communication Skills. Elective counseling groups, including Relapse Prevention, Emotion Management, Problem-Solving, Coping Skills, and related psycho educational topics are also offered. The Challenge Program is also available for inmates who are prone to substance abuse, mental illness, and violence.

Residential Drug Abuse Program (RDAP): USP Allenwood does not have the Residential Drug Abuse Program (RDAP), however RDAP is offered at FCI Allenwood Medium. USP Allenwood does offer a Drug Abuse Education program, the Non-Residential Drug Abuse Program (NR-DAP), Alcoholics Anonymous (AA), and Narcotics Anonymous (NA).

Education Services: USP Allenwood offers literacy, GED (in English and Spanish languages), and English-as-a-Second Language (ESL) programs. Classes are separated into pre-GED, GED, and Special Learning Needs levels. A parenting program and Adult Continuing Education (ACE) classes are also available. High school diplomas and post-secondary degrees are available through paid correspondence programs.

Advanced Occupational Education: USP Allenwood does not offer any advanced occupational education programs.

Vocational Training: USP Allenwood offers vocational training in Computer Word Processing and Computer Assisted Drafting, and the IC3 Internet Computing Core Certification.

Apprenticeship: USP Allenwood offers apprenticeships in Cook, Quality Control Technician, and Upholsterer.

Library Services: A law and leisure library are available to inmates at USP Allenwood. The TRULINCS Electronic Law Library includes an extensive range of information on federal legislative and case law, including the Federal Bureau of Prisons' Program Statements. Electric typewriters are available in the Library Research Center for inmate legal work. Inmates must provide the materials to utilize the electric typewriters (e.g., print wheel, ribbon, correction tape, paper, etc.). The leisure library offers fiction and nonfiction books, newspapers, and magazines.

UNICOR: The USP Allenwood UNICOR facility produces office furniture.

Commissary: USP Allenwood inmates are permitted to spend up to a specific dollar amount each month for regular purchases (currently $360.00), and an additional amount for special purchase items. SMU inmates are restricted to a $50.00 per week spending limit, excluding postage stamps and sneakers. Each inmate is responsible for knowing the amount of money available in his account. An inmate's Unit Manager can approve withdrawals from the trust fund account to send funds to dependents and other family members.

Recreation Services: USP Allenwood's Recreation Department consists of both indoor and outdoor areas. Activities range from individualized arts and crafts programs to intramural team sports such as softball, basketball, and volleyball. Physical fitness and weight reduction programs are also available. Musical Instruments and Hobbycraft programs are available for inmates. Inmates in the Special Management Unit (SMU) are offered a minimum of five hours of recreation per week. The Recreation Department at USP Allenwood is responsible for supplying the SMU with recreation equipment including games and fitness items. Inside the unit, board games and playing cards, abdominal benches, and other various exercise equipment are available. The outside recreation area consists of abdominal benches and other areas for inmate recreation.

Visitation Information: On Sunday, Friday, and Saturday visitation is held between 8:00 a.m. and 3:00 p.m. On federal holidays visitation is held between 8:00 a.m. and 3:00 p.m. See Chapter 1 for more information on visitation.

Prison Politics: This is a very political yard. Inmates are required to be part of an organized car in order to stay.

Level of Violence: There is a moderate level of violence at this facility. According to inmates, there is an average of one fight per week and a stabbing every few months.

Vulnerable Populations: Sex offenders, informants, and LGBT inmates are not allowed to stay at this prison.

Good: "None that I know of."

Bad: "Very old and dirty; significant politics."

Other Comments: "If you have clean paperwork, go. For a USP, it's really not that bad."

In the News: In February 2018, United States Penitentiary Allenwood prisoner Michael Moore was federally indicted for the possession of a weapon -- a sharpened piece of plastic.

In 2012, James Holmes killed 12 and injured 70 in the theater shooting in Aurora, Colorado. He was subsequently incarcerated at United States Penitentiary Florence, where he was attacked by fellow inmates. Shortly thereafter, he was secretly moved to USP Allenwood.

In 2008, a fight among prisoners at USP Allenwood resulted in eight of them being hospitalized.

In September 2005, Ritz D. Williams and Shawn Cooya, prisoners at USP Allenwood, stabbed and kicked fellow prisoner Alvin Allery repeatedly, killing him. Both were sentenced to life in prison for the murder in 2013.

FCI Allenwood Medium

Federal Correctional Institution Allenwood Medium | FCI Allenwood Medium

Facility Address & Contact Information

Federal Correctional Institution Allenwood Medium
Route 15
Allenwood, PA 17810

Phone: 570-547-7950
Fax: 570-547-7751
Email: ALX/ExecAssistant@bop.gov

BOP Website: https://www.bop.gov/locations/institutions/alm/
Wikipedia: https://en.wikipedia.org/wiki/Federal_Correctional_Institution%2C_Allenwood
ZCG Website: https://www.prisonerresource.com/resources/federal-prison-profiles/northeast-region-ner/federal-correctional-complex-allenwood-fcc-allenwood/federal-correctional-institution-allenwood-medium-fci-allenwood-medium/

Inmate Correspondence Address

Inmate Name and Registration Number
FCI Allenwood Medium
Federal Correctional Institution
P.O. Box 2000
White Deer, PA 17887

NOTE: Funds cannot be sent directly to federal inmates. See Chapter 1 for more information on sending funds to federal inmates.

Sex: Male

Security Level: Medium Security

Location: FCI Allenwood Medium is located 197 miles north of Washington, DC; 11 miles south of Williamsport, PA; 2 miles north of Allenwood, PA, on U.S. Route 15.

BOP Region: Northeast Region (NER)

BOP Institution Code: ALM for FCI Allenwood Medium, ALX for Allenwood Federal Correctional Complex

Judicial District: Middle District of Pennsylvania

Medical Care Level: Level 2/3. See Chapter 2 for more information on Medical Care and Mental Health Care Levels.

Mental Health Care Level: Level 3

Population (as of May 1, 2019): 1,258

Background: Federal Correctional Institution Allenwood Medium is a medium-security federal prison in Allenwood, Pennsylvania, which houses male inmates. It was opened in 1992 and is part of the Allenwood Federal Correctional Complex.

Notable inmates include former NSA employee Ronald Pelton (served 30 years for espionage), Kifha Jayyousi (served 12 years for murder conspiracy and providing material support for terrorism), and James Cromitie (serving 25 years for attempted use of weapons of mass destruction and attempted murder).

Media reports indicate that inmates have been charged with running an international drug smuggling operation from inside FCI Allenwood Medium.

Housing: Inmates at FCI Allenwood Medium are housed in two-person cells.

Health Services: All inmates entering FCI Allenwood Medium will have a mandatory, complete physical examination within 14 days of arrival. This examination may include laboratory studies, hearing and sight screening, dental examination, medical history, and physical examination. Sick call, dental sick call, physical examinations, annual immunizations/screenings, health promotion/disease prevention, and medications are provided to inmates. While emergency medical care is available 24 hours a day, inmates must submit a sick call form for non-emergency care. Health Services staff will assist with scheduling appointments outside of regular sick call time if necessary.

Psychology Services: FCI Allenwood Medium provides individual therapy, group therapy, and intake evaluations. Educational groups and a self-help library are also available to inmates.

Residential Drug Abuse Program (RDAP): FCI Allenwood Medium has the Residential Drug Abuse Program (RDAP). A Drug Abuse Education program, the Non-Residential Drug Abuse Program (NR-DAP) and self-help groups such as Alcoholics Anonymous (AA) and Narcotics Anonymous (NA) are also offered.

Education Services: FCI Allenwood Medium provides GED and English-as-a-Second Language (ESL) programs. Adult Continuing Education (ACE) classes, an Employment Readiness and Employment Resource Center (resources for job search techniques), a Breaking Barriers program (a video series creating an awareness that change is possible through the development of cognitive thinking skills), and a parenting program are also available. High school diplomas and post-secondary degrees are available through paid correspondence programs.

Advanced Occupational Education: FCI Allenwood Medium does not offer any advanced occupational education programs.

Vocational Training: FCI Allenwood Medium offers vocational training in Aquaculture Science, Carpentry, Computers (IC3 Computing Core Certification), and Electric.

Apprenticeship: FCI Allenwood Medium offers apprenticeships in Fishery Worker, Housekeeping, and QA Tech.

Library Services: The leisure library offers fiction and nonfiction books, magazines, and newspapers. The Education Department offers the TRULINCS Electronic Law Library for inmates researching federal caselaw. Typewriters and a copy machine are available for inmate use. The Education Department also has an interlibrary loan agreement with the Union County Public Library to expand its offerings.

UNICOR: The FCI Allenwood Medium UNICOR facility produces office furniture.

Commissary: FCI Allenwood Medium inmates are permitted to spend up to $360.00 each month for regular purchases, and an additional amount for special purchase items. Items include candy, snacks, food, clothing, shoes, and electronics. Each inmate is responsible for knowing the amount of money available in his account. An inmate's Unit Manager can approve withdrawals from an inmate's trust fund account to send funds to dependents and other family members.

Recreation Services: FCI Allenwood Medium's Recreation Department consists of both indoor and outdoor areas. Indoor activities include a gymnasium, T.V. viewing area, fitness equipment, games, hobbycrafts, ceramics, musical instruments, multi-purpose rooms, and a Wellness Resource Room. Outdoor activities include softball fields, flag football field, soccer field, sand volleyball pit, fitness stations, handball/racquetball courts, circular track, handicapped walking track, basketball courts, pavilion area, courtyard, bocce ball courts, and horseshoe pits.

Visitation Information: On Sunday, Friday, and Saturday visitation is held between 8:00 a.m. and 3:00 p.m. On federal holidays visitation is held between 8:00 a.m. and 3:00 p.m. See Chapter 1 for more information on visitation.

In the News: In 2005, Federal Correctional Institution Allenwood Medium prisoners Jose Orejuela and Jorge Figueroa were caught, along with 20 other people, for supervising a drug smuggling operation to import cocaine into the United States.

FCI Allenwood Low

Federal Correctional Institution Allenwood Low | FCI Allenwood Low

Facility Address & Contact Information

Federal Correctional Institution Allenwood Low
Route 15
Allenwood, PA 17810

Phone: 570-547-1990
Fax: 570-547-0343
Email: ALX/execassistant@bop.gov

BOP Website: https://www.bop.gov/locations/institutions/alf/
Wikipedia: https://en.wikipedia.org/wiki/Federal_Correctional_Institution%2C_Allenwood
ZCG Website: https://www.prisonerresource.com/resources/federal-prison-profiles/northeast-region-ner/federal-correctional-complex-allenwood-fcc-allenwood/federal-correctional-institution-allenwood-low-fci-allenwood-low/

Inmate Correspondence Address

Inmate Name and Registration Number
FCI Allenwood Low
Federal Correctional Institution
P.O. Box 1000
White Deer, PA 17887

NOTE: Funds cannot be sent directly to federal inmates. See Chapter 1 for more information on sending funds to federal inmates.

Sex: Male

Security Level: Low Security

Location: FCI Allenwood Low is located 197 miles north of Washington, DC; 11 miles south of Williamsport, PA; 2 miles North of Allenwood, PA, on U.S. Route 15.

BOP Region: Northeast Region (NER)

BOP Institution Code: ALF for FCI Allenwood Low, ALX for Allenwood Federal Correctional Complex

Judicial District: Middle District of Pennsylvania

Medical Care Level: Level 2. See Chapter 2 for more information on Medical Care and Mental Health Care Levels.

Mental Health Care Level: Level 3

Population (as of May 1, 2019): 1,323

Background: Federal Correctional Institution Allenwood Low is a low-security federal prison in Allenwood, Pennsylvania, which houses male inmates. It was opened in 1992 and is part of the Allenwood Federal Correctional Complex.

Media reports indicate that inmates have been charged with possession of weapons and running fraudulent government cooperation schemes from inside the prison.

Housing: Inmates are housed in dormitories in two and three-person cubicles.

Health Services: Routine medical and dental care is offered within the Health Services Department. Physical examinations, annual immunization/screening, emergency medical treatment, and medications are also provided. In order to seek routine care, inmates must submit a triage form. Emergency medical care can be obtained by approaching any staff member.

Psychology Services: All inmates at FCI Allenwood Low are seen for an intake interview with a psychologist. A psychologist is on call 24 hours a day, 7 days a week for crisis intervention and suicide prevention. Individual counseling services are available for any inmate experiencing family, interpersonal, adjustment, or other personal concerns. Educational and therapeutic groups addressing particular topics like stress management, anger management, and dealing with other people are also available. Medications for mental health problems are provided through Health Services. A treatment program for sex offenders is voluntary and is located at other facilities.

Residential Drug Abuse Program (RDAP): FCI Allenwood Low has the Residential Drug Abuse Program (RDAP). It also offers offer a Drug Abuse Education program, the Non-Residential Drug Abuse Program (NR-DAP), and self-help groups such as Alcoholics Anonymous (AA) and Narcotics Anonymous (NA).

Education Services: FCI Allenwood Low provides GED and English-as-a-Second Language (ESL) programs. Certificates and $25 credited to the student's commissary account are awarded for successful completion. A parenting program and Adult Continuing Education (ACE) classes are also available to the inmate population. High school diplomas and post-secondary degrees are available through paid correspondence programs.

Advanced Occupational Education: FCI Allenwood Low offers advanced occupational education in Culinary Arts, Office Automation, and Fiber Optics.

Vocational Training: FCI Allenwood Low offers vocational training in Computer Internet Computing Core Certification (IC3).

Apprenticeship: FCI Allenwood Low offers apprenticeship programs in Cooking and Housekeeping.

Library Services: The law/leisure library is located in the Education Department. All required legal books and policies are provided. Inmates also have access to the TRULINCS Electronic Law Library. Electric typewriters are provided; however, inmates must purchase typewriter ribbons and correction tape from the commissary. Manual typewriters are provided for inmates who do not purchase ribbons from the commissary. A copy machine is located in the law library for inmate use. In the leisure library inmates can check out newspapers, magazines, and fiction and nonfiction books.

UNICOR: The FCI Allenwood Low UNICOR facility produces office furniture.

Commissary: FCI Allenwood Low inmates are permitted to spend up to $360.00 each month for regular purchases, and an additional amount for special purchase items. Available items include snacks, food, clothing, shoes, and electronics. Over-the-counter medications can also be purchased. Each inmate is responsible for knowing the amount of money available in his account. Inmates tend to use their laundry bag to carry their purchases back to their cell.

Recreation Services: FCI Allenwood Low's Recreation Department consists of both indoor and outdoor areas. Programs include hobbycrafts (e.g., ceramics, painting, drawing, and crochet), instructional music classes, a wellness program (e.g., step aerobics, a jogging program, exercise fitness bikes, swiss ball, cardio, total body fitness, jump rope, yoga), and other activities such as fitness equipment, weight lifting, walking, jogging, handball, basketball, bocce ball, billiards, foosball, bingo, puzzles, chess, and board games. Athletic leagues are available in billiards, ping pong, floor hockey, softball, bocce ball, horseshoes, handball/racquetball, basketball, flag football, volleyball, and soccer.

Visitation Information: On Sunday, Friday, and Saturday visitation is held between 8:00 a.m. and 3:00 p.m. On federal holidays visitation is held between 8:00 a.m. and 3:00 p.m. See Chapter 1 for more information on visitation.

In the News: In February 2018, Jose Capriata and Lenelle Gray, prisoners at Federal Correctional Institution Allenwood Low, were indicted on charges of possession of a weapon.

In March 2017, TheArthur Duncan, who served 39 months at FCI Allenwood Low on drug charges, was admitted to practice law in federal court.

In 2000, George Gallego and Hamed Elbarki, prisoners at FCI Allenwood Low, were indicted in a scheme where families of other prisoners paid James Gallego, George's brother, thousands of dollars to help arrange cooperation agreements for sentence reductions. George Gallego had his own sentence reduced by informing on his co-conspirators.

FCI Berlin

Federal Correctional Institution Berlin | FCI Berlin

Facilities: FCI Berlin with an adjacent minimum-security satellite prison camp.

Facility Address & Contact Information

Federal Correctional Institution Berlin
1 Success Loop Road
Berlin, NH 03570

Phone: 604-342-4000
Fax: 603-342-4250
Email: BER/ExecAssistant@bop.gov

BOP Website: https://www.bop.gov/locations/institutions/ber/
Wikipedia: https://en.wikipedia.org/wiki/Federal_Correctional_Institution%2C_Berlin
ZCG Website: https://www.prisonerresource.com/resources/federal-prison-profiles/northeast-region-ner/federal-correctional-institution-berlin-fci-berlin/

Inmate Correspondence Address

For FCI Berlin

Inmate Name and Registration Number
FCI Berlin
Federal Correctional Institution
P.O. Box 9000
Berlin, NH 03570

For Satellite Prison Camp

Inmate Name and Registration Number
FCI Berlin
Satellite Prison Camp
P. O. Box 9000
Berlin, NH 03570

NOTE: Funds cannot be sent directly to federal inmates. See Chapter 1 for more information on sending funds to federal inmates.

Sex: Male

Security Level: Main: Medium Security; Camp: Minimum Security

Location: FCI Berlin is located in Coos County, in northern New Hampshire, 115 (185 km) North of Concord, New Hampshire, and 95 miles (153 km) Northwest of Portland, Maine. FCI Berlin is nestled on 707 acres just north of the White Mountains and east of the Androscoggin River. The expansive facility encompasses approximately 680,000 square feet of inside building area including the federal correctional institution, satellite prison camp, Garage, Warehouse, Powerhouse, Firing Range, and the Staff Training Center.

BOP Region: Northeast Region (NER)

BOP Institution Code: BER for FCI Berlin

Judicial District: District of New Hampshire

Medical Care Level: Level 1. See Chapter 2 for more information on Medical Care and Mental Health Care Levels.

Mental Health Care Level: Level 1

Population (as of May 1, 2019): Main: 840; Camp: 86

Background: Federal Correctional Institution Berlin is a medium-security federal prison in Berlin, New Hampshire, which houses male inmates. It was opened in 2012. Federal Correctional Institution Berlin Camp, which also houses male inmates, is located adjacent to the main institution.

FCI Berlin cost more than $270 million to build, and was completed in November 2010, but did not receive activation funds until almost a year later due to Congressional budget stalemates.

It officially opened on October 21, 2012, as the Bureau of Prisons' 118th facility, making it one of the newest prisons in the federal prison system.

Notable inmates include Kent Hovind (served eight years for tax evasion and tax noncompliance).

Media reports indicate that at least one guard and one camp inmate have been charged with smuggling contraband into the institution.

Housing: Inmates are assigned to one of twelve housing units, which primarily consist of two-person cells. A unit is a self-contained inmate living area that includes both inmate housing and office space for unit staff. Camp inmates are housed in dormitories.

Health Services: Inmates are given a social screening by Unit Management staff, medical screening by Health Services, and mental health screening by Mental Health staff at the time of arrival. Health services include chronic care, routine dental care, medical and dental emergency care for injuries and sudden illness, age-appropriate preventive care to promote optimal health and functional status, restorative care to promote achievable functional status, long-term care, and end-of-life care. Inmates are assigned to a specific Mid-Level Practitioner, who treats them for the duration of their stay.

Psychology Services: FCI Berlin inmates with previously identified mental health or drug abuse programming needs are scheduled for an interview with Psychology Services staff. The Psychology Services department also offers screening, assessment, and treatment of mental health problems, individual and/or group counseling, psycho-educational classes, self-help, and supportive services, or referral to Health Services for medical treatment of a mental illness. Psychology Services may refer inmates with severe emotional, cognitive, or behavioral problems to other institutions where they will receive appropriate care.

Residential Drug Abuse Program (RDAP): FCI Berlin has the Residential Drug Abuse Program (RDAP). A Drug Abuse Education course and a Non-Residential Drug Abuse Program (NR-DAP) are offered, as well as treatment options for inmates who have abused alcohol and/or drugs.

Education Services: FCI Berlin and the camp offers GED instruction in English and Spanish and the English-as-a-Second Language (ESL) program. Classes are separated into pre-GED, GED, Advanced GED, and Special Learning Needs levels. High school diplomas and post-secondary degrees are available through paid correspondence programs.

Advanced Occupational Education: FCI Berlin does not offer advanced occupational educational training aside from its vocational training.

Vocational Training: FCI Berlin offers vocational training in Administrative Assistant, Carpentry, Culinary Arts, Electrical Residential & Commercial, and Janitorial Maintenance. The camp offers Weatherization.

Apprenticeship: FCI Berlin does not offer any apprenticeship programs.

Library Services: The FCI Berlin leisure library offers inmates a variety of reading materials, including periodicals, newspapers, fiction, nonfiction, and reference books. The institution also participates in an interlibrary loan program. The TRULINCS Electronic Law Library provides inmates with access to legal materials and an opportunity to prepare legal documents. Inmates also have access to typewriters and a copy machine.

UNICOR: FCI Berlin does not have a UNICOR facility.

Commissary: Inmates may use funds in their account to purchase items at the institution commissary, place funds on their inmate phone account, purchase TRU-Units for their TRULINCS account, or send funds outside of the institution using Form BP-199. Inmates must have their commissary card in their possession at all times for identification purposes. The monthly spending limit is $360.00. Each inmate account is revalidated on a monthly basis. Inmates are permitted to purchase a wide variety of food and non-food items in the commissary.

Recreation Services: Leisure programs at FCI Berlin include organized and informal games, sports, physical fitness, table games, hobbycrafts, music programs, intramural activities, social and cultural organizations, and movies. Art activities include paintings and sketches using traditional methods (e.g., oils, pastels, crayons, pencils, inks, and charcoal). Hobbycraft activities include ceramics, mosaics, crochet, knitting, and sculptures. Wellness programs include screening, assessments, goal setting, fitness/nutrition plans, counseling, and classes. Inmates may also check out musical instruments such as guitars.

Visitation Information: On Sunday and Saturday visitation is held between 8:15 a.m. and 3:00 p.m. On federal holidays visitation is held between 8:15 a.m. and 3:00 p.m. See Chapter 1 for more information on visitation.

Prison Politics: This is a very political yard. Inmates have to be part of a car in order to stay.

Level of Violence: Inmates report a moderate level of violence.

Vulnerable Populations: No sex offenders, informants, or LGBT allowed to walk the yard.

Good: "Hallways carpeted and connected to everything, so you never have to go outside."

Bad: "Politics." "Very cold and lots of snow."

Other Comments: "This is a harder yard, so it is not sex offender-, informant-, or LGBT-friendly. Only go here if you like harder, more political time." "Unless you have clean paperwork, stay away." "Many younger inmates who cause trouble."

In the News: In January 2018, Latoya Sebree, a guard at the Federal Correctional Institution in Berlin, was sentenced to 15 months in prison for smuggling cell phones, marijuana, tobacco and other contraband into the facility.

Camp in the News: In April 2007, Christopher Beaudoin, a work release prisoner at Federal Correctional Institution Berlin Camp, was charged with trying to smuggle tobacco, which he stole from a construction worker, into the prison. He was later sentenced to one to three years of additional prison time.

MDC Brooklyn

Metropolitan Detention Center Brooklyn | MDC Brooklyn

Facility Address & Contact Information

Metropolitan Detention Center Brooklyn
80 – 29th Street
Brooklyn, NY 11232

Phone: 718-840-4200
Fax: 718-840-5001
Email: BRO/ExecAssistant@bop.gov

BOP Website: https://www.bop.gov/locations/institutions/bro/
Wikipedia: https://en.wikipedia.org/wiki/Metropolitan_Detention_Center%2C_Brooklyn
ZCG Website: https://www.prisonerresource.com/resources/federal-prison-profiles/northeast-region-ner/metropolitan-detention-center-brooklyn-mdc-brooklyn/

Inmate Correspondence Address

Inmate Name and Registration Number
MDC Brooklyn
Metropolitan Detention Center
P.O. Box 329002
Brooklyn, NY 11232

NOTE: Funds cannot be sent directly to federal inmates. See Chapter 1 for more information on sending funds to federal inmates.

Sex: Male and Female

Security Level: Administrative Security (Multiple Security Levels)

Location: MDC Brooklyn is located in the Sunset Park section of Brooklyn, one of the five boroughs of New York City.

BOP Region: Northeast Region (NER)

BOP Institution Code: BRO for MDC Brooklyn

Judicial District: Eastern District of New York

Medical Care Level: Level 2. See Chapter 2 for more information on Medical Care and Mental Health Care Levels.

Mental Health Care Level: Level 2

Population (as of May 1, 2019): 1,659

Background: Metropolitan Detention Center Brooklyn is an administrative-security federal prison in Brooklyn, New York, which houses both male and female inmates. It was opened in 1994.

MDC Brooklyn houses pre-trial and pre-sentence detainees. The National Association of Women Judges has described the conditions of confinement at MDC Brooklyn as "unconscionable."

Notable inmates include New York City mobster Vincent Asaro (convicted of car arson), Linda Weston (serving a life sentence for murder, racketeering, and hate crimes), and current MSNBC host Al Sharpton (served 90 days for trespassing on federal property).

Media reports have indicated that at least ten female and one male detainee have been sexually assaulted by several guards and three lieutenants at the facility. In addition, in the past several years, guards have been arrested for stealing money from inmates and, in one case, for hiring hitmen to attack a former spouse with a hammer. News reports also state that the Bureau paid out a multi-million-dollar settlement after one inmate suffered a stroke as a result of prolonged malnutrition at the facility and then died shortly after his release.

Housing: Inmates are housed in cells with two or more bunks.

Health Services: Sick call, dental sick call, emergency services and medications are all provided to inmates. Inmates must submit a Sick Call form in order to be evaluated by Health Services. Emergency care is available 24 hours a day.

Psychology Services: The Psychology Department at MDC Brooklyn provides mental health services to those inmates who have a history of mental illness and who have difficulty adjusting to incarceration. Staff members are assigned to individual floors in order to expedite addressing of inmate mental health concerns. Inmates are required to submit an "Inmate Request to Staff" form in non-emergency situations to the Psychology Department. Medication for psychiatric patients is usually continued upon admission to the institution. If there is a need for psychiatric medication the inmate will be placed on the list to see the psychiatrist.

Residential Drug Abuse Program (RDAP): MDC Brooklyn does not have the Residential Drug Abuse Program (RDAP). The Drug Education Class and the Non-Residential Drug Abuse Program (NR-DAP) are available.

Education Services: MDC Brooklyn provides GED and English-as-a-Second Language (ESL) programs. High school diplomas and post-secondary degrees are available through paid correspondence programs.

Advanced Occupational Education: MDC Brooklyn does not offer any advanced occupational education.

Vocational Training: MDC Brooklyn does not offer any vocational training programs.

Apprenticeship: MDC Brooklyn does not offer any apprenticeship programs.

Library Services: A leisure library and law library are available to inmates. Law books are for reference and may not be removed from the law library for any reason. A photocopy machine is available in the Education Department and can be utilized by inmates with the purchase of copy cards from the Commissary. Leisure books can be checked out of the main libraries during each floor's respective library session. Inmates confined in SHU can request leisure books through the appropriate request form.

UNICOR: MDC Brooklyn does not have a UNICOR facility.

Commissary: Inmates have the right to use funds for commissary and other purchases, consistent with institution security and good order, for opening bank and/or savings accounts, and for assisting family. Prisoners are permitted to spend up to $90 per week for regular and special purchases. Food, snacks, drinks, electronics, and other items can be purchased in the commissary.

Recreation Services: The MDC Brooklyn Recreation Department consists of indoor and outdoor areas. Leisure activities include participation in organized and informal games, wellness activities, curricular and extracurricular activities, sports, social activities, artwork, physical fitness, table games, and board games. Recreation staff are available to aid in planning and organizing recreational activities.

Visitation Information: On weekdays and federal holidays visitation is held between 12:00 and 3:00 p.m. as well as 5:00 to 7:30 p.m. On weekends visitation is held between 8:00 a.m. and 3:00 p.m. See Chapter 1 for more information on visitation.

In the News: In August 2018, George Gonzalez, a guard at the Metropolitan Detention Center in Brooklyn, pleaded guilty to hiring hitmen to severely injure his estranged wife and her boyfriend with a hammer to their spines.

Also in August 2018, a prisoner at MDC Brooklyn filed a lawsuit alleging numerous abuses at the facility, including sexual assaults and medical neglect.

In May 2018, Eugenio Perez, a lieutenant at MDC Brooklyn, was convicted of sexually assaulting five female inmates between 2013 and 2016.

In January 2018, Carlos Richard Martinez, a lieutenant at MDC Brooklyn, was found guilty of raping a female prisoner at least four times between December 2015 and April 2016.

In November 2017, MDC Brooklyn guard Armondo Moronta pleaded guilty to sexually abusing three female inmates.

In June 2016, members of the National Association of Women Judges visited MDC Brooklyn and described the conditions as "unconscionable."

In 2015, the Bureau of Prisons paid $2.9 million to the widow of Gerald Kapiloff, whose medical pleas were ignored until he suffered a massive seizure from malnutrition during his 16-month sentence at MDC Brooklyn. Kapiloff died a year after his release.

In May 2013, Debbie Austin, a guard at MDC Brooklyn, and her roommate Shamika Clarke were charged with stealing $1,600 that was sent to prisoners and supposed to be credited to their trust accounts.

In March 2013, Nancy Gonzalez, a guard at MDC Brooklyn, was arrested for having sex with Ronnell Wilson, a prisoner at the facility who was accused of killing two NYPD police officers. Gonzalez gave birth to Wilson's child, but lost custody of him after violating the conditions of her bail, specifically the condition to refrain from drinking alcohol.

In November 2001, Randy Denjen, a lieutenant at MDC Brooklyn, allegedly raped a female prisoner.

In 2000, Mamdouh Mahmud Salim was awaiting trial on terrorism charges at MDC Brooklyn when he shoved a comb into guard Louis Pepe's eye, leaving him brain damaged and nearly blind.

USP Canaan

United States Penitentiary Canaan | USP Canaan

Facilities: USP Canaan with an adjacent minimum-security satellite prison camp.

Facility Address & Contact Information

United States Penitentiary Canaan
3057 Eric J. Williams Memorial Drive
Waymart, PA 18472

Phone: 570-488-8000
Fax: 570-488-8130
Email: CAA/ExecAssistant@bop.gov

BOP Website: https://www.bop.gov/locations/institutions/caa/
Wikipedia: https://en.wikipedia.org/wiki/United_States_Penitentiary%2C_Canaan
ZCG Website: https://www.prisonerresource.com/resources/federal-prison-profiles/northeast-region-ner/united-states-penitentiary-canaan-usp-canaan/

Inmate Correspondence Address

For USP Canaan

Inmate Name and Registration Number
USP Canaan
U.S Penitentiary
P.O. Box 300
Waymart, PA 18472

For Satellite Prison Camp

Inmate Name and Registration Number
USP Canaan
Satellite Prison Camp
P.O. Box 200
Waymart, PA 18472

NOTE: Funds cannot be sent directly to federal inmates. See Chapter 1 for more information on sending funds to federal inmates.

Sex: Male

Security Level: Main: High Security; Camp: Minimum Security

Location: USP Canaan is located in northeast Pennsylvania, 20 miles east of Scranton and 134 miles north of Philadelphia.

BOP Region: Northeast Region (NER)

BOP Institution Code: CAA for USP Canaan

Judicial District: Middle District of Pennsylvania

Medical Care Level: Level 2. See Chapter 2 for more information on Medical Care and Mental Health Care Levels.

Mental Health Care Level: Level 2

Population (as of May 1, 2019): Main: 1,268; Camp: 111

Background: United States Penitentiary Canaan is a high-security federal prison in Waymart, Pennsylvania, which houses male inmates. It was opened in 2005. United States Penitentiary Canaan Camp, which also houses male inmates, is located adjacent to the main institution.

At least four murders have taken place at USP Canaan since its opening. Pennsylvania lawmakers have called the facility "one of the most dangerous penitentiaries in the country." In June 2011, one of the largest ever institutional salmonella poisoning outbreaks occurred when 300 inmates and several staff members became ill after eating chicken in the prison dining room.

Notable inmates include father and son executives John Rigas and Timothy Rigas (convicted of bank fraud); drug kingpin Juan Matta-Ballesteros (serving a life sentence for drug offenses); Somali pirate leader Mohammad Shibin (serving a life sentence); and former Army Ranger Luke Sommer (serving a 44-year sentence for bank robbery and soliciting murder).

Media reports indicate that at least one guard has been killed, two guards stabbed, and one inmate murdered at the facility. In addition, at least one guard has been indicted for smuggling contraband into the institution.

Housing: Inmates live in six housing units consisting of one and two-person cells. Inmates at the camp are housed in dormitories.

Health Services: Health services include preventative care, diagnosis or treatment for chronic conditions, emergency services, mental health care, substance abuse treatment, annual immunizations/screenings, physical examinations, and dental care. Inmates must submit a triage form in order to be evaluated for routine healthcare needs. Emergency care is available 24 hours a day.

Psychology Services: Priority psychology services include intake screenings, treatment of major mental disorders, crisis intervention, and suicide prevention. Other self-help, support, and lifestyle change programs are offered as resources and need dictate. Typical groups including anger management are offered.

Residential Drug Abuse Program (RDAP): USP Canaan has the Residential Drug Abuse Program (RDAP). It also offers a Drug Education class, the Non-Residential Drug Abuse Program (NR-DAP), Alcoholics Anonymous (AA), and Narcotics Anonymous (NA). The Challenge Program, which assists inmates in successfully reintegrating into the community through the elimination of drug abuse and elimination/management of mental illness, is also available.

Education Services: USP Canaan provides literacy, GED, and English-as-a-Second Language (ESL) programs. Adult Continuing Education (ACE) classes and a parenting program are also available. High school diplomas and post-secondary degrees are available through paid correspondence programs.

Advanced Occupational Education: USP Canaan offers advanced occupational education in Culinary Arts.

Vocational Training: USP Canaan and the satellite camp offer vocational training in Horticulture.

Apprenticeship: USP Canaan offers apprenticeships in Electrical, HVAC, and Plumbing. The camp offers an apprenticeship in Electrical.

Library Services: USP Canaan's Education Department provides a wide variety of reading material, including newspapers, magazines, and a broad selection of leisure reading books (westerns, fiction, nonfiction, biographies, reference, science, history, etc.). The TRULINCS Electronic Law Library is located in four stations throughout the institution, one in each pod, and one in SHU. Printers are located in the main law library, Commissary, and SHU.

UNICOR: The USP Canaan UNICOR facility handles bindery operations. The camp does not house a UNICOR facility.

Commissary: The Commissary provides a bank-type account for inmate money and for the procurement of items not issued regularly as part of the institution administration. Funds deposited by family, friends, or other sources are stored in the inmate's Trust Fund Account. This money may be used for purchasing approved sale items in the institution commissary, sent home for family support, or used for other approved purposes. The commissary shopping schedule is based on each housing unit, and the shopping days are rotated monthly.

Recreation Services: Leisure activities and recreation programs at USP Canaan are supervised by the Recreation Department. Programs include indoor and outdoor activities and range from individualized arts and crafts programs to intramural team sports, such as softball, basketball, and soccer. Physical fitness and weight reduction programs are important activities for inmates and contribute to good mental health, healthy interpersonal relations, and stress reduction. Various leisure classes and hobbycraft programs are also available for interested participants.

Visitation Information: On Sunday, Friday, and Saturday visitation is held between 8:00 a.m. and 3:00 p.m. On federal holidays visitation is held between 8:00 a.m. and 3:00 p.m. See Chapter 1 for more information on visitation.

In the News: In March 2018, Pennsylvania lawmakers wrote to Attorney General Jeff Sessions and then-BOP Director Mark Inch decrying prison staffing cuts, saying that USP Canaan "is one of the most dangerous penitentiaries in the country," citing 256 reported acts of violence in fiscal year 2017.

In August 2015, a prison employee and two guards were stabbed by a prisoner in the dining hall at USP Canaan.

In March 2015, Senator Bob Casey (D-PA), sponsored a bill in Congress as a result of the fatal 2013 stabbing of USP Canaan guard Eric Williams that would require Bureau of Prisons employees to carry pepper spray.

In December 2013, an unidentified guard at USP Canaan was quoted in the news as saying, "There's so many violent acts happening all the time," they run out of room in the SHU.

In February 2013, USP Canaan prisoner Jessie Con-Ui beat and stabbed prison guard Eric Williams to death. Williams was stabbed a total of 129 times. Con-Ui allegedly committed the attack because he felt disrespected after Williams allegedly ordered two guards to ransack his cell. Con-Ui, who was serving a life sentence, was sentenced to life again in July 2017.

In March 2012, Donald E. Lykon, a guard at USP Canaan, was charged with smuggling cell phones, tobacco and marijuana into the prison over a four-month period in 2011.

In April 2010, Allen Archie Hurley, a prisoner at USP Canaan who was serving time for bank robbery, killed Gambino crime family associate Joseph O'Kane, stabbing him 92 times.

FCI Danbury & FSL Danbury

Federal Correctional Institution Danbury | FCI Danbury

Facilities: FCI Danbury with an adjacent low-security satellite prison and an adjacent minimum-security satellite prison camp.

Facility Address & Contact Information

Federal Correctional Institution Danbury
Route 37
Danbury, CT 06811

Phone: 203-743-6471
Fax: 203-312-5110
Email: DAN/ExecAssistant@bop.gov

BOP Website: https://www.bop.gov/locations/institutions/dan/
Wikipedia: https://en.wikipedia.org/wiki/Federal_Correctional_Institution,_Danbury
ZCG Website: https://www.prisonerresource.com/resources/federal-prison-profiles/northeast-region-ner/federal-correctional-institution-danbury-fci-danbury/

Inmate Correspondence Address

For FCI Danbury

Inmate Name and Registration Number
FCI Danbury
Federal Correctional Institution
Route 37
Danbury, CT 06811

For Satellite Low

Inmate Name and Registration Number
FCI Danbury
Satellite Low
Route 37
Danbury, CT 06811

For Satellite Prison Camp

Inmate Name and Registration Number
FCI Danbury
Satellite Prison Camp
Route 37
Danbury, CT 06811

NOTE: Funds cannot be sent directly to federal inmates. See Chapter 1 for more information on sending funds to federal inmates.

Sex: Main: Male; Satellite Low: Female; Camp: Female

Security Level: Main: Low Security; Satellite Low: Low Security; Camp: Minimum Security

Location: FCI Danbury is located in southwestern Connecticut, 70 miles from New York City, three miles north of Danbury, on State Route 37.

BOP Region: Northeast Region (NER)

BOP Institution Code: DAN for FCI Danbury

Judicial District: District of Connecticut

Medical Care Level: Level 2. See Chapter 2 for more information on Medical Care and Mental Health Care Levels.

Mental Health Care Level: Level 3

Population (as of May 1, 2019): Main: 759; Satellite Low: 121; Camp: 162

Background: Federal Correctional Institution Danbury is a low-security federal prison located in Danbury, Connecticut, which houses male inmates. It was opened in 1940. Federal Satellite Low Danbury is a low-security federal prison which houses female inmates. Federal Correctional Institution Danbury Camp, which also houses female inmates, was opened in 1982 and is located adjacent to the main institution.

FCI Danbury was initially intended for both male and female prisoners. From 1993 to 2013, it was exclusively for female prisoners. It has transitioned back to an exclusively male prison, with female inmates now housed at the satellite camp and at the federal satellite low.

Notable inmates include leading real estate investor Leona Helmsley (served 21 months in 1993 and 1994 for tax evasion); leader of the Unification Church Sun Myung Moon (served 11 months for tax evasion); Piper Kerman (served 13 months for drug conspiracy);

Grammy-award-winning singer Lauryn Hill (served three months for intentionally failing to file tax returns); Bravo television star Teresa Giudice (served 12 months for bankruptcy and mail fraud); and Watergate burglars G. Gordon Liddy and Howard Hunt. Piper Kerman authored the book *Orange is the New Black: My Year in a Women's Prison* about her time at FCI Danbury, which is the basis for the hit Netflix series *Orange is the New Black*.

Media reports indicate that at least nine inmates have been sexually assaulted by guards. In addition, guards have also been indicted for smuggling contraband into the institution and accepting bribes. At least two inmates have also been charged with weapons possession.

Housing: Inmates are housed in one of 13 housing units. While most of the housing units consist of cubicles which have bunk beds, some housing units have cells. I Unit houses the Skills Program, L Unit houses RDAP, and M Unit is a general population unit, though it consists of cells. Currently, A, B, and K Units are closed. Inmates at the camp are housed in dormitories.

Health Services: Routine medical and dental care are offered within the Health Services Department at FCI Danbury. Health services include health promotion and disease prevention, annual immunizations/screening, treatment for on-the-job injuries, sick call, dental call, physical examinations, preventive health care, emergency medical treatment, and medications. Inmates are assigned to a specific health care provider who treats them for the duration of their stay. Pill and insulin lines are conducted at 6:00 a.m., 12:00 p.m., and 5:00 p.m.

Psychology Services: The Psychology Services Department offers basic mental health care to inmates. This care may include screening, assessment, and treatment of mental health or drug abuse problems, individual and/or group counseling, psycho-educational classes, self-help and supportive services, or referral to Health Services for medical treatment of a mental illness. Typical groups include anger management, Smart Recovery, and others. Inmates are notified of upcoming groups and other Psychology Department offerings through posted notices. The Resolve Program for inmates who are dealing with mental illness as a result of trauma, and the Skills Program, for inmates with intellectual disabilities and social deficiencies are also available.

Residential Drug Abuse Program (RDAP): FCI Danbury offers the Residential Drug Abuse Program (RDAP). The camp does not have the Residential Drug Abuse Program (RDAP). A Drug Abuse Education Course and the Non-Residential Drug Abuse Program (NR-DAP), Alcoholics Anonymous (AA), and Narcotics Anonymous (NA) are offered. Other non-residential groups are also available.

Education Services: FCI Danbury provides literacy, GED, and English-as-a-Second Language (ESL) programs. Incentive awards are utilized to recognize inmates making satisfactory progress and successfully completing the literacy program. Inmates may also receive incentives for progressing to various levels in the GED or ESL Programs. Graduation ceremonies recognize GED, ESL, and Occupational Education completions. Adult Continuing Education (ACE) classes and a parenting program are also offered. High school diplomas and post-secondary degrees are available through paid correspondence programs.

Advanced Occupational Education: FCI Danbury does not offer any advanced occupational education programs.

Vocational Training: FCI Danbury offers vocational training in Culinary Arts and Horticulture. The camp offers Puppies Behind Bars.

Apprenticeship: FCI Danbury and the satellite facilities offer apprenticeships in Baker, Carpenter, Chaplain Service Support, Cook, Dental Assistant, Education and Training, Electrician, Horticulturist, Housekeeper (Commercial, Residential, or Industrial), Landscape Management Technician, Legal Secretary, Material Coordinator, Office Manager/ Administrative Services, Painter, Plumber, Quality Control Inspector, Recreation Assistant, Teacher Aide, and Tool Machine Set-Up Operator. FCI Danbury offers apprenticeships in HVAC, Meat Cutter, Peer Specialist, and Stationary Engineer. The camp offers Animal Trainer, Baker, Career Development Technician, and Undercar Specialist.

Library Services: The leisure libraries at FCI Danbury and the adjacent facilities offer inmates a variety of reading materials, including periodicals, newspapers, fiction, nonfiction, and reference books. The institutions also participate in an interlibrary loan program. Inmates are provided access to legal materials and an opportunity to prepare legal documents through the use of the TRULINCS Electronic Law Library. A copy machine is available to reproduce materials needed for research. Typewriters are also available.

UNICOR: FCI Danbury does have a UNICOR facility, but it is not currently in operation. The camp does not house a UNICOR facility.

Commissary: Inmates at FCI Danbury may use funds in their account to purchase items at the institution commissary, place funds on their inmate phone account, purchase TRU-Units for their TRULINCS account, or send funds out of the institution using Form BP-199. Commissary and validation schedules are posted on the TRULINCS bulletin board. Each unit shops once a week on a designated shopping day based on the weekly unit inspection. Commissary is open Monday through Thursday from 6:00 to 7:45 a.m. Monday through Wednesday from 5:00 to 6:30 p.m. Funds are withdrawn after positive identification by commissary card or fingerprint identification. It is the inmate's responsibility to know the amount of money available in his or her account. Inmates must have their commissary card in their possession at all times for identification purposes.

Recreation Services: The FCI Danbury Recreation Department consists of indoor and outdoor areas, including leisure, wellness, sports, and music programs. Structured classes include a wide variety of hobbycraft and music programs. Non-structured leisure activities include puzzles, dominos, cards, board games, and billiard equipment. Art activities include oils, pastels, crayons, pencils, inks, and charcoal. Hobbycraft classes include art, plastic canvas, origami, crochet, knitting, and others. Wellness programs are offered, such as circuit training, aerobics, over 50 fitness, nutrition, yoga, and others. An annual Health Fair is held to provide services and information to the inmate population. Indoor and outdoor intramural sports leagues are offered year-round. Basketball, softball, volleyball, soccer, handball, and racquetball leagues are offered seasonally. Music programs such as musical theory concepts and how to play an instrument are available.

Visitation Information: On Sunday, Monday, Friday, and Saturday visitation is held between 8:30 a.m. and 3:00 p.m. On federal holidays visitation is held between 8:30 a.m. and 3:00 p.m. See Chapter 1 for more information on visitation.

Prison Politics: There is a very low level of politics at this prison.

Level of Violence: Inmates report a low level of violence, though a progressively increasing amount in late 2018.

Vulnerable Populations: Sex offenders, informants, and LGBT inmates are allowed to walk the yard. One respondent stated that "there is a huge population of sex offenders here." One inmate did note that sex offenders do not have a TV that they can control and that they must sit at one of four tables in the chow hall.

Bad: "The medical care is HORRIBLE!" "There are frequent lockdowns due to lack of staffing." "Ten-minute moves are enforced; no open compound." "No air conditioning in the housing units." "No bathrooms in either the leisure or law libraries, so inmates must wait until the activities move in order to use them elsewhere."

In the News: In July 2018, John Faucher, a prisoner at the Federal Correctional Institution at Danbury who is serving just under five years for robbery, pleaded guilty to possessing a weapon while in federal custody, for which he faces up to five additional years in prison.

Also in July 2018, FCI Danbury food service employee Eric Williams was charged with smuggling cell phones and other contraband into the prison.

In May 2018, John Durham, a prisoner at FCI Danbury, was indicted on a charge of weapons possession.

In January 2017, female prisoners returned to FCI Danbury after they were all moved to Metropolitan Detention Center Brooklyn in 2013 when the prison was converted into a men's facility.

In July 2015, Kisha Perkins, a case manager at the FCI Danbury, was sentenced to a year in prison for accepting bribes from prisoners under her supervision.

In March 2014, Steven Wolff, a repair foreman at FCI Danbury, was sentenced to five months in prison for having sexual relations with a prisoner and paying a lookout with contraband.

In June 2004, Gregory Webb, a guard at FCI Danbury, was sentenced to probation and community service for having oral sex with a female prisoner and lying to investigators about it.

In August 2003, Anthony Tortorella, an FCI Danbury guard, was sentenced to ten months in prison for having sex with six female prisoners between 1998 and 2001, and for harboring an illegal alien. Tortorella's sentence was particularly lenient because he agreed to testify against prison guard Richard Vasquez, who was also having sex with female prisoners at FCI Danbury.

In July 1977, a fire broke out at FCI Danbury killing five prisoners and injuring another 86 prisoners, staff and firefighters.

FMC Devens

Federal Medical Center Devens | FMC Devens

Facilities: FMC Devens with an adjacent minimum-security satellite prison camp.

Facility Address & Contact Information

Federal Medical Center Devens
42 Patton Road
Ayer, MA 01432

Phone: 978-796-1000
Fax: 978-796-1118
Email: DEV/ExecAssistant@bop.gov

BOP Website: https://www.bop.gov/locations/institutions/dev/
Wikipedia: https://en.wikipedia.org/wiki/Federal_Medical_Center,_Devens
ZCG Website: https://www.prisonerresource.com/resources/federal-prison-profiles/northeast-region-ner/federal-medical-center-devens-fmc-devens/

Inmate Correspondence Address

For FMC Devens

Inmate Name and Registration Number
FMC Devens
Federal Medical Center
P.O. Box 879
Ayer, MA 01432

For Satellite Prison Camp

Inmate Name and Registration Number
FMC Devens
Satellite Prison Camp
P.O. Box 879
Ayer, MA 01432

NOTE: Funds cannot be sent directly to federal inmates. See Chapter 1 for more information on sending funds to federal inmates.

Sex: Male

Security Level: Administrative Security (Multiple Security Levels)

Location: FMC Devens is located in north central Massachusetts, about 39 miles west of Boston and 20 miles north of Worcester on the decommissioned military base of Fort Devens.

BOP Region: Northeast Region (NER)

BOP Institution Code: DEV for FMC Devens

Judicial District: District of Massachusetts

Medical Care Level: Level 3/4. See Chapter 2 for more information on Medical Care and Mental Health Care Levels.

Mental Health Care Level: Level 4

Population (as of May 1, 2019): Main: 1,013; Camp: 116

Background: Federal Medical Center Devens is an administrative-security federal prison in Ayer, Massachusetts, which houses male inmates. It was opened in 1999. Federal Medical Center Devens Camp, which also houses male inmates, was opened in 1998 and is located adjacent to the main institution.

FMC Devens is a Sex Offender Management Program (SOMP) facility, which means that around 40 percent of the inmate population is incarcerated for a current or past sexual offense.

Current notable inmates include Peter Madoff (serving 10 years for conspiracy to commit securities fraud); former underboss of the Colombo crime family John Franzese (serving eight years for racketeering conspiracy); former underboss of the Gambino crime family Frank Locascio (serving a life sentence for racketeering and directing criminal activities); and former Congressman Anthony Weiner. Former notable inmates include John Gambino (convicted of drug trafficking and murder); billionaire and former director of Goldman Sachs Rajat Gupta (served two years for insider trading); former boss of the DeCalvacante crime family John Riggi (served 22 years for racketeering, extortion, and conspiracy to commit murder); former Massachusetts State Representative John George, Jr.; former New York State Assemblyman Daniel Van Pelt; and former federal prosecutor and state Republican Party Chairman Sam Currin.

Media reports indicate that guards have been arrested for embezzlement, sexual assault, and smuggling contraband into the prison.

Housing: Inmates are housed in differing housing variations based on their security level status. Medium-security inmates tend to be housed in two-person cells, though there are some four-, six-, and eight-person cells. Low-security inmates tend to be housed in dormitories divided into two-person cells, though there are also some eight-person rooms. Inmates at the facility due to medical or psychological treatment are housed in one-, two-, or four-person cells. Inmates in the camp are housed in open dormitories. There are 128 inmates in the camp dorms.

Health Services: Inmates receive a thorough physical examination and psychological tests during the orientation period. Health services include medical sick call, dental sick call, and all support services. Emergency health care services are available 24 hours each day. Routine dental and medical care are obtained by attending sick call at 7:30 a.m. on Monday, Tuesday, Thursday, and Friday. Pill and insulin line are conducted at 7:00 a.m., 12:00 p.m., and 7:00 p.m.

Psychology Services: New inmates at FCI Devens undergo psychological testing during their Admission & Orientation phase. Crisis counseling, coping skills, suicide prevention, mental health counseling, and spiritual counseling are all available for inmates. The Psychology Department also offers a Residential Sex Offender Treatment Program (SOTP-R) and a Sex Offender Management Program (SOMP). This department also offers self-development programs in both group and individual counseling. Classes include meditation, anger management, stress reduction, and victim impact.

Residential Drug Abuse Program (RDAP): FMC Devens does not offer the Residential Drug Abuse Program (RDAP). However, the Non-Residential Drug Abuse Program (NR-DAP) and the Drug Education class are offered.

Education Services: FMC Devens and the camp provide GED, parenting, and English-as-a-Second Language (ESL) programs. Certificates are awarded for completion of all programs. Adult Continuing Education (ACE) classes are also available, which are taught by fellow inmates and span a wide variety of topics. Parenting and the Back to Work Reentry Program are also available. High school diplomas and post-secondary degrees are available through paid correspondence programs. Hours of operation are Monday through Thursday from 8:30 a.m. to 8:30 p.m., Friday 8:30 a.m. to 3:30 p.m., and Saturday 7:30 a.m. to 3:30 p.m. All of these times exclude recalls for counts and meals.

Advanced Occupational Education: FMC Devens does not offer any advanced occupational education programs.

Vocation Training: FMC Devens offers vocational training in Computer Applications/MS Office (nine-month program including Word, Excel, and PowerPoint). and Culinary Arts.

Apprenticeship: FMC Devens offers apprenticeships in Education & Training and HVAC (limited to four inmates and takes three years to complete). The camp offers apprenticeships in Animal Trainer and Cook.

Library Services: A leisure and law library is available for inmates. An electronic law library has been added as part of the TRULINCS system, where inmates can conduct legal research from a database that contains the latest updates on case law from every federal district and circuit court in the United States, federal criminal/civil rules of procedure, sentencing guidelines, Bureau of Prisons Policy Statements, and more. Magazines, newspapers and basic reference books cannot be removed from the library, but fiction and nonfiction books can. An interlibrary loan program is also available, as are DVD movies. Typewriters are available for inmate use in preparing legal documents. A copy machine is also available for inmate use.

UNICOR: FMC Devens and the camp do not house a UNICOR facility.

Commissary: Funds deposited by an inmate's family, friends, or other sources are stored in the inmate's commissary account, which is administered by FMC Devens. Inmates can use the funds to make telephone calls, send and receive emails, and purchase commissary items. Commissary items include sodas, snacks, food, clothing, ice cream, and shoes. Inmates are permitted to shop once a week on their designated shopping day. A $360 monthly spending limit is imposed. Shopping is conducted at breakfast, 8:30 a.m., and lunch Monday through Thursday. At the camp, inmates must submit their order on Sunday. Purchases are then delivered on Thursday.

Recreation Services: FMC Devens recreation programs include indoor and outdoor activities that range from individualized hobbycraft programs to intramural team sports. The Inmate Recreation and Activity Center includes a multi-purpose room, outdoor recreation yard, and an indoor inmate Activity Center. The indoor Activity Center is located on the recreation yard and is intended for activities such as basketball, soccer, and floor hockey. Also indoors, inmate can use pull-up and dip bars, tables, TVs, ellipticals, treadmills, and stationary bikes. The Hobbycraft Shop and a music practice room are located in the Recreation Building, as is an art room. Outside, inmates can play softball, soccer, horseshoes, basketball, bocce ball, and handball, as well as walk the track. Hours of operation are 6:00 a.m. to 8:30 p.m., excluding count and mealtimes. The camp has far scaled down offerings, which consist of softball, handball, volleyball, bocce ball, stationary bikes, and treadmills.

Visitation Information: On Sunday, Friday, and Saturday visitation is held between 8:30 a.m. and 3:00 p.m. On federal holidays visitation is held between 8:30 a.m. and 3:00 p.m. See Chapter 1 for more information on visitation.

Prison Politics: There is a very low level of politics at this prison. According to one inmate, "This is a population management yard. There are very little, if any, political issues. Any outward signs of gangs or similar is normally met with staff intervention." Another respondent agreed, stating, "This is not a political yard at all."

Level of Violence: Violence is very infrequent at this facility. As explained by one inmate, "There is very little violence outside of a few rare events. Any violence is actually more typical amongst the mentally handicapped inmates than others. This seems to be due to psychological issues, not the culture of the yard." Another respondent stated, "There is hardly ever any violence. Level of safety is very great."

Vulnerable Populations: Sex offenders, informants, and LGBT inmates can walk the yard. According to one respondent, "This institution is designed for these three groups. While this is a Sex Offender Management Program (SOMP) facility, there is also the Residential Sex Offender Treatment Program (SOTP-R)." Another inmate agreed, stating, "If you don't put your business out there, you will rarely if ever be asked what you are in prison for. Those out in the open about being a sex offender might be somewhat shunned by a few individuals, but this would be the exception to the rule." As concisely put by another respondent, "Overall, anyone is able to walk this yard."

Good: "Cool place. Soft yard. Good medical." "For bedridden inmates, they can stay in the housing units and have their food brought to them." "It is a laid-back place with very few issues." "Socially, anyone can find a helpful, supportive crowd." "There is a very good rec program here." "Unit teams and medical are both good." "This is a good place for treatment of various kinds; psych treatment is good." "COs are pretty laid back for the most part." "We still have microwaves."

Bad: "Cubicle housing, common restrooms, cold, very few TVs." "There is very little respect and very little to do in terms of productive activities." "The food portions are poor, and the national menu is seldom followed." "The commissary stays out of soda." "Weather gets really cold in the winter."

Other Comments: "This is an ideal place for sex offenders. It is a very soft yard due to so many sex offenders." "This place is mellow, kind of like a retirement home."

In the News: In April 2018, National Fish & Seafood president Jack Ventola, who was sentenced to two years in prison for tax fraud, requested to be incarcerated at Federal Medical Center Devens.

In November 2017, former Congressman Anthony Weiner turned himself in to FMC Devens to begin serving his 21-month sentence.

In June 2014, it was reported that the founder of the $3.7 billion hedge fund Galleon Group Raj Rajaratnam had been making secret payments to certain prisoners at FMC Devens in exchange for special treatment and a top-floor room.

In 2009, former state court judge, federal prosecutor and state Republican Party Chairman Sam Currin, who was serving 70 months at FMC Devens for laundering $1.3 million, was released after his sentence was reduced by more than five years.

In November 2004, Jeffrey Holliday, a maintenance foreman at FMC Devens, was charged with embezzling $90,000 in federal funds.

In 2003, Jose Concepcion Benzor Espinoza, a mentally ill prisoner who had stabbed his nephew to death over the television volume, gouged his own eyes out while waiting to undergo a mental health evaluation at FMC Devens.

In 2001, Lisa Rennie, a communication technician at FMC Devens, gave a cell phone to a prisoner she was having sex with. Rennie was sentenced to six months probation for the contraband, but not charged with the sexual misconduct, nor required to register as a sex offender.

FCI Elkton & FSL Elkton

Federal Correctional Institution Elkton | FCI Elkton

Facilities: FCI Elkton and an adjacent low-security satellite prison.

Facility Address & Contact Information

Federal Correctional Institution Elkton
8730 Scroggs Road
Lisbon, OH 44415

Phone: 330-420-6200
Fax: 330-420-6436
Email: ELK/ExecAssistant@bop.gov

BOP Website: https://www.bop.gov/locations/institutions/elk/
Wikipedia: https://en.wikipedia.org/wiki/Federal_Correctional_Institution,_Elkton
ZCG Website: https://www.prisonerresource.com/resources/federal-prison-profiles/northeast-region-ner/federal-correctional-institution-elkton-fci-elkton/

Inmate Correspondence Address

For FCI Elkton

Inmate Name and Registration Number
FCI Elkton
Federal Correctional Institution
P.O. Box 10
Lisbon, OH 44432

For Satellite Low

Inmate Name and Registration Number
FCI Elkton
Satellite Low
P.O. Box 10
Lisbon, OH 44432

NOTE: Funds cannot be sent directly to federal inmates. See Chapter 1 for more information on sending funds to federal inmates.

Sex: Male

Security Level: Main: Low Security; Satellite Low: Low Security

Location: FCI Elkton is located in northeastern Ohio, less than one hour from Pittsburgh, Youngstown, and Canton.

BOP Region: Northeast Region (NER)

BOP Institution Code: ELK for FCI Elkton

Judicial District: Northern District of Ohio

Medical Care Level: Level 2. See Chapter 2 for more information on Medical Care and Mental Health Care Levels.

Mental Health Care Level: Level 2

Population (as of May 1, 2019): Main: 1,986; Satellite Low: 516

Background: Federal Correctional Institution Elkton is a low-security federal prison in Lisbon, Ohio, which houses male inmates. It was opened in 1997. Federal Satellite Low Elkton is also a low-security federal prison which houses male inmates. It is located adjacent to the main institution.

FCI Elkton is a Sex Offender Management Program (SOMP) facility, which means that the psychology department is more robust, and approximately 40 percent of the inmate population is incarcerated for a current or past sexual offense.

Notable inmates include former boss of the Gambino crime family Peter Gotti (serving 25 years for extortion and conspiracy to commit murder), and Joseph Vas (served six years for corruption and other federal criminal charges).

Media reports indicate that there has been one inmate murdered at and two escapes from the institution.

Housing: Inmates are housed in two- and three-person pods, with a total of six housing units. The satellite low has dormitory-style housing which consists of two- and three-person cubicle. There is a total of four housing units.

Health Services: On-site medical care is available 16 hours a day. Emergency care is available 24 hours a day. Services include intake evaluation, routine health care and dental care, and emergency care. Inmates must submit a triage form to Health Services in order to be scheduled for routine care. The triage form must be submitted between 6:30 and 6:45 a.m. Monday, Tuesday, Thursday, or Friday. Dental sick call is on Tuesday and Friday from 6:30 to 6:45 a.m. Pill and insulin line are held at 6:00 a.m. and 3:00 p.m.

Psychology Services: All inmates are reviewed by Psychology after their arrival at FCI Elkton and FSL Elkton. Various mental health classes and group counseling programs are available. Depending upon need and interest, individual counseling for mental health concerns is also available. Psychiatric medication is prescribed through Health Services. Self-image groups, and other voluntary groups are available for interested inmates. Groups include Cage Your Rage, Re-Entering on Firm Footing, Mentoring, Successful Living, Responsibility for Your Relationships, Attitude - the Choice is Yours, Positive Mental Attitude, Who Moved My Cheese, Memory Power, Seven Habits of Highly Successful People, Self-Discovery, Beat the Street, Anger Management, AA/NA, and Victim Awareness/Impact Panel. A Non-Residential Sex Offender Treatment Program (SOTP-NR) is also available at the satellite low.

Residential Drug Abuse Program (RDAP): FCI Elkton has the Residential Drug Abuse Program (RDAP). The satellite low does not have the Residential Drug Abuse Program (RDAP). Both facilities offer a Drug Abuse Program and the Non-Residential Drug Abuse Program (NR-DAP).

Education Services: FCI Elkton and the satellite low provide GED and English-as-a-Second Language (ESL) programs. A parenting program and Adult Continuing Education classes (ACE) are also available. At the satellite low, current ACE offerings include constitutional law, reentry, basic auto care and maintenance, Spanish, CDL, music theory, practical mythology, and others. High school diplomas and post-secondary degrees are available through paid correspondence programs. Hours of operation are 6:30 to 10:00 a.m., 12:30 to 2:50 p.m., and 5:15 to 8:00 p.m. Monday through Thursday, 6:30 to 10:30 a.m. and 11:30 a.m. to 3:00 p.m. Friday, and 6:00 to 9:30 a.m. and 11:00 a.m. to 3:00 p.m. Sunday.

Advanced Occupational Education: FCI Elkton offers advanced occupational education in Hospitality Management and Building Trades. The satellite low does not offer any advanced occupational education programs.

Vocational Training: FCI Elkton offers vocational training in Culinary Food Preparation and Serving Arts 1 & 2. The satellite low does not offer any vocational training programs.

Apprenticeship: FCI Elkton offers apprenticeships in Computer Operator, Cook, Electrician, and HVAC. The satellite low does not offer any apprenticeship programs.

Library Services: The law library is located in the Education Department and contains a variety of legal reference materials via the TRULINCS Electronic Law Library for use in preparing legal papers. Reference materials include the United States Code Annotated, Federal Reporter, Supreme Court Reporter, Bureau of Prisons Program Statements, institution supplements, indexes, and other legal materials. An inmate law library clerk is available to assist with basic legal research. Typewriters and a copy machine are also available. Legal materials are available to inmates in detention or segregation status, ordinarily through a delivery system or satellite collection. In the leisure library, inmates can check out books, magazines, and newspapers. Movies and DVDs are also available.

UNICOR: The FCI Elkton UNICOR facility is a data services factory which provides proofreading and editing services. FSL Elkton does not have a UNICOR facility.

Commissary: Inmates are permitted to spend up to $360.00 per month. Stamps, telephone credits, over-the-counter medications, items approved by the Chaplain for religious purposes, and items approved by the Supervisor of Education for educational purposes are exempted from the spending limitation. Inmates are allowed to purchase a wide variety of items from the commissary, including food, snacks, candy, soda, drink mixes, electronics, clothing, and shoes. Inmates can shop once a week on their assigned shopping day. Sales are currently conducted on Tuesday, Wednesday, and Thursday from 6:40 a.m. to 12:00 p.m.

Recreation Services: The Recreation Departments at FCI Elkton and FSL Elkton consist of both indoor and outdoor areas. Recreation wellness, leisure time, and health education programs are offered. Inmates can also participate in intramural sports leagues and hobbycraft programs. Group and individual activities are also available. Indoors, inmates have access to billiards, music room, guitars, piano, drums, ellipticals, treadmills, stationary bikes, foosball, ceramics, leathercraft, painting, stair steppers, and group workout classes (e.g., abs, cardio, yoga, over 45, etc.). Outdoors, inmates have access to softball, soccer, handball, racquetball, bocce ball, horseshoes, basketball, volleyball, pickleball, cornhole, and a track. Hours of operation are 8:45 to 10:00 a.m., 11:00 a.m. to 3:00 p.m., and 5:00 to 8:00 p.m. Monday through Friday. On the weekends, hours of operation are 11:00 a.m. to 3:00 p.m. and 5:00 to 8:00 p.m.

Visitation Information: On Sunday and Saturday visitation is held between 8:00 a.m. and 3:00 p.m. On Monday, Thursday, and Friday visitation is held between 5:00 and 9:00 p.m. On federal holidays visitation is held between 8:00 a.m. and 3:00 p.m. See Chapter 1 for more information on visitation.

Prison Politics: This facility has virtually no level of prison politics. According to several inmates, some of the smaller TV rooms are run by racial cars that require clean paperwork in order to enter. The same respondents noted that sex offenders aren't allowed to change the

TV channels in the day rooms, but that's about it for politics. As succinctly put by one inmate, "Politics are minimal. Races mix except for TV rooms."

Level of Violence: There is minimal violence at this prison. According to one respondent, "As long as people mind their own business and treat others with respect, they don't tend to have problems." Another inmate agreed, stating, "Violence is practically non-existent. The yard is very safe."

Vulnerable Populations: Sex offenders, informants, and LGBT inmates can walk the yard. There are many sex offenders on the compound. One inmate stated, "Anyone can walk the yard. There are large populations of sex offenders, gays, and transgenders prisoners."

Good: "The view from rec is amazing. Lots of hills and trees. The guards are fairly laid back if you stay out of the way. Food is pretty decent."

Bad: "The prison is very overcrowded, and the rec yard is small. There are only four computers and phones for 150+ inmates. No restroom in commissary, where you can be stuck for an hour." "Some of the RDAP guys are loudmouth morons." "The mailroom is hardcore against almost all photos if it is not clearly a family photo."

Other Comments: "All in all, this is a safe place."

FSL Prison Politics: This is generally not a political yard. One respondent noted that the only real politics concerns racially segregated TV rooms. Another stated that "there is very little political structure at all amongst the inmates." Another made the observation that "blacks tend to sit with blacks, Hispanics with Hispanics and non-sex offenders with non-sex offenders, but there are no off-limits areas to anyone and plenty of people from each group do talk to other groups."

FSL Level of Violence: There is minimal violence at this prison, with only a fight or so each month. An inmate explained that it is a "very safe compound" and that "you have to go looking for a fight to get in one." Another explained, "even loud verbal threats and arguing is heard less than once per month." Another inmate agreed, stating that there was "no violence" and that the institution was "extremely safe." Another respondent stated, "I have witnessed NO violence in the 9 months that I have been here. I would say that the FSL is very safe." Yet another inmate stated, "Violence is very rare; fairly safe."

FSL Vulnerable Populations: Sex offenders, informants, and LGBT inmates can walk the yard. There is a large population of sex offenders and transgender inmates due to it being a Sex Offender Management Program (SOMP) facility. One inmate stated that "sex offenders are the dominant majority on the compound with three of the four dorms primarily filled with them." He went on to state, "We have transgender and gay inmates as well with no issues." One inmate observed, "Everyone is allowed to walk the yard. There are a lot of gay men here and no one seems to have any problems. There is only one transgender woman here and while I have heard people say things behind her back, a lot of people are nice to her and she seems happy and safe." Another inmate stated that these groups "rarely have any problems."

FSL Good: "Very easy place to do time. Units are very quiet at night and reasonably quiet during the days." "Very safe place for sex offenders." "The staff is laid back and leaves you alone if you leave them alone." "The good thing about the prison is that it is very, very safe. There is no fear of fights or violence, and everyone gets along pretty well. There is a very open and laid-back feeling here." "Very calm and easy place to do time." "No real violence or major arguments." "Very quiet." "Very laid-back place to do time." "While this is a Low, it is treated a lot like a Camp."

FSL Bad: "Boring at times and there just isn't a lot to do in the winter months." "Only complaint is everyone snitches about anything and everything." "There are a lot of drugs, inmate overdosing, and a few cops have been indicted for smuggling." "Lack of programming, vocational opportunities, and recreational opportunities." "Nothing really to do." "We are starting to lose hours for rec and education as staff shortages continue." "While there are a few bad seeds -- both staff and inmates -- they really are nothing to worry about."

FSL Other Comments: "If you have to do time as a sex offender or person who just wants to do their time and go home and not have to deal with all the typical prison BS, FSL Elkton is the place to do your time. People who have been to other SOMP yards say that this is the easiest place to do time." "Generally, this is a crappy place unless you're into K2 or want a cell phone." "Overall, I'm not too unhappy with the situation here." "This is a safe place for sex offenders, gay men, and transgender inmates. There is a very high percentage of sex offenders here. It is a relaxed prison from what I understand. I feel lucky to be here."

In the News: In August 2018, Steven Merlak, the warden of Federal Correctional Institution Elkton, retired.

In December 2010, David A. Goetzke, a prisoner at FCI Elkton, who was sentenced to 235 months for a sex offense involving a minor, was beaten to death by other inmates.

In April 2008, Americ Joslin shot himself in the head as he was being driven to FCI Elkton to begin serving a five-year sentence for fraud.

In 2001, Rafael Herrera and Juan Gonzales Valencia, who were imprisoned at FCI Elkton, escaped.

FCI Fairton

Federal Correctional Institution Fairton | FCI Fairton

Facilities: FCI Fairton with an adjacent minimum-security satellite prison camp and a detention center.

Facility Address & Contact Information

Federal Correctional Institution Fairton
655 Fairton-Millville Road
Fairton, NJ 08320

Phone: 856-453-1177
Fax: 856-453-4015
Email: FAI/ExecAssistant@bop.gov

BOP Website: https://www.bop.gov/locations/institutions/fai/
Wikipedia: https://en.wikipedia.org/wiki/Federal_Correctional_Institution,_Fairton
ZCG Website: https://www.prisonerresource.com/resources/federal-prison-profiles/northeast-region-ner/federal-correctional-institution-fairton-fci-fairton/

Inmate Correspondence Address

For FCI Fairton

Inmate Name and Registration Number
FCI Fairton
Federal Correctional Institution
P.O. Box 420
Fairton, NJ 08320

For Satellite Prison Camp

Inmate Name and Registration Number
FCI Fairton
Satellite Prison Camp
P.O. Box 420
Fairton, NJ 08320

NOTE: Funds cannot be sent directly to federal inmates. See Chapter 1 for more information on sending funds to federal inmates.

Sex: Male

Security Level: Main: Medium Security; Camp: Minimum Security

Location: FCI Fairton is located 50 miles southeast of Philadelphia and 40 miles west of Atlantic City, off State Highway 55 at 655 Fairton-Millville Road.

BOP Region: Northeast Region (NER)

BOP Institution Code: FAI for FCI Fairton

Judicial District: District of New Jersey

Medical Care Level: Level 2. See Chapter 2 for more information on Medical Care and Mental Health Care Levels.

Mental Health Care Level: Level 3

Population (as of May 1, 2019): Main & Detention Center: 983; Camp: 110

Background: Federal Correctional Institution Fairton is a medium-security federal prison in Fairton, New Jersey, which houses male inmates. It was opened in 1990. Federal Correctional Institution Elkton Camp, which also houses male inmates, was opened in 1992 and is located adjacent to the main institution.

Notable inmates include Lucchese crime family member Nicodemo Scarfo, Jr. (serving a 30-year sentence for racketeering, conspiracy, and money laundering).

Media reports indicate that there has been one inmate murdered, two inmates airlifted to a local hospital following assaults, and two inmates taken to the hospital following a brawl involving 40 prisoners. Additionally, at least one guard has been indicted for smuggling contraband into the institution and one guard has committed suicide on prison grounds.

Housing: Inmates are housed in two-, three-, and four-person cells. Two-person cells are the most common. In the camp, inmates live in dormitory-style housing.

Health Services: FCI Fairton provides emergency services, dental sick call (for emergency care only, such as toothaches, abscesses, temporary/permanent fillings, etc.), medical sick call, routine dental treatment, and medications to inmates. While emergency care is available 24 hours a day, inmates must submit triage forms to be evaluated for routine health care needs.

Psychology Services: All inmates are screened by an FCI Fairton Psychology Services staff member during their first month at the institution. Psychology Department classes include Anger Management, Stress Management, HIV/AIDS awareness, basic cognitive skills, and Criminal Lifestyles. Certificates are provided for successful program completion. Inmates may also receive brief counseling, individual psychotherapy, and/or group psychotherapy for emotional, behavioral, and familial problems, or for other personal concerns that may arise. Psychology Services coordinates with Health Services in the area of psychiatric medication.

Residential Drug Abuse Program (RDAP): FCI Fairton has the Residential Drug Abuse Program (RDAP). The camp does not have the Residential Drug Abuse Program (RDAP). Both facilities offer the Drug Abuse Education Class, the Non-Residential Drug Abuse Program (NR-DAP), and self-help programs including Alcoholics Anonymous (AA), Narcotics Anonymous (NA), Thinking Skills, Parenting and Recovery, Nicotine Anonymous, Anger and Recovery, and Living Free.

Education Services: FCI Fairton and the satellite camp provide GED and English-as-a-Second Language (ESL) programs. Social education (Pre-Release Program) and career counseling are also available as are Adult Continuing Education (ACE) classes. ACE classes include smart investing, keyboarding, real estate investing, and CDL. High school diplomas and post-secondary degrees are available through paid correspondence programs.

Advanced Occupational Education: FCI Fairton offers advanced occupational education in Aquaculture and Horticulture. The camp does not offer any advanced occupational education programs.

Vocational Training: No vocational training is offered at FCI Fairton or the camp aside from the vocational training and apprenticeship programs.

Apprenticeship: FCI Fairton offers apprenticeships in Electrician, Gardener, HVAC, Landscape Management Technician, Landscape Technician, Plumber, Quality Assurer, and Building Maintenance Apprenticeship. The camp offers an apprenticeship in Dog Trainer for Hearing Impaired.

Library Services: The FCI Fairton education library is designed to support leisure reading, independent study, and academic programs. Resources include printed materials in various forms, as well as audiotapes, videotapes, listening laboratory media/study kits, reference materials, and a computer laboratory. Books, magazines, newspapers, and movies are also available. The law library provides inmates with access to legal research materials. This is primarily accomplished through the TRULINCS Electronic Law Library. Inmates also have access to a copy machine and electronic typewriters.

UNICOR: The FCI Fairton UNICOR facility produces electronics and plastics.

Commissary: Inmates are permitted to spend up to $360.00 each month for all purchases. The only items that are excluded from this spending limitation are stamps, phone credits, copy cards, over-the-counter medications, and computer/TRULINCS units. The total value of an inmate's accumulated commissary items (excluding special purchases) is limited to the respective monthly spending limit. Inmates tend to use their laundry bags to carry their commissary purchases from the store. Inmates can purchase a variety of items ranging from food, drinks, and cosmetics to shoes, electronics, and clothing.

Recreation Services: Leisure and recreation offerings at FCI Fairton include indoor and outdoor activities, ranging from individualized arts and crafts programs to intramural team sports, such as softball, basketball, volleyball, and others. Physical fitness and weight reduction programs are also offered. The yard also has a weight pile.

Visitation Information: On Sunday, Monday, Friday, and Saturday visitation is held between 8:15 a.m. and 3:15 p.m. On federal holidays visitation is held between 8:15 a.m. and 3:15 p.m. See Chapter 1 for more information on visitation.

Prison Politics: This yard is not very political. According to one respondent, "it's a drop-out yard now."

Level of Violence: There is a minimal level of violence.

Vulnerable Populations: Sex offenders, informants, and LGBT inmates can remain on the yard.

Good: "Nothing is good."

Bad: "Medical is particularly bad."

In the News: In February 2018, Salomon Hernandez-Vega, who was serving a 77-month sentence at the Federal Correctional Institution at Fairton, was found dead in his cell after an "altercation."

In December 2016, a prisoner at FCI Fairton was airlifted to a hospital after suffering head injuries.

In August 2013, FCI Fairton prisoner Alano-Martin was airlifted to a hospital after being assaulted on the recreation yard.

In September 2013, Robert Pyott, a guard at FCI Fairton, was found dead of an apparent self-inflicted gunshot outside the perimeter fence.

In June 2012, Job Brown, a guard at FCI Fairton, pleaded guilty to charges of accepting $3,600 to smuggle tobacco and vitamins into the facility between January and March 2012.

In June 2011, two prisoners at FCI Fairton were taken to the hospital after a fight broke out among 40 prisoners on the recreation yard.

FCI Fort Dix

Federal Correctional Institution Fort Dix | FCI Fort Dix

Facilities: FCI Fort Dix with an adjacent minimum-security satellite prison camp.

Facility Address & Contact Information

Federal Correctional Institution Fort Dix
5756 Hartford & Pointvile Road
Joint Base MDL, NJ 08640

Phone: 609-723-1100
Fax: 609-724-7557
Email: FTD/ExecAssistant@bop.gov

BOP website: https://www.bop.gov/locations/institutions/ftd/
Wikipedia: https://en.wikipedia.org/wiki/Federal_Correctional_Institution,_Fort_Dix
ZCG Website: https://www.prisonerresource.com/resources/federal-prison-profiles/northeast-region-ner/federal-correctional-institution-fort-dix-fci-fort-dix/

Inmate Correspondence Address

For FCI Dix

Inmate Name and Registration Number
FCI Fort Dix
Federal Correctional Institution
P.O. Box 2000
Joint Base MDL, NJ 08640

For Satellite Prison Camp

Inmate Name and Registration Number
FCI Fort Dix
Satellite Prison Camp
P.O. Box 2000
Joint Base MDL, NJ 08640

NOTE: Funds cannot be sent directly to federal inmates. See Chapter 1 for more information on sending funds to federal inmates.

Sex: Male

Security Level: Main: Low Security; Camp: Minimum Security

Location: FCI Fort Dix is located in central New Jersey, approximately 45 minutes east of Philadelphia, off Route 68.

BOP Region: Northeast Region (NER)

BOP Institution Code: FTD for FCI Fort Dix

Judicial District: District of New Jersey

Medical Care Level: Level 2. See Chapter 2 for more information on Medical Care and Mental Health Care Levels.

Mental Health Care Level: Level 2

Population (as of May 1, 2019): Main: 3,714; Camp: 332

Background: Federal Correctional Institution Fort Dix is a low-security federal prison located in Joint Base MDL, New Jersey, which houses male inmates. It was opened in 1992. Federal Correctional Institution Fort Dix Camp, which also houses male inmates, is located adjacent to the main institution.

FCI Fort Dix is the largest single federal prison in the United States by number of inmates. It is divided into two sides: East and West. The facility is known as a free-for-all where cell phones and drugs are rampant among the inmate population. In January 2018 alone, over a thousand cell phones were seized, as were dozens of bottles of liquor, cartons of cigarettes, and over a pound of K2.

Notable inmates include FBI-10-Most-Wanted fugitive Richard Goldberg (serving 20 years for production of child pornography); drug trafficker George Jung (served 19 years); former mayor of Providence (RI) Buddy Cianci (served four years for racketeering); former Detroit mayor Kwame Kilpatrick (serving 28 years for bribery, racketeering, and corruption); "Pharma Bro" Martin Shkreli who is serving seven years for fraud and stock manipulation; and Jamaican kingpin Christopher "Dudas" Coke.

Media reports indicate that at least one guard and one inmate have been indicted for smuggling, one inmate has been indicted in a murder-for-hire scheme, and another inmate who was formerly an elected official was assaulted in general population. In addition, eight inmates who were in prison on child pornography charges were indicted for using contraband cell phones to view and share child pornography.

Housing: Inmates are housed in two-, six, and 12-person rooms. The camp has dormitory-style housing.

Health Services: Health services include sick call, dental sick call, emergency medical services, medications, eye examinations, eyeglasses, physical examinations, preventive health care services, and diagnosis and treatment of chronic infectious diseases. Inmates at FCI Fort Dix can request medical care by attending sick call at 6:30 a.m. Monday, Tuesday, Thursday, or Friday. Emergency care, which is available 24 hours a day, can be obtained by approaching any staff member and asking for assistance. Pill line and insulin line are held in the morning, afternoon, and evening.

Psychology Services: Intake screening, individual counseling, and group services are available to inmates. Classes are also offered at various times throughout the year, including Criminal Thinking Errors, anger management, emotional awareness, HIV/AIDS Awareness, and others. Psychology Services notifies inmates of upcoming treatment programs. Open house is held on Wednesday at 12:30 p.m.

Residential Drug Abuse Program (RDAP): FCI Fort Dix has the Residential Drug Abuse Program (RDAP). The camp does not have the Residential Drug Abuse Program (RDAP). Both facilities offer a Drug Abuse Education class, the Non-Residential Drug Abuse Program (NR-DAP), Alcoholics Anonymous (AA), and Narcotics Anonymous (NA) groups.

Education Services: FCI Fort Dix and the satellite camp provide GED, English-as-a-Second Language (ESL), and parenting programs. Adult Continuing Education (ACE) classes are also available. High school diplomas and post-secondary degrees are available through paid correspondence programs. Mercer Community College also provides in-person, non-credit classes several nights each week. Hours of operation are 7:30 to 10:30 a.m., 12:30 to 3:30 p.m., and 5:30 to 8:00 p.m. Monday through Friday.

Advanced Occupational Education: FCI Fort Dix offers advanced occupational education in Commercial Driver's License.

Vocational Training: FCI Fort Dix offers vocational training in Computers, Electrical (Advanced), Electrical (Basic Level), Horticulture, Hydroponic, Woodworking, and House

Framing. The camp also offers vocational training in Turf Science and Floor Covering and Installation.

Apprenticeship: FCI Fort Dix offers apprenticeships in Alteration Tailor, Building Maintenance Repairer, Cook, HVAC, Industrial Housekeeping, Office Manager, Quality Control, and Teacher's Aide. The camp offers apprenticeships in Horticulturist and Landscaping.

Library Services: The leisure library and law library are open seven days a week. Legal and reference books are for inmates' reference and may not be removed from the law library for any reason. Most legal research is conducted via the TRULINCS Electronic Law Library. Inmates also have access to a copy machine and electronic typewriters. In the leisure library inmates can check out magazines, newspapers, and fiction and nonfiction books.

UNICOR: The FCI Fort Dix UNICOR facility handles recycling activities, services, and the production of clothing and textiles. The camp does not house a UNICOR facility.

Commissary: Inmates are permitted to spend up to $360.00 each month at the commissary on items such as food, drinks, clothing, radios, MP3 players, and shoes. Copy cards, postage stamps, and over-the-counter medications do not count against this spending limit. Depending on their registration number, inmates are assigned a specific day of the week to shop. Shopping is conducted Monday through Thursday, from 12:30 to 2:00 p.m.

Recreation Services: FCI Fort Dix offers both indoor and outdoor recreation areas. Indoor areas include a gymnasium, weightlifting rooms, stationary bicycles and exercise area, TVs, and music rooms. Table games and pool tables are available in all units. The outdoor recreation area consists of a softball field, soccer/football field, handball/racquetball courts, horseshoe pits, volleyball courts, bocce ball lanes, and a track. The hobbycraft program includes art activities (e.g., pencil drawing, pastel work to acrylic, oil painting), music, and leather craft. The music program offers instructional and practical lessons in piano and guitar, and a music room. The outside recreation yard is open year-round. Intramural sports programs include basketball, soccer, volleyball, and softball. Various classes are also available weekly, including spinning, HEAT, abs, and yoga. Hours of operation are 6:30 to 10:30 a.m., 11:30 a.m. to 3:30 p.m., and 5:00 to 8:30 p.m.

Visitation Information: On Sunday, Friday, and Saturday visitation is held between 8:30 a.m. and 3:00 p.m. On Monday visitation is held between 8:30 a.m. and 12:00 p.m. On federal holidays visitation is held between 8:30 a.m. and 3:00 p.m. See Chapter 1 for more information on visitation.

Prison Politics: For the most part, there is a low to moderate level of politics at this facility. This largely depends on the group that an inmate is affiliated with and what their charges are.

Level of Violence: There tends to be a low to moderate level of violence at this facility. According to respondents, this primarily consists of occasional fights. Sometimes vulnerable inmates are targeted. One inmate said, "inmates largely bring violence on themselves by doing stupid stuff, not as a result of politics." Another explained that "violence is mostly within gang issues. . . . I don't think this is the safest place to be, but it's not like a USP or Medium."

Vulnerable Populations: Respondents had mixed beliefs about sex offenders, informants, and LGBT inmates. Some said that all can stay, though they are sometimes targeted, while others felt that informants could not stay. More vulnerable sex offenders are sometimes bullied. As described by one respondent, "Sex offenders are sometimes made to stay out of their own room all day until count time or recall and a lot feel threatened with violence or extortion." Another expressed that "sex offenders are often excluded and shunned here and can and often will be victimized." According to one inmate, "This isn't a great place for these types of people."

Good: "Openness, do what you want to do, more privacy due to less cop presence." "We are able to be outdoors most of the time." "There are people who are not political, and the religious community looks out for each person."

Bad: "Lack of personal area privacy and security due to larger occupancy rooms." "The people sometimes suck, that is people who don't have the same criminal background or type of charges." "The Education Department is really sorry." "Half the time education and rec are closed due to staff shortages." "Often staff turn a blind eye to the abuse of vulnerable populations." "Staff here figure out ways to not work. They are abusive and lazy." "The drug issues and the drinking are quite bad here, and the atmosphere created by staff is very heavy-handed."

Other Comments: "Good place to go as long as you keep to your own business." "If you need a cell phone or some drugs, then this is the place to be. If you want to do your time and not be bothered with such nonsense, then this is the worst prison in the Federal Bureau of Prisons. I would take anywhere, including a penitentiary, rather than this place." "People say this is one of the worst-run places in the Northeast Region. Administratively, I'd say that's true!"

In the News: In June 2018, former Detroit Mayor Kwame Kilpatrick, who was sentenced to 28 years for bribery, racketeering and corruption, was moved to Federal Correctional Institution Fort Dix.

In April 2018, Martin Shkreli, the man who sparked an outrage after boosting the price of the life-saving AIDS drug Daraprim by more than 5,000 percent, was moved to the low-security FCI Fort Dix to serve out the remainder of his seven-year sentence for fraud and stock manipulation.

In April 2018, Paul Anton Wright, a guard at FCI Fort Dix, was arrested and indicted for smuggling suboxone and K2 into the facility.

Also in April 2018, Omar Adonis Guzman-Martinez, serving more than 16 years for drugs at FCI Fort Dix, was sentenced to an additional 30 years for using smuggled cell phones to arrange a 2016 slashing attack on his former girlfriend and the murder of her boyfriend -- while he was still in prison.

In January 2018, a stash of contraband, including 1,046 cell phones, dozens of bottles of liquor, over a pound of K2, and 95 cartons of cigarettes were found in a basement just outside the secure area of FCI Fort Dix. Prisoners allegedly were able to sneak out of the prison unnoticed, pick up contraband from this stash spot, and then sneak back into the prison undetected.

In September 2017, Angel Cordero, a prisoner at FCI Fort Dix, was indicted along with Ohio resident Eduardo Rios Velasquez in a murder-for-hire conspiracy.

In May 2017, eight federal prisoners, including Anthony C. Jeffries, 32, Christopher D. Roffler, 30, Jordan T. Allen, 31, Jacob S. Good, 26, William H. Noble, 52, Brian J. McKay, 47, Charles W. Bush, 38, and Erik M. Smith, 36, who were already serving time for child pornography at the FCI Fort Dix, were charged with using cell phones, memory cards, and cloud storage accounts to possess, sell and distribute child pornography on federal property. On May 8, 2018, Smith was the first to be sentenced. He received 13 additional years in prison.

Also in May 2017, Jamaican drug kingpin Christopher "Dudas" Coke, whose loyalists fought security forces to prevent his arrest and extradition resulting in over 70 people killed in the process, was sent to the low-security FCI Fort Dix.

In December 2016, Phil Hamilton, the first elected Virginia legislator to be convicted of public corruption, was attacked while he was sleeping on Christmas Eve by another prisoner at FCI Fort Dix with a lock in a sock. Following media and congressional attention, Hamilton was moved to FCI Schuylkill.

In 2016, more than 1,500 contraband cell phones were seized from inmates at the facility, which was up from 652 in 2015, and 217 in 2014.

In 2010, a joint FBI and Bureau of Prisons investigation found that Dimorio McDowell, an inmate at FCI Fort Dix, was operating a major identity theft ring from within the prison, along with eight co-conspirators. He was sentenced to an additional 14 years in prison was moved to FCI Terre Haute.

From 1999 to 2003, noted writer and documentarian Seth Ferranti spent about three years out of his 25-year sentence for an LSD conspiracy at FCI Fort Dix, which he considered to be "the best place to play soccer in the entire U.S. prison system."

In 1999, prisoner George Davis filed a lawsuit accusing officials at FCI Fort Dix of ignoring a medical condition that causes him to snore, which put him at risk of injury from other prisoners in his housing unit.

USP Lewisburg

United States Penitentiary Lewisburg | USP Lewisburg

Facilities: USP Lewisburg with an adjacent minimum-security satellite prison camp.

Facility Address & Contact Information

United States Penitentiary Lewisburg
2400 Robert F. Miller Drive
Lewisburg, PA 17837

Phone: 570-523-1251
Fax: 570-522-7745
Email: LEW/ExecAssistant@bop.gov

BOP Website: https://www.bop.gov/locations/institutions/lew/
Wikipedia: https://en.wikipedia.org/wiki/United_States_Penitentiary,_Lewisburg
ZCG Website: https://www.prisonerresource.com/resources/federal-prison-profiles/northeast-region-ner/united-states-penitentiary-lewisburg-usp-lewisburg/

Inmate Correspondence Address

For USP Lewisburg

Inmate Name and Registration Number
USP Lewisburg
U.S. Penitentiary
P.O. Box 1000
Lewisburg, PA 17837

For Satellite Prison Camp

Inmate Name and Registration Number
USP Lewisburg
Satellite Prison Camp
P.O. Box 2000
Lewisburg, PA 17837

NOTE: Funds cannot be sent directly to federal inmates. See Chapter 1 for more information on sending funds to federal inmates.

Sex: Male

Security Level: Main: High Security; Camp: Minimum Security

Location: USP Lewisburg is located in central Pennsylvania, 200 miles north of Washington D.C.; 170 miles north of Philadelphia, Pennsylvania; and 70 miles north of Harrisburg, Pennsylvania. The institution is located approximately 2 miles off of U.S. Route 15.

BOP Region: Northeast Region (NER)

BOP Institution Code: LEW for USP Lewisburg

Judicial District: Middle District of Pennsylvania

Medical Care Level: Level 2. See Chapter 2 for more information on Medical Care and Mental Health Care Levels.

Mental Health Care Level: Level 2

Population (as of May 1, 2019): Main: 771; Camp: 408

Background: United States Penitentiary Lewisburg is a high-security federal prison located in Lewisburg, Pennsylvania, which houses male inmates. It was opened in 1932. United States Penitentiary Lewisburg Camp, which also houses male inmates, is located adjacent to the main institution.

Initially named North Eastern Penitentiary, USP Lewisburg was one of four federal prisons to open in 1932. As of 2009, USP Lewisburg was designated as a Special Management Unit (SMU) intended to house the most violent and disruptive inmates in the Bureau of Prisons. Although most USP Lewisburg inmates are housed in the SMU, there remains a work cadre of approximately 200 inmates in the USP's general population. The Bureau has publicly stated that the SMU is being moved to AUSP Thomson in late 2018, but that institution's activation has been delayed. USP Lewisburg has been the subject of numerous lawsuits concerning conditions of confinement and lack of psychological treatment, as well as the subject of numerous reports detailing a significant level of violence at the facility. A joint investigation by NPR and The Marshall Project found that USP Lewisburg has six times more inmate-on-inmate assaults than other federal prisons.

Media reports indicate that there have been ten inmate murders, at least one suicide, at least one assault which required hospitalization, one unspecified death, one ordered gang hit, and over 800 fights since 2010. At least five inmates have been charged with weapon possession and one guard has been charged with theft of government property. One guard was also killed while transporting an inmate to a hospital.

Ironically, in 2012, CNBC named USP Lewisburg Camp one of the 12 best federal prisons in which to do time.

Housing: Inmates are housed in one and two-person cells, while inmates in the camp are housed in dormitories.

Health Services: USP Lewisburg and the satellite camp treat all medically necessary emergent and non-emergent conditions. Services include preventive health care, emergency treatment, and diagnosis or treatment of chronic infectious diseases, mental health care, and substance abuse treatment. Dental sick call, physical examinations, annual TB screening, influenza vaccination and medications are also available. While emergency care is available 24 hours a day, inmates must submit a sick call form to be evaluated for routine health care needs.

Psychology Services: At USP Lewisburg, every inmate will meet with a psychologist for a brief intake interview to review psychological history. Crisis intervention, available 24 hours a day, is provided to inmates with serious and immediate psychological concerns. For less urgent matters, Psychology Services offers brief counseling. The department has a small self-help library with books and videotapes related to various psychological issues. A psychiatrist is available for inmates who need medication for the management of psychological difficulties. For all but emergency situations, inmates must contact Psychology Services in writing or during an open house period. In the camp, Psychology Services is available for crisis intervention and brief counseling as deemed necessary. Psychology also performs mental health evaluations by staff referral. The Health Services department works with Psychology Services to access need for psychotropic medication. Other services, such as group therapy and mental health related classes, are made available as time permits.

Residential Drug Abuse Program (RDAP): The USP Lewisburg camp has the Residential Drug Abuse Program (RDAP), but the main institution does not. A Drug Education Class, and the Non-Residential Drug Abuse Program (NR-DAP) are also offered.

Education Services: USP Lewisburg provides literacy, GED, and English-as-a-Second Language (ESL) programs. A parenting program and Adult Continuing Education (ACE) classes are also available. High school diplomas and post-secondary degrees are available through paid correspondence programs.

Advanced Occupational Education: USP Lewisburg offers advanced occupational education in Business English/Information, Business English/Reading, Business Math, and Computer Fundamentals. The camp offers Desktop Publishing and Graphic Arts.

Vocational Training: USP Lewisburg and the camp do not offer any vocational training, aside from the advanced occupational education and apprenticeship programs.

Apprenticeship: USP Lewisburg offers apprenticeships in Commercial Housekeeping, Electrical, HVAC, and Plumbing. They camp does not offer any apprenticeship programs.

Library Services: A law and leisure library are available to inmates at USP Lewisburg. The law library provides legal research and legal document preparation. The library is open during the daytime and most evenings. Typewriters are provided for typing legal documents only. Inmate law clerks are on duty to assist in locating legal references. The Education Department maintains a leisure library which contains approximately 4,000 volumes, including magazines, newspapers, periodicals, fiction and nonfiction books, and reference books (i.e. encyclopedias, dictionaries, medical encyclopedias, college listings and synopses, recent volumes of "Books in Print", etc.). The leisure library also contains a well-stocked Hispanic library, including various books, magazines, and newspapers.

UNICOR: USP Lewisburg and the camp house UNICOR facilities.

Commissary: Inmates are allowed to spend up to $360.00 monthly in the commissary. Items include ice cream, food, candy, drink mixes, sodas, and other items. Clothing, shoes, and electronics can also be purchased. Inmates are only allowed to shop on their assigned day each week.

Recreation Services: Leisure and recreation programs at USP Lewisburg include indoor and outdoor areas. Leisure activities include cards, checkers, chess, dominoes, handball, and table tennis. A music room is available for enrolled inmates only. Approved bands may use the music rooms and participate in musical talent shows. The Arts & Crafts Program offers leather craft, ceramics, knitting, crocheting, acrylic painting, glass painting, pencil and ink sketching, and pastel drawing. Craft activities are restricted to the hobby shop area except for pencil and ink sketching and crocheting. These materials are permitted in quarters. A General Public Arts & Crafts Sale is available for marketing products finished through Arts & Crafts. Structured leagues in the Spring/Summer include basketball, bocce ball, horseshoes, sand volleyball, tennis, handball, soccer, and softball. In the Fall/Winter they include chess, dominoes, flag football, ping-pong, pinochle, pool, softball, and spades.

Visitation Information: On Sunday and Saturday visitation is held between 8:00 a.m. and 3:00 p.m. On federal holidays visitation is held between 8:00 a.m. and 3:00 p.m. See Chapter 1 for more information on visitation.

In the News: In June 2018, the Bureau of Prisons announced that the Special Management Unit (SMU) at USP Lewisburg would be moved to AUSP Thomson beginning in late 2018. It was not clear whether several lawsuits alleging mistreatment and torture in the SMU were a factor in the decision.

In May 2018, Richard Haynes, who was a prisoner at USP Lewisburg for less than a week, was found unresponsive in his cell and pronounced dead at a local hospital.

In February 2018, a total of five prisoners at USP Lewisburg were separately indicted for weapons possession: Jose Capriata, Lenelle Gray, Jorge Lopez-Cruz, Michael Moore, and Ernie Joseph Sandoval.

In July 2017, a report by the U.S. Department of Justice's Office of the Inspector General singled out USP Lewisburg in its criticism of the Bureau's failure to track the time prisoners spend in "restrictive housing" and its mistreatment of mentally ill prisoners.

In June 2017, the DC Prisoner's Project of the Washington Lawyer's Committee for Civil Rights and Urban Affairs filed a class action lawsuit against USP Lewisburg arguing that mentally ill prisoners were being given crossword and Sudoku puzzles, as well as coloring books, instead of counseling, treatment and medications.

In 2016, an investigation by NPR and the Marshall Project found that USP Lewisburg had six times as many prisoner-on-prisoner assaults than all other federal prisons, making it one of the most dangerous prisons in America. Federal incident report data showed that guards used pepper spray or restraints in response to 228 in-cell fights. There have been more than 800 recorded prisoner-on-prisoner assaults, with four prisoners killed, since 2010.

In November 2015, a report issued by the District of Columbia Corrections Information Council (CIC), an independent oversight group, noted that excessive force complaints at USP Lewisburg far outweigh those at other federal prisons where DC prisoners are housed. While the DC prisoners alleged unprovoked attacks in areas where there are no cameras, the BOP claimed that none of these incidents were reported or substantiated. The CIC made several recommendations for installing more cameras, reducing the time prisoners are kept in isolation and increasing independent monitoring of staff.

In October 2015, Gerardo Arche-Felix, a prisoner at USP Lewisburg who had been pleading with guards, staff, and his family to get himself moved, was strangled to death in his cell with a bed sheet. Arche's cellmate, Jose Hernandez-Vasquez, was charged with first-degree murder.

In August 2015, Jimmy Barker, a prisoner at USP Lewisburg, died after a fight with his cellmate.

In May 2015, Javier Oswaldo Jovel-Aguilar, a prisoner at USP Lewisburg incarcerated as a result of an expired visa, was sentenced to 30 additional years in prison after beating his cellmate, Arnold Smith, to death. The assault occurred in June 2010.

In April 2015, Renell Wooten, a prisoner at USP Lewisburg, who was only four months from release and expressed worries about being killed before he could get out and see his family again, was found dead in his cell, hanged by a bed sheet.

In March 2015, a prisoner at USP Lewisburg was assaulted by his cellmate, requiring treatment at an outside medical facility.

In 2015, Randall Spade, a prison guard at USP Lewisburg, sued the Department of Justice for negligence upon learning that they released his personal information to prisoners, unredacted, through a standard public records request.

In February 2013, Fred Hagenbuch, a senior officer specialist at USP Lewisburg, pleaded guilty to illegally removing property, such as electrical conduit, fencing and fence posts, from FCI Allenwood.

In late 2012, Andrew Cervantes, a Nuestra Familia gang member who was imprisoned at USP Lewisburg, ordered the murder of an inmate at USP McCreary. The inmate was assaulted and stabbed in March 2013 but survived.

In December 2011, the Pennsylvania Institutional Law Project filed a lawsuit against USP Lewisburg on behalf of prisoner Sebastian Richardson, who suffered being tightly shackled for weeks at a time because he refused to accept violent cellmates.

In July 2010, Adam Martin, a prisoner at USP Lewisburg, was killed after getting into a fight with another prisoner.

Between 2008 and July 2011, there were 272 prisoner-on-prisoner assaults reported at USP Lewisburg.

In January 1998, Jesse Tharp, a guard at USP Lewisburg, was indicted on charges of having indecent contact with a child under the age of eight and a child under the age of five on federal property outside the prison.

In 1997, Lewisburg prisoners Abdul Salaam and Frank Joyner were stabbed to death in a fight that left four other prisoners injured.

In October 1987, Robert F. Miller, a senior officer at USP Lewisburg, was shot and killed in an ambush as he and three other guards were transporting a prisoner to the hospital.

FCI Loretto

Federal Correctional Institution Loretto | FCI Loretto

Facilities: FCI Loretto with an adjacent minimum-security satellite prison camp.

Facility Address & Contact Information

Federal Correctional Institution Loretto
772 St. Joseph Street
Loretto, PA 15940

Phone: 814-472-4140
Fax: 814-472-6046
Email: LOR/ExecAssistant@bop.gov

BOP Website: https://www.bop.gov/locations/institutions/lor/
Wikipedia: https://en.wikipedia.org/wiki/Federal_Correctional_Institution,_Loretto
ZCG Website: https://www.prisonerresource.com/resources/federal-prison-profiles/northeast-region-ner/federal-correctional-institution-loretto-fci-loretto/

Inmate Correspondence Address

For FCI Loretto

Inmate Name and Registration Number
FCI Loretto
Federal Correctional Institution
P.O. Box 1000
Loretto, PA 15940

For Satellite Prison Camp

Inmate Name and Registration Number
FCI Loretto
Satellite Prison Camp
P.O. Box 1000
Loretto, PA 15940

NOTE: Funds cannot be sent directly to federal inmates. See Chapter 1 for more information on sending funds to federal inmates.

Sex: Male

Security Level: Main: Low Security; Camp: Minimum Security

Location: FCI Loretto is located in southwest Pennsylvania between Altoona and Johnstown, 90 miles east of Pittsburg, off Route 22, between I-80 and the Pennsylvania Turnpike via Route 220.

BOP Region: Northeast Region (NER)

BOP Institution Code: LOR is FCI Loretto

Judicial District: Western District of Pennsylvania

Medical Care Level: Level 2. See Chapter 2 for more information on Medical Care and Mental Health Care Levels.

Mental Health Care Level: Level 2

Population (as of May 1, 2019): Main: 914; Camp: 91

Background: Federal Correctional Institution Loretto is a low-security federal prison in Loretto, Pennsylvania, which houses male inmates. It was opened in 1984. Federal Correctional Institution Loretto Camp, which also houses male inmates, is located adjacent to the main institution.

FCI Loretto was formerly a Catholic seminary, which was built in 1960.

Notable inmates include Robert Kidane Phillipos (obstructed justice in connection with the Boston Marathon bombing); acting boss of the Patriarca crime family Anthony DiNunzio (served six years for racketeering); former New York State Assemblyman William Boyland, Jr. (convicted of extortion, bribery, and corruption charges); and Rafaello Follieri (convicted of fraud and money laundering).

Media reports indicate that at least three inmates have been indicted for drug possession and that at least two inmates from the camp have escaped.

Housing: Inmates are housed in four-, six-, and 24-person rooms (North and South units), as well as dormitories, which are divided into four- and six-person cubicles (Central Unit).

Health Services: Sick call, dental sick call, emergency treatment, medications, chronic care, eyeglasses, physical examinations, health education on infectious diseases, HIV testing, and annual TB testing are provided at FCI Loretto. Medical and dental sick call are held at 6:30 to 7:00 a.m. Monday, Tuesday, Thursday, and Friday.

Psychology Services: Psychology services include an initial psychological screening, individual and/or group counseling, crisis intervention, psycho-educational classes, self-help, and supportive services, or referral to Health Services for psycho-pharmacological medication. Groups include anger management, Smart Recovery, and HIV/AIDS Awareness. Self-help books and videos are available to the inmate population. Notices of upcoming groups are posted on inmate bulletin boards. Open house is conducted between 7:30 and 8:30 a.m. on Mondays.

Residential Drug Abuse Program (RDAP): FCI Loretto and the camp do not have the Residential Drug Abuse Program (RDAP), but referrals can be made to institutions which do offer RDAP. Both facilities provide the Drug Abuse Education Course, the Non-Residential Drug Abuse Program (NR-DAP), Alcohol Anonymous (AA), and Narcotics Anonymous (NA).

Education Services: FCI Loretto provides GED and English-as-a-Second Language (ESL) programs. Adult Basic Education is a program that is available for inmates who score lower than the fifth-grade level on the Test of Adult Basic Education (TABE). Adult Continuing Education (ACE) courses and a parenting program are also available. Current ACE offerings include Evolution, History of Western Film, and Creative Writing. High school diplomas and post-secondary programs are available through paid correspondence programs. Hours of operation are 7:00 a.m. to 2:30 p.m. Sunday, 6:00 a.m. to 4:00 p.m. Monday through Friday, and 6:00 a.m. to 8:00 p.m. Tuesday, Wednesday, and Thursday, excluding meals and counts.

Advanced Occupational Education: FCI Loretto offers advanced occupational education in Automotive Repair. The camp offers CDL, and both offer Personal Fitness Trainer.

Vocational Training: FCI Loretto offers training in Fiber Optics, Retail Sales, and Customer Service.

Apprenticeship: Both facilities offers apprenticeships in Cook and Teacher Aide.

Library Services: Both a leisure and law library are available to inmates at FCI Loretto. The leisure library contains a wide variety of newspapers, magazines, listening and video tapes, and fiction and nonfiction books. There is a wide variety of reference material. The law library is electronic and provides all of the required resource material. Inmates are permitted to be in the leisure and law library during their off-duty hours only. Typewriters and a copy machine are also available for inmate use.

UNICOR: FCI Loretto does not have a UNICOR facility.

Commissary: Inmates are allowed to spend up to $360.00 monthly in the commissary on items such as food, candy, snacks, drinks, clothing, shoes, and electronics (e.g., watches, radios, MP3 players, etc.). Copy cards, over-the-counter medications, and postage stamps do not count against the spending limit. Inmates are allowed to shop once a week on their assigned day. Sales are conducted after breakfast and after lunch.

Recreation Services: The recreation facilities at FCI Loretto provide inmates with both indoor and outdoor activities. The recreation center includes three pool tables, treadmills, ellipticals, a hobbycraft room (ceramics kiln, painting, leathercraft), a band room (piano and sound system), and a weight pile in a separate building. The yard has a full-sized football field, bocce ball, horseshoes, softball diamond, and a 1/3-mile track. Sports leagues include ultimate frisbee, soccer, softball, flag football, basketball, pool, bridge, and spades. Hobbycraft classes include origami, painting, drawing, card-making, leathercraft, digital photography, calligraphy, and crochet. Exercise classes include aerobic (beginner and advanced), yoga, nutrition, and "big boy" fitness. The music program includes individual and band practice slots, concerts, and lessons (guitar, bass, drums, music theory, and violin).

Visitation Information: On Sunday, Friday, and Saturday visitation is held between 8:15 a.m. and 2:15 p.m. On federal holidays visitation is held between 8:15 a.m. and 2:15 p.m. See Chapter 1 for more information on visitation.

Prison Politics: There is a low level of prison politics. Inmates are not required to be part of a car in order to stay. One respondent expressed, "This is not so much a political yard, as it is a bigoted one."

Level of Violence: There is a very low level of violence at this facility. One inmate reports a "fight every couple of months." Another respondent stated, "I'd rate the safety level as high." Another inmate explained, "There is very little violence, but MUCH barking. Most people are bullies here, but essentially afraid to get jammed up and get transferred."

Vulnerable Populations: Sex offenders, informants, and LGBT inmates are allowed to walk the yard. One respondent stated that "sex offenders have issues with extortion or not being allowed to stay in their rooms during the day," where they can sit in the chow hall, and have "restricted access to the weight pile and TV rooms." Another inmate observed that "there is a large and supportive LGBT community here, including a few transgenders who are currently transitioning. While there is some minor name calling, they really don't get hassled." Another inmate stated that "Sex offenders are completely ostracized and oppressed here. They are not allowed to be in their own assigned cell most of the day. They are not allowed to be in the TV room or even lay in their beds if they are sick." He continued, "They are bullied, and staff are aware of this but do nothing to intervene or prevent the situation."

Good: "Decent, clean facility." "There are plenty of benches to sit out at recreation." "Tons of musical instruments and a great band room." "Great selection in the library."

Bad: "Some staff apathy. The mail room is increasingly strict, now banning any colored envelopes or stickers from coming in. The mail room is also very prudish when it comes to erotica or art books." "The way staff and inmates treat sex offenders." "The nasty, disrespectful way about half of the staff talks to many of the inmates." "Some of the dorms don't have any air conditioning."

In the News: In June 2018, James Hickey, who was sentenced to 18 months in a fraud case involving more than a dozen people including former Mayor Ed Pawlowski and ex-mayor of Reading Vaughn Spencer, was designated to serve out his sentence at Federal Correctional Institution Loretto.

In August 2017, Edward R. Harris, a prisoner at FCI Loretto, was federally indicted for the possession of marijuana while in prison.

In June 2017, Christopher D. Rarick and Edwin Manuel Guzman, prisoners at FCI Loretto, were separately indicted for the possession of buprenorphine, a contraband opiate.

In February 2017, Charles Mack, a prisoner who was recently released from FCI Loretto, was pursuing a lawsuit accusing Jeffrey Stevens, trust fund supervisor; Douglas Roberts, commissary materials handler; and Samuel Veslosky, warehouse foreman, of harassment over his religious beliefs, leading to the loss of his prison job in the commissary.

Camp in the News: In March 2005, former Connecticut Governor John G. Rowland, who resigned amidst an investigation into corruption, was sentenced to a year and a day in federal prison. He served his period of incarceration at Federal Correctional Institution Loretto Camp.

In November 2002, Edward Calloway and another unidentified prisoner slipped away from FCI Loretto Camp to visit their girlfriends in a nearby motel. They were caught returning to the camp and charged with escape.

FCI McKean

Federal Correctional Institution McKean | FCI McKean

Facilities: FCI McKean with an adjacent minimum-security satellite prison camp.

Facility Address & Contact Information

Federal Correctional Institution McKean
6975 Route 59
Lewis Run, PA 16738

Phone: 814-362-8900
Fax: 814-363-6821
Email: MCK/ExecAssistant@bop.gov

BOP Website: https://www.bop.gov/locations/institutions/mck/
Wikipedia: https://en.wikipedia.org/wiki/Federal_Correctional_Institution,_McKean
ZCG Website: https://www.prisonerresource.com/resources/federal-prison-profiles/northeast-region-ner/federal-correctional-institution-mckean-fci-mckean/

Inmate Correspondence Address

For FCI McKean

Inmate Name and Registration Number
FCI McKean
Federal Correctional Institution
P.O. Box 8000
Bradford, PA 16701

For Satellite Prison Camp

Inmate Name and Registration Number
FCI McKean
Satellite Prison Camp
P.O. Box 8000
Bradford, PA 16701

NOTE: Funds cannot be sent directly to federal inmates. See Chapter 1 for more information on sending funds to federal inmates.

Sex: Male

Security Level: Main: Medium Security; Camp: Minimum Security

Location: FCI McKean is located in northwest Pennsylvania between Bradford and Kane, 90 miles south of Buffalo, off Route 59, one-fourth mile east of the intersection of State Route 59 and U.S. Route 219.

BOP Region: Northeast Region (NER)

BOP Institution Code: MCK for FCI McKean

Judicial District: Western District of Pennsylvania

Medical Care Level: Level 1. See Chapter 2 for more information on Medical Care and Mental Health Care Levels.

Mental Health Care Level: Level 1

Population (as of May 1, 2019): Main: 870; Camp: 220

Background: Federal Correctional Institution McKean is a medium-security federal prison in Lewis Run, Pennsylvania, which houses male inmates. It was opened in 1989. Federal Correctional Institution McKean Camp, which also houses male inmates, is located adjacent to the main institution.

Notable inmates include former acting boss of the Colombo crime family Alphonse Persico (serving a life sentence for murder); Philadelphia politician Chaka Fattah (sentenced to ten years for racketeering); actor Wesley Snipes (served two years at the camp for failing to file tax returns); and MLB pitcher Denny McLain (served six years for money laundering, conspiracy, theft, and mail fraud).

Media reports indicate that one inmate was indicted for assaulting a guard, two prisoners were indicted for drug conspiracy, at least one prisoner was charged with drug possession, and one guard was charged with a weapons violation after getting drunk at home and trying to shoot off his wedding ring. In addition, at least one inmate has escaped from the prison.

Housing: Inmates are housed in two-, four-, six-, eight-, and twelve-person cells. Inmates at the camp are housed in dorms, which are divided into two-person cubicles.

Health Services: Health services include medical and dental sick call, chronic care management, routine dental care, medical and dental emergency care for injuries and sudden illness, medications, age-appropriate preventive care to promote optimal health and functional status, restorative care to promote achievable functional status, long-term care, and end-of-life care. Inmates can request medical care by attending sick call between 7:30 and 8:00 a.m. on weekdays. Emergency medical care is available 24 hours a day. Pill line is conducted at 6:30 a.m. and 4:30 p.m.

Psychology Services: Psychology services include screening, assessment and treatment of mental health problems, individual and/or group counseling, psycho-educational classes, self-help and supportive services, and referral to Health Services for medical treatment of a mental illness. Inmates who are new or who have been previously identified as having mental health or drug abuse programming needs are scheduled for an interview with Psychology Services staff to review their history and identify their programming needs. Psychological programs offered at FCI McKean include Anger Management, Emotional Self-Regulation, Criminal Thinking, and Seeking Safety. Inmates can request placement in these programs by submitting an Inmate Request to Staff form.

Residential Drug Abuse Program (RDAP): FCI McKean does not have the Residential Drug Abuse Program (RDAP). The camp has the Residential Drug Abuse Program (RDAP). Both facilities offer the Drug Education Course and the Non-Residential Drug Abuse Program (NR-DAP).

Education Services: FCI McKean provides literacy, GED, and English-as-a-Second Language (ESL) programs. Incentive awards are provided to recognize inmates making satisfactory progress and successfully completing the literacy (i.e., GED and ESL) program. Inmates may also receive incentives for progressing to various levels in the GED or ESL programs. Graduation ceremonies recognize GED, ESL, and Occupational Education completions. Adult Continuing Education (ACE) classes and a parenting program are also available. High school diplomas and post-secondary degrees are available through paid correspondence programs.

Advanced Occupational Education: Advanced occupational education classes are offered at FCI McKean in Culinary Arts and NCCER Carpentry Level 1 & 2. The camp offers Teacher's Aide.

Vocational Training: FCI McKean and the satellite camp do not offer any vocational training aside from the advanced occupational education and apprenticeship programs.

Apprenticeship: FCI McKean offers apprenticeships in Career Technician, Cook, Electrician, Housekeeping, and Teacher's Aide. The camp does not offer any apprenticeship programs.

Library Services: FCI McKean offers both a leisure and law library to inmates. The leisure library offers magazines, newspapers, fiction, nonfiction, and reference books. An interlibrary loan program is available. DVD movies are also available for viewing. Inmates are provided access to legal materials and an opportunity to prepare legal documents through the use of the TRULINCS Electronic Law Library. A copy machine is available to reproduce materials needed for research. Electric typewriters are also available for inmate use.

UNICOR: FCI McKean does not have a UNICOR factory.

Commissary: Inmates are allowed to spend $360.00 monthly in the commissary on their assigned shopping days. Clothing, shoes, electronics, food, drink mixes, and other items are available for purchase. Spending limits on certain items may apply. In order to shop, inmates must go to the commissary, turn in their order form, and wait for their order to be filled. Sales are conducted at 6:00 a.m. and 10:30 a.m.

Recreation Services: Leisure activities at FCI McKean include organized and informal games, sports, table games, hobbycrafts, music programs, intramural activities, social and cultural organizations, and movies. Art activities include painting and sketches using traditional methods (e.g., oils, pastels, crayons, pencils, inks, and charcoal). Hobbycraft activities include ceramics, leatherwork, models, clay, mosaics, crochet, knitting, sculptures, woodworking, lapidary, and others. Wellness programs include screening, assessments, goal setting, fitness/nutrition plans, and counseling. Indoors, inmates have access to leathercraft, art room, band room, tables, musical instruments, TVs, stationary bikes, and ellipticals. Outdoors, inmates have access to softball, soccer, handball, pull-up bars, and a track.

Visitation Information: On Sunday and Saturday visitation is held between 8:15 a.m. and 3:00 p.m. On Friday visitation is held between 8:00 a.m. and 12:00 p.m. On federal holidays visitation is held between 8:15 a.m. and 3:00 p.m. See Chapter 1 for more information on visitation.

Prison Politics: This is a very political yard. Inmates must be part of a car or gang in order to stay.

Level of Violence: There is a moderate level of violence at this facility. Inmates report fights being common.

Vulnerable Populations: Sex offenders and LGBT inmates can't stay on the yard.

Good: "I can't think of a good thing about it except for the trees."

Bad: "Everything. Nothing is good." "No air conditioning."

Other Comments: "Don't go there. Unless you like it hot or like hard, political time, don't go."

Camp Prison Politics: There are no politics at this prison.

Camp Level of Violence: Inmates report virtually no violence. According to one inmate, "There is maybe one or two fights a year."

Camp Vulnerable Populations: While BOP policy prohibits sex offenders from being placed at a camp, informants and LGBT inmates do not have any problems staying at this facility.

Camp Bad: "Health Services is overwhelmed."

In the News: In January 2018, Rogelio Muniz-Valdez, a prisoner at Federal Correctional Institution McKean, was sentenced to an additional year and a day in prison for throwing urine at a guard in March 2017.

In July 2017, Malinda Penezich was indicted for an undisclosed incident at FCI McKean.

In May 2017, Josean Reyes-Pagan, a prisoner at FCI McKean, was convicted of possession of smuggled drugs.

In March 2013, Jose Cardenas-Covarrubias and Donaciano Contreras-Monje, prisoners at the FCI McKean, were charged, along with two outside accomplices, with organizing the sale of 13 pounds of methamphetamine to undercover police officers.

Also in March 2013, Alfredo Malespini III, a guard at FCI McKean, shot his own finger trying to get his wedding ring off in a drunken argument with his wife and was subsequently charged with a weapons violation and disorderly conduct.

In November 2017, Ghassan Saleh, a prisoner who escaped from FCI McKean in June 1997, was recaptured after U.S. Marshals found out he was scheduled to return to the U.S. on a flight from his home country of Lebanon.

In 2005, prisoners at FCI McKean protested a prison smoking ban with a work strike, resulting in a temporary lockdown.

Camp in the News: In December 2010, actor Wesley Snipes reported to Federal Correctional Institution McKean Camp to begin serving a three-year sentence for failing to file his taxes.

MCC New York

Metropolitan Correctional Center New York | MCC New York

Facility Address & Contact Information

Metropolitan Correctional Center New York
150 Park Row
New York, NY 10007

Phone: 646-836-6300
Fax: 646-836-7751
Email: NYM/ExecAssistant@bop.gov

BOP Website: https://www.bop.gov/locations/institutions/nym/
Wikipedia: https://en.wikipedia.org/wiki/Metropolitan_Correctional_Center,_New_York
ZCG Website: https://www.prisonerresource.com/resources/federal-prison-profiles/northeast-region-ner/metropolitan-correctional-center-new-york-mcc-new-york/

Inmate Correspondence Address

Inmate Name and Registration Number
MCC New York
Metropolitan Correctional Center
150 Park Row
New York, NY 10007

NOTE: Funds cannot be sent directly to federal inmates. See Chapter 1 for more information on sending funds to federal inmates.

Sex: Male and Female

Security Level: Administrative Security (Multiple Security Levels)

Location: MCC New York is located in downtown Manhattan, adjacent to Foley Square and across the street from the federal courthouse.

BOP Region: Northeast Region (NER)

BOP Institution Code: NYM for MCC New York

Judicial District: Southern District of New York

Medical Care Level: Level 2. See Chapter 2 for more information on Medical Care and Mental Health Care Levels.

Mental Health Care Level: Level 2

Population (as of May 1, 2019): 797

Background: Metropolitan Correctional Center New York is an administrative-security federal prison in New York, New York, which houses both male and female inmates. It was opened in 1975.

MCC New York is a 12-story high-rise housing primarily pre-trial and pre-sentence detainees, as well as holdover inmates. Most prisoners held at MCC New York have cases pending in the United States District Court for the Southern District of New York. The facility also holds prisoners serving brief sentences. According to the *Los Angeles Times*, the prison is often referred to as the "Guantanamo of New York," and *The New York Times* reported that its administrative segregation units have severe security measures. Amnesty International stated that the conditions of MCC New York "fall short of international standards for humane treatment."

Numerous high-profile individuals have been held at MCC New York during court proceedings, including Gambino crime family bosses John Gotti and Jackie D'Amico, Bonanno crime family member John Zancocchio, Turkish gold trader Reza Zarrab, drug kingpin Frank Lucas, Ponzi scheme mastermind Bernard Madoff, terrorists Omar Abdel Rahman and Ramzi Yousef, weapons trafficker Victor Bout, and multi-U.S. embassy bomber Ahmed Khalfan Ghailani. In January 2017, after being extradited to the United States, Mexican drug lord Joaquin "el Chapo" Guzman was housed in the facility.

Media reports indicate that one guard was indicted for raping a detainee, a lieutenant was charged with beating a handcuffed detainee, three guards were indicted for smuggling drugs into the institution, and one guard was indicted for applying for fraudulent unemployment benefits. In addition, at least one inmate who was assaulted required hospitalization and at least one inmate has been murdered at the facility.

Housing: Inmates are housed in one of 10 housing units. Two of the housing units have multiple 20-person dormitories, while the other eight consist of two-person cells.

Health Services: Health care includes general medical and dental treatment. Emergency medical care is available 24 hours a day. Inmates must submit sick call forms for routine health care needs.

Psychology Services: Psychology services include screening for signs of suicide and referral to the Psychology Department to address emergency concerns.

Residential Drug Abuse Program (RDAP): MCC New York does not have the Residential Drug Abuse Program (RDAP). The Drug Education Class and the Non-Residential Drug Abuse Program (NR-DAP) are available.

Education Services: GED courses are available to inmates at MCC New York.

Advanced Occupational Education: MCC New York does not offer any advanced occupational education programs.

Vocational Training: MCC New York does not offer any vocational training programs.

Apprenticeship: MCC New York does not offer any apprenticeship programs.

Library Services: Inmates at MCC New York are provided access to legal materials and an opportunity to prepare legal documents through the use of the TRULINCS Electronic Law Library. The library also provides a wide range of reading materials for educational and recreational purposes, including magazines and newspapers.

UNICOR: MCC New York does not house a UNICOR facility.

Commissary: Inmates are allowed to spend up to $360.00 on commissary purchases monthly. Popular items include food, beverages, radios, and other items.

Recreation Services: Inmates at MCC New York have limited access to recreation facilities. Most of the activities occur inside the facility, including watching movies.

Visitation Information: Visitation is held between 8:00 a.m. and 2:30 p.m. On federal holidays visitation is held between 8:00 a.m. and 2:30 p.m. Visitation is further segmented based on each inmate's housing unit. On Monday, Z-A (9 South/SHU) and B-A (Unit 2 - Females) Units are allowed visitation. On Tuesday, K-S Unit (11 South) has visitation. On Wednesday, G-S (7 South) and G-N (7 North) Units have visitation. On Thursday, I-N (9 North) and E-N (5 North) Units have visitation. On Friday, K-N Unit (11 North) and K-S (11 South) Units have visitation. And on Saturday and Sunday E-S Unit (5 South - CADRE) has visitation. See Chapter 1 for more information on visitation.

In the News: In August 2018, John Zancocchio of the Bonanno crime family, whose lawyer persuaded a federal judge to release him prior to trial because the food at Metropolitan Correctional Center New York "dangerously exasperates [sic] his condition," was caught on camera buying a hot dog from a Manhattan street vendor.

In April 2018, Victor Casado, a guard at MCC New York, was charged with taking more than $45,000 in bribes from wealthy Turkish gold trader Reza Zarrab to smuggle cell phones, alcohol and other contraband into the facility for him.

In February 2018, retired cop Nicholas Tartaglione, who was charged with the kidnapping and murder of Martin Santos-Luna, Urbano Morales-Santiago, Miguel Sosa-Luna and Hector Gutierrez, was attacked, hospitalized for two-and-a-half-weeks, and returned to solitary confinement at MCC New York.

In 2018, the Mexican drug lord known as El Chapo was held in the most secure section of MCC New York while awaiting trial.

In September 2017, civil rights attorney Andrew Laufer sued the Bureau of Prisons, alleging that after prisoner Robert Grant was beaten to death at MCC New York in May 2015, prison staff tried to cover it up, telling the man's family that he died of an overdose.

In January 2017, activist Martin Gottesfeld, who was in solitary confinement at MCC New York for his involvement in a cyber-attack of Boston health care facilities in defense of a patient, wrote an open letter to the Attorney General, the Department of Justice's Office of the Inspector General, the Bureau of Prisons' Acting Director, and the *Huffington Post* alleging prisoner mistreatment and inadequate medical care.

In June 2016, Andrew Kessler, a guard at MCC New York, was arrested and charged with applying for nearly $14,000 worth of fraudulent unemployment benefits.

In May 2016, Rudell Mullings, a guard at MCC New York, was sentenced to seven years in prison for forcibly raping a female prisoner.

In February 2016, *The Intercept* reported that MCC New York's pre-trial isolation practices are worse than Guantanamo, according to at least one prisoner who has been held at both facilities and an attorney who has represented clients at both locations.

In 2014, a report by Human Rights Watch noted the brutal nature of life and the extreme conditions of isolation at MCC New York.

In 2011, Amnesty International reported that the conditions of MCC New York "fall short of international standards for humane treatment."

In June 2009, Ahmed Khalfan Ghailani, who was being held at Guantanamo Bay since September 2006 for the bombings of U.S. embassies and the murder of 224 people, was transferred to MCC New York to face criminal prosecution.

In 2005, Edwin Williams, a guard at MCC New York, was arrested for taking thousands of dollars in bribes to smuggle contraband, such as marijuana, tobacco, and food to prisoners.

In 2003, Edward Mulroney, a lieutenant at MCC New York, beat a prisoner who was handcuffed and held down by two other guards, resulting in fractures to the prisoner's eye socket and cheekbone.

In 1998, Roy Thomas, a guard at MCC New York, was charged with conspiring with a jailed drug dealer to steal 100 kg of cocaine from a rival drug dealer and then sell the drugs himself. Thomas was also accused of taking $1,500 from the jailed drug dealer to smuggle in contraband.

FCI Otisville

Federal Correctional Institution Otisville | FCI Otisville

Facilities: FCI Otisville with an adjacent minimum-security satellite prison camp, and a detention center.

Facility Address & Contact Information

Federal Correctional Institution Otisville
Two Mile Drive
Otisville, NY 10963

Phone: 845-386-6700
Fax: 845-386-6727
Email: OTV/ExecAssistant@bop.gov

BOP Website: https://www.bop.gov/locations/institutions/otv/
Wikipedia: https://en.wikipedia.org/wiki/Federal_Correctional_Institution,_Otisville
ZCG Website: https://www.prisonerresource.com/resources/federal-prison-profiles/northeast-region-ner/federal-correctional-institution-otisville-fci-otisville/

Inmate Correspondence Address

For FCI Otisville

Inmate Name and Registration Number
FCI Otisville
Federal Correctional Institution
P.O. Box 1000
Otisville, NY 10963

For Satellite Prison Camp

Inmate Name and Registration Number
FCI Otisville
Satellite Prison Camp
P.O. Box 1000
Otisville, NY 10963

NOTE: Funds cannot be sent directly to federal inmates. See Chapter 1 for more information on sending funds to federal inmates.

Sex: Male

Security Level: Main: Medium Security; Camp: Minimum Security

Location: FCI Otisville is located in the southeastern part of New York, near the Pennsylvania and New Jersey borders; 70 miles northwest of New York City (NYC).

BOP Region: Northeast Region (NER)

BOP Institution Code: OTV for FCI Otisville

Judicial District: Southern District of New York

Medical Care Level: Level 2. See Chapter 2 for more information on Medical Care and Mental Health Care Levels.

Mental Health Care Level: Level 2

Population (as of May 1, 2019): Main: 732; Camp: 111

Background: Federal Correctional Institution Otisville is a medium-security federal prison in Otisville, New York, which houses male inmates. It was opened in 1980. Federal Correctional Institution Otisville Camp, which also houses male inmates, is located adjacent to the main institution.

FCI Otisville is based upon an open campus-style layout.

Notable inmates include Shalom Weiss (sentenced to 845 years for fraud, racketeering, and money laundering); Sholom Rubashkin (serving 27 years for fraud); and former financial advisor Kenneth Ira Starr (serving a seven-year sentence for fraud and money laundering).

Media reports indicate that at least one inmate has died from unknown causes and at least one guard has been indicted for sexually assaulting inmates and assisting them in escaping from the institution.

In 2012, CNBC named FCI Otisville and FCI Otisville Camp two of the 12 best federal prisons in which to do time. And in 2009, *Forbes* magazine named FCI Otisville one of the ten cushiest federal prisons in America.

Housing: Inmates are housed in two-person cells. Inmates in the camp are housed in cubes and dormitories, which are divided into two-person cubicles.

Health Services: Routine health care, physical examinations, emergency care, medications, eyeglasses, and dental services are available to inmates at FCI Otisville. Sick call is held Monday,

Tuesday, Thursday, and Friday at 7:00 a.m. Pill line is held during meals, and insulin line is conducted before breakfast and dinner. All inmates at the camp who wish to be seen for sick call must report to the common area during designated hours. In emergency situations, inmates must let the unit officer, unit team, or any other staff know, who will then contact Health Services.

Psychology Services: FCI Otisville psychology services include intake screening for designated inmates, evaluations requested by staff or the court, group and/or individual treatment, and crisis intervention. Current groups include anger management, criminal thinking, victim impact, and Doing Time with the Right Mind. Some individuals may be evaluated as a result of court orders, parole commission requests, or Unit Team referrals. Psychology Services also conducts halfway house interviews. In the camp, psychologists are available for individual and group psychotherapy. Inmates interested in services may submit an Inmate Request to Staff Member to Psychology Services. Mental health services are offered in areas of behavioral and emotional problems.

Residential Drug Abuse Program (RDAP): FCI Otisville and the camp do not have the Residential Drug Abuse Program (RDAP), but referrals can be made to institutions which do provide RDAP. A Drug Education Program, the Non-Residential Treatment Program (NR-DAP), Alcoholics Anonymous (AA) and Narcotics Anonymous (NA) are available.

Education Services: FCI Otisville provides literacy, GED, Spanish GED, and English-as-a-Second Language (ESL) programs. Parenting and Adult Continuing Education (ACE) classes are also available. Current ACE classes include astronomy, basic math business start-up, real estate, and forklift operation. High school diplomas and post-secondary degrees are available through paid correspondence programs.

Advanced Occupational Education: FCI Otisville offers advanced occupational education in Computer Skills, Floor Care Maintenance, Custodial Technician, Horticulture/Landscape, Textiles, and Production.

Vocational Training: FCI Otisville and the camp do not offer any vocational training programs.

Apprenticeship: FCI Otisville and the camp do not offer any apprenticeship programs.

Library Services: FCI Otisville offers both a leisure and law library. The leisure library contains reference materials, encyclopedias in English and Spanish, newspapers, videotapes, and periodicals. The law library provides access to legal materials and an opportunity to prepare legal documents through the use of the TRULINCS Electronic Law Library. A copying machine is available to reproduce materials needed for research. Electric typewriters are also available for inmate use.

UNICOR: FCI Otisville and the satellite camp do not have UNICOR facilities.

Commissary: A spending limitation of $360.00 per month enforced. Items exempt from the monthly limit are postage stamps, copy cards, over-the-counter medications, and TRUFONE credits. Commissary purchases can be made one time per week in accordance with the scheduled shopping days. Shopping is conducted Monday through Thursday at 6:30 to 8:30 a.m. and 11:00 a.m. to 12:30 p.m. A wide variety of items are available for inmate purchase. Larger purchases, such as shoes and sweat suits, are made on Fridays.

Recreation Services: Recreation and leisure activities at FCI Otisville include a variety of options. Weights, cardio equipment, bocce ball, soccer, flag football, cards, pool tables, movies, horseshoes, softball court, handball court, tennis area, baseball field, running, and walking are all available. A band room and TVs are also available. All recreation programs are posted on the Unit Bulletin Boards. Times and special events are also posted throughout the units and in the recreation/leisure times areas. Current hours of operation are 6:30 to 10:30 a.m., 12:30 to 3:30 p.m., and 4:30 to 8:30 p.m.

Visitation Information: On Sunday, Monday, Friday, and Saturday visitation is held between 8:00 a.m. and 2:45 p.m. On federal holidays visitation is held between 8:00 a.m. and 2:45 p.m. See Chapter 1 for more information on visitation.

Prison Politics: While some respondents felt that the yard is somewhat political, others felt that it is not political at all. One inmate referred to the prison as a "special needs yard" for gang drop-outs and other vulnerable populations.

Level of Violence: Inmates report a low level of violence at this prison. One inmate referred to the yard as having "low violence" and being "safe."

Vulnerable Populations: Sex offenders, informants, and LGBT inmates can stay, but they are somewhat ostracized. According to one respondent, "Sex offenders, gays, and transgenders can walk the yard, but staff do openly discriminate against all three groups (but not against the rats)."

Good: "Feels more like a college campus than a prison; windows that opened." "Very laid-back facility. Staff do not harass and are generally helpful. No politics or violence. Commissary is good. Lots of stuff to do in recreation." "Safe and laid back."

Bad: "Staff put people with messed up paperwork out there to the inmate population." "Not enough jobs, low pay, inadequate staffing which leads to recreation and education being closed a lot." "No real programs or jobs." "Staff are openly hostile to sex offenders." "Commissary is terrible, prices are inflated, and the selection is garbage." "Food is terrible." "Staff are lazy and unprofessional, there's no real programs to assist in transition back to society, and staff go out of their way to harass sex offenders and LGBT inmates."

Other Comments: "It's a soft yard, but not the best for sex offenders, LGBTs, or informants." "Overall, a very good facility, although it used to be better before a lot of the older staff retired.

Population change including influx of sex offenders has also had some negative effects." "If you are a sex offender, don't go. Ironically, it's the staff, not the inmates, who make this the case."

Camp Prison Politics: There are virtually no politics at this prison. According to one respondent, "As a Camp, everyone pretty much minds their own business, at least in a traditional prison politics sense. There really aren't any gangs or anything."

Camp Level of Violence: There is virtually no violence at this facility. According to one inmate, "When someone gets in a fight, they are transferred out to a Low."

Camp Vulnerable Populations: While sex offenders are barred from Camp placement due to BOP policy, informants and LGBT inmates are allowed to stay.

Camp Good: "It is quiet and fairly relaxed here."

Camp Bad: "Very boring."

In the News: In November 2016, Federal Correctional Institution Otisville prisoner Bertram Alexander was found unresponsive and pronounced dead at a local hospital.

In August 2009, Hope Spinato, a guard at FCI Otisville, was sentenced to eight months in prison for aiding an escape. Spinato admitted to driving an unidentified prisoner to her home on several occasions to have sex before returning him to the prison.

Sholam Weiss, who was sentenced to 845 years for racketeering, wire fraud and money laundering as the head of the National Heritage Life Insurance Company -- bilking over $450 million from its elderly clients, is serving his sentence at FCI Otisville.

Camp in the News: In May 2016, Sheldon Silver, New York Assembly speaker for more than 20 years, requested that he be sent to Federal Correctional Institution Otisville Camp after being convicted of corruption.

FDC Philadelphia

Federal Detention Center Philadelphia | FDC Philadelphia

Facility Address & Contact Information

Federal Detention Center Philadelphia
700 Arch Street
Philadelphia, PA 19105

Phone: 215-521-4000
Fax: 215-521-7220
Email: PHL/ExecAssistant@bop.gov

BOP Website: https://www.bop.gov/locations/institutions/phl/
Wikipedia: https://en.wikipedia.org/wiki/Federal_Detention_Center,_Philadelphia
ZCG Website: https://www.prisonerresource.com/resources/federal-prison-profiles/northeast-region-ner/federal-detention-center-philadelphia-fdc-philadelphia/

Inmate Correspondence Address

Inmate Name and Registration Number
FDC Philadelphia
Federal Detention Center
P.O. Box 562
Philadelphia, PA 19106

NOTE: Funds cannot be sent directly to federal inmates. See Chapter 1 for more information on sending funds to federal inmates.

Sex: Male and Female

Security Level: Administrative Security (Multiple Security Levels)

Location: FDC Philadelphia is located in the heart of the city of Philadelphia.

BOP Region: Northeast Region (NER)

BOP Institution Code: PHL for FDC Philadelphia

Judicial District: Eastern District of Pennsylvania

Medical Care Level: Level 2. See Chapter 2 for more information on Medical Care and Mental Health Care Levels.

Mental Health Care Level: Level 2

Population (as of May 1, 2019): 940

Background: Federal Detention Center Philadelphia is an administrative-security federal prison in Philadelphia, Pennsylvania, which houses both male and female inmates. It was opened in 2000.

FDC Philadelphia holds male and female detainees prior to or during court proceedings, as well as inmates serving brief sentences. The detention center is 12-stories high. It has 628 cells for United States Marshal Service pre-trial detainees, primarily from the following districts: Eastern District of Pennsylvania, Southern and Northern Districts of New Jersey, and the District of Delaware. FDC Philadelphia is also a United States Parole Commission Revocation Site. There are 120 prisoners, already sentenced, that serve as orderlies. The prison is connected by a tunnel to the James A. Byrne United States Courthouse.

Media reports indicate that one male guard was indicted for sexually assaulting male inmates, another guard was indicted for also sexual assaulting inmates, and a third guard was indicted for smuggling contraband into the institution.

Housing: Inmates are housed in either two- or three-person cells or dormitories.

Health Services: Health services at FDC Philadelphia include prenatal care, mental health assessments, eyeglasses, medical and dental sick call, and chronic care. Medical appointments are requested by submitting a sick call request form to the Health Services Unit for a fee of $2.00 per visit. Inmates without funds will still receive medical care by submitting a sick call request. Emergency medical care is available 24 hours a day.

Psychology Services: Psychology services include intake screening, group and individual treatment and counseling, mental health assessments, and crisis intervention. Inmates are screened upon arrival and referred to a psychologist, psychiatrist, or mental health specialist for follow-up evaluation and intervention as needed.

Residential Drug Abuse Program (RDAP): FDC Philadelphia does not have the Residential Drug Abuse Program (RDAP). A Drug Education Class and the Non-Residential Drug Abuse Program (NR-DAP) are both available.

Education Services: FDC Philadelphia provides GED, English-as-a-Second Language (ESL) programs, and Adult Continuing Education (ACE) courses. A parenting program, and re-entry programs such as Money Smart, Mock Job Fair, Resource Fairs, employment workshops, HIV seminars, Celebrate Recovery support program, financial planning, living on a budget, and other programs are also available. High school diplomas and post-secondary degrees are available through paid correspondence programs.

Advanced Occupational Education: FDC Philadelphia does not offer any advanced occupational education programs.

Vocational Training: FDC Philadelphia does not offer any vocational training programs.

Apprenticeship: FDC Philadelphia does not offer any apprenticeship programs.

Library Services: FDC Philadelphia offers both a leisure and law library to inmates. The leisure library offers magazines, newspapers, fiction, nonfiction, and reference books. Inmates are provided access to legal materials and an opportunity to prepare legal documents through the use of the TRULINCS Electronic Law Library. A copy machine is available to reproduce materials needed for research. Electric typewriters are also available for inmate use.

UNICOR: FDC Philadelphia does not have a UNICOR facility.

Commissary: Inmates are allowed to spend $360.00 monthly in the commissary on their assigned shopping days. Clothing, candies, food, drink mixes, and other items are available for purchase. Quantity limits on certain items may apply.

Recreation Services: Recreation Services available at FDC Philadelphia include both physical and leisure activities. Physical activities include basketball, mini soccer, handball, volleyball, and aerobic and yoga classes. Body fat analysis, fitness assessments, walking programs, health and wellness classes, and nutrition classes are also available. Leisure activities consist of board games, dominoes, card games, bingo, and music programming. The hobbycraft program includes drawing, calligraphy, watercolors, and crochet/knitting.

Visitation Information: On Sunday and Saturday visitation is held between 7:15 a.m. and 2:00 p.m. On Monday, Tuesday, Wednesday, Thursday, and Friday visitation is held between 6:15 a.m. and 2:30 p.m. On federal holidays visitation is held between 7:15 a.m. and 2:00 p.m. See Chapter 1 for more information on visitation.

In the News: In April 2018, Federal Detention Center Philadelphia announced that it would rescind its policy that barred visitors who were not immediate family. Around 100 detainees were prevented from seeing their own children under the old policy.

In July 2016, FDC Philadelphia changed its visitation policy to allow only immediate family members, which caused a fair amount of distress since many detainees have relationships and children with people they are not married to.

In June 2012, Richard Spisak, a guard at FDC Philadelphia, was sentenced to 32 months in prison for having male prisoners perform oral sex on him in his office.

In 2006, Delton Doran, a guard at FDC Philadelphia, was charged with having sex with a prisoner at the facility.

In 2005, FDC Philadelphia guard Matthew Sartin pleaded guilty to smuggling cell phones and liquor to five prisoners.

FCI Ray Brook

Federal Correctional Institution Ray Brook | FCI Ray Brook

Facilities: FCI Ray Brook with a detention center.

Facility Address & Contact Information

Federal Correctional Institution Ray Brook
128 Ray Brook Road
Ray Brook, NY 12977

Phone: 518-897-4000
Fax: 518-897-4216
Email: RBK/ExecAssistant@bop.gov

BOP Website: https://www.bop.gov/locations/institutions/rbk/
Wikipedia: https://en.wikipedia.org/wiki/Federal_Correctional_Institution,_Ray_Brook
ZCG Website: https://www.prisonerresource.com/resources/federal-prison-profiles/northeast-region-ner/federal-correctional-institution-ray-brook-fci-ray-brook/

Inmate Correspondence Address

Inmate Name and Registration Number
FCI Ray Brook
Federal Correctional Institution
P.O. Box 300
Ray Brook, NY 12977

NOTE: Funds cannot be sent directly to federal inmates. See Chapter 1 for more information on sending funds to federal inmates.

Sex: Male

Security Level: Medium Security

Location: FCI Ray Brook is located in upstate New York, midway between the villages of Lake Placid and Saranac Lake, off Route 86.

BOP Region: Northeast Region (NER)

BOP Institution Code: RBK for FCI Ray Brook

Judicial District: Northern District of New York

Medical Care: Level 1. See Chapter 2 for more information on Medical Care and Mental Health Care Levels.

Mental Health Care Level: Level 1

Population (as of May 1, 2019): 720

Background: Federal Correctional Institution Ray Brook is a medium-security federal prison in Ray Brook, New York, which houses male inmates. It was opened in 1981.

The site was formerly the Olympic Village for the 1980 Winter Olympic Games in Lake Placid. At the time, there was significant controversy concerning this planned transition from Olympic Village to federal prison. The Bureau of Prisons has received numerous complaints regarding conditions at FCI Ray Brook. The United States Court of Appeals for the Second Circuit reinstated a previously dismissed lawsuit filed against the Bureau of Prisons on behalf of six inmates who were allegedly housed in an extremely hot and cramped single room without adequate ventilation and cleaning supplies. The lawsuit is currently pending.

Media reports indicate that at least one guard has been indicted for bribery and smuggling contraband into the prison. Additionally, it has been reported that at least one prison protest has taken place.

Housing: Inmates are housed in two-, four-, and six-person cells.

Health Services: Medical and dental sick call, medical emergencies, medications, dental care, eyeglasses, physical examinations, chronic care, and preventive health care services are available to inmates. While emergency medical care is available 24 hours a day, inmates must submit a triage form to be evaluated for routine care needs.

Psychology Services: All inmates at FCI Ray Brook are screened by Psychology Services staff during the institution's Admission and Orientation Program. Screening may include an individual interview. Psychologists are available for individual and/or group psychotherapy. Inmates interested in psychology services should submit an "Inmate Request to a Staff" ("Cop-Out") to Psychology Services requesting placement in a particular program or class. Mental health services are offered for those suffering from behavioral or emotional problems. A self-help library is also available to the inmate population.

Residential Drug Abuse Program (RDAP): FCI Ray Brook does not have the Residential Drug Abuse Program (RDAP), but referrals can be made to institutions which do provide RDAP. A Drug Abuse Education Course, the Non-Residential Drug Abuse Treatment Program (NR-DAP), Alcoholics Anonymous (AA), and Narcotics Anonymous (NA) are available.

Education Services: FCI Ray Brook provides literacy, GED, and English-as-a-Second Language (ESL) programs. Parenting classes and Adult Continuing Education (ACE) classes are also available. FCI Ray Brook offers a Literacy Volunteers of America program. High school diplomas and post-secondary degrees are available through paid correspondence programs.

Advanced Occupational Education: FCI Ray Brook offers advanced occupational education in Associate Certified Electronics, Business Math 1 & 2, Business Word 1 & 2, Credentialed Alcohol Substance Abuse Counselor, Customer Service Specialist, Introduction to Customer Service Specialist, and Office Manager/Administrative Services.

Vocational Training: FCI Ray Brook does not offer any vocational training aside from the advanced occupational education and apprenticeship programs.

Apprenticeship: FCI Ray Brook offers apprenticeships in Building Maintenance Repair, Career Development Technician, Education and Training, Housekeeping, and Recreation Assistant.

Library Services: FCI Ray Brook offers both a law and leisure library. The law library is located in the Education Department and contains a variety of legal reference materials for use in preparing legal papers. Reference materials include the United States Code Annotated, Federal Reporter, Supreme Court Reporter, Bureau of Prisons Program Statements, institution supplements, indexes, and other legal materials. Most of these materials are available via the TRULINCS Electronic Law Library computers. A leisure library is available in the Education Department. Inmates may check out books, magazines, reference materials, and newspapers. A DVD movie program is also available.

UNICOR: The FCI Ray Brook UNICOR facility produces clothing and textiles.

Commissary: Inmates are allowed to spend $360.00 monthly in the commissary on their assigned shopping days. In addition, inmates are authorized to have three (3) books of stamps in their possession. Clothing, shoes, over-the-counter medications, food, drink mixes, and other items are available for purchase. Limits on certain items may apply.

Recreation Services: Recreation programs at FCI Ray Brook include indoor and outdoor activities. Intramural team sports, such as softball, soccer, basketball, and volleyball are available. The leisure art/craft programs include acrylic painting, pencil art, ceramic craft, oil painting, crochet/knitting, and beadwork. In addition to these programs, a housing unit art/hobbycraft program offers crochet/knitting, pencil art, beading, and paper art. Inside, inmates have access to band room, arts and crafts room, basketball, treadmills, ellipticals, stationary bikes, TVs, DVDs, rowing machines, TRULINCS mailing label printers, and pool tables. Outside, inmates have access to a track, weights, horseshoes, softball, basketball, handball, soccer, tables, and a track.

Visitation Information: On Sunday and Saturday visitation is held between 8:30 a.m. and 3:00 p.m. On federal holidays visitation is held between 8:30 a.m. and 3:00 p.m. See Chapter 1 for more information on visitation.

Prison Politics: This prison is very political. All inmates must be part of a gang or car.

Level of Violence: There is significant violence at this facility. According to inmate reports, two or three fights occur per month and there are periodic stabbings.

Vulnerable Populations: Sex offenders, informants, and LGBT inmates are not allowed to walk the yard.

Good: "Warm jackets with hoods issued. Good cold weather gear issued." "Nothing too great." "Level of respect amongst inmates, weights, quality and quantity of food, and microwaves."

Bad: "In the SHU, have to ask cops to flush toilets." "Politics, very cold, and lots of snow." "Politics and frequent two to four-day lockdowns in response to fights between inmates of different races."

Other Comments: "Don't go. Not informant- or sex offender-friendly." "This tends to be a political yard, especially for those from New York and the surrounding areas. If from these areas, and you have clean paperwork, you might like it here." "If your paperwork is good and you're not a sex offender and you like order, go. If your paperwork isn't clean, don't go. You won't be able to stay."

In the News: In August 2018, Federal Correctional Institution Ray Brook guard Carlos Ochoa pleaded guilty to bribery and smuggling a cell phone and charger to prisoner Richard Coleman.

In January 2017, Tracey I. Coleman was arrested after she left a stun gun in the lobby of FCI Ray Brook and was charged with introducing contraband and possession of a weapon on prison grounds.

In March 2011, FCI Ray Brook was temporarily locked down after prison staff observed large groups of prisoners congregating on the recreation yard.

FCI Schuylkill

Federal Correctional Institution Schuylkill | FCI Schuylkill

Facilities: FCI Schuylkill with an adjacent minimum-security satellite prison camp.

Facility Address & Contact Information

Federal Correctional Institution Schuylkill
Interstate 81 & 901 West
Minersville, PA 17954

Phone: 570-544-7100
Fax: 570-544-7350
Email: SCH/ExecAssistant@bop.gov

BOP Website: https://www.bop.gov/locations/institutions/sch/
Wikipedia: https://en.wikipedia.org/wiki/Federal_Correctional_Institution,_Schuylkill
ZCG Website: https://www.prisonerresource.com/resources/federal-prison-profiles/northeast-region-ner/federal-correctional-institution-schuylkill-fci-schuylkill/

Inmate Correspondence Address

For FCI Schuylkill

Inmate Name and Registration Number
FCI Schuylkill
Federal Correctional Institution
P.O. Box 759
Minersville, PA 17954

For Satellite Prison Camp

Inmate Name and Registration Number
FCI Schuylkill
Satellite Prison Camp
P.O. Box 670
Minersville, PA 17954

NOTE: Funds cannot be sent directly to federal inmates. See Chapter 1 for more information on sending funds to federal inmates.

Sex: Male

Security Level: Main: Medium Security; Camp: Minimum Security

Location: FCI Schuylkill is located 100 miles northwest of Philadelphia; 46 miles northeast of Harrisonburg; west of I-81 off State Highway 901.

BOP Region: Northeast Region (NER)

BOP Institution Code: SCH for FCI Schuylkill

Judicial District: Middle District of Pennsylvania

Medical Care Level: Level 2. See Chapter 2 for more information on Medical Care and Mental Health Care Levels.

Mental Health Care Level: Level 2

Population (as of May 1, 2019): Main: 964; Camp: 241

Background: Federal Correctional Institution Schuylkill is a medium-security federal prison in Minersville, Pennsylvania, which houses male inmates. It was opened in 1991. Federal Correctional Institution Schuylkill Camp, which also houses male inmates, is located adjacent to the main institution.

FCI Schuylkill includes a unit for pre-trial detainees that was opened in 1992.

Notable inmates include American rap artist Beanie Sigel (served two years for tax evasion); former boss of the Philadelphia Crime Family John Stanfa (serving a life sentence for multiple murders, kidnapping, and other crimes); and organized crime leader James Coonan (serving a 75 year sentence for murder, kidnapping, and other crimes, and for dominating the Hell's Kitchen area of New York City for over a 20-year period).

Media reports indicate that at least two prisoners have escaped from the camp.

Housing: Inmates are housed in one of four housing units, which contain a number of two-person cells. Inmates at the camp are housed in dormitories in two-person cubicles.

Health Services: Sick call, dental sick call, routine dental care, emergency medical treatment, medications, physical examinations upon admission and release, preventative health care examinations, optometry, and flu vaccines are available to inmates. Emergency medical care is available 24 hours a day. Sick call is conducted at 7:30 a.m. on weekdays.

Psychology Services: All FCI Schuylkill inmates must complete a Psychology Services screening. If a crisis exists, any staff member can contact a member of the Psychology Department for inmates. Inmates can also talk with a member of the Psychology Department during the lunch meal. Priority services include suicide prevention, intake screening, the treatment of major mental disorders, and crisis intervention. Other services include adjustment counseling, short-term individual counseling, and group therapy. The Psychology Department provides educational and therapeutic groups that address special concerns faced by inmates. The group classes vary and have previously included Criminal Lifestyles, Relapse Prevention, and Anger Management.

Residential Drug Abuse Program (RDAP): FCI Schuylkill have the Residential Drug Abuse Program (RDAP). The camp does not have a Residential Drug Abuse Program (RDAP). A Drug Abuse Program, Drug Abuse Education class, the Non-Residential Drug Abuse Program (NR-DAP), a 12-Step Group, and Alcoholics Anonymous (AA) are also available.

Education Services: FCI Schuylkill provides literacy, GED, and English-as-a-Second Language (ESL) programs. Pre-release, parenting, and Adult Continuing Education (ACE) programs are also available to the inmate population. An incentive award of $25.00 is given upon completion of both the GED and ESL programs. Graduates are given a graduation ceremony, certificates of achievement, a tassel, and two cap and gown photos. Additional certificates are given upon completion of specific achievement levels, or when selected as "Student of the Month." High school diplomas and post-secondary degrees are available through paid correspondence programs.

Advanced Occupational Education: FCI Schuylkill offers advanced occupational education in Basic Residential Wiring and Culinary Arts. The camp offers advanced occupational education in Commercial Driver's License Class A, Horticulture, and Landscaping.

Vocational Training: FCI Schuylkill and the camp do not offer any vocational training aside from the advanced occupational education and apprenticeship programs.

Apprenticeship: FCI Schuylkill and the camp offer an apprenticeship in Cooking.

Library Services: FCI Schuylkill provides both a leisure and law library. The leisure library includes newspapers, magazines, periodicals, and reference books. An interlibrary loan program is also available. Inmates can use the law library to conduct legal research through

TRULINCS Electronic Law Library terminals. Federal Register documents, institution supplements, and the Black's Law Dictionary are maintained in hard copy format in the main law library and in the Special Housing Unit. Typewriters and a photocopier are available for inmate use. Hours of operation are 7:30 to 11:00 a.m. and 12:30 to 3:15 p.m.

UNICOR: The FCI Schuylkill UNICOR facility disassembles electronic products. The camp does not house a UNICOR facility.

Commissary: Inmates are allowed to spend $360.00 monthly in the commissary on their assigned shopping days. Inmates can shop at 7:30 a.m., 8:30 a.m., and 12:00 p.m. Clothing, shoes, food, drink mixes, and other items are available for purchase. Quantity limits on certain items may apply.

Recreation Services: The Recreation Department at FCI Schuylkill consists of three areas: a gymnasium, outside recreation yard, and Leisure Center (arts and crafts/music). The Recreation Department offers activities including basketball, racquetball, bocce ball, soccer, handball, volleyball, horseshoes, jogging/walking, softball, wiffle ball, flag football, indoor floor hockey, physical fitness, and health education programs. Leisure activities include table games such as backgammon, bid whist, billiards, gin, checkers, dominoes, foosball, chess, spades, table tennis, bridge, and pinochle. A music program and arts and hobbycraft are available, as are special programs and activities throughout the year (e.g., movies, holiday sporting events, tournaments/contests, and inmate music shows). In the camp, the indoor recreation area has a hobbycraft area, weight room, a music room, and a game room with various table games. The outdoor recreation yard offers a softball field, basketball courts, bocce court, a weightlifting area, handball/racquetball courts, a volleyball court, and several horseshoe pits.

Visitation Information: On Sunday, Friday, and Saturday visitation is held between 8:30 a.m. and 3:00 p.m. On federal holidays visitation is held between 8:30 a.m. and 3:00 p.m. See Chapter 1 for more information on visitation.

Prison Politics: This is a moderately political yard. According to one respondent, "Everything is segregated by race or state."

Level of Violence: Inmates report a low level of violence. One inmate stated that it is "safe compared to other spots." Another respondent agreed, stating there is a "very small amount of violence."

Vulnerable Populations: While LGBT inmates are allowed to walk the yard, inmates report that sex offenders and informants are typically run off.

Good: "It is not violent."

Bad: "There are times that we stay locked down due to a fight even when there doesn't need to be a lockdown."

Other Comments: "The facility is breaking down with burst pipes, which makes it so the hot water sometimes goes out."

In the News: On September 16, 2001, Michael Hart, a guard at the Federal Correctional Institution at Schuylkill, was suspended and reassigned to a prison camp for hanging a small American flag in a window overlooking the recreation area.

Camp in the News: In March 2018, Raymond Collazo, a prisoner at Federal Correctional Institution Schuylkill Camp, escaped by walking away.

In December 2017, Harvey Shaner escaped from FCI Schuylkill Camp, but was recaptured in less than two weeks.

CHAPTER 8:

South Central Region Prisons

South Central Regional Office

The South Central Regional Office is an administrative office providing oversight and support to facilities located in the South Central Region (SCR). The South Central Region covers Federal Bureau of Prison facilities located in Arkansas, Louisiana, New Mexico, Oklahoma, and Texas. These facilities are overseen by a regional office that provides oversight, technical assistance, and other types of operational support. In addition, they conduct training programs for staff in their region and assist state and local criminal justice agencies.

Regional Director: Eric Wilson
SCR Population: 28,686

Facility Address & Contact Information

South Central Regional Office
Federal Bureau of Prisons
U.S. Armed Forces Reserve Complex
344 Marine Forces Drive
Grand Prairie, TX 75051

Email: SCRO/ExecAssistant@bop.gov

Phone: 972-730-8600

Fax: 972-730-8809

BOP Website: https://www.bop.gov/locations/regional_offices/scro/

Wikipedia: n/a

ZCG Website: https://prisonerresource.com/resources/federal-prison-profiles/federal-prison-regional-offices/south-central-regional-office-ser/

Staff Mail

Staff Name

South Central Regional Office

U.S. Armed Forces Reserve Complex

344 Marine Forces Drive

Grand Prairie, TX 75051

Freight and Non-USPS Parcels

Staff Name

South Central Regional Office

ATTN: Warehouse

U.S. Armed Forces Reserve Complex

344 Marine Forces Drive

Grand Prairie, TX 75051

South Central Region Prisons

FCI Bastrop (TX)
FCI Beaumont Low (TX)
FCI Beaumont Medium (TX)
USP Beaumont (TX)
FCI Big Spring (TX)
FPC Bryan (TX)
FMC Carswell (TX)
FCI El Reno (OK)
FCI Forrest City Low (AR)
FCI Forrest City Medium (AR)
FMC Fort Worth (TX)
FDC Houston (TX)
FCI La Tuna (TX)
FSL La Tuna (TX)
FCI Oakdale 1 (LA)
FCI Oakdale 2 (LA)
FTC Oklahoma City (OK)
FCI Pollock (LA)
USP Pollock (LA)
FCI Seagoville (TX)
FCI Texarkana (TX)
FCI Three Rivers (TX)

FCI Bastrop

Federal Correctional Institution Bastrop | FCI Bastrop

Facilities: FCI Bastrop with an adjacent minimum-security satellite prison camp.

Facility Address & Contact Information

Federal Correctional Institution Bastrop
1341 Highway 95 North
Bastrop, TX 78602

Phone: 512-321-3903
Fax: 512-304-0117
Email: BAS/ExecAssistant@bop.gov

BOP Website: https://www.bop.gov/locations/institutions/bas/
Wikipedia: https://en.wikipedia.org/wiki/Federal_Correctional_Institution,_Bastrop
ZCG Website: https://www.prisonerresource.com/resources/federal-prison-profiles/south-central-region-scr/federal-correctional-institution-bastrop-fci-bastrop/

Inmate Correspondence Address

For FCI Bastrop

Inmate Name and Registration Number
FCI Bastrop
Federal Correctional Institution
P.O. Box 1010
Bastrop, TX 78602-1010

For Satellite Prison Camp

Inmate Name and Registration Number
FCI Bastrop
Satellite Prison Camp
P.O. Box 1010
Bastrop, TX 78602

NOTE: Funds cannot be sent directly to federal inmates. See Chapter 1 for more information on sending funds to federal inmates.

Sex: Male

Security Level: Main: Low Security; Camp: Minimum Security

Location: FCI Bastrop is located 30 miles southeast of Austin, 8 miles south of Elgin, 8 miles north of Bastrop, off Highway 95.

BOP Region: South Central Region (SCR)

BOP Institution Code: BAS for FCI Bastrop

Judicial District: Western District of Texas

Medical Care Level: Level 2. See Chapter 2 for more information on Medical Care and Mental Health Care Levels.

Mental Health Care Level: Level 2

Population (as of May 1, 2019): Main: 1,242; Camp: 180

Background: Federal Correctional Institution Bastrop is a low-security federal prison in Bastrop, Texas, which houses male inmates. It was opened in 1979. Federal Correctional Institution Bastrop Camp, which also houses male inmates, is located adjacent to the main institution.

Notable inmates include Leandro Luna and Adan Chavez (convicted of narcotics offenses, escaped in 2009 by stealing a Federal Bureau of Prisons vehicle).

Media reports indicate that at least one guard has been federally indicted for bribery at the institution.

Housing: Inmates at FCI Bastrop are housed in two- and three-person cells within one of five dormitories. Inmates at the camp are housed in dormitories.

Health Services: Health services include sick call, dental sick call, physical examinations, emergency medical and dental care, diagnosis and treatment of chronic infectious diseases, and prescription medications (over-the-counter medications are available in the commissary). Inmates must submit a sick call form to be evaluated for non-emergency medical needs, and a $2.00 fee is charged to the Inmate Commissary Account for each health care visit. Sick call is held Monday through Friday at 6:30 a.m. Emergency medical care is available 24 hours a day at no fee. Insulin line and pill line are conducted during meals.

Psychology Services: Inmates at FCI Bastrop have access to psychologists who provide counseling and other mental health services. Each psychologist has an office inside the main institution, and at the camp, where they can be easily reached. Individual and group therapy are available along with a variety of substance abuse programs. Specialty groups for addictions, self-image, and other voluntary groups are also available (e.g., criminal thinking, cognitive skills, anger management, etc.). A contract psychiatrist is also available by referral from a psychologist.

Residential Drug Abuse Program (RDAP): FCI Bastrop has the Residential Drug Abuse Program (RDAP). Both facilities provide drug abuse programs, a Drug Abuse Education Course, Non-Residential Drug Abuse Program (NR-DAP), and Alcoholics Anonymous (AA).

Education Services: FCI Bastrop provides literacy, GED, English-as-a-Second Language (ESL) programs, Adult Continuing Education (ACE), and special learning needs courses. A parenting program is also available. High school diplomas and post-secondary degrees are available through paid correspondence programs.

Advanced Occupational Education: FCI Bastrop offers advanced occupational training in Building Trades, Culinary Arts, Horticulture, and Oil and Gas Field Technician. The camp does not offer any advanced occupational education.

Vocational Training: FCI Bastrop and the camp do not offer any vocational training programs aside from the advanced occupational education and apprenticeship programs.

Apprenticeship: FCI Bastrop offers apprenticeships in Baking, Carpentry, Cooking, Dental Assistant, Electrician, Electrician Maintenance, Heating and A/C Installer and Servicer, Maintenance Repairer, Painting, Plumbing, and Quality Control Technicians. The camp offers apprenticeships in Heating and A/C Installer Servicer, Stationary Engineer, and Welding.

Library Services: The leisure library and the law library are located in the Education Department. Inmate clerks are available to assist in research and preparation. All required legal materials are available for viewing in the law library. A copy machine is available to reproduce materials needed for research. The leisure library contains books, magazines, and newspapers for use during leisure time. The TRULINCS Electronic Law Library is also available to the inmate population in the Education Department.

UNICOR: The FCI Bastrop UNICOR factory retrofits vehicles for government agencies. The satellite camp does not have a UNICOR facility.

Commissary: Inmates may use funds in their account to purchase items at the institution commissary, place funds on their inmate phone account, purchase TRU-Units for their TRULINCS account, or send funds out of the institution using Form BP-199. Inmates are permitted to spend up to $180.00 biweekly for commissary purchases and Special Purchase Orders (SPOs). Inmates are only permitted to shop once a week on their designated shopping day. Remaining spending limit at the end of the period cannot be carried over into the next period. Withdrawals for education and leisure time items are approved by the Supervisor of Education up to $320.00.

Recreation Services: The FCI Bastrop Recreation Department offers both indoor and outdoor activities. Facilities include a gym, hobbycraft shop, weight area, and recreation yard. The satellite camp offers a fitness area and hobbycraft shop.

Visitation Information: On Sunday, Friday, and Saturday visitation is held between 8:00 a.m. and 3:00 p.m. On federal holidays visitation is held between 8:00 a.m. and 3:00 p.m. See Chapter 1 for more information on visitation.

Prison Politics: There is a low level of politics at this facility.

Level of Violence: There is very little violence at this prison. According to one inmate, "I have never feared for my safety."

Vulnerable Populations: Sex offenders, informants, and LGBT inmates can walk the yard. One respondent explained, "Everyone walks; there are lots of sex offenders and informants; plenty of gays as well."

Good: "The surroundings and landscape are good." "Very safe."

Bad: "The controlled movements are bad." "Some BS. Doors are locked for all counts and at night." "No open movement."

In the News: In May 2015, Shanon E. Frank and Mattheu Ellis Jones, prisoners at the Federal Correctional Institution in Bastrop, pleaded guilty to conspiring to bribe the prisoner's pharmacy technician, Eric Renaldo Telles, to smuggle contraband, which included watches, shirts and nutritional supplements, into the prison over a period of eight months.

In 2009, Leandro Luna and Adan Chavez, both inmates at FCI Bastrop, escaped by stealing a Bureau of Prisons vehicle and fleeing to Mexico. They were tracked by the Lone Star Fugitive Task Force, which consisted of local authorities, Texas Rangers, and U.S. Marshals. The public wasn't notified of their escape for two days, and the prison did not share any further details. Both men were apprehended by Mexican authorities six days after their escape.

FCC Beaumont

Federal Correctional Complex Beaumont | FCC Beaumont

Facilities: FCC Beaumont houses USP Beaumont with a minimum-security satellite prison camp, FCI Beaumont Medium and FCI Beaumont Low.

USP Beaumont

United States Penitentiary Beaumont | USP Beaumont

Facility Address & Contact Information

United States Penitentiary Beaumont
6200 Knauth Road
Beaumont, TX 77705

Phone: 409-727-8188
Fax: 409-626-3700
Email: BMP/ExecAssistant@bop.gov

BOP Website: https://www.bop.gov/locations/institutions/bmp/
Wikipedia: https://en.wikipedia.org/wiki/United_States_Penitentiary,_Beaumont
ZCG Website: https://www.prisonerresource.com/resources/federal-prison-profiles/south-central-region-scr/federal-correctional-complex-beaumont-fcc-beaumont/united-states-penitentiary-beaumont-usp-beaumont/

Inmate Correspondence Address

For USP Beaumont

Inmate Name and Registration Number
USP Beaumont
U.S. Penitentiary
P.O. Box 26030
Beaumont, TX 77720

For Satellite Prison Camp

Inmate Name and Registration Number
USP Beaumont
Satellite Prison Camp
P.O. Box 26030
Beaumont, TX 77720

NOTE: Funds cannot be sent directly to federal inmates. See Chapter 1 for more information on sending funds to federal inmates.

Sex: Male

Security Level: Main: High Security; Camp: Minimum Security

Location: USP Beaumont is located on the Texas Gulf coast, about 90 minutes from Houston.

BOP Region: South Central Region (SCR)

BOP Institution Code: BMP for USP Beaumont, BMX for Beaumont Federal Correctional Complex

Judicial District: Eastern District of Texas

Medical Care Level: Level 2. See Chapter 2 for more information on Medical Care and Mental Health Care Levels.

Mental Health Care Level: Level 2

Population: (as of May 1, 2019): Main: 1,032; Camp: 537

Background: United States Penitentiary Beaumont is a high-security federal prison in Beaumont, Texas, which houses male inmates. It was opened in 1997 and is part of the Beaumont Federal Correctional Complex. United States Penitentiary Beaumont Camp, which also houses male inmates, is located adjacent to the main institution.

The facility is informally known as "Bloody Beaumont." There have been at least three inmate murders at the prison.

Media reports indicate that several guards have been convicted of smuggling contraband and obstruction of justice for covering up guards' assaults on inmates. Several guards have also been assaulted and stabbed by inmates. Three prisoners have been murdered by fellow inmates.

In 2016, The Richest named USP Beaumont one of the 15 most dangerous prisons in America.

Housing: Inmates are housed in one- and two-person cells. There is a total of six housing units. Inmates at the camp are housed in two- or three-person cubicles in dormitory settings. There are approximately 150 inmates in each dorm.

Health Services: Sick call, eyeglasses, emergency medical treatment, physical examinations, medications, immunizations, and dental care are provided at USP Beaumont and the satellite camp. The camp has sick call at 6:30 a.m. on Monday, Tuesday, Thursday, and Friday, and pill and insulin lines are conducted during meals. Over-the-counter medications are available at the commissary. Inmates can access health care services for a fee of $2.00 per visit, charged to the inmate's commissary account. Emergency medical care is available 24 hours a day at no fee.

Psychology Services: Inmates are provided with an intake screening upon arrival at USP Beaumont and the camp. Psychology staff offer treatment programs addressing a full range of clinical disorders, provide self-help options, assess and treat behavioral and emotional problems, and facilitate overall adjustment. Crisis counseling, coping skills, suicide prevention, mental health counseling, and spiritual counseling are available. The Challenge Program is available for inmates who are prone to substance abuse, mental illness, and violence. Inmates can sign up for programs by submitting a cop-out or attending Psychology Services open house. Inmates can attend open house on Wednesdays from 10:30 to 11:00 a.m.

Residential Drug Abuse Program (RDAP): USP Beaumont and the camp have the Residential Drug Abuse Program (RDAP). Both facilities also provide a drug abuse program, a Drug Abuse Education Course, and the Non-Residential Drug Abuse Program (NR-DAP).

Education Services: USP Beaumont provides literacy, GED, and English-as-a-Second Language (ESL) programs. Adult Continuing Education (ACE) and parenting classes are also available. High school diplomas and post-secondary degrees are available through paid correspondence programs. While the camp generally has the same programs, availability and offerings are scaled back.

Advanced Occupational Education: USP Beaumont offers advanced occupational education in Advanced Microcomputer Office and Administrative Applications, Culinary Arts, Microcomputer Applications, Small Business Management, and Welding. The camp offers Basic Diesel Repair, Commercial Driver License, and Culinary Arts.

Vocational Training: USP Beaumont does not offer vocational training aside from the advanced occupational education and apprenticeship programs.

Apprenticeship: USP Beaumont offers apprenticeships in Carpentry and Electrician. Both the main prison and the camp offer apprenticeships in Electrician, HVAC, Painting, Plumbing, and Teacher Aide.

Library Services: A law library is located in the Education department and contains a variety of legal reference materials for use in preparing legal papers. The TRULINCS Electronic Law Library is available for inmate usage. Typewriters and a copier are also available in the library. The leisure library offers fiction and nonfiction books, magazines, and newspapers for the inmate population. While the camp has the same general offerings, they are much more limited. Survey respondents report mostly fiction books and no magazines.

UNICOR: The UNICOR at USP Beaumont produces clothing and textiles. The camp does not have a UNICOR facility.

Commissary: Inmates are given an activated account upon arrival, showing all deposits and withdrawals. Inmates are permitted to spend up to $90.00 weekly for commissary purchases and Special Purchase Orders (SPOs). Balances can be checked via the automated inquiry machine (AIM), through the Inmate Telephone System, or through the TRULINCS computers. Fingerprint identification is used for Commissary sales. Remaining spending limit at the end of the period cannot be carried over into the next period. At the camp, inmates are allowed to shop at 6:00 and 11:00 a.m. A $180 biweekly spending limitation is imposed. When shopping, camp inmates turn in their commissary form and wait for their order to be processed.

Recreation Services: The USP Beaumont Recreation Department includes of both indoor and outdoor components. Activities range from individualized arts and crafts programs to intramural team sports such as softball, basketball, and volleyball. Outside, inmates can play soccer, softball, horseshoes, handball, basketball, and football. There is also a track, dip bars, stationary bikes, and treadmills. Hours of operation are 6:00 to 10:30 a.m., 11:30 a.m. to 3:30 p.m., and 4:45 to 8:30 p.m. At the camp, inmates have access to both indoor and outdoor recreation. Inside, inmates can play pool, run on treadmills, and engage in various hobbycraft activities such as painting and leathercraft. There is also a band room where inmates have access to microphones, guitars, drums, and a piano.

Visitation Information: On Sunday and Saturday visitation is held between 8:30 a.m. and 3:00 p.m. On Friday visitation is held between 5:00 and 8:00 p.m. On federal holidays visitation is held between 8:30 a.m. and 3:00 p.m. See Chapter 1 for more information on visitation.

Camp Prison Politics: Due to being a Camp, there are virtually no politics, though some of the Hispanic groups do reportedly act political at times.

Camp Level of Violence: There is virtually no violence. One inmate suggested that the safety was a "9". Another respondent stated that he "hasn't seen or known of any violence" at the facility.

Camp Vulnerable Populations: Informants and LGBT inmates can stay, though sex offenders are precluded from Camp placement by Bureau of Prisons policy.

Camp Good: "It's laid back."

Camp Bad: "Staff is very rude, and they choose to solve problems by taking things away. They punish everyone for what one or a few do. It's a Camp with no fence, so people bring in contraband. When contraband is found in a common area, they take away the yard, commissary, visits, etc. They call it 'modified operations' and it's a huge bummer and will exacerbate your mental health issues if you have them." "Very bad medical through a private contractor." "Community service work details are no longer allowed to receive free world food, instead they have to bring their own bag lunch with them." "Poor education system and no furloughs for any reason. Even the death of a parent does not warrant a furlough even for those that would qualify at other camps." "The administration likes to punish everyone with communal sanctions when they find any contraband. This includes turning off the TVs." "Nothing that I know."

Camp Other Comments: "Due to a recent escape which made national news, the administration has taken a tougher, more punitive stance on the inmate population."

In the News: In July 2018, Reginald Edward Green, a prisoner at United States Penitentiary Beaumont, was found guilty of assaulting a federal officer after punching a guard in the face.

In June 2018, Ricky Fackrell and Christopher Cramer, members of the white supremacist gang Soldiers of the Aryan Culture at USP Beaumont, were sentenced to death for the fatal 2014 stabbing of prisoner Leo Johns, a member of the same group.

In September 2017, in the wake of Hurricane Harvey, families and relatives of prisoners at USP Beaumont worried about the health of their loved ones after hearing rumors of deaths, lack of food and unsanitary conditions despite reassurances from Bureau of Prisons officials that everything was fine. "People don't believe BOP because they have reason to distrust their claims already," said Azzurra Crispino, co-founder of Prison Abolition Prisoner Support.

In June 2017, Eric S. Patrick, a chaplain at USP Beaumont who was paid to smuggle tobacco and cigarettes into the prison, was sentenced to a year and a day in prison.

In May 2010, Edgar Balthazar Garcia and Mark Isaac Snarr, prisoners at USP Beaumont, were sentenced to death for the 2007 stabbing of two guards and the killing of another prisoner, Gabriel Rhone, who was stabbed more than 50 times.

In September 2001, a USP Beaumont guard, Gerald Galloway, was sentenced to 122 years in prison for smuggling cocaine and heroin into the facility.

In March 2001, Lieutenant Bryan Small pleaded guilty to obstruction of justice for approving false reports to cover up guards' attacks on USP Beaumont prisoners.

In 1999, prisoner Darryl Brown was stabbed to death at USP Beaumont.

Camp in the News: In January 2018, Joshua Hansen, a prisoner at Federal Correctional Institution Beaumont Camp, was captured after he left the facility to retrieve contraband, including alcohol, tobacco and freshly prepared food, so he could bring it back to the prison.

FCI Beaumont Medium

Federal Correctional Institution Beaumont Medium | FCI Beaumont Medium

Facility Address & Contact Information

Federal Correctional Institution Beaumont Medium
5830 Knauth Road
Beaumont, TX 77705

Phone: 409-721-0101
Fax: 409-720-5000
Email: BMM/ExecAssistant@bop.gov

BOP Website: https://www.bop.gov/locations/institutions/bmm/
Wikipedia: https://en.wikipedia.org/wiki/Federal_Correctional_Institution,_Beaumont
ZCG Website: https://www.prisonerresource.com/resources/federal-prison-profiles/south-central-region-scr/federal-correctional-complex-beaumont-fcc-beaumont/federal-correctional-institution-beaumont-medium-fci-beaumont-medium/

Inmate Correspondence Address

Inmate Name and Registration Number
FCI Beaumont Medium
Federal Correctional Institution
P.O. Box 26040
Beaumont, TX 77720-6040

NOTE: Funds cannot be sent directly to federal inmates. See Chapter 1 for more information on sending funds to federal inmates.

Sex: Male

Security Level: Medium Security

Location: FCI Beaumont Medium is located on the Texas Gulf coast, about 90 minutes from Houston.

BOP Region: South Central Region (SCR)

BOP Institution Code: BMM for FCI Beaumont Medium, BMX for Beaumont Federal Correctional Complex

Judicial District: Eastern District of Texas

Medical Care Level: Level 2. See Chapter 2 for more information on Medical Care and Mental Health Care Levels.

Mental Health Care Level: Level 2

Population: (as of May 1, 2019:): 1,502

Background: Federal Correctional Institution Beaumont Medium is a medium-security federal prison in Beaumont, Texas, which houses male inmates. It was opened in 1999 and is part of the Beaumont Federal Correctional Complex.

FCI Beaumont Medium, like USP Beaumont, is known as "Bloody Beaumont" due to commonplace violence. Two inmates have been murdered at the facility.

Media reports indicate that one prison guard was indicted for sexually abusing a child. News reports also indicate that at least two murders have taken place at the institution, as well as one skirmish in which several prisoners were injured.

Housing: Inmates are housed in one- and two-person cells. There is a total of 12 housing units.

Health Services: Health services include sick call, eyeglasses, emergency medical treatment, physical examinations, medications, immunizations, and dental care. Over-the-counter medications are available for purchase at the commissary. Inmates are assigned a specific health care provider who treats them for the duration of their stay. In order to be evaluated for a medical complaint, inmates must attend sick call at 6:00 a.m. on Monday, Tuesday, Thursday, or Friday. Pill and insulin line are conducted during meals. Emergency medical care is available 24 hours a day.

Psychology Services: FCI Beaumont Medium provides intake screening to inmates upon arrival. Psychology staff offer treatment programs addressing a full range of clinical disorders, provide self-help options, assess and treat behavioral and emotional problems, and facilitate overall adjustment. A variety of group therapy programs are offered, including anger management, criminal thinking, stress reduction, and others.

Residential Drug Abuse Program (RDAP): FCI Beaumont Medium has the Residential Drug Abuse Program (RDAP). The institution also provides a drug abuse program, a Drug Abuse Education Course, and the Non-Residential Drug Abuse Program (NR-DAP).

Education Services: FCI Beaumont Medium provides literacy, GED and English-as-a-Second Language (ESL) programs. By policy, with minor exceptions, all federal inmates who do not have a high school diploma or GED must enroll in the literacy program. High school diplomas and post-secondary degrees are available through paid correspondence programs. Lamar College currently offers a free program where inmates can earn an associate's degree, but in order to qualify, inmates must be within 10 years of release.

Advanced Occupational Education: FCI Beaumont Medium offers advanced occupational education in HVAC, Advanced HVAC, Advanced Microcomputer Office and Administrative Applications, Building Trades, Culinary Arts, Major Appliance, Microcomputer Applications, and Small Business Management.

Vocational Training: FCI Beaumont Medium does not offer vocational training aside from its advanced occupational education and apprenticeship programs.

Apprenticeship: FCI Beaumont Medium offers apprenticeships in Carpentry, Electrical, HVAC, Painting, Plumbing, and Teacher Aide.

Library Services: A law library is located in the Education Department, containing a variety of legal reference materials for use in preparing legal papers. A copy machine is available to reproduce materials needed for research. Electric typewriters are also available for inmate use. Inmates can check out fiction and nonfiction books, newspaper, and magazines from the leisure library.

UNICOR: The UNICOR at FCI Beaumont Medium produces clothing and textiles.

Commissary: Inmates at FCI Beaumont Medium are allowed to spend up to $360.00 each month on items such as food, beverages, clothing, shoes, and limited electronics. A weekly spending limit of $90 is enforced. Copy cards, postage stamps, and over-the-counter medications do not count against the spending limit. Inmates are allowed to shop once a week on their assigned day, from 7:00 a.m. to 2:00 p.m.

Recreation Services: The FCI Beaumont Medium Recreation Department offers both indoor and outdoor areas. Activities range from individualized arts and crafts programs (e.g. painting, drawing, leathercraft, etc.) to intramural team sports such as softball, basketball, volleyball, flag football, and Frisbee. A track is also available. The Recreation Department operates on a structured schedule. General operating hours are 8:30 a.m. to 3:30 p.m. and 5:30 to 8:15 p.m. The prison's administration enforces a split schedule where half of the housing units are allowed to attend recreation at certain times, while the other half is restricted from participating. The exception is 8:00 a.m. to 3:30 p.m. on Tuesday, Wednesday, and Thursday.

Visitation Information: On Sunday and Saturday visitation is held between 8:30 a.m. and 3:00 p.m. On Friday visitation is held between 5:00 and 8:00 p.m. On federal holidays visitation is held between 8:30 a.m. and 3:00 p.m. See Chapter 1 for more information on visitation.

Prison Politics: This is a very political yard. Inmates are required to be part of a car.

Level of Violence: There is a high level of violence at this prison. One respondent explained, "Put it this way, the level of security is all they talk about, but an individual got kicked to death here in 2013 and now in 2018 they still have the yard on modified operations."

Vulnerable Populations: Sex offenders, informants, and LGBT inmates cannot stay. According to one respondent, "If they are found out, they will be dealt with."

Good: "The only good thing about this institution is that the guards don't mess with you."

Bad: "The cops aren't going to do anything for you unless you get on the Warden and he makes them."

In the News: In October 2017, Shane Gotte, an employee at Federal Correctional Institution Beaumont Medium, was arrested after a video was discovered showing him sexually abusing a child.

In September 2017, rumors spread that two prisoners at FCI Beaumont Medium were dead as a result of flooding caused by Hurricane Harvey, which the Bureau of Prisons said were false. There were, however, at least two other deaths at FCC Beaumont in 2017: one the result of cancer in January and the other of a heart attack in March.

In 2009, Joseph Ebron, a prisoner at FCI Beaumont Medium, was sentenced to death for his part in the murder of fellow prisoner Keith Barnes. Ebron allegedly restrained Barnes while prisoner Marwin Mosley, who later killed himself, stabbed Barnes in the chest 106 times.

In 2005, prisoner Jose Jaimes-Martinez was stabbed to death by other unidentified prisoners at the medium-security FCI Beaumont.

In December 1999, five prisoners were injured in "skirmishes" at FCI Beaumont Medium.

FCI Beaumont Low

Federal Correctional Institution Beaumont Low | FCI Beaumont Low

Facility Address & Contact Information

Federal Correctional Institution Beaumont Low
5560 Knauth Road
Beaumont, TX 77705

Phone: 409-727-8172
Fax: 409-626-3500
Email: BML/ExecAssistant@bop.gov

BOP Website: https://www.bop.gov/locations/institutions/bml/
Wikipedia: https://en.wikipedia.org/wiki/Federal_Correctional_Institution,_Beaumont
ZCG Website: https://www.prisonerresource.com/resources/federal-prison-profiles/south-central-region-scr/federal-correctional-complex-beaumont-fcc-beaumont/federal-correctional-institution-beaumont-low-fci-beaumont-low/

Inmate Correspondence Address

Inmate Name and Registration Number
FCI Beaumont Low
Federal Correctional Institution
P.O. Box 2602
Beaumont, TX 77720

NOTE: Funds cannot be sent directly to federal inmates. See Chapter 1 for more information on sending funds to federal inmates.

Sex: Male

Security Level: Low Security

Location: FCI Beaumont Low is located on the Texas Gulf coast, about 90 minutes from Houston.

BOP Region: South Central Region (SCR)

BOP Institution Code: BMF for FCI Beaumont Low, BMX for Beaumont Federal Correctional Complex

Judicial District: Eastern District of Texas

Medical Care Level: Level 2. See Chapter 2 for more information on Medical Care and Mental Health Care Levels.

Mental Health Care Level: Level 2

Population: (as of May 1, 2019): 1,916

Background: Federal Correctional Institution Beaumont Low is a low-security federal prison in Beaumont, Texas, which houses male inmates. It was opened in 1996 and is part of the Beaumont Federal Correctional Complex.

Media reports indicate that at least three guards have been charged with accepting bribes in return for smuggling contraband into the institution, while a prison administrator was charged with operating an illicit fraud scheme in which she offered to reduce inmates' sentences for money. At least one inmate has escaped from the camp.

Housing: Inmates are housed in two- and three-person cubicles in dormitories. Each dorm houses approximately 150 inmates.

Health Services: FCI Beaumont Low offers the same health services as all FCC Beaumont institutions, including sick call, eyeglasses, emergency medical treatment, physical examinations, medications, immunizations and dental care. Over-the-counter medications are available for purchase at the commissary. While emergency medical care is available 24 hours a day, inmates must attend sick call for routine health care needs. Sick call is conducted Monday, Tuesday, Thursday, and Friday at 6:30 a.m. Pill and insulin lines are held during and after each meal.

Psychology Services: Intake screening is provided to inmates upon arrival. The psychology staff offer a variety of comprehensive treatment programs addressing a full range of clinical disorders, provide self-help options, assess and treat behavioral or emotional problems, and facilitate overall adjustment. Anger management, Smart Recovery, and other programs are available, as is a self-help lending library.

Residential Drug Abuse Program (RDAP): FCI Beaumont Low has the Residential Drug Abuse Program (RDAP). It also provides a Drug Abuse Education Course, the Non-Residential Drug Abuse Program (NR-DAP), Alcoholics Anonymous (AA), and Narcotics Anonymous (NA).

Education Services: The FCI Beaumont Low Education Department is open from 7:40 to 10:30 a.m., 12:40 to 3:30 p.m., and 5:00 to 8:30 p.m. on weekdays. The department provides literacy, GED, and English-as-a-Second Language (ESL) programs. Additional programs include parenting, Release Preparation Program (RPP), and Adult Continuing Education (ACE) courses. High school diplomas and post-secondary degrees are available through paid correspondence programs. The faculty also has a free college program through Lamar College, which allows inmates to earn an associate's degree.

Advanced Occupational Education: FCI Beaumont Low offers advanced occupational education in Advanced Microcomputer Applications, Basic Diesel, Building Trades, Culinary Arts, HVAC, Industrial Sewing, Major Appliance, and Microcomputer Applications. Each of these classes are taught by Lamar College and last four to six months.

Vocational Training: FCI Beaumont Low does not offer vocational training aside from its advanced occupational education and apprenticeship programs.

Apprenticeship: FCI Beaumont Low offers apprenticeships in Carpentry, Electrician, HVAC, Painting, Plumbing, and Teacher Aide.

Library Services: The Education Department houses the law library, which has a variety of legal reference materials available for use in preparing legal papers. Two inmate law clerks are available to help with legal research needs. A copier is available in the library to assist with making legal copies. Inmates also have access to the TRULINCS Electronic Law Library and to electronic typewriters. In the leisure library inmates can check out fiction and nonfiction books, several local and national newspapers, and approximately 20 different magazines. Inmates are allowed to walk amongst the stacks of books to make their selections.

UNICOR: The UNICOR at FCI Beaumont Low produces clothing and textiles. Specifically, inmates sew clothing for the U.S. government and military, as well as the Afghan military.

Commissary: Inmates at FCI Beaumont Low are allowed to spend $360.00 monthly in the commissary on their housing unit's assigned shopping day. Shopping is conducted Monday through Thursday between 6:30 and 9:00 a.m. and between 12:00 and 3:00 p.m. Inmates are only permitted to spend $180 biweekly. Clothing, shoes, electronics, food, drink mixes, and other items are available for purchase. Quantity limits on certain items may apply. It is commonplace for inmates to carry their purchases back to their housing units in laundry bags.

Recreation Services: The FCI Beaumont Low Recreation Department consists of both indoor and outdoor components. A band program is also active with drum, guitar, and piano classes taught. Indoors, inmates can engage in crafts such as origami, painting, drawing, and leather-craft. Stationary bikes, ellipticals, treadmills, and a label printer are available. Outside, inmates can participate in intramural team sports such as softball, basketball, frisbee, soccer, handball, and volleyball. There is also a track for inmates to run and walk. Hours of operation are 8:30 to 9:15 a.m., 10:30 to 3:15 p.m., and 4:45 to 8:00 p.m.

Visitation Information: On Sunday, Monday, Thursday, Friday, and Saturday visitation is held between 8:30 a.m. and 3:00 p.m. On federal holidays visitation is held between 8:30 a.m. and 3:00 p.m. See Chapter 1 for more information on visitation.

Prison Politics: This is a somewhat political yard. According to respondents, inmates don't have to be part of a car, but those who seek respect do have to join. Cars are often organized along racial lines. Independents are allowed, but inmates tend to segregate themselves along racial lines for both celling and control of certain TVs.

Level of Violence: Some violence, but not a lot. According to respondents, there are fights every now and then and occasional political jumpings. One inmate pegged the safety as a 5 out of 10.

Vulnerable Populations: While sex offenders, informants, and LGBT inmates can stay, they are often excluded from cars and are ostracized. Some inmates felt that there wasn't much ostracization and that everyone generally gets along.

Good: "Not a whole lot stands out." "It's fairly safe as far as prisons go. It's not as strict or structured as some places. You don't have to work." "RDAP dorm is clean, low population, and sex offenders can watch TVs and sit at the tables, whereas in some other dorms they have to sit in chairs along the walls to watch TVs. Lots of available TVs in housing units."

Bad: "Unnecessary politics. Mediocre food." "It's not as strict or structured as it should reasonably be. Petty guard policies and atmosphere. Arbitrary, asinine rules." "The food isn't good or plentiful. No fried foods. Diet sodas only." "It is really hot here." "No microwaves, and the ice machines are locked up until after 4:00 p.m."

Other Comments: "Not a bad place, but there are better Lows." "No weights, average commissary." "Honestly, everything is a mess here. The administrative atmosphere/culture is bad, and because of it, the compound culture is bad. While there are worse places to be as far as Lows go, this place is run like a Medium." "I would rate FCI Beaumont Low a 7.5 and a 9 in the RDAP unit."

In the News: In April 2018, Tanya L. Richard, an administrative employee at Federal Correctional Institution Beaumont Low, was indicted for running a $4 million fraud scheme in which families were told they could reduce the sentence of their loved ones by paying money.

In August 2017, Anqunett Vernetta Lewis, a guard at FCI Beaumont Low, was sentenced to 18 months for bribery. She was allegedly being paid by inmates to smuggle watches with cellular capability into the prison.

In January 2016, Lakista Lashau Davis, a contract nurse at FCI Beaumont Low, was sentenced to three years in federal prison for accepting $5,000 to smuggle heroin into the facility for a prisoner.

In 2003, Jamaal Landry, a guard at FCI Beaumont Low, was charged with bribery after being caught in a sting, agreeing to take $3,000 to smuggle four pounds of marijuana into the prison.

FCI Big Spring

Federal Correctional Institution Big Spring | FCI Big Spring

Facilities: FCI Big Spring with an adjacent minimum-security satellite prison camp.

Facility Address & Contact Information

Federal Correctional Institution Big Spring
1900 Simler Avenue
Big Spring, TX 79720

Phone: 432-266-2300
Fax: 432-466-2576
Email: BIG/ExecAssistant@bop.gov

BOP Website: https://www.bop.gov/locations/institutions/big/
Wikipedia: https://en.wikipedia.org/wiki/Federal_Correctional_Institution,_Big_Spring
ZCG Website: https://www.prisonerresource.com/resources/federal-prison-profiles/south-central-region-scr/federal-correctional-institution-big-spring-fci-big-spring/

Inmate Correspondence Address

For FCI Big Spring

Inmate Name and Registration Number
FCI Big Spring
Federal Correctional Institution
1900 Simler Avenue
Big Spring, TX 79720

For Satellite Prison Camp

Inmate Name and Registration Number
FCI Big Spring
Satellite Prison Camp
1900 Simler Avenue
Big Spring, TX 79720

NOTE: Funds cannot be sent directly to federal inmates. See Chapter 1 for more information on sending funds to federal inmates.

Sex: Male

Security Level: Main: Low Security; Camp: Minimum Security

Location: FCI Big Spring is located midway between Dallas and El Paso, on the southwest edge of Big Spring, at the intersection of I-20 and U.S. Highway 80.

BOP Region: South Central Region (SCR)

BOP Institution Code: BIG for FCI Big Spring

Judicial District: Northern District of Texas

Medical Care Level: Level 2. See Chapter 2 for more information on Medical Care and Mental Health Care Levels.

Mental Health Care Level: Level 2

Population (as of May 1, 2019): Main: 1,207; Camp: 182

Background: Federal Correctional Institution Big Spring is a low-security federal prison in Big Spring, Texas, which houses male inmates. It was opened in 1972. Federal Correctional Institution Big Spring Camp, which also houses male inmates, opened in 1992 and is located adjacent to the main institution.

FCI Big Spring initially opened as a Federal Prison Camp. FCI Big Spring buildings were previously used as the Webb Air Force Base before being converted into a prison. In 1990, it was converted to the low-security federal prison it is today.

Media reports indicate that in the past several years there has been one work stoppage and one racially motivated brawl at FCI Big Spring. News reports also state that one guard was indicted for accepting bribes to smuggle contraband while another male guard was indicted for raping a male prisoner.

Housing: Inmates are housed in two-person cells. There is a total of twelve housing units. Inmates in the camp are housed in dormitories.

Health Service: Sick call, dental sick call, emergency medical treatment, medications, physical examinations, and immunizations are provided at both FCI Big Spring and the satellite camp. Emergency medical care is available 24 hours a day by approaching any staff member. Routine care is available by submitting a sick call form to Health Services.

Psychology Services: All inmates are screened through a brief interview by Psychology Services staff within 14 days of arrival at FCI Big Spring. A psychologist is available to provide counseling and other mental health services to inmates experiencing behavioral, emotional, and/ or adjustment problems. These mental health services include crisis intervention, individual and group counseling, pre-release counseling, evaluation, and testing. A variety of special topic groups, such as Relationships, Living Free Values Development, Commitment to Change: Overcoming Errors in Thinking Group, Dealing with Anger, Stress Management, Breaking Barriers, Framework for Recovery, and Victim's Impact are offered by or co-sponsored by the department.

Residential Drug Abuse Program (RDAP): FCI Big Spring and the camp do not house a Residential Drug Abuse Program (RDAP). A variety of substance abuse services, such as a Living Sober group, are offered. A Drug Education Class is also provided. Individual and group counseling is provided by the drug treatment specialist through the Non-Residential Drug Abuse Program (NR-DAP).

Education Services: FCI Big Spring provides literacy, GED, and English-as-a-Second Language (ESL) programs. Inmates who obtain a GED while at the institution will receive $25.00 and a graduation photograph. Parenting and Adult Continuing Education (ACE) classes are also available. High school diplomas and post-secondary degrees are available through paid correspondence programs.

Advanced Occupational Education: FCI Big Spring offers Building Trades, Commercial Maintenance, Computer Skills/Desktop Publishing, Electrical Trades, Food Service Management, Green Insulation Technology, HVAC, High Reliability Soldering, Masonry Trades, Plumbing Trades, and Wind Energy Technician.

Vocational Training: FCI Big Spring does not offer any vocational training. The camp offers vocational training in Horticulture.

Apprenticeship: FCI Big Spring does not currently offer any apprenticeship training.

Library Services: In the leisure library inmates can check out hardcover books, paperback books, magazines, and newspapers. The law library is located in the east end of the Education Building. The law library contains the collection of legal reference materials required by the federal prison system. Most of these legal materials are on the TRULINCS Electronic Law Library Computers. Typewriters are available through a check out procedure. A Debitec copy machine is also available for inmate use. Inmate law library clerks are available to assist in locating legal materials. Legal reference material is available for preparation of legal documents in the law library.

UNICOR: The FCI Big Spring UNICOR facility produces electronics and plastics.

Commissary: Inmates are allowed to spend $360.00 monthly in the commissary on their assigned shopping days. This limit does not include telephone credits, nicotine replacement therapy patches, over-the-counter medications, copy cards or postage. Inmates can also purchase a number of other commissary items, including food, snacks, candy, ice cream, drinks, clothing, shoes, and more.

Recreation Services: Indoors, the FCI Big Spring Recreation Department offers a gym, weight room, track area, recreation center with pool tables, a ping pong table, TV viewing areas, free weights and cardio area, music rooms, an Issue Room with pool balls, guitars, board games, a gym, and hobbycraft area. Outdoor facilities include a softball/soccer field, 10 Handball/Racquetball courts, a quarter mile running track, sand volleyball court, horseshoe pits, a weight pavilion, bocce ball courts, and intramural leagues in a number of sports.

Visitation Information: On Sunday and Saturday visitation is held between 8:00 a.m. and 3:00 p.m. On federal holidays visitation is held between 8:00 a.m. and 3:00 p.m. See Chapter 1 for more information on visitation.

In the News: In June 2018, prisoners at Federal Correctional Institution Big Spring refused to go to work, resulting in a lockdown lasting more than a week.

In 2014, Matthew Castaneda, a guard at FCI Big Spring, was sentenced to six months in prison for making false statements in connection with his role in accepting bribes to smuggle cell phones and other contraband into the facility.

In August 2013, a fight broke out at FCI Big Spring, resulting in conflicting accounts of the situation: prisoners claimed it was a racially motivated gang fight with hostages, while the Bureau of Prisons said everything was locked down and under control.

In September 1997, Darren Humphries, a guard at FCI Big Spring, was indicted for raping a male prisoner earlier in the year.

FPC Bryan

Federal Prison Camp Bryan | FPC Bryan

Facility Address & Contact Information

Federal Prison Camp Bryan
1100 Ursuline Avenue
Bryan, TX 77805

Phone: 979-823-1879
Fax: 979-775-5681
Email: BRY/PublicInformation@bop.gov

BOP Website: https://www.bop.gov/locations/institutions/bry/
Wikipedia: https://en.wikipedia.org/wiki/Federal_Prison_Camp,_Bryan
ZCG Website: https://www.prisonerresource.com/resources/federal-prison-profiles/south-central-region-scr/federal-prison-camp-bryan-fpc-bryan/

Inmate Correspondence Address

Inmate Name and Registration Number
FPC Bryan
Federal Prison Camp
P.O. Box 2149
Bryan, TX 77805

NOTE: Funds cannot be sent directly to federal inmates. See Chapter 1 for more information on sending funds to federal inmates.

Sex: Female

Security Level: Minimum Security

Location: FPC Bryan is located 95 miles northwest of Houston and 165 miles south of Dallas, in the town of Bryan at the intersection of Ursuline Avenue and 23rd Street.

BOP Region: South Central Region (SCR)

BOP Institution Code: BRY for FPC Bryan

Judicial District: Southern District of Texas

Medical Care Level: Level 2. See Chapter 2 for more information on Medical Care and Mental Health Care Levels.

Mental Health Care Level: Level 2

Population (as of May 1, 2019): 853

Background: Federal Prison Camp Bryan is a minimum-security federal prison in Bryan, Texas, which houses female inmates. It was opened in 1989.

The facility partners with Canine Companions for Independence to allow inmates to train dogs to become personal assistance dogs.

Notable inmates include former Commissioner of Hidalgo County (TX) Sylvia Handy (convicted of hiring illegal aliens as county employees, personal caretakers, and then stealing their earnings to pay for personal expenses), and Ruby Jane McMillian (convicted of conspiracy as part of a methamphetamine distribution ring).

Media reports indicate that there have been at least three escapes at the institution and that at least seven female inmates have been sexually assaulted by prison guards.

In 2017, Insider Monkey named FPC Bryan one of the ten easiest federal prisons to do time.

Housing: Inmates are housed in four-person rooms. There are approximately 200 inmates per dormitory.

Health Services: Health services provided at FPC Bryan include, sick call, emergency health treatment, medications, physical examinations, chronic care, HIV testing, dental services and an initial screening. Emergency medical care is available 24 hours a day. Routine care is obtained by attending sick call on Monday, Tuesday, Thursday, and Friday at 6:30 a.m. Insulin line is also held at 6:30 a.m., while pill line is held at 8:00 a.m. and 3:00 p.m.

Psychology Services: FPC Bryan provides screening, assessment, and treatment of mental health and drug abuse problems, individual and group counseling, psycho-educational classes, self-help and supportive services, and referral to Health Services for medical treatment of a mental illness. Comprehensive assessments of each inmate's strengths and weaknesses are made, along with programming recommendations specific to meet psychological needs. Brief counseling and long-term therapy, as determined by the psychologist, is available. Medication monitoring and evaluation for medication referral are available. Mental health programs are designed to help inmates with severe emotional, cognitive, and behavioral problems are available for inmates who are having difficulty functioning in a mainline institution due to a psychological disorder. The STAGES Program for inmates with serious mental illness and personality disorders is also offered.

Residential Drug Abuse Program (RDAP): FPC Bryan has the Residential Drug Abuse Program (RDAP). It also provides a drug abuse program, Drug Abuse Education Course, and the Non-Residential Drug Abuse Program (NR-DAP).

Education Services: FPC Bryan provides literacy, GED, English-as-a-Second Language (ESL), Adult Continuing Education (ACE) courses, and parenting classes. Hours of operation are 7:30 to 10:30 a.m., 12:40 to 3:30 p.m., and 5:30 to 8:30 p.m. Incentive awards are provided to inmates making satisfactory progress and successfully completing the literacy programs. Inmates may also receive incentives for progressing to various levels in the GED or ESL programs. Graduation ceremonies recognize GED, ESL, and Occupational Education completions. High school diplomas and post-secondary degrees are available through paid correspondence programs. Blinn College also offers inmate on-site classes.

Advanced Occupational Education: FPC Bryan offers advanced occupational education in Accounting Technology, Administrative Assistant Specialist, Cosmetologist, HVAC, Horticulture, Medical Transcription and Coding Specialist, Microsoft-Business Applications, and Small Business Management.

Vocational Training: FPC Bryan does not offer vocational training programs aside from the advanced occupational education programs.

Apprenticeship: No apprenticeship training programs are currently available at FPC Bryan aside from the advanced occupational education programs.

Library Services: FPC Bryan offers both leisure and law libraries. The leisure libraries offer inmates a variety of reading materials, including periodicals, newspapers, fiction, nonfiction, and reference books. An interlibrary loan program is available. The TRULINCS Electronic Law Libraries provide inmates with access to legal materials and an opportunity to prepare legal documents. A copy machine and electric typewriters are also available for inmate usage.

UNICOR: The FPC Bryan UNICOR faculty is a call center.

Commissary: Inmates are allowed to spend $360.00 monthly in the commissary on their assigned shopping days. Commissary is open Monday through Thursday with shopping times of 6:30 a.m., 10:30 a.m., and 2:00 p.m. Inmates may use funds in their account to purchase items at the institution commissary, place funds on their inmate phone account, purchase TRU-Units for their TRULINCS account, or send funds out of the institution using Form BP-199. Often inmates carry their purchases in laundry bags back to their housing unit.

Recreation Services: Leisure activities at FPC Bryan include organized and informal games, sports, physical fitness, table games, hobbycrafts, music programs, intramural activities, social and cultural organizations, and movies. Art and hobbycraft programs, wellness programs and other recreation programs are also available. Indoors, inmates will find treadmills, ellipticals, Stairmasters, and various weights. Outdoors, inmates can participate in softball, volleyball, weightlifting, yoga, Pilates, and the Jumpstart weight loss program. Picnic tables, bleachers, and TVs are also available. Hours of operation are 6:00 a.m. to 8:30 p.m., excluding count times and recall for the noon meal.

Visitation Information: On Sunday and Saturday visitation is held between 8:00 a.m. and 5:00 p.m. On federal holidays visitation is held between 8:00 a.m. and 3:00 p.m. See Chapter 1 for more information on visitation.

Prison Politics: Because FPC Bryan is a Camp, there are virtually no prison politics.

Level of Violence: There is almost no violence. One inmate stated that the institution is "very safe" and that there "very rarely is an altercation."

Vulnerable Populations: While sex offenders are barred from Camp placement, informants and LGBT inmates don't have any problems walking this yard.

Good: "The programs offered and the opportunity to better yourself."

Bad: "The pettiness and the lack of professionalism of a few staff members."

Other Comments: "Stepping down from an FCI, here you have many more rights, but also many more rules." "As long as you do the right things in here, this place is easy. There are always worse places to bid your time."

In the News: In May 2017, three women -- Edith Lara, Ysenia Frausto and Brenda Rosas -- escaped from Federal Prison Camp Bryan. Frausto was picked up by the U.S. Marshals two days later.

In July 2016, James Graves, a guard at FPC Bryan, was sentenced to 21 months in prison for engaging in sexual contact with two female prisoners.

In May 2016, Kendrick Desmond Brooks, an employee at FPC Bryan, was sentenced to six months for having sex with female prisoners.

In April 2016, Deputy Attorney General Sally Yates visited FPC Bryan as part of National Reentry Week, designed to highlight the necessity of successful reintegration back into society.

Also in April 2016, Marshall Thomas, a guard at FPC Bryan, was sentenced to 18 months in prison and required to register as a sex offender after admitting to forcible intercourse with a female prisoner and vaginal penetration with his fingers of another prisoner in July 2014.

In April 2010, Canine Companions for Independence began operating a program at FPC Bryan to train puppies the skills to become assistance dogs.

In 1998, Charles Keith Alexander, a cook supervisor at FPC Bryan, was indicted on nine misdemeanor charges after sexually assaulting four female prisoners over a two-year period.

FMC Carswell

Federal Medical Center Carswell | FMC Carswell

Facilities: FMC Carswell and an adjacent minimum-security satellite prison camp.

Facility Address & Contact Information

Federal Medical Center Carswell
J Street, Building 3000
Fort Worth, TX 76127

Phone: 817-782-4000
Fax: 817-782-4875
Email: CRW/ExecAssistant@bop.gov

BOP Website: https://www.bop.gov/locations/institutions/crw/
Wikipedia: https://en.wikipedia.org/wiki/Federal_Medical_Center,_Carswell
ZCG Website: https://www.prisonerresource.com/resources/federal-prison-profiles/south-central-region-scr/federal-medical-center-carswell-fmc-carswell/

Inmate Correspondence Address

For FMC Carswell

Inmate Name and Registration Number
FMC Carswell
Federal Medical Center
P.O. Box 27137
Fort Worth, TX 76127

For Satellite Prison Camp

Inmate Name and Registration Number
FMC Carswell
Satellite Prison Camp
P.O. Box 27137
Fort Worth, TX 76127

NOTE: Funds cannot be sent directly to federal inmates. See Chapter 1 for more information on sending funds to federal inmates.

Sex: Female

Security Level: Main: Administrative Security (Multiple Security Levels); Camp: Minimum Security

Location: FMC Carswell is located in the northeast corner of the Naval Air Station, Joint Reserve Base; 1 mile from Highway 183 and 3 miles from I-30.

BOP Region: South Central Region (SCR)

BOP Institution Code: CRW for FMC Carswell

Judicial District: Northern District of Texas

Medical Care Level: Level 3/4. See Chapter 2 for more information on Medical Care and Mental Health Care Levels.

Mental Health Care Level: Level 3/4

Population: (as of May 1, 2019) Main: 1,293; Camp: 355

Background: Federal Medical Center Carswell is an administrative-security federal prison in Fort Worth, Texas, which houses female inmates. It was opened in 1994. Federal Medical Center Carswell Camp, which also houses female inmates, is located adjacent to the main institution.

FMC Carswell is the Federal Bureau of Prisons' medical and psychiatric center for female inmates and features the Bureau's only Administrative Unit for disruptive female federal prisoners. The Administrative Unit is a high-security unit for women classified with violence and/or escape attempts who are referred to as "special management concerns." The prison is also a Sex Offender Management Program (SOMP) facility.

Notable inmates include gold and bronze medal winning Olympian Marion Jones Thompson (convicted of fraud and use of performance enhancing drugs), and Lisa M. Montgomery (sentenced to death after kidnapping and murdering a pregnant woman).

Media reports indicate that at least three guards have been indicted for sexually assaulting inmates, while a prison employee was convicted of accepting kickbacks from a private prison healthcare company in exchange for contract preference.

Housing: Inmates are housed in a variety of configurations, from one- and two-person medical cell to dorms with four-person rooms. Inmates at the camp are housed in dormitories divided into two-person pods.

Health Services: Medical and dental sick call, medications, and medical and dental emergency services are available to inmates. Emergency medical care is available 24 hours a day. Inmates are assigned a health care provider who treats them for the duration of their stay. Sick call is held Monday, Tuesday, Thursday, and Friday at 6:00 a.m. Pill and insulin line are conducted before each meal.

Psychology Services: Psychology Services at FMC Carswell offers a wide variety of therapeutic programming. Clinical psychologists or Drug Abuse Treatment Specialists are available for evaluation, crisis intervention, and counseling. Consultant support is provided by community and staff psychiatrists. Psychology Services has organized its program for female offenders into four tracks as a means of efficiently offering a wide variety of self-improvement and recovery opportunities. The four tracks are Abuse Recovery, Addictions, Values, and Wellness. Other group classes include trauma, anger management, and cognitive thinking. FMC Carswell also offers outpatient psychiatric services. Inmates may submit an Inmate Request to Staff addressed to Psychiatry Services to request outpatient care. A Non-Residential Sex Offender Treatment Program (SOTP-NR) is also available. The facility also offers the STAGES Program for inmates with serious mental illness and personality disorders. And through the Religious Services Department, the Life Connections Program is offered for inmates who desire to grow as responsible persons.

Residential Drug Abuse Program (RDAP): FMC Carswell has the Residential Drug Abuse Program (RDAP). A Spanish RDAP program is also available. Drug abuse programs, the Non-Residential Drug Abuse Program (NR-DAP), a Drug Education class, Alcoholics Anonymous (AA), and nicotine dependence groups are offered.

Education Services: FMC Carswell provides literacy, GED, English-as-a-Second Language (ESL), and parenting programs. Also available are Adult Continuing Education (ACE) classes, which are taught by fellow inmates and on a variety of topics. High school diplomas and post-secondary degrees are available through paid correspondence programs. Hours of operation are 8:00 a.m. to 6:30 p.m. Monday through Friday. The Education Department is closed on the weekends.

Advanced Occupational Education: The main facility at FMC Carswell offers advanced occupational education in Cosmetology and Culinary Arts. The camp offers a Horticulture Master Gardener Program and a program for National Fitness Personal Trainers.

Vocational Training: FMC Carswell does not offer any vocational training aside from its advanced occupational education programs.

Apprenticeship: FMC Carswell does not currently offer any apprenticeship programs.

Library Services: The law library contains a collection of legal reference materials as required by the Federal Bureau of Prisons. Most of these reference materials, along with federal case law, are on the TRULINCS Electronic Law Library. In the leisure library inmates can check out both fiction and nonfiction books, newspapers, and magazines.

UNICOR: FMC Carswell does not have a UNICOR.

Commissary: Inmates at FMC Carswell are allowed to spend up to $360.00 per month on items such as food, drinks, clothing, shoes, and electronics. The spending limitation is further allocated to $180 every two weeks. Inmates are allowed to shop once a week on their assigned day. Commissary is open Monday through Thursday at 6:00 to 11:00 a.m. Inmates are issued a Commissary/I.D. card with their register number and picture on it. This card is to be used for Commissary purchases and identification purposes and must be in the inmate's possession at all times.

Recreation Services: The FMC Carswell Recreation Department offers a variety of leisure activities such as bingo, board games, cards, organized and informal sports, social activities, arts and hobbycrafts, physical fitness, and aerobic activities. Inmates also have access to a track.

Visitation Information: On Sunday and Saturday visitation is held between 8:00 a.m. and 3:00 p.m. On federal holidays visitation is held between 8:00 a.m. and 3:00 p.m. See Chapter 1 for more information on visitation.

Prison Politics: There are no politics at this prison due to being a medical center.

Level of Violence: There is a very low level of violence. According to one inmate, "Violence is sporadic at best and occurs mostly with younger inmates and/or new inmates trying to make themselves known." Another respondent agreed, stating, "Pretty safe overall."

Vulnerable Populations: Sex offenders, informants, and LGBT inmates can all walk the yard. According to one respondent, "There is even a residential sex offender treatment program." The same inmate also explained that "there are a lot of transgender and gay inmates here." Another inmate agreed, stating that transgender inmates and sex offenders are allowed in all of the housing units.

Good: "This place is ok overall. It's a medical facility, so the medical care is pretty good." "Psychology and recreation are both pretty good."

Bad: "They don't really offer much in the way of pre-release care or planning." "This is not a medical place. I have seen people die and families be lied to. A lot gets covered up."

In the News: In March 2018, a lawsuit brought by the conservative Christian legal group Alliance Defending Freedom and Rhonda Fleming (convicted in 2009 of a multimillion-dollar fraud scheme), trying to force transgender women out of the all-female Federal Medical

Center Carswell, failed to reach a negotiated settlement on time. The parties have asked the judge to set a new deadline.

In February 2018, the vice president of the American Federation of Government Workers (the federal prison guards' union) said that FMC Carswell would lose 71 positions because of the Trump Administration's policy to "rightsize" staffing levels in federal prisons.

In November 2017, Matthew McGaugh, a case manager at FMC Carswell, was sentenced to one year in prison for sexual abuse of a ward after forcing a female prisoner to perform multiple sex acts on him while she was under his supervisory authority. The conduct occurred in November 2016.

In October 2014, Cary Hudson, a financial administrator for the Bureau of Prisons at FMC Carswell, pleaded guilty to accepting kickbacks from Integrated Medical Solutions, Inc., in exchange for his assistance with federal contracts to provide health care to prisoners.

In 2014, Brady Michael Green, a guard at FMC Carswell, pleaded guilty to making a false statement -- for lying about having sex with a prisoner -- so he wouldn't have to register as a sex offender. Green was sentenced to three months in prison.

In 2012, Kraig D. Lavan, a guard at FMC Carswell, was indicted for and pleaded guilty to engaging in a "sexual act" with a female prisoner.

In 2007, Lisa M. Montgomery, who kidnapped and murdered a pregnant woman, then claimed the unborn baby as her own, was sentenced to death and is the only woman on federal death row.

FCI El Reno

Federal Correctional Institution El Reno | FCI El Reno

Facilities: FCI El Reno, with an adjacent minimum-security satellite prison camp.

Facility Address & Contact Information

Federal Correctional Institution El Reno
4205 Highway 66 West
El Reno, OK 73036

Phone: 405-262-4875
Fax: 405-319-7626
Email: ERE/ExecAssistant@bop.gov

BOP Website: https://www.bop.gov/locations/institutions/ere/
Wikipedia: https://en.wikipedia.org/wiki/Federal_Correctional_Institution,_El_Reno
ZCG Website: https://www.prisonerresource.com/resources/federal-prison-profiles/south-central-region-scr/federal-correctional-institution-el-reno-fci-el-reno/

Inmate Correspondence Address

For FCI El Reno

Inmate Name and Registration Number
FCI El Reno
Federal Correctional Institution
P.O. Box 1500
El Reno, OK 73036

For Satellite Prison Camp

Inmate Name and Registration Number
FCI El Reno
Satellite Prison Camp
P.O. Box 1500
El Reno, OK 73036

NOTE: Funds cannot be sent directly to federal inmates. See Chapter 1 for more information on sending funds to federal inmates.

Sex: Male

Security Level: Main: Medium Security; Camp: Minimum Security

Location: FCI El Reno is located 30 miles west of Oklahoma City.

BOP Region: South Central Region (SCR)

BOP Institution Code: ERE for FCI El Reno

Judicial District: Western District of Oklahoma

Medical Care Level: Level 2. See Chapter 2 for more information on Medical Care and Mental Health Care Levels.

Mental Health Care Level: Level 2

Population (as of May 1, 2019): Main: 941; Camp: 256

Background: Federal Correctional Institution El Reno is a medium-security federal prison in El Reno, Oklahoma, which houses male inmates. It was opened in 1933. Federal Correctional Institution El Reno Camp, which also houses male inmates, opened in 1980 and is located adjacent to the main institution.

FCI El Reno is located on the Fort Reno Military Reserve. FCI El Reno was initially designed to house younger prisoners aged 18 to 26, until the late 1970s, when it opened to all age groups. President Barack Obama visited FCI El Reno in July 2015, making him the first sitting U.S. president to ever visit a federal prison.

Media reports indicate that at least one guard has sexually assaulted an inmate at the prison.

Housing: Inmates are housed in two- and three-person cells. Inmates at the camp are housed in dormitories which are divided into two- and four-person cubicles.

Health Services: Sick call, dental care, emergency treatment, chronic care, preventive health care services, emergency services, diagnosis and treatment of chronic infectious diseases, mental health care, substance abuse treatment, and medications are all available at FCI El Reno. Emergency health care is available 24 hours a day. In order to be evaluated for routine care needs, inmates must attend sick call, which is held between 6:00 and 6:30 a.m. on Monday, Tuesday, Thursday, and Friday. Pill and insulin lines are conducted during breakfast and dinner.

Psychology Services: Psychologists are responsible for providing a full range of professional psychological services. Psychologists also aid staff members through program design, consultation, and training. Services for inmates include evaluations and therapy. Common treatment groups include anger management, HIV/AIDS awareness, and criminal thinking.

Residential Drug Abuse Program (RDAP): FCI El Reno has the Residential Drug Abuse Program (RDAP). The camp does not have the Residential Drug Abuse Program (RDAP). Both facilities offer the Drug Abuse Program, Drug Abuse Education Course, and Non-Residential Drug Abuse program (NR-DAP).

Education Services: FCI El Reno provides literacy, GED, and English-as-a-Second Language (ESL) programs. Other educational offerings include parenting and Adult Continuing Education (ACE) classes. High school diplomas and post-secondary degrees are available through paid correspondence programs.

Advanced Occupational Education: FCI El Reno offers advanced occupational education in Culinary Arts, Electric, Plumbing, Purchasing Agent, and Welding. The camp offers Diesel Repair and Horticulture.

Vocational Training: No vocational training is available at FCI El Reno aside from the advanced occupational education programs.

Apprenticeship: FCI El Reno offers apprenticeships in Dental Assistant, Drafting, Machinist, Millwright, Painter, Quality Control, Tool and Die Maker, and Welding. The camp offers an apprenticeship in Dental Assistant.

Library Services: FCI El Reno offers a legal and leisure library for inmates. The legal library primarily consists of the Bureau's TRULINCS Electronic Law Library computers. Typewriters and a copy machine are also available. The leisure library permits inmates to check out fiction and nonfiction books, newspapers, and magazines. There are also several educational DVDs that inmates can check out.

UNICOR: The FCI El Reno UNICOR facility handles metal fabrication and welding. The satellite camp does not house a UNICOR facility.

Commissary: Inmates at FCI El Reno are permitted to spend up to $360.00 per month in commissary purchases on their designated shopping days. This is further restricted to $180 every two weeks. Items such as food, drinks, clothing, and electronics can be purchased.

Inmates are allowed to shop twice a week. Sales are conducted Monday through Thursday at 1:00 and 3:00 p.m.

Recreation Services: Recreation services at FCI El Reno include areas for both indoor and outdoor activities, which include field games, court games, tabletop games, individual events, arts and crafts, team sports, space for music enthusiasts, pool tables, and television. Basketball, flag football, soccer, and Frisbee are all popular sports leagues. Yoga, a track, weights, ellipticals, treadmills, and stationary bikes are also available. In the afternoons and evenings, the administration imposes one-way moves to and from the Recreation Department.

Visitation Information: On Sunday, Monday, Friday, and Saturday visitation is held between 8:00 a.m. and 3:00 p.m. On federal holidays visitation is held between 8:00 a.m. and 3:00 p.m. See Chapter 1 for more information on visitation.

Prison Politics: While some inmates feel that this is a very political yard, others feel that it is only somewhat political. There is a general car requirement.

Level of Violence: There is a moderate level of violence at this facility. Inmates report periodic fights and some stabbings. This is especially prevalent amongst the Hispanic inmates.

Vulnerable Populations: Sex offenders and informants can't stay. LGBT inmates can remain, but they are somewhat ostracized and have to contend with an unfriendly and unsupportive environment.

Good: "Really big lockers." "Huge weight pile, great UNICOR apprenticeship in welding." "For the most part, this place is pretty calm."

Bad: "Very petty cops." "Few leisure resources, lots of in-car political bickering." "The officers like to harass people for nothing, and they will make up rules as they go. The cops also retaliate for filing grievances."

Other Comments: "It sucks shit. Do Not Go There!" "If you are from northern Texas or Oklahoma and have clean paperwork, then this is a good yard." "It's a better FCI in the area." "If you're just doing your time and you don't use drugs, this place is ok. Don't get caught with anything or they will give you a street charge."

In the News: In January 2018, former Arkansas State Senator Jake Files reported to Federal Correctional Institution El Reno to begin his 18-month sentence for fraud and money laundering.

In January 2017, Amanda Hock, a guard at FCI El Reno, was sentenced to probation and community service for engaging in sexual conduct with a male prisoner in December 2015.

In July 2015, President Barack Obama became the first sitting U.S. president to visit a federal prison when he met with prisoners and law enforcement officials at FCI El Reno.

Federal Correctional Complex Forrest City | FCC Forrest City

Facilities: FCC Forrest City houses FCI Forrest City Medium, as well as FCI Forrest City Low with an adjacent minimum-security satellite prison camp.

FCI Forrest City Medium

Federal Correctional Institution Forrest City Medium | FCI Forrest City Medium

Facility Address & Contact Information

Federal Correctional Institution Forrest City Medium
1400 Dale Bumpers Road
Forrest City, AR 72335

Phone: 870-494-4200
Fax: 870-494-4496
Email: FOM/ExecAssistant@bop.gov

BOP Website: https://www.bop.gov/locations/institutions/fom/
Wikipedia: https://en.wikipedia.org/wiki/Federal_Correctional_Institution,_Forrest_City
ZCG Website: https://www.prisonerresource.com/resources/federal-prison-profiles/south-central-region-scr/federal-correctional-complex-forrest-city-fcc-forrest-city/federal-correctional-institution-forrest-city-medium-fci-forrest-city-medium/

Inmate Correspondence Address

Inmate Name and Registration Number
FCI Forrest City Medium
Federal Correctional Institution
P.O. Box 3000
Forrest City, AR 72336

NOTE: Funds cannot be sent directly to federal inmates. See Chapter 1 for more information on sending funds to federal inmates.

Sex: Male

Security Level: Medium Security

Location: FCI Forrest City Medium is located in eastern Arkansas, between Little Rock (58 miles east) and Memphis (45 miles west), near I-40.

BOP Region: South Central Region (SCR)

BOP Institution Code: FOM for FCI Forrest City Medium, FOX for Forrest City Federal Correctional Complex

Judicial District: Eastern District of Arkansas

Medical Care Level: Level 2. See Chapter 2 for more information on Medical Care and Mental Health Care Levels.

Mental Health Care Level: Level 2

Population (as of May 1, 2019): 1,040

Background: Federal Correctional Institution Forrest City Medium is a medium-security federal prison in Forrest City, Arkansas, which houses male inmates. It is part of the Forrest City Federal Correctional Complex.

Media reports indicate that one guard was indicted for sexually abusing a child in the parking lot of an elementary school. Another guard was indicted for smuggling contraband into the institution.

Housing: Inmates are housed in two-person cells.

Health Services: Sick call, medical and dental emergency care, medications, periodic examinations, optometry, and eyeglasses are available at FCI Forrest City Medium. All inmates receive a physical examination within their first 14 days of arriving at the facility. Routine health care is available through the submission of triage forms. Emergency medical care is available 24 hours a day by contacting any member of the prison's staff.

Psychology Services: Psychology staff offer comprehensive individual and group therapy programs. These programs address a full range of clinical disorders, provide self-help options, assess and treat behavioral and emotional problems, and facilitate overall adjustment. Regular groups include criminal thinking, anger management, and others. Crisis intervention is available 24 hours, seven days a week by approaching any staff member and requesting Psychology Services to be contacted.

Residential Drug Abuse Program (RDAP): FCI Forrest City Medium has the Residential Drug Abuse Program (RDAP). The facility also provides the Drug Abuse Education Course, the Non-Residential Drug Abuse Program (NR-DAP), Alcoholics Anonymous (AA), and Narcotics Anonymous (NA).

Education Services: FCI Forrest Medium provides literacy, GED, and English-as-a-Second Language (ESL) programs. Instructors use the Adult Basic Learning Exam (ABLE), Test of Adult Basic Education (TABE), and Spanish Assessment of Basic Education (SABE) tests to determine each inmate's academic abilities. In order to request placement in any of these classes, inmates can wait until staff assign them to a class or expedite the process by submitting a cop-out or speaking to an Education Department staff member at the noon meal. Adult Continuing Education (ACE) and parenting classes are also available to the inmate population. High school diplomas and post-secondary degrees are available through paid correspondence programs.

Advanced Occupational Education: FCI Forrest City Medium offers advanced occupational education in Building Trades, Diesel Technology, and Office Technology.

Vocational Training: FCI Forrest City Medium does not offer any vocational training aside from the advanced occupational education programs.

Apprenticeship: FCI Forrest City Medium does not offer any apprenticeships.

Library Services: The leisure library contains a broad selection of fiction and nonfiction books, magazines, and newspapers, which inmates can check out. The law library contains a variety of legal reference materials for use in preparing legal papers. Reference materials include the United States Code Annotated, Federal Reporter, Supreme Court Reporter, Bureau of Prisons Program Statements, institution supplements, Code of Federal Regulations, federal case law, and other legal materials. The majority of these materials are accessible through the law library computers which offer a scaled-down, federal-only LexisNexis program. Typewriters are also available for inmate use. The law library is located in the Education Department.

UNICOR: The FCI Forrest City Medium UNICOR facility produces office furniture.

Commissary: Inmates at FCI Forrest City Medium are allowed to shop once per week on their designated shopping day. A $360.00 monthly spending limit is imposed. Inmates can purchase a wide variety of items. Items include ice cream, sodas, food, candy, and various snacks. Clothing, shoes, and electronics can also be purchased.

Recreation Services: FCI Forrest City Medium offers a variety of indoor and outdoor activities. A leisure center offers music rooms, TV (sports or news only), patio area, billiard table, foosball, ping-pong, table games and multi-purpose rooms, a hobbycraft area, a fitness area and a gym. The recreation yard offers a variety of outdoor activities, programs and classes, step aerobics, exercise classes, and spinning and circuit training on fitness equipment. Intramural and individual sports are also available to the general population. Basketball, softball, and football leagues are popular.

Visitation Information: On Sunday and Saturday visitation is held between 8:00 a.m. and 3:00 p.m. On federal holidays visitation is held between 8:00 a.m. and 3:00 p.m. See Chapter 1 for more information on visitation.

Prison Politics: There is a low level of politics at this prison. Inmates are not required to be part of a car in order to stay.

Level of Violence: Inmates report a low level of violence at this facility. One inmate referred to the prison as being "safe."

Vulnerable Populations: Sex offenders, informants, and LGBT inmates can remain. According to one respondent, "Sex offenders seem to be everywhere." He further explained, "The only place where sex offenders seem to have any problems are with the TVs. It's best for them to avoid TV rooms." Another inmate stated that "all are allowed on the yard."

Bad: "TVs can be problematic for sex offenders and other undesirables." "Visits are highly controlled, and families are sometimes sent away after a long trip to the prison due to stupid reasons. Sometimes no reason is given. The cops are also slow at calling people to visitation." "More programs are needed for the sex offender population."

In the News: In October 2011, Charles Witcher, a 24-year-old guard at Federal Correctional Institution Forrest City Medium, was arrested on a charge of statutory rape for having sexual contact with a 13-year-old girl in the parking lot of an elementary school.

In May 2005, Xavier Livingstone, a guard at FCI Forrest City Medium, was arrested while trying to smuggle contraband into the facility.

FCI Forrest City Low

Federal Correctional Institution Forrest City Low | FCI Forrest City Low

Facilities: FCI Elkton with an adjacent minimum-security satellite prison camp.

Facility Address & Contact Information

Federal Correctional Institution Forrest City Low
1400 Dale Bumpers Road
Forrest City, AR 72335

Phone: 870-630-6000
Fax: 870-494-4496
Email: FOR/ExecAssistant@bop.gov

BOP Website: https://www.bop.gov/locations/institutions/for/
Wikipedia: https://en.wikipedia.org/wiki/Federal_Correctional_Institution,_Forrest_City
ZCG Website: https://www.prisonerresource.com/resources/federal-prison-profiles/south-central-region-scr/federal-correctional-complex-forrest-city-fcc-forrest-city/federal-correctional-institution-forrest-city-low-fci-forrest-city-low/

Inmate Correspondence Address

For FCI Forrest City Low

Inmate Name and Registration Number
FCI Forrest City Low
Federal Correctional Institution
P.O. Box 9000
Forrest City, AR 72336

For Satellite Prison Camp

Inmate Name and Registration Number
FCI Forrest City Low
Satellite Prison Camp
P.O. Box 8000
Forrest City, AR 72336

NOTE: Funds cannot be sent directly to federal inmates. See Chapter 1 for more information on sending funds to federal inmates.

Sex: Male

Security Level: Main: Low Security; Camp: Minimum Security

Location: FCI Forrest City Low is located in eastern Arkansas, between Little Rock (85 miles east) and Memphis (45 miles west), near I-40.

BOP Region: South Central Region (SCR)

BOP Institution Code: FOR FCI Forrest City Low, FOX for Forrest City Federal Correctional Complex

Judicial District: Eastern District of Arkansas

Medical Care Level: Level 2. See Chapter 2 for more information on Medical Care and Mental Health Care Levels.

Mental Health Care Level: Level 2

Population (as of May 1, 2019): Main: 1,862; Camp: 274

Background: Federal Correctional Institution Forrest City Low is a low-security federal prison in Forrest City, Arkansas, which houses male inmates. It was opened in 1997 and is part of the Forrest City Federal Correctional Complex. Federal Correctional Institution Forrest City Camp, which also houses male inmates, was opened in 1997 and is located adjacent to the main institution.

Media reports indicate that two guards were arrested for possession with intent to distribute drugs in a school zone. Also, at least two inmates have escaped from the prison.

Housing: Inmates are housed in dormitories which are divided into two- and three-person cubicles. In each housing unit, there is also a room which houses 16 bunk beds for a total of 32 inmates. There is a total of 12 housing units, each which holds approximately 150 inmates.

Health Services: Sick call, medical and dental emergency care, medications, periodic examinations, optometry, and eyeglasses are available at FCI Forrest City Low. All inmates receive a physical examination within their first 14 days of arriving at the facility. Emergency medical care is available 24 hours a day. Routine care is available through the submission of a sick call, which is conducted at 7:15 a.m. on Monday, Tuesday, Thursday, and Friday. Insulin line is at

6:30 a.m. and 5:00 p.m. Pill line is at 7:00 a.m. and 7:30 p.m. There is also a noon self-carry medication pickup.

Psychology Services: Psychology staff at FCI Forrest City Low offer comprehensive individual and group therapy programs. These programs address the full range of clinical disorders, provide self-help options, assess and treat behavioral and emotional problems, and facilitate overall adjustment. Crisis intervention is also available 24 hours a day, seven days a week. Typical groups include anger management, criminal thinking, grief, PTSD, support, Seeking Safety, and others.

Residential Drug Abuse Program (RDAP): FCI Forrest City Low offers the Residential Drug Abuse Program (RDAP). The camp does not have the Residential Drug Abuse Program (RDAP). Both facilities provide various drug abuse programs, a Drug Abuse Education Course, and Non-Residential Drug Abuse Program (NR-DAP), and Alcoholics Anonymous (AA).

Education Services: FCI Forrest City Low provides GED and English-as-a-Second Language (ESL) programs. Instructors use the Adult Basic Learning Exam (ABLE), Test of Adult Basic Education (TABE), and Spanish Assessment of Basic Education (SABE) tests to determine each inmate's academic abilities. Adult Continuing Education (ACE) and parenting classes are also available to the inmate population. Current ACE offerings include public speaking, CDL, philosophy, HVAC, small engine repair, Spanish, debate, motivational speaking, and financial investments. High school diplomas and post-secondary degrees are available through paid correspondence programs. Hours of operation are 7:30 to 10:00 a.m., 12:00 to 3:00 p.m., and 5:00 to 8:00 p.m. Monday through Thursday, 7:30 to 10:00 a.m., 12:00 to 3:00 p.m. Friday, and 7:30 to 9:00 a.m. and 12:00 to 3:00 p.m. Saturday.

Advanced Occupational Education: FCI Forrest City Low offers advanced occupational education in Building Trades, Diesel Technology, and Drafting Technology. Both the main facility and the camp offer Drafting Technology and Office Technology.

Vocational Training: FCI Forrest City Low does not offer vocational training aside from the advanced occupational education programs.

Apprenticeship: FCI Forrest City Low does not offers any apprenticeships.

Library Services: The law library contains a variety of legal reference materials for use in preparing legal papers. Reference materials include the United States Code Annotated, Federal Reporter, Supreme Court Reporter, federal case law, Bureau of Prisons Program Statements, institution supplements, and other legal materials. All of these are available on the TRULINCS Electronic Law Library computers. Inmates also have access to six typewriters, a copy machine, and a computer (to view discovery materials). The law library is located in the Education Department. A leisure library is also available to inmates, where they can check out newspapers, magazines, and fiction and nonfiction books. An interlibrary loan program is available.

UNICOR: The FCI Forrest City Low UNICOR facility produces office furniture. The camp does not house a UNICOR facility.

Commissary: FCI Forrest City Low inmates are allowed to shop once per week on their designated shopping day. Shopping is held Monday through Thursday between 6:30 and 9:00 a.m., and 11:00 a.m. to 2:00 p.m. Inmates are allowed to spend up to $360.00 per month on items such as food, drinks, clothing, electronics, and more. In order to shop, inmates must line up, turn in their commissary forms, and wait for their orders to be filled.

Recreation Services: FCI Forrest City Low offers a variety of indoor and outdoor activities. Inmates have access to pool tables, stationary bikes, treadmills, leatherwork, drawing, chess, piano, guitar, yoga, painting, and ab classes. Outside, inmates have access to softball, football, soccer, pickleball, handball, volleyball, bag toss, horseshoes, bocce ball, basketball, Frisbee, and a track. Hours of operation are 6:30 a.m. to 3:00 p.m. (excluding counts and meals) and 5:00 p.m. to sundown Monday through Friday. On the weekends, the hours of operation are 7:30 to 9:00 a.m., 11:00 a.m. to 3:00 p.m., and 5:00 p.m. to sundown.

Visitation Information: On Sunday and Saturday visitation is held between 8:00 a.m. and 3:00 p.m. On federal holidays visitation is held between 8:00 a.m. and 3:00 p.m. See Chapter 1 for more information on visitation.

Prison Politics: There is a low to moderate level of politics at this facility. Inmates are not required to be part of a car. According to one respondent, "There is deep racial separation here."

Level of Violence: There is a low level of violence at this prison. One respondent pegged it as an "8 out of 10" for safety. Another stated that it was "good," while another referred to the prison as "safe." One respondent specified that when violence occurs, it "almost always involves money, drugs, cell phones or things related." Another inmate stated that "the level of violence is generally low. There are some fist fights and rare attacks with locks. For the most part, this is a safe compound."

Vulnerable Populations: Sex offenders, informants, and LGBT inmates can stay. Some respondents felt that all are somewhat ostracized and excluded from the TV rooms, while other respondents felt that this was not the case. All said that such vulnerable populations shouldn't have many problems, if any. One inmate in particular stated that "sex offenders are left alone for the most part, as are the gay guys." He also expressed that there is "a pretty robust gay community here," and the "five or so trans guys here have more problems with staff than with other inmates." Another inmate expressed that "anyone can walk the yard."

Good: "Low violence and cops mostly leave you alone." "If you have something coming your way, the medical/psychology relationship can be helpful." "The recreation department is good aside from the lack of dedication from staff. The UNICOR is also very good." "It is fundamentally safe, even for me, a gay sex offender."

Bad: "Very dysfunctionally run. Things are never on time and are always inconsistent. Rules change from staff to staff, day to day, and so on." "Medical is ineffective and slow to respond to health issues. The staff generally is unmotivated and do not do their work with any time schedule." "All of the food is filled with carbs and they almost never have salad." "The general maintenance of this place is dismal. It could be so much better with a change in staff and some money spent on general maintenance." "Overall, the facility is decent enough. Over the past 10 years it has shifted from a highly political yard to a very non-political one." "They have a penchant for mass punishment here due to the K2 and cell phone problems that they let get too out of control. If such contraband is found in a common area, everyone in the area loses phone and email privileges." "At times there is not a lot to do." "The staff is generally biased and lazy." "The administration has stopped allowing families to mail books or magazines directly to inmates. Also, kids can no longer mail cards that they have drawn on."

Other Comments: "Due to the amount of drugs, tobacco, and cell phones that have been found as of late in the Recreation Department, the administration has imposed special mass punishments on all inmates. This to include restrictions on recreation and incoming correspondence." "This facility used to be a good, well-run prison, but in the last three years it has gone from good to lousy. It's poor leadership at the top that is driving this place down." "Just because it is a safe yard doesn't mean that it is a good yard." "With 160 guys on a unit, it's going to be loud and tempers will flair, but everyone gets along and does just fine on the compound."

In the News: In December 2016, Devoy Nokes and George Robert were recaptured after escaping from Federal Correctional Institution Forrest City Low the day before.

In November 2002, Shannon L. Hendrickson and Charles Troup, Jr., guards at FCI Forrest City Low, were arrested for possessing and trying to sell 2.2 grams of cocaine and 40 grams of marijuana near a school.

FMC Fort Worth

Federal Medical Center Fort Worth | FMC Fort Worth

Facility Address & Contact Information

Federal Medical Center Fort Worth
3150 Horton Road
Fort Worth, TX 76119

Phone: 817-534-8400
Fax: 817-413-3350
Email: FTW/ExecAssistant@bop.gov

BOP Website: https://www.bop.gov/locations/institutions/ftw/
Wikipedia: https://en.wikipedia.org/wiki/Federal_Correctional_Institution,_Fort_Worth
ZCG Website: https://www.prisonerresource.com/resources/federal-prison-profiles/south-central-region-scr/federal-medical-center-fort-worth-fmc-fort-worth/

Inmate Correspondence Address

Inmate Name and Registration Number
FMC Fort Worth
Federal Medical Center
P.O. Box 15330
Fort Worth, TX 76119

NOTE: Funds cannot be sent directly to federal inmates. See Chapter 1 for more information on sending funds to federal inmates.

Sex: Male

Security Level: Administrative Security (Multiple Security Levels)

Location: Located in north central Texas, in southeast Fort Worth; north of I-20 and east of I-35.

BOP Region: South Central Region (SCR)

BOP Institution Code: FTW for FMC Fort Worth

Judicial District: Northern District of Texas

Medical Care Level: Level 3/4. See Chapter 2 for more information on Medical Care and Mental Health Care Levels.

Mental Health Care Level: Level 3

Population (as of May 1, 2019): 1,526

Background: Federal Medical Center Fort Worth is an administrative-security federal prison in Fort Worth, Texas, which houses male inmates. It opened in 1971

FMC Fort Worth was initially a low-security federal prison (FCI Fort Worth) but was converted to a Federal Medical Center in early 2017. Inmates at FMC Fort Worth have various security levels, as well as special medical and mental health needs.

Media reports indicate that at least three guards have been indicted for sexually assaulting inmates. Additionally, at least one guard has been convicted of smuggling drugs into the facility.

Housing: Inmates are housed in units which range from two-, three-, four-, six-, and eight-person cells to dormitories housing 20 to 30 inmates.

Health Services: Services at FMC Fort Worth include medical and dental triage, emergency medical services, medications, eyeglasses, physical examinations, and chronic care. Emergency medical services are available 24 hours a day. Inmates are assigned to a particular Mid-Level Practitioner, who serves as their primary point of contact with Health Services. Sick call is conducted on Monday, Tuesday, Thursday, and Friday at 7:00 a.m. Pill line and insulin line are held three times a day.

Psychology Services: The Psychology Department offers a broad spectrum of services including individual and group counseling, education, drug abuse treatment, a smoking cessation program, and psychological assessments. Emergency psychological services are available to inmates 24 hours a day, 365 days a year. The Psychology Department posts notices of upcoming offerings in inmate housing units. In order to request placement into particular programs inmates must submit cop-outs. Hours of operation are 8:00 a.m. to 3:00 p.m.

Residential Drug Abuse Program (RDAP): FMC Fort Worth has the Residential Drug Abuse Program (RDAP). FMC Fort Worth also provides inmates with the Drug Education class and the Non-Residential Drug Abuse Program (NR-DAP).

Education Services: FMC Fort Worth provides the Test of Adult Basic Education (TABE) to determine appropriate placement in the literacy, GED, and English-as-a-Second Language (ESL) programs. Adult Continuing Education (ACE) classes and a parenting program are also available. Current ACE offerings include World Religion, Used Car Sales, Astronomy, Stocks, Commodities, Greek and Roman Mythology, Creative Writing, Algebra 1 and 2, and Business Etiquette. Inmates can also participate in the Reading is Fundamental and Words Travel Programs. High school diplomas and post-secondary degrees are available through paid correspondence programs. Classes are also offered by Coastline and Lasson community colleges. The hours of operation are 7:00 to 10:00 a.m., 12:00 to 3:00 p.m., and 5:30 to 7:00 p.m. Monday through Friday.

Advanced Occupational Education: FMC Fort Worth offers advanced occupational education in Building Service Maintenance and Office Technology.

Vocational Training: No vocational training is available at FMC Fort Worth aside from the advanced occupational education programs.

Apprenticeship: An apprenticeship is offered in HVAC.

Library Services: The library at FMC Fort Worth has a collection of approximately 5,000 fiction and nonfiction books, which can be checked out by inmates. Newspapers, magazines, and reference books may be used only in the library. Inmates housed in the SHU have access to materials in the SHU inmate law library. Inmates also have access to the TRULINCS Electronic Law Library, where they can research federal case law, Bureau of Prisons Program Statements, and more. Typewriters and a copy machine are also available for inmate use.

UNICOR: FCI Fort Worth does not house a UNICOR facility.

Commissary: FMC Fort Worth inmates can spend up to $360.00 monthly on their specified shopping day. Shopping hours rotate on a quarterly basis and are posted in inmate housing units and the Commissary. Currently, shopping is conducted on Monday, Tuesday, and Wednesday between 6:00 to 7:00 a.m. and 11:00 a.m. to 1:00 p.m. Identification cards are mandatory for any purchases. Upon qualifying, inmates can open savings accounts at the Bureau of Prisons Federal Credit Union, which is located on the FMC Fort Worth grounds.

Recreation Services: The Recreation Department at FMC Fort Worth offers both indoor and outdoor facilities. The indoor facility houses a large hobbycraft program (e.g., leather, painting, drawing, and card-making), fitness equipment, card tables, music rooms, televisions, and pool and ping-pong tables. The outdoor facility includes a running/walking track, multipurpose courts, handball/racquetball courts, softball fields, soccer/football field, horseshoe pits, volleyball courts, and a weightlifting area. Inmates can also watch TV and check out DVDs.

Visitation Information: On Sunday, Monday, and Saturday visitation is held between 8:00 a.m. and 3:00 p.m. On federal holidays visitation is held between 8:00 a.m. and 3:00 p.m. See Chapter 1 for more information on visitation.

Prison Politics: Respondents had mixed feelings about the level of politics at this facility. Some said that this prison is "semi-political, but not real serious," while others felt that there are serious political overtones. All respondents stated that inmates are not required to be part of a car. Generally speaking, since it is a Federal Medical Center, the politics are not like what one would find at a harder medium or a softer high.

Level of Violence: There is a minimal level of violence at this prison. Inmates report few minor fights and no stabbings in the past few years.

Vulnerable Populations: Sex offenders, informants, and LGBT inmates can walk the yard. All are allowed to use the weight pile and participate in sports. One respondent stated that "sex offenders are not allowed in the TV rooms."

Good: "Nothing is good." ""Relatively safe."

Bad: "Bad food, bad medical policies, and lazy staff." "Unit teams and, in particular, unit managers are very bad."

Other Comments: "It's fairly laid back and most people get along with each other. Easy time."

In the News: In October 2016, Yvonne Marrufo, a cook supervisor at Federal Medical Center Fort Worth, was sentenced to three years of probation for sexual abuse of a ward. At the time of her sentencing, the judge crossed out the condition of probation that she register as a sex offender.

In April 2016, Rudy Ramon, a guard at FMC Fort Worth, was sentenced to four years of probation for sex with a prisoner, which occurred in 2014. Ramon was not required to register as a sex offender.

In November 2007, Vincent Inametti, a Catholic priest, pleaded guilty to sexually assaulting female prisoners at FMC Fort Worth.

In July 1998, Benicio Hoyos, a cook employed at FMC Fort Worth, was sentenced to 46 months in prison, the lowest sentence allowed, for smuggling cocaine, heroin, marijuana and liquor into the facility.

FDC Houston

Federal Detention Center Houston | FDC Houston

Facility Address & Contact Information

Federal Detention Center Houston
1200 Texas Avenue
Houston, TX 77002

Phone: 713-221-5400
Fax: 713-229-4200
Email: HOU/ExecAssistant@bop.gov

BOP Website: https://www.bop.gov/locations/institutions/hou/
Wikipedia: https://en.wikipedia.org/wiki/Federal_Detention_Center,_Houston
ZCG Website: https://www.prisonerresource.com/resources/federal-prison-profiles/south-central-region-scr/federal-detention-center-houston-fdc-houston/

Inmate Correspondence Address

Inmate Name and Registration Number
FDC Houston
Federal Detention Center
P.O. Box 526255
Houston, TX 77052

NOTE: Funds cannot be sent directly to federal inmates. See Chapter 1 for more information on sending funds to federal inmates.

Sex: Male and Female

Security Level: Administrative Security (Multiple Security Levels)

Location: FDC Houston is located in downtown Houston at the intersection of Texas Avenue and San Jacinto Avenue.

BOP Region: South Central Region (SCR)

BOP Institution Code: HOU for FDC Houston

Judicial District: Southern District of Texas

Medical Care Level: Level 2. See Chapter 2 for more information on Medical Care and Mental Health Care Levels.

Mental Health Care Level: Level 2

Population (as of May 1, 2019): 823

Background: Federal Detention Center Houston is an administrative-security federal prison in Houston, Texas, which houses both male and female inmates. It was opened in 1999.

FDC Houston houses male and female pre-trial and pre-sentence detainees, as well as hold-over inmates.

Notable inmates include Joel Lopez (after being sentenced to life in prison as a result of a federal drug offense, attempted to pay a soon-to-be-released inmate $2 million to kill her judge, U.S. District Court Judge Ricardo Hinojosa).

Media reports indicate that at least one guard sexually assaulted an inmate at the prison.

Housing: Inmates are housed in various formats, from two-person cells to dormitories. There are four total housing units.

Health Services: Inmates at FDC Houston have access to routine medical and dental evaluations, medications, preventive health care services, emergency services, prenatal care, and diagnosis and treatment of chronic infectious diseases. While emergency medical care is available 24 hours a day, inmates must submit a triage form for routine care.

Psychology Services: Short-term individual and group psychotherapy is available depending on individual needs and staff availability. Individual therapy for crisis resolution is available to all inmates at FDC Houston. Group sessions are also available. Notices of group offerings are posted in inmate housing units. Inmates must submit an Inmate Request to staff form to attend such groups. A smoking cessation program is available upon submitting a copout to Psychology services, as FDC Houston is a smoke-free environment.

Residential Drug Abuse Program (RDAP): FDC Houston does not have the Residential Drug Abuse Program (RDAP), however the facility does offer the Drug Education class and the Non-Residential Drug Abuse Program (NR-DAP).

Education Services: FDC Houston offers literacy, GED, English-as-a-Second Language (ESL), and Adult Continuing Education (ACE) programs. Education services focus on the self-study style of learning, with students' progress monitored by education staff. High school diplomas and post-secondary degrees are available through paid correspondence programs.

Advanced Occupational Education: FDC Houston does not offer any advanced occupational education programs.

Vocational Training: FDC Houston does not offer any vocational training programs.

Apprenticeship: FDC Houston does not offer any apprenticeship programs.

Library Services: Both a law library and wellness/leisure library are available to inmates at FDC Houston. In the law library, inmates have access to the TRULINCS Electronic Law Library. A wellness leisure library is also maintained in each unit's Activity Room. Various books, magazines, newspapers, and pamphlets are maintained for use by all inmates within the housing units. In addition to the unit libraries, a large selection of videotapes and reading materials are available for viewing in the institution Law Library. Access to the video library is coordinated with the Education Law Library schedule.

UNICOR: FDC Houston does not house a UNICOR facility.

Commissary: Inmates can spend up to $360.00 a month at the commissary on their designated shopping day once a week. Various items are available, such as clothing, shoes, electronics, food, drink mixes, and other items. A list with the price of each item can be obtained from the unit officer. Inmates must have funds in their account to purchase any goods from the Commissary.

Recreation Services: Recreation activities at FDC Houston include a wide range of physical and passive programs, including hobbycrafts activities and various sports. The schedules are updated each month and are posted throughout each housing unit. Movies are available for viewing.

Visitation Information: On Sunday, Friday, and Saturday visitation is held between 8:00 a.m. and 11:00 a.m. as well as 12:00 p.m. and 3:00 p.m. On Monday and Thursday visitation is held between 8:00 to 11:00 a.m., 12:00 and 3:00 p.m., and 5:00 and 8:00 p.m. On federal holidays visitation is held between 8:00 a.m. and 11:00 a.m. as well as 12:00 and 3:00 p.m. See Chapter 1 for more information on visitation.

In the News: In August 2017, seventeen staff members at the Federal Detention Center in Houston were unable to leave the facility because of extensive flooding by Hurricane Harvey. Staff volunteers from FMC Carswell, FMC Fort Worth, FCI Seagoville, and the U.S. Army helped deliver food, water and other necessities to the facility.

In May 2017, an unnamed former female prisoner at FDC Houston, who was having a consensual sexual relationship with a guard named Samuel Hawkins, sued Hawkins and the federal government for $10 million after Hawkins raped her just four days before she was released.

FCI La Tuna & FSL La Tuna

Federal Correctional Institution La Tuna | FCI La Tuna

Facilities: FCI La Tuna with an adjacent low-security satellite prison and a minimum-security satellite prison camp.

Facility Address & Contact Information

Federal Correctional Institution La Tuna
8500 Doniphan Road
Anthony, TX 88021

Phone: 915-791-9000
Fax: 915-791-9758
Email: LAT/ExecAssistant@bop.gov

BOP Website: https://www.bop.gov/locations/institutions/lat/
Wikipedia: https://en.wikipedia.org/wiki/Federal_Correctional_Institution,_La_Tuna
ZCG Website: https://www.prisonerresource.com/resources/federal-prison-profiles/south-central-region-scr/federal-correctional-institution-la-tuna-fci-la-tuna/

Inmate Correspondence Address

For FCI La Tuna

Inmate Name and Registration Number
FCI La Tuna
Federal Correctional Institution
P.O. Box 3000
Anthony, TX 88021

For FSL La Tuna Satellite Low

Inmate Name and Registration Number
FSL La Tuna
Federal Satellite Low
P.O. Box 6000
Anthony, TX 88021

For Satellite Prison Camp

Inmate Name and Registration Number
FCI La Tuna
Satellite Prison Camp
P.O. Box 8000
Anthony, TX 88021

NOTE: Funds cannot be sent directly to federal inmates. See Chapter 1 for more information on sending funds to federal inmates.

Sex: Male

Security Level: FCI: Low Security; Satellite: Low Security; Camp: Minimum Security

Location: FCI La Tuna is located on the Texas/New Mexico border, 12 miles north of the city limits of El Paso, off I-10 on State Highway 20.

BOP Region: South Central Region (SCR)

BOP Institution Code: LAT for FCI La Tuna

Judicial District: Western District of Texas

Medical Care Level: Level 2. See Chapter 2 for more information on Medical Care and Mental Health Care Levels.

Mental Health Care Level: Level 2

Population (as of May 1, 2019): FCI: 737; Satellite: 179; Camp: 249

Background: Federal Correctional Institution La Tuna is a low-security federal prison in Anthony, Texas, which houses male inmates. It was opened in 1932. Federal Satellite Low La Tuna and Federal Correctional Institution La Tuna Camp, which also houses male inmates, are both located adjacent to the main institution.

FCI La Tuna was originally called the El Paso Detention Farm and is located on the Texas-New Mexico border. Former inmate Bob Jones, an El Paso businessman who had been sentenced to 10 years for corruption and fraud, was known for writing letters to his family that were intended to warn loved ones to steer clear of misdeeds and illegal behavior, as the consequences were unbearable. A series of Jones' letters were published in the *El Paso Times* and were known as the "Letters from La Tuna." Jones died of kidney failure due to contracting E. Coli from the prison.

Notable inmates include George Jung (convicted of conspiracy and drug trafficking and who had his life profiled in the Johnny Depp film *Blow*). Jung had been a member of the Medellin Cartel and was a key player in the cocaine trade in the United States during the 1970s and 1980s. Jung was reportedly responsible for up to 89 percent of the cocaine smuggled into the United States.

Media reports indicate that the inmate population has protested over prison slave labor. Additionally, at least one inmate has escaped from the camp.

Housing: Inmates are housed in a variety of configurations ranging from three-person cubicles to open dormitory. Unit One houses inmates in three-person cubicles. Unit Two houses deportable aliens in an open bay dorm. Unit Three houses inmates in four-person cubicles. Unit Four houses inmates in an open bay dorm. Unit Five houses RDAP inmates in three-person cubicles. Unit Six houses inmates in four-person cubicles. The camp houses inmates in dormitories.

Health Services: All inmates at FCI La Tuna are provided health care services including medical and dental sick call, emergency medical and dental treatment, medications, eye exams, and eyeglasses. Emergency medical care is available 24 hours a day. Dental and medical sick call are held Monday, Tuesday, Thursday, and Friday from 6:00 to 6:30 a.m. Pill line is conducted at 6:00 a.m., 11:00 a.m., and 4:00 p.m. Insulin line coincides with breakfast and dinner.

Psychology Services: Psychology Services provides basic mental health care to inmates. This care may include screening, assessment and treatment of mental health and drug abuse problems, individual and/or group counseling, psycho-educational classes, self-help and supportive services, and referral to Health Services for medical treatment of a mental illness. Individual programming recommendations can also be made. Current class offerings include Emotional Self-Development, Communications, Cognitive Thinking Skills, Criminal Thinking, Anger Management, and Stress Reduction. A self-help library is also available.

Residential Drug Abuse Program (RDAP): FCI La Tuna has the Residential Drug Abuse Program (RDAP). The satellite low and the camp do not have the Residential Drug Abuse Program (RDAP). All La Tuna facilities provide a Drug Abuse Program, the Drug Education Class, and the Non-Residential Drug Abuse Program (NR-DAP).

Education Services: FCI La Tuna provides literacy, GED, and English-as-a-Second Language (ESL) programs. Incentive awards are provided to recognize inmates making satisfactory progress and successfully completing the literacy (i.e., GED and ESL) program. Graduation ceremonies recognize GED, ESL, and Occupational Education completions. Parenting and Adult Continuing Education (ACE) programs are also available. Current classroom-based ACE courses include Spanish, poetry, current events, CDL, math, OSHA, and home inspection. Current video-based ACE courses include Preparation for Parole, Job Search After Prison, and Making Good Choices. High school diplomas and post-secondary degrees are available through paid correspondence programs. Hours of operation are 7:30 to 10:30 a.m., 12:30 to 3:30 p.m., and 5:30 to 8:15 p.m. Monday through Thursday, as well as 7:30 to 10:30 a.m. and 12:30 to 3:30 p.m. Friday and Sunday. The Education Department is closed Saturday.

Advanced Occupational Education: FCI La Tuna offers advanced occupational education in HVAC, Microsoft Office, and Office Technology. The satellite low offers Microsoft Office and Office Technology. The camp does not offer any advanced occupational education.

Vocational Training: FCI La Tuna offers vocational training in Auto. The satellite low offers vocational training in Office Technology, and the camp offers vocational training in Building Trades, Auto, and Welding.

Apprenticeship: No apprenticeships are offered at FCI La Tuna.

Library Services: The leisure libraries offer inmates reading materials including periodicals, newspapers, fiction, nonfiction, and reference books. An interlibrary loan program with local, state, and college libraries and available bookmobile services is also available. The TRULINCS Electronic Law Library allows inmates access to legal materials and an opportunity to prepare legal documents. Inmates also have access to typewriters and a copy machine.

UNICOR: The FCI La Tuna UNICOR facility handles fleet management and vehicular components. Specifically, inmates customize vehicles for U.S. Border Patrol, U.S. Customs Services, U.S. Army, U.S. Forest Service fire trucks, and other government and law enforcement agencies. Approximately 130 inmates are employed at the FCI La Tuna UNICOR factory.

Commissary: Inmates have a monthly spending limit of $360.00 and items must not exceed the available storage space in the inmate's locker. Popular items include ice cream, candy, food, drinks, and clothing. Inmates may spend a maximum of $110.00 per week excluding stamps and phone OTC medicine. Inmates may not possess more than one watch, one radio, one photo/scrapbook, or one MP3 player. Sales are conducted Monday through Friday at 6:00 to 7:30 a.m. and during the noon meal. Inmates may only shop once a week on their assigned day.

Recreation Services: Indoor and outdoor activities at FCI La Tuna include organized and informal games, sports, physical fitness, table games, hobbycrafts, music programs, intramural activities, social and cultural organizations, and movies. Art and hobbycraft programs include ceramics, leatherwork, models, clay, mosaics, crochet, knitting, sculptures, woodworking, and lapidary. Wellness programs include screening, assessments, goal setting, fitness/nutrition plans and counseling. The recreation yard, located behind UNICOR, include three handball courts, a racquetball court, a basketball court, bocce ball lanes, multipurpose court, a soccer/softball field, a pickleball court, a volleyball court, a weight pile, and a quarter-mile run/walk track. Spin bikes, ping pong, guitars, and seating are also available. Hours of operation are 6:30 to 10:30 a.m., 11:30 a.m. to 3:30 p.m., and 5:00 to 8:30 p.m. Monday through Friday. On the weekend, recreation is open from 6:30 to 9:00 a.m., 10:30 a.m. to 3:30 p.m., and 5:00 to 8:30 p.m.

Visitation Information: On Sunday, Monday, and Saturday visitation is held between 8:00 a.m. and 3:00 p.m. On federal holidays visitation is held between 8:00 a.m. and 3:00 p.m. See Chapter 1 for more information on visitation.

Prison Politics: While most inmates said that there is a low to medium level of prison politics, one stated that the yard is "extremely political." Inmates are not required to be in a car, though many are. While some groups check paperwork, most don't. There are periodic visible car meetings on the yard.

Level of Violence: There is a low level of violence at this facility. According to one respondent, "I feel safe here and have not had any problems with anyone." According to another inmate, "This is a safe yard." In contrast to what others reported, one inmate did note that there are a "lot of fights over gambling and drug debts."

Vulnerable Populations: Sex offenders, informants, and LGBT inmates can walk the yard, though they will be found out and have to claim independent (meaning that they stand apart from any car, group, or gang). Respondents state that they are not accepted into the cars and are often excluded from TV areas, have limited housing options, and are restricted to only a few places on the yard. One respondent highlighted that there are not enough seats at the sex offender table for people to sit, so they must stand until an open seat becomes available at the designated table.

Good: "You can see the interstate from the rec yard. I like seeing the traffic, red lights, the McDonald's sign, the BBQ place down the road (you can also smell the food), and the hotel. The best thing going as far as the institution itself is UNICOR." "For the most part, this facility is run very well and maintained well." "Good food." "Most staff are ok."

Bad: "It's boring as hell and there is nothing productive for inmates to do but get in trouble. We are in the desert and there is a lot of dirt here. No grass, no trees and when there is a cool breeze outside, you must close the windows in the units because the dirt will consume your bed." "Staff condones the politics which makes things sour. When people want to get together to have a conversation, work out, or fix food, politics is always an issue." "The overcrowding in the rooms and moving about the facility can be like a traffic jam on the freeway." "The staff is pretty much the issue here. That and the lack of open compound." "BOP: Backwards on Purpose."

Other Comments: "This place sucks. It is boring every single day. The politics rule the inmate population and staff never does anything about it." "There is no racial diversity here." "If you are not a sex offender, you are probably ok here."

In the News: In June 2018, the Department of Justice and Immigration and Customs Enforcement began sending immigration detainees to five federal prisons, including setting aside 230 beds at Federal Correctional Institution La Tuna, as a result of the Trump Administration's "zero tolerance" policy.

In September 2016, inmates at FCI La Tuna participated in a nationwide prison strike against slave labor, along with at least 45 other state prisons.

Camp in the News: In September 2016, Christian H. Lara and Gustavo Corral escaped from Federal Correctional Institution La Tuna Camp.

FCC Oakdale

Federal Correctional Complex Oakdale | FCC Oakdale

Facilities: FCC Oakdale comprises FCI Oakdale 1 and FCI Oakdale 2, with an adjacent minimum-security satellite prison camp.

FCI Oakdale 1

Federal Correctional Institution Oakdale 1 | FCI Oakdale 1

Facility Address & Contact Information

Federal Correctional Institution Oakdale 1
1507 East Whatley Road
Oakdale, LA 71463

Phone: 318-335-4070
Fax: 318-215-2688
Email: OAK/ExecAssistant@bop.gov

BOP Website: https://www.bop.gov/locations/institutions/oak/
Wikipedia: https://en.wikipedia.org/wiki/Federal_Correctional_Institution,_Oakdale
ZCG Website: https://www.prisonerresource.com/resources/federal-prison-profiles/south-central-region-scr/federal-correctional-complex-oakdale-fcc-oakdale/federal-correctional-institution-oakdale-fci-oakdale/

Inmate Correspondence Address

Inmate Name and Registration Number
FCI Oakdale 1
Federal Correctional Institution
P.O. Box 5010
Oakdale, LA 71463

NOTE: Funds cannot be sent directly to federal inmates. See Chapter 1 for more information on sending funds to federal inmates.

Sex: Male

Security Level: Low Security

Location: FCI Oakdale 1 is located in central Louisiana, 35 miles south of Alexandria, 58 miles north of Lake Charles, off State Highway 165 on Whatley Road.

BOP Region: South Central Region (SCR)

BOP Institution Code: OAK for FCI Oakdale 1, OAX for Oakdale Federal Correctional Complex

Judicial District: Western District of Louisiana

Medical Care Level: Level 2. See Chapter 2 for more information on Medical Care and Mental Health Care Levels.

Mental Health Care Level: Level 2

Population (as of May 1, 2019): 1,125

Background: Federal Correctional Institution Oakdale 1 is a low-security federal prison in Oakdale, Louisiana, which houses male inmates. It opened in 1986 and is part of the Oakdale Federal Correctional Complex.

In 1987, only a year after it opened, the inmates rioted and burned most of FCI Oakdale 1 to the ground. The facility reopened in its current capacity in 1989.

Notable inmates include Louisiana Congressman William J. Jefferson (sentenced to 13 years for bribery, racketeering, and money laundering); Max Butner (sentenced to 13 years for computer hacking and wire fraud after stealing credit card information from two million customers and amounting $86 million in fraudulent charges); and former CEO of WorldCom Bernie Ebbers (sentenced to 25 years for securities fraud following his part in the company's collapse, which resulted in an estimated $100 billion in losses).

Media reports indicate that two inmates have been indicted for orchestrating an escape attempt, while a third inmate was indicted for filing fraudulent tax returns.

Housing: Inmates are housed in four housing units. Housing units are in a dorm structure, divided between two-person cells and four- to six-person rooms.

Health Services: Inmates at FCI Oakdale 1 are provided necessary medical, dental, and mental health services, emergency medical and dental care, medications, periodic health examinations, and eyeglasses. Inmates new to the institution with contact lenses will be evaluated for medical necessity of contact lenses. If contact lenses are not medically indicated, the inmate will be provided with eyeglasses. Emergency care is available 24 hours a day. Inmates must attend sick call at 6:30 a.m. on Monday, Tuesday, Wednesday, and Friday in order to be evaluated for routine care. Pill line and insulin line are conducted during breakfast and dinner.

Psychology Services: For inmates that require psychological care, FCI Oakdale 1 offers screening, assessment, and treatment of mental health and drug abuse problems, individual and group counseling, psycho-educational classes, self-help and supportive services, and referral to Health Services for medical treatment of a mental illness. Several residential mental health programs designed to help inmates with severe emotional, cognitive, and behavioral problems are available for those having difficulty functioning in a mainline Institution. Inmates requiring such care can be referred for such program placement. Open house hours are 11:00 a.m. to 1:00 p.m. on Tuesdays.

Residential Drug Abuse Program (RDAP): FCI Oakdale 1 does not have the Residential Drug Abuse Program (RDAP), but it does offer a Drug Abuse Education course and the Non-Residential Drug Abuse Program (NR-DAP).

Education Services: FCI Oakdale 1 provides literacy, GED and English-as-a-Second Language (ESL) programs. An incentive of $25.00 is awarded to inmates who complete a GED class by passing the Official General Education Development Examination (GED). A Certificate of Achievement is awarded for completion of levels 1 and 2 of the literacy program. An incentive of $25.00 is also awarded to inmates who complete the ESL class by passing the Comprehensive Adult Student Assessment System Examination (CASAS). A parenting program and Adult Continuing Education (ACE) classes are also offered. Current ACE classes include baking, Spanish, typing, construction, CDL, business, and real estate. Self-study courses are offered as a part of the ACE program. A high school diploma or GED is necessary for some programs. The facility also offers a sewing program. High school diplomas and post-secondary degrees are available through paid correspondence programs. Hours of operation are 7:30 a.m. to 7:30 p.m. Monday through Friday, with the exception of Friday night. On Saturday, the hours are 8:00 a.m. to 3:15 p.m. Excluded from these hours of operation are meals, counts, and other institutional recalls.

Advanced Occupational Education: FCI Oakdale 1 does not offer any advanced occupational education programs.

Vocational Training: FCI Oakdale 1 does not offer any vocational training aside from the apprenticeship programs.

Apprenticeship: FCI Oakdale 1 offers apprenticeships in the areas of Building Trade and Horticulture.

Library Services: FCI Oakdale 1 offers both a law and leisure library. The law library provides legal materials via the TRULINCS Electronic Law Library. Typewriters and a copy machine are also available. A leisure library offers inmates a variety of fiction and nonfiction books, newspapers, reference materials, and periodicals. Titles unavailable in the library may be obtained through the interlibrary loan services. Library services are extended to all inmates. Commissary cards are required to check out library materials.

UNICOR: The FCI Oakdale 1 UNICOR facility produces clothing and textiles.

Commissary: Inmates are allowed to shop once each week and are allowed to spend up to $360.00 per month. Inmates are further restricted to a $180 biweekly spending limitation. The shopping day is determined by the fourth and fifth digit of the inmate's BOP register number. A biometric fingerprint process is used to identify each inmate prior to commissary sales. Inmates who are fingerprint exempt must have in their possession their commissary card. A variety of items can be purchased in the commissary such as food, beverages, clothing, electronics, and more. Shopping is conducted Tuesday, Wednesday, and Thursday during breakfast and lunch.

Recreation Services: The FCI Oakdale 1 Recreation Department offers both indoor and outdoor activities. The gymnasium area comprises the Recreation Supervisor's office and the basketball court area. The inside recreation space includes a hobbycraft area. This area houses the tool room for the hobbycraft activities, an art room, and a classroom. Activities include leather craft, basket weaving, woodwork, yarn art, stick craft, free-lance painting, and drawing. Indoor activities also include dominoes, chess, card games, checkers, Yahtzee, backgammon, and Scrabble. The outside recreation yard has a running track, soccer and football fields, bocce ball lanes, horseshoe pits, four handball/racquetball courts, tennis/basketball court, softball field, and two volleyball courts. Court games such as handball, racquetball, tennis, horseshoes, basketball, bocce ball, and pickleball are available. The intramural sports program includes basketball, volleyball, soccer, flag football, and softball. Organized fitness programs include run/walk clubs, fitness clubs, and a Wellness Program. Music related activities and programs are also available for inmate participation. Instruction is available in guitar and various percussion instruments. TVs are also available for watching sports. Hours of operation are 6:00 to 10:00 a.m., 10:30 a.m. to 3:00 p.m., and 4:30 to 8:15 p.m. Monday through Friday. On the weekends, hours of operation are 6:45 to 9:15 a.m., 10:30 to 3:00 p.m., and 4:30 to 8:15 p.m.

Visitation Information: On Sunday and Saturday visitation is held between 8:15 a.m. and 3:00 p.m. On federal holidays visitation is held between 8:15 a.m. and 3:00 p.m. See Chapter 1 for more information on visitation.

Prison Politics: While some felt that this yard is moderately political, others felt that it was not political. Multiple respondents stated that Paisas cannot walk the yard, though. One respondent stated that "the racial groups sometimes gather in the yard for car meetings."

Level of Violence: There is a fairly low level of violence at this facility. According to one respondent, "there are perhaps a dozen fights per year." Another respondent stated that while there is minimal violence that he did "not feel safe" on the yard. The same respondent stated that the compound has been locked down two times in the past three months due to violence.

Vulnerable Populations: Sex offenders, informants, and LGBT inmates can walk the yard. According to one inmate, "It's a PC yard, so everyone can walk." Another respondent agreed, stating, "Sex offenders, snitches, transgenders, and gays can walk the yard. They tend to not have many problems due to there being so many of them."

Good: "Good quality food, but bad portions." "The food isn't too bad."

Bad: "The compound is run by the prison guard's union, so they are very reluctant to change anything from the way it was when it was a Medium years ago." "Very limited rec." "Staff and inmates have bad attitudes." "No rehabilitative programs for sex offenders." "Unit Teams are very disrespectful. When you try to speak with them, they blow you off and do all they can to not help."

Other Comments: "The administration is corrupt. Nepotism is everywhere and they simply mistreat people."

In the News: In March 2018, John Michael McConnell was arrested, accused of fraudulently obtaining over $170,000 in tax refunds between 2010 and 2017 while he was in prison, including at Federal Correctional Institution Oakdale 1.

In October 2003, David Lara and Heriberto Morales, prisoners at FCI Oakdale 1, were federally indicted after an informant revealed their plans to escape using homemade bombs and a distraction.

FCI Oakdale 2

Federal Correctional Institution Oakdale 2 | FCI Oakdale 2

Facilities: FCI Oakdale 2 with an adjacent minimum-security satellite prison camp.

Facility Address & Contact Information

Federal Correctional Institution Oakdale 2
2105 East Whatley Road
Oakdale, LA 71463

Phone: 318-335-4466
Fax: 318-215-2185
Email: OAD/ExecAssistant@bop.gov

BOP Website: https://www.bop.gov/locations/institutions/oad/
Wikipedia: https://en.wikipedia.org/wiki/Federal_Detention_Center,_Oakdale
ZCG Website: https://www.prisonerresource.com/resources/federal-prison-profiles/
south-central-region-scr/federal-correctional-complex-oakdale-fcc-oakdale/
federal-detention-center-oakdale-fdc-oakdale/

Inmate Correspondence Address

For FCI Oakdale 2

Inmate Name & Register Number
FCI Oakdale 2
Federal Correctional Institution
P.O. Box 5010
Oakdale, LA 71463

For Satellite Prison Camp

Inmate Name and Registration Number
FCI Oakdale 2
Satellite Prison Camp
P.O. Box 5010
Oakdale, LA 71463

NOTE: Funds cannot be sent directly to federal inmates. See Chapter 1 for more information on sending funds to federal inmates.

Sex: Male

Security Level: Main: Low Security; Camp: Minimum Security

Location: FCI Oakdale 2 is located in central Louisiana, 35 miles south of Alexandria, 58 miles north of Lake Charles, off State Highway 165 on Whatley Road.

BOP Region: South Central Region (SCR)

BOP Institution Code: OAD for FCI Oakdale 2, OAX for Oakdale Federal Correctional Complex

Judicial District: Western District of Louisiana

Medical Care Level: Level 2. See Chapter 2 for more information on Medical Care and Mental Health Care Levels.

Mental Health Care Level: Level 2

Population (as of May 1, 2019): Main: 892; Camp: 135

Background: Federal Correctional Institution Oakdale 2 is a low-security federal prison in Oakdale, Louisiana, which houses male inmates. It was opened in 1990 and is part of the Oakdale Federal Correctional Complex. Federal Correctional Institution Oakdale 2 Camp, which also houses male inmates, is located adjacent to the main institution.

Media reports indicate that at least two inmates have attempted to escape from the prison.

Housing: Inmates are housed in two-person cells. At the camp inmates are housed in dormitories.

Health Services: Health care at FCI Oakdale 2 includes medical, dental, and mental health services, emergency medical and dental care, medications, periodic health examinations, and eyeglasses. Dental and medical sick call are held several times a week.

Psychology Services: Services provided by the Psychology Department include crisis intervention (suicidal risk assessments), psychotherapy (individual and group), psychological assessments, and psycho-education (self-help and audio/visual material). All inmates/detainees must complete, sign, and date a Psychology Services Inmate Questionnaire (PSIQ), provided by medical staff, on their arrival at Receiving & Discharge (R&D). This is a mandatory assessment. Inmates/Detainees in the Special Housing Unit must receive mandatory 30-day reviews by Psychology Services. Assessment using psychological testing will be completed as determined by the psychologist. Additionally, the staff psychologists conduct the following programs: 40-hour Drug Education Program, Stress Management Group, Psychological-Educational Support Group, and Anger Management Group. Each of these groups meet weekly. The institution also offers a Reintegration Housing Unit (RHU) which acts as a SHU step-down/rehab program.

Residential Drug Abuse Program (RDAP): FCI Oakdale 2 does not have the Residential Drug Abuse Program (RDAP) but does offer the Drug Abuse Education Class and the Non-Residential Drug Abuse Program (NR-DAP).

Education Services: FCI Oakdale 2 provides literacy, GED, and English-as-a-Second Language (ESL) programs. A parenting program and Adult Continuing Education (ACE) courses taught by fellow prisoners, are also available. A self-paced ACE program offers inmates the opportunity to utilize handouts and a textbook to complete classes independently. High school diplomas and post-secondary degrees are available through paid correspondence programs.

Advanced Occupational Education: FCI Oakdale 2 does not offer any advanced occupational education programs.

Vocational Training: FCI Oakdale 2 does not offer any vocational training programs.

Apprenticeship: The satellite camp offers an apprenticeship program in Welding.

Library Services: FCI Oakdale 2 provides access to a legal library, where legal materials are available via the TRULINCS Electronic Law Library. A leisure library is also available which provides a variety of fiction and nonfiction books, newspapers, reference materials, and periodicals to the inmate population. Titles unavailable in the library may be obtained through the interlibrary loan program. Typewriters and a copy machine are available to inmates. Inmates are given 25 free legal copies per month and each additional legal copy costs fifteen cents. Inmates in the RHU have their own in-unit library.

UNICOR: FCI Oakdale 2 does not house a UNICOR facility.

Commissary: Inmates are allowed to spend up to $360.00 per month at the commissary. Shopping is permitted once each week. The shopping day is determined by the fourth and fifth digits of the inmate's BOP register number. Inmates must have their account card in their possession in order to shop at the commissary. Items such as food, sodas, snacks, ice cream, clothing, and electronics are available for purchase.

Recreation Services: The FCI Oakdale 2 recreation services include both indoor and outdoor activities. Indoors, inmates have access to pool tables, TVs, foosball, ping pong, ellipticals, treadmills, stationary bikes, art rooms, and a band room. Outdoors, inmates have access to pull-up bars, dip bars, stationary bikes, basketball, soccer, football, softball, handball, and volleyball.

Visitation Information: On Sunday and Saturday visitation is held between 8:15 a.m. and 3:00 p.m. On federal holidays visitation is held between 8:15 a.m. and 3:00 p.m. See Chapter 1 for more information on visitation.

Prison Politics: The Reintegration Housing Unit (RHU) is not political at all.

Level of Violence: There is little to no violence in the RHU.

Vulnerable Populations: Sex offenders, informants, and LGBT inmates can stay in the RHU.

Good: "The RHU allows inmates to be somewhere safe when stepping down from long-term SHU; great commissary."

Bad: "No complaints for the RHU."

Other Comments: "Go there if you are Hispanic." "Lots of safety and mental health reasons to go to the RHU. Good place if you've been in the hole for a long time. It helps a lot."

In the News: In October 2017, Lucas Gregory Woodard and Nicholas Bickle were discovered tangled in razor wire trying to escape from Federal Correctional Institution Oakdale 2.

In November 1987, after the U.S. signed an agreement with Cuba that would force many illegal Cuban immigrants back to Cuba under the dictatorship of Fidel Castro, the Cuban prisoners at FCI Oakdale 2 rioted, taking over the prison, setting fires and holding hostages.

FTC Oklahoma City

Federal Transfer Center Oklahoma City | FTC Oklahoma City

Facility Address & Contact Information

Federal Transfer Center Oklahoma City
7410 South MacArthur Boulevard
Oklahoma City, OK 73169

Phone: 405-682-4075
Fax: 405-680-4043
Email: OKL/ExecAssistant@bop.gov

BOP Website: https://www.bop.gov/locations/institutions/okl/
Wikipedia: https://en.wikipedia.org/wiki/Federal_Transfer_Center,_Oklahoma_City
ZCG Website: https://www.prisonerresource.com/resources/federal-prison-profiles/south-central-region-scr/federal-transfer-center-oklahoma-city-ftc-oklahoma-city/

Inmate Correspondence Address

Inmate Name and Registration Number
FTC Oklahoma City
Federal Transfer Center
P.O. Box 898801
Oklahoma City, OK 73189

NOTE: Funds cannot be sent directly to federal inmates. See Chapter 1 for more information on sending funds to federal inmates.

Sex: Male and Female

Security Level: Administrative Security (Multiple Security Levels)

Location: FTC Oklahoma City is located 3 miles west of I-44 and 4 miles south of I-40.

BOP Region: South Central Region (SCR)

BOP Institution Code: OKL for FTC Oklahoma City

Judicial District: Western District of Oklahoma

Medical Care Level: Level 2. See Chapter 2 for more information on Medical Care and Mental Health Care Levels.

Mental Health Care Level: Level 2

Population (as of May 1, 2019): 1,202

Background: Federal Transfer Center Oklahoma City is an administrative-security federal prison in Oklahoma City, Oklahoma, which houses both male and female inmates. It opened in 1995.

FTC Oklahoma City is the Federal Bureau of Prisons' transfer hub for male and female inmates. It serves as the main hub of the Justice Prisoner and Alien Transport System, popularly known as ConAir. A cadre of low-security inmates are assigned to FTC Oklahoma City to perform food service and maintenance duties. Piper Kerman, author of the Netflix series *Orange is the New Black*, stated in 2005 that the women's section was "spotlessly clean" and "subdued."

Media reports indicate that at least one inmate has died at the facility, though the cause of death was not publicly reported.

Housing: Inmates are housed in one and two-tier housing units which consist of cells with bunk beds inside them.

Health Services: Medical services are provided by FTC Oklahoma City medical staff and community consultants. All new cadre inmates receive a preventive health screening and dental screening which screens for viral hepatitis, HIV, TB, colon cancer, diabetes, and cholesterol. Dental sick call is for emergency care only. To obtain routine dental treatment inmates must submit an inmate request to staff to the Dental Department. Medications are also provided. Medical services are available to inmates on a 24-hour basis through routine medical programs and urgent emergency care.

Psychology Services: Psychology staff provide a full range of psychological services on an as-needed basis. Brief clinical assessments are completed on all newly committed cadre inmates. Brief counseling is available as well as specialty programs such as stress management, rational thinking, and dealing with grief, which are periodically offered and available to cadre inmates.

Psychologists are available 24 hours a day, year-round to respond to emergency mental health concerns.

Residential Drug Abuse Program (RDAP): FTC Oklahoma City does not have the Residential Drug Abuse Program (RDAP), however it does offer a Drug Education Class and the Non-Residential Drug Abuse Program (NR-DAP).

Education Services: FTC Oklahoma City provides literacy, GED, and English-as-a-Second Language (ESL) programs. Adult Continuing Education (ACE) classes and Release Preparation Program classes are also available. Release Preparation Classes focus on interview skills, resume writing, cultural diversity, locating jobs, and additional classes. Inmates can find notices of additional education classes on the cadre unit bulletin board. High school diplomas and post-secondary degrees are available through paid correspondence programs.

Advanced Occupational Education: FTC Oklahoma City does not offer any advanced occupational education programs.

Vocational Training: FTC Oklahoma City does not offer any vocational training programs.

Apprenticeship: FTC Oklahoma City does not offer any apprenticeship programs.

Library Services: An Electronic Law Library provides inmates with access to law library materials. Typewriters are available in the cadre unit for legal document preparation. A leisure library offers inmates fiction and nonfiction books, magazines, and newspapers.

UNICOR: FTC Oklahoma City does not house a UNICOR facility.

Commissary: Cadre inmates can spend up to $360.00 per month and may shop at the commissary once per week with an additional short line for stamps, hygiene and special purchase orders only. Commissary items include beverages, food, clothing, electronics, and others. Transferring inmates do not have access to commissary shopping while at FTC Oklahoma City.

Recreation Services: There are several hobbycraft programs offered to FTC Oklahoma City cadre inmates. Cadre inmates may also participate in structured fitness programs and activities such as basketball, handball, unit walking, and utilizing fitness equipment. Fitness programming is also part of the Release Preparation Program. A bulletin board is located in the cadre unit to keep inmates informed of recreation opportunities. Transferring inmates have access to a small outdoor recreation area, which is connected to each housing unit.

Visitation Information: On Sunday and Saturday visitation is held between 8:00 a.m. and 3:00 p.m. On federal holidays visitation is held between 8:00 a.m. and 3:00 p.m. See Chapter 1 for more information on visitation.

In the News: In October 2017, Darius Ghahary was found unresponsive in his cell at Federal Transfer Center Oklahoma City and was taken to the hospital where he was declared dead.

FCC Pollock

Federal Correctional Complex Pollock | FCC Pollock

Facilities: FCC Pollock comprises USP Pollock, with an adjacent minimum-security satellite prison camp, and FCI Pollock.

USP Pollock

United States Penitentiary Pollock | USP Pollock

Facilities: USP Pollock with an adjacent minimum-security satellite prison camp.

Facility Address & Contact Information

United States Penitentiary Pollock
1000 Airbase Road
Pollock, LA 71467

Phone: 318-561-5300
Fax: 318-561-5391
Email: POL/ExecAssistant@bop.gov

BOP Website: https://www.bop.gov/locations/institutions/pol/
Wikipedia:https://en.wikipedia.org/wiki/United_States_Penitentiary,_Pollock
ZCG Website: https://www.prisonerresource.com/resources/federal-prison-profiles/south-central-region-scr/federal-correctional-complex-pollock-fcc-pollock/united-states-penitentiary-pollock-usp-pollock/

Inmate Correspondence Address

For USP Pollock

Inmate Name and Registration Number
USP Pollock
U.S. Penitentiary
P.O. Box 2099
Pollock, LA 71467

For Satellite Prison Camp

Inmate Name and Registration Number
USP Pollock
Satellite Prison Camp
P.O. Box 2099
Pollock, LA 71467

NOTE: Funds cannot be sent directly to federal inmates. See Chapter 1 for more information on sending funds to federal inmates.

Sex: Male

Security Level: Main: High Security; Camp: Minimum Security

Location: USP Pollock is located in central Louisiana between Highways 165 and 167, approximately 12 miles north of Alexandria.

BOP Region: South Central Region (SCR)

BOP Institution Code: POL for USP Pollock, POX for Pollock Federal Correctional Complex

Judicial District: Western District of Louisiana

Medical Care Level: Level 1. See Chapter 2 for more information on Medical Care and Mental Health Care Levels.

Mental Health Care Level: Level 1

Population (as of May 1, 2019): Main: 1,111; Camp: 205

Background: United States Penitentiary Pollock is a high-security federal prison in Pollock, Louisiana, which houses male inmates. It was opened in 2000 and is part of the Pollock Federal

Correctional Complex. United States Penitentiary Pollock Camp, which also houses male inmates, is located adjacent to the main institution.

In 2018, Louisiana Senators Bill Cassidy and John Kennedy and U.S. Representatives Ralph Abraham and Mike Johnson sent a letter to the Bureau's Acting Director and Attorney General Jeff Sessions stating, in part, that "USP Pollock is one of the most dangerous facilities in the nation[.]"

Notable inmates include Richard Lee McNair (convicted of murder and robbery). McNair escaped from the prison in 2006 and was captured by the Royal Canadian Mounted Police in New Brunswick, Canada, 18 months later.

Media reports indicate that two guards have been killed by inmates, two additional guards were stabbed by an inmate, five inmates have been murdered, one inmate has escaped, and one guard was indicted for attempting to smuggle drugs into the prison.

In 2018, Trendrr named USP Pollock one of the 11 most dangerous prisons in the United States. And in 2016, The Richest named the facility as one of the most dangerous prisons in America.

Housing: Inmates are housed in two-, three-, and four-person cells. There are 11 housing units. Inmates at the camp are housed in dormitories.

Health Services: Shortly after arrival at the institution, all inmates receive a screening examination. Health services include sick call, routine medical and dental call, emergency medical treatment, and medications. Most medical care is provided through appointments, where inmates are placed on the institutional call-out list. Inmates must present their ID card each time they report to Health Services. Emergency care is available 24 hours a day.

Psychology Services: Inmates meet with a psychologist for a routine intake screening within 14 days of arrival. Psychologists are available for individual psychotherapy on an as-needed basis. Crisis intervention is also available. USP Pollock also offers the Challenge Program, a unit-based, residential treatment program stressing the acquisition and implementation of pro-social values and a non-criminal lifestyle. Group therapy and counseling, personal development groups, individual therapy and counseling, correctional counseling, crisis intervention, pre-release counseling, voluntary groups, and other programs deemed appropriate are available to inmates.

Residential Drug Abuse Program (RDAP): USP Pollock does not have the Residential Drug Abuse Program (RDAP). However, the Drug Education Class and the Non-Residential Drug Abuse Program (NR-DAP) are offered.

Education Services: USP Pollock provides literacy, GED, and English-as-a-Second Language (ESL) programs. Each student who successfully completes the General Educational Development Test or CASAS certification test will receive a $25.00 achievement award and will be recognized during the Education Department's graduation ceremony. Parenting and Adult Continuing Education (ACE) programs are also available. Inmates interested in ACE may sign up for various courses that are offered on a rotating basis throughout the year. Schedules of planned courses are posted on the TRULINCS system for review. Examples of ACE courses are Conversational Spanish, Prison to Paycheck, National Geographic Classics, and United States and World History. High school diplomas and post-secondary degrees are available through paid correspondence programs.

Advanced Occupational Education: USP Pollock offers advanced occupational educational in Building Trades and Culinary Arts. Both facilities also offer Business Management, Custodial Maintenance, and Microcomputer Applications.

Vocational Training: USP Pollock does not offer any vocational training programs aside from its advanced occupational education programs.

Apprenticeship: USP Pollock does not offer any apprenticeship programs.

Library Services: The leisure and law libraries offer a variety of services. Fiction and nonfiction books, magazines, and newspapers are available for inmate use. An Interlibrary Loan Program is also available. The law library offers legal material as mandated by federal law. The Education Department provides the TRULINCS Electronic Law Library which contains many legal research resources, including federal cases from every district court and circuit court. Inmates also have access to typewriters and a copy machine.

UNICOR: USP Pollock does not house a UNICOR facility.

Commissary: Inmates are permitted to spend a maximum of $360.00 a month, with a limit of $180.00 per week for regular purchases. Commissary access time is based on housing unit assignment. Inmates are only permitted to shop once a week. A point-of-sale computerized commissary withdrawal system is used at USP Pollock. The system simplifies purchasing and gives inmates an improved, up-to-date record of all account activity. Inmates must register their fingerprint with Commissary prior to shopping. All sales are conducted using fingerprint recognition. Commissary is delivered to inmates in their housing units.

Recreation Services: Recreation at USP Pollock offers both indoor and outdoor activities. Various sports leagues, wellness programs (such as health and fitness classes), and cardiovascular conditioning are available to inmates. A music program is also available. Inmates can also participate in hobbycrafts which include ceramics, leather craft, and art programs. Inside, inmates have access to an art room, leather room, basketball, stationary bikes, treadmills, rowing machines, ellipticals, tables, ping pong, and a band room. Outside, inmates have access to a small track, softball, basketball, bocce ball, horseshoes, handball, volleyball, and soccer.

Visitation Information: On Sunday, Monday, and Saturday visitation is held between 8:00 a.m. and 3:00 p.m. On federal holidays visitation is held between 8:00 a.m. and 3:00 p.m. See Chapter 1 for more information on visitation.

Prison Politics: There is a significant level of politics at this prison. According to one respondent, "While the yard is very political, it is good politics. Mostly independent whites and Texas Hispanic groups."

Level of Violence: Inmates report a significant level of violence.

Vulnerable Populations: Sex offenders, informants, and LGBT inmates cannot walk the yard. According to one inmate, "If you have a bad rap such as a sex crime or are a snitch or a check-in from another spot, don't come here. Life will be hard, and you can't stay."

Good: "The inmate population is straight from a political perspective." "The officers are respectful."

Bad: "Unit teams at times refuse to help people get the right amount of halfway house placement." "Not everyone gets to use the rec facility due to different housing units being assigned to specific rec yards, which have limited and different equipment from the other yards."

Other Comments: "If you have straight paperwork and don't mind political time, this isn't a bad spot. But if your paperwork isn't clean, then this isn't the place for you. You can't stay, and you might even get beat off the yard."

In the News: In July 2018, Charles White, who was already serving a life sentence at United States Penitentiary Pollock, was sentenced to an additional 20 years in prison for the stabbing and murder of guards Eric Farmer and Remington Steedley.

In June 2018, Louisiana Senators Bill Cassidy and John Kennedy and U.S. Representatives Ralph Abraham and Mike Johnson sent a letter to Bureau of Prisons Acting Director Hugh Hurwitz and Attorney General Jeff Sessions which stated, in part, "USP Pollock is one of the most dangerous facilities in the nation, and there have been many acts of violence involving inmates, including against staff."

In February 2018, Lee Adams, a prisoner at USP Pollock, was sentenced to two additional years in prison for involuntarily killing another prisoner when he struck the man, causing him to fall backwards and fracture his skull on the concrete floor.

In January 2017, Remington Steedley, a guard at USP Pollock, and counselor Eric Farmer were killed by prisoners Charles Lee White and Marco Damon Duncan, who were both serving life sentences, after Steedley and Farmer inspected Duncan's cell.

In May 2012, Brandon Ray Willis, a guard at USP Pollock, was sentenced to 71 months in prison after trying to conspire with an undercover agent to smuggle heroin and methamphetamines into the facility.

In November 2007, William Bullock and Donald Till, prisoners at USP Pollock, were killed in a prison fight.

In April 2007, two USP Pollock prisoners were stabbed to death.

In 2006, Richard McNair escaped from USP Pollock by hiding in a pile of mailbags, but was caught 18 months later in New Brunswick, Canada.

Camp in the News: In September 2017, Raphael Torres escaped from United States Penitentiary Pollock Camp and was recaptured in two hours.

In December 2016, Sadar Dakar Cade escaped from USP Pollock Camp.

In February 2013, Roland Castro escaped from the minimum-security prison camp at USP Pollock.

FCI Pollock

Federal Correctional Institution Pollock | FCI Pollock

Facility Address & Contact Information

Federal Correctional Institution Pollock
1000 Airbase Road
Pollock, LA 71467

Phone: 318-765-4400
Fax: 318-765-4476
Email: POL/ExecAssistant@bop.gov

BOP Website: https://www.bop.gov/locations/institutions/pom/
Wikipedia: https://en.wikipedia.org/wiki/Federal_Correctional_Institution,_Pollock
ZCG Website: https://www.prisonerresource.com/resources/federal-prison-profiles/south-central-region-scr/federal-correctional-complex-pollock-fcc-pollock/federal-correctional-institution-pollock-fci-pollock/

Inmate Correspondence Address

Inmate Name and Registration Number
FCI Pollock
Federal Correctional Institution
P.O. Box 4050
Pollock, LA 71467

NOTE: Funds cannot be sent directly to federal inmates. See Chapter 1 for more information on sending funds to federal inmates.

Sex: Male

Security Level: Medium Security

Location: FCI Pollock is located in central Louisiana between Highways 165 and 167, approximately 12 miles north of Alexandria.

BOP Region: South Central Region (SCR)

BOP Institution Code: POM for FCI Pollock, POX for Pollock Federal Correctional Complex

Judicial District: Western District of Louisiana

Medical Care Level: Level 1. See Chapter 2 for more information on Medical Care and Mental Health Care Levels.

Mental Health Care Level: Level 1

Population (as of May 1, 2019): 1,359

Background: Federal Correctional Institution Pollock is a medium-security federal prison in Pollock, Louisiana, which houses male inmates. It is part of the Pollock Federal Correctional Complex.

Notable inmates include Gambino crime family member Gene Gotti (sentenced to 50 years for running a multi-million dollar heroin ring), and FBI-Ten-Most-Wanted fugitive and head of security for the white supremacist group The Order Richard Scutari (convicted of armed car robbery in an attempt to finance an overthrow of the U.S. government).

Media reports indicate that at least one guard has been indicated for accepting bribes to smuggle contraband into the institution. Additionally, at least three inmates have escaped from the camp.

Housing: Inmates are housed in two-person cells.

Health Services: Within 14 days of arrival at FCI Pollock, inmates receive a health care examination. All inmates have access to sick call, routine medical and dental call, emergency medical treatment, and medications. In order to request routine health care, inmates must submit a sick call request to Health Services. Emergency care is available 24 hours a day.

Psychology Services: FCI Pollock offers inmates psychological programming groups, such as anger management, criminal thinking, HIV/AIDS awareness, and others. Crisis counseling is available on an as-needed basis. Notices of upcoming offerings are posted in inmate housing units.

Residential Drug Abuse Program (RDAP): FCI Pollock does not have the Residential Drug Abuse Program (RDAP) but does offer the Drug Abuse Education class and the Non-Residential Drug Abuse Program (NR-DAP).

Education Services: FCI Pollock provides literacy, GED, and English-as-a-Second Language (ESL) programs. A parenting program and Adult Continuing Education (ACE) classes are also available. High school diplomas and post-secondary degrees are available to inmates through paid correspondence programs.

Advanced Occupational Education: FCI Pollock offers advanced occupational education in Building Trades, Business Management, Culinary Arts, Custodial Maintenance, Outdoor Motors and Sewing.

Vocational Training: FCI Pollock does not offer any vocational training programs aside from the advanced occupational education programs.

Apprenticeship: FCI Pollock does not offer any apprenticeship programs.

Library Services: Inmates can utilize both the leisure and law libraries. Fiction and nonfiction books, magazines, and newspapers are available for inmate use. An Interlibrary Loan Program is also available. The law library offers legal material, typewriters, and a copy machine. The Education Department also has the TRULINCS Electronic Law Library.

UNICOR: The FCI Pollock UNICOR facility produces clothing and textiles.

Commissary: Inmates are allowed to shop once a week in the commissary on a designated day. While a monthly spending limit of $360.00 is imposed, inmates are only allowed to spend up to $180.00 every two weeks. Some items include ice cream, candy, food, snacks, sodas, and clothing. Shoes, electronics, and over-the-counter medications are also available.

Recreation Services: The FCI Pollock Recreation Department offers both indoor and outdoor areas. Indoor activities include artwork and hobbycraft projects. Outdoors are various sports and use of the track.

Visitation Information: On Sunday, Monday, and Saturday visitation is held between 8:00 a.m. and 3:00 p.m. On federal holidays visitation is held between 8:00 a.m. and 3:00 p.m. See Chapter 1 for more information on visitation.

Prison Politics: This is a very political yard. Inmates must be part of a car in order to remain.

Level of Violence: There is significant violence at this prison. Inmates report frequent fights, common stabbings, and lots of violence-induced lockdowns.

Vulnerable Populations: Some inmates report that sex offenders can stay if they are part of a car and are honest from the start, while informants and LGBT inmates can remain if they are undercover. Other inmates assert that sex offenders, informants, and LGBT inmates cannot walk the yard at all.

Good: "Issued tubs for extra storage which can be placed under your bunk." "Nothing, no pros to that place at all."

Bad: "Heavy Hispanic presence, with political implications." "Everything, food, everyone is strung out, cops put you out there." "Cops promote violence."

Other Comments: "An alright yard, but try to be solid and fly under the radar." "Stay away. Don't go."

In the News: In April 2018, Byron A. Wyatt, a guard at Federal Correctional Institution Pollock Medium, was convicted of accepting bribes to smuggle contraband.

FCI Seagoville

Federal Correctional Institution Seagoville | FCI Seagoville

Facilities: FCI Seagoville with a detention center and an adjacent minimum-security satellite prison camp.

Facility Address & Contact Information

Federal Correctional Institution Seagoville
2113 North Highway 175
Seagoville, TX 75159

Phone: 972-287-2911
Fax: 972-287-5466
Email: SEA/ExecAssistant@bop.gov

BOP Website: https://www.bop.gov/locations/institutions/sea/
Wikipedia: https://en.wikipedia.org/wiki/Federal_Correctional_Institution,_Seagoville
ZCG Website: https://www.prisonerresource.com/resources/federal-prison-profiles/south-central-region-scr/federal-correctional-institution-seagoville-fci-seagoville/

Inmate Correspondence Address

For FCI Seagoville

Inmate Name and Registration Number
FCI Seagoville
Federal Correctional Institution
P.O. Box 9000
Seagoville, TX 75159

For Satellite Prison Camp

FCI Seagoville
Satellite Prison Camp
P.O. Box 9000
Seagoville, TX 75159

NOTE: Funds cannot be sent directly to federal inmates. See Chapter 1 for more information on sending funds to federal inmates.

Sex: Male

Security Level: Main: Low Security; Camp: Minimum Security

Location: FCI Seagoville is located 11 miles southeast of Dallas, off Highway 175 (Hawn Freeway).

BOP Region: South Central Region (SCR)

BOP Institution Code: SEA for FCI Seagoville

Judicial District: Northern District of Texas

Medical Care Level: Level 2. See Chapter 2 for more information on Medical Care and Mental Health Care Levels.

Mental Health Care Level: Level 2

Population (as of May 1, 2019): FCI & FDC: 1,851; Camp: 167

Background: Federal Correctional Institution Seagoville is a low-security federal prison in Seagoville, Texas, which houses male inmates. It opened in 1938. Federal Correctional Institution Seagoville Camp, which also houses male inmates, is located adjacent to the main institution.

FCI Seagoville initially housed female inmates. During World War II, the prison housed Japanese, German, and Italian families who were considered national security risks. In 1945, it converted to the male federal prison it is today. The facility is a Sex Offender Management Program (SOMP) institution, which means that around 40 percent of the inmate population is incarcerated for a current or past sexual offense.

Media reports indicate that at least two guards have been indicted for smuggling contraband into the institution. Additionally, one inmate has escaped, and one inmate has been indicted for attacking a fellow prisoner he believed to be gay.

Housing: Inmates are housed in two-, three-, five-, and twelve-person rooms. B, D, and E housing units have air conditioning, while the others do not. There is a total of seven housing units. Inmates at the detention center are housed in two-person cells and those at the camp are housed in dormitories.

Health Services: Inmates at FCI Seagoville have access to sick call, dental care, dental emergency care, emergency medical care, eyeglasses, medications, chronic care and physical examinations. The Health Services waiting room offers educational videos on various health related concerns. Emergency medical care is available 24 hours a day. Sick call is held between 6:30 and 7:00 a.m. on Monday, Tuesday, Thursday, and Friday. Insulin and pill line are conducted at 6:30 a.m. and 5:30 p.m. on weekdays and 7:00 a.m. and 5:00 p.m. on weekends.

Psychology Services: Psychological services are available to the inmate population in both facilities in both English and Spanish. Individual consultation, counseling, and crisis intervention are readily available for all inmates. A Non-Residential Sex Offender Treatment Program (SOTP-NR) is also available to prisoners at FCI Seagoville. Other groups include anger management, mindfulness, basic cognitive skills, stress management, grief management, and emotional self-regulation.

Residential Drug Abuse Program (RDAP): FCI Seagoville has the Residential Drug Abuse Program (RDAP). The camp does not offer RDAP. Both institutions also offer the Drug Education Program and the Non-Residential Drug Abuse Program (NR-DAP).

Education Services: FCI Seagoville offers literacy, GED, and English-as-a-Second Language (ESL) programs to inmates. A certificate is given to students who achieve the eighth-grade functional literacy level. Students who achieve the state standards for GED receive a State of Texas diploma and a cash award up to $25, if funds are available. A parenting program and Adult Continuing Education (ACE) classes are also available. Current ACE classes include drafting technology, African American history, creative writing, introduction to law library, real estate, American civil war, everyday math, science, criminal justice, financial self-defense, and more. Institution Release Preparation Program sessions consisting of six core classes are also offered to inmates. High school diplomas and post-secondary degrees are available through paid correspondence programs. Cedar Valley College offers limited college classes. Hours of operation are 7:30 to 10:30 a.m., 11:30 a.m. to 2:50 p.m., and 5:00 to 7:50 p.m. Monday through Friday and 7:00 to 9:30 a.m., 11:00 a.m. to 2:50 p.m., and 5:00 to 7:50 p.m. on Saturday.

Advanced Occupational Education: FCI Seagoville offers advanced occupational education in Auto Mechanic, Automotive Technician, Computer Graphics and Design, Construction Tech, Core Construction, HVAC, Landscape Design, and Turfgrass. No advanced occupational education programs are available at the camp.

Vocational Training: Neither FCI Seagoville nor the camp offer any vocational training programs aside from the advanced occupational education programs.

Apprenticeship: FCI Seagoville does not offer any apprenticeship programs.

Library Services: Both leisure and law libraries are available to inmates at FCI Seagoville. Typewriters and a copy machine are available in the law library and are to be utilized for legal work only. Typewriter ribbons are available from the commissary. Legal research is conducted through the TRULINCS Electronic Law Library computers. In the leisure library, inmates have access to books and magazines. Current magazine subscriptions and newspapers are maintained for English and Spanish speaking inmates. The leisure library also provides a variety of educational, entertainment, and self-help videos and books on tape for inmates interested in personal enrichment. An interlibrary loan program is also available.

UNICOR: The FCI Seagoville UNICOR facility produces clothing and textiles.

Commissary: Inmates can spend up to $360.00 per month. This amount is increased during the Christmas holiday season. Popular items include food, beverages, and clothing. Shoes, electronics, ice cream, and over-the-counter medications are also available for purchase. Special Purchase Orders for sports equipment, hobbycraft items, etc., are limited each month. Commissary shopping hours are based on the fourth and fifth digits an inmate's registration number. The commissary is open Monday through Thursday, between 6:30 and 8:20 a.m., and 10:30 a.m. to 1:00 p.m. UNICOR inmates are allowed to shop on Wednesdays.

Recreation Services: Both indoor and outdoor facilities are available at FCI Seagoville depending on weather conditions. Television viewing rooms are located in each of the housing units for inmate use. Seven televisions are also available in the Recreation Department. There are a variety of organized sports including softball, flag football, soccer, Frisbee, volleyball, pickleball, handball, racquetball, and basketball. Varsity sports teams are chosen from the inmate population to compete in contests against outside teams. A hobby shop (e.g., painting, beading, art, leather, crochet, etc.), weightlifting/fitness area (with dumbbells, barbells, flat and decline benches, leg press, and shoulder rack), wellness program, track, and music room are also available for inmates. Hours of operation are 6:00 to 10:20 a.m., 11:00 a.m. to 3:15 p.m., and 5:00 to 7:30 p.m.

Visitation Information: On Sunday and Saturday visitation is held between 8:30 a.m. and 3:00 p.m. On federal holidays visitation is held between 8:30 a.m. and 3:00 p.m. See Chapter 1 for more information on visitation.

Prison Politics: There is a low level of politics at this prison. According to respondents, some parts of the yard and other areas (e.g., some TV rooms and tables) are claimed by different races or cars, but not too much of this occurs. According to one inmate, "the facility is extremely safe for all charges/groups." Another inmate stated, "Everyone talks to each other, but when it comes to watching TVs or eating in the chow hall, it is segregated by race and type of crime." Another inmate expressed, "We have some politics just to keep the peace, but it's a SOMP/PC Low."

Level of Violence: There is very little violence at this facility. One inmate explained that "it is a safe institution." Another rated it a 9 out of 10 for safety. Another respondent agreed, stating that there was a "low level of violence." One respondent colored this discussion by stating, "Safety is moderate only because we are vastly understaffed." Another inmate stated, "Violence is rare and serious injuries are almost unheard of. Fist fights happen, but most violence stops at pushing and shoving."

Vulnerable Populations: Sex offenders, informants, and LGBT inmates are allowed to walk the yard. One respondent referred to the yard as a "drop-out yard" where everyone can walk. Another expressed that it is a "sex offender and protective custody yard." He also stated that "transgender inmates are allowed to walk." Another inmate explained, "This is a SOMP yard, so it's 65-70% sex offender right now. Almost everyone else is either an informant or got run out of somewhere else for some reason."

Good: "This prison is very nice looking. The outdoor areas look like a park with lots of grass, trees, flower beds, and hedges. The buildings are all red brick and architecturally pleasing. There is even a gazebo which the inmates can use when the compound is open to free movement, which doesn't happen very often." "Very little theft or violence, just morons." "Beautiful campus, trees, shrubs, college-like campus." "Gazeboes and picnic tables on compound." "There are a lot of trees and vegetation because of the VT Landscape department." "Possibly the most laid-back prison in the BOP." "Food service is decent and is getting better." "The prison resembles a college campus with scores of mature live oak trees along with dozens of flower beds and hedges."

Bad: "The only bad thing about this prison is the COs who still want to use their authority to mistreat prisoners." "Not the best staff as far as individual problems are concerned." "Inmate-to-inmate respect level is very low compared to other places." "Not a place for wheelchairs and walkers due to being too bumpy and narrow." "Staff are terrible as a whole." "It used to be an open compound until someone shut that down." "There are a lot of bad things about this compound." "Huge drug problem here. K2 has inmates dropping like flies. It is so bad now that if an inmate is high, they don't even lock them up if they can walk and talk because there is no room in the SHU for them."

Other Comments: "Easy time." "Anyone can walk here no problem. Just don't expect it to be very 'prison-like.' It's more like a college campus (in layout), full of middle school maturity-level grown men." "Other than the heat, it's a great spot to do time." "If you have a choice in where to go, then don't come here." "This is not a bad spot, but it's not Club Fed either."

In the News: In June 2018, William Laurence Stanley escaped from Federal Correctional Seagoville and was recaptured the next day.

In May 2018, U.S. Senator John Cornyn and Bureau of Prisons Director Mark Inch took a tour of FCI Seagoville in the lead up to a federal criminal justice reform bill.

In April 2017, award-winning journalist Barrett Brown, who was released from FCI Seagoville to serve the remainder of his sentence on home confinement, was unexpectedly returned to FCI Seagoville because the Bureau of Prisons was unhappy that he was speaking to the media. Brown's attorney explained to the Bureau that BOP policy only requires prior authorization for interviews conducted in-person at Bureau institutions, not interviews conducted via telephone, email, or postal mail.

In March 2013, John Hall, a prisoner at FCI Seagoville and Aryan Brotherhood gang member, was sentenced to an additional 71 months in prison after beating and kicking another prisoner in December 2011 because he believed the victim was gay.

In February 2012, Michael Hopper, a guard at FCI Seagoville, was sentenced to two years in prison for smuggling alcohol, tobacco and nutritional supplements into the prison.

In 2009, Barry Kent Haatvedt, a guard at FCI Seagoville, received three-and-a-half years in prison for bribery after being paid approximately $10,000 to smuggle tobacco into the prison.

FCI Texarkana

Federal Correctional Institution Texarkana | FCI Texarkana

Facilities: FCI Texarkana with an adjacent minimum-security satellite prison camp.

Facility Address & Contact Information

Federal Correctional Institution Texarkana
4001 Leopard Drive
Texarkana, TX 75501

Phone: 903-838-4587
Fax: 903-223-4424
Email: TEX/ExecAssistant@bop.gov

BOP Website: https://www.bop.gov/locations/institutions/tex/
Wikipedia: https://en.wikipedia.org/wiki/Federal_Correctional_Institution,_Texarkana
ZCG Website: https://www.prisonerresource.com/resources/federal-prison-profiles/
south-central-region-scr/federal-correctional-institution-terminal-island-fci-terminal-island/

Inmate Correspondence Address

For FCI Texarkana

Inmate Name and Registration Number
FCI Texarkana
Federal Correctional Institution
P.O. Box 7000
Texarkana, TX 75505

For Satellite Prison Camp

Inmate Name and Registration Number
FCI Texarkana
Satellite Prison Camp
P.O. Box 9300
Texarkana, TX 75505

NOTE: Funds cannot be sent directly to federal inmates. See Chapter 1 for more information on sending funds to federal inmates.

Sex: Male

Security Level: Main: Low Security; Camp: Minimum Security

Location: FCI Texarkana is located in northeast Texas near the Arkansas border, 175 miles east of Dallas, 70 miles north of Shreveport, LA; off Route 59 South on Leopard Drive.

BOP Region: South Central Region (SCR)

BOP Institution Code: TEX for FCI Texarkana

Judicial District: Eastern District of Texas

Medical Care Level: Level 2. See Chapter 2 for more information on Medical Care and Mental Health Care Levels.

Mental Health Care Level: Level 2

Population (as of May 1, 2019): Main: 1,012; Camp: 274

Background: Federal Correctional Institution Texarkana is a low-security federal prison in Texarkana, Texas, which houses male inmates. It opened in 1940. Federal Correctional Institution Texarkana Camp, which also houses male inmates, is located adjacent to the main institution.

Notable inmates include Keith Judd (sentenced to 17 years for extortion). While incarcerated, Judd filed papers to run for president in the 2012 general election. He won 41 percent of the primary vote in West Virginia against incumbent Barack Obama.

Media reports indicate that at least nine guards have been indicted for sexually assaulting inmates and at least one guard has been convicted of smuggling contraband into the prison. Additionally, six inmates have been indicted for possessing contraband, four prisoners have been indicted for drug possession, and one inmate has been indicted for attempting to smuggle contraband into the institution.

In 2005, *The Kansas City Star* named FCI Texarkana Camp one of the five best federal prisons for white collar offenders.

Housing: Inmates are housed in several configurations ranging from two-, four-, and ten-person cells to dormitories with up to 40 inmates. In the camp, inmates are housed in dormitories.

Health Services: FCI Texarkana provides preventive health care, emergency medical care, chronic care, medications, physical examinations, annual TB testing, dental care, and eyeglasses. Emergency medical care is available 24 hours a day, while on-site medical care is available 16 hours a day. Inmates must submit a triage form to be evaluated for routine care needs. Sick call is held in the mornings at 6:30 a.m. Pill line is conducted during each meal, and insulin line is held before breakfast and dinner.

Psychology Services: All inmates are screened by a psychologist upon arrival to FCI Texarkana. Psychology staff offer brief individual counseling and comprehensive individual and group therapy programs. These programs address the full range of clinical disorders, provide self-help options, assess and treat behavioral and emotional problems, and facilitate overall adjustment. The Psychology Department also provides drug abuse treatment for those who have substance use disorders, helps to determine the need for psychotropic medication, consults with other staff about the mental health needs of inmates, and coordinates services with other departments as appropriate. Crisis intervention is available 24 hours a day, seven days a week, including holidays.

Residential Drug Abuse Program (RDAP): FCI Texarkana does not have the Residential Drug Abuse Program (RDAP). The camp does have the Residential Drug Abuse Program (RDAP). Both facilities offer a Drug Abuse Education program and the Non-Residential Drug Abuse Program (NR-DAP).

Education Services: Inmates at FCI Texarkana are offered literacy, GED, and English-as-a-Second Language (ESL) programs. Adult Continuing Education (ACE), a parenting program (Inside Out Dad), Language Lab, and a Resume Writing Workshop are also available. Current ACE classes include Start Your Own Business, Spanish (beginner, intermediate, and advanced), Civil War, and Our Universe. Information on course offerings and enrollment is posted on bulletin boards in the units, in the Education Department, and on TRULINCS. High school diplomas and post-secondary degrees are available through paid correspondence programs. Rosetta Stone programs are available in Spanish, German, French, Japanese, and Italian. Hours of operation are 7:00 a.m. to 8:00 p.m. Monday through Saturday, excluding Friday night, meals, and institutional recalls.

Advanced Occupational Education: FCI Texarkana offers advanced occupational education in Business Computer Applications, Introduction to Culinary Arts, Culinary Arts, Graphic Design, HVAC, Upholstery, and Welding. The camp offers advanced occupational education programs in Automotive/Diesel Mechanics, Building Trades, Business Computer Applications, HVAC, and Introduction to Culinary Arts.

Vocational Training: FCI Texarkana does not offer any vocational training programs aside from the advanced occupational education programs.

Apprenticeship: FCI Texarkana offers apprenticeships in Dental Assistant, Dental Technician, Electrical Apprenticeship, and HVAC. The camp offers Dental Assistant Apprenticeship, Dental Technician, Electrical Apprenticeship, and HVAC.

Library Services: The leisure library offers a wide variety of books including vocational and technical books, general reference (i.e., encyclopedias, dictionaries, etc.), college and high school texts, as well as fiction and nonfiction. Several magazines and daily newspapers are provided. An interlibrary loan program is also available. The law library utilizes the Lexis Nexis Electronic Law Library system. Inmates may research legal information through the available computer stations. Typewriters and a copy machine are available for inmate use.

UNICOR: The FCI Texarkana UNICOR facility handles recycling activities and services, and produces industrial products.

Commissary: Inmates are permitted to spend up to $360.00 per month on a variety of products. This is further restricted to $100 per week. The main commissary is located between the Hospital and the Dining Hall. The camp commissary is located behind the housing area in the Hospital and Commissary building. All monies sent or earned are deposited into the inmate's commissary account. Commissary hours and prices are posted on the bulletin board. UNICOR inmates are allowed to shop at 6:30 a.m. All other inmates can shop on any of the hourly activities moves.

Recreation Services: The Recreation Departments in both facilities provide a number of exercise programs based on cardiovascular exercise, which are 10 weeks in length and are available for all age groups. The classes vary in exercises and topics of instruction include health, nutrition, exercise, stretching, and personal training. A variety of sports programs are also available for the inmate population. Intramural leagues include volleyball, basketball, softball, Frisbee, soccer, horseshoes, bocce ball, micro-soccer, indoor volleyball, and indoor basketball. The gymnasium offers basketball, handball/racquetball, volleyball, and aerobic equipment (e.g., treadmills, stationary bikes, ellipticals) during the winter months. The outside recreation area offers a jogging/walking track, two outdoor exercise areas, two basketball courts, and two multi-purpose courts. Bocce ball courts, horseshoe pits, and an area for handball and racquetball are also available. A small recreation yard contains two handball courts and a covered weightlifting area. A large recreation yard has a softball field, soccer field, running track, six handball courts, two horseshoe pits, a bocce pit, two shuffleboard decks, a basketball court, and a weightlifting area. The Modular Unit (not available at the camp) offers a place for table and board games, music, billiard tables, ping pong table, TVs, and art and hobbycraft. An Activity Center provides an area for playing card games and various table games. The hobbycraft program offers inmates the opportunity to participate in leather craft, stick art, beads, and art (painting, drawing, and airbrushing). The prison's music program has two band rooms. Hours of operation are 6:30 a.m. to 8:15 p.m., excluding counts and meals.

Visitation Information: On Sunday and Saturday visitation is held between 8:00 a.m. and 3:00 p.m. On federal holidays visitation is held between 8:00 a.m. and 3:00 p.m. See Chapter 1 for more information on visitation.

Prison Politics: There is a low to moderate level of prison politics at this facility. According to inmates, this can be seen in the structure of seating in the chow hall and TV rooms. One inmate explained, "While there is a degree of politics, it's mostly for show." Another respondent agreed, stating, "To the most part, the racial politics are pretty relaxed. The chow hall and some of the TV rooms are segregated, and groups of different races, in general, segregate out. However, there is very little actual racial violence." According to another respondent, "Just about every race interacts with all the other races here." One inmate clarified, "Politics tend to be oriented more so along sex offender/non-sex offender grounds."

Level of Violence: There is a low level of violence at this prison. According to one respondent, "When there is violence, there are never any weapons involved, and it's often one-on-one and short-lived." Another inmate explained, "There is almost no violence here; it is very safe." Another respondent explained violence as follows: "Violence here isn't really that much of an issue. There're a few fights every now and then, but it's usually nothing more than a few bumps and bruises. The overall safety here is much better than at a lot of other places as long as you're respectful and don't run up debts that you can't pay."

Vulnerable Populations: Sex offenders, informants, and LGBT inmates are allowed to walk the yard. One inmate stated, "Sex offenders seem to be the majority of the compound." Another inmate explained, "Some units won't allow sex offenders to watch TV in the TV rooms, but it's kind of overlooked in some ways depending on the person." He also explained, "The staff don't really do anything to address the politics unless it's an issue that they are forced to deal with." Another respondent stated, "Informants are somewhat allowed. If a person isn't in a gang or affiliated with one, and is respectful, they usually don't get messed with. If a person is claiming they aren't an informant and is later found out, that can cause problems." Another inmate stated, "There's actually a former SIS lieutenant on the yard that doesn't seem to have any issues." Another respondent explained, "Overall, it's just a matter of circumstance and affiliation." Yet another inmate stated, "I'm a sex offender and haven't had any real problems in the 3+ years I've been here."

Good: "The best VT programs, good food, weights, and the TV rooms have five to eight TVs which are mostly newer." "The population is pretty low." "The staff is fairly professional." "Commissary." "The food is generally good." "The food here is better than most places, and the portions tend to be a bit more than typical." "The general consensus here is that this place is a good deal more laid back than most." "Most of the guards are just here to collect an easy check and don't really mess with people as long as they aren't being complete idiots." "The Chapel is really good."

Bad: "Pretty crowded, there is a bad K2 problem, no air conditioning in some housing units, and medical care is hit or miss on which MLP you are assigned to." "They just took the microwaves and our ice coolers." "There are frequent episodes of mass punishment due to the drug problems. The BOP lacks innovation and common sense when dealing with such issues." "There's a lot of petty activity here and some of the guards are on a personal quest to see just how far they can push the disrespect because they know the guys here are trying to point down to camp or home." "The worst aspects are the politics and guards' attitudes."

Other Comments: "We have a new warden. So far it seems to be an improvement, and the prison seems better managed." "The BOP in general seems to be on a downward spiral. As the budgets and staffing levels drop, overcrowding increases and program accessibility decreases. The same is true here as of elsewhere." "It's a pretty relaxed place overall. Just a bit petty at times." "Overall, this isn't too bad of a place to be. There is plenty to do to keep the time going by and the politics are manageable."

In the News: In July 2018, Kevin Tyler, a prisoner accused of attempting to smuggle contraband into Federal Correctional Institution Texarkana, asked the court to allow him access to over 1,000 pages of discovery necessary for his defense which prosecutors were trying to prevent in the name of prison security.

In March 2018, it was reported that FCI Texarkana had 41 staff positions eliminated, leaving 241 positions with 1,200 prisoners.

Also in March 2018, Jack Elton Willie, Kevin Tyler and Jeffery Lee Anderson were indicted for sending suboxone strips to Chester Brown, a prisoner at FCI Texarkana.

In January 2018, Chester Brown, Eric Wayne Grimes and Charles Webb, prisoners at FCI Texarkana, were separately indicted for the possession of contraband drugs.

In July 2017, Jasmer West, a prisoner at FCI Texarkana, was indicted for the possession of synthetic marijuana, or K2.

In November 2016, the Dallas News found that at least eight federal prison guards, including FCI Texarkana guard Jose Angel Rivas, committed sexual misconduct with prisoners since 2014, but some were allowed to plea to non-sexual crimes in order to stay off the state's sex offender registry.

In March 2016, Jose Angel Rivas, a guard at FCI Texarkana, was indicted for illegal sexual contact with and providing contraband to a male prisoner from May 2013 to February 2015.

In November 2015, six prisoners at FCI Texarkana -- Michael Chad Thompson, Ernest Allen McClain, Robert Abrego, Jesus Dozal, Scott McGarry and Eliezer Hernandez -- were separately indicted for possessing contraband such as cell phones, a knife, laptops and marijuana.

In November 2014, Shelonda Chares, a case manager at FCI Texarkana, was charged with engaging in a sexual act with a prisoner.

FCI Three Rivers

Federal Correctional Institution Three Rivers | FCI Three Rivers

Facilities: FCI Three Rivers with an adjacent minimum-security satellite prison camp.

Facility Address & Contact Information

Federal Correctional Institution Three Rivers
U.S. Highway 72 West
Three Rivers, TX 78071

Phone: 361-786-3576
Fax: 361-786-5051
Email: TRV/ExecAssistant@bop.gov

BOP Website: https://www.bop.gov/locations/institutions/trv/
Wikipedia: https://en.wikipedia.org/wiki/Federal_Correctional_Institution,_Three_Rivers
ZCG Website: https://www.prisonerresource.com/resources/federal-prison-profiles/south-central-region-scr/federal-correctional-institution-three-rivers-fci-three-rivers/

Inmate Correspondence Address

For FCI Three Rivers

Inmate Name and Registration Number
FCI Three Rivers
Federal Correctional Institution
P.O. Box 4200
Three Rivers, TX 78071

For Satellite Prison Camp

Inmate Name and Registration Number
FCI Three Rivers
Satellite Prison Camp
P.O. Box 4200
Three Rivers, TX 78071

NOTE: Funds cannot be sent directly to federal inmates. See Chapter 1 for more information on sending funds to federal inmates.

Sex: Male

Security Level: Main: Medium Security; Camp: Minimum Security

Location: FCI Three Rivers is located about 80 miles south of San Antonio and 73 miles northwest of Corpus Christi, off I-37 on Highway 72; 8 miles west of the town of Three Rivers, across from Choke Canyon Lake.

BOP Region: South Central Region (SCR)

BOP Institution Code: TRV for FCI Three Rivers

Judicial District: Southern District of Texas

Medical Care Level: Level 1. See Chapter 2 for more information on Medical Care and Mental Health Care Levels.

Mental Health Care Level: Level 1

Population (as of May 1, 2019): Main: 1,028; Camp: 285

Background: Federal Correctional Institution Three Rivers is a medium-security federal prison in Three Rivers, Texas, which houses male inmates. It was opened in 1990. Federal Correctional Institution Three Rivers Camp, which also houses male inmates, is located adjacent to the main institution.

Media reports indicate that one guard has been indicted for impersonating a police officer while he was off-duty, while another guard was indicted for smuggling contraband into the institution. News reports also indicate that there was a gang war in 2008, where one inmate was killed and another 22 injured.

Housing: Inmates are housed in two-person cells. Inmates at the camp are housed in dormitories.

Health Services: Within 14 days of arrival, inmates are given a complete physical examination. Sick call, dental care, emergency medical services, eyeglasses, chronic care, medications, physical examinations, HIV testing, and immunizations are all provided at FCI Three Rivers and the satellite camp. Emergency medical care is available 24 hours a day.

Psychology Services: Services provided by the psychology staff include crisis intervention, individual and group therapy, and psycho-educational programs (e.g., Anger Management, Stress Management, and Communication Skills). Notices of upcoming offerings are posted on bulletin boards in inmate housing units.

Residential Drug Abuse Program (RDAP): FCI Three Rivers and the camp do not house a Residential Drug Abuse Program (RDAP), but both do refer to facilities that do provide the program. Both facilities offer drug treatment programs, relapse prevention groups, a Drug Abuse Education Program, and the Non-Residential Drug Abuse Treatment Program (NR-DAP).

Education Services: FCI Three Rivers offers literacy, GED, and English-as-a-Second Language (ESL) programs. Graduation ceremonies are conducted once a year for students completing GED, ESL, and vocational training classes. A bonus of $25.00 is awarded for completion of GED, ESL or VT programs. Certificates from the institution are also awarded for completion of ACE, Parenting, GED, and ESL classes. In addition, a Student of the Month is chosen each month from classes in the Literacy program for significant progress as well as dedication and hard work. The Student of the Month is rewarded with a day off from school and work cleared through the Supervisor of Education and Unit Manager. Upon completion of each 240 hours of satisfactory progress, students are awarded a day off from school. Other incentives are awarded based on progress through the Literacy Program. A parenting program and Adult Continuing Education (ACE) courses are also offered. An employment resource center is also available to assist inmates within 24 months of release prepare for post-incarceration. High school diplomas and post-secondary degrees are available through paid correspondence programs.

Advanced Occupational Education: FCI Three Rivers and the camp offer advanced occupational education in Building Trades, HVAC, Microsoft Applications, and Welding. The camp offers General Automotive, HVAC, Microsoft Applications, and Wastewater Instruction.

Vocational Training: FCI Three Rivers does not offer any vocational training programs aside from the advanced occupational education programs.

Apprenticeship: FCI Three Rivers and the camp offer apprenticeships in Electrical Apprentice, HVAC, and Plumbing.

Library Services: Leisure and law libraries are available at both facilities. The leisure library has books available for checkout and DVDs available for viewing. Fiction and nonfiction books, newspapers, and magazines are available for inmate reading. Inmates are provided access to legal materials and an opportunity to prepare legal documents through the use of the TRULINCS Electronic Law Library. A copy machine is available to reproduce materials needed for research. Electric typewriters are also available for inmate use.

UNICOR: The FCI Three Rivers UNICOR facility handles fleet management and vehicular components. The camp does not have a UNICOR facility.

Commissary: The commissary spending limitation is $360.00 per month on a designated shopping day. The shopping day is based on the meal rotation roster generated by the Institution Duty Officer utilizing the weekly sanitation scores. Over-the-counter medications, copy cards, and postage stamps do not count against the spending limit. Foods, snacks, beverages, clothing, shoes, and electronics are also available for purchase.

Recreation Services: FCI Three Rivers recreation activities include hobbycraft (e.g., arts, leather craft, painting, beadwork), leisure, and fitness programs (e.g., walk/run club, abdominal fitness workout, yoga), intramural sports, and a band/music program. Activities including basketball, soccer, softball, flag football, handball/racquetball, bocce ball, horseshoes, and volleyball, are also offered.

Visitation Information: On Sunday and Saturday visitation is held between 8:15 a.m. and 3:00 p.m. On federal holidays visitation is held between 8:15 a.m. and 3:00 p.m. See Chapter 1 for more information on visitation.

In the News: In May 2017, David Cavazos, a guard at Federal Correctional Institution Three Rivers, was federally indicted for receiving a bribe to smuggle K2 into the prison.

In March 2017, FCI Three Rivers guard Justin Coates was arrested after he was seen pulling over another vehicle while he was armed and in uniform. He was charged with impersonating a police officer.

In November 2016, journalist Barrett Brown, who was prosecuted over stolen credit cards and fraudulent charges that he alleged he had nothing to do with, was released from FCI Three Rivers owing nearly $900,000 in restitution.

In March 2008, a gang war erupted between the Mexican Mafia and the Paisas at FCI Three Rivers resulting in one prisoner, Servando Rodriguez, dead and 22 others injured.

CHAPTER 9:

South East Region Prisons

Southeast Regional Office

The Southeast Regional Office is an administrative office providing oversight and support to facilities located in the Southeast Region (SER). The Southeast Region covers Federal Bureau of Prison facilities located in Alabama, Florida, Georgia, Mississippi, Puerto Rico, and South Carolina. These facilities are overseen by a regional office that provides oversight, technical assistance, and other types of operational support. In addition, they conduct training programs for staff in their region and assist state and local criminal justice agencies.

Regional Director: J.A. Keller
SER Population: 29,135

Facility Address & Contact Information

Southeast Regional Office
Federal Bureau of Prisons
3800 Camp Creek Parkway, SW
Building 2000
Atlanta, GA 30331

Email: SERO/ExecAssistant@bop.gov
Phone: 678-686-1200
Fax: 678-686-1229

BOP Website: https://www.bop.gov/locations/regional_offices/sero/
Wikipedia: n/a
ZCG Website: https://prisonerresource.com/resources/federal-prison-profiles/
federal-prison-regional-offices/southeast-regional-office-ser/

Staff Mail

Staff Name
Southeast Regional Office
3800 Camp Creek Parkway
Building 2000
Atlanta, GA 30331

Freight and Non-USPS Parcels

Staff Name
Southeast Regional Office
ATTN: Warehouse
3800 Camp Creek Parkway
Building 2000
Atlanta, GA 30331

Southeast Region Prisons

FCI Aliceville (AL)
USP Atlanta (GA)
FCI Bennettsville (SC)
FCI Coleman Low (FL)
FCI Coleman Medium (FL)
USP Coleman 1 (FL)
USP Coleman 2 (FL)
FCI Edgefield (SC)
FCI Estill (SC)
MDC Guaynabo (PR)
FCI Jesup (GA)
FSL Jesup (GA)
FCI Marianna (FL)
FCI Miami (FL)
FDC Miami (FL)
FPC Montgomery (AL)
FPC Pensacola (FL)
FCI Talladega (AL)
FCI Tallahassee (FL)
FCI Williamsburg (SC)
FCI Yazoo City Low (MS)
FCI Yazoo City Medium (MS)
USP Yazoo City (MS)

FCI Aliceville

Federal Correctional Institution Aliceville | FCI Aliceville

Facilities: FCI Aliceville with adjacent minimum-security satellite prison camp.

Facility Address & Contact Information

Federal Correctional Institution Aliceville
11070 Highway 14
Aliceville, AL 35442

Phone: 205-373-5000
Fax: 205-373-5020
Email: ALI/ExecAssistant@bop.gov

BOP Website: https://www.bop.gov/locations/institutions/ali/
Wikipedia: https://en.wikipedia.org/wiki/Federal_Correctional_Institution,_Aliceville
ZCG Website: https://www.prisonerresource.com/resources/federal-prison-profiles/southeast-region-ser/federal-correctional-institution-aliceville-fci-aliceville/

Inmate Correspondence Address

For FCI Aliceville

Inmate Name and Registration Number
FCI Aliceville
Federal Correctional Institution
P.O. Box 4000
Aliceville, AL 35442

For Satellite Prison Camp

Inmate Name and Registration Number
FCI Aliceville
Satellite Prison Camp
P.O. Box 487
Aliceville, AL 35442

NOTE: Funds cannot be sent directly to federal inmates. See Chapter 1 for more information on sending funds to federal inmates.

Sex: Female

Security Level: Main: Low Security; Camp: Minimum Security

Location: FCI Aliceville is located 100 miles from Birmingham, on the west side of Alabama.

BOP Region: Southeast Region (SER)

BOP Institution Code: ALI for FCI Aliceville

Judicial District: Northern District of Alabama

Medical Care Level: Level 2. See Chapter 2 for more information on Medical Care and Mental Health Care Levels.

Mental Health Care Level: Level 2

Population (as of May 1, 2019): Main: 1,344; Camp: 254

Background: Federal Correctional Institution Aliceville is a low-security federal prison in Aliceville, Alabama, which houses female inmates. The prison opened in 2013. Federal Correctional Institution Aliceville Camp, which also houses female inmates, is located adjacent to the main institution.

Construction on FCI Aliceville began in 2008 and it became operational in 2013. The prison is located between Aliceville and Pickensville.

Notable prisoners include Elaine Brown (serving a 35-year sentence after authorities found her stockpiling bombs, handguns, and high-powered rifles during an eight-month standoff over her and her husband's, Ed Brown, tax evasion charge).

Media reports indicate that guards have been charged with sexually assaulting female inmates, lying to federal investigators, and smuggling contraband into the institution.

Housing: Inmate are housed in two- and three-person cells, though regardless of occupancy, only two people are in any one cell. Only 16 of the 64 cells in each unit are three-person, which house new arrivals, inmates returning from the SHU, and those on IFRP refusal status. There is a total of 12 housing units. In each unit there are six TVs, six computers, two computers for video visits, two hot water dispensers, and one ice machine. Inmates at the camp are housed in dormitories. Those in the Special Housing Unit (SHU) are housed in cells.

Health Services: FCI Aliceville provides medical sick call services for routine, non-emergency conditions, dental sick call for dental emergencies, chronic care services, pharmacy services, prescription medications, tuberculosis testing, eye examinations once every two years, physical and periodic health examinations, and HIV testing. Sick call is held Monday, Tuesday, Thursday, and Friday at 8:00 a.m. Regular hours of operation are 8:00 a.m. to 3:30 p.m. Pill and insulin line are held at 6:00 a.m. and various times in the evening. Emergency medical care is available 24 hours a day.

Psychology Services: Inmates participate in Psychology Services A&O within a month of their arrival. Psychology Services staff work with inmates who have mental health and significant emotional and behavioral problems. Open house is held Wednesdays from 12:30 to 2:00 p.m. Psychology Services staff also encourage inmates without such problems to engage in self-improvement activities. Inmates who need to be seen by a psychiatrist for psychotropic medications are referred to Health Services, with input from Psychology Services. Groups offered include drug treatment and trauma treatment. Recent offerings include the Resolve program, Foundation, Assert Yourself for Females, and Women's Relationships. Brief counseling sessions are available to address individual needs. The facility also offers the STAGES program for inmates with serious mental illness and personality disorders.

Residential Drug Abuse Program (RDAP): FCI Aliceville and the satellite camp do not have the Residential Drug Abuse Program (RDAP). Both facilities offer the Drug Education class and the Non-Residential Drug Abuse Program (NR-DAP).

Education Services: The FCI Aliceville Education Department is open from 8:00 a.m. to 3:30 p.m. Monday through Friday, and 5:30 to 8:30 p.m. Monday through Thursday. It is also open from 8:00 to 9:30 a.m. and 12:00 to 3:30 p.m. Saturday and Sunday. The department offers literacy, GED and GED preparation classes, Spanish GED, English-as-a-Second Language (ESL), and a Special Learning Needs program. Adult Continuing Education (ACE) and parenting classes are also available. Inmates are allowed to sign up for one five-week long ACE class at a time. The Parenting Program meets for three hours each week for twelve weeks. A Release Preparation Program is offered, where inmates can take Staying Healthy, Budgeting, Housing & Transportation, Self-Esteem, Pathway to a Successful Reentry, and Key to Successful Employment. Each of these are four weeks long and are held on Tuesdays and Thursdays from 6:00 to 8:00 p.m. Inmate tutors teach skills including job searching, resume writing, budgeting, and buying a home. High school diplomas and post-secondary degrees are available through paid correspondence programs.

Advanced Occupational Education: FCI Aliceville does not offer any advanced occupational education programs.'

Vocational Training: FCI Aliceville offers vocational training programs in Carpentry, Cosmetology, Electrical. The Carpentry and Electrical programs are accredited by the National Center for Construction Education and Research. Both facilities also offer training in MS Office.

Apprenticeship: FCI Aliceville offers apprenticeships in Carpentry, Electrician, HVAC, and Plumbing.

Library Services: FCI Aliceville has both a leisure and law library with hundreds of reading and reference books in English and Spanish, newspapers, magazines, legal reference materials, Bureau of Prison policies, a copy machine, and typewriters. Inmates can conduct legal research on the TRULINCS Electronic Law Library computers. A law library clerk is available to assist inmates with legal typing needs.

UNICOR: FCI Aliceville does not have a UNICOR facility. The UNICOR building is currently used by the Mail Room and R & D.

Commissary: A $360.00 monthly spending limit is imposed. Inmates are allowed to shop once a week on a designated day. Currently, each housing unit has its own shopping day, during which inmates can shop from 6:00 to 10:30 a.m. Shopping is only conducted Monday, Tuesday, and Wednesday. Inmates can purchase a wide variety of items, including clothing, shoes, electronics, food, sodas, ice cream, and more.

Recreation Services: FCI Aliceville offers athletic and leisure time activities for the inmate population. The gymnasium, recreation yard, inside recreation areas, and hobbycraft are open from 6:00 to 10:30 a.m., 12:30 to 3:30 p.m., and 5:00 to 8:30 p.m. The Recreation Department also offers a variety of games, sports, social activities, arts and hobbycrafts, wellness, and other group and individual activities. Inside, offerings include crochet, knitting, beading, cardmaking, drawing, acrylic painting, step-aerobics, yoga, and Zuma. Outside, inmates can play softball, soccer, football, volleyball, and basketball. The camp has a recreation yard, a variety of games, sports, social activities, arts and hobbycrafts, wellness, and other group and individual activities.

Visitation Information: On Sunday and Saturday visitation is held between 8:00 a.m. and 3:00 p.m. On federal holidays visitation is held between 8:00 a.m. and 3:00 p.m. See Chapter 1 for more information on visitation.

Prison Politics: There are no reported prison politics at this facility.

Level of Violence: While most respondents felt that there is a very low level of violence at this prison, others stated that the level of violence is high for a low. One inmate who felt that there was a high level of violence stated that "the place is not under control at all" and that "older inmates are at high risk here."

Vulnerable Populations: Sex offenders, informants, and LGBT inmates can walk the yard. According to one respondent, "everyone is all put in here together and can mingle with everyone else."

Good: "It is very easy and relaxing being here."

Bad: "We need more programs." "Nothing is good about this prison." "Very bad medical care."

Other Comments: "This place needs to be completely shut down."

In the News: In May 2018, reality TV celebrity Kim Kardashian West met with President Donald Trump to advocate for a presidential pardon of Alice Marie Johnson, who was serving a life sentence at the Federal Correctional Institution at Aliceville for a first-time drug conspiracy offense. Johnson was subsequently pardoned by President Trump.

Also in May 2018, Jesse Bailey, a guard at FCI Aliceville, was sentenced to a year-and-a-half in prison for having sex with a female prisoner and lying about it to federal investigators.

In April 2017, Eric C. Walker, a materials handling supervisor at FCI Aliceville, was arrested and accused of smuggling tobacco and other contraband into the prison for cash bribes.

In January 2017, Patricia Bradley became warden of FCI Aliceville after serving as an associate warden at Federal Correctional Complex Yazoo City.

In September 2016, Brenda Montgomery and Cindy Tate were sentenced to 57 months in federal prison for stealing nearly $4 million from the bank where they were employed. Both were sent to FCI Aliceville.

In February 2016, a tornado tore through FCI Aliceville, ripping the roof off of a dorm building and leaving the female prisoners hiding under their bunks on the top floor and standing in four inches of water on the bottom floor.

USP Atlanta

United States Penitentiary Atlanta | USP Atlanta

Facilities: USP Atlanta with an adjacent minimum-security satellite prison camp and a detention center.

Facility Address & Contact Information

United States Penitentiary Atlanta
601 McDonough Boulevard, SE
Atlanta, GA 30315

Phone: 404-635-5100
Fax: 404-331-2403
Email: ATL/PublicInformation@bop.gov

BOP Website: https://www.bop.gov/locations/institutions/atl/
Wikipedia: https://en.wikipedia.org/wiki/United_States_Penitentiary,_Atlanta
ZCG Website: https://www.prisonerresource.com/resources/federal-prison-profiles/southeast-region-ser/united-states-penitentiary-atlanta-usp-atlanta/

Inmate Correspondence Address

For USP Atlanta

Inmate Name and Registration Number
USP Atlanta
U.S. Penitentiary
P.O. Box 150160
Atlanta, GA 30315

For Satellite Prison Camp

Inmate Name and Registration Number
USP Atlanta
Satellite Prison Camp
P.O. Box 150160
Atlanta, GA 30315

NOTE: Funds cannot be sent directly to federal inmates. See Chapter 1 for more information on sending funds to federal inmates.

Sex: Male

Security Level: Main: Medium Security; Camp: Minimum Security

Location: USP Atlanta is located southeast of Atlanta, at the junction of Boulevard SE and McDonough Boulevard SE; off I-20 (south on Boulevard) off I-285 (north on Moreland Avenue, left on McDonough Boulevard).

BOP Region: Southeast Region (SER)

BOP Institution Code: ATL for USP Atlanta

Judicial District: Northern District of Georgia

Medical Care Level: Level 2. See Chapter 2 for more information on Medical Care and Mental Health Care Levels.

Mental Health Care Level: Level 3

Population (as of May 1, 2019): Main: 1,815; Camp: 145

Background: United States Penitentiary Atlanta is a medium-security federal prison in Atlanta, Georgia, which houses male inmates. It opened in 1902. United States Penitentiary Atlanta Camp, which also houses male inmates, is located adjacent to the main institution.

USP Atlanta was the largest prison when it became operational, with 3,000 inmates. Documentation on every inmate was kept in a mini-documentary. Every detail was kept, from medical treatments to letters from the outside. Notable incidents include a 1987 bloody riot staged by Cuban detainees, who took dozens of hostages and set fire to the prison. Nearby hospitals reported that at least one inmate was killed, eight had gunshot wounds, and two guards were injured. The prison was rebuilt after the riot. In 1995, a new housing unit for pre-trial detainees was added.

Notable inmates include leader of the Chicago Outfit Al Capone (smuggled and bootlegged liquor during the 1920s prohibition and was convicted of tax evasion in 1931). Capone stayed at USP Atlanta until being transferred to Alcatraz Federal Penitentiary in 1934.

Media reports indicate that guards and a lieutenant have been indicted for assaulting inmates, bribery, theft of government funds, and filing false reports. Also, news media have reported numerous instances of inmates assaulting staff at the institution as well as inmates at the camp both escaping and leaving the institution only to return with duffle bags of contraband.

In 2011, News One named USP Atlanta one of the ten most notorious prisons in the United States.

Housing: Inmates are housed in one- and two-person cells and open dormitories. At the camp, inmates are housed in dormitories, which are divided into two-person cubicles.

Health Services: The USP Atlanta Health Services Department provides routine, urgent and chronic care to inmates as needed. Services include sick call, emergency medical treatment, medications, physical examinations, preventative health screening, HIV testing, treatment for on-the-job injuries, TB screening, and routine and emergency dental care. Emergency care is available 24 hours a day.

Psychology Services: USP Atlanta provides a psychological intake screening for all new inmates. General psychological services include individual and group psychotherapy. Regular groups include anger management, criminal thinking, and others. The Mental Health Step Down Program is also available for inmates with serious mental health issues who need to develop functional skills. Notices of groups are posted in inmate housing units.

Residential Drug Abuse Program (RDAP): USP Atlanta does not offer the Residential Drug Abuse Program (RDAP), but inmates can be referred to an institution that does have RDAP. The facility offers a drug program, Drug Education class, the Non-Residential Drug Abuse Program (NR-DAP), and Alcoholics Anonymous (AA).

Education Services: USP Atlanta offers literacy, GED, and English-as-a-second language (ESL) programs. An Adult Continuing Education (ACE) and parenting program are also available to inmates. High school diplomas and post-secondary degrees are available through paid correspondence programs.

Advanced Occupational Education: USP Atlanta offers advanced occupation education in Custodial Maintenance.

Vocational Training: USP Atlanta offers vocational training in Basic Custodial Maintenance, Electrical, and HVAC. The camp also offers Custodial Maintenance. Some work experiences available include cook, baker, butcher, electrician, plumber, painter, and carpenter.

Apprenticeship: USP Atlanta does not offer any apprenticeships.

Library Services: USP Atlanta offers both leisure and law libraries. In the leisure library, inmates can check out books, newspapers, and magazines. The law library primarily consists of the TRULINCS Electronic Law Library. Typewriters and a copy machine are also available. The law library is open Monday through Saturday.

UNICOR: The USP Atlanta UNICOR facility employs inmates as industry workers (mailbag, battle dress uniform, mattress), quality assurance workers, and clerk orderlies.

Commissary: The Commissary is located on the lower compound. Each inmate may spend a maximum of $360.00 per month on commissary items. Inmates may only shop once a week on their designated shopping day. It offers a variety of candies, beverages, toiletries, and other items for sale. Deposits are made through the centralized inmate lockbox.

Recreation Services: USP Atlanta recreation services consist of both indoor and outdoor activities and range from individualized arts and crafts programs to intramural team sports such as softball, basketball, soccer, and volleyball. Musical instruments are also available in the recreation area.

Visitation Information: On Sunday, Friday, and Saturday visitation is held between 8:00 a.m. and 3:00 p.m. On federal holidays visitation is held between 8:00 a.m. and 3:00 p.m. See Chapter 1 for more information on visitation.

In the News: In July 2018, Melvin Thomas, a guard at United States Penitentiary Atlanta, was sentenced to a year-and-a-day in prison after pleading guilty to bribery for selling tobacco to a prisoner.

In March 2018, Gregory McLeod, a lieutenant at USP Atlanta who repeatedly punched a prisoner in the face and then obstructed justice by writing two false reports about the incident, was sentenced to 20 months in prison.

In February 2018, Joe Fletcher, who was serving seven months at USP Atlanta for a supervised release violation, used a contraband cell phone to record a video of himself bragging that he murdered LaDonte Smith in 2010 and got away with it.

In February 2017, two guards were punched in the face and another was forcibly pushed in three separate incidents at USP Atlanta.

In October 2015, two prisoners in the pretrial/holdover housing unit at USP Atlanta assaulted two guards after getting into an argument with them.

In May 2014, a local news station reported that two prisoners at USP Atlanta, Cameron Braswell and Rex Whitlock, used a cell phone and social media to show off their shoes and tattoos.

In December 2010, Benjamin Montgomery, a guard at USP Atlanta, pleaded guilty to assaulting a prisoner and obstructing justice by writing a false report about the incident.

In May 2010, Michelle Dunmeyer, a contract specialist at USP Atlanta, pleaded guilty to using a government credit card to purchase more than $20,000 in electronics and gasoline for herself.

In April 2007, Christopher Holcomb, a guard at USP Atlanta, was sentenced to six months in jail for taking a bribe of $1,200 to smuggle a cell phone in for a prisoner.

In 1995, Gary Settle, Michael Rivers and Charles Harrelson, the hit man father of actor Woody Harrelson, attempted to escape USP Atlanta by climbing one of the walls. They surrendered after a guard fired a warning shot.

In November 1987, after the U.S. and Cuba agreed that many illegal Cubans fleeing the Castro regime would be returned to Cuba, 1,400 Cubans in USP Atlanta rioted, holding 89 people hostage for 11 days.

Camp In the News: In February 2018, Deldrick D. Jackson, serving ten years at United States Penitentiary Atlanta Camp, and Kelly Bass were sentenced to 18 months and six months, respectively, on charges relating to escape: Jackson worked with Bass to pick up Jackson and other prisoners, drive them around to hotels and restaurants, then bring them back to the prison with alcohol, cigarettes and other contraband to sell.

In September 2017, Jaye L. Thomas was indicted on three counts of escape for leaving the USP Atlanta Camp three times in 2016.

In February 2017, Justin Stinson left USP Atlanta Camp, retrieved a duffel bag containing a cell phone, alcohol, tobacco products and other contraband, and was arrested on his way back into the camp. In June 2017, he was sentenced to an additional 15 months incarceration. Atlanta Police have reportedly seen prisoners leaving the camp and returning with contraband since January 2013.

FCI Bennettsville

Federal Correctional Institution Bennettsville | FCI Bennettsville

Facilities: FCI Bennettsville with an adjacent minimum-security satellite prison camp.

Facility Address & Contact Information

Federal Correctional Institution Bennettsville
696 Muckerman Road
Bennettsville, SC 29512

Phone: 843-454-8200
Fax: 843-454-8219
Email: BEN/ExecAssistant@bop.gov

BOP Website: https://www.bop.gov/locations/institutions/ben/
Wikipedia: https://en.wikipedia.org/wiki/Federal_Correctional_Institution,_Bennettsville
ZCG Website: https://www.prisonerresource.com/resources/federal-prison-profiles/southeast-region-ser/federal-correctional-institution-bennettsville-fci-bennettsville/

Inmate Correspondence Address

For FCI Bennettsville

Inmate Name and Registration Number
FCI Bennettsville
Federal Correctional Institution
P.O. Box 52020
Bennettsville, SC 29512

For Satellite Prison Camp

Inmate Name and Registration Number
FCI Bennettsville
Satellite Prison Camp
P.O. Box 52020
Bennettsville, SC 29512

NOTE: Funds cannot be sent directly to federal inmates. See Chapter 1 for more information on sending funds to federal inmates.

Sex: Male

Security Level: Main: Medium Security; Camp: Minimum Security

Location: FCI Bennettsville is located in Marlboro County off Highway 9, 86 miles from Myrtle Beach.

BOP Region: Southeast Region (SER)

BOP Institution Code: BEN for FCI Bennettsville

Judicial District: District of South Carolina

Medical Care Level: Level 1. See Chapter 2 for more information on Medical Care and Mental Health Care Levels.

Mental Health Care Level: Level 1

Population (as of May 1, 2019): Main: 1,290; Camp: 150

Background: Federal Correctional Institution Bennettsville is a medium-security federal prison located in Bennettsville, South Carolina, which houses male inmates. Federal Correctional Institution Bennettsville Camp, which also houses male inmates, is located adjacent to the main institution.

FCI Bennettsville Camp is located near the main institution and contains a warehouse, facility maintenance, and a mechanics garage.

Media reports indicate that at least one inmate has been murdered at the institution and at least one guard has been charged with smuggling contraband into the institution.

Housing: Inmates are housed in two- and three-person cells. There is a total of 12 inmate housing units. The camp contains dormitory housing for up to 150 inmates.

Health Services: Shortly after arrival, all inmates at FCI Bennettsville receive an initial medical screening. Health services for all inmates include medical and dental sick call, medications, eyeglasses, and routine physical examinations. Inmates are assigned to a specific health care provider who treats them for the duration of their stay. FCI Bennettsville and camp inmates can complete an Inmate Request to Staff Member form (cop-out) for routine appointments. Emergency care is available 24 hours a day.

Psychology Services: FCI Bennettsville provides intake screening, crisis intervention, and individual and group counseling for all inmates. The intake interview gathers information to assess the inmate's current psychological functioning. Regular group counseling services include anger management, and criminal thinking. A self-help library is also available to the inmate population.

Residential Drug Abuse Program (RDAP): FCI Bennettsville does not offer the Residential Drug Abuse Program (RDAP), but inmates may be transferred to other institutions that offer RDAP. A Drug Education Class, the Non-Residential Drug Abuse Program (NR-DAP), Alcoholics Anonymous (AA), and Narcotics Anonymous (NA), are available.

Education Services: FCI Bennettsville offers literacy, GED instruction in English and Spanish languages and the English-as-a-Second Language (ESL) program. Classes are separated into pre-GED, Advanced GED, GED, and Special Learning Needs levels. Adult Continuing Education (ACE) classes and a parenting program are also available. Inmates can also complete high school diplomas and earn post-secondary degrees through paid correspondence courses. Inmates are allowed to type on AlphaSmart word processing units.

Advanced Occupational Education: FCI Bennettsville offers a Welding advanced occupational education program. Microsoft 2010 is also offered at the prison. The camp does not offer any advanced occupational education programs.

Vocational Training: FCI Bennettsville offers vocational training programs, which are approved by the Automotive Service Excellence, National Construction Center for Education and Research (NCCER), Green Clean Institute, and the National Restaurant Association. Course offerings include Automotive Service, Electrical Technology, Green Technology (NCCER), HVAC, Mechanical Maintenance and Systems, Construction and Extraction, NCCER Core, and Welding. The NCCER Core class is offered in English and Spanish. The camp offers Welding.

Apprenticeship: FCI Bennettsville does not currently offer any apprenticeship programs.

Library Services: The main library at FCI Bennettsville is located in the Education Department, and the auxiliary library is located in the Recreation Leisure Center. The library at the camp is located in the camp education area. Fiction and nonfiction books, newspapers, and magazines can be checked out. The law libraries primarily consist of the TRULINCS Electronic Law Library.

UNICOR: The FCI Bennettsville UNICOR facility handles fleet management and vehicular components. The satellite camp does not house a UNICOR facility.

Commissary: Inmates are permitted to spend up to $90 per week for regular and special purchases on their assigned shopping day. On their assigned shopping day, inmates submit their completed order form and wait for their order to be filled. Stamps and phone time are excluded from this spending limitation. Commissary deposits made through outside sources must include the inmates committed name and inmate number. Deposits can include money brought at time of arrival, sent from outside sources, or earned from work assignments. Requests for Withdrawal of Inmate's Personal Funds are processed within one (1) week of receipt by the Financial Management Department. Inmates are responsible for keeping track of balances and knowing the amount of money available in their commissary account. Balances can be checked via the Inmate Telephone System or on the TRULINCS computer system.

Recreation Services: FCI Bennettsville offers an outdoor recreation yard and an indoor recreation leisure center. Exercise activities include basketball, flag football, softball, soccer, racquetball/handball, walking/running track, bocce ball, horseshoe pits, and workout equipment (i.e., stationary bikes, treadmills, etc.). Other leisure and social activities include ceramics, art, crochet, board games, ping pong, playing cards, Dominoes, chess, checkers, and Scrabble. A music program is also available and consists of established inmate bands, self-taught practice sessions, and instructional books. The musical equipment includes drums, congas, electric guitars, amplifiers, speakers, brass instruments, microphones, and cords.

Visitation Information: On Sunday and Saturday visitation is held between 8:30 a.m. and 3:00 p.m. On Friday visitation is held between 5:00 to 8:00 p.m. On federal holidays visitation is held between 8:30 a.m. and 3:00 p.m. See Chapter 1 for more information on visitation.

Prison Politics: While some inmates reported that this is not a political yard and there is no car requirement, others disagreed, stating that this is a mostly political yard that does have a car requirement.

Level of Violence: While some inmates reported that there is a moderate level of violence, others reported a significant level of violence. Both groups agreed that there are a healthy number of fights.

Vulnerable Populations: Sex offenders and informants can't stay, but LGBT inmates can walk the yard.

Good: "Commissary selection." "The Education Department has a really robust career Education Resource Center. They really seem to care about their students."

Bad: "Lots of lockdowns due to fights." "Bad medical care and disrespectful cops."

Other Comments: "Not that bad of a spot." "Sex offenders should not go. They won't last." "If you want to be and live with members of your own race in a real way, go. Very racially oriented."

In the News: In August 2015, Toni Sawyer, Nia LaShay Mitchell and Leonard Javon Cooper were suspected of attempting to smuggle contraband into Federal Correctional Institution Bennettsville and were charged with trespassing and possession with intent to distribute marijuana.

Also in August 2015, FCI Bennettsville prisoner Larry Carter was found unresponsive and pronounced dead after an apparent assault by another prisoner.

In February 2015, Charlotte McLaughlin, a guard at FCI Bennettsville, was sentenced to 13 months in prison for smuggling tobacco and cell phones into the prison in 2012 and 2013.

In 2012, Dawud Adbullah Khalid, an inmate at FCI Bennettsville, escaped from the prison. He was recaptured and sentenced to an additional five years.

Federal Correctional Complex Coleman | FCC Coleman

Facilities: FCC Coleman comprises USP Coleman 1, USP Coleman 2, FCI Coleman Medium, and FCI Coleman Low with an adjacent minimum-security satellite prison camp.

USP Coleman 1

United States Penitentiary Coleman 1 | USP Coleman 1

Facility Address & Contact Information

United States Penitentiary Coleman 1
846 N.E. 54th Terrace
Coleman, FL 33521

Phone: 352-689-6000
Fax: 352-689-6012
Email: COA/PublicInformation@bop.gov

BOP Website: https://www.bop.gov/locations/institutions/cop/
Wikipedia: https://en.wikipedia.org/wiki/United_States_Penitentiary,_Coleman
ZCG Website: https://www.prisonerresource.com/resources/federal-prison-profiles/southeast-region-ser/federal-correctional-complex-coleman-fcc-coleman/united-states-penitentiary-coleman-1-usp-coleman-1/

Inmate Correspondence Address

Inmate Name and Registration Number
USP Coleman 1
U.S. Penitentiary
P.O. Box 1033
Coleman, FL 33521

NOTE: Funds cannot be sent directly to federal inmates. See Chapter 1 for more information on sending funds to federal inmates.

Sex: Male

Security Level: High Security

Location: USP Coleman 1 is located in central Florida, south of the town of Coleman, off Highway 301 on State Road 470 in Sumter County; about 50 miles northwest of Orlando, 60 miles northeast of Tampa, and 35 miles south of Ocala.

BOP Region: Southeast Region (SER)

BOP Institution Code: COP for USP Coleman 1, COX for Coleman Federal Correctional Complex

Judicial District: Middle District of Florida

Medical Care Level: Level 2/3. See Chapter 2 for more information on Medical Care and Mental Health Care Levels.

Mental Health Care Level: Level 3

Population (as of May 1, 2019): 1,420

Background: United States Penitentiary Coleman 1 is a high-security federal prison in Coleman, Florida, which houses male inmates. It was opened in 2001 and is part of the Coleman Federal Correctional Complex.

Media reports indicate that at least two guards have been indicted for smuggling contraband into the institution and 19 inmates have been indicted for smuggling drugs into the prison. Additionally, two inmates have been murdered at the institution. In one of the two inmate murders, staff staged the circumstances to allow the inmate to be murdered and were subsequently given life sentences for their involvement.

Housing: Inmates are housed in one- and two-person cells. There are approximately 110 inmates in each housing unit.

Health Services: USP Coleman 1 provides sick-call, first-aid, dental care, eyeglasses, physical examinations, emergency and routine treatment, and follow-up care. Prescription medications are available through the pharmacy. Sick call is held between 7:00 and 8:00 a.m. on weekdays. Emergency medical care is available 24 hours a day. Pill line is conducted at 7:00 to 8:00 a.m. and 2:00 to 3:00 p.m.

Psychology Services: USP Coleman 1 psychology services include an initial intake exam and services for emotional problems, sexual assault prevention, and the CODE program. The Challenge Program is also available for inmates who are prone to substance abuse, mental illness and violence. Upcoming treatment offerings are posted in inmate housing units. Currently, psychology classes include anger management, cognitive thinking skills, and criminal thinking.

Inmates must visit Psychology Services open house or file a cop-out to request program placement. Psychologists are available for individual and/or group psychotherapy as needed.

Residential Drug Abuse Program (RDAP): USP Coleman 1 does not have the Residential Drug Abuse Program (RDAP). A Drug Abuse Education class, the Non-Residential Drug Abuse Program (NR-DAP), Challenge Program, and referrals to the Residential Drug Abuse Program are available.

Education Services: USP Coleman 1 provides literacy, GED, and English-as-a-Second Language (ESL) programs in English and Spanish. Students who complete the GED tests are awarded $25, which is added to their commissary accounts, and are provided with an opportunity to participate in a graduation ceremony. Classes in business, Spanish, Commercial Driver's License, creative writing, parenting, public speaking, Pre-Release Programming, employment, and personal finance skills are also offered. High school diplomas and post-secondary degrees are available through paid correspondence programs.

Advanced Occupational Education: USP Coleman 1 offers a Culinary Arts advanced occupational education program.

Vocational Training: Vocational training classes include Culinary Arts, Custodial Maintenance, and MS Office.

Apprenticeship: USP Coleman 1 offers apprenticeships in Cook, Electrician, HVAC, and Plumbing.

Library Services: A law and leisure library are available to inmates at USP Coleman 1. The law library houses TRULINCS Electronic Law Library terminals, a copy machine, and typewriters. The leisure library has newspapers, periodicals, and fiction and nonfiction books. Both libraries are open from Monday through Saturday and closed on Sundays and holidays.

UNICOR: USP Coleman 1 does not house a UNICOR facility.

Commissary: Inmates with funds in their accounts are permitted to spend up to $360.00 per month on items such as food, snacks, candy, ice cream, electronics, clothing, and shoes. This spending limit is further reduced to a weekly limit of $90. Toothpaste, toothbrushes, combs, razors, and soap are issued by the institution. Inmates may purchase name brand items through the commissary. Designated shopping days take place once per week. In the Reintegration Housing Unit (RHU), commissary orders are delivered to the housing unit.

Recreation Services: USP Coleman 1 provides a recreation yard, hobbycraft center, leisure center, sports leagues, music center, a cards and games room, and a fitness area. The fitness area is set up with spinning bikes, treadmills, elliptical machines, rowing machines, step machines, and sit up boards. The games room includes table games such as foosball and ping pong. Outside, inmates have access to a track, basketball, softball, football, soccer, handball, horseshoes, and bocce ball. Inmates are allowed to participate in these activities during non-work hours. Inmates in the RHU have restricted access to recreation.

Visitation Information: On Sunday, Monday, and Saturday visitation is held between 8:00 a.m. and 3:00 p.m. On federal holidays visitation is held between 8:00 a.m. and 3:00 p.m. See Chapter 1 for more information on visitation.

Prison Politics: This is a very political yard where all inmates must be part of a car. Most cars are racially-oriented. According to one inmate, "The general population is highly political." The same inmate explained that there is a protective custody unit filled with "gang drop-outs" and "government cooperators." In this unit, time is reported as being easier.

Level of Violence: Inmates report significant violence at this facility. According to one respondent, "General population is very violent, even against staff members." Another explained, "The violence is terrible. People are regularly killed." Another inmate agreed, stating, "Violence is very high, and safety is very poor." As it pertains to the protective custody unit, "In the last two years there have been no stabbings and only one simple fist fight. I have yet to see a guard attacked in here."

Vulnerable Populations: Sex offenders, informants, and LGBT inmates are not allowed to stay at the facility. According to inmate respondents, these vulnerable populations are typically driven off. As explained by one inmate, "Transgender and gay inmates, as well as sex offenders, are not allowed to walk the yard." In the protective custody unit, all three groups are allowed to walk.

Good: "Efficient and extensive recreation department."

Bad: "Lockdowns happen all the time." "Staff known to put inmates out there or allow bad things to happen by turning a blind eye." "In the protective custody unit, we are stuck inside a small dorm all day, every day." "In the RHU, recreation, medical treatment, and religious services are either delayed or nonexistent. Likewise, we only receive cold meals in the evening."

Other Comments: "Only go if you have clean paperwork." "The protective custody unit has given me the chance to follow a genuine spiritual path. Nowhere else would that be possible at the penitentiary custody level. The RHU is a blessing overall."

In the News: In February 2018, Albert Larry Harris, a guard at United States Penitentiary Coleman 1, was sentenced to two years in prison for accepting a $5,000 bribe to smuggle drugs into the facility.

Between April 2014 and July 2015, Antwon Pitt, who had a long history of violent behavior and was serving two years at USP Coleman 1 for robbery, had 20 documented sexual offenses at the prison along with more than 20 other disciplinary offenses, including assault, refusing orders, destruction of property and fighting. In June 2016, less than a year after his release, Pitt was convicted of robbery, burglary, kidnapping, assault and first-degree sexual abuse.

In December 2010, Miguel Jimenez, a prisoner at USP Coleman 1, was stabbed to death in the recreation yard.

In July 2010, Michael Kennedy, a guard at USP Coleman 1, was found guilty of the fatal assault of prisoner Richard Delano after he and guard Erin Sharma placed Delano in a cell with a prisoner they knew would assault him. Sharma was found guilty in July 2009 and sentenced to life in prison in October 2009. The assault took place in March 2005.

In July 2004, 19 prisoners at USP Coleman 1 were indicted for smuggling drugs, which included marijuana and heroin, into the prison.

In 2004, USP Coleman 1 prison cook Charles West was sentenced to 15 months for smuggling drugs into the prison.

USP Coleman 2

United States Penitentiary Coleman 2 | USP Coleman 2

Facility Address & Contact Information

United States Penitentiary Coleman 2
846 N.E. 54th Terrace
Coleman, FL 33521

Phone: 352-689-7000
Fax: 352-689-7012
Email: COA/PublicInformation@bop.gov

BOP Website: https://www.bop.gov/locations/institutions/clp/
Wikipedia: https://en.wikipedia.org/wiki/United_States_Penitentiary,_Coleman
ZCG Website: https://www.prisonerresource.com/resources/federal-prison-profiles/southeast-region-ser/federal-correctional-complex-coleman-fcc-coleman/united-states-penitentiary-coleman-2-usp-coleman-2/

Inmate Correspondence Address

Inmate Name and Registration Number
USP Coleman 2
U.S. Penitentiary
P.O. Box 1034
Coleman, FL 33521

NOTE: Funds cannot be sent directly to federal inmates. See Chapter 1 for more information on sending funds to federal inmates.

Sex: Male

Security Level: High Security

Location: USP Coleman 2 is located in central Florida, south of the town of Coleman, off Highway 301 on State Road 470 in Sumter County; about 50 miles northwest of Orlando, 60 miles northeast of Tampa, and 35 miles south of Ocala.

BOP Region: South East Region (SER)

BOP Institution Code: CLP for USP Coleman 2, COX for Coleman Federal Correctional Complex

Judicial District: Middle District of Florida

Medical Care Level: Level 2/3. See Chapter 2 for more information on Medical Care and Mental Health Care Levels.

Mental Health Care Level: Level 3

Population (as of May 1, 2019): 1,352

Background: United States Penitentiary Coleman 2 is a high-security federal prison in Coleman, Florida, which houses male inmates. It is part of the Coleman Federal Correctional Complex.

According to writings from former prisoner Nate A. Lindell, USP Coleman 2 is "a so-called 'special-needs' prison -- a 'safe' facility where informants, former cops, ex-gang members, check-ins (prisoners who intentionally put themselves in solitary confinement to be safe), homosexuals, and sex offenders can all, supposedly, walk the Yard freely."

Media reports indicate that one guard was indicted for lying to federal investigators about sexually assaulting an inmate. Additionally, two inmates have been murdered at the prison.

Housing: Inmates are housed in one- and two-person cells. There is a total of 12 housing units which surround the recreation yard.

Health Services: USP Coleman 2 provides sick-call, first-aid, dental care, eyeglasses, physical exams, emergency and routine treatment, and follow-up care. Prescription medications are available through the pharmacy. Over-the-counter medications are available through the commissary. Inmates are assigned a specific health services provider who treats them throughout their stay. Sick call is held weekday mornings. Pill and insulin lines are conducted at 6:30 a.m., 2:00 p.m., and 5:30 p.m.

Psychology Services: Clinical psychologists provide assessment and treatment for problems such as depression, anxiety, and interpersonal issues. Treatment is offered through individual and group psychotherapy, as well as several self-help programs which utilize self-help books. Typical groups include anger management, and criminal thinking. A self-help library is also available to the inmate population.

Residential Drug Abuse Program (RDAP): USP Coleman 2 offers the Residential Drug Abuse Program (RDAP). The facility also offers the Drug Abuse Education class, the Non-Residential Drug Abuse Treatment (NR-DAP), Residential Challenge Program, and Alcoholics Anonymous (AA).

Education Services: USP Coleman 2 provides a literacy program in English and Spanish for inmates who do not have a high school diploma or a GED. English-as-a-Second Language (ESL) is also available. Students who complete the GED exam are awarded $25, which is added to their commissary accounts, and an opportunity to participate in a graduation ceremony. Students receiving a Student-of-the-Month award will receive a $5 cash award. Also offered is a robust Adult Continuing Education (ACE) program, with courses in business, Spanish, Commercial Driver's License, creative writing, parenting, public speaking, Pre-Release Programming, employment, and personal finance skills. High school diplomas and post-secondary programs are available through paid correspondence programs.

Advanced Occupational Education: USP Coleman 2 offers advanced occupational education in Culinary Arts, Electrical, Fundamentals of Maintenance, HVAC, MS Office, and Custodial Maintenance.

Vocational Training: USP Coleman 2 does not currently offer any vocational training programs.

Apprenticeship: USP Coleman 2 offers Cook, HVAC, Electrical, Cook: Hotel and Restaurant, and Plumbing apprenticeship programs.

Library Services: A law and leisure library is available to inmates at USP Coleman 2. The library allows inmates to check out books, magazines, and newspapers. There are also over 500 DVDs and 25 TVs that inmates can use. The law library offers typewriters, a copy machine, and the TRULINCS Electronic Law Library which is open Monday through Friday.

UNICOR: USP Coleman 2 does not house a UNICOR facility.

Commissary: A spending limit of $360.00 is imposed monthly, which is further structured into a $90 per week spending limitation. Inmates are allowed to shop in the commissary once a week on their designated shopping day. Schedules are posted in each housing unit. Currently, the commissary is open Monday through Thursday evenings. Inmates must submit their commissary order form the morning of the day they intend to shop. Popular items include ice cream, sodas, snacks, foods, and clothing.

Recreation Services: USP Coleman 2 provides a recreation yard, hobbycraft center, leisure center, sports leagues, music center, a cards and games room, and a fitness area. Music theory classes are offered in piano, drums, classical and saxophone.

Inside, inmates have access to basketball, volleyball, treadmills, stationary bikes, ellipticals, leather room, pottery room, art room, library, band room, tables, and a robust gaming program/ room. Outside, inmates have access to stationary bikes, ellipticals, skiing machine, basketball, softball, football, soccer, handball, horseshoes, bocce ball, and a track.

The Recreation Department is open seven days a week. Throughout the calendar year, the Recreation Department sponsors contests and tournaments on all recognized federal holidays. Prize bags (edibles) will be awarded as prizes for first place winners.

Visitation Information: On Sunday, Monday, and Saturday visitation is held between 8:00 a.m. and 3:00 p.m. On federal holidays visitation is held between 8:00 a.m. and 3:00 p.m. See Chapter 1 for more information on visitation.

Prison Politics: This is not a political yard. There is no car requirement. One inmate referred to it as a "special needs yard" for "gang drop-outs and high-profile cases."

Level of Violence: This prison has a low level of violence. Inmate estimates indicate one or so fights per month.

Vulnerable Populations: While one respondent advised that sex offenders aren't allowed to stay, another suggested that there are probably undercover sex offenders on the compound. All respondents agreed that informants and LGBT inmates can remain on the yard.

Good: "Allow flea markets all the time, theft from the kitchen institutionally accepted, good money on the compound." "Weather. No politics."

Other Comments: "Absolutely go, just don't tell that you have bad paperwork if that applies to you."

In the News: In April 2018, Heather Lee Kussoff, a guard at United States Penitentiary Coleman 2 (USP 2), was indicted for lying under oath about a romantic relationship she was having with a prisoner.

In January 2011, Wo 'Se Piankhi-Shabaki, a prisoner at USP Coleman 2 who was serving a life sentence, was killed by another prisoner.

In March 2008, Boyd Wallace Higginbotham, Jr., a prisoner at USP Coleman 2, stabbed fellow prisoner Steven Pritchard to death in the dining hall, for which he was later sentenced to life in prison.

FCI Coleman Medium

Federal Correctional Institution Coleman Medium | FCI Coleman Medium

Facilities: FCI Coleman Medium with an adjacent minimum-security satellite prison camp.

Facility Address & Contact Information

Federal Correctional Institution Coleman Medium
846 N.E. 54th Terrace
Coleman, FL 33521

Phone: 352-689-5000
Fax: 352-689-5027
Email: COA/PublicInformation@bop.gov

BOP Website: https://www.bop.gov/locations/institutions/com/
Wikipedia: https://en.wikipedia.org/wiki/Federal_Correctional_Institution,_Coleman
ZCG Website: https://www.prisonerresource.com/resources/federal-prison-profiles/southeast-region-ser/federal-correctional-complex-coleman-fcc-coleman/federal-correctional-institution-coleman-medium-fci-coleman-medium/

Inmate Correspondence Address

For FCI Coleman Medium

Inmate Name and Registration Number
FCI Coleman Medium
Federal Correctional Institution
P.O. Box 1032
Coleman, FL 33521

For Satellite Prison Camp

Inmate Name and Registration Number
FCI Coleman Medium
Satellite Prison Camp
P.O. Box 1027
Coleman, FL 33521

NOTE: Funds cannot be sent directly to federal inmates. See Chapter 1 for more information on sending funds to federal inmates.

Sex: Male

Security Level: Main: Medium Security; Camp: Minimum Security

Location: FCI Coleman Medium is located in central Florida, south of the town of Coleman, off Highway 301 on State Road 470 in Sumter County; about 50 miles northwest of Orlando, 60 miles northeast of Tampa, and 35 miles south of Ocala.

BOP Region: Southeast Region (SER)

BOP Institution Code: COM for FCI Coleman Medium, COX for Coleman Federal Correctional Complex

Judicial District: Middle District of Florida

Medical Care Level: Level 2/3. See Chapter 2 for more information on Medical Care and Mental Health Care Levels.

Mental Health Care Level: Level 3

Population (as of May 1, 2019): Main: 1,534; Camp: 467

Background: Federal Correctional Institution Coleman Medium is a medium-security federal prison in Coleman, Florida, which houses male inmates. It was opened in 1996 and is part of the Coleman Federal Correctional Complex. Federal Correctional Institution Coleman Camp, which also houses male inmates, is located adjacent to the main institution.

Media reports indicate that at least one guard has been indicted for taking bribes and smuggling contraband into the institution.

Housing: Inmates are housed in two-person cells. There is a total of twelve housing units. Camp inmates are housed in dormitories, which are divided into two-person cubicles.

Health Services: FCI Coleman Medium provides sick-call, first-aid, dental sick call, emergency and routine treatment, and follow-up care. The facility offers a pharmacy for prescription medications (over-the-counter medications are available through the commissary). Services also include health care staff referrals, health care staff-approved follow-up treatment for chronic conditions, preventive health care services, emergency services, diagnosis and treatment of chronic infectious diseases, and mental health care. Sick call is held at 7:00 a.m. on weekdays, and open house is held on Wednesdays at 1:30 p.m. Emergency medical care is available 24 hours a day at FCI Coleman Medium.

Psychology Services: In addition to conducting routine initial intake screenings for all inmates admitted to the facility, Psychology Services staff provide crisis intervention services, brief counseling, individual and group therapy, and psycho-educational groups. The Skills Program is available for inmates with intellectual disabilities and social deficiencies. The STAGES Program is available for camp inmates with serious mental illness and personality disorders. Inmates must either submit a request to staff or visit Psychology Services open house to sign up for available programs.

Residential Drug Abuse Program (RDAP): FCI Coleman Medium does not have the Residential Drug Abuse Program (RDAP). Drug education classes as well as the Non-Residential Transitional Services are available for inmates. The Non-Residential Drug Abuse Program (NR-DAP) is also available.

Education Services: FCI Coleman Medium offers literacy, GED, and English-as-a-Second Language (ESL) programs in English and Spanish. An Adult Basic Education (ABE) program is available for inmates without a high school diploma or GED. Adult Continuing Education (ACE) classes and a parenting program are also available. High school diplomas and post-secondary degrees are available through paid correspondence programs.

Advanced Occupational Education: FCI Coleman Medium offers advanced occupational education in Culinary Arts, HVAC, and Electrical, while the camp offers Cosmetology, Horticulture, HVAC, and Custodial Maintenance.

Vocational Training: Vocational training programs at FCI Coleman Medium are designed to meet the changing needs of the community workforce. Business Education (Computer Training), Culinary Arts, Home Health Care, Typing, Baking, Heating/Air Conditioning, Landscaping, and Electrical are offered at the prison.

Apprenticeship: Both FCI Coleman Medium and the satellite camp offer apprenticeships in Electrician, HVAC, Landscape Tech, and Plumbing.

Library Services: Inmates can access the law and leisure libraries at both the main prison and the camp seven days a week. The leisure library offers books, newspapers, and magazines to the inmate population. In the law library, inmates can access the TRULINCS Electronic Law Library, copy machine, and typewriters.

UNICOR: The FCI Coleman Medium UNICOR facility produces office furniture.

Commissary: Inmates are permitted to spend up to $360.00 per month in the main prison and in the camp. A weekly spending limitation of $90 is further imposed. The following items do not affect the spending limit: postage stamps (limit one book per week), Nicotine Replacement Therapy (NRT) patches, Kosher/Halal shelf-stable entrees for inmates who are FRP Refuse, copy cards, and copy paper. Commissary items include candy, cookies, ice cream, instant coffee, fresh fruit, and toiletries. The shopping schedule rotates quarterly and can be found posted on the commissary bulletin board. Currently, inmates shop from 12:30 to 3:30 p.m. on their designated shopping day. If all inmates haven't been served, then shopping continues after the 4:00 p.m. count.

Recreation Services: The FCI Coleman Medium prison and camp provide a recreation yard, hobbycraft center, leisure center, and sports leagues. Both the main prison and camp recreation yards offer basketball, bocce ball, handball, racquetball, horseshoe pits, softball and a jogging track. The main prison also has a music center, a cards and games room, and a fitness area. Additional offerings at the main prison include football, soccer, tennis, ping pong, and yoga.

Visitation Information: On Sunday, Monday, and Saturday visitation is held between 8:00 a.m. and 3:00 p.m. On federal holidays visitation is held between 8:00 a.m. and 3:00 p.m. See Chapter 1 for more information on visitation.

Prison Politics: There is a low to moderate level of politics. Inmates report that while there are cars, you don't necessarily have to be a part of one in order to stay, though it will make your time easier.

Level of Violence: There is a low to moderate level of violence at this facility. According to one inmate, "Safety is almost guaranteed." Others disagreed, stating that violence can be a problem, especially "if you get involved in politics or the drug trade."

Vulnerable Populations: One inmate reports there being no transgender inmates at the facility.

Good: "Prison is laid back."

In the News: In February 2017, 524 past and present female employees of Federal Correctional Complex Coleman, led by Tammy Padgett and Taronica White, won a $20 million settlement for decades of sexual harassment by prisoners and staff and the subsequent dismissiveness by prison managers.

In January 2016, William Houghton and Eddie Rodas-Castro, guards at Federal Correctional Institution Coleman Medium, pleaded guilty in a case involving the beating of a prisoner in the head and face and then falsifying reports in an attempt to cover it up. Houghton was sentenced to a year and a day in March 2016.

In July 2015, Roy Larry Lee, who was serving a life sentence for non-violent drug offenses at FCI Coleman Medium, was granted clemency by President Obama after spending 25 years in prison.

In January 2011, Ronnie Young, a guard at FCI Coleman Medium, was arrested after thousands of images and videos of child pornography were found on his home computer.

Camp in the News: In January 2018, former Florida Congresswoman Corrine Brown reported to Federal Correctional Institution Coleman Camp to begin serving her five-year sentence for fraud.

FCI Coleman Low

Federal Correctional Institution Coleman Low | FCI Coleman Low

Facility Address & Contact Information

Federal Correctional Institution Coleman Low
846 N.E. 54th Terrace
Coleman, FL 33521

Phone: 352-689-4000
Fax: 352-689-4008
Email: COA/PublicInformation@bop.gov

BOP Website: https://www.bop.gov/locations/institutions/col/
Wikipedia: https://en.wikipedia.org/wiki/Federal_Correctional_Institution,_Coleman
ZCG Website: https://www.prisonerresource.com/resources/federal-prison-profiles/southeast-region-ser/federal-correctional-complex-coleman-fcc-coleman/federal-correctional-institution-coleman-low-fci-coleman-low/

Inmate Correspondence Address

Inmate Name and Registration Number
FCI Coleman Low
Federal Correctional Institution
P.O. Box 1031
Coleman, FL 33521

NOTE: Funds cannot be sent directly to federal inmates. See Chapter 1 for more information on sending funds to federal inmates.

Sex: Male

Security Level: Low Security

Location: FCI Coleman Low is located in central Florida, south of the town of Coleman, off Highway 301 on State Road 471 in Sumter County; about 50 miles northwest of Orlando, 60 miles northeast of Tampa, and 35 miles south of Ocala.

BOP Region: Southeast Region (SER)

BOP Institution Code: COL for FCI Coleman Low, COX for Coleman Federal Correctional Complex

Judicial District: Middle District of Florida

Medical Care Level: Level 2. See Chapter 2 for more information on Medical Care and Mental Health Care Levels.

Mental Health Care Level: Level 3

Population (as of May 1, 2019): 2,082

Background: Federal Correctional Institution Coleman Low is a low-security federal prison in Coleman, Florida, which houses male inmates. It was opened in 1995 and is part of the Coleman Federal Correctional Complex.

Media reports indicate that one guard was indicted for possessing child pornography. Additionally, two guards have been indicted for assaulting an inmate and then falsifying reports concerning the beating.

Housing: Inmates are housed in dormitories which are divided into two- and three-person pods. There is a total of 12 housing units, each housing approximately 170 inmates.

Health Services: FCI Coleman Low provides sick call, emergency care, intake screening, physical examinations, medications, dental services, HIV testing, eye exams, and prescription glasses. No fees are charged for health care services based on health care staff referrals, health care staff-approved follow-up treatment for a chronic condition, preventive health care services, emergency services, diagnosis or treatment of chronic infectious diseases, mental health care, or substance abuse treatment. The $2.00 co-pay is also not charged when a health care provider orders or approves any of the following services: blood pressure monitoring, glucose monitoring, insulin injections, chronic care clinics, TB testing, vaccinations, wound care, or patient education. Sick call is held Monday, Tuesday, Thursday, and Friday at 7:00 a.m. Pill and insulin lines are held around mealtimes.

Psychology Services: FCI Coleman Low offers individual counseling, group counseling, psychological assessment, psychiatric consultation, crisis intervention, and AIDS counseling.

Upcoming group offerings are posted in inmate housing units. Inmates must submit a cop-out in order to request program placement. Self-help programs are also available including Sexually Abusive Behavior Prevention and Intervention.

Residential Drug Abuse Program (RDAP): FCI Coleman Low has the Residential Drug Abuse Program (RDAP). The facility also offers the Non-Residential Drug Abuse Treatment Program (NR-DAP), Drug Education class, Freedom from Drugs course, Alcoholics Anonymous (AA), and Narcotics Anonymous (NA).

Education Services: FCI Coleman Low offers literacy, GED, and English-as-a-Second Language (ESL) programs. Adult Continuing Education (ACE) classes and a parenting program are also available. High school diplomas and post-secondary degrees are available through paid correspondence programs.

Advanced Occupational Education: FCI Coleman Low offers advanced occupational education in Culinary Arts, Cook, HVAC, Electric, Custodial Maintenance, Horticulture, and the Mavis Beacon Typing program. The Horticulture and Culinary Arts Programs are operated by the University of Florida.

Vocational Training: FCI Coleman Low does not offer any vocational training programs.

Apprenticeship: FCI Coleman Low offers Dental Assistant, HVAC, Landscape Tech, and Plumber apprenticeship programs.

Library Services: FCI Coleman Low has both a leisure library and a law library. Both libraries are open six days a week, excluding Sundays and holidays. The leisure library allows inmates to check out fiction and nonfiction books, magazines, and newspapers. The law library provides inmates access to the TRULINCS Electronic Law Library and electronic typewriters. A photocopy machine is also available in the leisure library. Many housing units also have their own in-unit libraries.

UNICOR: The FCI Coleman Low UNICOR facility produces office furniture.

Commissary: The spending limit is $360.00 per month and $90 per week. Inmates are issued an identification card, which must be presented when shopping in the commissary. Account balances can be checked from TRULINCS computers in inmate housing units. Commissary items include food, drinks, clothing, shoes, radios, MP3 players, over-the-counter medications, and more. Inmates must turn in their orders the day prior to shopping. While each unit shops on a specific day, the commissary is only open Monday through Thursday from 12:00 to 3:30 p.m.

Recreation Services: The FCI Coleman Low Recreation Department offers both indoor and outdoor activities. The recreation yard includes a flag football/soccer field, volleyball court, handball/racquetball courts, shuffleboard, horseshoe pits, walking/running track, softball fields, basketball courts, a multi-purpose court, bocce courts, TVs, and fitness stations (e.g., pull-up and dip bars). Major and minor intramural leagues are offered for soccer, softball, volleyball, handball, flag football, basketball, tennis, horseshoes, bocce, and racquetball. There is also a music room, arts and crafts program, games (e.g., board games), movies, pool tables, fitness classes (e.g., yoga), rowing machines, ellipticals, and more.

Visitation Information: On Sunday, Monday, and Saturday visitation is held between 8:00 a.m. and 3:00 p.m. On federal holidays visitation is held between 8:00 a.m. and 3:00 p.m. See Chapter 1 for more information on visitation.

Prison Politics: There is a very low level of politics, if any at all. According to one respondent, "I expected more politics. Divides are obvious between Black, white, and Spanish inmates, but gangs don't necessarily run the yard or anything." Another inmate stated that "there are barely any politics at all, just the regular racial segregations amongst inmates."

Level of Violence: There is a low level of violence. According to one respondent, "Fights are rare here." Another inmate agreed, stating, "There are occasional fights, but they are rarely serious." One respondent stated that the institution is "safe."

Vulnerable Populations: Sex offenders, informants, and LGBT inmates can all walk the yard. According to one inmate, "I'm a sex offender and found I have no fear and walk/live freely everywhere." Another expanded on this, stating, "there are high sex offender, informant, gay, and transgender populations."

Good: "Low politics and typically laid back." "The facility is well [kept] compared to other Fed facilities." "Open compound on weekends and after evening meal on weekdays." "Relatively clean, decent food, very easy place to be if not interested in too many illicit activities." "The quality of the food is good, but the quantity leaves something to be desired."

Bad: "Visitation is treated like higher security compounds." "Lots of drug use." "There is little to no oversight of staff, to include even the Warden's staff. No accountability for staff. The staff is dysfunctional, don't communicate well with each other or the inmate population, and are surprisingly lazy." "The bulk of the staff are very unhappy in their roles here and may take this out on the inmate population." "It seems as though everything is deteriorating on a monthly basis. There are increasingly harsh regulations, less freedoms, less privileges, and poorer food." "Compound closes at a drop of rain, overcrowded, commissary consistently out of stock, and medical very slow." "All non-orderly inmates required to leave the unit from 7:40 a.m. work call until 9:30 a.m. recall, Monday through Friday." "In visitation, inmates have to wear a jump-suit instead of their regular uniform." "The Mail Room restricts greeting cards, colored paper, crayon and marker drawings, and other materials."

Other Comments: "I live in an all-veterans unit of 180 veterans. This is the safest, cleanest, and most organized example of what is possible." "Not a terrible place to do time, depending on what a person is interested in doing." "There is very little violence and next to no politics." "Moves are typically on time, and unless the weather is bad, the recreation yard is typically open." "I'd rate it 6.5 or 7 out of 10."

In the News: In April 2018, administrators at Federal Correctional Complex Coleman announced that prisoners would no longer be allowed to receive books, greeting cards or letters written in crayon or marker. Books would only be able to be purchased from internal prison suppliers, which incur a 30 percent mark-up and significant delays in delivery. The book policy was subsequently rescinded.

In August 2017, Albert Larry Harris, a guard at Federal Correctional Institution Coleman Low, was arrested for taking thousands of dollars in bribes to smuggle drugs and other contraband into the prison.

FCI Edgefield

Federal Correctional Institution Edgefield | FCI Edgefield

Facilities: FCI Edgefield with an adjacent minimum-security satellite prison camp.

Facility Address & Contact Information

Federal Correctional Institution Edgefield
501 Gary Hill Road
Edgefield, SC 29824

Phone: 803-637-1500
Fax: 803-637-9840
Email: EDG/ExecAssistant@bop.gov

BOP Website: https://www.bop.gov/locations/institutions/edg/
Wikipedia: https://en.wikipedia.org/wiki/Federal_Correctional_Institution,_Edgefield
ZCG Website: https://www.prisonerresource.com/resources/federal-prison-profiles/southeast-region-ser/federal-correctional-institution-edgefield-fci-edgefield/

Inmate Correspondence Address

For FCI Edgefield

Inmate Name and Registration Number
FCI Edgefield
Federal Correctional Institution
P.O. Box 725
Edgefield, SC 29824

For Satellite Prison Camp

Inmate Name and Registration Number
FCI Edgefield
Satellite Prison Camp
P.O. Box 725
Edgefield, SC 29824

NOTE: Funds cannot be sent directly to federal inmates. See Chapter 1 for more information on sending funds to federal inmates.

Sex: Male

Security Level: Main: Medium Security; Camp: Minimum Security

Location: FCI Edgefield is located on the South Carolina/Georgia border, northeast of Augusta, approximately 30 miles northeast of I-20 on Highway 25.

BOP Region: Southeast Region (SER)

BOP Institution Code: EDG for FCI Edgefield

Judicial District: District of South Carolina

Medical Care Level: Level 2. See Chapter 2 for more information on Medical Care and Mental Health Care Levels.

Mental Health Care Level: Level 2

Population (as of May 1, 2019): Main: 1,402; Camp: 532

Background: Federal Correctional Institution Edgefield is a medium-security federal prison in Edgefield, South Carolina, which houses male inmates. It opened in 1998. Federal Correctional Institution Edgefield Camp, which also houses male inmates, was opened in 1998 and is located adjacent to the main institution.

Media reports indicate that at least one prisoner has been indicted for conspiracy to smuggle drugs into the prison.

Housing: Inmates at FCI Edgefield are housed in two- and three-person cells. There is a total of six housing units. Inmates at the camp are housed in dormitories, which are divided into two-person pods.

Health Services: FCI Edgefield provides medical and dental sick call, emergency treatment, special housing unit sick call, prescription medications (over-the-counter medications are available through the commissary), voluntary HIV testing, and dental and eye care. Inmates must submit a sick call form to be evaluated for routine health care needs. Emergency medical care is available 24 hours a day. Pill line is at 6:30 a.m. and 7:00 p.m., though inmates can pick-up self-carry prescriptions at 3:00 p.m. Insulin line is conducted before breakfast and dinner.

Psychology Services: FCI Edgefield offers brief counseling, group treatment, Anger Management, Stress Management, and Criminal Thinking, as well as other programs. Notices of upcoming treatment offerings are posted in inmate housing units. Inmates must submit a cop-out in order to request program placement.

Residential Drug Abuse Program (RDAP): FCI Edgefield does not offer the Residential Drug Abuse Program (RDAP), but the camp does have the Residential Drug Abuse Program (RDAP). Both facilities also offer a Drug Education Program and the Non-Residential Drug Abuse Program (NR-DAP).

Education Services: Inmates are interviewed by an Education representative upon arrival at FCI Edgefield to determine what type of educational programming is appropriate. Both facilities offer literary, GED, English-as-a-Second Language (ESL), parenting, and Adult Continuing Education (ACE) programs. ACE classes include creative writing, world geography, basic real estate, GED math, entrepreneurial opportunities, creative thinking, business basics, advanced math, effective planning, political science, and barber basics. High school diplomas and post-secondary degrees are available through paid correspondence programs.

Advanced Occupational Education: Both FCI Edgefield and the camp offer advanced occupational education in Culinary Arts, ServeSafe, and General Services Automotive Technician. The camp also offers Forklift Operator.

Vocational Training: FCI Edgefield does not offer any vocational training aside from the advanced occupational education and apprenticeship programs.

Apprenticeship: FCI Edgefield offers an apprenticeship in Culinary Arts.

Library Services: FCI Edgefield offers a leisure and law library. In the leisure library inmates can check out fiction and nonfiction books, newspapers, and magazines. Inmates can also check out DVDs. The law library offers typewriters, a copy machine, and the TRULINCS Electronic Law Library. Both libraries are open six days a week.

UNICOR: The FCI Edgefield UNICOR facility produces clothing and textiles. The camp does not house a UNICOR facility.

Commissary: A monthly spending limit of $360.00 is imposed. Once each week, prisoners can make a visit to the commissary, where they can purchase foods, drinks, electronics, and more. The housing units shop on a rotating basis. The rotation schedule is based on inmates' registration numbers and is posted in the Commissary and all housing units. Inmates must have funds in their account to purchase goods. Stamps, Nicoderm, over-the-counter medications, and special purchase items are exempt from the spending limit. Shopping is conducted Monday through Thursday from 6:30 to 10:00 a.m. and 12:00 to 1:00 p.m.

Recreation Services: Recreation programs at FCI Edgefield include indoor and outdoor activities ranging from individualized arts and crafts programs to intramural team sports such as softball, basketball, volleyball, and soccer. Indoors, inmates have access to table games, arts and crafts, crochet, and some musical instruments. The institution's Recreation Departments are open seven days a week from 6:30 to 9:30 a.m., 12:00 to 3:30 p.m., and 5:00 to 8:00 p.m.

Visitation Information: On Sunday and Saturday visitation is held between 8:00 a.m. and 2:00 p.m. On Friday visitation is held between 5:00 and 8:00 p.m. On federal holidays visitation is held between 8:00 a.m. and 2:00 p.m. See Chapter 1 for more information on visitation.

Prison Politics: While most respondent said that there is a low level of prison politics, a limited number suggested that there was a medium level of racial politics and that cars are common. Paperwork concerns sometimes come into play as it concerns the racial groups, but not often. According to one respondent, "The white race and, in particular, the Aryan Brotherhood and Dirty White Boys can be bad about politics."

Level of Violence: Most respondents said that there is very little violence, though one respondent in particular stated that "Edgefield is right in the middle when it comes to violence." He explained "[there are] more stabbings and assaults here than I would have expected." While one inmate pegged it as a 4 out of 10 for safety, another felt it was a 6 out of 10. One respondent stated that "the violence is at a minimum." Another inmate explained that there is "a lot of talk, but minor violence."

Vulnerable Populations: Sex offenders, informants, and LGBT inmates are allowed to walk the yard. According to one inmate, "They are all allowed here, and the transgenders are treated fairly." Another inmate explained it as it being a "protective custody institution," though this appears to be a minority opinion.

Good: "Even though the prison is a warehouse, most officers are friendly." "There is no good thing at this prison." "Not good at all."

Bad: "Run loosely. Drug use is rampant. It is a very tempting environment to do wrong and nothing." "Very poor training and reentry preparation." "The staff are very lazy and lacking in their job performance." "The food is less than fair, and the portions are terrible." "The SHU is horrible. The staff heap abuses and limit privileges to those confined therein." "Rec is often cancelled, the food is horrible, and communication amongst inmates and the administration is very poor." "Staff lock us down for dumb reasons." "The compound officers are a bit crazy, and the administration is very bad at being on schedule with anything."

Other Comments: "This is the worst institution in the Southeast Region."

In the News: In July 2016, infamous poker cheat Christian Lusardi was sent to Federal Correctional Institution Edgefield after his parole from state prison to serve out his five-year sentence for the manufacture and sale of bootleg DVDs.

In December 2004, Kenneth Tager, a prisoner at FCI Edgefield, pleaded guilty to conspiracy to possess and intent to distribute in a marijuana smuggling scheme involving a woman, Pamela Forsyth, who was sentenced to probation for bringing it to him.

FCI Estill

Federal Correctional Institution Estill | FCI Estill

Facilities: FCI Estill with an adjacent minimum-security satellite prison camp.

Facility Address & Contact Information

Federal Correctional Institution Estill
100 Prison Road
Estill, SC 29918

Phone: 803-625-4607
Fax: 803-625-5635
Email: EST/ExecAssistant@bop.gov

BOP Website: https://www.bop.gov/locations/institutions/est/
Wikipedia: https://en.wikipedia.org/wiki/Federal_Correctional_Institution,_Estill
ZCG Website: https://www.prisonerresource.com/resources/federal-prison-profiles/southeast-region-ser/federal-correctional-institution-estill-fci-estill/

Inmate Correspondence Address

For FCI Estill

Inmate Name and Registration Number
FCI Estill
Federal Correctional Institution
P.O. Box 699
Estill, SC 29918

For Satellite Prison Camp

Inmate Name and Registration Number
FCI Estill
Satellite Prison Camp
P.O. BOX 699
Estill, SC 29918

NOTE: Funds cannot be sent directly to federal inmates. See Chapter 1 for more information on sending funds to federal inmates.

Sex: Male

Security Level: Main: Medium Security; Camp: Minimum Security

Location: FCI Estill is located in Hampton County, off State Road 321, about 3 miles south of Estill.

BOP Region: Southeast Region (SER)

BOP Institution Code: EST for FCI Estill

Judicial District: District of South Carolina

Medical Care Level: Level 2. See Chapter 2 for more information on Medical Care and Mental Health Care Levels.

Mental Health Care Level: Level 2

Population (as of May 1, 2019): Main: 981; Camp: 260

Background: Federal Correctional Institution Estill is a medium-security federal prison in Estill, South Carolina, which houses male inmates. It was opened in 1993. Federal Correctional Institution Estill Camp, which also houses male inmates, is located adjacent to the main institution.

Notable inmates include Peter Madoff, Bernie Madoff's younger brother.

Media reports indicate that at least one guard has been indicted for bribery and smuggling contraband and drugs into the prison.

Housing: Inmates are housed in two- and three-person cells. Inmates at the camp are housed in dormitories, in two-person cubicles.

Health Services: Inmates arriving at FCI Estill receive an initial medical screening during intake. Medical and dental sick call, routine sick call visits, medication, medical emergencies, eyeglasses, medically indicated footwear, and routine physical examinations are also provided. Emergency medical care is available 24 hours a day.

Psychology Services: Psychology services include intake screenings, crisis intervention, and group counseling. Regular treatment groups include criminal thinking, and anger management.

Residential Drug Abuse Program (RDAP): FCI Estill and the camp do not have the Residential Drug Abuse Program (RDAP), but inmates can be transferred to institutions that do offer the program. Both facilities offer a Drug Education class, the Non-Residential Drug Treatment Program (NR-DAP), Alcoholics Anonymous (AA), and Narcotics Anonymous (NA).

Education Services: FCI Estill provides literacy, GED, English-as-a-Second Language (ESL) programs, and pre-release training programs. Parenting and Adult Continuing Education (ACE) programs are also available. Twice a year, a graduation ceremony is scheduled for education classes (GED and ESL), as well as vocational occupation classes. Certificates and $25 are awarded for successful completion and participation. Achievement incentives, such as commissary-type items are also occasionally provided. Additional dollar incentives of $5 are given out for achieving a basic literacy level, and those who achieve a score of 500 or higher in each subject area of the practice GED examination are given $10. High school diplomas and post-secondary degrees are available through paid correspondence programs.

Advanced Occupational Education: FCI Estill offers advanced occupational education in Manage First, Carpentry, Electrical, and Welding. The camp offers Electrical and Plumbing. Both facilities also offer Serve Safe.

Vocational Training: FCI Estill does not offer any vocational training aside from the advanced occupational education and apprenticeship programs.

Apprenticeship: Both FCI Estill and the satellite camp offer apprenticeships in Baking, Cooking, Electrical, Housekeeping, HVAC, and Welding.

Library Services: Inmates can access a leisure and law library at both facilities. The law library contains the TRULINCS Electronic Law Library, typewriters, and a copy machine. The leisure library allows inmates to check out fiction and nonfiction books, newspapers, and magazines. The law library schedule is posted in the Education building.

UNICOR: FCI Estill and the camp do not have UNICOR facilities.

Commissary: Inmates at FCI Estill are permitted to spend up to $360.00 each month for regular and special purchases. Stamps, over-the-counter medicine, copy cards, TRULINCS units and phone time are excluded from this spending limitation. Ice cream, foods, beverages, electronics, clothing, and shoes can be purchased in the commissary.

Recreation Services: Inmates at both facilities have access to a recreation yard, hobbycraft program, sports and musical equipment, wellness classes, and a photo program. Table games, tournaments, and league events are available. Intramural team sports in softball, basketball, and volleyball are also available. The hobbycraft area is located in the recreation leisure center. Classes in leather, art, drawing, beadwork, and crochet are available. The Recreation Department is open seven days a week.

Visitation Information: On Sunday and Saturday visitation is held between 8:00 a.m. and 3:00 p.m. On federal holidays visitation is held between 8:00 a.m. and 3:00 p.m. See Chapter 1 for more information on visitation.

In the News: In November 2016, Anthony Jermaine Creech, a guard at Federal Correctional Institution Estill, was sentenced to six months in prison for smuggling marijuana and other contraband into the prison for bribes.

In February 2013, Peter Madoff, Bernie's younger brother, was sent to FCI Estill.

In 2010, a large-scale fight broke out on the FCI Estill recreation yard, ending with law enforcement showing up to the scene. Nine inmates were sent to the hospital with injuries. Ambulance staff reported that prisoners had been beaten with shovels, rakes, and hoes, and had wounds ranging from deep lacerations to possible broken bones.

In 2005, a former FCI Estill prison guard was sentenced to 10 years for possessing heroin with intent to distribute to an inmate in exchange for $100,000.

MDC Guaynabo

Metropolitan Detention Center Guaynabo | MDC Guaynabo

Facility Address & Contact Information

Metropolitan Detention Center Guaynabo
652 Carreta 28
Guaynabo, PR 00965

Phone: 787-749-4480
Fax: 787-775-7824
Email: GUA/ExecAssistant@bop.gov

BOP Website: https://www.bop.gov/locations/institutions/gua/
Wikipedia: https://en.wikipedia.org/wiki/Metropolitan_Detention_Center%2C_Guaynabo
ZCG Website: https://www.prisonerresource.com/resources/federal-prison-profiles/southeast-region-ser/metropolitan-detention-center-guaynabo-mdc-guaynabo/

Inmate Correspondence Address

Inmate Name and Registration Number
MDC Guaynabo
Metropolitan Detention Center
P.O. Box 2005
Catano, PR 00963

NOTE: Funds cannot be sent directly to federal inmates. See Chapter 1 for more information on sending funds to federal inmates.

Sex: Male and Female

Security Level: Administrative Security (Multiple Security Levels)

Location: MDC Guaynabo is located 6 miles west of San Juan, Puerto Rico, off Highway 22, at the intersection of Road 165 and Road 28.

BOP Region: Southeast Region (SER)

BOP Institution Code: GUA for MDC Guaynabo

Judicial District: District of Puerto Rico

Medical Care Level: Level 2. See Chapter 2 for more information on Medical Care and Mental Health Care Levels.

Mental Health Care Level: Level 2

Population (as of May 1, 2019): 1,319

Background: Metropolitan Detention Center Guaynabo is an administrative-security federal prison in Guaynabo, Puerto Rico, which houses both male and female inmates. In opened in 1992.

MDC Guaynabo holds male and female detainees of all security levels who are awaiting trial or sentencing. In recent years, the institution has been under fire for inhumane conditions and deplorable treatment of inmates in the wake of Hurricane Maria.

Notable inmates include Puerto Rico's most wanted fugitive Jose Figueroa-Agosto (apprehended in 2010 for drug trafficking conspiracy and money laundering), and Alberto Goachet (a former aide to a Puerto Rico Senator who was convicted of money laundering).

Media reports indicate that there has been a mass outbreak of gastroenteritis, one prisoner has been murdered, nine prisoners have been indicted for the planning and murder of a lieutenant, and one guard has been charged with possession and solicitation of child pornography.

Housing: Inmates are housed in two-person cells.

Health Services: MDC Guaynabo provides physical examinations, sick call, dental care, prescriptions through the pharmacy, dental care, female health care services, HIV testing, and Sexually Transmitted Diseases (STD) education. Emergency medical care is available 24 hours a day.

Psychology Services: MDC Guaynabo offers psychological assessments, crisis intervention, individual and group counseling, and referrals to Health Services. Notices of upcoming treatment offerings are posted in inmate housing units.

Residential Drug Abuse Program (RDAP): MDC Guaynabo does not have the Residential Drug Abuse Program (RDAP). However, the institution does offer screening for RDAP. It also offers a Drug Education class and the Non-Residential Drug Abuse Program (NR-DAP). Inmates who complete NR-DAP receive $30.

Education Services: MDC Guaynabo offers literary, GED, and English-as-a-Second Language (ESL) classes. Adult Continuing Education (ACE) courses, often taught by inmate instructors under the direction of Education Department staff, are also offered. ACE courses include Small Business, College Board, and Advanced Math. High school diplomas and post-secondary degrees are available through paid correspondence programs.

Advanced Occupational Education: MDC Guaynabo does not offer any advanced occupational education programs.

Vocational Training: MDC Guaynabo does not offer any vocational training programs.

Apprenticeship: MDC Guaynabo does not offer any apprenticeship programs.

Library Services: Leisure and law libraries are available for inmates. In the leisure library, inmates can check out fiction and nonfiction books, magazines, and newspapers. In the law library, inmates have access to the TRULINCS Electronic Law Library.

UNICOR: MDC Guaynabo does not house a UNICOR facility.

Commissary: Inmates are allowed to spend $360.00 per month on designated shopping days. Approved special purchase items, over-the-counter medications, and postage stamps are not counted against the spending limit. Items such as food, snacks, drinks, and radios can be purchased.

Recreation Services: MDC Guaynabo offers a hobbycraft program, structured classes (e.g., fitness, nutrition, human anatomy, exercise physiology, and smoking cessation), a variety of sport clinics (e.g., basketball), table games (e.g., chess, dominoes, pool), a sewing program for the female population, and special activities during the holidays.

Visitation Information: On Sunday, Thursday, and Friday visitation is held between 7:00 and 10:00 a.m. as well as 12:00 and 3:00 p.m. On Wednesday and Saturday visitation is held between 7:00 and 10:00 a.m., 12:00 and 3:00 p.m., and 5:00 and 8:00 p.m. See Chapter 1 for more information on visitation.

In the News: In March 2018, a lawsuit was filed in Puerto Rico's federal court against Metropolitan Detention Center Guaynabo by staff alleging severe mistreatment and violation of basic human rights following the destruction caused by Hurricane Maria.

In September 2017, MDC Guaynabo lost its electricity and running water after it was hit by Hurricane Maria. More than 100 prisoners were kept locked in their cells for nearly a week with no showers, no toilets and limited drinking water.

In December 2015, at least 49 prisoners at MDC Guaynabo became ill during an outbreak of gastroenteritis.

In January 2015, nine prisoners at MDC Guaynabo were indicted and charged with conspiring to murder Guaynabo Lieutenant Osvaldo Albarati-Casanas, who was shot and killed while driving on the Jose Diego expressway. It was thought at the time that one of the prisoners used a contraband cell phone to order the hit.

In May 2013, Angel Marreno Hernandez, a prison guard, was arrested and held in MDC Guaynabo on child pornography charges after encouraging a 15-year-old girl to exchange nude photos with him.

In April 2013, Glaston Smith, a prisoner at MDC Guaynabo who was awaiting deportation, was stabbed to death by other prisoners, the third ICE detainee death at Guaynabo in 2013.

In March 2009, Alberto Goachet, an aide to former Puerto Rico Sen. Jorge De Castro Font, was sentenced to three months in prison for money laundering and instructed to report to MDC Guaynabo within 30 days to begin serving his sentence.

FCI Jesup & FSL Jesup

Federal Correctional Institution Jesup | FCI Jesup

Facilities: FCI Jesup with an adjacent low-security satellite prison and minimum-security satellite prison camp.

Facility Address & Contact Information

Federal Correctional Institution Jesup
2600 Highway 301 South
Jesup, GA 31599

Phone: 912-427-0870
Fax: 912-427-1125
Email: JES/ExecAssistant@bop.gov

BOP Website: https://www.bop.gov/locations/institutions/jes/
Wikipedia: https://en.wikipedia.org/wiki/Federal_Correctional_Institution,_Jesup
ZCG Website: https://www.prisonerresource.com/resources/federal-prison-profiles/southeast-region-ser/federal-correctional-institution-jesup-fci-jesup/

Inmate Correspondence Address

For FCI Jesup

Inmate Name and Registration Number
FCI Jesup
Federal Correctional Institution
2680 301 South
Jesup, GA 31599

For FSL Jesup Satellite Low

Inmate Name and Registration Number
FSL Jesup
Federal Satellite Low
2680 301 South
Jesup, GA 31599

For Satellite Prison Camp

Inmate Name and Registration Number
FCI Jesup
Satellite Prison Camp
2650 301 South
Jesup, GA 31599

NOTE: Funds cannot be sent directly to federal inmates. See Chapter 1 for more information on sending funds to federal inmates.

Sex: Male

Security Level: Main: Medium Security; Satellite: Low Security; Camp: Minimum Security

Location: FCI Jesup is located in southern Georgia on Route 301, 65 miles southwest of Savannah, 40 miles northwest of Brunswick, and 105 miles northwest of Jacksonville, Florida.

BOP Region: Southeast Region (SER)

BOP Institution Code: JES for all facilities

Judicial District: Southern District of Georgia

Medical Care Level: Level 2. See Chapter 2 for more information on Medical Care and Mental Health Care Levels.

Mental Health Care Level: Level 2

Population (as of May 1, 2019): Main: 949; Satellite Low: 530; Minimum: 155

Background: Federal Correctional Institution Jesup is a medium-security federal prison in Jesup, Georgia, which houses male inmates. It was opened in 1990. Federal Satellite Low Jesup, which was opened in 2003, and Federal Correctional Institution Jesup Camp, which was opened in 1989, are located adjacent to the main institution.

Notable inmates include computer hacker Christopher Chainey (sentenced to 10 years for gaining unauthorized access to protected computers by breaking into the personal online accounts of Scarlett Johansson and Christina Aguilera and posting revealing photos of them online), former Pennsylvania State Senator Robert J. Mellow (housed at the camp), and televangelist Jim Bakker (also housed at the camp).

Media reports indicate that three prisoners have been indicted for filing fraudulent tax returns.

Housing: Inmates are housed in two-, three-, and four-person cells. Inmates at the satellite low and camp are housed in dormitories.

Health Services: FCI Jesup provides sick call, emergency services, clinic appointments, intake screening, physical examinations, chronic care, medications, dental services, eyeglasses, and HIV testing. Contact lenses and hearing aids are only permitted when medically approved. Emergency care is available 24 hours a day. Inmates must submit a triage form in order to be evaluated for routine care needs.

Psychology Services: FCI Jesup offers intake screening, crisis intervention, individual and group counseling, and medication management. Typical programs include anger management, criminal thinking, and HIV/AIDS Awareness. A self-help library is also available to the inmate population. Inmates must submit a request to staff (cop-out) in order to seek placement in any desired program.

Residential Drug Abuse Program (RDAP): FCI Jesup has the Residential Drug Abuse Program (RDAP). The facility also offers a Drug Abuse Education Program, the Non-Residential Drug Abuse Program (NR-DAP) and Alcoholics Anonymous (AA).

Education Services: FCI Jesup offers literacy, GED, and English-as-a-Second Language (ESL) programs. Adult Continuing Education classes are also offered at all facilities, including Commercial Driver's License (CDL), Legal Research, Writing and Analysis, Spanish I, Basic Finance, Resume Writing, and Parenting. A mock job fair is held annually. Altamaha Technical College, through the FCI/FSL Jesup Education Department, offers a wide variety of educational courses designed to develop academic and occupational skills. High school diplomas and post-secondary degrees are available through paid correspondence programs.

Advanced Occupational Education: FCI Jesup offers Commercial Wiring, Air Conditioning Technology (HVAC), Information Technology, Electrical Construction Maintenance, and Microsoft Office Applications Professional advanced occupational education programs.

Apprenticeship: FCI Jesup does not offer any apprenticeship programs.

Library Services: Law and leisure libraries are available to FCI Jesup inmates. A variety of reading materials, magazines, newspapers, books, and media are available for inmate use. An interlibrary-loan program is available through the local public library. Inmates can also watch movies on DVD. The law library offers typewriters, a copy machine, and the TRULINCS Electronic Law Library.

UNICOR: The FCI Jesup UNICOR facility produces clothing and textiles.

Commissary: The monthly spending limit at FCI Jesup is $360.00. The commissary has designated shopping days and times. Each inmate must have his commissary list completed, possess his inmate Identification Card, and have his nylon commissary shopping bag with him prior to entering the sales unit. Inmates can purchase a variety of items, including clothing, shoes, food, sodas, snacks, electronics, and more.

Recreation Services: FCI Jesup facilities provide a recreation yard, leisure games, intramural leagues, music, hobbycraft, fitness and wellness, and a movie program. Inside, inmates have access to a gym, stationary bikes, stair steppers, tables, arts and crafts, musical equipment, pool tables, and basketball. Outside, inmates have access to TVs, volleyball, bocce ball, softball, football, soccer, handball, basketball, and a track.

Visitation Information: On Sunday and Saturday visitation is held between 8:00 a.m. and 3:00 p.m. On federal holidays visitation is held between 8:00 a.m. and 3:00 p.m. See Chapter 1 for more information on visitation.

Prison Politics: This is a somewhat political yard, but there is no car requirement.

Level of Violence: There is a moderate level of violence at this prison. Respondents report that there are one or two fights each month which frequently result in lockdowns.

Vulnerable Populations: Sex offenders, informants, and LGBT inmates can stay if they are honest from the start.

Good: "Great weather, short winters, felt like a college campus, and trees on the yard."

Bad: "Very poor programming."

Other Comments: "Go there and don't lie about charges or personal characteristics; laid back yard."

In the News: In August 2013, former Pennsylvania State Senator Robert J. Mellow was moved from the minimum-security camp at FCI Williamsburg to the medium-security Federal Correctional Institution Jesup after new state charges were filed against him.

In August 2003, Michael Little, Gary Barnes and Ricky Davis, prisoners at FCI Jesup, along with Davis' wife Angie, were indicted for filing $2.4 million in fraudulent income tax returns.

Camp in the News: In 1993, televangelist Jim Bakker was transferred from Federal Medical Center Rochester, where he spent about three years, to Federal Correctional Institution Jesup Camp.

FCI Marianna

Federal Correctional Institution Marianna | FCI Marianna

Facilities: FCI Marianna and an adjacent minimum-security satellite prison camp.

Facility Address & Contact Information

Federal Correctional Institution Marianna
3625 FCI Road
Marianna, FL 32446

Phone: 850-526-2313
Fax: 850-718-2014
Email: MNA/ExecAssistant@bop.gov

BOP Website: https://www.bop.gov/locations/institutions/mna/
Wikipedia: https://en.wikipedia.org/wiki/Federal_Correctional_Institution,_Marianna
ZCG Website: https://www.prisonerresource.com/resources/federal-prison-profiles/southeast-region-ser/federal-correctional-institution-marianna-fci-marianna/

Inmate Correspondence Address

For FCI Marianna

Inmate Name and Registration Number
FCI Marianna
Federal Correctional Institution
P.O. Box 7007
Marianna, FL 32447

For Satellite Prison Camp

Inmate Name and Registration Number
FCI Marianna
Satellite Prison Camp
P.O. Box 7006
Marianna, FL 32447

NOTE: Funds cannot be sent directly to federal inmates. See Chapter 1 for more information on sending funds to federal inmates.

Sex: Main: Male; Camp: Female

Security Level: Main: Medium Security; Camp: Minimum Security

Location: FCI Marianna is located in the Florida panhandle, 65 miles west of Tallahassee and 5 miles north of the town of Marianna, off Highway 167.

BOP Region: Southeast Region (SER)

BOP Institution Code: MNA for FCI Marianna

Judicial District: Northern District of Florida

Medical Care Level: Level 2. See Chapter 2 for more information on Medical Care and Mental Health Care Levels.

Mental Health Care Level: Level 3

Population (as of May 1, 2019): Main: 0; Camp: 42

Background: Federal Correctional Institution Marianna is a medium-security federal prison in Marianna, Florida, which houses male inmates. It was opened in 1988. Federal Correctional Institution Marianna Camp, which houses female inmates, was opened the same year and is located adjacent to the main institution.

In October 2018, Hurricane Michael, a Category 4 storm, inflicted significant damage on FCI Marianna. Due to the extensive damage, all inmates were evacuated after the storm. The facility is not currently housing inmates.

FCI Marianna is a Sex Offender Management Program (SOMP) facility, which means that approximately 40 percent of the prison's population is incarcerated for either a current or past sexual offense.

Media reports indicate that at least two guards have been indicted for smuggling contraband into the institution.

Housing: Inmates are housed in two- and three-person cells. There is a total of eight housing units. Inmates at the camp are housed in dormitories, which are divided into two-person cubicles.

Health Services: FCI Marianna provides medical sick call, emergency medical care, physical examinations, immunizations, dental care, and medication through the pharmacy (over-the-counter medications are available through the commissary). Mammograms, MRIs, and CT scans are performed at facilities in the local community. Emergency medical care is available 24 hours a day. Sick call is held during breakfast. Pill line is conducted at 6:45 a.m., 4:15 p.m., and 7:30 p.m. on the weekdays. On the weekends, the morning session is at 8:30 a.m. Insulin line is held during breakfast and dinner.

Psychology Services: FCI Marianna offers intake screenings, crisis intervention and individual and group counseling. The Non-Residential Sex Offender Treatment Program (SOTP-NR) is available. Other groups include anger management, rational thinking, and a transgender support group. The F.I.S.H. (Finding Insight Self-Help) program allows inmates to complete self-study packets on a variety of topics, including depression, PTSD, gang violence, anxiety, guilt, shame, and anger. Self-help books and DVD videos are also available. At the camp, the STAGES Program is available for inmates with serious mental illness and personality disorders. Open house is held on Tuesdays and Thursdays from 11:00 a.m. to 12:00 p.m.

Residential Drug Abuse Program (RDAP): FCI Marianna offers the Residential Drug Abuse Program (RDAP). It also offers a Drug Education Course, the Non-Residential Drug Abuse Program (NR-DAP), Alcoholics Anonymous (AA), and Narcotics Anonymous (NA).

Education Services: FCI Marianna offers literacy, GED, and English-as-a-Second Language (ESL) programs. The GED classes are offered in English and Spanish. Adult Continuing Education (ACE) classes include parenting, Financial Management, Conversational Spanish, Health Education, Career Planning, Career Counseling, and Basic Study Skills. A reentry resource center is also available. High school diplomas and post-secondary programs are available through paid correspondence programs. Inmates also have access to a specialized pilot program. The Inmate Comprehensive Academic Network, or iCAN, allowed educated inmates with real world experience to create and conduct classes on their area of expertise. Current offerings include Better Man Series, Going Home Series, Family Fundamentals, Changing Your Thinking, 12-Steps, Legal Research, and Cognitive Behavioral Therapy. Hours of operation are 7:30 to 10:30 a.m., 12:30 to 3:15 p.m., and 6:30 to 8:15 p.m. Monday through Friday, with the exception of Friday night, when the department is closed.

Advanced Occupational Education: FCI Marianna offers advanced occupational education in K-9 training, Business Foundations, Electrical Helper and Refrigerant Certification. The camp offers K-9 training, Building Maintenance, Cosmetology, Culinary Arts, Lube Technician, Mechanic Technician, Safety Technician, Horticulture, Building and Trades Core, and Plumbing Helper.

Vocational Training: FCI Marianna does not offer any vocational programs aside from the advanced occupational education and apprenticeship programs.

Apprenticeship: FCI Marianna offers apprenticeships in HVAC, HVAC Helper, Electrician, and Plumbing.

Library Services: FCI Marianna houses both a leisure library and a law library for inmate use. The leisure library offers fiction and nonfiction books, newspapers, and magazines. The DVD movie program has been cancelled. The law library offers the TRULINCS Electronic Law Library on eight computers, six typewriters, and a copy machine.

UNICOR: FCI Marianna does not have a UNICOR facility.

Commissary: Inmates can spend up to $360.00 per month in the commissary on their designated weekly shopping day. This limit is further restricted to $180 every two weeks. Over-the-counter (OTC) medications, telephone credits, and postage stamps do not count against the monthly spending limit. Popular items include food, drinks, ice cream, and electronics. Sales are conducted Monday through Thursday during breakfast and lunch. Funds are retained by the institution in a trust fund account, from which the inmate may withdraw money for personal spending in the institution commissary, family support, or other approved purposes. Accumulated institutional earnings and monies sent from outside are given to the inmate upon release or may be mailed home.

Recreation Services: FCI Marianna offers both recreation and hobbycraft areas where inmates can engage in a wide variety of leisure activities. In the recreation yard, inmates can play sports such as basketball, softball, horseshoes, handball, flag football, bocce ball, volleyball, soccer and frisbee. In the hobbycraft areas, inmates can paint, draw, and engage in any other number of hobbycraft and artwork activities (e.g., crochet, basket weaving, charcoal, acrylic, and oil painting). A band room, track, ellipticals, stationary bikes, treadmills, TVs, ab machines, and more also available. The gym and leisure center are open during all operational hours. Changes in the hours of operation are posted on inmate bulletin boards in the housing units.

Visitation Information: On Sunday, Monday, and Saturday visitation is held between 8:15 a.m. and 3:00 p.m. On federal holidays visitation is held between 8:15 a.m. and 3:00 p.m. See Chapter 1 for more information on visitation.

Prison Politics: This is not a political yard. According to one respondent, "This is a sex offender, drop-out, and check-in yard."

Level of Violence: There is minimal violence at this prison, though there are some fights. According to one inmate, "For the most part, this is a safe yard except for the drop-out drug-gies fighting amongst themselves over debts and drugs." Another concurred, stating, "There is very little violence. That which does occur is centered around drug use and drug bills." Another inmate explained that the violence is getting worse "due to the drugs and what comes with them." One respondent stated that he would "rate the safety at roughly an 8 out of 10."

Vulnerable Populations: Sex offenders, informants, and LGBT inmates can stay. According to one inmate, "They are all safe here." Another inmate stated, "Sex offenders, informants, gays, and transgenders are all allowed to walk here. There is actually a pretty high population of transgender and gay inmates." One respondent did note that "staff sometimes discriminate against sex offenders when it comes to employment, medical, and commissary."

Good: "Great recreation department. Good chapel and psychology services." "The scenery and landscape are great." "Good food and medical care." "Safe, calm yard; nothing going on."

Bad: "Staff disrespectful, poor commissary selection, and bad food." "Pay is crap all over, nothing going on."

Other Comments: "Overall, fine for anyone. Lots of sex offenders, so a very soft yard." "FCI Marianna is generally horrible." "Overall, it's a nice yard, fairly slow-paced and somewhat boring at times, just the place to finish a bid." "Lack of politics means the staff have free reign and sometimes make off-the-wall proclamations that nobody stands up against." "It's safe to a point but getting worse due to all of the drugs."

In the News: In June 2012, Steven M. Smith and Mary S. Summers, guards at the Federal Correctional Institution in Marianna, were indicted for a smuggling operation that involved cell phones, tobacco, a lighter, an MP3 player and synthetic marijuana.

In 2012, several dozen prison guards filed lawsuits against FCI Marianna's UNICOR facility seeking compensation for illnesses and resulting quality of life losses they say they suffered from exposure to toxic dust generated in the process of recycling computers, which have components containing lead, cadmium, beryllium, mercury, and possibly other toxic substances.

FCI Miami

Federal Correctional Institution Miami | FCI Miami

Facilities: FCI Miami with an adjacent minimum-security satellite prison camp.

Facility Address & Contact Information

Federal Correctional Institution Miami
15801 S.W. 137th Avenue
Miami, FL 33177

Phone: 305-259-2100
Fax: 305-259-2160
Email: MIA/ExecAssistant@bop.gov

BOP Website: https://www.bop.gov/locations/institutions/mia/
Wikipedia: https://en.wikipedia.org/wiki/Federal_Correctional_Institution,_Miami
ZCG Website: https://www.prisonerresource.com/resources/federal-prison-profiles/southeast-region-ser/federal-correctional-institution-miami-fci-miami/

Inmate Correspondence Address

For FCI Miami

Inmate Name and Registration Number
FCI Miami
Federal Correctional Institution
P.O. Box 779800
Miami, FL 33177

For Satellite Prison Camp

Inmate Name and Registration Number
FCI Miami
Satellite Prison Camp
P.O. Box 779800
Miami, FL 33177

NOTE: Funds cannot be sent directly to federal inmates. See Chapter 1 for more information on sending funds to federal inmates.

Sex: Male

Security Level: Main: Low Security; Camp: Minimum Security

Location: FCI Miami is located in southwest Dade County, 30 miles from downtown Miami, off the Florida Turnpike (Homestead Extension, 152nd Street exit), 2.5 miles to 137th Street South.

BOP Region: Southeast Region (SER)

BOP Institution Code: MIA for FCI Miami

Judicial District: Southern District of Florida

Medical Care Level: Level 2. See Chapter 2 for more information on Medical Care and Mental Health Care Levels.

Mental Health Care Level: Level 2

Population (as of May 1, 2019): Main: 894; Camp: 364

Background: Federal Correctional Institution Miami is a low-security federal prison in Miami, Florida, which houses male inmates. It was opened in 1976. Federal Correctional Institution Miami Camp, which also houses male inmates, was opened in 1992 and is located adjacent to the main institution.

The prison originally housed refugees from Cuba, many of which had criminal records. In 1980, during the Mariel Boatlift, over 100,000 refugees were housed in FCI Miami. In 1992, Hurricane Andrew destroyed much of FCI Miami. In 2018, OSHA issued a report detailing numerous safety and security violations at the prison.

Notable inmate Lou Pearlman, a well-known music producer and manager who made Backstreet Boys and N'SNYC famous, was sentenced to 25 years for orchestrating a Ponzi scheme which caused investors to lose $200 million. He died in 2016 while serving his sentence. Another notable inmate was NFL quarterback Shane Matthews who was sentenced to three months as part of a $20 million health care fraud conspiracy. He was housed at FCI Miami Camp.

Media reports indicate that at least two guards have been assaulted by inmates and one guard has been indicted for sexually abusing an inmate.

Housing: Inmates are housed in two- and three-person cells. Inmates at the camp are housed in dormitories, which are divided into two-person cubicles.

Health Services: FCI Miami provide sick call, physical examinations, prescription medication, dental and eye care, and HIV, TB, and Hepatitis testing. While emergency care is available 24 hours a day, inmates must attend sick call at 7:00 a.m. on Monday, Tuesday, Thursday, or Friday in order to be evaluated for routine care needs.

Psychology Services: FCI Miami provides psychological evaluations, crisis consultation, referrals to Health Services, and individual and group counseling services in English and Spanish. Psychology Services staff post notices of upcoming treatment offerings in inmate housing units. Inmates must submit a request to staff or visit the open house in order to request program placement.

Residential Drug Abuse Program (RDAP): Both FCI Miami and the camp have the Residential Drug Abuse Program (RDAP). The RDAP program at FCI Miami is conducted in Spanish. Drug abuse programming, including a Drug Abuse Education Course and the Non-Residential Drug Abuse Treatment program (NR-DAP), is also available.

Education Services: FCI Miami provides literacy, GED, GED prep, and English-as-a-Second Language (ESL) programs. An incentive award of $5 is given to an inmate who completes the Test of Adult Basic Education (TABE), while $25 is awarded to those who pass the GED or ESL examinations. Also offered are courses on parenting, janitorial, Pre-Release Preparation, college, and other correspondence courses. High school diplomas and post-secondary degrees are available through paid correspondence programs.

Advanced Occupational Education: FCI Miami offers advanced occupational education in Custodial Maintenance and HVAC-1.

Vocational Training: FCI Miami offers vocational training in Drafting in the main building.

Apprenticeship: FCI Miami and the camp offer apprenticeships in Electrical and HVAC. The main building also offers a Plumbing apprenticeship.

Library Services: FCI Miami provides a leisure library, and a media lab. Inmates can check out newspapers, magazines, and books. Inmates are provided access to legal materials and an opportunity to prepare legal documents through the use of the TRULINCS Electronic Law Library. A copy machine is available to reproduce materials needed for research. Electric typewriters are also available for inmate use.

UNICOR: The FCI Miami UNICOR facility produces clothing and textiles.

Commissary: Inmates who have funds posted in their commissary account are permitted to spend up to $360.00 monthly for a variety of commissary items. Stamps and over-the-counter (OTC) medical items are not counted against the monthly spending limit. Each inmate must have an identification card to shop. Shopping is conducted during breakfast. Inmates must carry their I.D. card at all times. Inmates may check their account balance using the TRULINCS computers located in the housing units. PIN numbers can be obtained in the Business Office, Inmate's Account Section, on Tuesdays and Thursdays from 11:00 A.M. to noon. Account balances can also be obtained via the inmate telephone system.

Recreation Services: FCI Miami provides a recreation yard, as well as structured and unstructured recreational activities. The yard allows for recreational and group exercises and sports. Inmates are also allowed to participate in a wide variety of art and hobbycraft activities. Chess, musical instruments, ceramic classes, and leathercraft are popular activities.

Visitation Information: On Sunday, Friday, and Saturday visitation is held between 8:00 a.m. and 3:00 p.m. On federal holidays visitation is held between 8:00 a.m. and 3:00 p.m. See Chapter 1 for more information on visitation.

Prison Politics: This prison has a low level of politics.

Level of Violence: Inmates report very little violence at this facility.

Vulnerable Populations: Sex offenders, informants, and LGBT inmates can walk the yard. According to one respondent, these groups "don't have many problems."

Bad: "Lots of black mold." "The paper is talking about the prison possibly closing due to health concerns."

Other Comments: "Stay the hell away and pray that you don't come here." "To me it is like paradise. I like it here a lot."

In the News: In June 2018, the Occupational Health and Safety Administration (OSHA) issued a report detailing numerous workplace violations at Federal Correctional Institution Miami that endangered prisoners and staff, including mold, water leakage and a lack of basic security equipment. OSHA also warned that violent prisoners were being moved to FCI Miami where guards were not sufficiently trained or equipped to deal with them.

In April 2018, the American Federation of Government Employees Local 506, a central Florida prison guard's union, complained after guards from other federal prisons were sent to FCI Miami during Hurricane Irma, when they felt the whole facility should have been evacuated. During the hurricane, the building flooded, and power was lost for several days. In previous years, the Bureau of Prisons has pulled people out of FCI Miami before a major storm.

In March 2018, one prisoner at FCI Miami attacked a guard during a search for contraband. The same month, another prisoner attacked a guard, pinning him to the ground.

In February 2018, NFL quarterback Shane Matthews was sentenced to three months for his unwitting role as a spokesperson in a $20 million health care fraud conspiracy. His teammate, Monty Grow, was sentenced in April 2018 to 22 years. Matthews was incarcerated at FCI Miami and Grow was sent to Federal Detention Center Miami.

In December 2011, Jack Chris Jackson, a guard at FCI Miami, pleaded guilty to the sexual abuse of a ward.

In 1992, Hurricane Andrew destroyed much of FCI Miami.

FDC Miami

Federal Detention Center Miami | FDC Miami

Facility Address & Contact Information

Federal Detention Center Miami
33 N.E. 4th Street
Miami, FL 33132

Phone: 305-577-0010
Fax: 305-536-7368
Email: MIM/ExecAssistant@bop.gov

BOP Website: https://www.bop.gov/locations/institutions/mim/
Wikipedia: https://en.wikipedia.org/wiki/Federal_Detention_Center,_Miami
ZCG Website: https://www.prisonerresource.com/resources/federal-prison-profiles/southeast-region-ser/federal-detention-center-miami-fdc-miami/

Inmate Correspondence Address

Inmate Name and Registration Number
FDC Miami
Federal Detention Center
P.O. Box 019120
Miami, FL 33101

NOTE: Funds cannot be sent directly to federal inmates. See Chapter 1 for more information on sending funds to federal inmates.

Sex: Male and Female

Security Level: Administrative Security (Multiple Security Levels).

Location: FDC Miami is located east of Miami International Airport in downtown Miami, at the corner of N.E. 4th Street and N. Miami Avenue.

BOP Region: Southeast Region (SER)

BOP Institution Code: MIM for FDC Miami

Judicial District: Southern District of Florida

Medical Care Level: Level 2. See Chapter 2 for more information on Medical Care and Mental Health Care Levels.

Mental Health Care Level: Level 2

Population (as of May 1, 2019): 999

Background: Federal Detention Center Miami is an administrative-security federal prison in Miami, Florida, which houses both male and female inmates. It was opened in 1985.

FDC Miami houses pre-trial and pre-sentence detainees of the U.S. Marshals Service. Many of the detainees are involved in federal court proceedings in the Southern District of Florida.

Media reports indicate that at least one guard has been indicted for sexually assaulting a female detainee, at least one guard has been charged with smuggling contraband, and two prisoners have been indicted for a mail and wire fraud scheme. Additionally, at least one inmate has committed suicide at the prison.

Housing: Inmates are housed in two-person cells.

Health Services: Services available to inmates include sick call, x-rays, lab, dental, pharmacy, female health care, and emergency treatment. The clinic is open 24 hours a day for emergency care needs.

Psychology Services: FDC Miami offers crisis intervention, brief counseling sessions, individual counseling, and follow-ups with inmates who are prescribed psychotropic medication. Psychology Services also offers a number of specialized programs dealing with mental health care, including The Resolve Program (focuses on physical and/or sexual abuse) and nonresidential counseling groups, which focus on coping skills, building healthy relationships, and enhancing emotional stability. Inmates can request program placement by submitting an Inmate Request to Staff form (also known as a cop-out).

Residential Drug Abuse Program (RDAP): FDC Miami does not offer the Residential Drug Abuse Program (RDAP). However, the institution does offer drug abuse programming, including a Drug Abuse Education Course and Non-Residential Drug Abuse Treatment Program (NR-DAP).

Education Services: FDC Miami provides mandatory literacy, GED, and English-as-a-Second Language (ESL) programs. High school diplomas and post-secondary degrees are available through paid correspondence programs.

Advanced Occupational Education: FDC Miami offers advanced occupational education in Computerized Engraving, Custodial Technician, and Food Handler programs.

Vocational Treatment: FDC Miami does not offer any vocational training programs aside from the advanced occupational education offerings.

Apprenticeship: FDC Miami does not offer any apprenticeship programs.

Library Services: Leisure and law libraries are available at FDC Miami. The leisure library offers magazines, newspapers, fiction, nonfiction, and reference books. Inmates are provided access to legal materials and an opportunity to prepare legal documents through the use of the TRULINCS Electronic Law Library. A copy machine is available to reproduce materials needed for research. Electric typewriters are also available for inmate use.

UNICOR: FDC Miami does not house a UNICOR facility.

Commissary: Inmates can spend up to $360.00 per month on items such as sodas, ice cream, food, clothing, electronics, and shoes. Each inmate at FDC Miami receives a commissary card upon arrival. They must have their commissary ID card in their possession at all times.

Recreation Services: Inmates at FDC Miami have access to organized and informal games, wellness activities, curricular and extracurricular activities, sports, social activities, artwork, hobbycrafts, table games, and board games. Board games include chess, checkers, dominoes, table tennis, Monopoly, Uno, Scrabble, Risk, Parcheesi, backgammon, and card games. Leisure activities for inmates include crocheting, step aerobics, stair stepping machines, calisthenics, and exercise bikes. Competitive tournaments take place weekly in basketball, soccer, handball, dominoes, spades, bingo, and bowling.

Visitation Information: On Sunday and Saturday visitation is held between 7:00 a.m. and 9:00 p.m. On federal holidays visitation is held between 7:00 a.m. and 9:00 p.m. See Chapter 1 for more information on visitation.

Prison Politics: This is a very political Federal Detention Center (FDC).

Level of Violence: The violence is high at this facility. According to one inmate, "there is an altercation every day and the use of weapons (e.g., knives, locks, etc.) are not uncommon." Theft is also reported to be a problem.

Vulnerable Populations: Sex offenders and transgender inmates are generally checked-in, while homosexual inmates can generally stay.

Bad: "Food sucks. COs laugh at inmates' problems." "Floors bare concrete in many rooms." "Frequent lockdowns." "Medieval attitudes."

Other Comments: "Most of the staff here act unprofessional. It appears as though since they don't show each other respect, they don't feel the need to show respect to the inmates."

In the News: In June 2018, Federal Detention Center Miami guard Michael Mazar was sentenced to five years in prison and nearly $9 million in restitution for his role in a $9 million prison-based fraud scheme, which involved smuggling a cell phone and other contraband into con man Jimmy Sabatino.

In November 2017, Jimmy Sabatino, who was serving time at FDC Miami for skipping out on bills for luxury hotels and goods while pretending to be a music industry bigwig, was sentenced to 20 years for a $9 million fraud scheme, in which luxury goods were sent to Valerie Kay Hunt and Denise Siksha Lewis on the outside, that he ran from his cell. Sabatino, fellow prisoner George Duquen, Hunt, and Lewis had also impersonated employees of Sony Music Entertainment and Roc Nation as part of this scam.

Also in November 2017, Damon Coleman, a guard at FDC Miami, was sentenced to eight months for the sexual assault of a female pretrial detainee.

In September 2006, immigration agents arrested 15 illegal aliens originating from Mexico and Guatemala who were hired to fix the roof of FDC Miami.

In January 2005, Richard Hirshfield, who was imprisoned for securities fraud in 1991 and was being held at FDC Miami awaiting trial on additional charges, hanged himself in the detention center's laundry room.

FPC Montgomery

Federal Prison Camp Montgomery | FPC Montgomery

Facility Address & Contact Information

Federal Prison Camp Montgomery
Maxwell Air Force Base
Montgomery, AL 36112

Phone: 334-293-2100
Fax: 334-293-2326
Email: MON/ExecAssistant@bop.gov

BOP Website: https://www.bop.gov/locations/institutions/mon/
Wikipedia: https://en.wikipedia.org/wiki/Federal_Prison_Camp,_Montgomery
ZCG Website: https://www.prisonerresource.com/resources/federal-prison-profiles/southeast-region-ser/federal-prison-camp-montgomery-fpc-montgomery/

Inmate Correspondence Address

Inmate Name and Registration Number
FPC Montgomery
Federal Prison Camp
Maxwell Air Force Base
Montgomery, AL 36112

NOTE: Funds cannot be sent directly to federal inmates. See Chapter 1 for more information on sending funds to federal inmates.

Sex: Male

Security Level: Minimum Security

Location: FPC Montgomery is located on Maxwell Air Force Base, off I-65 and I-85.

BOP Region: Southeast Region (SER)

BOP Institution Code: MON for FPC Montgomery

Judicial District: Middle District of Alabama

Medical Care Level: Level 2. See Chapter 2 for more information on Medical Care and Mental Health Care Levels.

Mental Health Care Level: Level 2

Population (as of May 1, 2019): 763

Background: Federal Prison Camp Montgomery is a minimum-security federal prison in Montgomery, Alabama, which houses male inmates. It was opened in 1930.

FPC Montgomery is the oldest federal prison camp in operation. It was originally named Federal Prison Camp Maxwell Field.

Notable inmates include Jesse Jackson, Jr. (served 29 months for conspiracy to commit wire fraud, mail fraud, and making false statements); former Fifth Circuit Judge Robert Frederick Collins (served five years for bribery); IndyCar driver John Paul, Jr. (served 28 months for racketeering); former New England Patriots receiver Reche Caldwell (sentenced to 27 months for drug possession with intent to distribute); former Enron Corporation CEO Jeff Skilling (sentenced to 24 years for conspiracy, insider trading, making false statements to auditors, and securities fraud); U.S. Representative Richard Alvin Tonry (served six months for campaign finance violations); Watergate co-conspirator Charles Colson (served seven months for obstruction of justice); and Attorney General and Watergate co-conspirator John Mitchell (served 19 months for corruption).

Media reports indicate that at least one prisoner has been indicted for smuggling contraband and attempted vehicular assault, while another inmate was charged with possessing contraband.

In 2017, Insider Monkey named FPC Montgomery one of the ten easiest federal prisons to do time. In 2012, CNBC named the institution one of the 12 best federal prisons in which to do time. And in 2009, *Forbes* magazine named the facility one of the ten cushiest federal prisons in America.

Housing: Inmates are housed in dorms, divided into two-person cubicles. There is a total of three housing units.

Health Services: FPC Montgomery provides sick call, dental sick call, emergency medical services, and medications. Inmates must submit a sick call form in order to be evaluated for routine care needs. Emergency medical care is available 24 hours a day.

Psychology Services: Psychology services at FPC Montgomery include screening, assessment, and treatment of mental health problems, individual and group counseling, psycho-educational classes, self-help and supportive services, and referral to Health Services for medical treatment of a mental illness. Regular treatment groups include anger management, HIV/AIDS awareness, stress management, and criminal thinking.

Residential Drug Abuse Program (RDAP): FPC Montgomery offers the Residential Drug Abuse Program (RDAP). Drug abuse programming, a Drug Abuse Education course, and the Non-Residential Drug Abuse Program (NR-DAP) are also offered.

Education Services: FPC Montgomery provides literacy, GED, and English-as-a-Second Language (ESL) programs. A parenting class is also available. High school diplomas and post-secondary degrees are available through paid correspondence programs.

Advanced Occupational Education: FPC Montgomery offers Building and Grounds Cleaning, Horticulture, Mechanics, Computer Applications, A+ Certification, WordPerfect, and Culinary Arts advanced occupational education programs.

Vocational Training: FPC Montgomery offers a Commercial Driver's License vocational training program.

Apprenticeship: FPC Montgomery offers apprenticeship programs in Electric Technician, Greens Keeper, Small Engine Repair, Plumber, Horticulture, Housekeeping, HVAC, and Landscaping.

Library Services: Both a leisure and law library are available to the inmate population. The leisure library offers nonfiction and fiction books, newspapers, and magazines. The law library primarily consists of the TRULINCS Electronic Law Library. Both libraries are open six days a week.

UNICOR: The FPC Montgomery UNICOR facility handles laundry services.

Commissary: Inmates are permitted to purchase items not to exceed the $360.00 monthly spending limitation. Over-the-counter medications and postage stamps do not count against the monthly spending limit. A maximum of 30 first class stamps can be purchased during regular sales. The equivalent in international and single stamps can be purchased. Popular commissary items include ice cream, drink mixes, food, electronics, clothing, and shoes.

Recreation Services: The FPC Montgomery Recreation Department provides activities and services, such as wellness classes, a music room, pool tables, and various fitness equipment. FPC Montgomery also offers the Inmates Providing Animal Care and Training (IMPACT)

Program, in which inmates raise puppies to become Service Dogs for Canine Companions for Independence, a non-profit service organization.

Visitation Information: On Sunday and Saturday visitation is held between 8:00 a.m. and 3:00 p.m. On federal holidays visitation is held between 8:00 a.m. and 3:00 p.m. See Chapter 1 for more information on visitation.

In the News: In August 2018, Elvis Mark Hartrick, a prisoner at Federal Prison Camp Montgomery, was sentenced to seven years in prison for trying to drive a work truck into a guard after he was spotted picking up packages of contraband, including cell phones, tobacco and alcohol. His passenger, prisoner Marvin Nathaniel Mobley, was sentenced to two months for possession of contraband.

In September 2017, former winery owner Charles Banks, who was sentenced to four years in prison for fraud, reported to FPC Montgomery to begin serving his time.

In early 2015, former New England Patriots receiver Reche Caldwell served 27 months at FPC Montgomery for transporting drugs in interstate commerce.

In 2006, former ENRON CEO Jeffrey Skilling was convicted of insider trading and securities fraud and sent to FPC Montgomery to serve out his sentence. He is scheduled for release in 2019.

FPC Pensacola

Federal Prison Camp Pensacola | FPC Pensacola

Facility Address & Contact Information

Federal Prison Camp Pensacola
110 Raby Avenue
Pensacola, FL 32509

Phone: 850-457-1911
Fax: 850-458-7291
Email: PEN/ExecAssistant@bop.gov

BOP Website: https://www.bop.gov/locations/institutions/pen/
Wikipedia: https://en.wikipedia.org/wiki/Federal_Prison_Camp,_Pensacola
ZCG Website: https://www.prisonerresource.com/resources/federal-prison-profiles/southeast-region-ser/federal-prison-camp-pensacola-fpc-pensacola/

Inmate Correspondence Address

Inmate Name and Registration Number
FPC Pensacola
Federal Prison Camp
P.O. Box 3949
Pensacola, FL 32516

NOTE: Funds cannot be sent directly to federal inmates. See Chapter 1 for more information on sending funds to federal inmates.

Sex: Male

Security Level: Minimum Security

Location: FPC Pensacola is located 175 miles west of Tallahassee, 50 miles east of Mobile, Alabama on Saufley Field, off I-10.

BOP Region: Southeast Region (SER)

BOP Institution Code: PEN for FPC Pensacola

Judicial District: Northern District of Florida

Medical Care Level: Level 2. See Chapter 2 for more information on Medical Care and Mental Health Care Levels.

Mental Health Care Level: Level 2

Population (as of May 1, 2019): 573

Background: Federal Prison Camp Pensacola is a minimum-security federal prison in Pensacola, Florida, which houses male inmates. It was opened in 1988.

FPC Pensacola was established in 1988 to provide prisoner labor for the Pensacola Naval Complex.

Notable inmates include NFL running back Jamal Lewis (served four months), NBA referee Tim Donaghy (served 15 months), and Goldman Sachs partner Robert Freeman (served four months).

Media reports indicate that at least one inmate has escaped from the prison.

In 2017, Insider Monkey named FPC Pensacola one of the ten easiest federal prisons to do time in. In 2012, CNBC named the facility one of the 12 best federal prisons in which to do time. In 2009, *Forbes* magazine named the institution one of the ten cushiest federal prisons. And in 2005, *The Kansas City Star* named FPC Pensacola one of the five best federal prisons for white collar offenders.

Housing: Inmates are housed in open dorms divided into two-person cubicles or eight-person rooms.

Health Services: FPC Pensacola provides sick call, emergency treatment, pharmacy services, physical examinations, dental services, and immunizations. Inmates are assigned to a specific health care provider who treats them for the duration of their stay. Emergency medical care is available 24 hours a day.

Psychology Services: FPC Pensacola provides intake screenings, referrals, acute crisis intervention, suicide prevention and intervention, sexually abusive behavior prevention and intervention, brief counseling, individual and group therapy, mental health evaluation (by staff referral only), and a psychology self-help resource library where inmates can check out books/videos, etc.

Residential Drug Abuse Program (RDAP): FPC Pensacola offers the Residential Drug Abuse Program (RDAP). A Drug Abuse Treatment Program, a Drug Abuse Education Program, and the Non-Residential Drug Abuse Treatment Program (NR-DAP) are also available.

Education Services: FPC Pensacola provides literacy, GED, and English-as-a-Second Language (ESL) programs. A parenting program and Adult Continuing Education (ACE) programs are also available. High school diplomas and post-secondary degrees are available through paid correspondence programs.

Advanced Occupational Education: FPC Pensacola does not offer any advanced occupational education programs.

Vocational Training: FPC Pensacola offers Computer Applications, Microsoft Office 2003, and A+ Computer Technician vocational training programs.

Apprenticeship: FPC Pensacola and offers apprenticeships in Cooking, Baker, Carpenter, Electrician, Greenskeeper II, Horticulturist, HVAC Technician, Landscape Technician, Marine Outboard Mechanic, Plumber, Small Engine Mechanic, and Welder.

Library Services: A law library and leisure library are available for inmates. In the law library inmates can conduct legal research on the TRULINCS Electronic Law Library computers. Typewriters and a copy machine are also available for inmate use. The leisure library offers newspapers, fiction and nonfiction books, and magazines for inmates to check out.

UNICOR: FPC Pensacola does not have a UNICOR facility.

Commissary: Inmates at FPC Pensacola are allowed to shop in the commissary once a week on their designated day. A monthly spending limitation of $360.00 is imposed. A wide variety of commissary items are available for inmate purchase.

Recreation Services: The Recreation Department offers a wide variety of leisure time activities. Intramural sports such as softball, basketball, flag football, soccer, volleyball, weight training, and fitness (abs/stretching, step aerobics, Presidential Sports Award Program, wellness) activities are available. Additional activities include music, hobbycraft (art, leather, wood), racquetball, bocce ball, and horseshoes.

Visitation Information: On Sunday and Saturday visitation is held between 8:00 a.m. and 3:00 p.m. On Friday visitation is held between 5:00 and 8:30 p.m. On federal holidays visitation is held between 8:00 a.m. and 3:00 p.m. See Chapter 1 for more information on visitation.

In the News: In April 2017, Hector Mulero-Algarin, a prisoner at Federal Prison Camp Pensacola, was discovered missing during an institutional count.

In 2008, NBA referee Tim Donaghy was sentenced to 15 months for betting on NBA games and was sent to FPC Pensacola.

FCI Talladega

Federal Correctional Institution Talladega | FCI Talladega

Facilities: FCI Talladega with an adjacent minimum-security satellite prison camp.

Facility Address & Contact Information

Federal Correctional Institution Talladega
565 E. Renfroe Road
Talladega, AL 35160

Phone: 256-315-4100
Fax: 256-315-4495
Email: TDG/ExecAssistant@bop.gov

BOP Website: https://www.bop.gov/locations/institutions/tdg/
Wikipedia: https://en.wikipedia.org/wiki/Federal_Correctional_Institution,_Talladega
ZCG Website: https://www.prisonerresource.com/resources/federal-prison-profiles/southeast-region-ser/federal-correctional-institution-talladega-fci-talladega/

Inmate Correspondence Address

For FCI Talladega

Inmate Name and Registration Number
FCI Talladega
Federal Correctional Institution
P.O. Box 1000
Talladega, AL 35160

For Satellite Prison Camp

Inmate Name and Registration Number
FCI Talladega
Satellite Prison Camp
P.O. Box 2000
Talladega, AL 35160

NOTE: Funds cannot be sent directly to federal inmates. See Chapter 1 for more information on sending funds to federal inmates.

Sex: Male

Security Level: Main: Medium Security; Camp: Minimum Security

Location: FCI Talladega is located in northeast Alabama, 50 miles east of Birmingham, 100 miles west of Atlanta, Georgia; off the 275 bypass on Renfroe Road.

BOP Region: Southeast Region (SER)

BOP Institution Code: TDG for FCI Talladega

Judicial District: Northern District of Alabama

Medical Care Level: Level 2. See Chapter 2 for more information on Medical Care and Mental Health Care Levels.

Mental Health Care Level: Level 2

Population (as of May 1, 2019): Main 841; Camp: 256

Background: Federal Correctional Institution Talladega is a medium-security federal prison in Talladega, Alabama, which houses male inmates. It was opened in 1979. Federal Correctional Institution Talladega Camp, which also houses male inmates, was opened in 1989 and is located adjacent to the main institution.

In 1991, approximately 120 Cuban detainees rioted and took seven Bureau of Prisons employees and three INS employees hostage.

Media reports indicate that at least two guards have been indicted for smuggling drugs into the prison.

Housing: Inmates are housed in five different housing units in two- or three-person cells. Inmates at the camp are housed in dormitories, which are divided into two-person cells.

Health Services: Intake screening, routine medical and dental care, emergency medical care, physical examinations, and medications are available to the inmate population. Inmates must submit a sick call form in order to be evaluated for routine care needs. Emergency medical care is available 24 hours a day. Insulin line is held before breakfast and dinner. Pill line is conducted three times a day.

Psychology Services: Psychological services include crisis counseling, suicide prevention, and individual and group counseling. Available groups include anger management, HIV/AIDS Awareness, and criminal thinking. Inmates can request program placement through the submission of an Inmate Request to Staff.

Residential Drug Abuse Program (RDAP): FCI Talladega does not have the Residential Drug Abuse Program (RDAP). The camp does have the Residential Drug Abuse Program (RDAP). Both facilities offer the Drug Education class, the Non-Residential Drug Abuse Program (NR-DAP), and Alcoholics Anonymous (AA).

Education Services: FCI Talladega provides literacy, GED, and English-as-a-Second Language (ESL) programs. Adult Continuing Education (ACE) classes taught by fellow inmates on a wide variety of topics and parenting programs are also available. High school diplomas and post-secondary degrees are available through paid correspondence programs.

Advanced Occupational Education: FCI Talladega offers Electrical 1 & 2, Forklift, HVAC 2, Job Readiness, Mason 1, 2, & 3, NCEER Core, Office Technology, ServSafe, and Welding.

Vocational Training: FCI Talladega does not offer any vocational training aside from its advanced occupational education programs. The camp offers vocational training in ServSafe, Carpentry 1 & 2, and Forklift.

Apprenticeship: FCI Talladega offers apprenticeships in the following occupations: Baker, Barber, Carpentry, Cook, Dental Assistant, Electrician, HVAC, Landscape Tech, Masonry, Painter, Plumber, Quality Assurance, Sheet Metal, Teacher's Aide, and Welding.

Library Services: A leisure and law library are available to inmates in the general population. The leisure library offers newspapers, fiction and nonfiction books, and magazines. The law library has the TRULINCS Electronic Law Library, a copy machine, and electric typewriters.

UNICOR: The FCI Talladega UNICOR facility produces military uniforms.

Commissary: Inmates are permitted to spend up to $360.00 per month on a wide variety of items. Such items include ice cream, radios, MP3 players, food, clothing, and more. Inmates are allowed to shop once a week on their designated shopping day.

Recreation Services: FCI Talladega and the camp offer indoor and outdoor recreational activities, including a hobbycraft program (e.g., art, leather, and wood), leisure and fitness programs, intramural sports, TVs, and a music program. The Recreation Department is open seven days a week from 7:00 a.m. to 8:00 p.m., excluding counts and meals.

Visitation Information: On Sunday, Friday, and Saturday visitation is held between 8:30 a.m. and 3:00 p.m. On federal holidays visitation is held between 8:30 a.m. and 3:00 p.m. See Chapter 1 for more information on visitation.

Prison Politics: This is not a political yard.

Level of Violence: There is very little violence at this facility.

Vulnerable Populations: Sex offenders, informants, and LGBT inmates can walk this yard.

Good: "Lazy COs that don't do anything." "They have programs to help you get ahead in the free world."

Bad: "Lazy administrators that don't do anything." "They have snitches and sex offenders trying to run the yard."

Other Comments: "Good place to retire."

In the News: In April 2016, Attorney General Loretta Lynch visited Federal Correctional Institution Talladega as part of the Obama Administration's "Reentry Week."

In December 2015, Bureau of Prisons Director Charles Samuels Jr., who was at one time a guard at FCI Talladega, announced his plans to retire in January 2016.

In July 2015, Marlon McNealy, who was serving a life sentence at FCI Talladega for non-violent drug offenses, was granted clemency by President Obama after spending 23 years in prison.

In March 2013, Belinda Keith, a training officer at FCI Talladega, was sentenced to two years of probation after pleading guilty to smuggling tobacco into the prison.

In January 2006, Ronald Hammonds, a guard at FCI Talladega, was arrested on charges of smuggling marijuana into the facility for prisoners.

In August 1991, approximately 121 Cuban detainees rioted after their concerns were ignored by staff, taking seven Bureau of Prisons employees and three INS employees hostage for ten days because they did not want to be returned to Cuba. Approximately 200 specially trained agents converged on the cell building and used explosives to break open doors after hearing several loud explosions inside the section of the prison where the hostages were being held. All hostages were rescued, and 121 detainees were taken into custody.

FCI Tallahassee

Federal Correctional Institution Tallahassee | FCI Tallahassee

Facilities: FCI Tallahassee with a detention center.

Facility Address & Contact Information

Federal Correctional Institution Tallahassee
501 Capital Circle, NE
Tallahassee, FL 32301

Phone: 850-878-2173
Fax: 850-671-6105
Email: TAL/ExecAssistant@bop.gov

BOP Website: https://www.bop.gov/locations/institutions/tal/
Wikipedia: https://en.wikipedia.org/wiki/Federal_Correctional_Institution,_Tallahassee
ZCG Website: https://www.prisonerresource.com/resources/federal-prison-profiles/southeast-region-ser/federal-correctional-institution-tallahassee-fci-tallahassee/

Inmate Correspondence Address

Inmate Name and Registration Number
FCI Tallahassee
Federal Correctional Institution
501 Capital Circle, NE
Tallahassee, FL 32301

NOTE: Funds cannot be sent directly to federal inmates. See Chapter 1 for more information on sending funds to federal inmates.

Sex: Main: Female; Detention Center: Male and Female

Security Level: Main: Low Security; Detention Center: Administrative Security (Multiple Security Levels)

Location: FCI Tallahassee is located 3 miles east of downtown Tallahassee, on Highway 319 at its intersection with Park Avenue and Conner Boulevard.

BOP Region: Southeast Region (SER)

BOP Institution Code: TAL for FCI Tallahassee

Judicial District: Northern District of Florida

Medical Care Level: Level 2. See Chapter 2 for more information on Medical Care and Mental Health Care Levels.

Mental Health Care Level: Level 2

Population (as of May 1, 2019): 836

Background: Federal Correctional Institution Tallahassee is a low-security federal prison in Tallahassee, Florida, which houses male inmates. It was opened in 1938.

FCI Tallahassee also has an adjacent detention center that houses both male and female administrative-security level detainees and inmates.

Notable inmates include terrorist Colleen LaRose (serving ten years for conspiracy to provide material support to terrorism and conspiracy to kill in a foreign country), and Earth Liberation Front member Chelsea Gerlach (served six years for arson).

Media reports indicate that at least eight prison guards have been indicted for sexually assaulting female prisoners at the facility.

Housing: Inmates are housed in two-person cells (RDAP) and dormitories, which are divided into two- and three-person cubicles. Detention center inmates are housed in cells.

Health Services: FCI Tallahassee provides emergency medical services, physical exams, periodic health exams, female health care, TB and HIV testing, medications, dental services, and eyeglasses. The detention center provides sick call, medication refills, emergency medical services, physical exams, TB and HIV testing, and dental services. Emergency medical care is available 24 hours a day. Sick call is available at 10:30 a.m. Monday, Tuesday, Thursday, and Friday.

Psychology Services: All inmates at FCI Tallahassee are screened by Psychology Services staff during the institution's Admission and Orientation Program. Each housing unit also has a unit counselor and psychologist on staff to provide guidance, counseling, and other mental health services to unit inmates. In the detention center, psychology services are available in the form of short-term supportive counseling for those who are identified by themselves, or by staff, as having difficulty handling their current circumstances. Requests can also be made to speak to a psychologist. Voluntary groups such as self-image, anger management, Trauma in Life, Seeking Safety, and Thinking for a Change are also available. The STAGES Program is available for inmates with serious mental illness and personality disorders.

Residential Drug Abuse Program (RDAP): FCI Tallahassee offers the Residential Drug Abuse Program (RDAP). The Drug Abuse Program, the Non-Residential Drug Abuse Program (NR-DAP), and Alcoholic Anonymous (AA) are also available.

Education Services: FCI Tallahassee offers literacy, GED, and English-as-a-Second Language (ESL) programs. Adult Continuing Education (ACE), marketable skills training, and parenting courses are also available. Due to the short-term nature of the Detention Center, educational opportunities are limited. High school diplomas and post-secondary degrees are available through paid correspondence programs.

Advanced Occupational Education: Advanced occupational education programs at FCI Tallahassee include Business Education I & II, Building Trades I & II, Cosmetology, Horticulture, and a Custodial Maintenance Technician Program.

Vocational Training: FCI Tallahassee offers Building Trades, Business Education, and Horticulture vocational training programs.

Apprenticeship: Apprenticeship programs at FCI Tallahassee are available to inmates in Construction, Electrician, Baker, Cook, Horticulturist, Housekeeper, Landscape Management Tech, Landscape Technician, Material Coordinator, Metal Fabricator, Office Apprenticeship, Painter, Plumber, Quality Control Inspector, Refrigeration Apprenticeship, Stationary Engineer, Teacher Aide 1, and Wood Machinist.

Library Services: A leisure and law library are available to inmates in the main prison. In the detention center, reading materials are available in the housing units. The leisure library offers fiction and nonfiction books, newspapers, and magazines. The law libraries offer typewriters, copy machines, and the TRULINCS Electronic Law Library.

UNICOR: The FCI Tallahassee UNICOR facility handles services.

Commissary: Inmates are permitted to spend $360.00 per month for regular purchases. Postage stamps and over-the-counter medication are exempt from the spending limit. Inmates may shop once a week on their designated shopping day. Shopping is conducted Monday through Thursday. Inmate funds are retained by the institution in a trust fund from which the inmate may withdraw money for personal spending in the institution Commissary, family support, or other approved purposes. Accumulated institutional earnings and money sent from outside are given to the inmate upon release or may be mailed home.

Recreation Services: Recreational programs at FCI Tallahassee and the detention center include both indoor and outdoor activities. Indoors, inmates can participate in various artwork and hobbycraft programs, talent shows, movies, and lectures on health and exercise. Outdoors, inmates can engage in individual and group exercises, sports, and other leisure activities. Popular activities include yoga, Pilates, weights, softball, flag football, and Frisbee. There is also a track. Hours of operation are 6:00 to 10:30 a.m., 12:00 to 3:30 p.m., and 5:00 to 8:30 p.m.

Visitation Information: On Sunday, Friday, and Saturday visitation is held between 8:30 a.m. and 3:00 p.m. On federal holidays visitation is held between 8:30 a.m. and 3:00 p.m. See Chapter 1 for more information on visitation.

Prison Politics: There is a low level of politics at this facility. According to one inmate, "Due to the yard being for women, there really isn't any politics." Another respondent explained, "Everyone works out together and helps each other."

Level of Violence: While most inmates felt that there is little to no violence at this prison, others felt that there was a low to moderate level of violence. As explained by one respondent, "There is no violence. I have never felt unsafe." Another inmate stated, "Due to the inmate population's age being so young, I would peg it as a 5 to 7 out of 10 for safety. It's not 100 percent safe, but the staff manage it very well."

Vulnerable Populations: Sex offenders, informants, and LGBT inmates can walk the yard. According to one respondent, "Sex offenders can walk the yard. I also have a transgender cellie. Neither group seems to have problems." Another inmate stated, "Everybody can walk, even women who killed their children or other people's children. Nobody cares. And nobody cares about informants either." Another respondent explained, "Everyone and anyone is allowed to walk the yard."

Good: "There is nothing good." "They offer a variety of programming to those who really want it." "This is a good place to program."

Bad: "We have to wear pants even when it is 100 degrees outside." "We need more good staff members that are consistent and caring about their job." "Medical care is pretty deplorable."

Other Comments: "The warden is not inmate friendly and that shows everywhere. Sadly, I am a repeat offender and was actually released from this facility in 2010. At the time, there were many more programs available and medical was way better than it is now."

542

In the News: In April 2014, Angel Santiago, a guard at Federal Correctional Institution Tallahassee, pleaded guilty to engaging in a sexual act with a prisoner.

In June 2006, Ralph Hill, a guard at FCI Tallahassee, opened fire on FBI agents who came to arrest him and five other guards -- Alfred Barnes, Gregory Dixon, Vincent Johnson, Alan Moore and E. Lavon Spence -- in a sex-for-contraband scheme. Hill was killed along with Inspector General Agent William Sentner.

In June 1998, William Hock, a guard at FCI Tallahassee, was convicted of having sex with female prisoners.

FCI Williamsburg

Federal Correctional Institution Williamsburg | FCI Williamsburg

Facilities: FCI Williamsburg with an adjacent minimum-security satellite prison camp.

Facility Address & Contact Information

Federal Correctional Institution Williamsburg
8301 Highway 521
Salters, SC 29590

Phone: 843-387-9400
Fax: 843-387-6961
Email: WIL/ExecAssistant@bop.gov

BOP Website: https://www.bop.gov/locations/institutions/wil/
Wikipedia: https://en.wikipedia.org/wiki/Federal_Correctional_Institution,_Williamsburg
ZCG Website: https://www.prisonerresource.com/resources/federal-prison-profiles/southeast-region-ser/federal-correctional-institution-williamsburg-fci-williamsburg/

Inmate Correspondence Address

For FCI Williamsburg

Inmate Name and Registration Number
FCI Williamsburg
Federal Correctional Institution
P.O. Box 340
Salters, SC 29590

For Satellite Prison Camp

Inmate Name and Registration Number
FCI Williamsburg
Satellite Prison Camp
P.O. Box 340
Salters, SC 29590

NOTE: Funds cannot be sent directly to federal inmates. See Chapter 1 for more information on sending funds to federal inmates.

Sex: Male

Security Level: Main: Medium Security; Camp: Minimum Security

Location: FCI Williamsburg is located in Williamsburg County off Highway 521.

BOP Region: Southeast Region (SER)

BOP Institution Code: WIL for FCI Williamsburg

Judicial District: District of South Carolina

Medical Care Level: Level 2. See Chapter 2 for more information on Medical Care and Mental Health Care Levels.

Mental Health Care Level: Level 2

Population (as of May 1, 2019): Main: 1,174; Camp: 144

Background: Federal Correctional Institution Williamsburg is a medium-security federal prison in Salters, South Carolina, which houses male inmates. Federal Correctional Institution Williamsburg Camp, which also houses male inmates, is located adjacent to the main institution.

FCI Williamsburg is located in the town of Salters, 90 miles southeast of Columbia, the state capital.

Media reports indicate that at least three inmates have escaped from the camp.

Housing: Inmates are housed in two- and three-person cells. In the camp, they are housed in dormitories.

Health Services: FCI Williamsburg and the satellite camp provide sick call, clinical and dental care, physical exams, chronic care, emergency medical care and pharmacy services. Eyeglasses and hearing aids are available when clinically indicated. Emergency medical care is available 24 hours a day. Sick call is held Monday, Tuesday, Thursday, and Friday at 7:00 a.m. Both medical and dental concerns are addressed at this time.

Psychology Services: FCI Williamsburg offers intake exams, psycho-educational classes such as Anger and Stress Management, and a focus on sexual abuse/assault prevention and intervention. Additional programs include Smoking Sensation, People in Prison Entering Sobriety, self-image groups, and other voluntary groups. A self-help library and relaxation CDs are also available.

Residential Drug Abuse Program (RDAP): FCI Williamsburg does not have the Residential Drug Abuse Program (RDAP). A Drug Education class, the Non-Residential Drug Abuse Program (NR-DP), Alcoholics Anonymous (AA), Narcotics Anonymous (NA) are available.

Education Services: FCI Williamsburg offers GED and English-as-a-Second Language (ESL) programs. Social education, life skills, parenting, Adult Continuing Education (ACE), and career counseling/release preparation programs are also available. High school diplomas and post-secondary degrees are available through paid correspondence programs.

Advanced Occupational Education: FCI Williamsburg advanced occupational education programs include Culinary Arts, NCCER Core, Residential Carpentry, and ServSafe.

Vocational Education: There is no vocational training at FCI Williamsburg aside from the advanced occupational education and apprenticeship programs.

Apprenticeship: FCI Williamsburg offers apprenticeships in Custodial Maintenance, HVAC, and Plumbing.

Library Services: The leisure library offers reference books, magazines, newspapers, music CDs, and DVD movies that are available for checkout in the library only. Fiction and nonfiction books can be checked out for two weeks at a time. An Interlibrary Loan program is offered in conjunction with the South Carolina State Library System. A law library is available, in which inmates may use the TRULINCS Electronic Law Library, typewriters, and a copy machine.

UNICOR: FCI Williamsburg does not house a UNICOR facility.

Commissary: Inmates can spend a maximum of $360.00 per month on items such as food, beverages, radios, MP3 players, clothing, and more. All inmates must be in possession of their Inmate Account card for all transactions associated with the Trust Fund Sales Unit. Copy cards, postage stamps, and over-the-counter medications do not count against this spending limit.

Sales hours are posted by memorandum for both FCI Williamsburg and the camp in the housing units. Sales are conducted Monday through Wednesday.

Recreation Services: Indoor and outdoor recreational activities are available for inmates at FCI Williamsburg. Programs include intramural sports, community-based sports (at the discretion of the Executive Staff), informal sports, physical fitness and wellness, special events, hobbycraft, music, movies, and other leisure time activities. Specific interests and additional recreational activities are considered when a demand appears to be sufficient to make other programs feasible. A gymnasium, softball fields, jogging track, soccer field, handball, bocce ball, basketball, and volleyball courts are available. A leisure recreation area for board games, a wellness resource library, and sports television viewing are also available. Inside, inmates have access to pool tables, ping pong, stationary bikes, stair steppers, basketball, leather room, art room, band room, tables, a library, and an ice machine. Outside, inmates have access to TVs, ellipticals, stair steppers, treadmills, stationary bikes, rowing machines, softball, soccer, football, shuffleboard, handball, volleyball, horseshoes, tennis, and two tracks.

Visitation Information: On Sunday and Saturday visitation is held between 8:00 a.m. and 3:00 p.m. On federal holidays visitation is held between 8:00 a.m. and 3:00 p.m. See Chapter 1 for more information on visitation.

Prison Politics: This is not a political yard. No car requirement. As put by one respondent, "There are no real political problems here; everyone generally gets along."

Level of Violence: There is a minimal level of violence. One inmate said, "There is very little fighting. Not much violence to speak of at all." Another inmate agreed, stating, "Ain't no violence here."

Vulnerable Populations: Sex offenders, informants, and LGBT inmates can walk the yard. According to one respondent, "All of these groups are here on the yard."

Good: "Quality and quantity of food, respectful staff, no politics, and clean." "Laid back staff." "This is a laid-back spot."

Bad: "Not much." "There are no jobs available for someone who has no funds coming in from the outside." "Lousy jobs and lousy medical." "The Captain and Warden are very special sorts."

Other Comments: "If you're going to do time, go to FCI Williamsburg. I loved it as much as one can love a prison." "I wouldn't change a thing; it's almost as if you were in college." "A laid back and safe environment to serve your time."

Camp in the News: In May 2017, three prisoners at Federal Correctional Institution Williamsburg Camp were discovered missing at 6:30 p.m., before they returned at 8:00 p.m.

In January 2013, former Pennsylvania State Senator Robert J. Mellow reported to FCI Williamsburg Camp to begin his 16-month sentence for utilizing senate staff to perform campaign work.

FCC Yazoo City

Federal Correctional Complex Yazoo City | FCC Yazoo City

Facilities: FCC Yazoo City houses FCI Yazoo City Low with an adjacent minimum-security satellite prison camp, FCI Yazoo City Medium, and USP Yazoo City.

USP Yazoo City

United States Penitentiary Yazoo City | USP Yazoo City

Facility Address & Contact Information

United States Penitentiary Yazoo City
2225 Haley Barbour Parkway
Yazoo City, MS 39194

Phone: 662-716-1020
Fax: 662-716-1036
Email: YAZ/PublicInformation@bop.gov

BOP Website: https://www.bop.gov/locations/institutions/yap/
Wikipedia: https://en.wikipedia.org/wiki/Federal_Correctional_Institution,_Yazoo_City
ZCG Website: https://www.prisonerresource.com/resources/federal-prison-profiles/southeast-region-ser/federal-correctional-complex-yazoo-city-fcc-yahoo-city/united-states-penitentiary-yazoo-city-usp-yazoo-city/

Inmate Correspondence Address

Inmate Name and Registration Number
USP Yazoo City
United States Penitentiary
P.O. Box 5888
Yazoo City, MS 39194

NOTE: Funds cannot be sent directly to federal inmates. See Chapter 1 for more information on sending funds to federal inmates.

Sex: Male

Security Level: High Security

Location: USP Yazoo City is located 36 miles north of Jackson, Mississippi, off Highway 49.

BOP Region: Southeast Region (SER)

BOP Institution Code: YAP for USP Yazoo City

Judicial District: Southern District of Mississippi

Medical Care Level: Level 1. See Chapter 2 for more information on Medical Care and Mental Health Care Levels.

Mental Health Care Level: Level 1

Population (as of May 1, 2019): 748

Background: United States Penitentiary Yazoo City is a high-security federal prison located in Yazoo City, Mississippi, which houses male inmates. It is part of the Yazoo City Federal Correctional Complex.

Media reports indicate that at least one guard has been indicted for smuggling contraband into the prison.

Housing: Inmates are housed in one- and two-person cells.

Health Services: USP Yazoo City provides primary health care for acute and chronic conditions including diagnosis, treatment, education, and counseling for inmates. Physical examinations, dental services, pharmacy services, immunizations and special care items (e.g., eyeglasses) are available. Staff includes physicians, mid-level practitioners, nurses, dentists, a pharmacist, and administrative support staff. Most radiological procedures are done onsite with the support of a consultant radiologist. Medical professionals who specialize in optometry, surgery, dermatology, psychiatry, ophthalmology, internal medicine, and a dietician evaluate patients at the institution on a regularly scheduled basis. Any additional care needs, as determined by the Clinical Director, will be provided in the local community or by a Federal Medical Center. Inmates must present their ID card to receive any health services. Emergency medical services are available 24 hours a day.

Psychology Services: Psychology services include intake screening, crisis intervention and individual and group counseling. Typical groups include anger management, stress management, and others.

Residential Drug Abuse Program (RDAP): USP Yazoo City does not have the Residential Drug Abuse Program (RDAP) however inmates can be referred to an institution that does provide RDAP. A Drug Education Course, the Non-Residential Drug Abuse Programs (NR-DAP), Alcoholics Anonymous (AA), and Narcotics Anonymous are available.

Education Services: USP Yazoo City provides literacy, GED, and English as a Second Language (ESL) programs. Adult Continuing Education (ACE) classes and a parenting program are also offered. Special interest courses such as Spanish, Real Estate, assorted business courses, and Release Preparation are also available. High school diplomas and post-secondary degrees are available through paid correspondence programs.

Advanced Occupational Education: USP Yazoo City does not offer any advanced occupational education programs.

Vocational Training: USP Yazoo City does not offer any vocational training aside from the Apprenticeship programs.

Apprenticeship: USP Yazoo City offers apprenticeships in Custodial Maintenance, Teacher's Aide, Teacher's Assistant, and Welding.

Library Services: Leisure and law library services are available for inmates. Inmates are allowed to checkout newspapers, magazines, and books from the leisure library. In the law library, inmates can use the TRULINCS Electronic Law Library, typewriters, and a copy machine.

UNICOR: USP Yazoo City UNICOR facility produces clothing and textiles.

Commissary: Inmates receive a total validation of $360.00 per month to spend at the institutional commissary. Inmates are allowed to shop once a week on their designated shopping day. Shopping days rotate quarterly, and the schedule is posted at the commissary. Inmates can purchase a wide variety of items from the commissary.

Recreation Services: USP Yazoo City offers indoor and outdoor activities. Leisure and social activities include board games, acrylic painting, bocce ball, horseshoes, band performances, watercolor painting, art and leather craft, and games tables for playing cards, dominoes, chess, checkers, backgammon, and Scrabble. Also available are pool tables, ping-pong tables, bumper pool, and television viewing. The recreation yard has a covered patio, walking/jogging track, stair steppers, one softball field, basketball courts, two bocce ball courts, two horseshoe pits, and outside pool tables. Intramural programs are offered in basketball, softball, soccer, and volleyball. Fitness and instructional programs include aerobics, racquetball/handball, music, calisthenics classes, stationary bikes, walking/cycling club, exercise mats, stair steppers, and abdominal benches.

Visitation Information: On Sunday and Saturday visitation is held between 8:00 a.m. and 3:00 p.m. On federal holidays visitation is held between 8:00 a.m. and 3:00 p.m. See Chapter 1 for more information on visitation.

In the News: In October 2017, approximately 1,200 prisoners from MDC Guaynabo in Puerto Rico were expected to be sent to Federal Correctional Complex Yazoo City because of the difficult conditions caused by Hurricane Maria.

FCI Yazoo City Medium

Federal Correctional Institution Yazoo City Medium | FCI Yazoo City Medium

Facility Address & Contact Information

Federal Correctional Institution Yazoo City Medium
2225 Haley Barbour Parkway
Yazoo City, MS 39194

Phone: 662-716-1020
Fax: 662-716-1036
Email: YAZ/PublicInformation@bop.gov

BOP Website: https://www.bop.gov/locations/institutions/yam/
Wikipedia: https://en.wikipedia.org/wiki/Federal_Correctional_Complex,_Yazoo_City
ZCG Website: https://www.prisonerresource.com/resources/federal-prison-profiles/southeast-region-ser/federal-correctional-complex-yazoo-city-fcc-yahoo-city/federal-correctional-institution-yazoo-city-medium-fci-yazoo-city-medium/

Inmate Correspondence Address

Inmate Name and Registration Number
FCI Yazoo City Medium
Federal Correctional Institution
P.O. Box 5888
Yazoo City, MS 39194

NOTE: Funds cannot be sent directly to federal inmates. See Chapter 1 for more information on sending funds to federal inmates.

Sex: Male

Security Level: Medium Security

Location: FCI Yazoo City Medium is located 36 miles north of Jackson, Mississippi, off Highway 49.

BOP Region: Southeast Region (SER)

BOP Institution Code: YAM for FCI Yazoo City Medium, YAX for Yazoo City Federal Correctional Complex

Judicial District: Southern District of Mississippi

Medical Care Level: Level 1. See Chapter 2 for more information on Medical Care and Mental Health Care Levels.

Mental Health Care Level: Level 1

Population (as of May 1, 2019): 1,337

Background: Federal Correctional Institution Yazoo City Medium is a medium-security federal prison in Yazoo City, Mississippi, which houses male inmates. It was opened in 2005 and is part of the Yazoo City Federal Correctional Complex.

Media reports indicate that at least one guard has been indicted for smuggling contraband into the institution. Additionally, at one point 17 prisoners had to be hospitalized after drinking contaminated prison-made alcohol.

Housing: Inmates are housed in two-person cells.

Health Services: FCI Yazoo City Medium provides primary health care for acute and chronic conditions including diagnosis, treatment, education, and counseling for inmates. Physical examinations, dental services, pharmacy services, immunizations, and special care items (e.g., eyeglasses) are also provided. While emergency care is available 24 hours a day, inmates must submit a sick call form in order to be evaluated for routine care needs.

Psychology Services: Psychology services include intake screening, crisis intervention, and individual and group counseling. Inmates must submit a cop-out or visit Psychology Services open house in order to sign up for treatment programs. Group counseling includes stress management, grief group, effective communication, Beat the Streets, and more. These groups are offered on a rotating basis depending upon the needs of the inmate population.

Residential Drug Abuse Program (RDAP): FCI Yazoo City Medium does not have the Residential Drug Abuse Program (RDAP), but inmates can be referred to an institution that does provide RDAP. A Drug Education Course, Alcoholics Anonymous (AA), and the Non-Residential Drug Abuse Treatment Program (NR-DAP) are available.

Education Services: FCI Yazoo City Medium provides literacy, GED, and English-as-a Second Language (ESL) programs. Adult Continuing Education (ACE) classes are taught by inmates. ACE classes include Spanish, Real Estate, and assorted Business courses. Release Preparation and parenting programs are also available. The Education Department offers a Special Learning Needs Program for inmates who demonstrate learning difficulties. High school diplomas and post-secondary degrees are available through paid correspondence programs.

Advanced Occupational Education: FCI Yazoo City Medium does not offer any advanced occupational education programs.

Vocational Training: FCI Yazoo City Medium does not offer any vocational training aside from the apprenticeship programs.

Apprenticeship: FCI Yazoo City Medium offers apprenticeships in Custodial Maintenance, Teacher's Aide, Teacher's Assistant, and Welding.

Library Services: Leisure and law library services are available for inmates. In the law library, inmates can use the TRULINCS Electronic Law Library, typewriters, and a copy machine. The leisure library offers books, newspapers, and magazines.

UNICOR: The FCI Yazoo City Medium UNICOR facility produces clothing and textiles.

Commissary: Inmates are allowed to spend up to $360.00 per month on a variety of commissary items. Inmates are allowed to shop once a week on their designated shopping day. Shopping days rotate quarterly. Inmates typically use their laundry bag to carry their purchases back to their housing units. Inmates may purchase their own hygiene items from the institution commissary.

Recreation Services: FCI Yazoo City Medium offers both indoor and outdoor activities, including a recreation yard with a covered patio, walking/jogging track, stair steppers, one softball field, basketball courts, two bocce ball courts, two horseshoe pits, and outside pool tables. Intramural programs are offered in basketball, softball, soccer, and volleyball. Fitness and instructional programs include aerobics, racquetball/handball, music, calisthenics classes, stationary bikes, walking/cycling club, exercise mats, stair steppers, and abdominal benches. Other leisure and social activities include board games, acrylic painting, bocce ball, horseshoes, band performances, watercolor painting, art and leather craft, and games tables for playing cards, dominoes, chess, checkers, backgammon, and Scrabble. Also available are pool tables, ping-pong tables, bumper pool, and television viewing.

Visitation Information: On Sunday and Saturday visitation is held between 8:00 a.m. and 3:00 p.m. On Friday visitation is held between 5:00 and 8:30 p.m. On federal holidays visitation is held between 8:00 a.m. and 3:00 p.m. See Chapter 1 for more information on visitation.

In the News: In September 2017, James P. Cheatham III, a guard at the medium-security Federal Correctional Institution at Yazoo City, was sentenced to 15 months in prison for smuggling contraband to prisoners in exchange for $10,000.

In June 2016, around 17 prisoners at FCI Yazoo City Medium were hospitalized after drinking homemade alcohol which was believed to contain botulism.

FCI Yazoo City Low

Federal Correctional Institution Yazoo City Low | FCI Yazoo City Low

Facilities: FCI Yazoo City Low with a minimum-security satellite prison camp.

Facility Address & Contact Information

Federal Correctional Institution Yazoo City Low
2225 Haley Barbour Parkway
Yazoo City, MS 39194

Phone: 662-751-4800
Fax: 662-716-1036
Email: YAZ/PublicInformation@bop.gov

BOP Website: https://www.bop.gov/locations/institutions/yaz/
Wikipedia: https://en.wikipedia.org/wiki/Federal_Correctional_Institution,_Yazoo_City
ZCG Website: https://www.prisonerresource.com/resources/federal-prison-profiles/southeast-region-ser/federal-correctional-complex-yazoo-city-fcc-yahoo-city/federal-correctional-institution-yazoo-city-low-fci-yazoo-city-low/

Inmate Correspondence Address

For FCI Yazoo City Low

Inmate Name and Registration Number
FCI Yazoo City Low
Federal Correctional Institution
P.O. Box 5000
Yazoo City, MS 39194

For Satellite Prison Camp

Inmate Name and Registration Number
FCI Yazoo City Low
Satellite Prison Camp
P.O. Box 5000
Yazoo City, MS 39194

NOTE: Funds cannot be sent directly to federal inmates. See Chapter 1 for more information on sending funds to federal inmates.

Sex: Male

Security Level: Main: Low Security; Camp: Minimum Security

Location: FCI Yazoo City Low is located 36 miles north of Jackson, Mississippi, off Highway 49.

BOP Region: Southeast Region (SER)

BOP Institution Code: YAZ for FCI Yazoo City Low, YAX for Yazoo City Federal Correctional Complex

Judicial District: Southern District of Mississippi

Medical Care Level: Level 1. See Chapter 2 for more information on Medical Care and Mental Health Care Levels.

Mental Health Care Level: Level 1

Population (as of May 1, 2019): Main: 1,993; Camp: 190

Background: Federal Correctional Institution Yazoo City Low is a low-security federal prison in Yazoo City, Mississippi, which houses male inmates. It opened in 1996 and is part of the Yazoo City Federal Correctional Complex. Federal Correctional Institution Yazoo City Camp, which also houses male inmates, was opened in 2001 and is located adjacent to the main institution.

Notable inmates include Karey Lee Woolsey (served 13 years for attempting to distribute more than 7,000 pounds of marijuana and released an album while incarcerated at FCI Yazoo City Low which reached a top 10 ranking on Billboard charts).

Media reports indicate that one inmate has been indicted for operating a drug trafficking scheme and another inmate was indicted for operating a tax fraud scheme. Two guards were treated for heat-related medical emergencies after the institution went without power for ten days. Additionally, at least one guard has been indicted for accepting a bribe.

Housing: Inmates are housed in one of 12 housing units which are separated into dormitories consisting of two-person cubicles, along with a six-person room in each housing unit. Camp prisoners are housed in dormitories.

Health Services: FCI Yazoo City Low provides primary health care for acute and chronic conditions including diagnosis, treatment, education, and counseling for inmates. Physical examinations, dental services, pharmacy services, immunizations, and special care items (e.g., eyeglasses) are provided. Inmates are assigned to a primary care provider who will treat them for the duration of their stay. Emergency medical care is available 24 hours a day by approaching any staff member and requesting assistance. Sick call is conducted between 6:00 and 6:30 a.m. Insulin and pill line are held at 6:30 a.m., 9:30 a.m., and 5:00 p.m.

Psychology Services: Psychology services include intake screening, crisis intervention, and individual and group counseling. Group therapy tends to include anger management, HIV/AIDS Awareness, criminal thinking, and other similar programs. A self-help is also available. Notices of upcoming treatment groups are posted in inmate housing units. Suicidal inmates can approach any staff member and request to be seen by a psychologist. Emergency care is available 24 hours a day. Open house is on Wednesday at 11:00 a.m.

Residential Drug Abuse Program (RDAP): FCI Yazoo City Low offers the Residential Drug Abuse Program (RDAP). The camp does not have the Residential Drug Abuse Program (RDAP). A Drug Education Class and Non-Residential Drug Abuse Treatment Programs (NR-DAP) are also offered.

Education Services: FCI Yazoo City Low provides literacy, GED, and English-as-a Second Language (ESL) programs. An incentive award of $25.00 will be given to inmates upon completion of the GED, ESL, or apprenticeship programs. Adult Continuing Education (ACE) classes and other special interest courses are taught by inmates. Current ACE classes include Spanish, Buying a Home, Buying an Automobile, Music Theory, American History, Marketing, and Investing. A Release Preparation and parenting classes are also available. High school diplomas and post-secondary degrees are available through paid correspondence programs.

Advanced Occupational Education: FCI Yazoo City Low does not offer any advanced occupational education programs.

Vocational Training: At FCI Yazoo City Low vocational training is available in Microsoft Office, Cabinetry, Restaurant Management, Drafting, AutoCAD, and Heating and Air Conditioning. The camp does not offer any vocational training.

Apprenticeship: FCI Yazoo City Low offers apprenticeships in Cabinet Making (8,000 hours), HVAC (6,000 hours), Teacher's Assistant (4,000 hours), and Custodial Maintenance (2,000 hours). The camp does not offer any apprenticeships.

Library Services: Leisure and law library services are available for inmates. In the leisure library inmates can check out newspapers, magazines, and fiction and nonfiction books. DVD movies and an interlibrary loan program are also available. In the law library inmates can use a copy machine, typewriters, and the TRULINCS Electronic Law Library. The law library is located in the Education Department.

UNICOR: The FCI Yazoo City Low UNICOR facility produces clothing and textiles.

Commissary: Inmates are allowed to spend $360.00 per month. This is further restricted to $90 per week. This is further restricted to $90 per week. Inmates are allowed to shop once a week on their designated shopping day. Shopping days rotate quarterly, and the schedule is posted at the commissary. Items such as food, beverages, clothing, and electronics can be purchased. Sales are conducted Monday through Wednesday from breakfast to 2:00 p.m. UNICOR inmates are allowed to shop first each morning.

Recreation Services: FCI Yazoo City Low offers both indoor and outdoor activities. Inmates can play board and card games, paint, draw, and engage in other art and crafts projects. Inmates can also exercise, play sports, walk or run on the track, and participate in a number of structured and unstructured activities. Inside, inmates have access to leathercraft, paint shop, pool tables, ping pong, foosball, tables, yoga, treadmills, stationary bikes, and TVs. Outside, inmates have access to softball, football, soccer, handball, horseshoes, bocce ball, basketball, volleyball, and a track. Past classes have included Abs 1 and 2, Spin Class, Biggest Loser, and more. Hours of operation are 6:00 to 8:00 a.m., 10:30 a.m. to 3:20 p.m., and 5:00 to 8:00 p.m.

Visitation Information: On Sunday and Saturday visitation is held between 8:00 a.m. and 3:00 p.m. On Friday visitation is held between 5:00 and 8:30 p.m. On federal holidays visitation is held between 8:00 a.m. and 3:00 p.m. See Chapter 1 for more information on visitation.

Prison Politics: While some said that this is a moderately political yard, others felt that politics are limited. Inmates are not required to be in a car. According to one inmate, "All inmates are free to use the Rec yard, work in UNICOR, and even use the TV room (depending on housing unit)." Another explained that the extent of the politics is where people sit in the chow hall.

Level of Violence: There is a low to moderate level of violence, with two or so fights per month. According to one respondent, "Violence is only evident amongst those who incur debts without repayment or who 'disrespect' another inmate. Depending on who you hang out with, I would consider this a pretty safe yard."

Vulnerable Populations: Sex offenders, informants, and LGBT inmates can stay, though they will be somewhat ostracized. While all can walk, one inmate explained that "if they go about trying to hide their charges (or are vocal about them) or hang with certain crowds and then get found out, then problems such as checking in could arise." Another inmate noted that "sex offenders and gays are generally left alone but are almost always excluded from organized sports."

Good: "Lazy cops." "COs are pretty lazy so don't expect a lot of locker searches and such." "It doesn't snow much here." "Not sure there's anything good here other than the officers generally leave the inmates alone and limited politics."

Bad: "Poor and lazy medical care." "The guard laziness can cut against you if you need something done. Writing someone up is largely the only way to get anything done." "Five-minute inbound moves and five-minute outbound moves." "Food quality and quantity are well below expectations." "Education and rec tend to open at the officer's whim on evenings and weekends." "Religious services tend to be more closed than open." "Lots of fog counts." "Showers are sometimes closed during the daytime." "Inmates are expected to be in khakis throughout the day, even in the housing units." "The only consistent thing about this place is its inconsistency. Nothing seems to be done the same way. Even varies by shift!" "Since the officers leave the inmates alone, there are lots and lots of drugs, cell phones, gambling, hustling, etc." "There is no maintenance and upkeep, so the place is falling apart." "The air conditioning goes out every summer."

Other Comments: "It's a good spot to do time. Cops fuck with you. Lots of Hispanics." "Generally, this is a crappy place unless you're into spice and want a cell phone. We've had an OD death and a murder (over a cell phone charger) in the last 18 months, plus dozens of hospitalizations due to spice."

In the News: In June 2018, Keith Mullen, a prisoner at Federal Correctional Institution Yazoo City Low, pleaded guilty after helping to arrange the purchase and delivery of 30 kilograms of methamphetamine with outside co-conspirators Allen Smith, Vincent Taylor McGee and Jose Pacheco.

In August 2016, Henry Lamont Jones, a prisoner at FCI Yazoo City Low, was indicted along with an outside co-conspirator, Toni Chinwah, for running a tax fraud scheme.

In June 2014, two employees at the low-security Federal Correctional Institution Yazoo City were treated for heat-related medical emergencies after the facility lost power for ten days, from the 15th to the 25th.

In February 2013, Robert Kale Johnson, a guard at FCI Yazoo City Low, was sentenced to 15 months in prison for accepting a $5,000 bribe.

CHAPTER 10:

Western Region Prisons

Western Regional Office

The Western Regional Office is an administrative office providing oversight and support to facilities located in the Western Region (WXR). The Western Region covers Federal Bureau of Prison facilities located in Alaska, Arizona, California, Hawaii, Idaho, Montana, Nevada, Oregon, Washington, Wyoming, and Utah. These facilities are overseen by a regional office that provides oversight, technical assistance, and other types of operational support. In addition, they conduct training programs for staff in their region and assist state and local criminal justice agencies.

Regional Director: Juan Baltazar, Jr.
WXR Population: 20,902

Facility Address & Contact Information

Western Regional Office
Federal Bureau of Prisons
7338 Shoreline Drive
Stockton, CA 95219

Email: WXRO/ExecAssistant@bop.gov
Phone: 209-956-9700
Fax: 209-956-9793

BOP Website: https://www.bop.gov/locations/regional_offices/wxro/
Wikipedia: n/a
ZCG Website: https://prisonerresource.com/resources/federal-prison-profiles/federal-prison-regional-offices/western-regional-office-wxr/

Staff Mail

Staff Name
Western Regional Office
7338 Shoreline Drive
Stockton, CA 95219

Freight and Non-USPS Parcels

Staff Name
Western Regional Office
ATTN: Warehouse
7338 Shoreline Drive
Stockton, CA 95219

Western Region Prisons

USP Atwater (CA)
FCI Dublin (CA)
FCI Herlong (CA)
FDC Honolulu (HI)
FCI Lompoc (CA)
USP Lompoc (CA)
MDC Los Angeles (CA)
FCI Mendota (CA)
FCI Phoenix (AZ)
FCI Safford (AZ)
MCC San Diego (CA)
FDC SeaTac (WA)
FCI Sheridan (OR)
FCI Terminal Island (CA)
FCI Tucson (AZ)
USP Tucson (AZ)
FCI Victorville Medium 1 (CA)
FCI Victorville Medium 2 (CA)
USP Victorville (CA)

USP Atwater

United States Penitentiary Atwater | USP Atwater

Facilities: USP Atwater with an adjacent minimum-security satellite prison camp.

Facility Address & Contact Information

United States Penitentiary Atwater
1 Federal Way
Atwater, CA 95301

Phone: 209-386-0257
Fax: 209-386-4635
Email: ATW/ExecAssistant@bop.gov

BOP Website: https://www.bop.gov/locations/institutions/atw/
Wikipedia: https://en.wikipedia.org/wiki/United_States_Penitentiary,_Atwater
ZCG Website: https://www.prisonerresource.com/resources/federal-prison-profiles/western-region-wxr/united-states-penitentiary-atwater-usp-atwater/

Inmate Correspondence Address

For USP Atwater

Inmate Name and Registration Number
USP Atwater
U.S. Penitentiary
P.O. Box 019001
Atwater, CA 95301

For Satellite Prison Camp

Inmate Name and Registration Number
USP Atwater
Satellite Prison Camp
P.O. Box 019001
Atwater, CA 95301

NOTE: Funds cannot be sent directly to federal inmates. See Chapter 1 for more information on sending funds to federal inmates.

Sex: Male

Security Level: Main: High Security; Camp: Minimum Security

Location: USP Atwater is located on a portion of the former Castle Air Force Base, about 130 miles from San Francisco.

BOP Region: Western Region (WXR)

BOP Institution Code: ATW for USP Atwater

Judicial District: Eastern District of California

Medical Care Level: Level 1. See Chapter 2 for more information on Medical Care and Mental Health Care Levels.

Mental Health Care Level: Level 1

Population (as of May 1, 2019): Main: 1,095; Camp: 97

Background: United States Penitentiary Atwater is a high-security federal prison in Atwater, California, which houses male inmates. United States Penitentiary Atwater Camp, which also houses male inmates, is located adjacent to the main institution.

USP Atwater is located on land formerly part of Castle Air Force Base, which the Air Force has verified was used to store nuclear weapons.

Notable inmates include leader of the Crips street gang Bobby Banks (sentenced to 55 years for conspiracy and drug trafficking for operating a large-scale crack cocaine distribution operation). Banks was featured in HBO's *Gang War: Bangin' In Little Rock*.

Media reports indicate that there have been at least two inmate murders, one inmate suicide, and two unspecified inmate deaths at the facility. In addition, multiple inmates and guards have been transported to local area hospitals for treatment of stab and other wounds as the result of assaults. One guard has also been murdered at the facility in the past decade.

Housing: Inmates are housed in one- and two-person cells. Inmates at the camp are housed in dormitories.

Health Services: Health services at USP Atwater include emergency medical services, physical examinations, examinations for inmates 50 and older, medication, dental sick call, and reading glasses. Inmates are assigned to a specific medical care provider who treats them for the duration of their stay. Emergency medical care is available 24 hours a day.

Psychology Services: USP Atwater provides intake screening, assessment, treatment of mental health and drug abuse problems, individual and group counseling, psycho-educational classes, self-help and supportive services, and referral to Health Services for medical treatment of a mental illness. The department also offers specialized mental health programs and the Challenge Program (an intensive, residential program for inmates with mental health problems).

Residential Drug Abuse Program (RDAP): USP Atwater and the camp do not have the Residential Drug Abuse Program (RDAP), but referrals can be made to institutions which do provide RDAP. Both facilities provide drug abuse programs, a Drug Abuse Education Course, and the Non-Residential Drug Abuse Program (NR-DAP).

Education Services: USP Atwater offers literacy, GED (in English and Spanish), and English-as-a-Second Language (ESL) programs. Incentive awards are provided to recognize inmates making satisfactory progress and successfully completing the literacy (i.e., GED and ESL) program. Inmates may also receive incentives for progressing to various levels in the GED or ESL programs. Graduation ceremonies recognize GED, ESL, and Occupational Education completions. A parenting program is available, and Adult Continuing Education (ACE) classes are also offered in subjects such as typing, computer literacy, foreign language, and business skills. High school diplomas and post-secondary degrees are available through paid correspondence programs.

Advanced Occupational Education: USP Atwater and the camp do not offer any advanced occupational education programs.

Vocational Training: USP Atwater offers vocational training in Building Trades/Landscaping and Computer Skills - Illustrator and MS Office. The camp does not offer vocational training programs.

Apprenticeship: USP Atwater offers apprenticeships for the following occupations: Electrician, Cook, HVAC, and Teacher's Aide. The camp offers apprenticeships for the following occupations: Landscape Technician, Stationary Engineer, and Teacher's Aide.

Library Services: Leisure and law libraries are available to inmates. A variety of reading materials, including periodicals, newspapers, fiction, nonfiction, and reference books are available at the leisure library. An interlibrary loan program with local, state, and college libraries and available bookmobile services is available. The TRULINCS Electronic Law Library offers inmates access to legal materials and preparation of legal documents. Typewriters and a copy machine are available for inmate use.

UNICOR: The USP Atwater and camp UNICOR facilities handle recycling.

Commissary: A spending limit of $360.00 per month is imposed. Inmates must have their commissary card in their possession at all times for identification purposes. Popular commissary items include ice cream, snacks, foods, electronics, clothing, drinks, and shoes.

Recreation Services: Leisure activities at USP Atwater include organized and informal games, sports, physical fitness, table games, hobbycrafts, music programs, intramural activities, social and cultural organizations, and movies. Art activities include painting and sketching using traditional methods (e.g., pastels, crayons, pencils, and charcoal). Hobbycraft activities include crochet and knitting. The camp also offers a number of recreation activities including leather craft, painting, sketching, and bead craft. The housing unit common area is where inmates can play cards, table games, etc. The recreation field hosts many structured activities throughout the year, including softball, track and field, soccer, volleyball, and wellness classes.

Visitation Information: On Sunday and Saturday visitation is held between 8:00 a.m. and 3:00 p.m. On federal holidays visitation is held between 8:00 a.m. and 3:00 p.m. See Chapter 1 for more information on visitation.

In the News: In August 2018, Juan Flores, who was serving a six-month sentence at United States Penitentiary Atwater, was found unresponsive in his cell and pronounced dead at a local hospital.

In July 2018, Raul Ortega was found unresponsive in his cell at USP Atwater in what officials believed to be a suicide.

In June 2018, "multiple incidents" reportedly took place at USP Atwater and a prisoner and staff member were taken to the hospital and treated. Earlier in June, one prisoner was taken to a hospital for treatment after being assaulted by two other prisoners.

In March 2018, Thomas Douglas Smith, a prisoner at USP Atwater, was found unresponsive in his cell and pronounced dead at a local hospital.

In October 2017, several prisoners at USP Atwater assaulted a staff member with a sharpened blade. Three staff members were treated at a local hospital, another received minor injuries and no prisoners were injured.

In May 2017, unmanned guard towers may have helped a prisoner escape from USP Atwater.

In March 2012, Samuel Stone, who was already serving a life sentence at USP Atwater, was charged with murdering his cellmate, Michael Anita, in July 2003.

In 2012, the Bureau of Prisons instituted a policy change allowing guards at seven federal facilities to carry pepper spray to use against violent prisoners. This was in response to the 2008 fatal stabbing of Jose Rivera, a guard at USP Atwater, by prisoners Leon Guerrero and Joseph Cabrera Sablan

In June 2008, USP Atwater guard Jose Rivera was chased down and stabbed to death by prisoners James Ninete, Leon Guerrero and Jose Cabrera Sablan. Guerrero, who was already serving a life sentence, was given another life sentence in May 2014.

In July 2003, prisoner Michael Anita was found stabbed to death in his cell in the Special Housing Unit (SHU) at USP Atwater, the first murder at the prison since it opened in 2002.

In June 2003, the Air Force verified that it stored nuclear weapons where USP Atwater now stands, meaning that nuclear waste is likely still present at the site.

In March 2003, two prisoners on the recreation yard of USP Atwater refused to stop attacking a third prisoner after they were ordered to stop, resulting in one of the men being shot in the torso by a guard. None of the prisoners' injuries were life-threatening.

FCI Dublin

Federal Correctional Institution Dublin | FCI Dublin

Facilities: FCI Dublin with an adjacent minimum-security satellite prison camp.

Facility Address & Contact Information

Federal Correctional Institution Dublin
5701 8th Street - Camp Parks
Dublin, CA 94568

Phone: 925-833-7500
Fax: 925-833-7599
Email: DUB/ExecAssistant@bop.gov

BOP Website: https://www.bop.gov/locations/institutions/dub/
Wikipedia: https://en.wikipedia.org/wiki/Federal_Correctional_Institution%2
C_Dublin
ZCG Website: https://www.prisonerresource.com/resources/federal-prison-profiles/
western-region-wxr/federal-correctional-institution-dublin-fci-dublin/

Inmate Correspondence Address

For FCI Dublin

Inmate Name and Registration Number
FCI Dublin
Federal Correctional Institution
5701 8th Street - Camp Parks
Dublin, CA 94568

For Satellite Prison Camp

Inmate Name and Registration Number
FCI Dublin
Satellite Prison Camp
5675 8th Street - Camp Parks
Dublin, CA 94568

NOTE: Funds cannot be sent directly to federal inmates. See Chapter 1 for more information on sending funds to federal inmates.

Sex: Female

Security Level: Main: Low Security; Camp: Minimum Security

Location: FCI Dublin is located 20 miles southeast of Oakland, off I-580.

BOP Region: Western Region (WXR)

BOP Institution Code: DUB for FCI Dublin

Judicial District: Northern District of California

Medical Care Level: Level 2. See Chapter 2 for more information on Medical Care and Mental Health Care Levels.

Mental Health Care Level: Level 3

Population (as of May 1, 2019): Main: 1,081; Camp: 204

Background: Federal Correctional Institution Dublin is a low-security federal prison in Dublin, California, which houses female inmates. It was opened in 1974. Federal Correctional Institution Dublin Camp, which also houses female inmates, was opened in 1980 and is located adjacent to the main institution.

FCI Dublin became a female-only prison in 2012 and is now one of only three federal prisons for women in the country.

Notable inmates include Patricia Hearst (served 21 months for bank robbery); former LAPD officers Stacey Koon and Laurence Powell (served 24 months after being convicted of civil rights violations in connection with the beating of Rodney King); Heidi Fleiss (served 20 months for money laundering and tax evasion); and former Prime Minister of the Ukraine Pavlo Lazarenko (served eight years after being convicted of money laundering).

Media reports indicate that at least nine female inmates have been sexually assaulted by guards. Additionally, at least three prisoners have escaped from the institution.

In 2017, Insider Monkey named FCI Dublin one of the ten easiest federal prisons to do time. In 2012, CNBC named the facility one of the 12 best federal prisons in which to do time. And in 2009, *Forbes* magazine named the institution one of the ten cushiest federal prisons in America.

Housing: Inmates are housed in two-person rooms. Inmates at the camp are housed in both cells and dormitories.

Health Services: Services offered include basic health education, intake, periodic health examinations, dental care, specific preventive health examinations (e.g., cancer screening), routine care, medications, emergency care, and specialty care. In addition, female inmates are eligible for pregnancy tests, pap smears, pelvic examinations, and breast examinations during intakes and at routine intervals.

Psychology Services: The FCI Dublin Psychology Services Department consists of the Chief Psychologist, Drug Abuse Program Coordinator, Staff Psychologists and Drug Treatment Specialists. The camp offers psychotherapy and personal development groups, along with crisis intervention and chemical abuse programming. The STAGES Program is also available for inmates with serious mental illness and personality disorders. There are also specialty groups for addiction, self-image groups, and other voluntary groups.

Residential Drug Abuse Program (RDAP): FCI Dublin and the camp have the Residential Drug Abuse Program (RDAP), the Non-Residential Drug Abuse Program (NR-DAP), and Alcoholics Anonymous (AA). The camp also offers the Drug Education class.

Education Services: FCI Dublin provides GED and English-as-a-Second-Language (ESL) classes. Parenting and Adult Education Classes (ACE) are also available. High school diplomas and post-secondary degrees are available through paid correspondence programs.

Advanced Occupational Education: FCI Dublin offers advanced occupational education in Custodial Maintenance, HVAC, Office Technology, and ServSafe. The camp does not offer any advanced occupational education programs.

Vocational Training: FCI Dublin does not provide any vocational training aside from the advanced occupational education and apprenticeship programs. The camp does not offer any vocational training programs.

Apprenticeship: FCI Dublin offers apprenticeships in the following occupations: Carpentry, Customer Service Representative, Dental Assistant, Electrician, Building and Grounds Cleaning, General Maintenance, HVAC, Plumbing, and Welding. The camp does not offer any apprenticeship programs.

Library Services: The FCI Dublin law library offers inmates access to supplies and services related to legal matters. Inmates can find relevant and up-to-date constitutional, statutory, and case law materials, as well as applicable court rules. Most of these materials are available on the TRULINCS Electronic Law Library. General library services are offered daily. A variety of reading materials, including newspapers, magazines, books, periodicals, reference sources, and audio-visual materials can be found in the Recreation Barn.

UNICOR: The FCI Dublin UNICOR facility handles directory assistance phone call services. The camp does not have a UNICOR facility.

Commissary: Inmates must have a photo identification inmate account card to shop at the commissary. Inmates may shop only once a week. Inmates with funds in their accounts are permitted to spend up to $360.00 per month for a variety of articles including candy, cookies, ice cream, instant coffee, toiletries, and greeting cards.

Recreation Services: The FCI Dublin Recreation Department is comprised of both indoor and outdoor components, ranging from individualized arts and craft programs to intramural team sports such as softball and volleyball. A variety of sports activities and exercise programs are offered. Hobbycraft activities are also made available through the Recreation staff. Small projects such as needlepoint, crochet, knitting, etc., may be worked on in the housing units, while most other activities will be conducted in the Arts & Crafts rooms.

Visitation Information: On Sunday and Saturday visitation is held between 8:00 a.m. and 2:00 p.m. On federal holidays visitation is held between 8:00 a.m. and 2:00 p.m. See Chapter 1 for more information on visitation.

In the News: In August 2003, Carlos Rodarte, a guard at Federal Correctional Institution Dublin, was sentenced to six months in prison for sexually assaulting two female prisoners in 2002 and for lying about it to federal investigators.

In 1999, Jon Hyson, a guard at FCI Dublin, pleaded guilty to four counts of engaging in illicit sexual acts with female prisoners.

In 1999, FCI Dublin guard Donnell Hawthorne pleaded guilty to engaging in sexual activities with three female prisoners. This was the fourth such case within the prior two years.

Camp in the News: In September 2017, Anna Armstrong and Irene Michell, who were both serving sentences for methamphetamine possession, walked away from Federal Correctional Institution Dublin Camp.

In August 1998, prisoner Astarte Rice-Davis escaped from FCI Dublin Camp by walking away.

FCI Herlong

Federal Correctional Institution Herlong | FCI Herlong

Facilities: FCI Herlong with an adjacent minimum-security satellite prison camp.

Facility Address & Contact Information

Federal Correctional Institution Herlong
741-925 Access Road A-25
Herlong, CA 96113

Phone: 530-827-8000
Fax: 530-827-8024
Email: HER/ExecAssistant@bop.gov

BOP Website: https://www.bop.gov/locations/institutions/her/
Wikipedia: https://en.wikipedia.org/wiki/Federal_Correctional_Institution%2C_Herlong
ZGC Website: https://www.prisonerresource.com/resources/federal-prison-profiles/western-region-wxr/federal-correctional-institution-herlong-fci-herlong/

Inmate Correspondence Address

For FCI Herlong

Inmate Name and Registration Number
FCI Herlong
Federal Correctional Institution
P.O. Box 800
Herlong, CA 96113

For Satellite Prison Camp

Inmate Name and Registration Number
FCI Herlong
Satellite Prison Camp
P.O. Box 800
Herlong, CA 96113

NOTE: Funds cannot be sent directly to federal inmates. See Chapter 1 for more information on sending funds to federal inmates.

Sex: Male

Security Level: Main: Medium Security; Camp: Minimum Security

Location: FCI Herlong is located in the Sierra highlands of northern California, 50 miles northwest of Reno, Nevada and about 30 miles south of Susanville, California.

BOP Region: Western Region (WXR)

BOP Institution Code: HER for FCI Herlong

Judicial District: Eastern District of California

Medical Care Level: Level 1. See Chapter 2 for more information on Medical Care and Mental Health Care Levels.

Mental Health Care Level: Level 1

Population (as of May 1, 2019): Main: 882; Camp: 84

Background: Federal Correctional Institution Herlong is a medium-security federal prison in Herlong, California, which houses male inmates. It opened in 2007. Federal Correctional Institution Herlong Camp, which also houses male inmates, is located adjacent to the main institution.

Notable inmates include Earth Liberation Front member Tre Arrow (served five years for arson), and co-founder of the environmental group Peaceful Uprising Tim DeChristopher (served two years for false representation).

Media reports indicate that at least one guard has been indicted for smuggling contraband into the prison.

Housing: Inmates are housed in two- and three-person cells. There are approximately 200 inmates in each housing unit. In the camp, inmates are housed in dormitories.

Health Services: FCI Herlong provides routine medical care for inmates. This care includes intake examinations, emergency care, and sick calls. While emergency care is available 24 hours a day, inmates must attend sick call on weekdays from 7:00 to 8:00 a.m. to be evaluated for non-emergency care. Pill line and insulin line are held at 6:30 a.m. and 4:50 p.m.

Psychology Services: FCI Herlong offers crisis counseling, individual and group therapy, and medication treatment in conjunction with Health Services. Typical treatment groups include anger management, stress reduction, and AIDS/HIV Awareness. Open house is held on Tuesday and Friday.

Residential Drug Abuse Program (RDAP): FCI Herlong offers the Residential Drug Abuse Program (RDAP). The Drug Education class, the Non-Residential Drug Abuse Program (NR-DAP), and Alcoholics Anonymous (AA) are also available.

Education Services: FCI Herlong offers inmates GED and English-as-a-Second Language (ESL) programs. Adult Continuing Education (ACE) and parenting programs are also available to the inmate population. High school diplomas and college correspondence courses are also available, but inmates must pay for them.

Advanced Occupational Education: FCI Herlong does not offer any advanced occupational education programs.

Vocational Training: The FCI Herlong camp has many vocational training programs which enable inmates to work outside the camp in the local community.

Apprenticeship: FCI Herlong does not offer any apprenticeship programs.

Library Services: Leisure and law libraries are available to the inmate population. In the leisure library inmates can check out fiction and nonfiction books, newspapers, and magazines. Inmates can also check-out NEO word processors. The law library primarily consists of the TRULINCS Electronic Law Library. Inmates also have access to typewriters and a copy machine.

UNICOR: The FCI Herlong UNICOR facility handles fleet management and vehicular components.

Commissary: Inmates are allowed to spend up to $360.00 per month in the commissary. They can shop once a week on their designated shopping day. Shopping is conducted Monday through Friday from 6:45 a.m. to 12:30 p.m. Copy cards, postage stamps, and over-the-counter medications do not count against this spending limit. Popular items include snacks, candy, drinks, food, ice cream, clothing, and electronics.

Recreation Services: FCI Herlong's Recreation Department offers both indoor and outdoor activities. Inside, inmates have access to an indoor gym with a basketball court and various workout machines (e.g., treadmills, ladder climbers, ellipticals, etc.), workout courses, music classes, art and craft programs, and more. Outside, inmates have access to a track, football/soccer field, basketball courts, softball field, tables, and more. The hours of operation are 6:45

to 11:00 a.m., 12:30 to 3:30 p.m., and 4:45 to 8:45 p.m. on weekdays. On weekends, the morning hours are 6:45 to 9:30 a.m.

Visitation Information: On Sunday and Saturday visitation is held between 8:00 a.m. and 3:00 p.m. On federal holidays visitation is held between 8:00 a.m. and 3:00 p.m. See Chapter 1 for more information on visitation.

Prison Politics: There is a low level of prison politics at this facility. Inmates are not required to be in a car.

Level of Violence: There is a low level of violence at this prison. According to one respondent, "it's safe." Another respondent stated, "This spot is cool, safe and low on violence."

Vulnerable Populations: Sex offenders, informants, and LGBT inmates can walk the yard.

Good: "Education, programs, recreation, and the moves are all good."

Bad: "The yard is split for recreation. So, all of the downstairs blocks rec together and the upstairs blocks rec together." "The lack of empathy is bad and the administration's attitude in dealing with grievances is also bad."

Other Comments: "Herlong is ok." "There are some problems with mental health on this yard and the lack of treatment, but this is also the same at other spots."

In the News: In September 2008, Michael Megill, a cook at the Federal Correctional Institution at Herlong, and his brother Jeremy were both sentenced to a year in prison for smuggling tobacco products into the facility for the prisoners.

FDC Honolulu

Federal Detention Center Honolulu | FDC Honolulu

Facility Address & Contact Information

Federal Detention Center Honolulu
351 Elliott Street
Honolulu, HI 96819

Phone: 808-838-4200
Fax: 808-838-4507
Email: HON/ExecAssistant@bop.gov

BOP Website: https://www.bop.gov/locations/institutions/hon/
Wikipedia: https://en.wikipedia.org/wiki/Federal_Detention_Center%2C_Honolulu
ZCG Website: https://www.prisonerresource.com/resources/federal-prison-profiles/western-region-wxr/federal-detention-center-honolulu-fdc-honolulu/

Inmate Correspondence Address

Inmate Name and Registration Number
FDC Honolulu
Federal Detention Center
P.O. Box 30080
Honolulu, HI 96820

NOTE: Funds cannot be sent directly to federal inmates. See Chapter 1 for more information on sending funds to federal inmates.

Sex: Male and Female

Security Level: Administrative Security (Multiple Security Levels)

Location: FDC Honolulu is located adjacent to Honolulu International Airport on the Hawaiian Airlines side.

BOP Region: Western Region (WXR)

BOP Institution Code: HON for FDC Honolulu

Judicial District: District of Hawaii

Medical Care Level: Level 2. See Chapter 2 for more information on Medical Care and Mental Health Care Levels.

Mental Health Care Level: Level 2

Population (as of May 1, 2019): 378

Background: Federal Detention Center Honolulu is an administrative-security federal prison in Honolulu, Hawaii, which houses both male and female inmates. It was opened in 2001.

FDC Honolulu houses pre-trial and pre-sentence detainees, as well as holdover inmates within its 12-story structure.

Notable inmates include stars of the reality TV show *Dog: The Bounty Hunter* Duane "Dog" Chapman, Leland Chapman, and Tim Chapman, all of whom were arrested on September 14, 2006 for illegal bounty hunting. All were released the following day.

Media reports indicate that two guards have been indicted for sexually assaulting three female detainees, at least one guard has been indicted for smuggling drugs into the prison, and four detainees were charged with smuggling drugs into the institution. Additionally, prisoners have participated in at least one hunger strike to protest conditions of confinement.

Housing: Inmates are housed in two-person cells.

Health Services: Health services at FDC Honolulu include sick call, emergency care, medications, chronic care management, routine dental care, medical and dental emergency care for injuries and sudden illness, age-appropriate preventive care to promote optimal health and functional status, restorative care to promote achievable functional status, long-term care, and end-of-life care. Emergency medical services are available 24 hours a day.

Psychology Services: FDC Honolulu's psychology services include screening, assessment, and treatment of mental health issues, individual and group counseling, psycho-educational classes, self-help and supportive services, and referral to Health Services for medical treatment of a mental illness. Inmates can request program placement by submitting an Inmate Request to Staff form.

Residential Drug Abuse Program (RDAP): FDC Honolulu does not offer the Residential Drug Abuse Program (RDAP), but referrals can be made to institutions that do provide RDAP. A Drug Abuse Education Course and the Non-Residential Drug Abuse Treatment Program (NR-DAP) are available.

Education Services: FDC Honolulu provides literacy, GED, and English-as-a-Second Language (ESL) programs. Incentive awards are provided to recognize inmates making satisfactory progress and successfully completing the literacy (i.e., GED and ESL) program. Inmates may also receive incentives for progressing to various levels in the GED or ESL programs. Graduation ceremonies recognize GED, ESL, and Occupational Education completions. High school diplomas and post-secondary degrees are available through paid correspondence programs.

Advanced Occupational Education: FDC Honolulu does not offer any advanced occupational education programs.

Vocational Training: FDC Honolulu does not offer any vocational training programs.

Apprenticeship: FDC Honolulu does not offer any apprenticeship programs.

Library Services: The leisure library offers inmates a variety of reading materials, including periodicals, newspapers, fiction, nonfiction, and reference books. There is also an interlibrary loan program with local, state, and college libraries and available bookmobile services. Inmates are also afforded access to legal materials and an opportunity to prepare legal documents with the assistance of the TRULINCS Electronic Law Library.

UNICOR: FDC Honolulu does not house a UNICOR facility.

Commissary: The monthly spending limit is $360.00. Inmates are allowed to shop once a week on their designated shopping day. Inmates may use funds in their account to purchase items at the institution commissary, place funds on their inmate phone account, purchase TRU-Units for their TRULINCS account, or send funds outside of the institution using Form BP-199. Inmates are allowed to purchase a wide variety of products at the commissary.

Recreation Services: FDC Honolulu offers a variety of recreation, leisure, wellness, and social programs. Leisure activities include organized and informal games, sports, physical fitness, table games, hobbycrafts, social and cultural organizations, and movies. Art activities include painting and sketching rendered in any of the usual media (e.g., oils, pastels, crayons, pencils, inks, and charcoal).

Visitation Information: On Monday, Tuesday, and Friday visitation is held between 7:30 a.m. and 1:30 p.m. as well as 2:15 and 8:15 p.m. On Sunday, Saturday, and federal holidays visitation is held between 6:15 and 8:15 a.m., 8:45 and 10:45 a.m., and 2:45 and 4:45 p.m., 5:15 and 7:15 p.m., and 7:45 and 9:45 p.m. See Chapter 1 for more information on visitation.

In the News: In June 2017, Diego Contreras, a guard at Federal Detention Center Honolulu, was sentenced to a year in prison for having inappropriate relationships with two female inmates and lying about it to federal investigators.

In April 2014, an estimated eight prisoners in the segregation unit at FDC Honolulu began a hunger strike to protest conditions that included maggots in the food, loss of family visits and lack of clean underwear.

In January 2014, Mark Damas, a guard at Hawaii's Halawa Correctional Facility, was arrested for intent to distribute more than five grams of methamphetamine and sent to FDC Honolulu to await trial.

In 2013, a female prisoner at the Women's Community Correctional Center who accused guard Irwin Ah-Hoy of sexual assault was moved to FDC Honolulu to protect her from potential retaliation, as Ah-Hoy retained his employment after being indicted for the sex crime.

In 2005, Akoni Sandoval, a guard at FDC Honolulu, along with four prisoners and two of their relatives, were charged with conspiring to smuggle marijuana and methamphetamines into the facility.

FCC Lompoc

Federal Correctional Complex Lompoc | FCC Lompoc

Facilities: USP Lompoc with an adjacent minimum-security satellite prison camp, FCI Lompoc.

USP Lompoc

United States Penitentiary Lompoc | USP Lompoc

Facilities: USP Lompoc with an adjacent minimum-security satellite prison camp.

Facility Address & Contact Information

United States Penitentiary Lompoc
3901 Klein Boulevard
Lompoc, CA 93436

Phone: 805-735-2771
Fax: 805-736-1292
Email: LOX/ExecAssistant@bop.gov

BOP Website: https://www.bop.gov/locations/institutions/lom/
Wikipedia: https://en.wikipedia.org/wiki/United_States_Penitentiary,_Lompoc
ZCG Website: https://www.prisonerresource.com/resources/federal-prison-profiles/western-region-wxr/federal-correctional-complex-lompoc-fcc-lompoc/united-states-penitentiary-lompoc-usp-lompoc/

Inmate Correspondence Address

For USP Lompoc

Inmate Name and Registration Number
USP Lompoc
U.S. Penitentiary
3901 Klein Boulevard
Lompoc, CA 93436

For Satellite Prison Camp

Inmate Name and Registration Number
USP Lompoc
Satellite Prison Camp
3705 West Farm Road
Lompoc, CA 93436

NOTE: Funds cannot be sent directly to federal inmates. See Chapter 1 for more information on sending funds to federal inmates.

Sex: Male

Security Level: Main: Medium Security; Camp: Minimum Security

Location: USP Lompoc is located 175 miles northwest of Los Angeles, adjacent to Vandenberg Air Force Base.

BOP Region: Western Region (WXR)

BOP Institution Code: LOM for USP Lompoc, LOX for Lompoc Federal Correctional Complex

Judicial District: Central District of California

Medical Care Level: Level 2. See Chapter 2 for more information on Medical Care and Mental Health Care Levels.

Mental Health Care Level: Level 2

Population (as of May 1, 2019): Main: 1,261; Camp: 483

Background: United States Penitentiary Lompoc is a medium-security federal prison in Lompoc, California, which houses male inmates. It was opened in 1959 and is part of the

Lompoc Federal Correctional Complex. United States Penitentiary Lompoc Camp, which also houses male inmates, is located adjacent to the main institution.

The prison was initially opened as Federal Correctional Institution Lompoc. In 1981, it was converted to USP Lompoc.

Notable inmates include White House Chief of Staff H.R. Haldeman (served 18 months for conspiracy and corruption charges related to the Watergate scandal); co-founder of EarthLink Reed Slatkin (served 14 years for mail fraud, wire fraud, money laundering, and conspiracy to obstruct justice); and co-founder of the Black Mafia Family Demetrius Flenory (serving 30 years for leading a national drug trafficking operation).

Media reports indicate that there have been at least two riots at the prison: one in which two guards and four inmates were injured, and another racially-motivated riot which consisted of 30 to 50 total inmates. Additionally, one prison guard has been killed and at least four stabbed by inmates, at least one guard has been indicted for smuggling drugs into the institution, and at least two inmates have escaped from the camp.

Housing: Inmates are housed in one and two-person cells. There is a total of eleven housing units. Inmates at the camp are housed in open dormitories.

Health Services: USP Lompoc offers sick call, chronic care, medications, routine dental care, medical and dental emergency care for injuries and sudden illness, eyeglasses, age-appropriate preventive care to promote optimal health and functional status, restorative care to promote achievable functional status, long-term care, and end-of-life care. Inmates must submit a triage form to be evaluated for non-emergency health care needs. Inmates can also speak with medical staff in the dining room during breakfast. Emergency medical services are available 24 hours a day.

Psychology Services: USP Lompoc inmates have access to intake screening, assessment, and treatment of mental health and drug abuse problems, individual and group counseling, psycho-educational classes, self-help, supportive services, and referral to Health Services for medical treatment of a mental illness. Regular treatment groups include anger management, HIV/AIDS Awareness, and criminal thinking. Inmates in the SHU also have access to classes which are delivered in paper packets. One such program is Cognitive Thinking.

Residential Drug Abuse Program (RDAP): USP Lompoc does not offer the Residential Drug Abuse Program (RDAP). The facility does provide a Drug Abuse Education Course, the Non-Residential Drug Abuse Program (NR-DAP), and Alcoholics Anonymous (AA).

Education Services: USP Lompoc provides literacy, GED, and English-as-a-Second Language (ESL) programs. Incentive awards are provided to recognize inmates making satisfactory progress and successfully completing the literacy (i.e., GED and ESL) program. Inmates may also receive incentives for progressing to various levels in the GED or ESL programs. Graduation ceremonies recognize GED, ESL, and Occupational Education completions. Adult Continuing Education (ACE) and parenting classes are also available. High school diplomas and post-secondary degrees are available through paid correspondence programs.

Advanced Occupational Education: USP Lompoc offers advanced occupational education in the following occupations: Welding, Barber, and Construction.

Vocational Training: USP Lompoc offers vocational training in hydroponics and construction.

Apprenticeship: USP Lompoc does not offer any apprenticeship programs.

Library Services: USP Lompoc houses both leisure and law libraries. The leisure library offers magazines, newspapers, fiction, nonfiction, and reference books. Inmates also have access to DVD movies. Inmates are provided access to legal materials and an opportunity to prepare legal documents through the use of the TRULINCS Electronic Law Library. A copying machine is available to reproduce materials needed for research. Electric typewriters are also available for inmate use.

UNICOR: The USP Lompoc UNICOR facility produces electronics and plastics and handles services.

Commissary: Inmates are permitted to spend up to $360.00 per month. Inmates may only shop once a week on their designated shopping day. Copy cards, postage stamps, and over-the-counter medications do not count against the spending limitation. Popular items include drinks, electronics, snacks, and shoes. Inmates must turn in their orders in the morning, then collect their purchases in the evenings.

Recreation Services: Recreation, leisure, wellness, and social programs are available to USP Lompoc inmates. Leisure activities include organized and informal games, sports, physical fitness, table games, hobbycrafts, music programs, intramural activities, social and cultural organizations, and movies. Art activities include painting and sketching using traditional methods (e.g., oils, pastels, crayons, pencils, inks, and charcoal). Hobbycraft activities include ceramics, leatherwork, models, clay, mosaics, crochet, knitting, sculptures, and woodworking. Wellness programs include screening, assessments, goal setting, fitness/nutrition plans, and counseling.

Visitation Information: On Sunday and Saturday visitation is held between 8:30 a.m. and 3:00 p.m. On federal holidays visitation is held between 8:30 a.m. and 3:00 p.m. See Chapter 1 for more information on visitation.

In the News: In February 2017, Armando Chavez-Tapia, a prisoner at United States Penitentiary Lompoc, filed a lawsuit against prison officials for medical negligence. Chavez-Tapia claimed that he was diagnosed with cancer and suffering excruciating pain, but the first Bureau of Prisons doctor just ridiculed him, and a second doctor prescribed him ibuprofen.

In May 2004, Julio Vega, a guard at USP Lompoc, pleaded guilty to attempting to smuggle three grams of heroin into the prison after getting caught in a sting operation.

In 2003, prisoners at USP Lompoc rioted, leaving two prisoners and four guards injured.

In 1998, a fight broke out involving 30 to 50 black and white prisoners in the recreation yard after a football game at USP Lompoc.

In 1997, an unnamed prisoner at USP Lompoc stabbed guard Scott Williams to death and injured four other guards who responded to the attack.

FCI Lompoc

Federal Correctional Institution Lompoc | FCI Lompoc

Facility Address & Contact Information

Federal Correctional Institution Lompoc
3600 Guard Road
Lompoc, CA 93436

Phone: 805-736-4154
Fax: 805-736-1292
Email: LOX/ExecAssistant@bop.gov

BOP Website: https://www.bop.gov/locations/institutions/lof/
Wikipedia: https://en.wikipedia.org/wiki/Federal_Correctional_Institution,_Lompoc
ZCG Website: https://www.prisonerresource.com/resources/federal-prison-profiles/western-region-wxr/federal-correctional-complex-lompoc-fcc-lompoc/federal-correctional-institution-lompoc-fci-lompoc/

Inmate Correspondence Address

Inmate Name and Registration Number
FCI Lompoc
Federal Correctional Institution
3600 Guard Road
Lompoc, CA 93436

NOTE: Funds cannot be sent directly to federal inmates. See Chapter 1 for more information on sending funds to federal inmates.

Sex: Male

Security Level: Low Security

Location: FCI Lompoc is located 175 miles northwest of Los Angeles, adjacent to Vandenberg Air Force Base.

BOP Region: Western Region (WXR)

BOP Institution Code: LOF is FCI Lompoc, LOX for Lompoc Federal Correctional Complex

Judicial District: Central District of California

Medical Care Level: Level 2. See Chapter 2 for more information on Medical Care and Mental Health Care Levels.

Mental Health Care Level: Level 2

Population (as of May 1, 2019): 1,217

Background: Federal Correctional Institution Lompoc is a low-security federal prison in Lompoc, California, which houses male inmates. It opened in 1970 and is part of the Lompoc Federal Correctional Complex.

FCI Lompoc was originally opened as Federal Prison Camp Lompoc. In 1990, it was converted into the low-security federal prison it is today.

Notable inmates include former record company executive Henry Uliomereyon Jones (serving 20 years for mail fraud, wire fraud, and securities fraud); former Boeing engineer Chi Mak (serving a 24-year sentence for conspiracy to commit economic espionage); and former IRS agent Steven Martinez (serving a 24-year sentence for mail fraud, identity theft, money laundering, and murder-for-hire).

Media reports indicate that nine prisoners and three guards had to be transported to a local hospital following a brawl in 2017. Two other prisoners required immediate medical attention following severe assaults, one in which a pipe was used as a weapon. News reports also indicate that one guard was indicted for second-degree murder for shooting and killing another guard while off-duty. The two guards were allegedly under the influence of illegal drugs at the time.

Housing: Inmates are housed in both open dormitories, which contain 76 inmates in the old dorms and 250 inmates in the new dorms, and a limited number of eight-person rooms. There is a total of nine dormitories.

Health Services: FCI Lompoc offers sick call, chronic care, medications, routine dental care, medical and dental emergency care for injuries and sudden illness, eye care, age-appropriate preventive care to promote optimal health and functional status, restorative care to promote achievable functional status, long-term care, and end-of-life care. Medical and dental sick call is held Monday, Tuesday, Thursday, and Friday between 6:00 and 7:00 a.m. Pill and insulin lines are conducted at 6:00 a.m. and 6:00 p.m. Emergency medical care is available 24 hours a day.

Psychology Services: FCI Lompoc inmates have access to intake screening, assessment, and treatment of mental health and drug abuse problems, individual and group counseling, psycho-educational classes (e.g., anger management, victim impact, etc.), self-help and supportive services, and referral for medical treatment of a mental illness. Notices of upcoming treatment groups are posted in inmate housing units. There is also a self-help library with books and DVDs. Inmates must submit a cop-out to request program placement.

Residential Drug Abuse Program (RDAP): FCI Lompoc offers the Residential Drug Abuse Program (RDAP). Drug abuse programs, a Drug Abuse Education Course, and a Non-Residential Drug Abuse Treatment Program (NR-DAP) are also available.

Education Services: FCI Lompoc offers literacy, GED, and English-as-a-Second Language (ESL) programs. Incentive awards are provided to recognize inmates making satisfactory progress and successfully completing the literacy (i.e., GED and ESL) program. Inmates may also receive incentives for progressing to various levels in the GED or ESL programs. Graduation ceremonies recognize GED, ESL, and Occupational Education completions. Adult Continuing Education (ACE) and parenting programs are also available. Current ACE offerings include basic electronics, geography, world history, business, solar electric, landscape design, real estate, money smart, CDL, and others. High school diplomas and post-secondary degrees are available through paid correspondence courses. Coastline Community College offers six free associate's degrees via correspondence and Allan Hancock College offers three on-site associate's degrees. Hours of operation are 8:00 a.m. to 8:00 p.m. on weekdays and 8:00 a.m. to 3:00 p.m. on Friday and Saturday, all of these times excluding counts and meals.

Advanced Occupational Education: FCI Lompoc does not offer any advanced occupational education programs.

Vocational Training: FCI Lompoc offers vocational training in Landscape Tech.

Apprenticeship: FCI Lompoc does not offer any apprenticeship programs.

Library Services: The leisure library offers inmates a variety of reading materials, including periodicals, newspapers, magazines, fiction, nonfiction, and reference books. An interlibrary loan program is also available. Inmates have access to educational DVDs and NEO word processors. The TRULINCS Electronic Law Library provides inmates access to legal materials and an opportunity to prepare legal documents. The FCI Lompoc law library also has a copy machine and typewriters for inmate use.

UNICOR: FCI Lompoc does not have a UNICOR factory.

Commissary: Inmates are permitted to spend up to $360.00 per month in the institutional commissary. This is further limited to $180 every two weeks. A wide variety of items can be purchased, including food, drinks, radios, MP3 players, clothing, shoes, and more. Shopping is conducted Monday through Friday at 5:00 p.m. Inmates are only allowed to shop once a week on their designated shopping day. On this day, inmates go to the commissary, turn in their order, and wait for it to be filled.

Recreation Services: The FCI Lompoc Recreation Department offers both indoor and outdoor activities. Inside, inmates can engage in a variety of arts and crafts activities (e.g., card-making, beading, drawing, painting, leatherwork, etc..), along with a music program (e.g., guitars, bass, accordion, etc.), gym, ellipticals, stationary bikes, stair steppers, ping pong, card tables, and

table games. Outside, inmates can play tennis, horseshoes, bocce ball, soccer, flag football, basketball, softball, volleyball, handball, and racquetball. A track and a large weight pile are also available. Hours of operation are 6:00 a.m. to 8:00 p.m., excluding counts and meals.

Visitation Information: On Sunday and Saturday visitation is held between 8:30 a.m. and 3:00 p.m. On federal holidays visitation is held between 8:30 a.m. and 3:00 p.m. See Chapter 1 for more information on visitation.

Prison Politics: There is a significant level of politics at this facility. Inmates are required to be in a car, which is generally organized along racial lines. One inmate reports, "They told me on my first day that I wasn't allowed to speak to anyone who wasn't white. Within a day, the car came in with knives to tell me to produce my paperwork." Others report that the chow hall and even work assignments are segregated. One inmate stated that things have "calmed down" since the June 2017 riot. Another inmate stated that "the Mexicans pretty much run the place."

Level of Violence: There is a low level of violence at this prison. Inmates report few fights, but a significant amount of intimidation and political posturing. One respondent stated that it is "basically very safe." Other inmates stated that it is "seldom violent" and that "violence is low but does happen."

Vulnerable Populations: While some inmates report that sex offenders, informants, and LGBT inmates can't remain on the yard, others say that all three can stay and that they have their own tables in the chow hall and have access to the weight pile. One respondent stated that sex offenders are typically driven out of two of the dorms, are not allowed in the TV rooms, and cannot use the pool hall. Another respondent stated that sex offenders are "subjected to constant verbal attacks, threats, and are not allowed to sit at most chow hall tables." Another inmate advised that there is a "large gay community here which is safe." Another respondent stated that sex offenders "roam free unbothered, but are barred from TVs and the good jobs." One respondent stated that there is one transgender inmate who doesn't appear to be harassed.

Good: "I really like the buildings because everything is in the same building (e.g., commissary, chow hall, theater, housing units, etc.). You don't have to go outside if you don't want to." "It's safe. The food is mostly decent. Recreation is plentiful. And the dorms are mostly quiet." "The yard is large and has tables. There are a number of nice communities (gamers, musicians, students, etc.) that can make time easier." "The food is ok, and the weather is windy but for the most part quite mild." "Ok weather, weight pile, decent yard." "Get to watch rocket launches from Vandenberg Air Force Base." "The food is mostly edible. Nice weather. Part of the visiting room is outdoors."

Bad: "Staff and politics. Very poor selection in the Library." "Chaotic, enclosed prison atmosphere, confining, horrible staff who lie and are disrespectful." "While it didn't used to be this way, now there are controlled movements." "There is almost no job training, so inmates lack any viable skills when they get out." "The place is run by the gangs. The staff seem to allow, if not support, this." "Medical care is worse than third world countries although there are a few staff who do try." "The best jobs are given to very select groups." "Many guards have an attitude and are disrespectful. No TV for sex offenders. More controlled moves than needed." "Most of the staff are assholes and lie to, harass, and steal from inmates. There are individual moves for each housing unit." "No microwaves." "Complete disrespect from most staff and common belittling and insults." "The water and medical care are very bad." "Overcrowded." "Medical doctor is a quack."

Other Comments: "If you're a sex offender, homosexual, or rat, don't come here. If you're a stand-up guy who has straight paperwork, you'll be fine and might even appreciate the culture." "I would not recommend it for sex offenders." "This is the highest security Low I've ever been in, and the most restrictive mail room operations, recreation and education movements, and getting responses from inmate staff request forms." "Could be worse places." "There is major corruption here amongst the staff." "There are many Spanish inmates at this prison." "Overall, it's ok here. There are just too many Spanish inmates and the politics that comes with them." "Poor management; hostile, aggressive, and untrained staff."

In the News: In June 2017, Federal Correctional Institution Lompoc was placed on lockdown following a brawl in which nine prisoners and three staff members were injured. A total of four ambulances were called to the scene to transport the injured to local hospitals.

In January 2015, Victor L. Curry, a prisoner at FCI Lompoc, was assaulted by fellow prisoner Kenyan Payne, resulting in a broken jaw and blindness in his left eye. Curry later sued FCI Lompoc's warden and medical director for medical neglect after he was thrown into solitary confinement while still bleeding from his ears, eye, nose and mouth as well as internally instead of being immediately treated.

In May 2004, David Sablan, a prisoner at FCI Lompoc, was indicted for attacking another prisoner with a pipe. The incident occurred in April 2003.

In March 2002, FCI Lompoc prison employee Timothy McNally shot and killed Federal Correctional Complex Victorville federal prison guard Gary Bent in a hotel room where they were attending joint training at FCI Lompoc. An investigation revealed that they both may have been using illegal drugs and were "playing" with a 9mm pistol at the time. McNally was charged with second-degree murder.

MDC Los Angeles

Metropolitan Detention Center Los Angeles | MDC Los Angeles

Facility Address & Contact Information

Metropolitan Detention Center Los Angeles
535 N. Alameda Street
Los Angeles, CA 90012

Phone: 213-485-0439
Fax: 213-253-9510
Email: LOS/ExecAssistant@bop.gov

BOP Website: https://www.bop.gov/locations/institutions/los/
Wikipedia: https://en.wikipedia.org/wiki/Metropolitan_Detention_Center,_Los_Angeles
ZCG Website: https://www.prisonerresource.com/resources/federal-prison-profiles/western-region-wxr/metropolitan-detention-center-los-angeles-mdc-los-angeles/

Inmate Correspondence Address

Inmate Name and Registration Number
MDC Los Angeles
Metropolitan Detention Center
P.O. Box 1500
Los Angeles, CA 90053

NOTE: Funds cannot be sent directly to federal inmates. See Chapter 1 for more information on sending funds to federal inmates.

Sex: Male and Female

Security: Administrative Security (Multiple Security Levels)

Location: MDC Los Angeles is located in downtown Los Angeles, off Hollywood Freeway (Highway 101), on the corner of Alameda Street and Aliso Street.

BOP Region: Western Region (WXR)

BOP Institution Code: LOS for MDC Los Angeles

Judicial District: Central District of California

Medical Care Level: Level 2. See Chapter 2 for more information on Medical Care and Mental Health Care Levels.

Mental Health Care Level: Level 2

Population (as of May 1, 2019): 624

Background: Metropolitan Detention Center Los Angeles is an administrative-security federal prison in Los Angeles, California, which houses both male and female inmates. It opened in 1989.

MDC Los Angeles primarily houses pre-trial and pre-sentence detainees and holdover inmates. The prison has a distinct design, referring to housing areas as rooms rather than cells, using wooden doors instead of iron bars on cell doors, and having plate glass windows, balconies, and atriums.

Notable inmates include Jose Cabrera Sablan (serving a life sentence for murdering a guard at USP Atwater in 2008), and Vianna Roman and Aaron Soto (charged with directing gang activities, extortion, robbery, truck trafficking, and murder).

Media reports indicate that at least four guards have been indicted for smuggling contraband into the facility.

Housing: Inmates are housed in two- and four-person cells.

Health Services: Intake screening is provided for each inmate upon arrival at the facility. An initial assessment by medical staff includes TB testing. Other services include physical examinations, HIV testing, and dental services. Emergency medical care is available 24 hours a day.

Psychology Services: The mental health services available include crisis intervention, suicide prevention, limited group therapy, limited individual therapy, limited substance abuse treatment, and psychiatric medication consultation.

Residential Drug Abuse Program (RDAP): MDC Los Angeles does not offer the Residential Drug Abuse Program (RDAP). However, crisis intervention and support to those detoxing from drugs or alcohol, as well as drug and alcohol education groups are available. The

Drug Education class, the Non-Residential Drug Abuse Program (NR-DAP), and Alcoholics Anonymous (AA) are also available.

Education Services: MDC Los Angeles offers literacy, GED, and English-as-a-Second Language (ESL) programs for inmates. Successful completion of the GED program results in the awarding of a state-issued diploma and other incentives. These may include participation in a graduation ceremony, photos, or a monetary award (max $25.00). High school diplomas and post-secondary degrees are available through paid correspondence programs.

Advanced Occupational Education: MDC Los Angeles does not offer any advanced occupational education programs.

Vocational Training: MDC Los Angeles does not offer any vocational training programs.

Apprenticeship: MDC Los Angeles does not offer any apprenticeship programs.

Library Services: Inmates are provided access to legal materials and an opportunity to prepare legal documents through the use of the TRULINCS Electronic Law Library located in the Education Department. A copying machine is available to reproduce materials needed for research. Electric typewriters are also available for inmate use. Inmates also have access to newspapers, magazines, and fiction and nonfiction books.

UNICOR: MDC Los Angeles does not house a UNICOR facility.

Commissary: Commissary spending is limited to $360.00 monthly (excluding special purchase items). Inmates can purchase a wide variety of commissary products on their weekly designated shopping day.

Recreation Services: Indoor and outdoor recreation is available to MDC Los Angeles inmates, including recreation areas and indoor activities such as ping-pong, pool, and board games. Each floor has a recreation deck where inmates can play basketball, exercise, and otherwise be partially outside, though in an enclosure.

Visitation Information: On Sunday and Saturday visitation is held between 8:00 a.m. and 1:00 p.m. On Monday, Tuesday, Wednesday, and Friday visitation is held between 2:30 and 8:00 p.m. On federal holidays visitation is held between 8:00 a.m. and 1:00 p.m. See Chapter 1 for more information on visitation.

Prison Politics: There is very minimal, if any, politics at this facility. This is in large part due to the institution being a Metropolitan Detention Center and not a regular prison.

Level of Violence: There is virtually no violence at this facility.

Vulnerable Populations: Sex offenders, informants, and LGBT inmates can stay.

Good: "As many food helpings as you want."

Bad: "Boring." "The facility is in disrepair; work orders take months."

Other Comments: "Prepare to be bored, but not go hungry." "This facility is a nightmare compared to regular BOP."

In the News: In February 2006, four guards at the Metropolitan Correctional Center in Los Angeles -- Juan Cortes, Anthony Robuffo, Ricardo Campos and Juan Nieto -- were arrested for smuggling cell phones and cigarettes to prisoners in exchange for payments of thousands of dollars.

FCI Mendota

Federal Correctional Institution Mendota | FCI Mendota

Facilities: FCI Mendota with an adjacent minimum-security satellite prison camp.

Facility Address & Contact Information

Federal Correctional Institution Mendota
33500 West California Avenue
Mendota, CA 93640

Phone: 559-274-4000
Fax: 559-274-4223
Email: MEN/ExecAssistant@bop.gov

BOP Website: https://www.bop.gov/locations/institutions/men/
Wikipedia: https://en.wikipedia.org/wiki/Federal_Correctional_Institution%2C_Mendota
ZCG Website: https://www.prisonerresource.com/resources/federal-prison-profiles/western-region-wxr/federal-correctional-institution-mendota-fci-mendota/

Inmate Correspondence Address

For FCI Mendota

Inmate Name and Registration Number
FCI Mendota
Federal Correctional Institution
P.O. Box 9
Mendota, CA 93640

For Satellite Prison Camp

Inmate Name and Registration Number
FCI Mendota
Satellite Prison Camp
P.O. Box 9
Mendota, CA 93640

NOTE: Funds cannot be sent directly to federal inmates. See Chapter 1 for more information on sending funds to federal inmates.

Sex: Male

Security Level: Main: Medium Security; Camp: Minimum Security

Location: Four miles south of Mendota, California; 37 miles west of Fresno, California.

BOP Region: Western Region (WXR)

BOP Institution Code: MEN for FCI Mendota

Judicial District: Eastern District of California

Medical Care Level: Level 1. See Chapter 2 for more information on Medical Care and Mental Health Care Levels.

Mental Health Care Level: Level 2

Population (as of May 1, 2019): Main: 853; Camp: 67

Background: Federal Correctional Institution Mendota is a medium-security federal prison in Mendota, California, which houses male inmates. It opened in 2012. Federal Correctional Institution Mendota Camp, which also houses male inmates, is located adjacent to the main institution.

FCI Mendota opened in January 2012 after years of funding delays. The final cost of construction was $235 million.

Notable inmates include Frankie Maybee (serving an 11-year sentence for hate crimes).

Media reports indicate that at least two guards have been attacked by inmates and at least one inmate has had to be transported to a local hospital for treatment of injuries suffered as a result of an assault.

Housing: Inmates are housed in two-person cells. At the camp inmates are housed in dormitories.

Health Services: FCI Mendota provides sick call, medications, physical examinations, dental care, and emergency care. Inmates must submit a sick call form in order to be evaluated for routine care needs. Emergency medical care is available 24 hours a day. Pill line is conducted at 6:30 a.m. and 4:30 p.m.

Psychology Services: Crisis counseling, coping skills, suicide prevention, mental health counseling, and spiritual counseling are all available to FCI Mendota prisoners. Treatment options include self-image groups, and other groups such as anger management, criminal thinking, and HIV/AIDS Awareness.

Residential Drug Abuse Program (RDAP): Neither FCI Mendota nor the camp have the RDAP program. However, they do offer a Drug Education class, the Non-Residential Drug Abuse Program (NR-DAP), and Alcoholics Anonymous (AA).

Education Services: FCI Mendota provide GED and English-as-a-Second Language programs. All inmates undergo education testing and counseling. The Education Department offers non-credit courses in a variety of subjects. Some of the courses include parenting, language lab, Adult Continuing Education (ACE) classes, and career resources. High school diplomas and post-secondary degrees are available through paid correspondence programs. Coastline Community College also offers several associate's degrees for inmates.

Advanced Occupational Education: FCI Mendota does not offer any advanced occupational education programs.

Vocational Training: FCI Mendota offers vocational training in Building Trades, Automotive, Warehouse, Recycling, and Computer Literacy.

Apprenticeship: FCI Mendota does not offer any apprenticeship programs.

Library Services: An inmate leisure library and law library are available to prisoners. The leisure library offers a wide variety of books including general reference (i.e. encyclopedias, dictionaries, etc.), fiction, and nonfiction. Inmates are allowed to walk amongst the bookshelves to make their selections. Several magazines and daily newspapers are provided. Inmates can also watch movies on DVD. The TRULINCS Electronic Law Library is available for inmate legal use. Typewriters are available for legal material only. A copy machine is also available.

UNICOR: Neither FCI Mendota nor the camp have a UNICOR facility.

Commissary: A commissary is available for prisoners to supplement their regular meals. Food, snacks, candy, ice cream, clothing, shoes, and electronics are available for purchase. A monthly spending limit of $360.00 is imposed, which is further structured into $90 weekly limits. Inmates may only shop once a week on their designated shopping day. Inmates must have a number stamped on their commissary sheet the day before shopping. Then, on their shopping day, this number is used to facilitate sales.

Recreation Services: The FCI Mendota Recreation Department provides indoor and outdoor recreation opportunities. The outdoor recreation yard has six handball/racquetball courts, two softball fields, five basketball courts, one soccer field, football, tennis, horseshoes, and one quarter mile track. The gymnasium has structured exercise and wellness activities such as spinning, aerobics, stretching, yoga, physical agility, sports agility, calisthenics, and officiating classes. Sit-up benches and glute/hamstring stations are located on the patio in front of the leisure center. The indoor leisure center has checker/backgammon tables, board games, ping pong, table soccer, treadmills, stair climbers, stair steppers, hobbycraft programs, TVS, pool tables, and a music program. The music program consists of three band rooms with structured classes offered in basic guitar, advanced guitar, basic drums, advanced drums, music theory, advanced music theory, and accordion. The hobbycraft programs consist of leather (kits only), ceramics, stick art, crochet, beading, and pencil/pastel/chalk drawing.

Visitation Information: On Sunday and Saturday visitation is held between 8:15 a.m. and 3:00 p.m. On federal holidays visitation is held between 8:15 a.m. and 3:00 p.m. See Chapter 1 for more information on visitation.

Prison Politics: This is a very political yard. Inmates are required to be part of a car in order to stay. In contrast to the majority, one respondent stated that "there is very little politics for a California yard." This refers to Western Region prisons being more violent and political than those in other regions.

Level of Violence: While most respondents stated that there is moderate to serious violence at this facility, one inmate felt that there was "very little violence." This appears to be the minority opinion. A number of inmates reported several fights each week.

Vulnerable Populations: While some respondents said that sex offenders and informants can't walk the yard, others felt that informants could walk if they were under the radar.

Good: "The violence isn't too bad, and the recreation is good." "Less political than other Western Region facilities." "No lockdowns."

Bad: "Politics, gravel everywhere, and no grass." "Nothing of life." "Staff wants respect but gives none."

Other Comments: "Unless you have clean paperwork, don't go." "Overall, it's an ok facility." "Bad location." "Easy time here at FCI Mendota. Very little going on."

In the News: In August 2018, two staff members at Federal Correctional Institution Mendota sustained minor injuries after a prisoner physically assaulted a staff member inside a housing unit.

In June 2018, a guard at FCI Mendota filed a whistleblower complaint about toxic mold growing in the control room, making some guards ill.

In January 2018, several prisoners at FCI Mendota were involved in an altercation, resulting in one being sent to the hospital for a non-life-threatening injury,

FCI Phoenix

Federal Correctional Institution Phoenix | FCI Phoenix

Facilities: FCI Phoenix with an adjacent minimum-security satellite prison camp.

Facility Address & Contact Information

Federal Correctional Institution Phoenix
37900 N. 45th Avenue
Phoenix, CA 85086

Phone: 623-465-9757
Fax: 623-465-5199
Email: PHX/ExecAssistant@bop.gov

BOP Website: https://www.bop.gov/locations/institutions/phx/
Wikipedia: https://en.wikipedia.org/wiki/Federal_Correctional_Institution%2C_Phoenix
ZCG Website: https://www.prisonerresource.com/resources/federal-prison-profiles/western-region-wxr/federal-correctional-institution-phoenix-fci-phoenix/

Inmate Correspondence Address

For FCI Phoenix

Inmate Name and Registration Number
FCI Phoenix
Federal Correctional Institution
37910 N. 45th Avenue
Phoenix, AZ 85086

For Satellite Prison Camp

Inmate Name and Registration Number
FCI Phoenix
Satellite Prison Camp
37930 N. 45th Avenue
Phoenix, AZ 85086

NOTE: Funds cannot be sent directly to federal inmates. See Chapter 1 for more information on sending funds to federal inmates.

Sex: Main: Male; Camp: Female

Security Level: Main: Medium Security; Camp: Minimum Security

Location: FCI Phoenix is located 30 miles north of downtown Phoenix, off I-17, Pioneer Road exit.

BOP Region: Western Region (WXR)

BOP Institution Code: PHX is FCI Phoenix

Judicial District: District of Arizona

Medical Care Level: Level 2. See Chapter 2 for more information on Medical Care and Mental Health Care Levels.

Mental Health Care Level: Level 2

Population (as of May 1, 2019): Main: 1,026; Camp: 288

Background: Federal Correctional Institution Phoenix is a medium-security federal prison in Phoenix, Arizona, which houses male inmates. It opened in 1985. Federal Correctional Institution Phoenix Camp, which houses female inmates, opened in 1989 and is located adjacent to the main institution.

FCI Phoenix includes a jail unit which houses holdover inmates.

Notable inmates include former Steppenwolf drummer Jerry Posin, who served five years.

Media reports indicate that at least six guards have been indicted for sexually assaulting prisoners. Additionally, another guard was indicted for raping a girl starting when she was six years old. The abuse allegedly continued for seven years.

Housing: Inmates are housed in two- and three-person cells. There is a total of four housing units. Inmates at the camp are housed in dormitories, which are divided into two-person cubicles.

Health Services: FCI Phoenix provides medical and dental sick call, emergency care, eye care, physical examinations, and medications. Emergency medical care is available 24 hours a day.

Inmates are assigned to a primary care provider who treats them for the duration of their stay. Sick call is held between 6:15 and 7:00 a.m. on Monday, Tuesday, Thursday, and Friday.

Psychology Services: Intake screening, individual psychotherapy, group psychotherapy, personal development groups, and crisis intervention are offered to inmates. Regular groups include criminal thinking, cognitive behavior, anger management, and others.

Residential Drug Abuse Program (RDAP): Both FCI Phoenix and the camp offer the Residential Drug Abuse Program (RDAP). Both facilities also offer a Drug Education class, the Non-Residential Drug Abuse Program (NR-DAP), and Alcoholics Anonymous (AA).

Education Services: FCI Phoenix provides pre-GED, GED (English and Spanish), and English-as-a-Second Language (ESL) programs. Inmates who successfully complete the GED and ESL programs, and who pass the GED and CASAS Certification exams respectively, are awarded a financial incentive award (usually $25.00). Adult Continuing Education (ACE) and parenting courses are also available to the inmate population. High school diplomas and post-secondary degrees are available through paid correspondence programs.

Advanced Occupational Education: FCI Phoenix offers advanced occupational education in Principles of Construction. The camp does not offer any advanced occupational education programs.

Vocational Training: Both FCI Phoenix and the camp offer vocational training in Carpentry. The main prison also offers vocational training in Electrical, Plumbing, and ServSafe.

Apprenticeship: FCI Phoenix and the camp offer apprenticeships in Cooking, Electrical, Electronics Tester, Electronics Utility Worker, HVAC, Landscape Tech, Plumbing, Quality Control, and Recreation Assistant. The camp also offers apprenticeships in Front-End Mechanic.

Library Services: A law and leisure library is available to inmates. The TRULINCS Electronic Law Library contains case law from the federal districts, circuits, and U.S. Supreme Court for reference during the library hours of operation. Inmates also have access to typewriters and a copy machine. FCI Phoenix maintains a leisure library with a large variety of books, including reference and general interest. The leisure library also participates in an interlibrary loan program with the City of Phoenix Public Library.

UNICOR: The FCI Phoenix UNICOR facility produces electronics and plastics. The camp does not house a UNICOR facility.

Commissary: Upon arrival, inmates are given commissary cards. Inmate commissary/ ID cards must be in possession of the inmate at all times when out of the housing unit. A spending limit of $360.00 per month is imposed. This is further divided into $180 biweekly limits. Postage stamps, some over-the-counter medicine, copy cards, funds transferred to ITS (phone credits), and TRULINCS account unit purchases (inmate email) are exempt from the spending limit. Inmates may only shop on their designated shopping day each week. Commissary sales are conducted Monday through Thursday. Inmates must turn in their order the day before shopping so that they can be assigned a number. Then, the next morning, inmates go to the commissary to pick up their purchases.

Recreation Services: Indoor and outdoor recreational activities are available at FCI Phoenix. A comprehensive program of sports activities including varsity and intramural teams is available for inmate participation. There are leagues for basketball, soccer, football, and softball, which include varsity, intramural, and over-35 teams. Tournaments are held on a regular basis in addition to the normal end-of-season tournaments for league playoffs and championships. Weightlifting, walking/running, and stationary bicycles are also available. Hobbycraft activities are available in both facilities. The main prison also has a music room and pool tables. The department opens at 6:00 a.m.

Visitation Information: On Sunday, Monday, and Saturday visitation is held between 8:00 a.m. and 3:00 p.m. On federal holidays visitation is held between 8:00 a.m. and 3:00 p.m. See Chapter 1 for more information on visitation.

Prison Politics: There is a low level of politics at this prison. As stated by one inmate, "Politics on this yard are very light, but the racial politics can be mild. There are also a good number of Paisas and Southsiders."

Level of Violence: There is no real violence at this facility. According to one respondent, "It's pretty safe here." Another agreed, stating, "There is no violence on this yard. It is safe here compared to the USP where I came from." Another respondent pegged the level of violence at a 2 out of 10.

Vulnerable Populations: Sex offenders, informants, and LGBT inmates can walk the yard. According to one inmate, "This place is full of informants. They seem to be the majority. Gay people also have no problems here."

Good: "You can do your own time. The Psychology Department is also good." "There are lots of palm trees."

Bad: "Since staff think that it is a soft yard, they are very disrespectful." "No type of computer training or any other training for that matter." "Education and medical leave a lot to be desired." "The food is horrible." "The staff seem to have political issues with one another."

Other Comments: "FCI Phoenix has the potential to be nice." "Soft yard." "This is a good and clean yard. It reminds me of a college campus." "You are able to do your own time here, but respect -- from inmates and staff -- does tend to be lacking."

In the News: In May 2013, Jose Arnulfo Martinez, an employee at Federal Correctional Institution Phoenix, was convicted of sexually abusing one female prisoner on three occasions in 2008 and another female prisoner three times in 2010.

In August 2012, Carl David Evans, a kitchen supervisor at FCI Phoenix, was arrested and charged with sexual abuse of a ward and providing contraband to prisoners after he was caught on an FBI surveillance camera engaging in sexual acts with two male prisoners.

In June 2007, Loren Williamson, a guard at FCI Phoenix, was arrested on charges that he raped a girl repeatedly from the time she was six years old until his arrest when she was twelve.

Camp in the News: In March 2017, Edward Mendoza, a guard at the federal women's camp in Phoenix, was sentenced to 16 months for having sex with one of the prisoners on several occasions in 2015.

In July 2016, James Toadvine Jr., a recreation specialist at FCI Phoenix Camp, was sentenced to a year in prison for engaging in sexual contact with a female prisoner.

FCI Safford

Federal Correctional Institution Safford | FCI Safford

Facility Address & Contact Information

Federal Correctional Institution Safford
1529 West Highway 366
Safford, AZ 85546

Phone: 928-428-6600
Fax: 928-348-1331
Email: SAF/ExecAssistant@bop.gov

BOP Website: https://www.bop.gov/locations/institutions/saf/
Wikipedia: https://en.wikipedia.org/wiki/Federal_Correctional_Institution,_Safford
ZCG Website: https://www.prisonerresource.com/resources/federal-prison-profiles/western-region-wxr/federal-correctional-institution-safford-fci-safford/

Inmate Correspondence Address

Inmate Name and Registration Number
FCI Safford
Federal Correctional Institution
P.O. Box 9000
Safford, AZ 85548

NOTE: Funds cannot be sent directly to federal inmates. See Chapter 1 for more information on sending funds to federal inmates.

Sex: Male

Security Level: Low Security

Location: FCI Safford is located in southeastern Arizona, 127 miles northeast of Tucson, 165 miles east of Phoenix, off Highway 191, 7 miles south of the town of Safford.

BOP Region: Western Region (WXR)

BOP Institution Code: SAF for FCI Safford

Judicial District: District of Arizona

Medical Care Level: Level 1. See Chapter 2 for more information on Medical Care and Mental Health Care Levels.

Mental Health Care Level: Level 1

Population (as of May 1, 2019): 834

Background: Federal Correctional Institution Safford is a low-security federal prison in Safford, Arizona, which houses male inmates. It was opened in 1974.

FCI Safford was originally opened in 1974 as Federal Prison Camp Safford. In 1985, it was converted into the low-security federal prison it is today.

Notable inmates include Earth Liberation Front member Kevin Tubbs (served 12 years for arson), Allen Pace (serving 24 years for armed robbery), and former police officer Karl Thompson (served 51 months for the beating death of Otto Zehm).

Housing: Inmates are housed in dormitories, which are divided into six- to eight-person cubicles. There are three total housing units.

Health Services: FCI Safford health services include sick call, medications, medical emergencies, dental sick call, routine dental care, eyeglasses, hearing aids, physical examinations, and HIV testing. Inmates are assigned to a particular mid-level practitioner (MLP) who treats them for the duration of their stay. Emergency medical care is available 24 hours a day. Sick call is held at 6:30 a.m. Pill line is conducted at 6:30 a.m., 11:00 a.m., and 4:30 p.m. on weekdays and 9:30 a.m. and 4:30 p.m. on weekends. Insulin line is held before breakfast and dinner.

Psychology Services: All inmates are screened by a psychologist during the institution's admission and orientation program. If there is a demonstrated need, services are offered in the areas of substance abuse treatment as well as treatment for other behavioral and emotional problems. Crisis counseling is available by contacting any staff member and asking for Psychology Services to be contacted. Groups and a self-help library containing books and videos are also available.

Residential Drug Abuse Program (RDAP): FCI Safford offers the Residential Drug Abuse Program (RDAP). The Drug Education class and the Non-Residential Drug Abuse Program (NR-DAP) are also available.

Education Services: FCI Safford provides literacy, GED, and English-as-a-Second Language (ESL) programs to inmates. Adult Continuing Education (ACE) and parenting classes are also available. A computer lab is also available where inmates can take classes such as typing. High school diplomas and post-secondary degrees are available through paid correspondence programs. Eastern Carolina College offers a program where inmates can earn an associate's degree in business.

Advanced Occupational Education: FCI Safford offers advanced occupational education in Carpentry, Business, Retail Sales, and HVAC.

Vocational Training: FCI Safford offers vocational training in Business, Carpentry, and HVAC.

Apprenticeship: FCI Safford offers apprenticeships in Cabinet Making, Culinary Arts, Dental Assistant, Electrical, HVAC, Plumbing, Commercial Driver's License, and Small Gas Engine.

Library Services: The FCI Safford leisure library includes a variety of magazines, newspapers, reference materials, and fiction and nonfiction books necessary for meeting inmates' educational, cultural, and leisure needs. Inmates are able to prepare legal documents and access legal materials via the TRULINCS Electronic Law Library (LexisNexis). The law library contains required legal publications, general legal reference materials, and a selection of Bureau of Prisons policies. A copy machine and electronic typewriters are also available.

UNICOR: The FCI Safford UNICOR facility produces clothing and textiles.

Commissary: Inmates may use funds in their account to purchase items at the institution commissary, place funds on their inmate phone account, purchase TRU-Units for their TRULINCS account, or send funds out of the institution using Form BP-199. Inmates must have their commissary card in their possession at all times for identification purposes. All purchases are limited to $180.00 every two weeks, for a total of $360 monthly, with the exception of over-the-counter medications, Nicotine Replacement Therapy patches, and postage stamps. An additional $50.00 is added to the spending limit during the November/December period to allow for holiday item purchases. Commissary is open Monday through Thursday between 6:00 and 8:00 a.m., and 10:30 a.m. to 12:00 p.m. Inmates may only shop once a week on their designated shopping day.

Recreation Services: The FCI Stafford Recreation Department consists of the equipment issue room, hobby shop, music room, weightlifting area, auditorium, and outdoor activities. The department offers organized intramural leagues throughout the calendar year. The hobbycraft programs include drawing, painting, leather craft kits, crochet, airbrush, and beading. Feature length movies are shown in the auditorium on weekends and holidays.

Inside, inmates have access to treadmills, stationary bikes, ellipticals, and rowing machines. Outside, inmates have access to a weight pile, track, six handball courts, two tennis courts, softball, basketball, soccer, volleyball, and ping pong. Hours of operation are 6:00 to 10:00 a.m., 12:00 to 3:30 p.m., and 4:30 to 8:30 p.m. on weekdays and 6:30 to 9:30 a.m., 10:30 to 3:30 p.m., and 4:30 to 8:30 p.m. on weekends.

Visitation Information: On Sunday and Saturday visitation is held between 8:00 a.m. and 3:00 p.m. On federal holidays visitation is held between 8:00 a.m. and 3:00 p.m. See Chapter 1 for more information on visitation.

Prison Politics: This is a somewhat political yard, though it appears that all can walk. According to inmate reports, if an inmate has bad paperwork, they will suffer from some ostracization, but not violence. There is no gang or car requirement.

Level of Violence: There is very little violence at this prison. One respondent stated, "Over the past two years the prison has become progressively soft and softer." Another inmate expressed that "overall this is a safe yard, no random acts of violence." One inmate pegged the violence level at a 1 out of 10, explaining, "There is no real violence here."

Vulnerable Populations: Sex offenders, informants, and LGBT inmates can stay, though, according to one inmate, they are "tormented and taken advantage of." The same person explained that "staff is just as hard on sex offenders as inmates are." Another inmate expressed that "sex offenders have segregated seating in the chow hall and their own TV to watch." Another inmate somewhat disagreed, stating that all three groups could stay and that it's "all cool."

Good: "Education, particularly college program; open compound on the evenings and weekends; trees, tables, and palm trees." "Food, rec, and UNICOR are good." "Food is pretty good, lots of sunshine, and beautiful mountains to look at." "The freedom and so many things to do." "The guards are helpful."

Bad: "Tense politics amongst the whites." "The way staff treat inmates, and sex offenders in particular, is bad." "The administration is getting rid of some of the shade trees and seating in the recreation area."

Other Comments: "Non-sex offenders will like this yard. Sex offenders and informants will be excluded from some areas, such as the weight pile. Laid back staff. Very pro-education." "Overall a good yard, and safe yard for all." "It's a good, kick-back yard."

In the News: In February 2016, former police officer Karl Thompson was released from Federal Correctional Institution Safford after completing his 51-month sentence for the beating death of janitor Otto Zehm.

MCC San Diego

Metropolitan Correctional Center San Diego | MCC San Diego

Facility Address & Contact Information

Metropolitan Correctional Center San Diego
808 Union Street
San Diego, CA 92101

Phone: 619-232-4311
Fax: 619-595-0390
Email: SDC/ExecAssistant@bop.gov

BOP Website: https://www.bop.gov/locations/institutions/sdc/
Wikipedia: https://en.wikipedia.org/wiki/Metropolitan_Correctional_Center,_San_Diego
ZCG Website: https://www.prisonerresource.com/resources/federal-prison-profiles/western-region-wxr/metropolitan-correctional-center-san-diego-mcc-san-diego/

Inmate Correspondence Address

Inmate Name and Registration Number
MCC San Diego
Metropolitan Correctional Center
808 Union Street
San Diego, CA 92101

NOTE: Funds cannot be sent directly to federal inmates. See Chapter 1 for more information on sending funds to federal inmates.

Sex: Male and Female

Security Level: Administrative Security (Multiple Security Levels)

Location: MCC San Diego is located in downtown San Diego, adjacent to the federal courthouse.

BOP Region: Western Region (WXR)

BOP Institution Code: SDC for MCC San Diego

Judicial District: Southern District of California

Medical Care Level: Level 2. See Chapter 2 for more information on Medical Care and Mental Health Care Levels.

Mental Health Care Level: Level 2

Population (as of May 1, 2019): 941

Background: Metropolitan Correctional Center San Diego is an administrative-security federal prison in San Diego, California, which houses both male and female inmates. It was opened in 1974.

MCC San Diego was the Federal Bureau of Prisons' first high-rise.

Notable inmates include brothers and former U.S. Border Patrol agents Fidel and Raul Villarreal (serving sentences of 30 and 35 years respectively for operating a human smuggling ring), and MLB all-star Esteban Loaiza (charged with possession with intent to distribute more than 40 pounds of cocaine).

Media reports indicate that 32 federal misdemeanor charges had to be dismissed following a computer glitch in which 37 detainees were delayed in seeing a judge for arraignment.

Housing: Inmates are housed in one of nine housing units. Each housing unit contains 48 cells, which are either divided into dormitories or two-person cells.

Health Services: Sick call, chronic care, physical examinations, eyeglasses, medications, and emergency care are available. Inmates must submit a sick call form in order to be evaluated for routine care needs. Emergency health care is available 24 hours a day.

Psychology Services: Intake screening, evaluations requested by staff or the court, group and individual treatment, crisis intervention, and psychiatric consultation are available to inmates. Notices are posted in inmate housing units of upcoming treatment groups. In order to participate, inmates must submit an Inmate Request to Staff requesting program placement.

Residential Drug Abuse Program (RDAP): MCC San Diego does not offer the Residential Drug Abuse Program (RDAP), but referrals can be made to institutions that do provide RDAP. A Drug Education class and the Non-Residential Drug Abuse Program (NR-DAP) are available.

Education Services: MCC San Diego provides GED and English-as-a-Second Language (ESL) programs to inmates. Inmates who do not have a GED or high school diploma are required to participate in such classes. Parenting and release preparation classes are also available to inmates. High school diplomas and post-secondary degrees are available through paid correspondence programs.

Advanced Occupational Education: MCC San Diego does not offer any advanced occupational education programs.

Vocational Training: MCC San Diego does not offer any vocational training programs.

Apprenticeship: MCC San Diego does not offer any apprenticeship programs.

Library Services: MCC San Diego offers both a leisure and law library. The leisure library offers magazines, newspapers, fiction, nonfiction, and reference books. Inmates are provided access to legal materials and an opportunity to prepare legal documents through the use of the TRULINCS Electronic Law Library. A copy machine is available to reproduce materials needed for research. Electric typewriters are also available for inmate use.

UNICOR: MCC San Diego does not house a UNICOR facility.

Commissary: Inmates can purchase commissary items on a weekly basis by submitting a commissary sheet. The commissary spending limit is $360.00 per month. Items such as food, snacks, ice cream, electronics, and other items can be purchased. Postage stamps and over-the-counter medications do not count against the spending limit.

Recreation Services: Recreation equipment is available within each MCC San Diego housing unit and on the roof recreation area. Various board games are also available in each housing unit.

Visitation Information: On Sunday and Saturday visitation is held between 8:00 a.m. and 3:30 p.m. On Monday, Thursday, and Friday visitation is held between 4:45 and 9:00 p.m. On federal holidays visitation is held between 8:00 a.m. and 3:30 p.m. See Chapter 1 for more information on visitation.

In the News: In May 2018, computer problems delayed 37 detainees at Metropolitan Correctional Center San Diego from seeing a judge in a timely manner, resulting in 32 misdemeanor charges being dismissed.

In March 2018, Major League Baseball All-Star Esteban Loaiza was federally indicted for the possession of more than 40 pounds of cocaine with intent to distribute and taken to MCC San Diego to await trial.

FDC SeaTac

Federal Detention Center SeaTac | FDC SeaTac

Facility Address & Contact Information

Federal Detention Center SeaTac
2425 South 200th Street
Seattle, WA 98198

Phone: 206-870-5700
Fax: 206-870-5717
Email: SET/ExecAssistant@bop.gov

BOP Website: https://www.bop.gov/locations/institutions/set/
Wikipedia: https://en.wikipedia.org/wiki/Federal_Detention_Center,_SeaTac
ZCG Website: https://www.prisonerresource.com/resources/federal-prison-profiles/western-region-wxr/federal-detention-center-seatac-fdc-seatac/

Inmate Correspondence Address

Inmate Name and Registration Number
FDC SeaTac
Federal Detention Center
P.O. Box 13900
Seattle, WA 98198

NOTE: Funds cannot be sent directly to federal inmates. See Chapter 1 for more information on sending funds to federal inmates.

Sex: Male and Female

Security Level: Administrative Security (Multiple Security Levels)

Location: FDC SeaTac is located 12 miles south of Seattle, 16 miles north of Tacoma, 1 mile west of I-5 (200th Street exit).

BOP Region: Western Region (WXR)

BOP Institution Code: SET for FDC SeaTac

Judicial District: Western District of Washington

Medical Care Level: Level 2. See Chapter 2 for more information on Medical Care and Mental Health Care Levels.

Mental Health Care Level: Level 2

Population (as of May 1, 2019): 667

Background: Federal Detention Center SeaTac is an administrative-security federal prison in Seattle, Washington, which houses both male and female inmates. It was opened in 1988.

FDC SeaTac primarily houses pre-trial and pre-sentence detainees, as well as holdover inmates.

Notable inmates include Colton Harris-Moore (served time for theft and burglary), cannabis advocate Marc Emery, and drug lord Clayton Roueche.

Media reports indicate that one guard was indicted for possession of child pornography, another guard was indicted for threatening to kill his wife after he learned about a Jerry Springer tape, and one woman was indicted for mailing greeting cards to inmates which contained methamphetamines.

Housing: Inmates are housed either in two-person cells or dormitories.

Health Services: Medical and dental sick call, physical examinations, x-rays, TB tests, medications, chronic care, urgent medical and dental care, routine care, and dentures are all provided at FDC SeaTac. Emergency medical care is available 24 hours a day.

Psychology Services: Psychology services at FDC SeaTac include crisis intervention, suicide prevention, brief individual counseling, biblio-therapy (self-help reading material), medication referrals, and forensic evaluations (for select inmates). Group counseling services are also periodically available for inmates. Groups have been offered in anger management, stress management, coping skills, and dealing with trauma (which includes female inmates with histories of physical and/or sexual abuse).

Residential Drug Abuse Program (RDAP): FDC SeaTac does not offer the Residential Drug Abuse Program (RDAP), but referrals can be made to institutions that do provide RDAP. The facility does provide a Drug Education Class and the Non-Residential Drug Abuse Program (NR-DAP).

Education Services: FDC SeaTac provides GED and English-as-a-Second Language (ESL) programs. High school diplomas and post-secondary degrees are available through paid correspondence programs.

Advanced Occupational Education: FDC SeaTac does not offer any advanced occupational education programs.

Vocational Training: FDC SeaTac does not offer any vocational training programs.

Apprenticeship: FDC SeaTac does not offer any apprenticeship programs.

Library Services: The Education Department maintains a mobile leisure book cart in all housing units, including the Special Housing Unit (SHU). The carts are rotated bi-weekly. The Education Department also provides a wide variety of magazines and newspapers (English and Spanish) that are distributed to the units. The law library is contained in an electronic law database accessible via computer workstations in each unit. Most legal materials can be located by performing a search on the TRULINCS Electronic Law Library database.

UNICOR: FDC SeaTac does not house a UNICOR facility.

Commissary: FDC SeaTac operates a commissary which provides numerous items for inmate purchase. Inmates are not limited to the amount of money they may spend at any one time but may not spend more $360.00 per month. Inmates are permitted to shop once a week on their designated shopping day.

Recreation Services: Indoor and outdoor activities are available, including aerobics, ping pong, hobbycraft classes, chess club/chess class, wellness and nutrition programs, screenwriting class, movies, and abs class. There are 10 federal holidays in which additional activities are offered. During these specific holidays special tournaments are held (e.g., bingo, card tournaments, pool, ping pong, basketball, and volleyball).

Visitation Information: On Sunday and Saturday visitation is held between 7:30 a.m. and 2:30 p.m. On Monday and Friday visitation is held between 2:00 and 9:00 p.m. On federal holidays visitation is held between 7:30 a.m. and 2:30 p.m. See Chapter 1 for more information on visitation.

In the News: In July 2018, Yolany Padilla, one of 55 parents at Federal Detention Center SeaTac who were separated from their children at the border as part of the Trump Administration's "zero tolerance" policy, was the first to be released, though without her child.

In June 2018, thousands of people protested outside FDC SeaTac, where more than 150 migrant detainees were being held. The protesters opposed the Trump Administration's "zero tolerance" policy and the separation of immigrant parents from their children.

In October 2014, William Cline, a guard at FDC SeaTac, admitted to downloading child pornography and was placed on administrative leave.

In June 2011, Lakewood, Washington, resident Michael A. Tharp was brought to FDC SeaTac after being charged with possession of child pornography. Tharp was also suspected of sending child porn to civilly committed sex offenders being held at Washington State's McNeil Island Special Commitment Center.

In May 2008, the director of the Southeast Asian Ceramics Museum in Bangkok, Thailand, who was being held at FDC SeaTac for wire fraud, died there as a result of peritonitis.

In December 2003, the Drug Enforcement Agency arrested Kristina Landry for sending cards laced with methamphetamine to a prisoner being held at FDC SeaTac.

In February 2003, Dennis Fontenot, a guard at FDC SeaTac, was charged with felony harassment after threatening to kill his wife over a Jerry Springer tape.

FCI Sheridan

Federal Correctional Institution Sheridan | FCI Sheridan

Facilities: FCI Sheridan including a detention center, and an adjacent minimum-security satellite prison camp.

Facility Address & Contact Information

Federal Correctional Institution Sheridan
27072 Ballston Road
Sheridan, OR 97378

Phone: 503-843-4442
Fax: 503-843-3408
Email: SHE/ExecAssistant@bop.gov

BOP Website: https://www.bop.gov/locations/institutions/she/
Wikipedia: https://en.wikipedia.org/wiki/Federal_Correctional_Institution,_Sheridan
ZCG Website: https://www.prisonerresource.com/resources/federal-prison-profiles/western-region-wxr/federal-correctional-institution-sheridan-fci-sheridan/

Inmate Correspondence Address

For FCI Sheridan and Detention Center

Inmate Name and Registration Number
FCI Sheridan
Federal Correctional Institution
P.O. Box 5000
Sheridan, OR 97378

For Satellite Prison Camp

Inmate Name and Registration Number
FCI Sheridan
Satellite Prison Camp
P.O. Box 6000
Sheridan, OR 97378

NOTE: Funds cannot be sent directly to federal inmates. See Chapter 1 for more information on sending funds to federal inmates.

Sex: Male

Security Level: Main: Medium Security; Detention Center: Administrative Security (Multiple Security Levels); Camp: Minimum Security

Location: FCI Sheridan is located in northwestern Oregon, 90 minutes south of Portland, off Highway 18 on Ballston Road.

BOP Region: Western Region (WXR)

BOP Institution Code: SHE for FCI Sheridan

Judicial District: District of Oregon

Medical Care Level: Level 2. See Chapter 2 for more information on Medical Care and Mental Health Care Levels.

Mental Health Care Level: Level 2

Population (as of May 1, 2019): Main & Detention Center: 1,271; Camp: 521

Background: Federal Correctional Institution Sheridan is a medium-security federal prison in Sheridan, Oregon, which houses male inmates. It was opened in 1989. Federal Correctional Institution Sheridan Camp, which also houses male inmates, was opened in 1989 and is located adjacent to the main institution.

FCI Sheridan also includes a detention center. This is the only federal prison in Oregon. The facility is designed in a style that resembles a college campus, with the concrete, two-story structures modeled after dormitories.

Notable inmates include former FBI-Ten-Most-Wanted fugitive Leslie Rogge (serving a 65-year sentence for bank robbery), Robert Gomez (serving 21 years for orchestrating the Miracle cars scam), and Earth Liberation Front member Tre Arrow (served 78 months for arson).

Media reports indicate that there has been one inmate murdered, five prisoners indicted for assaults, two guards stabbed, one inmate charged with money laundering, one guard indicted for smuggling drugs into the prison, and one guard indicted for kidnapping, raping, and choking a woman while off-duty. Additionally, news reports state that a large fight occurred at the camp in 2014.

In 2012, CNBC named FCI Sheridan one of the 12 best federal prisons in which to do time. In 2009, *Forbes* magazine named the facility one of the ten cushiest federal prisons in America. And in 2005, *The Kansas City Star* named the institution one of the five best federal prisons for white collar offenders.

Housing: Inmates are housed in two-person cells. There are four housing units. Inmates at the camp are housed in dormitories, which are divided into four-person cubicles.

Health Services: Sick call, dental care, physical examinations, emergency care, medications, and testing for infectious diseases are available. Inmates are assigned to a specific health care provider who treats them for the duration of their stay. Emergency medical care is available 24 hours a day.

Psychology Services: A psychologist is available to diagnose, provide therapy services, and evaluate prisoners. Regular group therapy classes include anger management, stress management, HIV/AIDS awareness, and criminal thinking.

Residential Drug Abuse Program (RDAP): Both FCI Sheridan and the camp offer the Residential Drug Abuse Program (RDAP). Drug Education programs, the Non-Residential Drug Abuse Program (NR-DAP), and Alcoholics Anonymous (AA) are also available.

Education Services: FCI Sheridan provides GED and English-as-a-Second Language (ESL) programs to inmates. Parenting and Adult Continuing Education (ACE) programs are also available. High school diplomas and post-secondary degrees are available through paid correspondence programs. At FDC Sheridan, inmates can complete educational packets on topics such as anger management, math, government, poetry, and others.

Advanced Occupational Education: FCI Sheridan and the camp offer advanced occupational education programs in Basic Woodworking, Building Trades, Desktop Publisher, Microsoft Excel, Microsoft PowerPoint, Microsoft Publisher, Microsoft Windows, Microsoft Word, Microsoft Word 2, and QuickBooks. The camp also offers Computer-Aided Design and Landscape Design.

Vocational Training: FCI Sheridan and the camp offer vocational training in Google Sketchup, Microsoft Excel, Microsoft PowerPoint/Publisher, Microsoft Word, Personal Fitness Trainer, and QuickBooks. The camp also offers vocational training in Basic Horticulture and Pesticide Applications.

Apprenticeship: FCI Sheridan offers apprenticeships in Baking, Barber, Building Maintenance, Cabinet Worker, Call Center Clerk, Cook, Landscape Management Technician, Office Management Clerk, Plumber, Sanitation Technician, Solar Technician, and Wood Turning Lathe Operator. The camp offers apprenticeships in Career Clerk, Dental Assistant, Farmworker, and Landscape Technician. Both facilities offer apprenticeships in Electrical, HVAC, Personal Fitness Trainer, and Teacher Aide.

Library Services: Both a leisure and law library are available for inmate use. The leisure library offers fiction and nonfiction books, magazines, and newspapers. The law library contains a variety of legal reference materials for use in preparing legal papers. Reference materials include the United States Code Annotated, Federal Reporter, Supreme Court Reporter, Bureau of Prisons Program Statements, institution supplements, indexes, and other legal materials. Most of these are available on the TRULINCS Electronic Law Library. The law library also houses typewriters and a copy machine.

UNICOR: The FCI Sheridan UNICOR facility produces electronics and plastics. The camp does not have a UNICOR facility.

Commissary: The Commissary Card is also an identification card. If an inmate leaves the housing unit, they must have the Commissary/I.D. Card in their possession. The monthly spending limit is $360, which is further restricted to $180 every two weeks. Inmates can purchase a wide variety of items from the commissary. Inmates can only shop once a week in the commissary on their designated shopping day.

Recreation Services: A wide variety of recreational activities are offered at FCI Sheridan. Sports and games are offered, including softball, flag football, soccer, bocce ball, horseshoes, volleyball, handball, racquetball, and basketball. Fitness equipment (e.g., ellipticals, treadmills, and stationary bikes), a hobby shop, and a central Recreation Area with ping pong tables, exercise equipment, and band room are also available. In the main prison, games (e.g. dominoes) are on the unit, and there is also an Inmate Photo Program. There is also a track. Inmates at FDC Sheridan have access to a small outdoor area for one hour each day.

Visitation Information: On Sunday, Friday, and Saturday visitation is held between 8:30 a.m. and 3:00 p.m. On federal holidays visitation is held between 8:30 a.m. and 3:00 p.m. See Chapter 1 for more information on visitation.

Prison Politics: This is a somewhat political yard.

Level of Violence: There is minimal violence at this prison. According to one respondent, "You have tough guys everywhere."

Vulnerable Populations: While some respondents stated that sex offenders and informants can't stay, others said that both groups, as well as LGBT inmates could stay. According to one inmate, "In the FDC, sex offenders, informants, LGBT inmates, and check-ins can walk in the J1 dorm." One respondent stated that in both the FCI and FDC that sex offenders sometimes pay the racial group's shot callers in order to stay.

Good: "Good college campus atmosphere, very nicely appointed cells, and trees." "Nice yard." "Skylights in day room."

Bad: "Nothing is good about any prison. Life stops for most locked up."

Other Comments: "I would endorse it."

In the News: In June 2018, District Judge Michael Simon approved an emergency temporary restraining order against Immigration and Customs Enforcement and the Bureau of Prisons after more than 100 immigration detainees at Federal Correctional Institution Sheridan were refused access to legal counsel in violation of their constitutional due process rights.

In July 2017, Shannon Jones, who pleaded guilty to defrauding 43 people out of $1.4 million, reported to FCI Sheridan to begin his two-and-a-half-year sentence.

In 2017, Emanuel Astacio-Arriagathe, a known Puerto Rican Netas gang member, was sentenced to 26 years and eight months in prison for the murder of Hector Orlando Salgado-Valderrama. In 2014, while a prisoner at FCI Sheridan, Astacio-Arriagathe had beat Salgado-Valderrama to death with a mop handle. When the mop handle broke, Astacio-Arriagathe kicked Salgado-Valderrama in the head while wearing his steel-toed work boots.

In June 2016, Victor Alas-Felix, a prisoner at FCI Sheridan who participated in a gang-related assault in May 2015, was sentenced to 40 months in prison.

In May 2015, four prisoners at FCI Sheridan -- Jose Carlos Acosta Jr., Omar Mendoza, Javier Rodriguez Tijerina Jr., and Victor Alas-Felix -- punched and kicked an unnamed prisoner unconscious, then attacked him again after he regained consciousness and tried to leave.

In October 2014, Sajoh C. Yates, a prisoner at FCI Sheridan who was diagnosed with paranoid schizophrenia, attacked and slashed the faces of two guards with a razor and was subsequently sent back to Federal Medical Center Springfield.

In January 2011, Harold James Nicholson, who was serving a 283-month sentence at FCI Sheridan for espionage, was sentenced to an additional eight years for conspiring to launder money while in prison.

In March 2008, James Rolan, a guard at FCI Sheridan, was sentenced to two years in prison for possession of heroin with intent to distribute by smuggling it into the prison.

In April 2005, Robert Stamper, a guard at FCI Sheridan, was sentenced to 61 years in state prison after being convicted of kidnapping an 18-year-old woman at gunpoint, raping her, choking her unconscious and leaving her for dead.

Camp in the News: In September 2014, a fight broke out among a group of prisoners at FCI Sheridan Camp.

FCI Terminal Island

Federal Correctional Institution Terminal Island | FCI Terminal Island

Facility Address & Contact Information

Federal Correctional Institution Terminal Island
1299 Seaside Avenue
San Pedro, CA 90731

Phone: 310-831-8961
Fax: 310-732-5325
Email: TRM/ExecAssistant@bop.gov

BOP Website: https://www.bop.gov/locations/institutions/trm/
Wikipedia: https://en.wikipedia.org/wiki/Federal_Correctional_Institution%2C_Terminal_Island
ZCG Website: https://www.prisonerresource.com/resources/federal-prison-profiles/western-region-wxr/federal-correctional-institution-terminal-island-fci-terminal-island/

Inmate Correspondence Address

Inmate Name and Registration Number
FCI Terminal Island
Federal Correctional Institution
P. O. Box 3007
San Pedro, CA 90733

NOTE: Funds cannot be sent directly to federal inmates. See Chapter 1 for more information on sending funds to federal inmates.

Sex: Male

Security Level: Low Security

Location: FCI Terminal Island is located in Los Angeles Harbor, between San Pedro and Long Beach; off Harbor Freeway (110 South) at the Terminal Island exit.

BOP Region: Western Region (WXR)

BOP Institution Code: TRM for FCI Terminal Island

Judicial District: Central District of California

Medical Care Level: Level 2/3. See Chapter 2 for more information on Medical Care and Mental Health Care Levels.

Mental Health Care Level: Level 3

Population (as of May 1, 2019): 1,142

Background: Federal Correctional Institution Terminal Island is a low-security federal prison in San Pedro, California, which houses male inmates. It was opened in 1938.

FCI Terminal Island served as the Naval Disciplinary Barracks from 1942 to 1950. For a period, it was also a medical facility for the California Department of Corrections. In 1995, it was converted into the low-security federal prison it is today. FCI Terminal Island serves as a medical facility for the Federal Bureau of Prisons.

Notable inmates include internet music entrepreneur Mouli Cohen (serving 22 years for wire fraud, money laundering, and tax evasion); Earth Liberation Front member Eric McDavid (served 10 years for conspiracy to destroy a dam, a lab, and other targets); former stockbroker Anthony Elgindy (served eight years for racketeering conspiracy, wire fraud, securities fraud, and extortion); Admiral Robert Gilbeau (served 18 months for lying to investigators); and former LAPD detective Randy Adair (convicted of bank robbery).

Media reports indicate that at least one guard has been indicted for smuggling contraband into the prison.

Housing: Inmates are housed in various housing structures ranging from dormitories to one- and two-person cells. E, F, and J Units have two-person cells (E and J Units also have toilets in the cell). A, B, C, D, and K Units are open dormitories (only K Unit has air conditioning).

Health Services: On-site emergency medical care, sick call, dental care, and medication are all provided at FCI Terminal Island. Emergency care is available 24 hours a day. Sick call is conducted at 6:30 a.m. on Monday, Tuesday, and Thursday.

Psychology Services: FCI Terminal Island offers screening, assessment, and treatment of mental health and drug abuse problems, individual and group counseling, psycho-educational classes, self-help and supportive services, and referral to Health Services for medical treatment of a mental illness. Notices of upcoming treatment programs are posted in inmate housing units. Inmates must submit a cop-out requesting program placement.

Residential Drug Abuse Program (RDAP): FCI Terminal Island offers the Residential Drug Abuse Program (RDAP). The facility also provides drug education classes and a Non-Residential Drug Abuse Program (NR-DAP).

Education Services: FCI Terminal Island offers literacy, GED, and English-as-a-Second Language (ESL) programs to inmates. Incentive awards are provided to recognize inmates making satisfactory progress and successfully completing the literacy (i.e., GED and ESL) program. Inmates may also receive incentives for progressing to various levels in the GED or ESL programs. Graduation ceremonies recognize GED, ESL, and Occupational Education completions. A parenting program, Release Preparation Program (RPP), and Adult Continuing Education (ACE) classes are also available. High school diplomas and post-secondary degrees are available through paid correspondence programs. Coastline Community College also offers classes to inmates. Hours of operation are 7:30 a.m. to 3:30 p.m. and 5:00 to 7:00 p.m. Monday through Thursday, and 7:30 a.m. to 3:30 p.m. Friday and Saturday, excluding meals and counts.

Advanced Occupational Education: FCI Terminal Island offers advanced occupational education in Carpentry, CFC, Electrical Home Wiring, Home Inspection, Plumbing, and Welding.

Vocational Training: FCI Terminal Island does not offer any vocational training aside from its advanced occupational education programs and apprenticeships.

Apprenticeship: FCI Terminal Island offers apprenticeships in Baking, Cooking, AutoCAD, Cabinet Making, Dental Assistant, Electrical, Electrostatic Powder Paint Machine, Engraver, HVAC, Industrial Truck Mechanic, Machine Setter, Maintenance Repairer, Material Coordinator, Pipefitter, Plumbing, Production Planner-Shipping Clerk, Quality Control, Stationary Engineer, and Tool and Die (Machinist).

Library Services: The leisure library offers inmates a variety of reading materials, including periodicals, newspapers, fiction, nonfiction, and reference books. An interlibrary loan program is also available. The TRULINCS Electronic Law Library allows inmates to access to legal materials and an opportunity to prepare legal documents. Typewriters and a copy machine are also available for inmate use.

UNICOR: FCI Terminal Island does not have a UNICOR facility.

Commissary: Inmates may use funds in their account to purchase items at the institution commissary, place funds on their inmate phone account, purchase TRU-Units for their TRULINCS account, or send funds out of the institution using Form BP-199. The spending limit is $360.00 per month. Inmates may only shop on their designated shopping day each week. Regular sales are conducted at 12:00 and 3:30 p.m. Monday through Thursday. Over-the-counter medications are sold on Friday to all inmates.

Recreation Services: FCI Terminal Island provides a variety of leisure, wellness, and social programs to inmates. Leisure activities include organized and informal games, sports,

physical fitness, table games, hobbycrafts, music programs, intramural activities, social and cultural organizations, and movies. Art activities include paintings and sketches using traditional methods (e.g., oils, pastels, crayons, pencils, inks, and charcoal). Hobbycraft activities include ceramics, leatherwork, models, clay, mosaics, crochet, knitting, sculptures, woodworking, and lapidary. Wellness programs include screening, assessments, goal setting, fitness/nutrition plans, and counseling. Inside, inmates have access to yoga, pool tables, TVs, and more. Outside, inmates have access to a weight pile, track, basketball, handball, shuffleboard, bocce ball, horseshoes, softball, flag football, soccer, and volleyball.

Visitation Information: On Sunday, Monday, and Saturday visitation is held between 8:00 a.m. and 3:00 p.m. On federal holidays visitation is held between 8:00 a.m. and 3:00 p.m. See Chapter 1 for more information on visitation.

Prison Politics: There is a low level of prison politics at this facility. According to one respondent, "this is a wannabe political yard." Another inmate explained, "There are some politics. The chow hall is segregated by race and political group." One respondent explained, "The politics are a joke from a bunch of gang drop-outs, snitches, gays, and sex offenders who all want to act like they are still solid gang members."

Level of Violence: While some inmates stated that there was no violence, others assert that there is a moderate level of violence. As put by one inmate, "not too violent, but more than most Lows." Another explained, "While there are occasional fights, they don't seem to be anything to worry about as long as you are respectful and mind your own business."

Vulnerable Populations: Sex offenders, informants, and LGBT inmates can walk the yard. One respondent explained that "it is their yard." Another stated, "They can all walk the yard, but they can't watch TV." One inmate explained, "They can do any programs, classes, or jobs that they want." The same inmate disagreed about the TVs, stating that they can "even watch the TVs."

Good: "The food and location are great." "It's by the water." "Lack of violence." "The food isn't too bad."

Bad: "Bad medical, and dental services are horrible." "The staff are extremely unprofessional." "Medical care is horrible." "Lots of fake politics and idiots who bark but who couldn't make it elsewhere." "The compound is falling apart; the buildings all look like they are abandoned."

Other Comments: "Most of the departments and programs are on par with other facilities in lack of care or benefit from participation." "The place is staffed with rejects from everywhere else. They are about the least professional group you're going to find."

In the News: In July 2015, Randy Adair, aka the Snowbird Bandit, a former LAPD detective who decided to start robbing banks in his retirement, was arrested, convicted, and sent to Federal Correctional Institution Terminal Island.

In February 2015, Luis Borjon, a guard at FCI Terminal Island, was sentenced to two days in jail with time served, 160 hours of community service and two years of supervised release for his role in smuggling cell phones into the facility.

FCC Tucson

Federal Correctional Complex Tucson | FCC Tucson

Facilities: FCC Tucson houses USP Tucson and an adjacent minimum-security satellite prison camp, and FCI Tucson with a detention center.

USP Tucson

United States Penitentiary Tucson | USP Tucson

Facilities: USP Tucson and an adjacent minimum-security satellite prison camp.

Facility Address & Contact Information

United States Penitentiary Tucson
9300 South Wilmot Road
Tucson, AZ 85756

Phone: 520-663-5000
Fax: 520-663-5024
Email: TCP/ExecAssistant@bop.gov

BOP Website: https://www.bop.gov/locations/institutions/tcp/
Wikipedia: https://en.wikipedia.org/wiki/United_States_Penitentiary,_Tucson
ZCG Website: https://www.prisonerresource.com/resources/federal-prison-profiles/western-region-wxr/federal-correctional-complex-tucson-fcc-tucson/united-states-penitentiary-tucson-usp-tucson/

Inmate Correspondence Address

For USP Tucson

Inmate Name and Registration Number
USP Tucson
U.S. Penitentiary
P.O. Box 24550
Tucson, AZ 85734

For Satellite Prison Camp

Inmate Name and Registration Number
USP Tucson
Satellite Prison Camp
P.O. Box 24549
Tucson, AZ 85734

NOTE: Funds cannot be sent directly to federal inmates. See Chapter 1 for more information on sending funds to federal inmates.

Sex: Male

Security Level: Main: High Security; Camp: Minimum Security

Location: USP Tucson is located in southern Arizona, 10 miles southeast of Tucson, near I-10 and Wilmot Road.

BOP Region: Western Region (WXR)

BOP Institution Code: TCP for USP Tucson and the camp, TCX for Tucson Federal Correctional Complex (FCC)

Judicial District: District of Arizona

Medical Care Level: Level 2/3. See Chapter 2 for more information on Medical Care and Mental Health Care Levels.

Mental Health Care Level: Level 3

Population (as of May 1, 2019): Main: 1,357; Camp: 143

Background: United States Penitentiary Tucson is a high-security federal prison in Tucson, Arizona, which houses male inmates. It is part of the Tucson Federal Correctional Complex. United States Penitentiary Tucson Camp, which also houses male inmates, is located adjacent to the main institution.

USP Tucson is a Sex Offender Management Program (SOMP) facility, which means that approximately 40 percent of the inmate population is incarcerated for either a current or past sexual offense.

Notable inmates include former USA Gymnastics doctor Larry Nasser (serving 60 years for production of child pornography and other sexual offenses), James "Whitey" Bulger, and Elizabeth Smart's kidnapper.

Media reports indicate that Larry Nasser was assaulted in a coordinated attack while at the prison. Inmates at the facility reported that the multi-person and multi-location assaults were designed to draw staff to one area of the prison while other inmates attempted to kill Nasser.

Housing: Inmates are housed in one and two-person cells. There is a total of 12 housing units. Inmates in the camp are housed in dormitories.

Health Services: Sick call, dental care, physical examinations, chronic care, medical and dental emergency care, medication, HIV testing, and eyeglasses, are available to the inmate population. Emergency medical care is available 24 hours a day. Medical sick call is held at 12:30 p.m. on Monday, Wednesday, Thursday, and Friday. Dental sick call is held on Monday and Friday at 7:00 a.m. Medication refills can be collected on Monday, Wednesday, Thursday, and Friday during the noon meal.

Psychology Services: USP Tucson offers screening, assessment, and treatment of mental health and drug abuse problems, individual and group counseling, psycho-educational classes (e.g., anger management, PTSD, etc.), self-help and supportive services, and referral to Health Services for medical treatment of mental illness. A self-help library is available. A Non-Residential Sex Offender Treatment Program (SOTP-NR) is available, as is the Challenge Program for inmates who are prone to substance abuse, mental illness, and violence.

Residential Drug Abuse Program (RDAP): Neither USP Tucson nor the camp offer the Residential Drug Abuse Program (RDAP), but referrals can be made to institutions that do provide RDAP. Both facilities provide Drug Education classes and a Non-Residential Drug Abuse Program (NR-DAP).

Education Services: USP Tucson offers GED and English-as-a-Second Language (ESL). Inmates who do not possess a GED or high school diploma are required to attend educational programming. Parenting and Adult Continuing Education (ACE) programs are also available.

ACE classes are both classroom- and video-based. INEA-Mexican High School Diploma Program students can have concurrent enrollment in GED literacy and in INEA-Mexican High School Diploma Program. The Mexican Consulate offers certificates in primary and secondary education through the Education Department. The Mexican curriculum is a voluntary program open to any student wishing to receive accreditation from the Mexican Government in either program. The Education Department offers a variety of re-entry classes to assist inmates in making a productive reintegration into society. High school diplomas and post-secondary degrees are available through paid correspondence programs. Pima Community College also offers a business certificate program.

Advanced Occupational Education: USP Tucson and the camp provide advanced occupational education in Basic & Advanced Baking, Business Management, and ServSafe.

Vocational Training: USP Tucson does not offer any vocational training programs.

Apprenticeship: USP Tucson offers apprenticeships in Cooking, Custodial Maintenance, Electrician, HVAC, Plumbing, and Pastry Cook. The camp does not offer any apprenticeships.

Library: USP Tucson offers both a leisure and law library to inmates. The leisure library offers magazines, newspapers, fiction, nonfiction, and reference books. An interlibrary loan program is also available. Inmates are provided access to legal materials and an opportunity to prepare legal documents through the use of the TRULINCS Electronic Law Library. A copy machine is available to reproduce materials needed for research. Electric typewriters and NEO word processors are also available for inmate use.

UNICOR: USP Tucson does not house a UNICOR facility.

Commissary: Inmates may use funds in their account to purchase items at the institution commissary, place funds on their inmate phone account, purchase TRU-Units for their TRULINCS account, or send funds out of the institution using Form BP-199. The monthly spending limit is $360.00, which is further restricted to $180 biweekly. Popular items include ice cream, sodas, candy, food, clothing, electronics, and shoes. Over-the-counter medications, copy cards, and postage stamps do not count against this limit. Commissary is open Monday through Thursday from 8:00 a.m. to 2:00 p.m. Inmates are only permitted to shop once a week, with their housing unit.

Recreation Services: USP Tucson provides a variety of leisure, wellness, and social programs to inmates. Leisure activities include organized and informal games, sports, physical fitness, table games, hobbycrafts, music programs, intramural activities, social and cultural organizations, and movies. Art activities include paintings and sketches using traditional methods (e.g., oils, pastels, crayons, pencils, inks, and charcoal). Hobbycraft activities include models, crochet, knitting, mini sticks, beading, origami, etc. Wellness programs include screening, assessments, goal setting, and fitness/nutrition plans and counseling. Inside, inmates have access to pool tables, TVs, band room, art room, yoga room, piano room, barber shop, ping pong, tables, darts, basketball, ellipticals, treadmills, stair steppers, stationary bikes, and a gaming program. Outside, inmates have access to soccer, basketball, bocce ball, softball, horseshoes, football, handball, stationary bikes, and track. Hours of operation are 8:00 to 10:00 a.m., 1:00 to 3:00 p.m., and 6:00 to 8:00 p.m. On the weekdays, both North and South sides rec together. On weekends, rec times rotates between the two sides.

Visitation Information: On Sunday and Saturday visitation is held between 8:15 a.m. and 3:00 p.m. On Friday visitation is held between 5:00 and 8:00 p.m. On federal holidays visitation is held between 8:15 a.m. and 3:00 p.m. See Chapter 1 for more information on visitation.

Prison Politics: Different inmates report that this is either a somewhat political yard or not political at all. There is a consensus that there are a lot of sex offenders and gang drop-outs. As reported by one inmate, "This is only a political yard if you want it to be. There are no actual politics here." While there is no car requirement, this is still a USP and cars are prevalent.

Level of Violence: Depending on respondent, there is either very little, moderate, or a high level of violence at this prison. This seems to be highly dependent on what group the inmate associates with. Most respondents said that there was a low level of violence, especially considering that this is a USP. Of the reported violence, most was the result of "dope fiends not paying their bills" or "someone looking to check-in by hitting someone." One respondent summed it up by saying that "there is no real violence here unless you click up and go out on dummy missions." One inmate did report that there were frequent fights, but fewer stabbings. This appears to be the minority opinion.

Vulnerable Populations: Sex offenders, informants, and LGBT inmates can walk the yard. Since the institution is a SOMP yard, there is a higher sex offender population.

Good: "The weather is so good that you can wear shorts year-round, people are respectful, and the food is good." "Non-political, nothing else good." "The food is not bad, and lockdowns are infrequent."

Bad: "Hot and violent. The reason for violence is often sex-oriented." "No grass, no green, and surrounded by a wall." "Everything, really hot weather, intolerant staff attitude, sexual assaults amongst inmates." "SIS has so little to do that they write up a lot of petty and bullshit shots to fill their quotas." "People here go to the SHU for the most stupid things possible. If you use any pen pal site, you get a 200-series shot." "The mail room often loses your mail and it's otherwise always very late." "Many normal magazines are banned here." "The staff here do as little as possible to help anyone." "Health care is awful and understaffed. A lot of inmates die from neglect and poor treatment." "There is no UNICOR so there is minimal money to be made here."

Other Comments: "While a USP, softer than some others. This depends in large part on who you associate with. Harder groups equate to harder time." "Not the worst USP around, but still a USP. You don't have to roll with a car. Your time here will depend greatly on the group that you affiliate with." "As far as USPs go, not a bad or violent place." "Don't go unless you are a sex offender and have to be in a USP. Softer than other USPs." "There is more good than bad here, but it's very petty." "This is a laid-back yard. There is no 'posting-up' for showers, rooms, or anything. We can walk in flip-flop shower shoes if we want. A lot of the staff are here because they cannot 'walk' other yards."

In the News: In May 2018, former USA Gymnastics doctor Larry Nasser, who was sentenced to 60 years in prison for the production of child pornography, was assaulted by other prisoners at United States Penitentiary Tucson, a higher-security protective custody yard.

In early 2016, civil rights activist and revolutionary Jamil Al-Amin (formerly H. Rap Brown), who is serving a life sentence for the killing of a police officer, was moved to USP Tucson. Al-Amin was a federal political target for decades before his murder conviction and has been blocked from speaking to journalists for the past 17 years because the Bureau still considers him to be a "security risk." He spent seven years in solitary confinement at ADX Florence before being sent to Federal Medical Center Butner, United States Penitentiary Canaan and finally USP Tucson.

Camp in the News: In July 2018, Oscar Delgado and Oscar Estrada, both serving time at Federal Correctional Institution Tucson Camp for possession with intent to distribute drugs, were discovered missing.

In March 2018, Juan Carlos Dorado, who was being held at FCI Tucson Camp for money laundering and intent to distribute methamphetamines, went missing.

FCI Tucson

Federal Correctional Institution Tucson | FCI Tucson

Facilities: FCI Tucson with a detention center.

Facility Address & Contact Information

Federal Correctional Institution Tucson
8901 South Wilmot Road
Tucson, AZ 85706

Phone: 520-574-7100
Fax: 520-574-4206
Email: TCN/ExecAssistant@bop.gov

BOP Website: https://www.bop.gov/locations/institutions/tcn/
Wikipedia: https://en.wikipedia.org/wiki/Federal_Correctional_Institution,_Tucson
ZCG Website: https://www.prisonerresource.com/resources/federal-prison-profiles/western-region-wxr/federal-correctional-complex-tucson-fcc-tucson/federal-correctional-institution-tucson-fci-tucson/

Inmate Correspondence Address

Inmate Name and Registration Number
FCI Tucson
Federal Correctional Institution
P.O. Box 23811
Tucson, AZ 85734

NOTE: Funds cannot be sent directly to federal inmates. See Chapter 1 for more information on sending funds to federal inmates.

Sex: Main: Male; Detention Center: Male and Female

Security Level: Main: Medium Security; Detention Center: Administrative Security (Multiple Security Levels)

Location: FCI Tucson is located in southern Arizona, 10 miles southeast of Tucson, near I-10 and Wilmot Road.

BOP Region: Western Region (WXR)

BOP Institution Code: TCN for FCI Tucson, TCX for Tucson Federal Correctional Complex

Judicial District: District of Arizona

Medical Care Level: Level 2. See Chapter 2 for more information on Medical Care and Mental Health Care Levels.

Mental Health Care Level: Level 3

Population (as of May 1, 2019): 594

Background: Federal Correctional Institution Tucson is a medium-security federal prison in Tucson, Arizona, which houses male inmates. It was opened in 1982 and is part of the Tucson Federal Correctional Complex. FCI Tucson includes a detention center which houses male and female detainees.

Notable inmates include Charles Keating (served five years for bankruptcy and wire fraud), and Abu Khalid Abdul-Latif (serving 18 years for conspiracy to murder U.S. officers).

Media reports indicate that at least three inmates have escaped from the camp.

Housing: Inmates are housed in two and four-person cells.

Health Services: Sick call, dental care, medication, physical examinations, eyeglasses, and emergency medical care are all available to inmates at FCI Tucson. Inmates are assigned to a specific health care provider who treats them for the duration of their stay. Inmates must submit a sick call form in order to be evaluated for routine health care needs. Emergency care is available 24 hours a day.

Psychology Services: The FCI Tucson Psychology Services Department provides screening, assessment, and treatment of mental health conditions, individual and group counseling, psycho-educational classes, self-help and supportive services, and referral to Health Services for medical treatment of a mental illness. Available groups include anger management and stress management. Notices of upcoming treatment offerings are posted in inmate housing units.

Residential Drug Abuse Program (RDAP): FCI Tucson does not offer the Residential Drug Abuse Program (RDAP), but referrals can be made to institutions that do provide

RDAP. The facility provides other drug abuse programs, a Drug Abuse Education Course, the Non-Residential Drug Abuse Program (NR-DAP), Alcoholics Anonymous (AA), and Narcotics Anonymous (NA).

Education Services: FCI Tucson offers GED and English-as-a-Second Language (ESL). Inmates who do not possess a GED or high school diploma are required to attend educational programming. Inmate Performance Pay is regulated by the inmate's level of education. Those not having a verified GED/High School Diploma are restricted to Grade 4 compensation for their inmate work assignment. INEA-Mexican High School Diploma Program students can have concurrent enrollment in GED literacy and in INEA-Mexican High School Diploma Program. The Mexican Consulate offers certificates in primary and secondary education through the Education Department. The Mexican curriculum is a voluntary program open to any student wishing to receive accreditation from the Mexican Government in either program. The Education Department offers a variety of re-entry classes to assist inmates in making a productive reintegration into society. High school diplomas and post-secondary degrees are available through paid correspondence programs. Inmates can also earn a business certificate from Pima Community College.

Advanced Occupational Education: FCI Tucson offers advanced occupational education in Custodial Maintenance, Basic & Advanced Baking, Serve Safe, NRAEF, and Business & Accounting.

Vocational Training: FCI Tucson offers vocational training programs in Electrical, HVAC, Plumbing, and Cooking/Baking.

Apprenticeship: FCI Tucson offers apprenticeships in Cook, Electrician, HVAC, Pastry Cook, and Plumber.

Library Services: FCI Tucson provides leisure and law libraries to inmates at both facilities. The leisure library contains newspapers, magazines, reference materials, and general circulation books. Inmates may check out fiction or nonfiction books for 14 days. The law library provides inmates with access to the TRULINCS Electronic Law Library, typewriters, and a copy machine.

UNICOR: The FCI Tucson UNICOR facility handles recycling activities.

Commissary: Inmates are allowed to spend up to $360.00 per month on items such as snacks, food, ice cream, radios, MP3 players, sodas, and more. Inmates can shop once a week on their designated shopping day. Postage stamps, copy cards, and over-the-counter medications do not count against the spending limitation.

Recreation Services: FCI Tucson provides inmates the opportunity to engage in both indoor and outdoor recreation. Inside, inmates can play music, cards, and board games. Inmates can also paint, draw, and engage in other art and craft activities. Outside, inmates can exercise, run the tracks, play sports, and socialize. Popular sports include football, basketball, soccer, and softball. A weight pile is also available.

Visitation Information: On Sunday and Saturday visitation is held between 8:15 a.m. and 3:00 p.m. On federal holidays visitation is held between 8:15 a.m. and 3:00 p.m. See Chapter 1 for more information on visitation.

FCC Victorville

Federal Correctional Complex Victorville | FCC Victorville

Facilities: FCC Victorville houses USP Victorville, FCI Victorville Medium 1, and FCI Victorville Medium 2, with an adjacent minimum-security satellite prison camp.

USP Victorville

United States Penitentiary Victorville | USP Victorville

Facility Address & Contact Information

United States Penitentiary Victorville
13777 Air Expressway Boulevard
Victorville, CA 92394

Phone: 760-530-5000
Fax: 760-530-5103
Email: VIP/ExecAssistant@bop.gov

BOP Website: https://www.bop.gov/locations/institutions/vip/
Wikipedia: https://en.wikipedia.org/wiki/United_States_Penitentiary%2C_Victorville
ZCG Website: https://www.prisonerresource.com/resources/federal-prison-profiles/western-region-wxr/federal-correctional-complex-victorville-fcc-victorville/united-states-penitentiary-victorville-usp-victorville/

Inmate Correspondence Address

Inmate Name and Registration Number
USP Victorville
U.S. Penitentiary
P.O. Box 3900
Adelanto, CA 92301

NOTE: Funds cannot be sent directly to federal inmates. See Chapter 1 for more information on sending funds to federal inmates.

Sex: Male

Security Level: High Security

Location: USP Victorville is located in San Bernardino County, approximately 85 miles north-west of Los Angeles, on Interstate 15.

BOP Region: Western Region (WXR)

BOP Institution Code: VIP for USP Victorville, VIX for Victorville Federal Correctional Complex

Judicial District: Central District of California

Medical Care Level: Level 2/3. See Chapter 2 for more information on Medical Care and Mental Health Care Levels.

Mental Health Care Level: Level 2

Population (as of May 1, 2019): 1,284

Background: United States Penitentiary Victorville is a high-security federal prison in Victorville, California, which houses male inmates. It was opened in 2004 and is part of the Victorville Federal Correctional Complex.

USP Victorville is informally known as "Victimville" due to the severe culture of violence amongst the inmate population.

Notable inmates include leader of the Cuban Five Gerardo Hernandez (serving a life sentence for conspiracy to commit murder and espionage), leader of the Chicago Latin Kings Augustin Zambrano (serving 60 years for racketeering conspiracy), and former MLB player Lenny Dykstra (served six months for grand theft auto and providing false financial statements).

Media reports indicate that at least five inmates have been murdered at the prison. Additionally, at least one guard has been indicted for smuggling contraband and a drone was discovered transporting contraband into the facility.

Housing: Inmates are housed in one- and two-person cells.

Health Services: Emergency medical care, sick call, physical examinations, annual TB testing, medication, dental services, and eyeglasses are all provided at USP Victorville. While emergency medical care is available 24 hours a day, inmates must submit a sick call form in order to be evaluated for routine care needs.

Psychology Services: Intake screening is provided for each inmate upon arrival at USP Victorville. Inmates can also speak with a psychologist briefly during open house hours or at main line. Psychologists conduct various groups and workshops for inmates, such as anger management and stress management.

Residential Drug Abuse Program (RDAP): USP Victorville does not offer the Residential Drug Abuse Program (RDAP), but referrals can be made to institutions that do provide RDAP. A Drug Education class, the Non-Residential Drug Abuse Program (NR-DAP), Alcoholics Anonymous (AA), and Narcotics Anonymous (NA) are available.

Education Services: USP Victorville offers literacy, GED, and English-as-a-Second Language (ESL) courses. Inmates that do not possess a high school diploma or GED are required to participate in the literacy program for a minimum of 240 hours. Adult Continuing Education (ACE) and parenting classes are also available. High school diplomas and post-secondary degrees are available through paid correspondence courses. Coastline Community College enables inmates to obtain an associate's degree in either liberal arts or specialized business.

Advanced Occupational Education: USP Victorville offers advanced occupational education in Automotive Service Excellence, Microsoft Office 2010, Recycling/Solid Waste Construction and Extraction Management, and ServSafe.

Vocational Training: USP Victorville does not offer any vocational training programs.

Apprenticeship: USP Victorville offers apprenticeships in HVAC and Plumbing.

Library Services: Leisure and law libraries are available for the inmate population complex-wide. The law library contains the TRULINCS Electronic Law Library terminals, typewriters, and a copy machine. The leisure library offers newspapers, magazines, and fiction and nonfiction books to the inmate population.

UNICOR: The USP Victorville UNICOR facility handles fleet management and vehicular components.

Commissary: USP Victorville operates a commissary which provides inmates an opportunity to purchase items not issued or delivered as basic care by the institution, as well as items of a higher quality. The monthly spending limit is $360.00. Inmates may only shop once a week on their designated shopping day.

Recreation Services: The USP Victorville Recreation Department offers a variety of hobby-craft programs, sports programs and leagues, leisure and holiday programs, music programs, and structured exercise/wellness programs. Inmates are afforded the opportunity to enroll in a housing unit art/hobbycraft program. The recreation resource library offers literature, DVDs, and videos related to fitness/wellness. An Inmate Photo Program is also offered to inmates. The program provides inmates the opportunity to have photos taken of themselves and their visitors on scheduled visiting days.

Visitation Information: On Sunday, Monday, and Saturday visitation is held between 8:30 a.m. and 3:00 p.m. On federal holidays visitation is held between 8:30 a.m. and 3:00 p.m. See Chapter 1 for more information on visitation.

In the News: In February 2017, Ignacio Adrian Sobers, Jr., a guard at the United States Penitentiary in Victorville, pleaded guilty to accepting a bribe for his role in smuggling MP3 players and pornographic material into the facility for a prisoner.

In March 2015, an unmanned drone was used to smuggle two cell phones into USP Victorville.

In June 2014, prisoners Brian Kountz and Robert Howard Ferguson were killed at USP Victorville. At least three other prisoners died within less than a year of Kountz's death at what is familiarly known as "Victimville."

In April 2005, prisoner Peter Scopazzi, who was in a fight with five other prisoners at USP Victorville, was stabbed several times and subsequently died.

FCI Victorville Medium 1

Federal Correctional Institution Victorville Medium 1 | FCI Victorville Medium 1

Facility Address & Contact Information

Federal Correctional Institution Victorville Medium 1
13777 Air Expressway Boulevard
Victorville, CA 92394

Phone: 760-246-2400
Fax: 760-246-2621
Email: VIM/ExecAssistant@bop.gov

BOP Website: https://www.bop.gov/locations/institutions/vim/
Wikipedia: https://en.wikipedia.org/wiki/Federal_Correctional_Institution,_Victorville
ZCG Website: https://www.prisonerresource.com/resources/federal-prison-profiles/western-region-wxr/federal-correctional-complex-victorville-fcc-victorville/federal-correctional-institution-victorville-medium-1-fci-victorville-medium-1/

Inmate Correspondence Address

Inmate Name and Registration Number
FCI Victorville Medium 1
Federal Correctional Institution
P.O. Box 3725
Adelanto, CA 92301

NOTE: Funds cannot be sent directly to federal inmates. See Chapter 1 for more information on sending funds to federal inmates.

Sex: Male

Security Level: Medium Security

Location: FCI Victorville is located in San Bernardino County, approximately 85 miles northwest of Los Angeles, on Interstate 15.

BOP Region: Western Region (WXR)

BOP Institution Code: VIM for FCI Victorville Medium 1, VIX for Victorville Federal Correctional Complex

Judicial District: Central District of California

Medical Care Level: Level 2. See Chapter 2 for more information on Medical Care and Mental Health Care Levels.

Mental Health Care Level: Level 2

Population (as of May 1, 2019): 1,326

Background: Federal Correctional Institution Victorville Medium 1 is a medium-security federal prison in Victorville, California, which houses male inmates. It was opened in 2004 and is part of the Victorville Federal Correctional Complex.

Notable inmates include Auburn Callowan (serving two life sentences for attempted murder and attempted hijacking of a FedEx flight).

Media reports indicate that at least one inmate has been murdered at the prison and that at least one guard has been assaulted by an inmate. Additionally, the institution has experienced numerous lockdowns as a result of inmate disturbances.

Housing: Inmates are housed in two-person cells.

Health Services: Emergency medical care, sick call, physical examinations, annual TB testing, medication, dental services, and eyeglasses are all provided at FCI Victorville Medium 1. Inmates are assigned to a primary care provider who treats them for the duration of their stay. Emergency medical care is available 24 hours a day.

Psychology Services: Intake screening is provided for each inmate upon arrival at the facility. Inmates can also speak with a psychologist briefly during open house hours or at main line. Psychologists conduct various groups and workshops for inmates. The Bureau Rehabilitation and Values Enhancement (BRAVE) Program at FCI Victorville Medium 1 is a unit-based residential treatment program which facilitates the adjustment of young, medium-security, first-time male inmate offenders into the Bureau. It is specifically focused on first-time federal offenders who are 32 years of age or younger, and who have a sentence of 60 months or more.

The goals of the program are to facilitate the adjustment of medium-security inmates entering the BOP for the first time, improve institution security, reduce recidivism and the rate of misconduct, and enhance early identification and appropriate clinical intervention of psychological disorders which may contribute to criminal activity and poor institution adjustment.

Residential Drug Abuse Program (RDAP): FCI Victorville Medium 1 does not offer the Residential Drug Abuse Program (RDAP), but referrals can be made to institutions that do provide RDAP. The institution does offer Alcoholics Anonymous (AA), Narcotics Anonymous (NA), a Drug Education class, and the Non-Residential Drug Abuse Program (NR-DAP).

Education Services: FCI Victorville Medium 1 offers GED and English-as-a-Second Language (ESL) programs to inmates. Those who earn a GED are awarded an incentive of $25. High school diplomas and post-secondary degrees are available through paid correspondence programs. Coastline Community College enables inmates to obtain an associate's degree in either liberal arts or specialized business.

Advanced Occupational Education: FCI Victorville Medium 1 offers advanced occupational education in Automotive Service Excellence, Construction & Building Trades, Microsoft Office 2010, Recycling/Solid Waste Management, and Solar Panel Installation.

Vocational Training: FCI Victorville Medium 1 does not offer any vocational training programs.

Apprenticeship: FCI Victorville Medium 1 offers apprenticeship programs in Dental Assistant, HVAC Mechanic/Installer, and Plumbing.

Library Services: Leisure and law Libraries are available for the inmate population complex-wide. The leisure library offers fiction and nonfiction books, newspapers, and periodicals. Inmates are provided access to legal materials and an opportunity to prepare legal documents through the use of the TRULINCS Electronic Law Library. A copy machine is available to reproduce materials needed for research. Electric typewriters are also available for inmate use.

UNICOR: The FCI Victorville Medium 1 UNICOR facility handles fleet management and vehicular components.

Commissary: FCI Victorville Medium 1 operates a Commissary where inmates can purchase clothing, shoes, electronics, drinks mixes, sodas, ice cream, and more. A monthly spending limitation of $360.00 is imposed.

Recreation Services: The FCI Victorville Medium 1 Recreation Department offers a variety of activities for the inmate population. These include sports, an art/hobbycraft program, individualized exercise, structured group exercise classes, and more. A recreation resource library is also available, in which inmates can access DVDs, tapes, and literature on health and exercise.

Visitation Information: On Sunday, Monday, and Saturday visitation is held between 8:30 a.m. and 3:00 p.m. On federal holidays visitation is held between 8:30 a.m. and 3:00 p.m. See Chapter 1 for more information on visitation.

In the News: In June 2018, a U.S. District Court judge approved a restraining order requested by the ACLU allowing immigrant detainees being held at Federal Correctional Institution Victorville Medium 1 to contact legal representatives.

In December 2017, FCI Victorville Medium 1 was locked down after a group of prisoners became "disruptive," the third lockdown since May of 2017.

In May 2017, a prisoner at FCI Victorville Medium 1 attempted to assault a staff member and was subdued with pepper spray.

In August 2006, Tony Padilla, a prisoner at FCI Victorville Medium 1, died of his injuries after a fight with another prisoner.

FCI Victorville Medium 2

Federal Correctional Institution Victorville Medium 2 | FCI Victorville Medium 2

Facilities: FCI Victorville Medium 2 with an adjacent minimum-security satellite prison camp.

Facility Address & Contact Information

Federal Correctional Institution Victorville Medium 2
13777 Air Expressway Boulevard
Victorville, CA 92394

Phone: 760-530-5700
Fax: 760-560-5706
Email: VVM/ExecAssistant@bop.gov

BOP Website: https://www.bop.gov/locations/institutions/vvm/
Wikipedia: https://en.wikipedia.org/wiki/Federal_Correctional_Institution,_Victorville
ZCG Website: https://www.prisonerresource.com/resources/federal-prison-profiles/western-region-wxr/federal-correctional-complex-victorville-fcc-victorville/federal-correctional-institution-victorville-medium-2-victorville-medium-2/

Inmate Correspondence Address

For FCI Victorville Medium 2

Inmate Name and Registration Number
FCI Victorville Medium 2
Federal Correctional Institution
P.O. Box 3850
Adelanto, CA 92301

For Satellite Prison Camp

Inmate Name and Registration Number
FCI Victorville Medium 2
Satellite Prison Camp
P.O. Box 5300
Adelanto, CA 92301

NOTE: Funds cannot be sent directly to federal inmates. See Chapter 1 for more information on sending funds to federal inmates.

Sex: Main: Male; Camp: Female

Security Level: Main: Medium Security; Camp: Minimum Security

Location: FCI Victorville Medium 2 is located in San Bernardino County, approximately 85 miles northwest of Los Angeles, on Interstate 15.

BOP Region: Western Region (WXR)

BOP Institution Code: VMM for FCI Victorville Medium 2, VIX for Victorville Federal Correctional Complex

Judicial District: Central District of California

Medical Care Level: Level 2. See Chapter 2 for more information on Medical Care and Mental Health Care Levels.

Mental Health Care Level: Level 2

Population (as of May 1, 2019): Main: 885; Camp: 297

Background: Federal Correctional Institution Victorville Medium 2 is a medium-security federal prison in Victorville, California, which houses male inmates. It was opened in 2004 and is part of the Victorville Federal Correctional Complex. Federal Correctional Institution Victorville Camp, which houses female inmates, was opened in 2004 and is located adjacent to the main institution.

Notable inmates include Mohamed Osman Mohamud (serving 30 years for attempted use of a weapon of mass destruction), and former leader of the now-defunct Sonora Cartel Muguel Caro-Quintero (serving 17 years for drug trafficking). Reality TV star Abby Lee Miller (convicted of bankruptcy fraud), and president of Discovery Home Builders Ayman Shahid who (sentenced to 46 months for mortgage fraud, wire fraud, and bank fraud) were both housed at the camp.

Media reports indicate that at least three guards have been assaulted by inmates and that several prisoners have been indicted for assaults on fellow prisoners. Additionally, one inmate had to be transported to a local hospital following a disturbance which resulted in the prison being locked down. At least one guard has been indicted for sexually assaulting two female prisoners at the camp.

Housing: Inmates are housed in two-, three-, and four-person cells. Those in the BRAVE program are housed in one- and two-person cells. There is a total of 12 housing units. Inmates in the camp are housed in dormitories, which are divided into two-person cubicles.

Health Services: Emergency medical care, sick call, physical examinations, annual TB testing, medication, dental services, and eyeglasses are all provided at FCI Victorville Medium 2. Inmates must submit a triage form in order to be evaluated for routine care concerns. Emergency medical care is available 24 hours a day by approaching any staff member.

Psychology Services: Intake screening is provided for each inmate upon arrival at FCI Victorville Medium 2. Inmates can also speak with a psychologist briefly during open house hours or at main line. Psychologists conduct various groups and workshops for inmates. These tend to include stress management and anger management. A self-help library is available. Suicide and other crisis counseling are available 24 hours a day if an emergency exists. The camp offers the STAGES Program for inmates with serious mental illness and personality disorders.

Residential Drug Abuse Program (RDAP): FCI Victorville Medium 2 does not offer the Residential Drug Abuse Program (RDAP), but referrals can be made to institutions that do provide RDAP. The institution offers Alcoholics Anonymous (AA), Narcotics Anonymous (NA), a Drug Education class, and the Non-Residential Drug Abuse Program (NR-DAP).

Education Services: FCI Victorville Medium 2 offers literacy, GED, and English as-a-Second Language (ESL) programs to inmates. Both parenting and Adult Continuing Education (ACE) programs are also available. Coastline Community College enables inmates to obtain an associate's degree in either liberal arts or specialized business. High school diplomas and post-secondary degrees are available through paid correspondence programs.

Advanced Occupational Education: FCI Victorville Medium 2 offers advanced occupational education in Automotive Service Excellence, Bicycle Repair, Horticulture, Microsoft Office 2010, Recycling/Solid Waste Management, ServSafe, and Solar Panel Installation. The camp offers Automotive Service Excellence, Horticulture, Microsoft Office 2010, Recycling/Solid Waste Management, ServSafe, and Wheelchair Repair.

Vocational Training: FCI Victorville Medium 2 does not offer any vocational training programs.

Apprenticeship: FCI Victorville Medium 2 offers apprenticeships in Plumbing and HVAC. The camp offers an apprenticeship in Dental Assistant.

Library Services: A leisure and law library is available for the inmate population. Inmates can check out a wide variety of books, magazines, and newspapers. Books can be checked out for two weeks at a time. A DVD movie program is also available. Inmates are provided access to legal materials and an opportunity to prepare legal documents through the use of the TRULINCS Electronic Law Library. A copy machine is available to reproduce materials needed for research. Electric typewriters are also available for inmate use. The library is open six days a week.

UNICOR: The FCI Victorville Medium 2 UNICOR facility handles vehicle management and vehicular components.

Commissary: Inmates have the opportunity to purchase items not issued or delivered as basic care by the institution, or items of a different higher quality. The monthly spending limit is $360.00. Inmates are allowed to shop once a week on their designated shopping day. Copy cards, postage stamps, and over-the-counter medications do not count against the spending limitation. Inmates tend to carry their purchases back to their housing units in laundry bags.

Recreation Services: The FCI Victorville Medium 2 Recreation Department offers a variety of indoor and outdoor activities for the inmate population. Inside, inmates can participate in arts and crafts programs. Outside, inmates can work out, play sports, take fitness classes, or socialize. A photo program is also available which allows inmates to have their photos taken.

Indoors, inmates have access to basketball, leathercraft, painting, tables, TVs, foosball, band room, ellipticals, treadmills, and stationary bikes. Outdoors, inmates have access to soccer, bocce ball, basketball, softball, handball, and a track.

Visitation Information: On Sunday, Monday, and Saturday visitation is held between 8:30 a.m. and 3:00 p.m. On federal holidays visitation is held between 8:30 a.m. and 3:00 p.m. See Chapter 1 for more information on visitation.

Prison Politics: This is a very political yard where inmates are required to be part of a racially-oriented car in order to stay. According to one inmate, "A car is required for personal safety."

Level of Violence: There is a significant level of violence at this prison. According to one respondent, "Fights are a regular occurrence and stabbings are not uncommon."

Vulnerable Populations: Sex offenders, informants, and LGBT inmates cannot walk the yard. According to one inmate, "If you are one of these sorts, you will be run-off and perhaps receive a boot party. If you make it and fly under the radar, staff will print off your PSR and hand it to your unit racial shot caller. Staff actively put these populations in harm's way."

Good: "Great vocational training." "Not much."

Bad: "Politics and violence." "Staff force sex offenders to walk the yard until they are checked-in. Merely asking to be placed in protective custody when you first get there won't stop this. The lieutenants actively try to get sex offenders killed." "LGBT inmates who do manage to stay belong to somebody. They are effectively their property and must do as they are told. Communal sexual violence is common in such unwilful agreements."

Other Comments: "If you are LGBT or a sex offender, this is not the yard for you to be on. This is a notably violent, political yard. Stay away." "The guards are just as bad as the inmates when it comes to politics. Don't trust them. If you have dirty paperwork, they will try to get you maimed."

In the News: In December 2017, Federal Correctional Institution Victorville Medium 2 was temporarily locked down after a group of prisoners became "disruptive." News reports indicate that one inmate was transported to the hospital with non-life-threatening injuries.

In September 2017, a guard at FCI Victorville Medium 2 was assaulted by a prisoner.

In August 2017, two guards at FCI Victorville Medium 2 were assaulted by three prisoners.

In May 2017, Fazliddin Kurbanov, a prisoner at FCI Victorville Medium 2, was indicted on charges of attempted murder of a federal officer after stabbing the warden, Calvin Johnson, with a shank, requiring more than 80 staples to close the wounds.

In July 2003, Richard Dale Morrison, an FCI Victorville Medium 2 prisoner, was charged with misdemeanor assault for his attack on former Taliban member John Walker Lindh in the prison chapel.

Camp in the News: In March 2018, Apolonio Gamez, a guard at Federal Correctional Institution Victorville Medium 2 Camp, was arrested on charges of sexually abusing two female prisoners.

CHAPTER II:

Private Contract Facilities

Private Contract Facilities

The Bureau of Prisons contracts with several private prison companies to house primarily low-security inmates. While any low-security inmate is eligible for private prison placement, deportable aliens are more likely to be housed in such facilities. These facilities are located across the country and are supervised by the regional office which governs the local geographic region.

Private Prison Population: 18,411
ZCG Website: https://www.prisonerresource.com/resources/federal-prison-profiles/private-prisons/

Private Prisons

CI Adams County (MS)
CI Big Spring (TX)
CI D. Ray James (GA)
CI Dalby (TX)
CI Great Plains (OK)
CI McRae (GA)
CI Moshannon Valley (PA)
CI Reeves 1 & 2
DC Reeves (TX)
CI Rivers (NC)
CI Taft (CA)
CI Taft Camp (CA)

CI Adams County

Correctional Institution Adams County | CI Adams County

Facility Address & Contact Information

Correctional Institution Adams County
20 Hobo Fork Road
Natchez, MS 39120

Phone: 601-304-2500
Fax: 601-446-5224
Email: ACC/General@bop.gov

BOP Website: https://www.bop.gov/locations/ci/acc/
CoreCivic Website: http://www.CoreCivic.com/facilities/adams-county-correctional-center
Wikipedia: https://en.wikipedia.org/wiki/Adams_County_Correctional_Center
ZCG Website: https://www.prisonerresource.com/resources/federal-prison-profiles/private-prisons/correctional-institution-adams-county-ci-adams-county/

Inmate Correspondence Address

Inmate Name and Registration Number
CI Adams County
Correctional Institution
P.O. Box 1600
Washington, MS 39190

NOTE: Funds cannot be sent directly to inmates. In order to deposit funds via mail, mail a money order with the inmate's name and registration number affixed to the following address:

CCA Inmate Trust
Facility: Adams
[Last Name, First Name, Inmate Registration Number]
P.O. Box 933488
Atlanta, GA 31193-3488

Funds can also be sent via Western Union (www.westernunion.com/corrections or 1-800-634-3442). See Chapter 1 for more information on sending funds to federal inmates.

Sex: Male

Security Level: Low Security

Location: CI Adams County is located 12 miles outside Natchez, Mississippi on U.S. Highways 61 and 98.

BOP Region: Southeast Region (SER)

BOP Institution Code: ACC for CI Adams County

Judicial District: Southern District of Mississippi

Medical Care Level: Information not available. See Chapter 2 for more information on Medical Care and Mental Health Care Levels.

Mental Health Care Level: Information not available.

Population (as of May 1, 2019): 2,213

Background: CI Adams County is owned and operated by CoreCivic (formerly known as the Corrections Corporation of America (CCA)) under contract with the U.S. Federal Bureau of Prisons. The facility has a capacity of 2,567 inmates. Most of its prisoners are illegal immigrants charged with re-entering the United States after a deportation. CoreCivic has owned the prison since 2007; the facility did not open until late in 2009.

Housing: Inmates are housed in units that are divided into three pods with bunks.

Health Services: CI Adams County has a medical unit where physicians, registered nurses, licensed practical nurses, and medical assistants provide routine check-ups, manage sick call, and address non-emergency needs. Private correctional health care facilities typically include a dental clinic as well. Emergency medical care is available 24 hours a day.

Psychology Services: Inmates are screened upon arrival at CI Adams County, and referred to a psychologist, psychiatrist or mental health specialist for follow-up evaluation and intervention if necessary. For inmates who experience mental health problems, from emotional conflict to mental illness, a team of qualified mental health professionals is available to assist them with their needs. Medications, therapeutic community activities, and group and individual counseling are provided if needed. All CoreCivic staff receive training in the identification of mental health crises, and they refer inmates to the professional staff whenever they suspect someone is experiencing a problem. Staff are directed to monitor inmates for signs of declining mental health and suicide risk, working actively to assist troubled inmates in their time of need.

Residential Drug Abuse Program (RDAP): CI Adams County provides the Residential Drug Abuse Program (RDAP).

Education Services: CI Adams offers inmates literacy and GED programs. High school diplomas and post-secondary degrees are available through paid correspondence programs. CoreCivic has partnered with the National Institute for Adult Education (Instituto Nacional de Educación para los Adultos, or INEA), an entity of the Mexican government, to provide adult education in Spanish.

Advanced Occupational Education: CI Adams County does not offer any advanced occupational education programs.

Vocational & Apprenticeship Training: CI Adams County offers vocational programs in Carpentry, Commercial Driver's License (CDL), Computer applications, Construction and building trades, Culinary Arts, Electrical, Horticulture and landscaping, HVAC, Masonry, Painting, Plumbing, Workforce Readiness, and Veterinary Technician.

Library Services: CI Adams County libraries contain periodicals, newspapers, fiction and nonfiction books, reference materials, and more. They also feature legal resources and related tools commonly sought by inmates.

UNICOR: CI Adams County does not house a UNICOR facility.

Commissary: Inmates have regular access to the commissary service to support their health and wellness. Inmates can purchase a selection of beverages, light meals and snacks, over-the-counter medications, stationery, clothing, personal hygiene products, religious items, and other miscellaneous products.

Recreational Services: A variety of sports and activities such as basketball, board games, creative writing, knitting, and more, are available to inmates at CI Adams County.

Visitation Information: On Sunday and Saturday visitation is held between 8:00 a.m. and 3:00 p.m. On federal holidays visitation is held between 8:00 a.m. and 3:00 p.m. See Chapter 1 for more information on visitation.

CI Big Spring

Correctional Institution Big Spring | CI Big Spring

Facility Address & Contact Information

Correctional Institution Big Spring
1701 Apron Drive
Big Spring, TX 79720

Phone: 432-264-0060 (Concerning Staff) / 432-267-7911 (Concerning Inmates)
Fax: 432-267-6522
Email: BSC/General@bop.gov

BOP Website: https://www.bop.gov/locations/ci/bsc/
GEO Group Website: https://www.geogroup.com/FacilityDetail/FacilityID/34
Wikipedia: https://en.wikipedia.org/wiki/Big_Spring_Correctional_Center
ZCG Website: https://www.prisonerresource.com/resources/federal-prison-profiles/private-prisons/correctional-institution-big-spring-ci-big-spring/

Inmate Correspondence Address

Inmate Name and Registration Number
CI Big Spring
Correctional Institution
2001 Rickabaugh Drive
Big Spring, TX 79720

NOTE: Funds can be sent directly to inmates in the form of a money order which has the inmate's name and registration number affixed. Family members can also call 1-866-345-1884 to deposit funds via telephone or go to www.accesscorrections.com to deposit funds online. See Chapter 1 for more information on sending funds to federal inmates.

Sex: Male

Security Level: Low Security

Location: Approximately four miles west of Big Spring, TX.

BOP Region: South Central Region (SCR)

BOP Institution Code: BSC for CI Big Spring

Judicial District: Northern District of Texas

Medical Care Level: Information not available. See Chapter 2 for more information on Medical Care and Mental Health Care Levels.

Mental Health Care Level: Information not available.

Population (as of May 1, 2019): 3,327

Background: CI Big Spring is a private prison. It is owned and operated by Geo Group and houses federal "deportable alien" detainees. The facility achieved initial accreditation through the American Correctional Association in 2010 and re-accreditation in 2012 and 2015. The current facility delivers all levels of services providing an environment for prisoners working their way through the judicial system.

Housing: The facility is comprised of four separate facilities, Interstate, Airpark, Flightline, and Cedar Hill.

Health Services: Inmates are initially provided with an intake examination. Routine and emergency health care and dental care are also available to the inmate population. While emergency care is available 24 hours a day, inmates must submit a sick call form in order to be evaluated for routine or chronic health care concerns.

Psychology Services: CI Big Spring offers psychological evaluations and treatment to inmates. Services include counseling and programs created to have rehabilitative impact. A Living in Balance program is also offered. Inmates are provided with access to a variety of behavioral treatment groups. These include stress management, anger management, life skills training, parenting techniques, conflict resolution, and preparation for re-entry into society.

Residential Drug Abuse Program (RDAP): CI Big Spring does not offer the Residential Drug Abuse Program (RDAP). Drug and alcohol abuse counseling is available. The program is delivered in four phases: aspects of substance abuse, life and living skills, obsessive and compulsive behaviors, and core issues in substance abuse. Some Geo Group facilities offer treatment groups including Alcoholics Anonymous (AA) and Narcotics Anonymous (NA).

Education Services: CI Big Spring offers GED, English-as-a-Second Language (ESL), and both American and Spanish Adult Basic Education (ABE) courses to the inmate population. Inmates without a GED or high school diploma are required to attend courses. Inmates are also provided with life skills classes to enhance parenting skills. High school diplomas and post-secondary degrees are available through paid correspondence programs.

Advanced Occupational Education: CI Big Spring not does offer any advanced occupational education programs.

Vocational Training: CI Big Spring offers vocational training in Custodial Maintenance, Barbering, Horticulture, Electrical, Building Trades, Auto Mechanics, Upholstery, Weaving, Heating, Ventilation, and Air Conditioning (HVAC), Small Engine Repair, Masonry, Plumbing, Culinary Arts, Computer Repair, Carpentry, and Welding.

Apprenticeship: CI Big Spring does not offer any apprenticeship programs.

Library Services: CI Big Spring offers a full legal library, as well as a leisure library. In the leisure library inmates can check out fiction and nonfiction books, newspapers, and magazines. In the law library inmates can conduct legal research and prepare legal filings.

UNICOR: CI Big Spring does not house a UNICOR facility.

Commissary: Inmates have access to an institutional commissary where they can purchase drinks, food, snacks, shoes, and limited electronics.

Recreation Services: Indoor and outdoor recreation opportunities are available at CI Big Spring. These include organized sports, individual exercise, board and card games, and arts and crafts projects.

Visitation Information: On Sunday and Saturday visitation is held between 8:30 a.m. and 3:30 p.m. On federal holidays visitation is held between 8:30 a.m. and 3:30 p.m. See Chapter 1 for more information on visitation.

CI D. Ray James

Correctional Institution D. Ray James | CI D. Ray James

Facility Address & Contact Information

Correctional Institution D. Ray James
3262 Highway 252 East
Folkston, GA 31537

Phone: 912-496-6242
Fax: 912-496-7806
Email: DRJ/General@bop.gov

BOP Website: https://www.bop.gov/locations/ci/drj
GEO Group Website: https://www.geogroup.com/FacilityDetail/FacilityID/45
Wikipedia: https://en.wikipedia.org/wiki/D._Ray_James_Correctional_Institution
ZCG Website: https://www.prisonerresource.com/resources/federal-prison-profiles/private-prisons/correctional-institution-d-ray-james-ci-d-ray-james/

Inmate Correspondence Address

Inmate Name and Registration Number
CI D. Ray James
Correctional Institution
P.O. Box 2000
Folkston, GA 31537

NOTE: Funds cannot be sent directly to inmates. Family members can use Access Corrections (www.accesscorrections.com or 1-866-345-1884) or Western Union (www.westernunion.com/corrections or 1-800-634-3442) to deposit funds on inmate accounts. See Chapter 1 for more information on sending funds to federal inmates.

Sex: Male

Security Level: Medium Security

Location: 3262 Highway 252, Folkston, GA 31537

BOP Region: Southeast Region (SEC)

BOP Institution Code: DRJ for CI D. Ray James

Judicial District: Southern District of Georgia

Medical Care Level: Information not available. See Chapter 2 for more information on Medical Care and Mental Health Care Levels.

Mental Health Care Level: Information not available.

Population (as of May 1, 2019): 1,728

Background: CI D. Ray James is a private prison. In January 2010, the D. Ray James Correctional Facility was awarded a contract to house adult males sentenced by the Federal Bureau of Prisons (BOP) and is now owned and operated by The GEO Group, Inc. The current facility delivers all levels of services providing an environment for prisoners working their way through the judicial system.

Housing: Inmates are housed in dormitories.

Health Services: CI D. Ray James inmates are initially provided with an intake examination. Routine and emergency health care and dental care are also available to the inmate population. While emergency care is available 24 hours a day, inmates must submit a sick call form in order to be evaluated for routine or chronic health care concerns.

Psychology Services: CI D. Ray James offers correctional mental health care. Services include counseling and programs created to have a rehabilitative impact. A Living in Balance program is also offered. Inmates are provided with access to a variety of behavioral treatment groups. These include stress management, anger management, life skills training, parenting techniques, conflict resolution, and preparation for re-entry into society.

Residential Drug Abuse Program (RDAP): CI D. Ray James does not have the Residential Drug Abuse Program (RDAP). Most Geo Group facilities offer RDAP as well as addiction programs including Alcoholics Anonymous (AA) and Narcotics Anonymous (NA). Additional substance abuse programming is offered.

Education Services: CI D. Ray James provides Pre-GED, GED, literacy training, English-as-a-Second Language (ESL), and Special Education programs for the inmate population. High school diplomas and post-secondary degrees are available through paid correspondence programs. Inmates are also provided with life skills classes to enhance parenting skills.

Advanced Occupational Education: CI D. Ray James offers advanced occupational education in smart board technology, customized learning through individual education plans, dynamic grouping, and technology-based learning.

Vocational Training: CI D. Ray James offers vocational training in Custodial Maintenance, Barbering, Horticulture, Electrical, Building Trades, Auto Mechanics, Upholstery, Weaving, Heating, Ventilation, and Air Conditioning (HVAC), Small Engine Repair, Masonry, Plumbing, Culinary Arts, Computer Repair, Carpentry, and Welding. The facility also offers the Teaching Animals and Inmate Life Skills (TAILS) program, which is in partnership with Pit Sisters. This program helps to rehabilitate and train dogs.

Apprenticeship: CI D. Ray James does not offer any apprenticeship programs to inmates.

Library Services: A law and leisure library are available for inmate use at CI D. Ray James. Inmates can check out fiction and nonfiction books, newspapers, and magazines. In the law library inmates can conduct legal research and prepare legal filings.

UNICOR: CI D. Ray James does not house a UNICOR facility.

Commissary: Inmates are allowed to shop in the institution's commissary once a week. Items such as clothing, shoes, food, snacks, electronics, and drink mixes are available for purchase.

Recreational Services: CI D. Jay James provides both indoor and outdoor recreation opportunities to the inmate population. Inmates are allowed to exercise, play sports, create art, and engage in various craft projects.

Visitation Information: Visitation is conducted on Sunday, Thursday, Friday, and Saturday between 8:30 a.m. and 3:30 p.m. On federal holidays visitation is held between 8:30 a.m. and 3:30 p.m. See Chapter 1 for more information on visitation.

CI Giles W. Dalby

Correctional Institution Giles W. Dalby | CI Giles W. Dalby

Facility Address & Contact Information

Giles W. Dalby Correctional Institution
805 North Avenue F
Post, TX 79356

Phone: 806-495-2175
Fax: 806-495-3157
Email: DAL/General@bop.gov

BOP Website: https://www.bop.gov/locations/ci/dal/
M&TC Website: www.mtctrains.com/family-friends-dalby-correctional-facility/
Wikipedia: https://en.wikipedia.org/wiki/Giles_W._Dalby_Correctional_Institution
ZCG Website: https://www.prisonerresource.com/resources/federal-prison-profiles/private-prisons/correctional-institution-giles-w-dalby-ci-giles-w-dalby/

Inmate Correspondence Address

Inmate Name and Registration Number
Giles W. Dalby
Correctional Institution
805 North Avenue F
Post, TX 79356

NOTE: Funds cannot be sent directly to inmates. In order to deposit funds via mail, mail a money order with the inmate's name and registration number affixed to the following address ($300 maximum; $3 fee per transaction):

Secure Deposits
MTC Giles Dalby
P.O. Box 12486
St. Louis, MO 63132

Family members can also call 1-866-345-1884 to deposit funds via telephone or go to www.accesscorrections.com to deposit funds online. See Chapter 1 for more information on sending funds to federal inmates.

Sex: Male

Security Level: Low Security

Location: Approximately 41 miles southeast of Lubbock, Texas.

BOP Region: South Central Region (SCR)

BOP Institution Code: DAL for Giles W. Dalby

Judicial District: Northern District of Texas

Medical Care Level: Information not available. See Chapter 2 for more information on Medical Care and Mental Health Care Levels.

Mental Health Care Level: Information not available.

Population (as of May 1, 2019): 1,602

Background: CI Dalby is a private prison. It is owned and operated by Management and Training Corporation.

Housing: Inmates are housed in one- or two-person cells.

Health Services: The Health Services Department at CI Dalby offers routine medical, dental and mental-health services to all inmates. This includes diagnostic physical and medical exams, as well as dental evaluations. Inmates must submit a sick call form in order to receive routine care. Emergency care is available 24 hours a day.

Psychology Services: Inmates at CI Dalby have access to a Psychology Services department where they can participate in various treatment groups including Choice and Change, Victim Impact, SAMHSA Anger Management, Thinking for Good, Foundations for a Drug Free World, and others. Specialized group therapy and counseling is also offered.

Residential Drug Abuse Program (RDAP): CI Dalby does not offer the Residential Drug Abuse Program (RDAP). However, the Non-Residential Drug Abuse Program (NR-DAP), Alcoholics Anonymous (AA), and Narcotics Anonymous (NA) are available. Foundations for a drug free world and additional substance abuse programs are also available.

Education Services: CI Dalby provides GED, English-as-a-second-Language (ESL) Programs, Adult Basic Education (ABE), INEA courses, computer skills training. Entrepreneurship, small business, and financial classes are available, as is the Inside Out Dads parenting program. High school diplomas and post-secondary degrees are available through paid correspondence programs.

Advanced Occupational Education: CI Dalby does not offer any vocational training programs.

Vocational Training: CI Dalby offers vocational training in AutoCAD, Building Trades, Electrical Trades, Entrepreneurship & Small Business, and Open Office Computer Apps. The facility also participates in the Post Animal Refuge Center (PARC) in which inmates make dog collars and leashes for dogs.

Apprenticeship: CI Dalby does not offer any apprenticeship programs.

Library Services: CI Dalby offers both a leisure and law library to inmates. In the leisure library, inmates can check out fiction and nonfiction books, newspapers, and magazines. In the law library, inmates can conduct legal research.

UNICOR: CI Dalby does not house a UNICOR facility.

Commissary: Inmates at CI Dalby have access to a commissary where they can shop once a week on their designated shopping day. A wide variety of items can be purchased, such as food, snacks, drinks, clothing, and limited electronics. A monthly spending limit of $360.00 is imposed.

Recreational Services: The Recreation Department at CI Dalby consists of both indoor and outdoor activities. Indoor leisure activities include hobbycrafts, leather crafting, and other art and craft projects. Outdoor activities include a variety of individual exercise and group sporting activities.

Visitation Information: On Sunday, Thursday, Friday, and Saturday visitation is held between 8:30 a.m. and 3:30 p.m. On federal holidays visitation is held from 8:30 a.m. and 3:30 p.m. See Chapter 1 for more information on visitation.

CI Great Plains

Correctional Institution Great Plains | CI Great Plains

Facility Address & Contact Information

Great Plains Correctional Institution
700 Sugar Creek Drive
Hinton, OK 73047

Phone: 405-542-3711
Fax: 405-542-3710
Email: GPC/General@bop.gov

BOP Website: https://www.bop.gov/locations/ci/gpc/
GEO Group Website: https://www.geogroup.com/FacilityDetail/FacilityID/54
Wikipedia: https://en.wikipedia.org/wiki/Great_Plains_Correctional_Institution
ZCG Website: https://www.prisonerresource.com/resources/federal-prison-profiles/private-prisons/correctional-institution-great-plains-ci-great-plains/

Inmate Correspondence Address

Inmate Name and Registration Number
CI Great Plains
Correctional Institution
P.O. Box 400
Hinton, OK 73047

NOTE: Funds cannot be sent directly to federal inmates. Family members can call 1-866-345-1884 to deposit funds via telephone or go to www.accesscorrections.com to deposit funds online. See Chapter 1 for more information on sending funds to federal inmates.

Sex: Male

Security Level: Low Security

Location: CI Great Plains is located in Hinton, Caddo County, Oklahoma, approximately 56 miles west of Oklahoma City.

BOP Region: South Central Region (SCR)

BOP Institution Code: GPC for Great Plains CI

Judicial District: Western District of Oklahoma

Medical Care Level: Information not available. See Chapter 2 for more information on Medical Care and Mental Health Care Levels.

Mental Health Care Level: Information not available.

Population (as of May 1, 2019): 1,753

Background: CI Great Plains is a contracted correctional institution, operated by private prison corporation The GEO Group, Inc. The facility opened in 1991 as the state's first private prison. The facility achieved initial accreditation through the American Correctional Association (ACA) in 2017.

Housing: Inmates are housed in a dormitory- style setting.

Health Services: CI Great Plains provides inmates with routine and emergency dental and health care. Inmates can obtain emergency health care 24 hours a day by approaching any staff member and requesting assistance. In order to obtain routine care, inmates must submit a sick call form and wait to be scheduled for an appointment.

Psychology Services: CI Great Plains provides inmates with an intake interview, substance abuse counseling, life skills, and employment assistance. Typical treatment groups include stress management, anger management, and others. Crisis intervention is available 24 hours a day.

Residential Drug Abuse Program (RDAP): CI Great Plains does not offer the Residential Drug Abuse Program (RDAP). However, Alcoholics Anonymous (AA) and Narcotics Anonymous (NA) are available.

Education Services: CI Great Plains offers GED, English-as-a-Second Language (ESL), and Adult Basic Education (ABE) courses to the inmate population. Inmates without a GED or high school diploma are required to attend courses. High school diplomas and post-secondary degrees are available through paid correspondence programs.

Advanced Occupational Education: CI Great Plains offers academic programs in smart board technology, customized learning through individual education plans, dynamic grouping, and technology-based learning.

Vocational Training: CI Great Plains offers vocational training in Custodial Maintenance, Barbering, Horticulture, Electrical, Building Trades, Auto Mechanics, Upholstery, Weaving, Heating, Ventilation, and Air Conditioning (HVAC), Small Engine Repair, Masonry, Plumbing, Culinary Arts, Computer Repair, Carpentry, and Welding.

Apprenticeship: CI Great Plains does not offer any apprenticeship programs to inmates.

Library Services: Inmates have access to a law library, leisure library, general interest library, and religious services. In the leisure library, inmates can check out fiction and nonfiction books, newspapers, and magazines. In the law library, inmates can conduct legal research and prepare legal filings.

UNICOR: CI Great Plains does not house UNICOR facilities.

Commissary: Inmates can shop once per week at the institution's Commissary. Items such as food, drinks, hygiene products, and electronics can be purchased.

Recreation Services: CI Great Plains offers indoor and outdoor recreation opportunities. These include arts and crafts, physical fitness, sports, board and card games, and more.

Visitation Information: On Sunday and Saturday visitation is held between 8:30 a.m. and 3:00 p.m. On federal holidays visitation is held between 8:30 a.m. and 3:00 p.m. See Chapter 1 for more information on visitation.

CI McRae

Correctional Institution McRae | CI McRae

Facility Address & Contact Information

Correctional Institution McRae
1000 Jim Hammock Drive
McRae, GA 31055

Phone: 229-868-7778
Fax: 229-868-7640
Email: MCA/General@bop.gov

BOP Website: https://www.bop.gov/locations/ci/mca/
CoreCivic Website: http://www.CoreCivic.com/facilities/mcrae-correctional-facility
Wikipedia: https://en.wikipedia.org/wiki/McRae_Correctional_Institution
ZCG Website: https://www.prisonerresource.com/resources/federal-prison-profiles/private-prisons/correctional-institution-mcrae-ci-mcrae/

Inmate Correspondence Address

Inmate Name and Registration Number
CI McRae
Correctional Institution
P.O. Drawer 30
McRae, GA 31055

NOTE: Funds cannot be sent directly to inmates. In order to deposit funds via mail, mail a money order with the inmate's name and registration number affixed to the following address:

CCA Inmate Trust
Facility: McRae
[Last Name, First Name, Inmate Registration Number]
P.O. Box 933488
Atlanta, GA 31193-3488

Funds can also be sent via Western Union (www.westernunion.com/corrections or 1-800-634-3442). See Chapter 1 for more information on sending funds to federal inmates.

Sex: Male

Security Level: Low Security

Location: Within McRae-Helena, Telfair County, Georgia.

BOP Region: Southeast Region (SER)

BOP Institution Code: MCA for CI McRae

Judicial District: Southern District of Georgia

Medical Care Level: Information not available. See Chapter 2 for more information on Medical Care and Mental Health Care Levels.

Mental Health Care Level: Information not available.

Population (as of May 1, 2019): 1,521

Background: CI McRae is a private prison. It is owned and operated by CoreCivic (formerly known as the Corrections Corporation of America (CCA)). In 2014, the ACLU of Georgia reported that CI McRae and another private federal prison in Georgia showed, "a record of violations of constitutional and Bureau of Prisons standards governing the medical treatment of prisoners" and other issues.

Housing: Inmates are housed in dormitories.

Health Services: CI McRae has a medical unit where physicians, registered nurses, licensed practical nurses, and medical assistants provide routine check-ups, manage sick call, and address non-emergency needs. Private correctional health care facilities typically include a dental clinic, as well.

Psychology Services: CI McRae has a team of qualified mental health professionals to assist inmates who experience mental health problems, from emotional conflict to mental illness. Inmates are screened upon arrival, and if needed, referred to a psychologist, psychiatrist, or mental health specialist for follow-up evaluation and intervention. Treatment in the form of medication is provided when needed, as well as group and individual counseling. All CoreCivic staff receive training in the identification of mental health crises and refer inmates to the professional staff whenever they suspect someone is experiencing a problem. Staff are directed to monitor the offender population for signs of declining mental health and suicide risk, working actively to assist a troubled offender in his or her time of need.

Residential Drug Abuse Program (RDAP): Th Residential Drug Abuse Program (RDAP) is offered at CI McRae.

Education Services: CI McRae offers GED instruction. CoreCivic has partnered with the National Institute for Adult Education (Instituto Nacional de Educación para los Adultos, or INEA), an entity of the Mexican government, to provide adult education in Spanish. High school diplomas and post-secondary degrees are available through paid correspondence programs.

Advanced Occupational Education: CI McRae does not offer any advanced occupational education programs.

Vocational & Apprenticeship Training: CI McRae vocational training programs include Carpentry, Commercial Driver's License (CDL), Computer Applications, Construction and Building Trades, Culinary Arts, Electrical, Horticulture and Landscaping, HVAC, Masonry, Painting, Plumbing, Workforce Readiness, and Veterinary Technician.

Library Services: The CI McRae library contains many periodicals, newspapers, fiction and nonfiction books, reference materials, and more. The law library features legal resources and related tools commonly sought by inmates.

UNICOR: CI McRae does not house a UNICOR facility.

Commissary: Inmates and detainees at CI McRae have regular access to commissary services to support their health and wellness. Individuals have the opportunity to purchase a selection of beverages, light meals and snacks, over-the-counter medications, stationery, clothing, personal hygiene products, religious items, and other miscellaneous products.

Recreational Services: CI McRae offers a variety of sports and activities such as basketball, board games, creative writing, knitting, and other activities to inmates.

Visitation Information: On Sunday and Saturday visitation is held between 8:30 a.m. and 3:30 p.m. On federal holidays visitation is held between 8:30 a.m. and 3:30 p.m. See Chapter 1 for more information on visitation.

CI Moshannon Valley

Correctional Institution Moshannon Valley | CI Moshannon Valley

Facility Address & Contact Information

Correctional Institution Moshannon Valley
555 Geo Drive
Philipsburg, PA 16866

Phone: 814-768-1200
Fax: 814-342-5900
Email: MVC/General@bop.gov

BOP Website: https://www.bop.gov/locations/ci/mvc/
GEO Group Website: https://www.geogroup.com/FacilityDetail/FacilityID/67
Wikipedia: https://en.wikipedia.org/wiki/Moshannon_Valley_Correctional_Center
ZCG Website: https://www.prisonerresource.com/resources/federal-prison-profiles/private-prisons/correctional-institution-moshannon-valley-ci-moshannon-valley/

Inmate Correspondence Address

Inmate Name and Registration Number
CI Moshannon Valley
Correctional Institution
555 Geo Drive
Philipsburg, PA 16866

NOTE: Funds cannot be sent directly to federal inmates. Funds can be deposited either through JPay (www.jpay.com or 1-800-574-5729) or Western Union (www.westernunion.com/corrections or 1-800-634-3442). See Chapter 1 for more information on sending funds to federal inmates.

Sex: Male

Security Level: Low Security

Location: CI Moshannon Valley is located in central Pennsylvania, 131 miles east of Pittsburg, two miles northwest of Philipsburg, PA.

BOP Region: Northeast Region (NER)

BOP Institution Code: MVC for CI Moshannon Valley

Judicial District: Western District of Pennsylvania

Medical Care Level: Information not available. See Chapter 2 for more information on Medical Care and Mental Health Care Levels.

Mental Health Care Level: Information not available.

Population (as of May 1, 2019): 1,755

Background: CI Moshannon Valley is a private prison. It is owned and operated by the GEO Group. Since 2006 CI Moshannon Valley has provided correctional services on behalf of the Federal Bureau of Prisons (BOP). The facility achieved initial accreditation through the American Correctional Association in 2008 and re-accreditation in 2011 and 2014 with a score of 99.80%. The facility was also accredited by The Joint Commission (TJC) in 2008 and was re-accredited in 2017. Notable inmates include David Radler (sentenced to 29 months for mail fraud) and Kareem Serageldin (released in 2016 after serving 30 months for conspiracy to artificially inflate subprime mortgage bond prices).

Housing: Inmates are housed in dormitories.

Health Services: CI Moshannon Valley provides inmates with routine and emergency dental and health care. Inmates can obtain emergency health care 24 hours a day by approaching any staff member and requesting assistance. In order to obtain routine care, inmates must submit a sick call form and wait to be scheduled for an appointment.

Psychology Services: Inmates are provided with an intake interview, substance abuse counseling, life skills, and employment assistance. Typical treatment groups include stress management, anger management, and others. Crisis intervention is available 24 hours a day.

Residential Drug Abuse Program (RDAP): CI Moshannon Valley does not offer the Residential Drug Abuse Program (RDAP). However, Alcoholics Anonymous (AA) and Narcotics Anonymous (NA) groups are provided.

Education Services: CI Moshannon Valley provides literacy, GED, Adult Basic Education (ABE), and English-as-a-Second Language (ESL) programs. High school diplomas and post-secondary degrees are available through paid correspondence programs.

Advanced Occupational Education: CI Moshannon Valley offers the BARKS Service Dog advanced occupational education programs. In this program, inmates receive training on how to care for and train dogs, then actually train dogs. This program partners with United Disability Services (UDS) of Lancaster, Pennsylvania.

Vocational Training: CI Moshannon Valley not does offer any vocational training programs.

Apprenticeship: CI Moshannon Valley does not offer any apprenticeship programs.

Library Services: CI Moshannon Valley inmates have access to a law library, leisure library, general interest library, and religious services. In the leisure library, inmates can check out fiction and nonfiction books, newspapers, and magazines. In the law library, inmates can conduct legal research and prepare legal filings.

UNICOR: CI Moshannon Valley does not house a UNICOR facility.

Commissary: Inmates can shop once per week at the institution's Commissary. Items such as food, drinks, hygiene products, and electronics can be purchased.

Recreation Services: CI Moshannon Valley offers indoor and outdoor recreation opportunities. These include arts and crafts, physical fitness, sports, board and card games, and more.

Visitation Information: On Saturday, Thursday, and Friday visitation is held between 8:00 a.m. and 4:00 p.m. On Friday visitation is held between 12:30 and 8:00 p.m. On federal holidays visitation is held between 8:00 a.m. and 4:00 p.m. See Chapter 1 for more information on visitation.

CI Reeves 1 & 2

Correctional Institution Reeves 1 & 2 | CI Reeves 1 & 2

Facility Address & Contact Information

Correctional Institution Reeves 1 & 2
100 West Country Road #204
Pecos, TX 79772

Phone: 432-447-2926
Fax: 432-447-9224
Email: REE/General@bop.gov

BOP Website: https://www.bop.gov/locations/ci/ree/
GEO Group Website: https://www.geogroup.com/FacilityDetail/FacilityID/74
Wikipedia: https://en.wikipedia.org/wiki/Reeves_County_Detention_Complex
ZCG Website: https://www.prisonerresource.com/resources/federal-prison-profiles/private-prisons/correctional-institution-reeves-ci-reeves-1-2/

Inmate Correspondence Address

Inmate Name and Registration Number
CI Reeves 1 & 2
Correctional Institution
P.O Box 2038
Pecos, TX 79772

NOTE: Funds cannot be sent directly to federal inmates. Family members can call 1-866-345-1884 to deposit funds via telephone or go to www.accesscorrections.com to deposit funds online. See Chapter 1 for more information on sending funds to federal inmates.

Sex: Male

Security Level: Low Security

Location: Southwest Texas, approximately 210 miles southwest of Lubbock, Texas, three miles from the Pecos Municipal Airport and 150 miles from the Mexican border.

BOP Region: South Central Region (SCR)

BOP Institution Code: RVS for CI Reeves

Judicial District: South Central Region (SCR)

Medical Care Level: Information not available. See Chapter 2 for more information on Medical Care and Mental Health Care Levels.

Mental Health Care Level: Information not available.

Population (as of May 1, 2019): 2,387

Background: CI Reeves 1 & 2 are private prisons. They are owned and operated by GEO Group.

Housing: Inmates are housed in a dormitory-style setting.

Health Services: CI Reeves 1 & 2 offer correctional health care.

Psychology Services: CI Reeves 1 & 2 offer correctional mental health care.

Residential Drug Abuse Program (RDAP): Neither facility offers the Residential Drug Abuse Program (RDAP), however programs such as Alcoholics Anonymous (AA) and Narcotics Anonymous (NA) are provided.

Education Services: CI Reeves 1 & 2 provide literacy, GED, English-as-a-Second Language (ESL), and Special Education. High school diplomas and post-secondary degrees are available through paid correspondence programs.

Advanced Occupational Education: CI Reeves 1 & 2 offer academic programs in smart board technology, customized learning through individual education plans, dynamic grouping, and technology-based learning.

Vocational Training: CI Reeves 1 & 2 offer vocational training in Custodial Maintenance, Barbering, Horticulture, Electrical, Building Trades, Auto Mechanics, Upholstery, Weaving, Heating, Ventilation, and Air Conditioning (HVAC), Small Engine Repair, Masonry, Plumbing, Culinary Arts, Computer Repair, Carpentry, and Welding.

Apprenticeship: CI Reeves 1 & 2 do not offer any apprenticeship programs to inmates.

Library Services: Inmates have access to both leisure and law libraries. In the law library, inmates are provided with a number of legal research resources. In the leisure library, inmates can check out newspapers, magazines, and fiction and nonfiction books.

UNICOR: CI Reeves 1 & 2 do not house UNICOR facilities.

Commissary: Inmates at CI Reeves 1 & 2 are allowed to shop once a week in the Commissary, where they can purchase food, drinks, clothing, electronics, and more.

Recreation Services: Recreation services at CI Reeves 1 & 2 include both indoor and outdoor activities. These include arts and crafts, individual exercise, and sports leagues.

Visitation Information: On Sunday and Saturday visitation is held between 8:00 a.m. and 3:30 p.m. On federal holidays visitation is held between 8:00 a.m. and 3:30 p.m. See Chapter 1 for more information on visitation.

DC Reeves

Detention Complex Reeves | DC Reeves

Facility Address & Contact Information

Detention Complex Reeves
100 County Road #204
Pecos, TX 79772

Phone: 432-447-2926
Fax: 432-447-9224
Email: REE/General@bop.gov

BOP Website: https://www.bop.gov/locations/ci/rvs/
GEO Group Website: https://www.geogroup.com/FacilityDetail/FacilityID/75
Wikipedia: https://en.wikipedia.org/wiki/Reeves_County_Detention_Complex
ZCG Website: https://www.prisonerresource.com/resources/federal-prison-profiles/south-central-region-scr/detention-complex-reeves-dc-reeves/

Inmate Correspondence Address

Inmate Name and Registration Number
Detention Complex Reeves
P.O Box 2038
Pecos, TX 79772

NOTE: Funds cannot be sent directly to federal inmates. Family members can call 1-866-345-1884 to deposit funds via telephone or go to www.accesscorrections.com to deposit funds online. See Chapter 1 for more information on sending funds to federal inmates.

Sex: Male

Security Level: Low Security

Location: Southwest Texas, just outside of Pecos, Texas.

BOP Region: South Central Region (SCR)

BOP Institution Code: RVS for DC Reeves

Judicial District: South Central Region (SCR)

Medical Care Level: Information not available. See Chapter 2 for more information on Medical Care and Mental Health Care Levels.

Mental Health Care Level: Information not available.

Population (as of May 1, 2019): 1,153

Background: DC Reeves is a private prison owned and operated by GEO Group. Now referred to as the Reeves County Detention Complex, most prisoners at the complex are low-security criminal aliens, serving sentences of one to five years for drug offenses or immigration violations. The R-3 compound is a separate facility consisting of three housing units with support buildings for centralized programs, food service, laundry, infirmary, and indoor/outdoor recreation.

Housing: Inmates are housed in a dormitory-style setting.

Health Services: DC Reeves provides inmates with routine and emergency dental and health care. Inmates can obtain emergency health care 24 hours a day by approaching any staff member and requesting assistance. In order to obtain routine care, inmates must submit a sick call form and wait to be scheduled for an appointment.

Psychology Services: DC Reeves offers several group-based therapeutic programs. While offerings rotate, these tend to focus on substance abuse counseling, life skills, stress management, anger management, and others. Crisis intervention is available 24 hours a day.

Residential Drug Abuse Program (RDAP): DC Reeves does not offer the Residential Drug Abuse Program (RDAP).

Education Services: DC Reeves provides literacy, GED, English-as-a-Second Language (ESL), and Special Education programs. High school diplomas and post-secondary degrees are available through paid correspondence programs.

Advanced Occupational Education: DC Reeves offers advanced occupational education in smart board technology, customized learning through individual education plans, dynamic grouping, and technology-based learning.

Vocational Training: DC Reeves offers vocational training in Custodial Maintenance, Barbering, Horticulture, Electrical, Building Trades, Auto Mechanics, Upholstery, Weaving, Heating, Ventilation, and Air Conditioning (HVAC), Small Engine Repair, Masonry, Plumbing, Culinary Arts, Computer Repair, Carpentry, and Welding.

Apprenticeship: DC Reeves does not offer any apprenticeship programs to inmates.

Library Services: Inmates at DC Reeves have access to a law library and leisure library. In the leisure library, inmates can check out fiction and nonfiction books, newspapers, and magazines. In the law library, inmates can conduct legal research and prepare legal filings. A copy machine and typewriters are available to the inmate population.

UNICOR: DC Reeves does not house a UNICOR facility.

Commissary: Inmates can shop once per week at the institution's Commissary. Items such as shoes, radios, food, drinks, snacks, candy, electronics, and more can be purchased.

Recreation Services: Indoor and outdoor recreation opportunities are available at DC Reeves. These include organized sports, individual exercise, board and card games, and arts and crafts projects.

Visitation Information: On Sunday and Saturday visitation is held between 8:00 a.m. and 3:30 p.m. On federal holidays visitation is held between 8:00 a.m. and 3:30 p.m. See Chapter 1 for more information on visitation.

CI Rivers

Correctional Institution Rivers | CI Rivers

Facility Address & Contact Information

Correctional Institution Rivers
145 Parker's Fishery Road
Winton, NC 27986

Phone: 252-358-5200
Fax: 252-358-5202
Email: RIV/General@bop.gov

BOP Website: https://www.bop.gov/locations/ci/riv/
GEO Group Website: https://www.geogroup.com/FacilityDetail/FacilityID/78
Wikipedia: https://en.wikipedia.org/wiki/Rivers_Correctional_Institution
ZCG Website: https://www.prisonerresource.com/resources/federal-prison-profiles/private-prisons/correctional-institution-rivers-ci-rivers/

Inmate Correspondence Address

Inmate Name and Registration Number
CI Rivers
Correctional Institution
P.O. Box 630
Winton, NC 27986

NOTE: Funds cannot be sent directly to inmates. In order to deposit funds via mail, mail a money order with the inmate's name and registration number affixed to the following address:

[Last Name, First Name]
[Inmate Registration Number]
P.O. Box 99
Winton, NC 27986

Funds can also be sent via Access Corrections (www.accesscorrections.com or 1-866-345-1884) or via Western Union (www.westernunion.com/corrections or 1-800-634-3442). See Chapter 1 for more information on sending funds to federal inmates.

Sex: Male

Security Level: Low Security

Location: CI Rivers is located in northeast North Carolina, about 30 miles south of Suffolk, Virginia and 130 miles northeast of Raleigh, North Carolina.

BOP Region: Mid-Atlantic Region (MXR)

BOP Institution Code: RIV for CI Rivers

Judicial District: Eastern District of North Carolina

Medical Care Level: Information not available. See Chapter 2 for more information on Medical Care and Mental Health Care Levels.

Mental Health Care Level: Information not available.

Population (as of May 1, 2019): 1,317

Background: CI Rivers is a contracted correctional institution, operated by the private corporation GEO Group, Inc. The facility received initial accreditation from the American Correctional Association (ACA) in 2003 and was re-accredited in 2006, 2009 and 2012. Accreditation was received from the Joint Commission (also known as JCAHO) in January 2003 and the institution was re-accredited in 2006 and 2009. CI Rivers houses U.S. citizens who were convicted of violating federal law.

Housing: Inmates at CI Rivers are housed in two-person cells.

Health Services: Inmates are initially provided with an intake examination. Routine and emergency health care and dental care are both available to the inmate population. While emergency care is available 24 hours a day, inmates must submit a sick call form in order to be evaluated for routine or chronic health care concerns.

Psychology Services: CI Rivers provides inmates with access to a variety of treatment groups. These include stress management, anger management, life skills training, parenting techniques, and "Doing Time with the Right Mind" - a program designed to teach inmates time management, conflict resolution, and preparation for re-entry into society.

Residential Drug Abuse Program (RDAP): CI Rivers offers the Residential Drug Abuse Program (RDAP). CI Rivers also offers Alcoholics Anonymous (AA) and Narcotics Anonymous (NA).

Education Services: CI Rivers offers GED, English-as-a-Second Language (ESL), and Adult Basic Education (ABE) courses to the inmate population. Inmates without a GED or high school diploma are required to attend courses. High school diplomas and post-secondary degrees are available through paid correspondence programs.

Advanced Occupational Education: CI Rivers not does offer any advanced occupational education programs.

Vocational Training: CI Rivers offers vocational training in Building Construction, Commercial Driving, and Computer Technology.

Apprenticeship: CI Rivers does not offer any apprenticeship programs.

Library Services: CI Rivers inmates have access to a law library, leisure library, general interest library, and religious services. In the leisure library, inmates can check out fiction and nonfiction books, newspapers, and magazines. In the law library, inmates can conduct legal research and prepare legal filings.

UNICOR: CI Rivers does not house a UNICOR facility.

Commissary: Inmates can shop once per week at the institution's Commissary. Items such as food, drinks, hygiene products, and electronics can be purchased.

Recreation Services: CI Rivers offers indoor and outdoor recreation opportunities. These include arts and crafts, physical fitness, sports, board and card games, and more.

Visitation Information: On Sunday, Thursday, Friday, and Saturday visitation is held between 8:30 a.m. and 3:00 p.m. On federal holidays visitation is held between 8:30 a.m. and 3:00 p.m. See Chapter 1 for more information on visitation.

CI Taft & CI Taft Camp

Correctional Institution Taft | CI Taft

Facilities: CI Taft with an adjacent satellite prison camp.

Facility Address & Contact Information

Correctional Institution Taft
1500 Cadet Road
Taft, CA 93268

Phone: 661-763-2510
Fax: 661-765-3034
Email: TAF/General@bop.gov

BOP Websites: https://www.bop.gov/locations/ci/taf/
M&TC Website: http://www.mtctrains.com/family-friends-taft-correctional-institution/
Wikipedia: https://en.wikipedia.org/wiki/Taft_Correctional_Institution
ZCG Website: https://www.prisonerresource.com/resources/federal-prison-profiles/private-prisons/correctional-institution-taft-ci-taft/

Inmate Correspondence Address

For CI Taft

Inmate Name and Registration NumberCI Taft
Correctional Institution
P.O. Box 7001
Taft, CA 93268

For Satellite Prison Camp

Inmate Name and Registration Number
CI Taft
Satellite Prison Camp
P.O. Box 7001
Taft, CA 93268

NOTE: Funds cannot be sent directly to inmates. In order to deposit funds via mail, mail a money order with the inmate's name and registration number affixed to the following address:

[Last Name, First Name]
[Inmate Registration Number]
P.O. Box 7001
Taft, CA 93268

Funds can also be sent via JPay (www.jpay.com or 1-800-574-5729). See Chapter 1 for more information on sending funds to federal inmates.

Sex: Male

Security Level: Main: Low Security; Camp: Minimum Security

Location: CI Taft is located in Eastern California, 47 Miles west of Bakersfield.

BOP Region: Western Region (WXR)

BOP Institution Code: TAF for CI Taft

Judicial District: Eastern District of California

Medical Care Level: Information not available. See Chapter 2 for more information on Medical Care and Mental Health Care Levels.

Mental Health Care Level: Information not available.

Population (as of May 1, 2019): 2,042

Background: CI Taft was opened in 1997. It is a private prison which is owned and operated by the Management & Training Corporation. It houses male inmates at low- and minimum-security levels.

Housing: Inmates are housed in dormitories, which are divided into cubicles.

Health Services: Health Services at CI Taft include routine medical, dental and mental health services to all inmates. This includes diagnostic physical and medical exams and dental evaluations. Inmates must submit a sick call form in order to receive routine care. Emergency care is available 24 hours a day.

Psychology Services: Mental health services including telepsychiatry, among other services available at CI Taft. Inmates can participate in treatment groups including Choice and Change, Victim Impact, Anger Management, Thinking for Good, Man in the Mirror, Breaking the Cycle, Cage Your Rage, Those Outspoken, Freedom from Drugs, and many others. Specialized group therapy and counseling is also offered.

Residential Drug Abuse Program (RDAP): CI Taft does not offer the Residential Drug Abuse Program (RDAP). However, the Non-Residential Drug Abuse Program (NR-DAP), Alcoholics Anonymous (AA), and Narcotics Anonymous (NA) are available. Foundations for a drug free world and additional substance abuse programs are available as well.

Education Services: CI Taft provides GED, English-as-a-second Language (ESL) Programs, and Adult Basic Education (ABE). INEA, VT Math, parenting, computer, and truck driving courses are also available. High school diplomas and post-secondary degrees are available through paid correspondence programs.

Advanced Occupational Education: CI Taft offers a variety of programs.

Vocational Training: CI Taft offers vocational training in Culinary Arts, NCCER, Open Office Computer Apps, ServSafe, Truck Driving, and Wheels for the World.

Apprenticeship: CI Taft does not offer any apprenticeship programs

Library Services: CI Taft offers both a leisure and law library to inmates. In the leisure library inmates can check out fiction and nonfiction books, newspapers, and magazines. In the law library inmates can conduct legal research.

UNICOR: CI Taft does not house a UNICOR facility.

Commissary: Inmates at CI Taft have access to a commissary where they can shop once a week on their designated shopping day. A wide variety of items can be purchased, such as food, snacks, drinks, clothing, and limited electronics. A monthly spending limit of $360.00 is imposed.

Recreation Services: Indoor and outdoor recreation opportunities are available at CI Taft. Indoor leisure activities include hobbycrafts, leather crafting, and other art and craft projects. Outdoor activities include a variety of individual exercise and group sporting activities.

Visitation Information: CI Taft: Sunday, Monday, Thursday, and Saturday visitation are held between 8:00 a.m. and 3:00 p.m. CI Taft Camp: Sunday, Friday, and Saturday visitation are held between 8:00 a.m. and 3:00 p.m. On federal holidays visitation is held between 8:00 a.m. and 3:00 p.m. See Chapter 1 for more information on visitation.

PART THREE

Appendices

This section presents ancillary information of interest to prisoners, their families, and counsel. These appendices include federal prisons listed in varying useful groupings, suggestions for further reading, our references, and other information of general interest.

Appendix 1: Federal Prisons by Region

Appendix 2: Federal Prisons Alphabetically

Appendix 3: Federal Prisons by Security Level

Appendix 4: Federal Prisons by State

Appendix 5: Federal Prisons for Female Inmates

Appendix 6: Further Reading

Bibliography

Call for Submissions

About Zoukis Consulting Group

About Christopher Zoukis

Appendix 1:
Federal Prisons by Region

MID-ATLANTIC REGION

FPC Alderson (WV)*
FCI Ashland (KY)
FCI Ashland Camp (KY)
FCI Beckley (WV)
FCI Beckley Camp (WV)
USP Big Sandy (KY)
USP Big Sandy Camp (KY)
FCI Butner Low (NC)
FCI Butner Medium 1 (NC)
FCI Butner Medium 2 (NC)
FMC Butner (NC)
FCI Butner Camp (NC)
FCI Cumberland (MD)
FCI Cumberland Camp (MD)
FCI Gilmer (WV)
FCI Gilmer Camp (WV)
FCI Hazelton (WV)
FCI Hazelton Secure Female Facility (WV)*
FCI Hazelton Camp (WV)
USP Hazelton (WV)
USP Lee (VA)
USP Lee Camp (VA)
FMC Lexington (KY)
FMC Lexington Camp (KY)*
FCI Manchester (KY)
FCI Manchester Camp (KY)
USP McCreary (KY)
USP McCreary Camp (KY)
FCI McDowell (WV)
FCI McDowell Camp (WV)
FCI Memphis (TN)
FCI Memphis Camp (TN)
FCI Morgantown (WV)
FCI Petersburg Low (VA)

FCI Petersburg Medium (VA)
FCI Petersburg Camp (VA)

NORTH CENTRAL REGION

MCC Chicago (IL)**
FPC Duluth (MN)
FCI Englewood (CO)
FCI Englewood Camp (CO)
FCI Florence (CO)
FCI Florence Camp (CO)
USP Florence (CO)
ADX Florence (CO)
FCI Greenville (IL)
FCI Greenville Camp (IL)*
USP Leavenworth (KS)
USP Leavenworth Camp (KS)
USP Marion (IL)
USP Marion Camp (IL)
FCI Milan (MI)
FCI Oxford (WI)
FCI Oxford Camp (WI)
FCI Pekin (IL)
FCI Pekin Camp (IL)
FMC Rochester (MN)
FCI Sandstone (MN)
MCFP Springfield (MO)
FCI Terre Haute (IN)
FCI Terre Haute Camp (IN)
USP Terre Haute (IN)
AUSP Thomson Camp (IL)
FCI Waseca (MN)*
FPC Yankton (SD)

NORTHEAST REGION

FCI Allenwood Low (PA)
FCI Allenwood Medium (PA)
USP Allenwood (PA)
FCI Berlin (NH)
FCI Berlin Camp (NH)

MDC Brooklyn (NY)**
USP Canaan (PA)
USP Canaan Camp (PA)
FCI Danbury (CT)
FSL Danbury (CT)*
FCI Danbury Camp (CT)*
FMC Devens (MA)
FMC Devens Camp (MA)
FCI Elkton (OH)
FSL Elkton (OH)
FCI Fairton (NJ)
FCI Fairton Camp (NJ)
FCI Fort Dix (NJ)
FCI Fort Dix Camp (NJ)
USP Lewisburg (PA)
USP Lewisburg Camp (PA)
FCI Loretto (PA)
FCI Loretto Camp (PA)
FCI McKean (PA)
FCI McKean Camp (PA)
MCC New York (NY)**
FCI Otisville (NY)
FCI Otisville Camp (NY)
FDC Philadelphia (PA)**
FCI Ray Brook (NY)
FCI Schuylkill (PA)
FCI Schuylkill Camp (PA)

SOUTH CENTRAL REGION

FCI Bastrop (TX)
FCI Bastrop Camp (TX)
FCI Beaumont Low (TX)
FCI Beaumont Medium (TX)
FCI Beaumont Camp (TX)
USP Beaumont (TX)
FCI Big Spring (TX)
FCI Big Spring Camp (TX)
FPC Bryan (TX)*
FMC Carswell (TX)*
FMC Carswell Camp (TX)*

FCI El Reno (OK)
FCI El Reno Camp (OK)
FCI Forrest City Low (AR)
FCI Forrest City Medium (AR)
FCI Forrest City Camp (AR)
FMC Fort Worth (TX)
FDC Houston (TX)**
FCI La Tuna (TX)
FCI La Tuna Camp (TX)
FSL La Tuna (TX)
FCI Oakdale 1 (LA)
FCI Oakdale 2 (LA)
FCI Oakdale 2 Camp (LA)
FTC Oklahoma City (OK)**
FCI Pollock (LA)
USP Pollock (LA)
USP Pollock Camp (LA)
FCI Seagoville (TX)
FCI Seagoville Camp (TX)
FCI Texarkana (TX)
FCI Texarkana Camp (TX)
FCI Three Rivers (TX)
FCI Three Rivers Camp (TX)

SOUTHEAST REGION

FCI Aliceville (AL)*
FCI Aliceville Camp (AL)
USP Atlanta (GA)
USP Atlanta Camp (GA)
FCI Bennettsville (SC)
FCI Bennettsville Camp (SC)
FCI Coleman Low (FL)
FCI Coleman Medium (FL)
FCI Coleman Camp (FL)
USP Coleman 1 (FL)
USP Coleman 2 (FL)
FCI Edgefield (SC)
FCI Edgefield Camp (SC)
FCI Estill (SC)
FCI Estill Camp (SC)

MDC Guaynabo (PR)**
FCI Jesup (GA)
FCI Jesup Camp (GA)
FSL Jesup (GA)
FCI Marianna (FL)
FCI Marianna Camp (FL)*
FCI Miami (FL)
FCI Miami Camp (FL)
FDC Miami (FL)**
FPC Montgomery (AL)
FPC Pensacola (FL)
FCI Talladega (AL)
FCI Talladega Camp (AL)
FCI Tallahassee (FL)*
FCI Williamsburg (SC)
FCI Williamsburg Camp (SC)
FCI Yazoo City Low (MS)
FCI Yazoo City Medium (MS)
FCI Yazoo City Camp (MS)
USP Yazoo City (MS)

WESTERN REGION

USP Atwater (CA)
USP Atwater Camp (CA)
FCI Dublin (CA)*
FCI Dublin Camp (CA)
FCI Herlong (CA)
FCI Herlong Camp (CA)
FDC Honolulu (HI)**
FCI Lompoc (CA)
FCI Lompoc Camp (CA)
USP Lompoc (CA)
USP Lompoc Camp (CA)
MDC Los Angeles (CA)**
FCI Mendota (CA)
FCI Mendota Camp (CA)
FCI Phoenix (AZ)
FCI Phoenix Camp (AZ)*
FCI Safford (AZ)
MCC San Diego (CA)**

FDC SeaTac (WA)**
FCI Sheridan (OR)
FCI Sheridan Camp (OR)
FCI Terminal Island (CA)
FCI Tucson (AZ)
FCI Tucson Camp (AZ)
USP Tucson (AZ)
FCI Victorville Medium 1 (CA)
FCI Victorville Medium 2 (CA)
FCI Victorville Camp (CA)*
USP Victorville (CA)

PRIVATE PRISONS

CI Adams County (MS)
CI Big Spring (TX)
CI D. Ray James (GA)
CI Dalby (TX)
CI Great Plains (OK)
CI McRae (GA)
CI Moshannon Valley (PA)
CI Reeves 1 & 2 (TX)
DC Reeves (TX)
CI Rivers (NC)
CI Taft (CA)
CI Taft Camp (CA)

*Prisons housing only female inmates.

**Facilities housing both male and female inmates.

Appendix 2:
Federal Prisons Alphabetically

CI Adams County (MS)
FPC Alderson (WV)*
FCI Aliceville (AL)
FCI Aliceville Camp (AL)
FCI Allenwood Low (PA)
FCI Allenwood Medium (PA)
USP Allenwood (PA)
FCI Ashland (KY)
FCI Ashland Camp (KY)
USP Atlanta (GA)
USP Atlanta Camp (GA)
USP Atwater (CA)
USP Atwater Camp (CA)
FCI Bastrop (TX)
FCI Bastrop Camp (TX)
FCI Beaumont Low (TX)
FCI Beaumont Medium (TX)
FCI Beaumont Camp (TX)
USP Beaumont (TX)
FCI Beckley (WV)
FCI Beckley Camp (WV)
FCI Bennettsville (SC)
FCI Bennettsville Camp (SC)
FCI Berlin (NH)
FCI Berlin Camp (NH)
USP Big Sandy (KY)
USP Big Sandy Camp (KY)
CI Big Spring (TX)
FCI Big Spring (TX)
FCI Big Spring Camp (TX)
MDC Brooklyn (NY)**
FPC Bryan (TX)*
FCI Butner Low (NC)
FCI Butner Medium 1 (NC)
FCI Butner Medium 2 (NC)
FCI Butner Camp (NC)

FMC Butner (NC)
USP Canaan (PA)
USP Canaan Camp (PA)
FMC Carswell (TX)*
FMC Carswell Camp (TX)*
MCC Chicago (IL)**
FCI Coleman Low (FL)
FCI Coleman Medium (FL)
FCI Coleman Camp (FL)
USP Coleman 1 (FL)
USP Coleman 2 (FL)
FCI Cumberland (MD)
FCI Cumberland Camp (MD)
CI D. Ray James (GA)
CI Dalby (TX)
FCI Danbury (CT)
FCI Danbury Camp (CT)*
FSL Danbury (CT)*
FMC Devens (MA)
FMC Devens Camp (MA)
FCI Dublin (CA)*
FCI Dublin Camp (CA)
FPC Duluth (MN)
FCI Edgefield (SC)
FCI Edgefield Camp (SC)
FCI El Reno (OK)
FCI El Reno Camp (OK)
FCI Elkton (OH)
FSL Elkton (OH)
FCI Englewood (CO)
FCI Englewood Camp (CO)
FCI Estill (SC)
FCI Estill Camp (SC)
FCI Fairton (NJ)
FCI Fairton Camp (NJ)
FCI Florence (CO)
FCI Florence Camp (CO)
USP Florence (CO)
ADX Florence (CO)
FCI Forrest City Low (AR)
FCI Forrest City Medium (AR)

FCI Forrest City Camp (AR)
FCI Fort Dix (NJ)
FCI Fort Dix Camp (NJ)
FMC Fort Worth (TX)
FCI Gilmer (WV)
FCI Gilmer Camp (WV)
CI Great Plains (OK)
FCI Greenville (IL)
FCI Greenville Camp (IL)*
MDC Guaynabo (PR)**
FCI Hazelton (WV)
FCI Hazelton Secure Female Facility (WV)*
FCI Hazelton Camp (WV)
USP Hazelton (WV)
FCI Herlong (CA)
FCI Herlong Camp (CA)
FDC Honolulu (HI)**
FDC Houston (TX)**
FCI Jesup (GA)
FCI Jesup Camp (GA)
FSL Jesup (GA)
FCI La Tuna (TX)
FCI La Tuna Camp (TX)
FSL La Tuna (TX)
USP Leavenworth (KS)
USP Leavenworth Camp (KS)
USP Lee (VA)
USP Lee Camp (VA)
USP Lewisburg (PA)
USP Lewisburg Camp (PA)
FMC Lexington (KY)
FMC Lexington Camp (KY)*
FCI Lompoc (CA)
FCI Lompoc Camp (CA)
USP Lompoc (CA)
USP Lompoc Camp (CA)
FCI Loretto (PA)
FCI Loretto Camp (PA)
MDC Los Angeles (CA)**
FCI Manchester (KY)
FCI Manchester Camp (KY)

FCI Marianna (FL)
FCI Marianna Camp (FL)*
USP Marion (IL)
USP Marion Camp (IL)
USP McCreary (KY)
USP McCreary Camp (KY)
FCI McDowell (WV)
FCI McDowell Camp (WV)
FCI McKean (PA)
FCI McKean Camp (PA)
CI McRae (GA)
FCI Memphis (TN)
FCI Memphis Camp (TN)
FCI Mendota (CA)
FCI Mendota Camp (CA)
FCI Miami (FL)
FCI Miami Camp (FL)
FDC Miami (FL)**
FCI Milan (MI)
FPC Montgomery (AL)
FCI Morgantown (WV)
CI Moshannon Valley (PA)
MCC New York (NY)**
FCI Oakdale 1 (LA)
FCI Oakdale 2 (LA)
FCI Oakdale 2 Camp (LA)
FTC Oklahoma City (OK)**
FCI Otisville (NY)
FCI Otisville Camp (NY)
FCI Oxford (WI)
FCI Oxford Camp (WI)
FCI Pekin (IL)
FCI Pekin Camp (IL)
FPC Pensacola (FL)
FCI Petersburg Low (VA)
FCI Petersburg Medium (VA)
FCI Petersburg Camp (VA)
FDC Philadelphia (PA)**
FCI Phoenix (AZ)
FCI Phoenix Camp (AZ)*
FCI Pollock Medium (LA)

USP Pollock (LA)

USP Pollock Camp (LA)

FCI Ray Brook (NY)

CI Reeves 1 & 2 (TX)

DC Reeves (TX)

CI Rivers (NC)

FMC Rochester (MN)

FCI Safford (AZ)

MCC San Diego (CA)**

FCI Sandstone (MN)

FCI Schuylkill (PA)

FCI Schuylkill Camp (PA)

FCI Seagoville (TX)

FCI Seagoville Camp (TX)

FDC SeaTac (WA)**

FCI Sheridan (OR)

FCI Sheridan Camp (OR)

USMCFP Springfield (MO)

CI Taft (CA)

CI Taft Camp (CA)

FCI Talladega (AL)

FCI Talladega Camp (AL)

FCI Tallahassee (FL)*

FCI Terminal Island (CA)

FCI Terre Haute (IN)

FCI Terre Haute Camp (IN)

USP Terre Haute (IN)

FCI Texarkana (TX)

FCI Texarkana Camp (TX)

AUSP Thompson Camp (IL)

FCI Three Rivers (TX)

FCI Three Rivers Camp (TX)

FCI Tucson (AZ)

FCI Tucson Camp (AZ)

USP Tucson (AZ)

FCI Victorville Medium 1 (CA)

FCI Victorville Medium 2 (CA)

FCI Victorville Camp (CA)*

USP Victorville (CA)

FCI Waseca (MN)*

FCI Williamsburg (SC)

FCI Williamsburg Camp (SC)
FPC Yankton (SD)
FCI Yazoo City Low (MS)
FCI Yazoo City Medium (MS)
FCI Yazoo City Camp (MS)
USP Yazoo City (MS)

*Prisons housing only female inmates.

**Facilities housing both male and female inmates.

Appendix 3:
Federal Prisons by Security Level

MINIMUM

FPC Alderson (WV)*
FCI Aliceville Camp (AL)
FCI Ashland Camp (KY)
USP Atlanta Camp (GA)
USP Atwater Camp (CA)
FCI Bastrop Camp (TX)
FCI Beaumont Camp (TX)
FCI Beckley Camp (WV)
FCI Bennettsville Camp (SC)
FCI Berlin Camp (NH)
FCI Big Sandy Camp (KY)
FCI Big Spring Camp (TX)
FPC Bryan (TX)*
FCI Butner Camp (NC)
USP Canaan Camp (PA)
FMC Carswell Camp (TX)*
FCI Coleman Camp (FL)
FCI Cumberland Camp (MD)
FCI Danbury Camp (CT)*
FMC Devens Camp (MA)
FCI Dublin Camp (CA)
FPC Duluth (MN)
FCI Edgefield Camp (SC)
FCI El Reno Camp (OK)
FCI Englewood Camp (CO)
FCI Estill Camp (SC)
FCI Fairton Camp (NJ)
FCI Florence Camp (CO)
FCI Forrest City Camp (AR)
FCI Fort Dix Camp (NJ)
FCI Gilmer Camp (WV)
FCI Greenville Camp (IL)*
FCI Hazelton Camp (WV)
FCI Herlong Camp (CA)

FCI Jesup Camp (GA)

FCI La Tuna Camp (TX)

USP Leavenworth Camp (KS)

USP Lee Camp (VA)

USP Lewisburg Camp (PA)

FMC Lexington Camp (KY)*

FCI Lompoc Camp (CA)

USP Lompoc Camp (CA)

FCI Loretto Camp (PA)

FCI Manchester Camp (KY)

FCI Marianna Camp (FL)*

USP Marion Camp (IL)

USP McCreary Camp (KY)

FCI McDowell Camp (WV)

FCI McKean Camp (PA)

FCI Memphis Camp (TN)

FCI Mendota Camp (CA)

FCI Miami Camp (FL)

FPC Montgomery (AL)

FCI Morgantown (WV)

FCI Oakdale II Camp (LA)

FCI Otisville Camp (NY)

FCI Oxford Camp (WI)

FCI Pekin Camp (IL)

FPC Pensacola (FL)

FCI Petersburg Camp (VA)

FCI Phoenix Camp (AZ)*

USP Pollock Camp (LA)

FCI Schuylkill Camp (PA)

FCI Seagoville Camp (TX)

FCI Sheridan Camp (OR)

CI Taft Camp (CA)

FCI Talladega Camp (AL)

FCI Terre Haute Camp (IN)

FCI Texarkana Camp (TX)

AUSP Thomson Camp (IL)

FCI Three Rivers Camp (TX)

USP Tucson Camp (AZ)

FCI Victorville Camp (CA)*

FCI Williamsburg Camp (SC)

FPC Yankton (SD)
FCI Yazoo City Camp (MS)

LOW

CI Adams County (MS)
FCI Aliceville (AL)*
FCI Allenwood (PA)
FCI Ashland (WV)
FCI Bastrop (TX)
FCI Beaumont Low (TX)
CI Big Spring (TX)
FCI Big Spring (TX)
FCI Butner Low (NC)
FCI Coleman Low (FL)
CI D. Ray James (GA)
CI Dalby (TX)
FCI Danbury (CT)
FSL Danbury (CT)*
FCI Dublin (CA)*
FCI Elkton (OH)
FSL Elkton (OH)
FCI Englewood (CO)
FCI Forrest City Low (AR)
FCI Fort Dix (NJ)
CI Great Plains (OK)
FSL Jesup (GA)
FCI La Tuna (TX)
FSL La Tuna (TX)
FCI Lompoc (CA)
FCI Loretto (PA)
CI McRae (GA)
FCI Miami (FL)
FCI Milan (MI)
CI Moshannon Valley (PA)
FCI Oakdale 1 (LA)
FCI Petersburg Low (VA)
CI Reeves 1 & 2 (TX)
CI Rivers (NC)
FCI Safford (AZ)
FCI Sandstone (MN)

FCI Seagoville (TX)

CI Taft (CA)

FCI Tallahassee (FL)*

FCI Terminal Island (CA)

FCI Texarkana (TX)

FCI Waseca (SD)*

FCI Yazoo City Low (MS)

MEDIUM

FCI Allenwood Medium (PA)

USP Atlanta (GA)

FCI Beaumont Medium (TX)

FCI Beckley (KY)

FCI Bennettsville (SC)

FCI Berlin (NH)

FCI Butner Medium 1 (NC)

FCI Butner Medium 2 (NC)

FCI Coleman Medium (FL)

FCI Cumberland (MD)

FCI Edgefield (SC)

FCI El Reno (OK)

FCI Estill (SC)

FCI Fairton (NJ)

FCI Florence (CO)

FCI Forrest City Medium (AR)

FCI Gilmer (WV)

FCI Greenville (IL)

FCI Hazelton Secure Female Facility (WV)*

FCI Hazelton (WV)

FCI Herlong (CA)

FCI Jesup (GA)

USP Leavenworth (KS)

USP Lompoc (CA)

FCI Manchester (KY)

FCI Marianna (FL)

USP Marion (IL)

FCI McDowell (WV)

FCI McKean (PA)

FCI Memphis (TN)

FCI Mendota (CA)

FCI Oakdale 2 (LA)
FCI Otisville (NY)
FCI Oxford (WI)
FCI Pekin (IL)
FCI Petersburg Medium (VA)
FCI Phoenix (AZ)
FCI Pollock (LA)
FCI Ray Brook (NY)
FCI Schuylkill (PA)
FCI Sheridan (OR)
FCI Talladega
FCI Terre Haute (IN)
FCI Three Rivers (TX)
FCI Tucson (AZ)
FCI Victorville Medium 1 (CA)
FCI Victorville Medium 2 (CA)
FCI Williamsburg (SC)
FCI Yazoo City Medium (MS)

HIGH

USP Allenwood (PA)
USP Atwater (CA)
USP Beaumont (TX)
USP Big Sandy (KY)
USP Canaan (PA)
USP Coleman 1 (FL)
USP Coleman 2 (FL)
USP Florence (AR)
USP Hazelton (WV)
USP Lee (VA)
USP Lewisburg (PA)
USP McCreary (KY)
USP Pollock (LA)
USP Terre Haute (IN)
USP Tucson (AZ)
USP Victorville (CA)
USP Yazoo City (MS)

ADMINISTRATIVE

MDC Brooklyn (NY)**
FMC Butner (NC)
FMC Carswell (TX)*
MCC Chicago (IL)**
FMC Devens (MA)
ADX Florence (CO)
FMC Fort Worth (TX)
MDC Guaynabo (PR)**
FDC Honolulu (HI)**
FDC Houston (TX)**
FMC Lexington (KY)
MDC Los Angeles (CA)**
FDC Miami (FL)**
MCC New York (NY)**
FTC Oklahoma City (OK)**
FDC Philadelphia (PA)**
DC Reeves (TX)
FMC Rochester (MN)
MCC San Diego (CA)**
FDC SeaTac (WA)**
USMCFP Springfield (MO)

*Prisons housing only female inmates.

**Facilities housing both male and female inmates.

Appendix 4:
Federal Prisons by State

AL

FCI Aliceville*
FCI Aliceville Camp
FPC Montgomery
FCI Talladega
FCI Talladega Camp

AR

FCI Forrest City Low
FCI Forrest City Medium
FCI Forrest City Camp

AZ

FCI Phoenix
FCI Phoenix Camp*
FCI Safford
FCI Tucson
FCI Tucson Camp
USP Tucson

CA

USP Atwater
USP Atwater Camp
FCI Dublin*
FCI Dublin Camp
FCI Herlong
FCI Herlong Camp
FCI Lompoc
FCI Lompoc Camp
USP Lompoc
USP Lompoc Camp
MDC Los Angeles**
FCI Mendota

FCI Mendota Camp
MCC San Diego**
CI Taft
CI Taft Camp
FCI Terminal Island
FCI Victorville Medium 1
FCI Victorville Medium 2
FCI Victorville Camp*
USP Victorville

CO

FCI Englewood
FCI Englewood Camp
FCI Florence
FCI Florence Camp
USP Florence
ADX Florence

CT

FCI Danbury
FCI Danbury Camp*
FSL Danbury*

FL

FCI Coleman Low
FCI Coleman Medium
FCI Coleman Camp
USP Coleman 1
USP Coleman 2
FCI Marianna
FCI Marianna Camp*
FCI Miami
FCI Miami Camp
FDC Miami**
FPC Pensacola
FCI Tallahassee*

GA

USP Atlanta
USP Atlanta Camp
CI D. Ray James
FCI Jesup
FCI Jesup Camp
FSL Jesup
CI McRae

HI

FDC Honolulu**

IL

MCC Chicago**
FCI Greenville
FCI Greenville Camp*
USP Marion
USP Marion Camp
FCI Pekin
FCI Pekin Camp
AUSP Thomson Camp

IN

FCI Terre Haute
FCI Terre Haute Camp
USP Terre Haute

KS

USP Leavenworth
USP Leavenworth Camp

KY

FCI Ashland
FCI Ashland Camp
USP Big Sandy
USP Big Sandy Camp

FMC Lexington
FMC Lexington Camp*
FCI Manchester
FCI Manchester Camp
USP McCreary
USP McCreary Camp

LA

FCI Oakdale 1
FCI Oakdale 2
FCI Oakdale 2 Camp
FCI Pollock Medium
USP Pollock
USP Pollock Camp

MA

FMC Devens
FMC Devens Camp

MD

FCI Cumberland
FCI Cumberland Camp

MI

FCI Milan

MN

FPC Duluth
FMC Rochester
FCI Sandstone
FCI Waseca*

MO

USMCFP Springfield

MS

CI Adams County
FCI Yazoo City Low
FCI Yazoo City Medium
FCI Yazoo City Camp
USP Yazoo City

NC

FCI Butner Low
FCI Butner Medium 1
FCI Butner Medium 2
FCI Butner Camp
FMC Butner
CI Rivers

NH

FCI Berlin
FCI Berlin Camp

NJ

FCI Fairton
FCI Fairton Camp
FCI Fort Dix
FCI Fort Dix Camp

NY

MDC Brooklyn**
MCC New York**
FCI Otisville
FCI Otisville Camp
FCI Ray Brook

OH

FCI Elkton
FSL Elkton

OK

FCI El Reno
FCI El Reno Camp
CI Great Plains
FTC Oklahoma City**

OR

FCI Sheridan
FCI Sheridan Camp

PA

FCI Allenwood Low
FCI Allenwood Medium
USP Allenwood
USP Canaan
USP Canaan Camp
USP Lewisburg
USP Lewisburg Camp
FCI Loretto
FCI Loretto Camp
FCI McKean
FCI McKean Camp
CI Moshannon Valley
FDC Philadelphia**
FCI Schuylkill
FCI Schuylkill Camp

PR

MDC Guaynabo**

SC

FCI Bennettsville
FCI Bennettsville Camp
FCI Edgefield
FCI Edgefield Camp
FCI Estill
FCI Estill Camp

FCI Williamsburg
FCI Williamsburg Camp

SD

FPC Yankton

TN

FCI Memphis
FCI Memphis Camp

TX

FCI Bastrop
FCI Bastrop Camp
FCI Beaumont Low
FCI Beaumont Medium
FCI Beaumont Camp
USP Beaumont
CI Big Spring
FCI Big Spring
FCI Big Spring Camp
FPC Bryan*
FMC Carswell*
FMC Carswell Camp*
CI Dalby
FMC Fort Worth
FDC Houston**
FCI La Tuna
FCI La Tuna Camp
FSL La Tuna
CI Reeves 1 & 2
DC Reeves
FCI Seagoville
FCI Seagoville Camp
FCI Texarkana
FCI Texarkana Camp
FCI Three Rivers
FCI Three Rivers Camp

VA

USP Lee
USP Lee Camp
FCI Petersburg Low
FCI Petersburg Medium
FCI Petersburg Camp

WA

FDC SeaTac**

WI

FCI Oxford
FCI Oxford Camp

WV

FPC Alderson*
FCI Beckley
FCI Beckley Camp
FCI Gilmer
FCI Gilmer Camp
FCI Hazelton
FCI Hazelton Secure Female Facility*
FCI Hazelton Camp
USP Hazelton
FCI McDowell
FCI McDowell Camp
FCI Morgantown

*Prisons housing only female inmates.

**Facilities housing both male and female inmates.

Appendix 5:
Federal Prisons for Female Inmates

MID-ATLANTIC REGION

FPC Alderson (MINIMUM, WV)
FCI Hazelton Secure Female Facility (MEDIUM, WV)
FMC Lexington Camp (MINIMUM, KY)

NORTH CENTRAL REGION

MCC Chicago (ADMINISTRATIVE, IL)*
FCI Greenville Camp (MINIMUM, IL)
FCI Waseca (LOW, MN)

NORTHEAST REGION

MDC Brooklyn (ADMINISTRATIVE, NY)*
FCI Danbury Camp (MINIMUM, CT)
FSL Danbury (LOW, CT)
MCC New York (ADMINISTRATIVE, NY)*
FDC Philadelphia (ADMINISTRATIVE, PA)*

SOUTH CENTRAL REGION

FPC Bryan (MINIMUM, TX)
FMC Carswell (ADMINISTRATIVE, TX)
FMC Carswell Camp (MINIMUM, TX)
FDC Houston (ADMINISTRATIVE, TX)*
FTC Oklahoma City (ADMINISTRATIVE, OK)*

SOUTHEAST REGION

FCI Aliceville (LOW, AL)
MDC Guaynabo (ADMINISTRATIVE, PR)*
FCI Marianna Camp (MINIMUM, FL)
FDC Miami (ADMINISTRATIVE, FL)*
FCI Tallahassee (LOW, FL)

WESTERN REGION

FCI Dublin (MINIMUM, CA)
FDC Honolulu (ADMINISTRATIVE, HI)
MDC Los Angeles (ADMINISTRATIVE, CA)*
FCI Phoenix Camp (MINIMUM, AZ)
MCC San Diego (ADMINISTRATIVE, CA)*
FDC SeaTac (ADMINISTRATIVE, WA)*
FCI Victorville Camp (MINIMUM, CA)

*Facilities also housing male inmates.

Appendix 6:
Further Reading

Books

Federal Prison Handbook: The Definitive Guide to Surviving the Federal Bureau of Prisons
by Christopher Zoukis (Middle Street Publishing, 2017)

Incarceration can be cruel for prisoners and their loved ones. Learn what to expect and make the best of this time by staying safe and building a life behind bars. The *Federal Prison Handbook* teaches everything you need to know to protect yourself and your rights, compiled by a college-educated inmate currently serving time at a federal prison. His insider's view of this unknown world will guide you through the mental stresses of confinement and keep you physically safe by explaining how to avoid the near-constant conflicts found inside federal prisons in the United States today.

Federal Prison Handbook is the recipient of numerous industry awards, including the IndieReader Nonfiction Discovery Award, Foreword Indie Social Sciences Book of the Year, National Indie Excellence Awards, and Next Generation Indie Book Awards. It is the top-rated federal prison survival book available today.

Whereas the *Directory of Federal Prisons* assists inmates in understanding designation, classification, and individual federal prisons, the *Federal Prison Handbook* is a companion book which assists prisoners in understanding life inside federal prison and the policies governing all aspects of such.

Prison Education Guide **by Christopher Zoukis (Prison Legal News Publishing, 2016)**

Prison Education Guide is the most comprehensive guide to correspondence programs for prisoners available today. This book provides the reader with step-by-step instructions to find the right educational program, enroll in courses, and complete classes to meet their academic goals. It is perfect for the incarcerated student who lacks internet access or the ability to attend education classes in person.

Prison Education Guide is the latest and best resource on the market for the incarcerated nontraditional student. It includes a detailed analysis of the quality, cost, and course offerings of all correspondence programs available to prisoners. This includes correspondence courses at the graduate, undergraduate, religious college, career, high school, personal enrichment, fee-based Bible study, and free Bible study levels. In a time when so many academic opportunities in prisons have been eliminated, this book is an invaluable reentry tool for prisoners who seek to further their education while incarcerated in order to help them prepare for life and work following their release.

Prison Education Guide has enjoyed favorable reviews from Foreword Reviews, the San Francisco Book Review, and Blasting News. It is the top-rated correspondence guidebook for prisoners available today.

The Habeas Citebook: Ineffective Assistance of Counsel by Brandon Sample and Alissa Hull (2nd Edition)(Prison Legal News Publishing, 2016)

The Habeas Citebook: Ineffective Assistance of Counsel is a neatly-organized resource designed to assist litigants in advancing claims of ineffective assistance of counsel, the most common claim presented in post-conviction, habeas corpus proceedings. Citing cases from the United States Courts of Appeals and United States District Courts, both published and unpublished, *The Habeas Citebook* breaks down ineffective assistance of counsel cases into 40 categories. From cases describing lawyers failing to investigate a defense, to conflicts of interests and misadvise on appeal, *The Habeas Citebook* is an essential resource for those examining former counsel's performance, as well as for the formulation of well-supported claims of ineffective assistance.

The Habeas Citebook also contains extensive resource information for the prisoner putting together a habeas petition or other collateral attack on their conviction, including various rules and procedural codes in their entirety, sample briefs, and informed advice on procedural matters.

As one would expect from a text published by *Prison Legal News, The Habeas Citebook* is a quality, well-researched resource for both prisoners and attorneys alike.

Pardons and Commutations of Sentences: The Complete Guidebook to Applying for Clemency by David L. Mathis and Brandon Sample (Prisology Press, 2019)

The President of the United States and the Governor of each state are empowered to grant pardons and commutations. A pardon can eliminate the collateral consequences of a conviction. A commutation can reduce the length of a sentence. In general, a pardon is sought after release from prison. A commutation, on the other hand, is used by prisoners to lessen their sentence. This easy-to-read guidebook is designed to assist individuals who want to apply for a pardon or commutation of sentence. The guidebook gives practical information about the process for applying for clemency, what to include in your petition, and provides answers about executive clemency in general. The guidebook is a "must have" for any individual who wants to navigate the complex process of applying for a pardon or commutation of sentence.

Publications

Prison Legal News

Prison Legal News, a project of the Human Rights Defense Center, is an award-winning 72-page monthly publication that reports on news, court rulings, verdicts and settlements related to criminal justice-related issues, including prisons, jails and other detention facilities. PLN has published continuously since 1990.

Prison Legal News
P.O. Box 1151
Lake Worth, FL 33460
https://www.prisonlegalnews.org
info@prisonlegalnews.com

Criminal Legal News

Criminal Legal News, also a project of the Human Rights Defense Center, is a 48-page monthly magazine available in print and online that provides timely review and analysis of individual rights, court rulings, and news concerning criminal justice-related issues. CLN provides information that enables prisoners and other concerned individuals and organizations to gain a better understanding of a broad range of criminal justice topics.

Criminal Legal News
P.O. Box 1151
Lake Worth, FL 33460
https://www.criminallegalnews.org
info@criminallegalnews.org

Corrlinks.com News Services

Law Office of Brandon Sample

The Law Office of Brandon Sample distributes a weekly newsletter, as well as breaking news alerts, concerning legal matters of interest to federal prisoners. Written by Brandon Sample, the author of *The Habeas Citebook: Ineffective Assistance of Counsel* (2nd Edition)(Prison Legal News Publishing, 2016) and *Pardons and Commutations of Sentences (Prisology Press, 2019)*, this news service provides the best legal analysis in the field. Sample is an expert attorney who has significant experience with 2255s and is able to provide on-point analysis of legal cases as they occur. Subscribing to this news service is a must for all federal prisoners.

Law Office of Brandon Sample
P.O. Box 250
Rutland, VT 05702
news@BrandonSample.com
Sentencing.net

Law Office of Jeremy Gordon

The Law Offices of Jeremy Gordon, in partnership with their affiliated non-profit Prisology. org, sends out an exceptional weekly newsletter with the latest legal news of interest to federal prisoners. What sets this newsletter apart from all others is the extremely valuable legal analysis provided by attorney Jeremy Gordon. This is essential reading for all jailhouse lawyers and those interested in staying up-to-date on the latest breaking legal news.

Law Office of Jeremy Gordon
P.O. Box 2275
Mansfield, TX 44857
info@topfederallawyer.com
www.gordondefense.com

Legal Information Service

Legal Information Service sends out a weekly newsletter consisting of various articles and legal updates. This electronic newsletter provides a good range of articles of interest to federal prisoners. The articles focus on legal developments, along with information about criminal justice reform efforts by leading organizations and news about the prison systems.

Legal Information Service
P.O. Box 636
Norwalk, OH 44857
newsletter@lisa-legalinfo.com
www.lisa-legalinfo.com

Bibliography

Bosworth, Mary. *The U.S. Federal Prison System*. Thousand Oaks, CA: Sage Publications, 2002.

Bureau of Prisons. "About Our Agency." Bureau of Prisons Website. Last accessed May 1, 2019. www.bop.gov/about/agency/organization.jsp.

---. *A Directory of Bureau of Prisons' National Programs*. Washington, DC: Bureau of Prisons, 2015.

---. "Central Office." Bureau of Prisons Website. Last accessed May 1, 2019. www.bop.gov/locations/central_office/.

---. "Designations." Bureau of Prisons Website. Last accessed May 1, 2019. www.bop.gov/inmates/custody_and_care/designations.jsp.

---. *Directory of Federal Prisons*. Washington, DC: Bureau of Prisons, 1993.

---. "Inmate Age." Bureau of Prisons Website. Last accessed May 1, 2019. www.bop.gov/about/statistics/statistics_inmate_age.jsp.

---. "Inmate Citizenship." Bureau of Prisons Website. Last accessed May 1, 2019. www.bop.gov/about/statistics/statistics_inmate_citizenship.jsp.

---. "Inmate Ethnicity." Bureau of Prisons Website. Last accessed May 1, 2019. www.bop.gov/about/statistics/statistics_inmate_ethnicity.jsp.

---. "Inmate Gender." Bureau of Prisons Website. Last accessed May 1, 2019. www.bop.gov/about/statistics/statistics_inmate_gender.jsp.

---. *Inmate Occupational Training Directory*. Washington, DC: Bureau of Prisons, 2016.

---. "Inmate Race." Bureau of Prisons Website. Last accessed May 1, 2019. www.bop.gov/about/statistics/statistics_inmate_race.jsp.

---. *Legal Resource Guide to the Federal Bureau of Prisons*. Washington, DC: Bureau of Prisons, 2014.

---. "Mid-Atlantic Regional Office." Bureau of Prisons Website. Last accessed May 1, 2019. https://www.bop.gov/locations/regional_offices/mxro/.

---. "North Central Regional Office." Bureau of Prisons Website. Last accessed May 1, 2019. https://www.bop.gov/locations/regional_offices/ncro/.

---. "Northeast Regional Office." Bureau of Prisons Website. Last accessed May 1, 2019. www.bop.gov/locations/regional_offices/nero/.

---. "Offenses." Bureau of Prisons Website. Last accessed May 1, 2019. www.bop.gov/about/statistics/statistics_inmate_offenses.jsp.

---. "Prison Security Levels." Bureau of Prisons Website. Last accessed May 1, 2019. www.bop.gov/about/statistics/statistics_inmate_sec_levels.jsp.

---. *Program Statement P5100.08, Inmate Security Designation and Custody Classification*. Washington, DC: Bureau of Prisons, 2006.

---. *Program Statement P5180.05, Central Inmate Monitoring System*. Washington, DC: Bureau of Prisons, 1996.

---. "Residential Drug Treatment Programs and Locations." Bureau of Prisons Website. Last accessed March 24, 2018. www.bop.gov/inmates/custody_and_care/substance_abuse_treatment.jsp.

---. "Sentence Imposed." Bureau of Prisons Website. Last accessed May 1, 2019. www.bop.gov/about/statistics/statistics_inmate_sentences.jsp.

---. "South Central Regional Office." Bureau of Prisons Website. Last accessed May 1, 2019. www.bop.gov/locations/regional_offices/scro/.

---. "Southeast Regional Office." Bureau of Prisons Website. Last accessed May 1, 2019. www.bop.gov/locations/regional_offices/sero/.

---. "Staff Ethnicity/Race." Bureau of Prisons Website. Last accessed May 1, 2019. www.bop.gov/about/statistics/statistics_staff_ethnicity_race.jsp.

---. "Staff Gender." Bureau of Prisons Website. Last accessed May 1, 2019. www.bop.gov/about/statistics/statistics_staff_gender.jsp.

---. *State of the Bureau*. Washington, DC: Bureau of Prisons, 2010.

---. "Substance Abuse Treatment." Bureau of Prisons Website. Last accessed March 24, 2018. www.bop.gov.inmates/custody_and_care/substance_abuse_treatment.jsp.

---. "Western Regional Office." Bureau of Prisons Website. Last accessed May 1, 2019. www. bop.gov/locations/regional_offices/wxro/.

Bussert, Todd. "The Federal Bureau of Prisons." In *Defending a Federal Criminal Case*, 2016 ed., edited by Federal Public Defenders of San Diego, Inc., 809-844. San Diego, CA: Federal Public Defenders of San Diego, Inc., 2016.

Donson, Jack. "Prison Designation: Custody Level." Prisonology. Last accessed May 14, 2018. http://prisonologyx.com/preparation/prison-designation/custody-level/.

---. "Prison Designation: Management Variable." Prisonology. Last accessed May 14, 2018. http://prisonologyx.com/preparation/prison-designation/management-variable/.

Ellis, Alan. "BOP Designations Based on Medical Needs." *Criminal Justice*, Fall 2008: 60.

---. "Health Care in the Federal Prison System." *Criminal Justice*, Summer 2008: 43.

---. "INSIGHT: Tips on Getting Your Client Into the Best Prison and Released at the Earliest Possible Opportunity." *BNA Criminal Law Reporter* 103, no. 18 (2018): 475-478.

Ellis, Alan, and J. Michael Henderson. *Federal Prison Guidebook: Sentencing and Post-Conviction Remedies*. Revision 4. Costa Mesa, CA: James Publishing, 2017.

Ellis, Alan, J. Michael Henderson, and James H. Feldman. "Securing a Favorable Prison Placement." *The Champion*, April 2006: 22-27.

Fassler, Larry. *Busted by the Feds*. 18th ed. Tucson, AZ: Southwest Legal Services, 2018.

Government Accountability Office. *Bureau of Prisons: Better Planning and Evaluation Needed to Understand and Control Rising Inmate Health Care Costs*. Washington, DC: Government Accountability Office, June 2017.

---. *Bureau of Prisons: Growing Inmate Crowding Negatively Affects Inmates, Staff, and Infrastructure*. Washington, DC: Government Accountability Office, 2012.

---. *Bureau of Prisons: Timelier Reviews, Plan for Evaluations, and Updated Policies Could Improve Inmate Mental Health Services Oversight.* Washington, DC: Government Accountability Office, July 2013.

Vasquez, Alicia and Todd Bussert. "How Federal Prisoners are Placed: Shedding Light on the BOP's Inmate Classification and Designation Process." *Criminal Justice*, Spring 1996: 19-22.

Zoukis, Christopher. *Federal Prison Handbook: The Definitive Guide to Surviving the Federal Bureau of Prisons.* Sullivan's Island, SC: Middle Street Publishing, 2017.

---. "How to Send Funds to Federal Inmates." Zoukis Prisoner Resources. Last accessed August 26, 2018. https://www.prisonerresource.com/prison-survival-guide/communication/send-funds-federal-inmates/.

---. "Medical Care Levels in Federal Prison." Zoukis Prisoner Resources. Last accessed August 26, 2018. https://www.prisonerresource.com/medical-care-levels-federal-prison/.

---. "Security Levels." Zoukis Prisoner Resources. Last accessed August 22, 2018. https://www.prisonerresource.com/security-levels/.

---. "Violence and Sexual Assault in Prison." Zoukis Prisoner Resources. Last accessed August 26, 2018. https://www.prisonerresource.com/prison-survival-guide/special-tactics/violence-sexual-assault/.

Call for Submissions

If you are currently incarcerated within any Federal Bureau of Prisons or private contract facility, we want to hear from you. Please write or email to let us know if any of the information contained in your prison's profile is out of date or if there is anything you feel should be included in the next edition. We are particularly interested in hearing about program changes, cultural issues at your facility, and a general review of the facility. Any information that you submit will be considered for inclusion in the next annual edition.

If possible, we would appreciate answers to the following culture-oriented questions as they concern your institution:

1. Is your prison political? If so, to what degree and do inmates generally have to be part of a car in order to stay?

2. What is the level of violence? How many fights and/or stabbings do you observe each week or month?

3. Can sex offenders, informants, or LGBT walk your yard? If some can stay but others must go, please clarify which.

4. What do you particularly like about your facility? What do you particularly dislike?

5. A general review of your facility would also be helpful. Within this, please explain who should or shouldn't go to your prison. Any general review information would be appreciated.

Please address all correspondence to the following email address: Info@PrisonerResource.com

About Zoukis Consulting Group

If, after reading this book, you find that you would like to retain a prison expert or attorney to assist you, please don't hesitate to contact us at the Zoukis Consulting Group. Our consultants and attorneys have decades of experience and a proven track record of helping clients make it through the criminal justice system in the best way possible.

We take particular pride in our prison preparation, in-prison, and reentry planning services. We can help you prepare for prison by providing informational services and referrals, resolve matters in prison as they arise (e.g., education, discipline, health care, transfers, etc.), and help you reintegrate back into society at the end of your term of imprisonment. Through our wealth of experience and reputation with the Bureau of Prisons, we can help you overcome any obstacle and approach every situation in an informed manner.

We can be found online at https://www.PrisonerResource.com and easily reached at info@PrisonerResource.com.

About Christopher Zoukis

Christopher Zoukis, MBA, managing director of Zoukis Consulting Group, LLC, is the author of *Directory of Federal Prisons* (Middle Street Publishing, 2019), *Federal Prison Handbook* (Middle Street Publishing, 2017), *Prison Education Guide* (PLN Publishing, 2016), and *College for Convicts* (McFarland & Co., 2014). He regularly contributes to *The Huffington Post*, *New York Daily News*, *Prison Legal News*, *Criminal Legal News*, and the *New York Journal of Books*.

During his twelve years of incarceration, Zoukis earned his Bachelor's Degree in Interdisciplinary Studies (Business Administration/Legal Studies) and Masters of Business Administration from Adams State University, where he is currently an adjunct professor in their Prison College Program. He has also received recognition and awards for his writing from the American Bar Association, Society of Professional Journalists, Pen America Center, Foreword Magazine, IndieReader, and other book and writing organizations.

Through his consulting firm, Mr. Zoukis regularly advises attorneys, prison consultants, criminal defendants, and their families about legal issues, prison preparation, in-prison matters, and reentry concerns. Through his firm's breadth of experience and proven track record, he is able to assist clients make the best of bad situations and come out in the best shape possible.

He can be found online at PrisonerResource.com and contacted at Info@PrisonerResource.com.

Index

W

Waseca
  Federal Correctional Institution 247
Western Regional Office 563
  List of Prisons 693
Williamsburg
  Federal Correctional Institution 544
Work Details 12
  Inmate Pay 12
  UNICOR 12

Y

Yankton
  Federal Prison Camp 251
Yazoo City
  Federal Correctional Institution Low 557
  Federal Correctional Institution Medium 553
  United States Penitentiary 549

Made in the USA
Las Vegas, NV
18 November 2023

81121010R00420